W9-BOO-929

MADISON-JEFFERSON COUNTY PUBLIC LIBRARY

ISABEL THE QUEEN

Isabel, Queen of Castile.
[*Collection of Stanley Moss, Riverdale-on-Hudson, New York.*]

Isabel
the
Queen
Life and Times

PEGGY K. LISS

New York Oxford
OXFORD UNIVERSITY PRESS
1992

MADISON-JEFFERSON COUNTY PUBLIC LIBRARY

Oxford University Press

Oxford   New York   Toronto
Delhi   Bombay   Calcutta   Madras   Karachi
Kuala Lumpur   Singapore   Hong Kong   Tokyo
Nairobi   Dar es Salaam   Cape Town
Melbourne   Auckland

and associated companies in
Berlin   Ibadan

Copyright © 1992 by Peggy K. Liss

Published by Oxford University Press, Inc.
200 Madison Avenue, New York, New York 10016

Oxford is a registered trademark of Oxford University Press

All rights reserved. No part of this publication may be reproduced,
stored in a retrieval system, or transmitted, in any form or by any means,
electronic, mechanical, photocopying, recording, or otherwise,
without the prior permission of Oxford University Press.

Library of Congress Cataloging-in-Publication Data
Liss, Peggy K.
Isabel the Queen : life and times / Peggy K. Liss.
p.   cm.   Includes bibliographical reference and index.
ISBN 0-19-507356-8
1. Isabella I, Queen of Spain, 1451–1504.
2. Spain—History—Ferdinand and Isabella, 1479—1516.
3. Spain—Kings and rulers—Biography.
I. Title.   DP163.L48   1992   946'.03'092—dc20   [B]   91-46645

946.03
LIS

The Publisher gratefully acknowledges the financial support of
The Program for Cultural Cooperation Between Spain's Ministry of Culture
and United States' Universities.

2 4 6 8 9 7 5 3 1

Printed in the United States of America
on acid-free paper

For Peter
and Sarah

Preface

This is the story of Isabel of Spain, who 500 years ago had tremendous impact on her realm and, though not then so apparent, on the entire world. Since then, she has lain in a small unadorned coffin in Granada. Is it too unimposing for so much glory, as her grandson, the emperor Charles V, reputedly said? Or is it larger than deserved by the monarch who introduced the Spanish Inquisition, took over the Muslim kingdom of Granada, expelled the Jews, and set in motion events that devastated the populace of the Caribbean?

This will be her story. It has to be told within the context of her times. It is a tale like its subject rich in fame and glory, tragedy and irony. It is also the narrative of a search for Isabel and an encounter with her. That encounter has resulted most of all in reaffirming the breadth and depth of individual complexity and confirming that human beings and human relations were no simpler in the past than they are today.

Her name was Isabel. Over the centuries in English she has been Izabell, Isabeau, Isabella. The Latin equivalent of Isabel is Elizabeth, and so she appears on the coins of her realm. Isabella seems an attempt to distinguish her from England's own Elizabeth I, even an awareness of her equal potency as a sovereign queen in the substitution to undercut it. It is high time to drop the latter-day diminutive and restore the strong original, Isabel, most consonant with her personality.

Scholars may question the numerous variations or revisions of standard interpretation here. I have returned to the vivid chronicles of her reign—those looking glasses tinted by their times and authors. I have also considered the accreted histories of five centuries and the wealth of recent work based on fifteenth-century documents, and some of those documents as well. I have traveled into literature and letters, into Isabelline geography, architecture, and art. It is a beginning.

My appreciation to everyone who offered help, advice, and criticism, who in one way or another kept me at it, to Inés Azar, Jonathan Brown, Bill Christian, Tom Colchie, Vicenta Cortés, Kathleen Deagan, John Elliott, Susan Freeman, Michael Gill, Annette Gordon, David Henige, Carole Horn, Richard Kagan, Ronda Kasl, Peter Korn, Angus Mackay, Linda Martz, Helen Nader, Joseph O'Callaghan, Beatrice Patt, William Phillips, Jack Pole, Jim Sacksteder, Joyce Seltzer, Matías Verna, and Stephen Weissman;

Sara Wolper, Jack Viebrock; to Miguel Angel Ladero Quesada for his careful reading of the entire penultimate draft; to Nancy Lane, Edward Harcourt, and Rosemary Wellner; and all the others at Oxford University Press who worked on the book; to Sandra Sider at the Hispanic Society of America, to Everette Larsen, Georgette Dorn, and Dolores Martin at the Library of Congress; to those who helped at the Archivo General de Simancas, the Biblioteca Nacional, the British Library, the Fitzwilliam Museum Library, the Fundación Lázaro Galdiano, the Morgan Library, the Newberry Library, the New York Public Library; and the many others over the years. I particularly want to thank the John Simon Guggenheim Memorial Foundation for a fellowship spurring completion of this book.

Washington, D.C.   P.K.L.
January 1992

Contents

Prologue

An Embassy to Egypt
1502

Yo no digo esta canción sino á quien conmigo va.

Conde Arnaldos

[I will not tell this song except to those who go with me.]

R ETURNING from an embassy to Egypt in September 1502, Pedro Mártir exulted in having reached once more the most secure port of all,
the Queen. Where, he asked a friend, could be found among the ancients,
"among the Queens and the powerful, such a one, who does not lack either
the valor to undertake great endeavors, or the constancy to carry them
through, or an enchantment with honesty?" She was a woman "stronger
than a strong man, more constant than any human soul, a marvelous example of honesty and virtue; Nature has made no other woman like her."[1]

He was not alone in his opinion. A consensus existed among her contemporaries that the Queen of Castile was an extraordinary woman who was
also an extraordinary monarch, one of the most powerful the world had
ever known. Truly extraordinary is the extent to which her powerful intellect and powerful will interacted with her will to power in becoming the
monarch she sought to be. Europe had no queen as great until the advent
of England's Elizabeth I.

Yet, that said, Isabel remains a mystery. Possibly because, unlike Elizabeth, she was no virgin queen, but shared the governing of the realm with
her husband, Fernando, King of Aragón. She alone was proprietary monarch of Castile, he of Aragón much smaller and, one-tenth as populous, the
two kingdoms from which modern Spain emerged, yet Isabel made certain
that the rule they exercised was viewed as seamlessly joint and the great
harmony prevailing between them was perceived as absolutely flawless, to
the point where her most astute chronicler, Fernando del Pulgar, could not,

on Isabel's having given birth, resist the comment that "the King and Queen had been delivered of a daughter." That show of joint authority continues to confound some people who should know better. Thus, the British Library in its subject catalogue of 1985 exactly reversed the monarchs' true roles in listing her as "Isabella. Queen. Consort of Ferdinand V of Spain."

Yet there are other reasons for the relative lack of prominence of this preeminent queen. To biographers, who on the whole have until recently preferred to take on subjects more exemplary than not, Isabel surely has appeared a hopelessly jumbled mass of both admirable and deplorable qualities. It was assuredly Isabel who introduced the Spanish Inquisition, conquered the kingdom of Granada, and expelled the Jews. Today, descendants of peoples then inhabiting America put in the same condemnatory category her sending out of Christopher Columbus.

For most of the 500 intervening years and with some notable exceptions, interest in her has been shown chiefly by rather myopic writers in Spanish of a romantic or pious disposition. Relatively recently, Francisco Franco, retaining the piety but not traditionally romantic, held out the joint reign of Fernando and Isabel as precedent for his own: they were the Catholic Kings who had unified Spain, championed the faith, and steered a course toward empire. During his regime there was a movement, gaining force in the 1960s, to have *Isabel la Católica* proclaimed a saint; and another emerged, fueled by reaction to the first, to look elsewhere, at Spain's society, at its economy, at anything but its rulers, and especially at anything but her. Today the pendulum is swinging back: most recently the eminent Spanish historian, Miguel Angel Ladero Quesada, has striven for balance in an overview of the crown and Spanish unity in her times. Beyond Spain, the one thorough history of her in English dates from the nineteenth century. The Bostonian, William H. Prescott, admired her strength and determination, but he assumed Fernando's complete joint authority and limited his narrative to war and politics.

Isabel herself has remained elusive. Although she signed thousands of the documents now stored in Spain's archives, and most are of an impersonal nature, their difficult fifteenth-century hand has been a deterrent to readers. She can, however, be more intimately encountered through the few surviving letters she exchanged with Fernando, through the chronicles and letters of her contemporaries, and through the literature, art, and architecture of her reign. This biography comes of seeking her in all those places; that search has yielded as well an appreciation of those contemporaries through whose eyes she appears.

One of the most articulate of them was the ambassador who returned from Egypt in 1502. Pietro Martire d'Anghiera, a native of Milan and a humanist, a teacher of the liberal arts, who came to Spain to tutor noble youths and stayed, to become known as Pedro Mártir, a fixture at court. Mártir sopped up the atmosphere there and relayed it in several hundred letters to friends and benefactors. His arrival coincided with the siege of Granada's principal port, Málaga, in 1487. His enthusiastic letters from then on reveal him instantly caught up in the prevailing spirit of militant, high-minded endeavor and dazzled by the ability and resolve of the King and Queen—so caught up that he became a soldier in the campaign against Granada. He wrote of being present at Granada's surrender in January 1492, of the expulsion of Spain's Jews that March, and of the commissioning of a fellow Italian in April to attempt to reach the Far East by sailing westward into the Atlantic. Mártir's was the first account of the discoveries of the Genoese who had become a Spanish admiral, Christopher Columbus.

Mártir felt himself a part of great events. He exulted in the atmosphere of religious conviction, and in the energetic and effective pursuit of ideals that he shared; he delighted in the power and the glory of the monarchs he served. He was particularly devoted to the Queen and became attached to her court. His mission to Egypt as her ambassador, though coming late in her life, can set the stage for her and for some of her principal goals, their scope, context, and pursuit, for what Isabel wanted for Spain and how she presented it.

Pedro Mártir left Granada in August 1501, lost three servants to plague, braved wartorn Italy where the Spanish fought the French, took ship in Venice, eluded Mediterranean pirates, and arrived in Alexandria only to find the Sultan had gone to Babylon or, as it was coming to be called, Cairo. He followed, waited weeks, and then, February 2, 1502, al-Ashraf Qānṣūh al-Ghawrī, Sultan of Babylon, Lord of Egypt, Syria, and Palestine, summoned the Spanish ambassador into his presence, secretly, to ensure that the many and influential Muslims and Jews who were emigrants from Spain not know.

Mártir had come to dissuade the Sultan from his threat to treat Christians in his domains as Spain's sovereigns were treating non-Christians in theirs. And, since the Sultan held Jerusalem, he had also to be dissuaded from withdrawing his protection from its Christian holy places. The Sultan's attitude was not auspicious. Why, Qānṣūh asked, should he not retaliate? For the Spanish monarchs had not only taken the Muslim kingdom of Granada, but after agreeing that its people might stay and keep their religion, they had forced them to become Christians. And why had they expelled the Jews?

Mártir replied that he had not been sent to render account. His monarchs were so powerful they feared no lord or king, for their empire extended from the pillars of Hercules to the Sultan's coasts. Still, he would satisfy his curiosity. Many years ago, when the Visigoths ruled Spain, there was a count named Julian, whose daughter having "received an injury" from Rodrigo, the King of Spain, had in revenge called in Muslims from Africa. They swept ruthlessly through Iberia, except for its forbidding northern mountains, in the kingdom of Asturias, where many Christians had sought refuge. Those Christians, taking as their captain one Pelayo, fought back valiantly, the women contributing to victory, hurling stones and shooting arrows from on high. And from then on, over centuries, the land had slowly been recovered, until the present monarchs had completed its reconquest. And so they had injured no one, for they had regained from cruel usurpers what their ancestors had lost.

As for their going back on their word, it was not so. Many Muslims and Jews had been allowed to leave; rather than forcing them to turn Christian, the monarchs had emulated Christ who spurned force. Even when the entire kingdom of Granada had revolted two years ago, its Muslims killing many Christians and deserving death, the monarchs had shown mercy, allowing them to become Christian or providing ships for those who preferred to go to Africa. In two of their highnesses' many kingdoms, Aragón and Valencia, there yet lived many more thousands of Muslims than Christians, peacefully, with no less liberty and protected by law, attending their mosques, riding horses, possessing arms, building houses, cultivating fields, owning cattle.

He then embarked on an explanation outraging today's sensibilities but further illuminating the official stance within Spain. As for the Jews, Mártir explained, his monarchs had expelled them because they were "a putrid pestilence," infecting Christians and breeding heresy, and if the Sultan but knew the contagion they spread, he would again throw them out of Egypt, as had the Pharoahs, for they dirtied what they touched, corrupted what they looked upon, and destroyed all by their words, disrupting the divine and the human. Merely to expel such abominable people had been mild and merciful.

Mártir's account to that point was faithful to perceptions widespread in Isabel's Spain, a vision of reality she fostered there as well as exported, although it was a distortion of the way things were or had happened. How that vision arose, the royal role in promoting it, how perception and events differed, and finally how comprehension of the past had affected the course of subsequent history, events, and attitudes are all part of Isabel's story.

"What the Western Christians who made the Crusades possessed," it has been observed, "was above all an image of Jerusalem."[2] Abroad in fifteenth-century Spain was a vision, a prophecy that a Spanish ruler would regain the holy places and usher in a final, golden age of the world, and in that last great crusade the ally was to be Babylon-Egypt. That the purported author and seer was Merlin attests to an unexpected and even more lofty international collaboration.

Mártir, as instructed, next turned to discussion of alliance with the Sultan, but in far more mundane terms, mindful that Egypt stood in effect as Spain's bastion against the Turks, who threatened Europe. Indeed, as has been said, "confrontation between Latin Christendom and Ottoman Islam . . . was the decisive political and cultural reality of the era, the one conditioning all others." Moreover, he not only reminded the Sultan that they shared a powerful enemy in the Ottoman Turks, but that they also shared participation in a vital trading network linking Europe, Africa, and Asia, connecting the Indian Sea with the Mediterranean and through it with the Atlantic Ocean. Between them they controlled the great hubs of commerce at either end of the Mediterranean Sea: Seville, Valencia, Barcelona, and Sicily in the West, and Alexandria in the East with its connections to Asia. Both men knew that even while warring against the Muslims of Granada, Spaniards had traded in Alexandria, and that a favorable balance of trade, helped by a flow of gold from Muslim Africa had contributed to Spanish victory. They knew that they shared military and economic interests. The Sultan, greatly admiring the power of the Spanish sovereigns and recognizing their value as allies against their mutual enemy, was won over. He would do all they asked, but their envoy must leave as he came, secretly.

The Castile of Isabel's birth calls to mind a kingdom much like a closed crusader fortress. Yet was it? Within its walls there lived the avowed religious archenemies, Muslims and Jews, and, fortress or not, its commodious gates opened to trade with many other nations and peoples and it had formed surprising, quiet alliances. And there was much more paradox, both obvious and hidden, to be found in that Castile by a child born in 1451.

I

PRINCESS

❦ 1 ❦

On the *Meseta*
1451–1460

On Thursday, April 22, at four and two-thirds hours after midday in the
year of our Lord 1451 was born the Holy Catholic Queen, Doña Isabel,
daughter of the King, Don Juan II, and of the Queen, Doña Isabel, his second wife.

Cronicón de Valladolid

The Queen, Our Lady, from childhood was without a father, and we can
even say a mother. . . . She had work and cares, and an extreme lack of
necessary things.

Fernando del Pulgar[1]

A GIFT FOR AN INFANTA

IN 1451 the town council of Murcia heard from the king, Juan II, of the
birth on April 22 of an *infante*. An *infante* could be male or female, but
the more specific term for a princess other than the heir-presumptive is
infanta. Such recourse to ambiguity, while undoubtedly cleared up by the
royal messenger, carried notice that the king and his queen consort, Isabel
of Portugal, had had a child who could inherit the crown of Castile. This
infante was indeed an *infanta*, and was given the name of Isabel. At birth
she was second in line of royal succession after her half-brother, Enrique,
King Juan's son by his first queen, María of Aragón. And Enrique, though
26 years old and married for quite a while, remained childless, making Isabel's succession not improbable.

Murcia's councillors quickly organized a procession and mass of thanksgiving for the arrival of the royal child and the health of the Queen. They
took longer to comply with the order accompanying the king's announcement that they honor the occasion with a gift to a certain royal secretary

and treasurer. Faced with what to give and how to pay for it, the town fathers found 10,000 *maravedís* through mortgaging of income from municipal sales taxes on meat and fish, then decided that a fitting present to the royal functionary would be an *esclava mora*, a female Muslim slave. When the woman selected died of plague, and Murcia's *corregidor*, the royal official imposed on most municipal councils to oversee and expedite their business, simply appropriated another, an irate couple complained to the council, arguing that their Miriem had been seized against her will. There is no record that Miriem was ever consulted, even when her masters agreed to sell her for the 10,000 *maravedís* budgeted by the council and paid through Abraham de Aloxas and Mose Axarques, Jews who either handled its funds or made advances against future revenues. With so much invested, the councilmen also hired a man and mule to deliver Miriem to her new owner.[2]

Plague and Muslims were facts of life in this Castilian town near the western edge of the Mediterranean Sea and had long represented a twin-pronged threat to Europe. In 1451, the year of Isabel's birth, the most dreaded Muslims were the Ottoman Turks who, under the Grand Turk, Mehmet II, began moving westward in earnest; Constantinople would fall two years later. Bubonic plague had arrived in Europe from the eastern Mediterranean a century earlier, carried by fleas on rats that infested ships docking in Italian and southeastern Spanish ports. Thousands, perhaps hundreds of thousands, of people had died of it, among them the King of Castile, Alfonso XI, while he was besieging Muslim Gibraltar, his death triggering a series of events leading to the reign of a new dynasty, which was Isabel's. Now, in the mid-fifteenth century, although the devastated populace and economy were recovering, epidemics still occurred sporadically. A younger brother's death, purportedly caused by bubonic plague, would open for Isabel the way to the crown. And during her reign, metaphors for evil, of pestilence and defilement, would proliferate, and diatribes against Jews similar to the one Pedro Mártir delivered to the Sultan of Egypt would be couched in plague terminology. But that is getting ahead of the story.

MADRIGAL DE LAS ALTAS TORRES

Isabel was born far inland, behind the high walls of Madrigal de las Altas Torres—Madrigal of the High Towers—in the heart of the *meseta*, the flat tableland at the heart of Castile. The forty-eight *altas torres* rising along the 40-foot-high walls ringing the town spoke of safety in a world geared to war. And they posed paradox as well, for they were of *mudéjar* construction, brick and rubble, of Arabic inspiration. Madrigal, like other places on Spain's central plateau, had been alternately occupied by Christians and Muslims until well into the eleventh century, and it was home to some inhabitants of Muslim culture afterwards. In the great house (called the royal palace) abutting those walls, Isabel toddled under intricately worked wooden ceilings, *artesonados*, carved by Muslim subjects of Castile's king, *mudéjares*. And tradition has it that she was baptized in Madrigal's church of San Nicolás, in its baptismal font thickly encrusted with gold from Muslim Africa.

The redbrown soil around Madrigal is fertile, in the summer a landscape of wheat, grapevines, and Mediterranean light, irrigated by the Zapardiel river to the east, the Trabancas river to the west. In 1451 it was essentially an agricultural town, with roughly 900 *vecinos*, or householders, translatable as between 3000 and 4500 inhabitants. Outside its four gates, the land had been worked in concentric circles of garden plots, vineyards, and fields of grain; beyond lay deep woods. The forests provided firewood and game—"with the help of Madrigal the king's table held many partridges"—as well as acorns to feed pigs and cattle and sustain the numerous sheep until some trekked northwards to spring and summer pasture. The vineyards yielded Madrigal's white wine, "renowned for its good bouquet and better taste," celebrated in Castile and sought after abroad, so celebrated that the poet, Jorge Manrique, could freely allude to it. "*¡O, Beata Madrigal/ ora pro nobis a Díos!*"—"O blessed Madrigal, pray for us to God," he has a drunken widow in a tavern toast irreverently, punning on supplication to Mary, mother of Jesus Christ.[3]

DARKNESS AND LIGHT

Only an occasional reference sheds light on Isabel's childhood. At 17, she wrote to her half-brother the king Enrique IV accusing him of having treated her badly; she came to present herself as a semi-orphan raised in obscurity and kept in want by him. Her court chronicler, Fernando del Pulgar, was to state that her early years were spent "in extreme lack of necessary things," and that she was without a father and "we can even say a mother."

Isabel was three when her father, Juan II of Castile, died. Enrique succeeded him. He was 30 years old. He had had no children with his first wife, Blanca of Navarre, and his second, Juana of Portugal, would have none until Isabel was ten; until then she grew up seeing her younger brother, Alfonso, born in November 1453, when she was two, as the heir-apparent to Castile's crown and herself as second in line. The new king, since childless, looked upon her as a potential problem. Seemingly, she was left in highly insecure circumstances.

The young dowager-queen, Isabel of Portugal, 27 years old at her husband's death, and her children then took up residence in the nearby town of Arévalo. Shortly thereafter, Enrique called on her accompanied by a favorite, Pedro Girón, Master of the military order of Calatrava. Girón, according to chronicler, Alonso de Palencia, made some indecent suggestions, shocking to her. Palencia, who is generally vitriolic about both

Enrique and Girón, went on to conclude that the importuning of this over-hasty, unwelcome (and, patently, not sufficiently noble) suitor threw Isabel of Portugal into so profound a sadness and horror of the outside world, that she then "closed herself into a dark room, self-condemned to silence, and dominated by such depression that it degenerated into a form of madness."[4]

Yet a chronicler more in touch with events at the time dates her retreat into darkness earlier, from her daughter's birth. Whatever the date, Isabel grew up with a deeply disturbed mother who locked herself away from the light of day. The child may well have dreaded becoming like her, and suffered tension between that dread and affection for her mother. Surely too she was aware that her own birth was among the causes rumored for her mother's madness. It is tempting to conjecture that qualities she displayed as an adult—love of order and the striving for it, a no-nonsense, highly rational stance, and a sharply defined personality—were honed in reaction to her mother's condition, and even to think that her dedication to light in all its forms, especially its religious associations—her abhorrence of dark forces, her determination to cleanse the body politic and rid the land of defilement—were not unrelated to the circumstances of her childhood.

Isabel, then, was raised in several sorts of obscurity, her quest toward light a motif running through her life. She began as a Cinderella figure, her early obscurity a sort of purgatory and a test of moral fiber she passed magnificently. Such has been the accepted version of her early years; it was her own version. It is incomplete.

Arévalo, 15 miles from Madrigal and like it a market town, was known as the best fortified of royal towns. There, her mother's condition notwithstanding, Isabel spent her early years in great stability and familial warmth. For when she was two and her mother again pregnant, her widowed grandmother, Isabel de Barcelos, arrived from Portugal. Tellingly, when first mentioned in the chronicles Isabel de Barcelos is in her forties and sitting, at Juan's request, in his privy council. Contemporaries, among them the chronicler Diego de Valera, recognized in her "a notable woman of great counsel and great help and consolation to her daughter"; Valera added that her death, in 1465, "was very harmful."[5] Surely she ran her daughter's household. Children like Isabel who go on to propel themselves beyond their earlier circumstances often see as a model someone in addition to their parents. Isabel of Castile had her grandmother. Later, as queen, she enjoyed keeping about her elderly women of good repute and good family.

Isabel de Barcelos came of royal Portuguese stock with a history of going for the throne and of doing it with claims far weaker than would be those of her Castilian grandchild. Daughter of Portugal's most powerful noble, the first Duke of Braganza, who was an illegitimate son of the King, João I, she had married her uncle, the *infante* dom João, that king's namesake and one of his five sons with Philippa, his Queen. Philippa's father was John of Gaunt, Duke of Lancaster; her mother Costanza was a Castilian *infanta*. Young Isabel's was the royal blood of Castile, Portugal, and England, and dynastic pride is apparent in the name Isabel having been repeated through seven generations, beginning with the thirteenth-century Portuguese queen canonized as Santa Isabel for the miracles she performed.

Isabel's *aya* or nurse-governess in Arévalo was also Portuguese. She was Clara Alvarnaez, the wife of Gonzalo Chacón, to whom Juan II had consigned his childrens' education and who was the dowager-queen's *camerero*, or administrator of household. Oddly enough, Chacón had earlier filled the same post for Juan II's *privado*, or favorite, Alvaro de Luna, an adversary of the Queen, Isabel of Portugal. Chacón and Clara Alvarnaez remained close to Isabel throughout their lifetimes. Nonetheless, Chacón had stayed loyal to Luna while he lived and venerated his memory afterwards: attributed to him is a chronicle of Luna's life, written during Isabel's early years. It is permeated with the prevailing ideals of absolute royal authority. The subsequent behavior of Chacón's young royal charges, Isabel and Alfonso, amply demonstrated that from the outset they both held lofty opinions of the meaning of royal sovereignty.

Between Chacón and her grandmother Isabel was raised in a household imparting to her a self-esteem bound up with high station in life and a firm belief in her own royal lineage as worthy of a crown and supportive of a vision of that crown gleaming with the luster of near-divine monarchy. Moreover, the circumstances of her childhood were such as to stimulate idealizing her royal parents and imagining them in their prime, just as she would have them sculpted on their tombs at Miraflores, where they lay side by side, resplendant in full regalia, amid symbols of worldly power and divine majesty. Even so, over the household's warmth and enhancing of self-worth hovered the shadow of her mother's illness, and, beyond, lay an uncertainty as to how a wider world, known to be wary of *infantes*, would treat her.

VISITORS AND OTHERS

A child growing up in that *meseta* town would know there was more to it than met the eye. The town's size did not equal its strategic importance. He who wants to be Lord of Castile, it was said, had to hold Arévalo. And Arévalo took outsized pride in being a theatre of Castile's glorious past. Hercules himself reputedly had founded it, *el gran Hércules* who, coming through Africa had brought Egyptians and Chaldeans to settle there, had founded Segovia, Avila, and Salamanca as well, and had left as memorials to his achievements the arches of an aqueduct (in fact, Roman in origin), statues of himself, and bulls carved of stone recalling those he had bested in Libya. In 1454 Arévalo had at least two such *toros*, and in its churches were to be seen some ancient caskets of hewn stone, revered as "caves of Hercules." That designation surely referred to the widespread legend that Spain had been destroyed by Muslim invaders because its Visigothic king Rodrigo had opened a charmed casket hidden in Hercules' cave beneath the Gothic capital, Toledo. And just outside the town's walls stood a circle of arched boulders where, as everyone knew, Hercules, that demigod claimed as illustrious ancestor by Castile's kings and nobles, had revealed the secrets of the movement of the stars and their influence on the world below.

That the venerated Visigoths too had found the area to their liking was remembered in the name of the nearby hamlet, Palacio de Goda. Arévalo also recalled Saint James himself, the apostle of Jesus Christ, having preached there. Arévalo's device was an armed knight sallying forth from a castle, commemorating its men who had fought the Moors in the crucial battle of Las Navas de Tolosa, opening Andalusia to reconquest by Castile. Such then was that small town, mindful of a large past and a present importance to the crown, where Isabel spent her childhood, in a *caserón* abutting its thick walls.

Although Isabel did not live at court after her father's death, her isolation was relative, for court figures came to Arévalo. Shortly after Juan died his sister, María, Queen of Aragón, arrived, visibly saddened. This aunt of Isabel's was powerful in her own right; for nearly 20 years she had effectively ruled Aragón while her husband its king, Alfonso V, known as the Magnanimous, held court in Naples. Alfonso's sister, also named María, had been Juan of Castile's first wife. Those queens, cousins married to cousins, at crucial junctures had mediated in the turbulent relations between Castile and Aragón, that is, between brothers, husbands, and sons. At the time it was said that if the queen of Castile were king, there would be peace and well-being in the realm. Now in 1454, Aragón's queen stayed on in Arévalo to negotiate with her nephew, Enrique IV, on behalf of her husband's brother, Juan, king of Navarre. It was agreed that Juan make formal renunciation of some Castilian claims of his in return for 3.5 million *maravedís* annually. It would be the last of her many good offices, for she died the next year. Enrique never paid. In 1459 Juan of Navarre succeeded to the crown of Aragón; he would more than compensate for his losses in Castile, dynastically, through the marriage of his son, Fernando, to its future queen, Isabel.

Enrique, Castile's new king, and his court also came to Arévalo, and stayed from September 1454 to January 1455. He undoubtedly lived in its castle and welcomed the aid, or anyway the image as family, of the dowager-queen and her mother in his negotiations with Portugal for the hand of their cousin Juana, the sister of Portugal's king, Afonso, to become his second wife. And from Arévalo, soon after his accession, Enrique had war cried against Muslim Granada.

"Enrique ordered those of his council and his *contadores mayores* to Arévalo," recounted Diego de Valera, reflecting an expectancy in the air, "because there would be drawn up the *libranza* of lands and *mercedes* and *raciones* and *quitáciones* and alms and salaries for the people he had ordered to carry war to the Moors."[6] (*Libranzas* were lists of disbursements. Lands were payments to nobles for providing military units. *Mercedes* were royal privileges. *Quitaciones* were recompense for public services. *Raciones* were stipends for maintaining men-at-arms ready for war.) The reconquest was to be resumed. Whatever the preparations for war that winter meant to a three year old, marshaling for war would recur throughout her youth and eventually become a way of life. But she would not again be present to see it directed against Muslims until she herself took up the reconquest.

The royal court and the dowager queen, then, arrived in Arévalo at about the same time and when, shortly thereafter, Enrique and Girón had called on the young and recent widow, it was most probably because Girón, with Enrique's approval, wanted to control through their mother the *infantes*. And there was Juan's will, leaving to his wife an allowance and towns, including Madrigal and Arévalo, and stipulating she have custody of the children "as long as she remained chaste."[7] Girón was clearly proposing she should not do so. That encounter could have done nothing to endear Enrique to Isabel's mother and grandmother, nor to alter their refusal to allow the children to become part of Enrique's entourage.

AN EDUCATION

Isabel of Portugal was devout. Having been unable to conceive a child in the early years of her marriage, she did so shortly after making a vow to Holy Mary, which she fulfilled by a barefoot pilgrimage to the shrine of Santa María de la Vega outside the town of Toro. In Arévalo, her household was in touch with Franciscans whose convent stood just beyond the town's walls and who belonged to the austere Observant branch of that religious order. Tradition has it that those friars had a reputation for sanctity and learning and a hand in Isabel's education, and that the convent had a fine library, for, Franciscan vows not to own anything notwithstanding, one Gonzalo de Madrigal, a teacher of theology, had collected its books, then solicited and received from the pope an order against its ever being broken up. There too a cynosure of spirituality and learning, Alfonso de Madrigal, known as *El Tostado*, had begun his own career as a student, and there his death in 1455 was surely mourned. Years later, Isabel supported publication of his writings. Whatever the extent of her contact with those Franciscans, she was always partial to that religious order, although not exclusively. She was remembered as having sent gifts to at least one of its friars, "whom she had known well when she was growing up in Arévalo,"[8] and, as she instructed in her will, she was buried in Franciscan habit, a shroud favored by some of her royal progenitors and thought to facilitate entry into heaven. In Arévalo too, with Enrique's court, was an old confessor and advisor highly esteemed by her father, Lope de Barrientos, Bishop of Cuenca. Juan had charged Barrientos in his will with overseeing the education of Isabel and Alfonso. Whatever the extent to which he did so, Barrientos had written a treatise against magic, and Isabel would later own a copy of it and express a similar abhorrence of divination, a belief in Divine Providence active directly in human affairs, and a faith in the efficacy of a disciplined and free will, in God's power, and human initiative.

There with the court too was Rodrigo Sánchez de Arévalo, diplomat, writer, and priest, Enrique's counselor and secretary, who, although his name speaks of a family connection to the town, had become accustomed to life in Burgos and at the courts of France and the papacy and did not much like wintering in what he termed "*esta desierto villa de Arévalo.*" He not only provides an example as to why Isabel's childhood came to be seen as shut away, but faced with enforced country life he passed time, as would a Florentine in the same predicament, by writing on politics and the education of the prince. And, if Sánchez de Arévalo interested himself in the education of the royal children encountered there, his views and experience supported schooling for Isabel; he had himself attended an elementary school for both boys and girls, the free school of the Dominicans at Santa María de Nieva, whose patron was Isabel's paternal grandmother, Queen Čatalina (remembered as formidable). And he avowedly held in high esteem one woman in particular, whom Juan II had also greatly admired, Joan of Arc, known in Castile as *la poucella*, the virgin; Sánchez de Arévalo had been in France during her meteoric career. His admiration of her was equalled by Chacón, whose chronicle of Luna recalled glowingly the grand reception accorded her envoys by Juan of Castile and Luna, so taken by her great deeds that he carried about a letter from her and displayed it at court as though it were a holy relic. All in all, it is unlikely that as a child Isabel, while hearing tales of those more usual exemplars for girls, nonviolent women saints failed to learn that passivity was to be scorned, a strong, assertive, disciplined will admired, and of the deeds of that devout and intrepid woman warrior and the great esteem she enjoyed in Spain. Moreover, Chacón, at pains to counter allegations that Luna had been in league with the Devil and to discount all superstition *per se*, stated in the chronicle that God alone had inspired Joan of Arc, that He performed marvels, but that generally He acted in reassuringly rational ways. Chacón's essentially moral and commonsensical outlook, one he shared with Juan's principal advisors, accorded with views Isabel later displayed and surely had influence in shaping them.

Just what Isabel was taught is unknown; as she later demonstrated, she received the usual female training in domestic arts. She surely too learned the Portuguese spoken at home, and she reportedly rode well. The upbringing of her younger brother, Alfonso, is more easily retrieved, from a description of the essentially chivalric education customary to highborn Castilian boys in the chronicle of Pero Niño, Count of Buelna, who was a follower of Luna's. Before the age of 14 Pero Niño had learned from the *ayo* provided him by the king that "knights have not been chosen to ride an ass or mule," that they must, rather, excel in jousting, be courteous and well spoken, and, preferably, well built and well dressed, indeed the model of fashion. A knight had to know all about armor, saddles, and horses, and to shine with sword, lance, and crossbow, as well as at games of darts, bowls, discs, and stones. He was to avoid women and greed, be sober, think before speaking, trust to experience, and value good advice and friends. Above all, he must master himself: "Plato says we should go against our appetite," the soul restrain the body. All extremes were evil. His heart was to be governed by the virtues. He had to have great faith in God and uphold Holy Mother Church. He was not to believe in the false prophecies of Merlin and others and he was to beware of alchemists. He might see in Hercules a paragon of knightly virtue.[9] From his later behavior it is certain that Alfonso would have argued with none of those injunctions, and, from that of Isabel, that she herself held to many of those chivalric precepts.

For six or seven years, during most of her childhood, Isabel lived in Arévalo. It was the longest she was ever to stay in any one place. Whatever her formal education there, children in fifteenth-century Europe were seldom sheltered from any aspect of life. And Isabel, highly intelligent, curious, and observant, was undoubtedly aware of much of what came within Arévalo's purview. In that upcountry town, as everywhere in Europe, religion, its holy days, its ceremony and ritual, marked time and events and the cycles of the year. It impinged upon behavior, intellect, and emotions, and it explained human relationships, the natural world, and the universe. Through it filtered all acceptable varieties of knowledge and speculation. Living in a pious household, in contact with devout friars, very familiar with worship in Arévalo's churches, the hours of her days noted by their bells, Isabel was immersed in the Christianity of time and place.

It was no secret that Arévalo's principal church, San Miguel, was built on the remains of mosque, reflecting a time-honored practice in Castile of reconsecrating mosques as churches and often dedicating them to Saint Michael the militant archangel. Often too, they were dedicated, as was another in the town, to Santa María de la Encarnación, Holy Mary of the Incarnation—the doctrine of Incarnation, since so hated by Muslims, signifying Christian triumph over the infidel. Isabel would see to it that Granada's mosques bore those same holy names, and she would not forget those particular cults in her own devotions.

Yet even while becoming steeped in a Roman Catholicism militantly opposed to Islam, the royal child became accustomed to a Christianity borrowing culturally and materially from Muslims. For Arévalo was among the most *mudéjar* of Castilian towns. Its churches, its walls and towers, its bridges and houses, and the porticoed arches over its streets had all been constructed in *mudéjar* style, of *ladrillo*, bricks and rubble. (Examples of that architecture still stand in Arévalo today; among them the church of San Juan adjoining the site of the royal palace, the Muslim-inspired belltower of the church of San Nicolás, and the church of San Martín with its two *mudéjar* Romanesque towers.)

Isabel was also accustomed to the physical presence in the town of people of Muslim culture and of Jews, to other peoples of other customs and religions, thought of as racially different, looked down upon, but there, a fact of daily life. In the 1450s among Arévalo's inhabitants was one of the largest concentrations in any Castilian town of *mudéjares*, Muslim subjects, and a Jewish *aljama* whose rabbi, Tsaddic of Arévalo (who died in 1454) and his historian son Josef were distinguished afar for their learning. In Castile's towns at that time Muslims and Jews generally lived, not in closed-off precincts, but alongside Christians. Yet while the young *infanta* became accustomed to the polycultural life of Castile, it was most likely at a distance. For although she may have seen and observed them, and been served by them, it is unlikely that she mingled with Jews or Muslims, or with any of the other townspeople.

That was not true regarding another sort of Muslim who came to Arévalo, highborn Granadans, honored guests at the Castilian court. In Isabel's childhood, an embassy arrived in Castile led by Abū al-Ḥasan ᶜAlī, the son of Granada's king, Abū Naṣr Saᶜd. Juan II and then Enrique enjoyed watching the prince and his retinue riding Moorish fashion, *a la jineta*, on a low saddle, short-stirruped, knees high, on small fast horses, a manner preferred by Enrique and other Castilians as well. Reputedly a splendid rider herself, did Isabel when very young watch too? Yet if she had firsthand experience of the reality of the mixed population of Iberia and of the elegance of Muslim knights, she also encountered, very close to home, constant reminders of the royal obligation to Christian reconquest.

Enrique had, immediately after his father died, ostensibly "to prevent rumblings and all suspicion," asked the Archbishop of Toledo, Alfonso Carrillo, to persuade the dowager queen to come to court, in vain. While acknowledging herself and her children in the king's power and subject to his will, she stoutly refused. Her determination, or perhaps her mother's, won out and, instead, Enrique posted in Arévalo 200 men to guard his stepmother and her children, that is, to ensure control of them. The children's proximate world included those guards, and among them were old border fighters, undoubtedly with inflated memories of campaign against Granada, a contest still thought of as unfinished. One, Fernando de Villasaña, had raided Granadan border forts and been with a force succoring the Christian outpost of Huelma, its conquest fifteen years earlier still celebrated. Too, such bygone campaigns remained vivid through the popular ballads and legends commemorating the feats of Christian knights and even then becoming fashionable at court. Those ballads, and veterans' tales of glorious exploits, *hazañas*, against the infidel who was also worthy adversary, all imparting a nostalgia for more heroic times and dedication to high purpose, were part of the ambience of growing up in Castile. So were, in obvious contrast, mounting complaints of Enrique's annual and far less glorious forays against Granada. Even so, Isabel favored their purpose, presented as a religious one. It is recorded that, in 1458, the *infanta* Isabel received a bull of indulgence for her contribution of 200 *maravedís* to that year's Granadan campaign.

A young captain of the Arévalo guards, Pedro Puertocarrero, a grandson of the Lord of Moguer, represented another facet of Castilian reconquest. Moguer was a thriving port of Andalusia. Its seamen would one day join those of nearby Palos on an Atlantic expedition that Isabel would sponsor and place under the command of one of the Genoese so familiar in southern Spanish ports, Christopher Columbus. Indeed, the heritage of such Andalusians included Atlantic venturing and the war of reconquest waged at sea; remembered were the great battles Christian navies had fought against African Muslims in the Strait of Gibraltar. Moreover, while Isabel was growing up in Arévalo, men out of Andalusian ports sometimes competed, sometimes cooperated with the Portuguese in seeking to profit from cargoes of African slaves and, even more, from African gold. Andalusians were known to be audaciously, and often extralegally, gaining a foothold in North Africa, sailing out into the Atlantic, and raiding and trading along the West African coast.

Isabel de Barcelos would have had a different, Portuguese version of Christian reconquest, one not focused on Granada but extending overseas. Her father-in-law, João I of Portugal, led expeditions against strategic Ceuta opposite Gibralter—and in a North African mosque-become-church knighted his sons, among them, João, whom she was to marry. Another was Henrique, known to history as Henry the Navigator, who was devoted to both chivalry and crusade and during Isabel's childhood was gaining renown for avidly promoting West African exploration. He asserted that his horoscope revealed that destiny called him to discover hidden secrets, and that he hoped through contacting the legendary Prester John and his Christian kingdom in Asia to outflank Islam and recover Jerusalem.

Isabel, it is well to remember, had not only a Spanish but a Portuguese heritage. To her mother, her grandmother, her great-uncle, Henrique, and to her *aya*, Clara Alvarnaez, belonged a vision of reconquest more farflung than the Spanish. For to the Portuguese, no longer sharing a land border with Muslims, reconquest had become an aggressive campaign against Islam at sea and overseas, one for Christianity and commerce, ever more focused upon the Atlantic Ocean. Rumor ran of their ever greater wealth in gold and slaves. Theirs was a national enterprise directed to far lands, noble savages—Henrique spoke of hostile people encountered as *homines silvestri*, suitably noble opponents for Christian knights—and to hidden Christians, and fueled by the dream of one day regaining Jerusalem. It was a vision with which Isabel was to demonstrate great familiarity.

Did she hear when she was seven of the campaign to conquer Morocco, to which Dom Henrique had persuaded his admiring nephew, Portugal's new king Afonso V? And did Isabel de Barcelos tell her grandchildren of the pilgrimages her father and her brother had made to that holiest of cities, Jerusalem? Or of the travels of another of João of Portugal's sons, Dom Pedro, and the legends that instantly arose of Pedro's encounters in far lands with marvels and monsters, and with Amazons, widows of a band of Goths and subjects of the Christian ruler, Prester John, in India? Did they hear about a letter that brother-in-law of hers reportedly brought back from Prester John to their father, Juan of Castile? Did Isabel as a child catch the excitement aroused by the quest then being pursued for unknown—hidden—lands and their fabled wealth? If so, it could help to explain her later interest in Africa, the Atlantic, the East and Jerusalem, and her inclination against much learned opinion to back Columbus. Whether or no, throughout her life, Portugal was important to her: sometimes enemy, sometimes competitor, always family.

Whatever else she learned within the household at Arévalo, the assumptions that the Castilian monarchy had a twin commitment to the faith and to reconquest, that wars against the Muslims were the proper business of the king and his people, and that Muslim and Jewish residents were a tolerated anomaly belonged to her early education.

IMPRESSIONS

At 17, Isabel wrote to Enrique accusing him of having treated her badly, much as Pulgar stated that her early years were spent "in extreme lack of necessary things," inferring that Enrique had strapped his father's second family by not honoring the provisions Juan had made for them. Still, Enrique's feelings were known to vacillate. A letter he wrote to her in 1463, before they fell out, is very warm—"you do not have any person in this world who loves you as much as I do"—but could also be construed as implying she was listening to his enemies.[10] Otherwise, the terms of affection with which he addressed her were largely formulaic, yet even formula had basis in the strong sense of familial attachment current among the powerful in fifteenth-century Castile, and she and Alfonso were after all the king's closest relatives, which of course cut two ways. Still, Enrique's most sympathetic chronicler, Diego Enríquez del Castillo, sounds defensive in stating that "the King always treated them [Isabel and Alfonso] with much love and great honor, and showed no less to the Queen their mother"; and goes on to say that he *held* them in safe places.[11] And, unless Enrique made unrecorded trips to Arévalo, after his initial stay there he saw little of them, for he is known to have returned only five years later, in the summer of 1459 and then again the following April. When, in 1461, he brought Isabel and her younger brother to court, as shall be seen, it was not through unalloyed family feeling.

Whatever Enrique's sentiments, the gap heretofore assumed between neglected, deprived child and powerful indeed brilliant monarch is clearly erroneous. Isabel's childhood, if relatively austere by later fifteenth-century standards, was no more than that. Why has it been thought otherwise? Pulgar admired Isabel greatly and, even when critical of her policies, as he was of the Inquisition, he defended her as well intended. Rightmindedness he associated with strength of character. And it was only in considering the formation of her character that he mentioned her early years, leaving the impression that solely through inner strength and firm faith did this neglected child develop into a peerless monarch. For him, and for Isabel herself, a principal explanation for depicting her childhood as unrelievedly dismal is a desire to show that adversity, compelling self-discipline, was the nursery of heroism, just as it was for saints and knights, indeed that tribulation indicated God's special attention and His favor. Thus, the impression conveyed of poor shunted-aside orphan was an image superimposed on reality; while not completely false neither was it true. What was true, and important to her later life is how she herself came to view her childhood, that Isabel saw herself as having triumphed over early adversity, and that she came to understand the worth of presenting the fortitude and will-power to do so as the principal theme of her young years. It is true, too, that latter-day celebrants of her life have tended to mistake that quality of fortitude, which indeed she possessed, for religious piety.

That self-image of hers, of misfortune overcome through her own efforts, owed much to the concept of ideal monarch given cogency during her father's reign. Luna's chronicler, her mentor Chacón, and other men close to him criticized Juan II severely, as Isabel had to be aware, for shirking responsibility and lacking moral fiber. Her own chroniclers—Diego de Valera who spanned the reigns, caustic Alonso de Palencia, and finely attuned Pulgar—saw in Isabel most of the very sterling qualities Juan had lacked, qualities associated with wielding strong personal monarchy, within a universe ordered by Providence and wherein much depended on the rectitude evinced by the monarch of Castile. Traits consonant with the qualities they endorsed as kingly, was their point, traits demonstrated by Isabel as queen, among them moral certitude, decisiveness, ambition, curiosity, piety, prudence, and a firm sense of both royal prerogative and royal obligation, had firm basis in her youth. It was well taken.

Arévalo's isolation was relative. And there she learned a good deal about being ruler of Castile, including that it was encumbent upon the monarch to carry out the reconquest, that royal subjects included Christians, Muslims, and Jews, and that the monarch was expected to develop and display a character in accord with concepts of good kingship. Nor is it surprising that, as Queen, her public image and her own vision of herself, including of her childhood, would come to coincide remarkably.

Growing up in Arévalo, she gained a self-possession, a pride in royal lineage, a sense of both entitlement and responsibility, a regal bearing, and a high morality inseparable from religion and ruling well. At ten, before Enrique finally brought her and her younger brother to court, she had had a more intimate family life, more attention, and more stability of people and place than most royal children ever received. In her veins, she had learned, ran the blood of warriors, of heroic Goths and Moorfighters, of monarchs and saints, of powerful men and women. Hers was a heritage for a queen.

GOD'S DESIGN

Childhood began a definition of self, a self formed through learned moral imperatives: ideals of royalty and chivalry, character-building values, a proud genealogy and history, and beyond all else, reliance on God's design, much of it still hidden, yet to be brought to light.

Light was tenuous. For there was too the internal war of the soul, the stain of original sin, especially dark for women, the daughters of Eve. Light was Eve's counterpart, Holy Mary. Light was Christ. Darkness was ever present in the tricks and enticements of Lucifer, the threat of Antichrist and of descent into the abyss, to be headed off only by militant vigilance and unrelenting personal effort. The battle between the forces of God and the Devil was waged in this world, eternally. The contrast of blackness and radiance was frightening and yet exciting, and it provided high relief, and boundaries, shaping and ordering a cosmos endowed with finiteness and the certitude, ultimately comforting, of God's design.

At some point Chacón took Isabel and Alfonso to Toledo, the old ceremonial capital of the Visigoths, to visit the cathedral and, in it, "the rich and marvelous chapel" where Luna lay. In that chapel they may have seen decorations such as would appeal to children: one tomb is ringed with a frieze of *salvajes*, totally naked except for the turbans on their heads. Such savages, imaginary inhabitants of Prester John's kingdom, equated with chivalrous Saracens by Dom Henrique and by many Castilians as well, represented as well wildmen of those far lands as yet hidden in darkness, which held the key to the reconquest of all Christendom.

More marvels were to be seen outside the chapel. Enclosing the choir, fifty-eight scenes carved in wood presented a late fourteenth-century vision of the universe, of God's design, of paradise lost and the promise of redemption. They recalled the stuff of liturgical plays and countless sermons, projecting a common fund of belief. There were (and still are) to be seen there such scenes as the separation of darkness and light beginning Genesis, Adam and Eve in the Garden of Eden, the adoration of the law received by Moses, and numerous prophecies drawn from everywhere: the Bible, the apocrypha, pronouncements of Roman Sibyls, legend, and the Jewish cabala and hagadah.

What was to be made of it all? A boy being educated as a knight, and his older sister, would know. Castilians were in the habit of seeing in the books of the Old Testament their own ancient history. The royal children would know of the Creation, original sin, and Lucifer, the angel who fell from heaven into hell. God it is, they would learn as had Pero Niño, "who frees us and takes us from the power of the Devil." A *caballero* though had to do his utmost: fight for *ley y fe*, heed the poor, and follow the example of Santiago who, though his members were cut off one by one, never denied Jesus Christ. Both the boy and his sister were to show themselves resolved to do their utmost.

2

A Royal Heritage
Perception and Reality

I'm the king . . . when I pray God answers.

Henry VIII in Maxwell Anderson's
"Anne of the Thousand Days"

. . . the inner turmoil suffered by the king, of which I cannot speak, for if I spoke about it, it would be outer, not inner, and keeping the inner *in* is the very essence of kingship.

Arthur, in Donald Barthelme, *The King*

THE SETTING

ISABEL'S Castile was not simply a kingdom on the western frontier of the known world of Christian Europe, a largely inward-turned frontier society dedicated to Christian advance against the Muslims. Rather, it was a far country from that fifteenth-century view still widespread today. It was above all a land ringed with myth, legend, misperception, and paradox. The enigma that has been Isabel for five centuries is rooted in the image of Castile prevailing at her birth, a view projected by the court.

As has been said, "The stories people believe about what happened in the past will often govern the way they lead their lives." So it was for Isabel, and so this chapter-long look at both the past she inherited and the stories of it current at her birth. It must be at the same time a look at Castile's monarchs and the traditions they elaborated concerning themselves and their kingdom, in the doing defining Spanish monarchy.

In the mid-fifteenth century, amid the rich farmlands of the central Castilian *meseta*, Arévalo and Madrigal at a distance appeared enclosed by turreted walls; yet a closer look revealed gates through which merchants, cattle, sheep, and produce came and went, as did the royal court. Although

Isabel has been said to have been born and raised in the upcountry towns cut off from the wider world, those towns were in fact royal seats housing a mélange of cultures and within a network of wider contact with other peoples and places. Arévalo and Madrigal lay athwart well-traveled trade routes, close to Medina del Campo, the site of one of Europe's greatest semi-annual fairs, an event Isabel much enjoyed. Those routes provided *meseta* towns with extended connections throughout Castile and beyond: to the west, with Portugal; to the north through the mercantile center of Burgos to the Cantabrian coast; to the east with the Mediterranean world through the ports of Aragonese-held Valencia and Murcian Cartagena, and to the south through Seville and its subsidiary Andalusian ports with Mediterranean and Atlantic commercial networks, and with Africa.

If the walls of Madrigal and Arévalo's castle point to a militant society, dedicated to internal crusade, to the enterprise known today as the *Reconquista*—the recovery by Christians of territory from Muslims—their wide gates can stand as metaphor for a less-heralded Castile that was a crossroads of cultural, technological, and commercial exchange. For centuries, Isabel's royal forebears had often participated in them all, even led the way, especially in war and trade. Yet with few exceptions they presented themselves and their kingdom as dedicated only to reconquest, even while more quietly implementing profitable interchange with the wider world, including adversaries. As it turned out, their attitudes and activities, and their presentation of them, had much to do with the world as Isabel saw it. The complex impetus for Pedro Mártir's embassy had long precedent.

A cavalcade of Mediterranean peoples, and Celts from the north, had settled areas of the Iberian peninsula before Rome imposed its law and administration and, eventually, introduced Christianity. As the Roman empire fell away, Visigoths—West Goths—arrived and took over towns, governing from Toledo and locally relying heavily on the most efficacious administrative system in place, that of the church. In 711, Arabs and Berbers crossed the Strait of Gibraltar from Africa to Spain. The Visigoth king, Rodrigo, died battling them, and—the growth of the legend, conveyed by Pedro Mártir to the Sultan, of fierce resistance notwithstanding—thereafter "the conquest of Spain appears to have been a gradual walk-through . . . Muslim columns followed the Roman roads, obtaining the surrenders of key towns, and in many cases leaving Jewish garrisons behind."[1] Remnants of the Visigothic aristocracy retreated into the mountains of Asturias and Cantabria in the far north. From there, Christian chieftains led raids for booty against Muslim-held territory and promoted settlements along frontiers, first in the intervening no-man's land north of the Duero river, then beyond, founding towns such as Madrigal, and, moving ever southwards, gained sway over lands won back from the Muslims. Such endeavor, over the centuries creating Christian kingdoms from Asturias to León to Castile, and then from Castile into La Mancha, Extremadura, and Andalusia, united nobles, clergy, and commoners in a common purpose, political, social, and religious, one promising reward on earth and in heaven, and one identified with royal leadership.

Castilian society evolved within this context. Nobles were defined by owning horses and armor; peasants were relatively free to take advantage of moving frontiers; and kings enjoyed civil, military, and religious authority. They were chief justices, head administrators, war leaders of the armed host, and champions against an enemy whom by the tenth century Christians tended to identify with the minions of Antichrist. Against infidel and demons Isabel's predecessors raised the banner of Santiago Matamoros, St. James the Moorslayer, he who appeared miraculously during battle to ensure Christian victory. And, with advance into Andalusia, they unfurled beside it the standard of Holy Mary, Protectress of the Armies.

Yet, from the first, militant ideal and reality diverged. Initially, advance had been not against the enemy but through settlement in a no-man's land, a conquest of space; war when waged was sporadic. That reality had allowed communities to form, towns to grow, and a complex relationship between Christians and Muslims to evolve. Christians sometimes fought Christians as well as Moors or allied across religious lines. Such was the ambience of Spain's great medieval hero, Rodrigo Díaz de Vivar, El Cid, so known from the Arabic word meaning 'lord,' whose actions and values as relayed in epic poetry are at once so entrancing to latter-day readers and so jarring to their preconceptions, for El Cid did not behave as is expected of an epic hero. A Christian considering himself a loyal vassal of the king of Castile, El Cid hires out as military chief to Muslim lords. He takes Valencia as his own domain, and, says the poet, he leads his men in exploits both highly valorous and part of a day's work "to gain one's bread"—"ganarse el pan." Wealth, as he says to his wife, Jimena, "marvelous and grand wealth is what comes to us"; and it is to be spent on dowering daughters, that is, on aggrandizing family and enhancing lineage. (El Cid had no sons.) He was to serve as exemplar to later nobles who looked to the crown for riches and position and saw no disloyalty to the king in accruing as much independent power of their own as possible. For Isabel, he would exemplify the conquering caballero; she would honor Vivar as his birthplace and, in referring to Valencia, take obvious pleasure in speaking of it as "Valencia del Cid." She too would, like his daughters, come into an inheritance in the absence of a male heir.

But it was El Cid's king, Alfonso VI, whose activity offered closer precedent to Isabel. In 1085 Alfonso, in taking Toledo from his own erstwhile Muslim ally, al-Qadir, who found Christian control preferable to that by internal enemies, did not make major changes: "The new pobladores came to bathe in its Islamic public baths, and to bake their bread in the old ovens."[2] Under Christian domination Toledo remained a city culturally and religiously mixed. Moreover, Alfonso, with no surviving son, left an expanded Castile to his daughter, Urraca, and, in the surrounding region opened by domination of Toledo, her husband, Raimundo of Burgundy, founded and fortified Avila, and in its hinterland one settlement then established was Isabel's birthplace, Madrigal, on a site repeatedly occupied and destroyed by both Muslims and Christians. Madrigal's eleventh-century Christian founders received a royal charter, built a church dedicated to Holy Mary on the foundations of a Muslim fortress, and organized a governing council. On this new frontier between the Duero and Tajo rivers, places like Madrigal were relatively self-governing with fewer priests, monks, and lords than to the north; even so, in common with northern places, leading inhabitants soon came to dominate the towns and their councils. And settling before long in Madrigal and elsewhere were *mudéjares* and Jews.

Such was the reality of the reconquest in the central *meseta*. It brought Isabel's progenitors, Castile's monarchs, authority over vast stretches of land. It brought them jurisdication, attendant revenues, the right to a share of all booty, and the wealth and power assuring royal strength relative to that of the nobles. It also multiplied everyone's opportunity for riches and standing. *Caballeros,* the knights who soon came to control the towns, seasonally rode forth from behind the walls of Avila and other places to join parties raiding Muslims (and sometimes neighboring Christians) for cattle, treasure, slaves, captives to be held for ransom, and to gain royal preferment. Over time they ventured ever further southwards under Castilian lords and kings to take Extremadura, to form the military orders holding that region's vast expanses, and to conquer all Muslim al-Andalus except the kingdom of Granada. Plague arrrived in the mid-fourtheenth century. As it receded, throughout a Castile that now commanded the greatest population and expanse of territory in the Iberian peninsula, nobles took over depopulated places. With labor scarce, less land was cultivated and they turned to raising more sheep, producing more wool.

During Isabel's childhood, population was recovering and abandoned fields were being planted to meet the mounting demand of nearby towns and long-distance trade; peasants were working under contract and seignorial rents were rising. Towns too were prospering. But their councils had literally lost ground, as well as labor, to the great nobles. Those aristocrats were intervening in urban affairs and benefiting from economic upswing, including the growth of trade and its revenues, as was the crown.

Still, service to the king continued to promise them the greatest rewards, which came in the form of lands and jurisdiction, revenues and cash, and titles. The king bestowed them all in the form of *mercedes,* grants made for services, and he could do so at his discretion. While the best rewarded of such services were military, it was enough to have at ready contingents of armed knights and foot soldiers and to convince the monarch that one was in some way deserving. Even so, much of the background to Isabel's reign is explained by the tension between towns and nobles, and by the energy expended by nobles, who, although prospering, were increasingly faced with inflation and fixed rents, and who competed ever more fiercely for royal *mercedes,* sometimes combining to pressure the monarch for generous grants, or at others simply appropriating them. In short, contests for urban power, mercantile enterprise, and infighting for *mercedes* were principal realities of aristocratic life, even though greatly at variance with that aristocracy's vision of itself as devoted to militant activity and ideals tied up with fighting the Moor. There was also another divergence between reality and perception that bears upon our story.

Through the centuries, Spaniards had both pursued Christian advance and, within it, lived alongside Muslims and Jews, as in the Toledo taken by Alfonso VI. Non-Christians resided principally in cities, towns, and villages, but within their own largely self-governing communities directly under royal authority. Travelers in Isabel's youth reported large stretches of the *meseta* inhabited by *"infieles,"* infidels, Muslims and even pagans. Murcia and other places had both Muslim slaves and Muslim communities. El Cid had fought both for and against Muslims, and in the epic poem had both borrowed from and prided himself on cheating Jews. The gap between the perception of Castile as an advancing frontier and the reality of Castile as a land of three cultures, was yet another paradox bequethed to Isabel.

Shifting frontiers and Christian advance, then, had reinforced in the Castile of her birth a polycultural reality, a society made up of disparate religiously defined communities. In all of them culture and religion were inseparable and the individual was a unit within a group united in one faith, whether Christian, Muslim, or Jewish. Bridging those three separate cultures and making some sense of their uneasy coexistence, at the political apex of each, was the authority of the king, who functioned as overlord of all three groups and ultimate mediator among them. The king was, accordingly, looked to both as Christian champion and as defender of non-Christian minorities.

Reflecting this situation, inscribed on the sumptuous tomb of Fernando III are eulogies of him in Hebrew and Arabic, Latin and Castilian, or Spanish. The tomb is in the cathedral of the Seville he conquered in 1248. The Muslim kingdom of Seville had encompassed most of Andalusia; Fernando is said on his deathbed there to have told his son, Alfonso: "I leave you the whole realm from the sea hither that the Moors won from Rodrigo, king of Spain." Fernando also on occasion "had hanged many people and boiled many in cauldrons" for heresy. In the seventeenth century he would be canonized as San Fernando. But before that another Fernando, a descendant and namesake of his, born in Aragón, would carry his sword into battle again, taking up a tradition and its imperatives.

TWO MORE KINGS NAMED ALFONSO AND VISIONS OF MONARCHY

From the perspective of Isabel's reign, particularly important to understanding the scope and terms of monarchy in Castile are the activities and attitudes of Alfonso X, the son who rode into Seville in triumph beside Fernando III and shortly after succeeded to the crown, and those of Alfonso XI, a century later. As a consequence of conquest, Alfonso X was faced with imposing royal authority over vast stretches of land and a heterogenous populace, and desirous that his reign receive due acclaim. His consequent activities—cultural, legal, military, mercantile, and religious—would have lasting impact on monarchy and how it was viewed in Castile.

Alfonso X took up the goal of his predecessors, to drive the Muslims into the sea, but felt he had to go farther for defense and reputation. Impelled by an imperial vision, he strove to make Castile a maritime power, by confronting Muslims at sea as well as on land, extending reconquest into North Africa, controlling the Strait of Gibraltar, and stimulating trade between Mediterranean and Atlantic ports.

With royal encouragement, commerce, from his reign on, was a principal source of royal income, crucial to defense, expansion, and the largesse vital to royal power. Royal income derived principally from customs duties and from sales taxes collected on trade. Commerce in Cantabria's iron with northern Europe was longstanding, and Castilian ships and seamen, most of them from northern coasts, carried to England, France, and Flanders the wool and wines of the *meseta* and the figs and almonds, the olive oil, wines, and cereals, the leather goods, dyestuffs, and African re-exports of Andalusia. Castilians traded too with Germany, Genoa, Venice, Florence, and Catalonia. Basques especially transported much of the merchandise of the western Mediterranean, sailing in and out of Marseilles, Barcelona, Valencia, Almería, Seville, and ports of Italy and North Africa; they and others ventured eastwards, bringing back Asian exports, notably precious cloths and spices, often paid for with the silver so valued in the Far East. Italian ships and merchants were also part of that wider network which, centering on Christian Spain and including Muslim Granada, linked Europe, Africa, and Asia. Within it the most tantilizing and lucrative commerce of all was in African gold.

The longstanding Castilian affection for gold is strikingly visible in the royal clothing and spoils of war housed in the monastery of Las Huelgas, that pantheon of medieval kings. Gold came to those kings as booty, as tribute and gifts from Muslim rulers, and in other ways. While accretion of bullion was the avowed goal, it was not necessarily to royal disadvantage if gold and silver coined in the realm left it, for the crown derived income from the trade in precious metals, as well as from minting, and on occasion from counterfeiting. Castile was in fact a hub of their global exchange.

Nowhere in Europe was silver known to command a higher exchange ratio in relation to gold than in Spain. From Seville and other ports of al-Andalus, major distribution centers, before and after Christian conquest, gold tended to flow to Europe, drawing silver in exchange. Silver then traveled eastwards. Castile's kings profited, quietly and mightily, from that exchange and its attendant activities. The flow of metals seldom appears on customs receipts and minting arrangements were very quiet indeed, as was the prodigious royal activity within the metals trade and the revenue realized from it.

Yet Alfonso X is best remembered as Alfonso *el sabio,* the Learned, who, impelled by curiosity and love of knowledge, and taking into account how badly educated were the Castilian clergy and how wretched their Latin, surrounded himself with Muslim and Jewish scholars and translators and sought to satisfy his own curiosity and educate his realm through retrieving the wisdom stored in Arabic sources. From his court came translations into the vernacular of classical knowledge and oriental learning, of "the whole sect of the Moors and all Jewish law and their very secret science, Cabala." Alfonso brought western and eastern cultural traditions into a particularly Spanish synthesis, potent in Isabel's day.

Still, there were more pragmatic reasons for his intellectual pursuits. Alfonso, perched on a frontier of many sorts, geographical, cultural, and spiritual, felt the tension between the attraction of the complex civilization he found in al-Andalus and its threat to his faith. He sought, as his nephew put it, to know the great errors of Islam and Judaism. Moreover, his delving into Islamic science, history, morality, legend, and lore, and into Arabic astronomy and astrology, culling them all for moral wisdom and the secrets of the universe, was a way to fathom and so carry out the divine plan. It was commonly assumed that secrets of the universe had to be uncovered before the Day of Judgment. Consequently his learning responded to a happy combination of religious imperative, intellectual interest, and royal policy, as well as to an awareness of the international prestige accreting to a learned monarch with a cultured court.

Alfonso founded the University of Salamanca, to add the luster to his reign that would come with cultural flowering, and to train men in canon and civil law, to produce *letrados* who would staff and strengthen royal government. To extend royal authority over a vastly expanded realm, Alfonso set jurists to countering the jumble of local law and custom. He had them draw up a uniform royal law code, the *Fuero Real,* and he personally oversaw the compiling of an encyclopedic treatise on law and government, the *Siete Partidas,* or *Seven Divisions,* that presented the king as near-sacred and his authority as immense.

Over time, the *Partidas* became supplementary law, bolstering monarchy. While owing much to the jurisprudence of imperial Rome and concepts of social order associated with Roman Catholicism, they borrowed as well from Islamic and Jewish legal formulation. They imparted a vision of a well-ordered earthly kingdom, at its head a paragon of virtue, devoted to justice, the near-absolute king: "Kings," they stated, "are vicars of God, each put in his kingdom over its people to maintain them in justice and in truth in temporal matters, just as an emperor in his empire." The king was to guide the people as the head does the members of a body; the king should be elegant; the king is the soul of the people. He had been designated by God as his alter-ego on earth, his viceroy, his mirror image.[3] Isabel would make certain the *Partidas* became the law of the land.

The *Partidas* portrayed an ideal monarch who was the realm's strongest link to God and whose chief duty was to do justice. The well-being of the kingdom, dependent on its right relationship with God, was possible only when the monarch, its head, was virtuous, a state requiring continual exercise of the royal will. The king's conscience, synonymous with his heart, was expected to perceive the will of God.

That concept of divine monarchy was all the more potent in a Spain where there was little pure theology, but, rather, a religious emphasis on applied faith, good works, and Christian morality, and a reliance on God's will as revealed through the prophets, the pope, church doctrine, history, law, and, not least, the royal conscience. Castile's clergy shared and disseminated the royal views on the intimate relationship of the ruler and God, the clergy sanctioned the imperative of reconquest, abetting the fusing of religion and national identity. Conversely, kings often behaved much like high priests. Alfonso X, particularly devoted to Holy Mary, carried her standard into battle, endowed her cult, and served as her troubadour. In his *Cántigas de Santa María—Songs of Holy Mary,* over 400 of them—he praised her and celebrated her miracles, which were often performed in favor of kings. Isabel would own a sumptuously illuminated manuscript of the *Cántigas* and esteem highly the cult of Mary.

Closely related, among the literary projects Alfonso X sponsored were two histories: one of the universe, the other of Spain, both revelatory of the workings of providence and presenting Spain as central to them. In Isabel's library were six manuscript copies of Alfonso's *General estoria,* or *General History,* and seven of his *Primera crónica general,* or *History of Spain.* Both chronicles had eastern and western roots, and they presented Castile's monarchy as the culmination of human history in accord with God's design. Alfonso, as customary in rulers with imperial pretensions, had the past narrated as suitable prelude to his own reign and realm. His histories assumed Castilian hegemony over all Spain and fit the kingdom and its rulers prominently within a universal context that attested to the unfolding of the divine plan. Those histories of his connected Spain with the ancient world through the adventures of the demigod, Hercules. They told of Hercules coming from Troy, conquering Africa, landing at Cadiz, setting up the pillars bearing his name, then traveling through the peninsula and founding Seville and a number of other cities. Among numerous feats, Hercules vanquished Penthesileia, the Queen of the Amazons, women warriors whom some Castilian chronicles identified as the widows of a band of slain Goths. Hercules was a great prince and lord. He had conquered much of Spain and originated the monarchy. He had made his nephew, Hispalis, Spain's king and from him succession had come down to the present, through the native *Hispani* rulers and the Visigothic kings. Moreover, Hercules was a descendant of Noah and thus within both Christian and classical heritage, Alfonso's histories made the longstanding Neoplatonic connections between figures of the Bible and Greek myth. Moreover they fit Spain within a broader Mediterranean tradition, having Spain stem from Troy as did Rome and so possess an equally prestigious origin.

Those histories gave to Spaniards a classical antiquity of their own, a golden age lost and worth restoring, an implicit Eden of simple virtues and natural morality, that of the Goths, the noble barbarians pure in spirit whose descent too was traced from Noah and who had vanquished the Roman empire. Isidore of Seville, writing in the seventh century, had set the tone in the prologue to his history of the Goths: "Of all lands from the West to India, you are the most beautiful, O Spain, sacred and ever-blessed mother of princes and peoples . . . glory and ornament of the earth, home of the famed and gloriously fecund Goths."

While a recipient of the fruits of Alfonso X's labors, Isabel particularly admired another Alfonso, Alfonso XI, who, in the early fourteenth century, had announced God's commending to him of sovereignty and his consequent debt to no earthly power by having himself crowned by the moving arm of a statue of Santiago. This Alfonso went on to gain renown as a mighty warrior in turning back the last Muslim invaders from Africa in the battle of Salado, then fulfilled a battlefield vow by endowing the then-inconsequential shrine of Holy Mary at Guadalupe. He also had the *Partidas* recognized as supplementary law. Not to be emulated was the fact that by 1350, when he died of the black plague while besieging Gibraltar, he had sired 10 children, only one of them, Pedro, by his queen. One of the others, Enrique de Trastámara, rebelled against Pedro, known to history as *el Cruel*, who had murdered Enrique's mother, his brothers, his friends, and even some strangers. Enrique at length killed Pedro in hand-to-hand combat, and so began a new dynasty, the Trastámara, which was Isabel's.

Among the books in Arabic that Alfonso the Learned had had translated was *The Secret of Secrets*, supposedly a collection of the deepest mysteries that Aristotle had revealed to his pupil, Alexander the Great; aside from imparting occult knowledge, it counseled practical wisdom above virtue, though the prince should appear virtuous, and put high value upon control of emotions, upon external show, guarding against revolt and revenge, and strong rule. A century later, Alfonso XI, perhaps aware of his proclivities, commissioned a guide to princely behavior for young Pedro. Adapted from a Latin *Mirror for Princes*, it advised the king-to-be to exercise self-control and free will, and to form himself through meditation, good habits, and a right relationship with God. It purveyed a vision of strong, personal, virtuous monarchy, one much like that in the *Partidas* and royal chronicles. By Isabel's time, such works had become a literary genre and the ideal of a perfect prince and perfect hero elucidated in them a commonplace. The good ruler, they advised, was a divine instrument, a leader in war, a dispenser of justice, and was committed to recovering the land from the Muslims. Yet not forgotten was the injunction Aristotle purportedly made to Alexander, to value practical wisdom above virtue, and to give the appearance of virtue. Isabel inherited a deep respect for public opinion, along with lessons in how to mold it.

PROPHECY AND MONARCHY

Most highly valued in the monarch by Isabel's time was dedication to reconquest. Nor was it considered a secular virtue. The idea of reconquest as a sacred duty had originated over 500 years before she was born. It was alive when a *Prophetic Chronicle* written at the court of Alfonso III of Asturias-León predicted that he would take the lead in recovering the realm of the Goths from the Moors. The author, a *mozárabe*, a Christian of Muslim culture, who was a priest and a refugee from Muslim Spain, based his prognosis on Christian, Jewish, and Muslim sources: on prophecies found in the Old Testament, in the Book of Revelation (or the Apocalypse) of John the Evangelist, and on astrological signs, as well as applying prophecy found in the books of Daniel and Ezekiel to identify Muslim-held Spain, al-Andalus, with the land of Gog and Magog, the giants who were to govern as the Last Judgment neared and until the advent of a liberating warrior-king would usher in a final, golden age. The reign of Gog and Magog was ending, the chronicle said; Alfonso III would soon free the subjugated land and restore the Gothic kingdom. He was, by implication, that divinely chosen warrior-king. Alfonso III did not sweep the Moors from Spain, but royal courts continued to produce such prophecies of the imminent approach of the apocalypse ending the world, and to find in the monarch at hand the prophesied King of the Last Days, a messianic figure heralding the world's final age. And the monarchy of Castile remained identified with recovering the land of Spain from the people known as *moros,* Moors.

Castile's kings continued to receive prophecies, usually at birth, and, as time went on, often attributed to Merlin, who was plucked from Arthur's Britain to become the preferred seer of European monarchs. Compilations ascribed to Merlin drew on the Apocalypse of St. John and they linked royal aspiration, the chivalric values of the Round Table, and revealed religion. In particular, there persisted a hybrid prophecy, reminiscent of the *Prophetic Chronicle* but laid to *el sabio Merlín,* predicting that a king from Spain, born "in the cave of Hercules," would escape it like a lion, would emulate David, Solomon, and Alexander the Great but surpass them all, conquer barbrians, subjugate Africa, and destroy Egypt; then, by regaining Jerusalem, usher in the final golden days. Indeed, Merlin was a prescient standby not only in Spain but in France and Germany, whose warring rulers outdid one another in being hailed as the prophesied last emperor and likened to the returning messiah, so that in Castile such prophecies not only wrapped its kings in a divine mantle but also announced them in international competition for primary position among Europe's crowned heads.

At the birth of Isabel's father, Juan II, in 1405 and again at his accession, such prophecies announced that reconquering Spain was to be the first step and that the time was at hand. Those predictions dovetailed nicely with the avowed intention of Juan's father, Enrique III, to halt westward Muslim advance by taking Granada and then to encircle Islam. Accordingly, that grandfather of Isabel's sent an ambassador to Tamerlane in Samarkand, at the back of the Muslim world, to propose an alliance. Nothing had come of it when Enrique died, not yet 30, within months of his son's birth. He left the campaign against Granada to his brother, Fernando, as well as the guardianship of the infant Juan, jointly with the child's mother, Queen Catalina. Those regents in turn supported a notable wielder of prophecies of Armageddon as imminent.

Throughout Europe at the dawn of the fifteenth century, prophecy was considered eminently respectable, a part of knowledge, among the most reliable of guides to the past and the future, pointing to truths unknowable by rational means, to matters hidden within the design of Divine Providence. And prophesying itself was democratic, for according to church doctrine anyone at all might be a true prophet. The trick was to distinguish truth from falsehood. The rewards were comprehension, acclaim, and a view through the dark mirror. The danger was that prophecy paralleled and sometimes merged with unsanctioned routes to hidden secrets, the occult sciences; among them, suspect but not forbidden, the astrology so entrancing to Alfonso X, viewed as a way of predicting the future based upon the influence of the movement of forms and images in the heavens.

The crusades and the Muslim conquest of Jerusalem in 1244 had given grist to prophecies of the imminence of the last days, usually preached by friars, Franciscans and Dominicans, members of mendicant orders who spread the word of urgent need to choose between doom and salvation. A Dominican preacher, Vicente Ferrer, traveled through Spain during Juan II's minority, holding crowds spellbound with his sermons, all on the same theme, all interpretations of prophecies in the Apocalypse and of the dream recounted in the Book of Daniel: The time was at hand for Antichrist to appear.

Persecuted Christians in ninth-century Muslim Córdoba had identified Antichrist with Muhammad; one such *mozárabe* had taken that notion north, inserting it within the Book of Prophecies he produced at Alfonso III's court. Another identified the Beast of 10 horns found in both Daniel and the Apocalypse with Antichrist, the Devil, and the Muslims as well. Particularly awful, magnificent, and indelible is the imagery in the tenth-century illustrations to the commentaries on the Apocalypse of John the Evangelist by Beatus de Liebana and other monks, illustrations whose popularity was enduring. Always, there lurked the Devil. Lucifer, the fallen angel, was central to the medieval European imagination. He waged a contest for human souls with God; the world was their battleground. God the Father was envisioned as old and bearded, and sternly, fearfully, just. As for the Devil, an early church council in Toledo described him as "a large, black, monstrous apparition with horns on his head, cloven hooves, ass's ears, claws, fiery eyes, gnashing teeth, a hugh phallus and a sulphurous smell."[4] All sinners aided him, belonged to him. He too, like Christ, had a mystical body, but sinners were its limbs; heretics were literally his members. He was also Antichrist, or Antichrist was his son by the Jewish whore of Babylon. The original sin of Adam and Eve had put humanity in the Devil's power; Christ had come to free those who followed Him. People had to choose, and the Devil was wily; they had to beware, always. Antichrist might present himself in the guise of the King of the Last Days or as the Messiah. All of this apocalyptic Christian belief was reflected by Alfonso X in his laws and his songs. The *Partidas* note safeguards: the Devil finds it difficult to harm the souls of those buried in hallowed ground, and in the *Songs of Mary* he is no match for her.

At the beginning of the fifteenth century, Vicente Ferrer's message was urgent and specific: If Antichrist had not yet arrived, he would come at any moment. He was to reign for three years, when Christ would come again and kill him, inaugurating a final age, a time when the clergy would return to poverty and all nations become Christian. The world would end forty-five days later. Sinners had little time left to repent. Like other forceful interpreters of prophecy, Ferrer had gained a wide reputation as a prophet in his own right. When, much later, he was declared a saint, the bull of canonization, echoing his legion of admirers, compared him to the Angel of the Evangel in the Apocalypse. That book was the part of the Bible everyone knew best. For throughout late medieval Europe, the Bible as a whole and especially the complete New Testament was a rarity. Much more common were illustrated manuscripts of the Evangelists and *Evangeliarios* containing passages from them read in Mass; the most popular excerpts were from the *Book of Revelation*. Revealed religion, Christ militant, and the vision of apocalypse were especially influential in a Castile lacking advanced studies in theology. Moreover, John the Evangelist was the patron saint of Castile's king, his namesake, Juan II. He would also, to more telling effect, be the patron of that king's daughter.

JEWS AND *CONVERSOS*

Jews had come to Iberia as early as Roman times, possibly even earlier; Spain's Jewish population was the largest in Europe. They lived principally, though not exclusively, in cities, and some of their communal leaders served kings as advisors, diplomats, financiers, physicians, and scholars. Even so, they were eternally on sufferance. Alfonso's *Partidas* state that Jews may live among Christians "so that they may live forever in captivity in order that men may remember they come from the lineage of those who crucified our Lord Jesus Christ." If less hostile than the medieval European norm, still the *Partidas* assumed that, since Adam and Eve had brought original sin upon human beings, putting them in the power of the Devil, and Christ had then come to liberate them all, that Jews only existed because they had refused to be freed; thus, they were still in thrall to the Devil, indeed prominent among those sinners who positively aided him and swelled his army in the battle for souls.

Alfonso X and his successors treated Jewish communities as royal protectorates, royally taxed, separate in culture and in many administrative matters from Christians. Until 1391, disdainful toleration was the norm; riots against Jews that did occur were local in nature. But that year, in Seville, with superior power weak (the king, Juan I, was a child) or nonexistent (the Archbishop had just died), in the aftermath of plague and amid hard times and an upsurge in popular religious enthusiasm, a rabble-rousing preacher fanned an outburst of violence against Jews; mobs in Seville invaded the Jewish quarter, the *aljama*, killing perhaps 4000 people. Anti-

Jewish violence spread rapidly throughout all Spain. Jews were attacked, robbed, slain, driven out of major cities. The Castilian royal council and the king of Aragón protested but did nothing. "All this," wrote the moralizing chronicler, Pero López de Ayala, "was done out of a thirst for plunder rather than piety. The people also wanted to do the same to the Moors . . . but they did not dare . . . because they were afraid that Christians held in Granada or overseas might be killed." Many Jews fled the country. At least a third of the Jews remaining in Spain were baptized, including many Jewish communal leaders. A generation later Vicente Ferrer stimulated a second wave.

Ferrer preached at court in 1411, during Juan II's minority. The regents backed his having Jewish men, women, and children in cities and towns under royal jurisdication forced to attend his sermons. Ferrer told them that as Jews they were cohorts of the Devil and Antichrist, clever, warped, and doomed, that like demons they tempted people to sin, and that they stole Christian children. Ferrer, drawing crowds and employing popular lore and language, played exquisitely on fears that the world was ending. Mobs often attacked Jews after his sermons. An anonymous author of a manuscript on Juan's reign written about 1500 told of hearing from his grandfather of Ferrer's preaching having incited the slaughter of nineteen of Toledo's most eminent Jews, men, women, and children, who were beheaded in a mill-run: it was "a thing sad to see, the wheel turned human blood instead of water."[5]

Within a month after Ferrer's visit, the royal regents issued or reissued stringent ordinances: Jews and Muslims must not live in urban centers. Jews must dress modestly, let their hair and beards grow, wear identifying red patches, and not take Christian names nor be addressed as *Don* or *Dõna*. Jewish physicians were not to have Christian patients; Jews were not to sell medicines nor foods to Christians, nor act as brokers or money-changers to them, and they were not to employ Christian tenant farmers or day laborers. They could not move to noble jurisdictions or go abroad. Those ordinances separated Jews from Christians as though cordoning off contagion, and pressured Jews mightily to convert. Benedict XIII added papal weight, issuing a bull prohibiting Jews having Talmuds or Hebrew books, or speaking of God. They must hear three Christian sermons annually. There was to be only one synagogue to a city.

Spanish Jews fled to Granada, to North Africa, to Portugal and elsewhere abroad, but principally they moved to the greater protection of noble domains; many converted. Restrictions were eased after Juan became king, especially those against Jews renting or collecting royal taxes, and Talmuds and synagogues were permitted. But there were fewer Jews. Some, artisans and shopkeepers in the main, returned to their homes. But, uprooted from major cities, communities shattered, autonomy and old leaders gone, for most of those remaining in Spain the issue was survival. They had become a far less significant social element than their brethren who had converted and so become eligible to hold public office, and to whom, along with Italians and south Germans, the crown turned for services Jews had formerly performed.

Mass conversion left uninstructed converts who retained great faith in their own theological instincts. And some became established at the royal court, including among the literati. Avowedly Christian, some converts from Judaism, or *conversos,* nonetheless questioned Christian doctrines logically difficult, the same ones Jews questioned—the Trinity, the Incarnation, salvation, and predestination. And they did so in a manner reminiscent of talmudic argument within Judaism. Disputatious, skeptical, and ironic, they raised, chiefly in poetry, rational arguments: If God wanted to save the world, why was he so slow about it? Did not Adam suffer enough in being sent from Eden into a life of hardship, had he to bear the guilt of bringing sin on future generations as well? Honor was outraged in one instance: since a married man sins who wishes to take another man's wife, how could God who is Our Lord do what he did to Joseph, who had only recently married Holy Mary? One *converso* poet ventured beyond all sect and community: Human beings, he said, do the work of spiders, weaving webs, their life is vanities. God is laughing at their behavior.[6]

Still, many of the recent converts were patently trying to be Christian and in that quest some were especially attracted to the fervent certainty of prophecy-wielding friars, of whom the greatest celebrity was Ferrer, who in turn embraced converts.

From 1391, *conversos* served at court not only as poets and scholars, but filled key posts in royal administration, finance, and diplomacy. Others became prominent on city councils. Yet others joined the regular and secular clergy, some achieving high position. And from the early years of the fifteenth century, converts who had gained entree into Christian society, to the court, and some into royal confidence, were in the forefront of proponents of strong monarchy.

When Juan II came of age at 14, in 1419, the idea was widespread that, regarding faith, simple was best, that a good heart and native wit may receive divine grace, and that a good heart may be divinely inspired, enlightened by God. In that fuzzy religious climate, *converso* court poets joined others in celebrating Juan's majority, engaged further in freewheeling theological discourse and displayed confidence in their own abilities to interpret prophecy; one praised both Ferrer and the young king, whom he compared to Merlin's lion-king bursting from Hercules' cave.

JUAN II AND ALVARO DE LUNA

By then, Spain's monarchs had invested themselves with a hallowed tradition of divine election avowedly based on the Bible and the church fathers, prophecy and its interpretation, royal chronicles, and the two laws, canon and civil. Restrictions on royal power were held to exist only in the king's conscience, in custom, in the limited length of the royal reach, and in the strength of the nobility. The chief theoretical limitation on monarchy in medieval Europe, that the king had been elected by the sovereign community, surfaced only occasionally. Most people found the nobles closer and more oppressive. The king was more distant and possessed an aura of holiness, an aura that the royal court was instrumental in creating and cultivating. Moreover, about the time that Isabel was born, this political theory was being tested with, it was to turn out, great significance for her.

At six, Juan II had been given as his page Alvaro de Luna, of obscure but well-connected Aragonese family and some years older than himself, from whom the boy soon refused to be separated. Luna became his *privado*, his most intimate friend and advisor, and after Juan came of age he appointed Luna Constable of Castile and handed him the reins of government. Luna, relying as little as possible on other nobles, thereafter acted like a king in the name of the king and himself became the wealthiest and most powerful of grandes, an effective (if avaricious) administrator who established a governing apparatus bent on centralizing power. He put able men in charge, many of them *conversos,* and allowed them sufficient latitude to run Castile for royal benefit and his own. He enlarged the royal chancery and its staff of *letrados,* men who knew, as he did, that their own standing, wealth, and power, were dependent on the prestige of the monarchy. Such people had drawn up the *Partidas* for Alfonso X, and now with their help Luna expanded royal administration and authority in theory and practice. Thus it was that, during the reign of so ineffective a king as Juan II, the principles and apparatus of strong monarchy nevertheless received tremendous impulse. Under Luna's direction, chancery documents ceaselessly referred to royal prerogatives in the most absolute terms, and to the king as patently above the civil law. On occasion the deputies of the Cortes or parliament, who were drawn from towns striving to limit the grasp of the nobility, linked royal power and the common good. And some of those same *letrados,* so assiduous in producing absolutist documents under Juan II, would compile law, equally regalist, for Isabel.

Luna, courtly and golden-tongued, won women's hearts, men's envy, and held the king in thrall for much of his long reign. Juan, it was observed, had an excessive and wondrous fondness for him. He loved Luna, said a contemporary, like no other, that "for thirty-five years he lived happy at his side and submissive to his will," and that while some saw it as due to the artifice and malice of sorcery, yet it was God's doing, past human understanding. Rumor abounded of "lascivious business" between king and constable.[7] Still, if attracted to men, or one man, Juan delighted in women, especially in the wife of his last years, Isabel of Portugal.

After Juan's first queen, María of Aragón, died, he married again, in 1447. His bride, chosen by Luna, was Isabel, the 19-year-old niece of the Portuguese king. During Juan's first marriage, averred the chronicler Alonso de Palencia, "the greatest marvel had been that even in the natural acts he followed the orders of the Constable, and though young and of good constitution and having a young and beautiful queen, if the Constable said not to, he would not go to her room, nor dally with other women, although naturally enough inclined to them."[8] But now Luna met resistance. Juan became completely infatuated with his bride and would no longer tolerate Luna's control of his private life, especially his regulation of connubial sexual relations.

So matters stood when Isabel of Portugal, Queen of Castile, fell into depression at about the time of the birth of her daughter and namesake. Rumor spread that Luna was trying to poison her. Certainly she had allied with his adversaries, and soon afterwards she persuaded the king to have Luna arrested. By then, Castile had suffered years of civil strife, centered on Luna and exacerbated by the king's dashing cousins, the *infantes* of Aragón, who had inherited vast property and high position in Castile. Luna was arrested, charged with high treason, and beheaded on June 2, 1453. His enemies hailed the Queen as a heroine—another Judith, another Esther, and worthy of comparison to Holy Mary.

Letrados of the royal chancery that Luna had built up had then put their experience to finding law to support the king's right to move against their mentor, to justify indicting and executing so great and powerful a noble and confiscating most of his estate. In the process, the regalism of the *Partidas,* the ideals of the mirrors for princes, the precedent of Biblical kingship, and the general belief that nothing could deceive the heart of the well-intended monarch were cited as operative principles. Thus in 1453, in the order for Luna's arrest Juan reminded his subjects of "the place of God which I hold on earth, with regard to justice, in order to administer and exercise it as properly and principally as every Christian Catholic king must do who wants to pay his due and discharge his conscience."[9] A decree of the Cortes sitting at Burgos that same year backed him up: the king, as head to the body that was the kingdom, was above all a judge who might pass judgment on the other parts of that body. A letter Juan signed stated it most simply: that to serve the king is to please God.

Yet for years Juan had stayed clear of governance and instead devoted himself to hunting, music, tourneys and other pleasures of court life. Like his Trastámara predecessors preferring the *meseta,* he lived as honored guest of great nobles or in the various royal great houses called palaces, and he enjoyed reading and having about him wise and educated men. Juan's interest in knowing the world's secrets was a pale reflection of that of his sage ancestor, Alfonso X, and he was more exclusively inclined to Western, European culture and to rational philosophy. Under his patronage, it was not manuscripts in Arabic but classics in Latin that received translation into Castilian, especially those of Christian stoicism. His philosophical bent is known to have extended to at least one instance of rational introspection: his puzzling over his own deficiencies in observing that "certain it is that steadfastness is the root of goodness, and a very strange evil is power combined with weakness." And he welcomed at court some well-informed critics, who lectured him roundly.

At midcentury, a coterie of powerful and highly respected men, *letrados* and nobles, bureaucrats and poets, laymen and high clergy, were voicing ever stronger feelings of a pressing need to cure the kingdom's ills, to stem civil strife, to remedy communal misery, and to redeem Castile through moral regeneration and strong personal monarchy. They believed Castile's only prospect of salvation lay in rousing Juan II to assert himself. Yet they deflected direct blame for the realm's sorry state from him by the assumption that while evils had come to Castile through Juan's inertia, it was in turn caused by God's anger at all the people. Juan's behavior and their reactions to it were to have much to do with Isabel's reaching the throne, with the advice she received, and with her view of herself and her reign.

Among the most vociferous advocates of strong personal monarchy was Iñigo López de Mendoza, Marqués de Santillana, who hated Luna. Santillana's fortune had been assured when his grandfather, Pedro González de Mendoza, had perished in battle against Portugal after giving his horse to the king, as well as by his own reputation for valor in service on the Muslim frontier and during Juan II's few forays against the Moors. Santillana also distinguished himself in letters: he is remembered as among the century's foremost poets. Yet he chose prose for voicing "a lamentation made in prophecy of the second destruction of Spain." In it he recalled the earlier Muslim conquest as the first destruction, invoked the august heritage of the Goths, and saw Spaniards as a chosen people being punished by an angry God—the implication being because of Luna's power and Juan II's inactivity. That remarkable diatribe of Scriptural cadence, reminiscent of the prophet Jeremiah's lament for Jerusalem, indeed seeing Spain as an analogue of the Holy City, conveys the rhetoric and spirit of a generation of worried but loyal critics, who saw national deliverance in reconquest led by the King.

Santillana asserted that Spain, having lost all sense of national purpose, was about to be destroyed again as in 711. "How great can be your blindness," he asked the personified nation,

> that you do not see the terrible evils coming, or the ferocious divine fires that will burn you? Why do you not see your people turned against your people, brothers against brothers, parents against children, and all in discord and evil around you, and all peace, love, truth, and security fled? Your people are sheep without a shepherd. Churches will tumble, the cursed name of Mahomat will be exalted, the sign of Christ will lie in the dust, the glorious lands of Hercules will be afflicted, and Trojan fires will consume the walls of cities.[10]

The people, he lamented, had fallen into avarice and luxury. God, the great sovereign, was full of vengeance. And he entreated Juan to bestir himself and exercise his will, to govern righteously and to go against the Moor. Juan's daughter would be far more successful in achieving those goals, and to do so she would rely heavily on Santillana's son, another Pedro González de Mendoza.

Juan's hairshirt extraordinary was Diego de Valera, knight-errant, political adventurer, scholar, poet, royal counselor, and *converso*, who, perhaps
because his father had been royal physician, was remarkably at ease with
the king and felt impelled to prescribe for "the common good of our
wretched Spain."[11] "Try to remember," Valera lectured Juan, "that you are
king . . . that you reign in God's stead on earth."[12] We shall see that Valera
continued to offer advice to kings; and a queen, for another thirty-odd
years.

Juan de Mena, poet and royal secretary, put the appeal to Juan within
the context of opposing forces of good and evil, heaven and hell. He coupled
the civil strife then so endemic and so deplored with disloyal and greedy
nobles, sin, black magic, and the vagaries of Fortune. Resorting to earlier
prophecies, changing them from salutation to injunction, it was, he said,
caused by the minions of Antichrist, demons; Muslims were their instruments. Against that lot he placed reconquest, divine providence, loyal
counselors, fame, and, ideally, the king. Mena exhorted Juan to show
strength and courage, "for you were made king of earth by He of the heavens, so that you and those you command/ Turn His wrath, God's wrath,
against the Moors." (The Spanish, staccato, rises to a crescendo: "*¡por ende,
vostros, essos que mandades, / la yra yra, la yra bolued en los moros!*")[13]

Juan's spine-stiffeners urged that the king actively exercise the free will
God gave him and insisted upon the impotence of fate and that popular
pagan deity, Fortune, her invocation so useful for sidestepping personal
responsibility. Juan appeared to concur in authorizing another advisor,
Lope de Barrientos, Bishop of Cuenca, to battle the Devil by burning books
on fortune-telling and astrology, the science associated with the fateful
influence of the stars. (Whether or not Barrientos, as Juan instructed, oversaw her education, Isabel's outlook was strikingly similar, with no room
for fateful passivity.)

After Luna's execution, although he still did not govern personally, Juan
entrusted the kingdom to two towers of moral strength, the Bishop of
Cuenca and the prior of the monastery of Guadalupe, and royal policy
indeed returned to reconquest. Little had been achieved against the Moors
since, in Juan's childhood, his uncle, the regent Fernando, had taken the
Granadan bastion of Antequera. Luna as Constable of Castile had led an
expedition against Granada in 1431, but nobles had sabotaged it, preferring
that Luna fail, even should it mean the Moors stay. Yet previous Trastámara
kings, while not assiduous in pursuing reconquest militarily, had enhanced
it theoretically through claiming as theirs by ancient right, based on Visigothic domination, North Africa and the Atlantic islands as well as the
kingdom of Granada. An advisor of Juan's, Alfonso de Cartagena, the *converso* Bishop of Burgos, had advanced it legally. So when papal bulls in 1452
confirmed Portuguese domination of all contested Africa and Atlantic
islands except the Canaries, Juan and his new governors objected and
planned to return to reconquest.

Portuguese activities had become increasingly worrisome. The *infante* of
Portugal, Henrique, had been sponsoring voyages of discovery. He held

lucrative trade monopolies in African lands and Atlantic islands and profited from agriculture—principally sugar—and the gold and slave trades. He sent out a third of all Portuguese voyages; the rest were dispatched by the king or other individuals. By 1450 the Portuguese were profiting in the trade with black Africa and Spaniards believed those profits were enormous. And it was then too that an event to the east reinvigorated Iberian interest in war against the Moor.

In 1451, the year Isabel was born, the Ottoman Sultan, Murād II, died, and his son and successor, Mehmet II, known as the Terror of Europe, took up his westward campaign, heeding old prophecies—says Palencia—that Constantinople would fall and then Rome: *Constantina cadent et alta palatia Romae.* Through Italy the awful words, *Constantina cadent,* "ran from mouth to mouth." When Isabel was two, in May 1453 Mehmet II indeed took Constantinople, and opinion swelled for a European crusade to counter the Turk.[14] Constantinople's fall, instilling in Roman Catholics the fear that the fate of what had been the chief eastern city of the Roman empire could be theirs as well, evoked a threat that would endure into the next century. This dread became so familiar that Niccolò Machiavelli alluded to its grip on the popular imagination in a salacious exchange in a play, *Mandragola*: "Do you think the Turk will come into Italy this year?/ Yes, if you do not say your prayers." Far less facetious were the verses a Castilian, Fernán Pérez de Guzmán, wrote to his cousin Santillana, lamenting the loss of "Noble Constantinople . . . the second Jerusalem."[15]

Muslim Cairo then held captive Jerusalem, Christendom's core, so often coupled in Castilian prophecies and sermons with Spain's future greatness, even with achievement of world empire. Jerusalem, like Spain having once been destroyed, served as its analogue, the lodestar of Castilian chivalric ideals and messianic hope, the ultimate goal of reconquest. Its restoration to Christian rule was an obligation laid by God upon Castile's monarch. The grandiose vision long inflated by royal panegyrists of the lion-king from Spain who would conquer barbarians, subjugate Africa, destroy Egypt, and regain Jerusalem, with Constantinople's fall spilled over into imperative: Spain, in the west, now had to balance the loss to the east. And to do it, Spain needed a strong ruler.

When, six months later, in mid-November 1453, the Queen gave birth to a son, he was given the tradition-laden name Alfonso. The King sought his horoscope and received the disquieting word that the stars threatened the boy's life before he was 15, but that if he lived, he would be the happiest prince of the century. Rumor ran that Juan II hoped to make this son his heir. But Juan, whether through regret for having executed Luna, or because Luna's restraining hand was gone, was no longer moderate in the pleasures of love and table, fell ill with severe quarternary fevers, and, although believing prophecies that he would live to 90, died within the year, on July 21, 1454—he was 49, the longest-lived king of his dynasty in five generations—and the crown passed to his elder son, Enrique, Isabel's half-brother.

※ 3 ※

The Wrong King
1461–1467

It is bittersweet to reign.

Motto of Enrique IV

ENRIQUE IV

ISABEL and Alfonso were at court in late 1461. Isabel was then ten, Alfonso eight. Their residing elsewhere was too risky for a king feeling increasingly uneasy about dissident nobles and their foreign allies, particularly Aragón, for Enrique was supporting the Catalans against their king, Juan of Aragón, and Juan was encouraging Enrique's increasingly powerful disaffected grandes. After a decade of prosperity, that coalition was gaining broader support, for Castilians were feeling the adverse effects of government by royal favorites, *privados*, adept at management but uninspired by the welfare of the realm and unconcerned with the broader and longer-ranging consequences of financial expediency. Among the more immediate consequences of that situation were inflation and devaluation of money and nobles encroaching on lands and intervening in urban affairs. Great nobles themselves were both players and pawns in kaleidoscopic coalitions, some of them intent on bettering Castile's situation and all on furthering their own. Throughout much of the reign of Juan II noble factions had battled for control of the king and his largesse, yet the difference was great. Even in a Europe where individualism was being newly rediscovered, Enrique as king was *sui generis*.

At his accession in 1454 Enrique IV was "a most powerful king," among Europe's most opulent.[1] He had inherited a royal fortune, one made up of the huge wealth reclaimed from Luna, income from the new taxes instituted by Luna on an expanding economy, and the revenues of the military orders of Santiago and Alcántara. Despite the euphoria tending to attach itself to the beginning of a reign, he soon aroused criticism for what he did, which was no more palatable because it was within a European-wide pattern of change, and he exacerbated opposition by how he did it.

Monarchs throughout a Europe grappling with the problems of their time, were intent upon extending central administration, especially in two principal royal spheres, justice and revenue, through expanding royal bureaucracies, and engaged in becoming more efficient in a third, the business of waging war. The resulting greater consolidation of central power would transform kingdoms into nation-states. Those pursuits went forward through sagacious and aggressive wielding of royal authority, and with the building for the monarch of a widespread respect, made up of a mix of esteem, fear, and awe. And they were usually attended by the redefining of the concept of nobility in order to shift emphasis from birth and military prowess *per se* to talent and service to the crown. Enrique undertook to initiate his versions of those trends during the years of Isabel's childhood in Arévalo, and it was to a great extent how he went about it and how he lived—for in mid-fifteenth century Europe the public and private life of monarchs were almost inseparable—that laid him low and provided prime negative example for her reign. A monarch needed a strong personality, an impressive bearing, and the ability to convince people it was in their best interests to follow him (or her), and his political success was often measured by deducting the square miles he ceded from those he had acquired.[2] The tenor of the times and Enrique's behavior within it would, during Isabel's subsequent years at his court, have much to do with how she chose to gain power, how she wielded it, and, ultimately, the constituting of Spain as a nation-state.

At a time when some of Spain's best minds and most engaged public servants were calling for a strong and resolute monarch, Enrique quickly became immensely unpopular with Castile's magnates and many other people by behaving as anything but that. He responded to the widespread sense of changing times, and to his personal avatars, chiefly by exhibiting flagrant disregard for some hallowed old ways under siege. To his subjects he was anything but a reassuring figure of a leader providing continuity in bridging old and new. Moreover, his lack of an heir promised instability and factional battles over succession. And having no progeny, Enrique had no impelling reason to think in terms of augmenting or even protecting his inheritance, and less reason to expect the perpetuation of his own name and renown. His motto expressed his ambivalence to being king at all: It is bittersweet to reign.

From his youth, Enrique's character had not inspired confidence. He had been a difficult child, the despair of his tutor, Barrientos, and often at odds with his father the king. Palencia, cryptically, for he said no more, even questioned his paternity, writing that Juan II of Castile was held by some to be father of Enrique IV and by all of Alfonso and Isabel. The rumor certainly did nothing for Enrique's self-esteem. He had been married young

but introduced to homosexuality even younger, reputedly at Luna's insti-
gation, as a way to keep him amused and controllable, and dependent on
favorites. Whatever their relations, among the earliest of his intimates was
Juan Pacheco, whose advice continued to sway him and whose displeasure
he continued to fear. As Enrique's on-and-off *privado*, Pacheco emulated his
own mentor, Luna, to the extent that he could, but Enrique, who was
stronger willed and wilier than his father, and had had the benefit of his
bad example, made sporadic efforts to stand up to Pacheco and offset his
influence by relying on other powerful barons.

Enrique made more decisions himself than had Juan but, to everyone's
consternation, frequently changed his mind. He was also more maladroit
in human relations. He was moody, unpredictable, devious, and given to
amusing himself at someone else's expense. He seems to have devoted himself more to governing than did Juan of Castile, but not much more, preferring the pleasures of music, hunting in the forests of Segovia and
Madrid, collecting a zoo, and the company of favorites who were not nobles
of first rank. His appearance was off-putting. His official and friendliest
chronicler, Diego Enríquez del Castillo, described him as tall and corpulent
with very large hands, red eyelids, and jutting chin. Palencia, who despised
him, wrote that he was always lugubrious of aspect and carelessly dressed,
without collar or any royal distinction, that he wore common stockings,
coarse leggings, and high shoes, his attire conveying his state of mind,
which tended to melancholy; that his eyes were fierce, never still and with
a hunted look. His aspect, Palencia declared, was dissolute, his skin white,
his hair red, and then added the detail he meant as metaphor for Enrique's
character: he hated agreeable odors, and he enjoyed the smell of burnt
leather, heads cut from horses, and other emanations of "the fetidness of
corruption."[3] It was a portrait of an anti-king, drawn with implicit parallel
to conceptions of Antichrist.

Just before coming to the throne, Enrique had put aside his wife of 13
years, Blanca, the daughter of the Queen of Navarre and its King-Consort,
Juan of Aragón. Enrique and Blanca had never had sexual intercourse, the
papal annulment read, through no fault of either but because their union
was diabolically bewitched by a demonic spell; the Devil had worked to prevent procreation. Blanca had been medically examined and found capable
of child-bearing and several women, prostitutes, had testified that Enrique
had achieved intercourse with them. It was an unconsummated marriage;
and such was the papal reasoning as to allow each to remarry.[4] Enrique did,
in May 1455, wed Juana, sister to Portugal's king, Afonso, who had begun
to profit mightily from the commerce with Africa resulting from the enterprise of his uncle, Henrique.

Amid lavish wedding festivities in Córdoba, the high-spirited 16-year-old
bride and her women displayed the audacious style of the newly prospering
court they came from, powdering their bodies white, baring much of their
breasts, and flirting unabashedly. They dazzled and scandalized the more
circumspect Castilians. Equally shocking and inappropriate, if very differ-

ent, was the attire of the bridegroom, for Enrique wore somber clothes of poor quality and a broad-brimmed black hat, which no one ever saw him take off. The night they were married, says Valera, although the king and queen slept in the same bed, the next morning the Queen was as virginal as she arrived, to everyone's chagrin. The customary bedsheet with the customary stain was not displayed. The story went around that a wit of Seville was heard to say that first among those things he would not bother stooping to pick up if he saw them laying in the street was Enrique's virility.

Isabel's partisans subsequently claimed Enrique's impotence as basis for her right to the crown. Regarding that right, the key question repeatedly raised throughout the intervening centuries has been: When Juana did have a child seven years later, was it Enrique's? Because if it was, it superseded Isabel and everyone else in line of succession. Pulgar insisted that "the impotence of the king to engender was notorious."[5] But he gave no evidence, and only several years after the child's birth, within the rhetoric of full civil war, did Enrique's opponents first level the charge formally. During Isabel's reign, Hieronymus Münzer, a German physician visiting Spain who talked to court figures, came away with the generally accepted explanation that Enrique's "member was thin and weak at the base but large at the head, so that he could not have an erection," that doctors had made a golden tube and placing it in the queen's vagina, introduced semen, to no effect, and that the king's semen was watery and sterile.[6]

There are not one but two questions to be answered about Enrique: Could he have the ordinary form of sexual intercourse and, if so, were his sperm fertile? Enríquez del Castillo and even the hostile Palencia state that it was established medically that he had had some sort of sexual relations with at least two women, the testifying prostitutes. Yet while the women were examined by physicians, Enrique was not. The entire discussion has remained in the realm of high gossip. Yet clearly Enrique had physical cause for unhappiness. Whatever the problem, problem there was, complicating an already complex personality. Whether or not Enrique was physically malformed or impotent or both, though no doubt mattering immensely to him, only when coupled with his general behavior did it provide sufficient basis for being viewed as the antithesis of what Castilians had come to assume a king should be; and it was this confluence of unacceptable behavior and questionable sexuality that was to matter most both to Isabel's succession and her reign.

REVIVING RECONQUEST

At the outset of his reign, Enrique did do the anticipated. He embarked on a campaign against Muslim Granada, but very quickly put an original stamp upon it. Coming to the throne in 1454 just after Constantinople fell to the Ottoman Turks and amid a shortlived but potent European revival of crusading fervor, among his first acts as king was to invoke the traditional rallying device of Castile's monarchs, "a cleansing war" against the Muslims of the kingdom of Granada. It was a timely, holy, and popular summons, one long urged by Castilian proponents of strong monarchy and one, as he and his advisors foresaw, enthusiastically heeded by Castile's magnates as promising employ, honor, and great profit. Indeed, some of them proposed the war in the first place and Enrique took it up as an ideal way to busy his truculent barons and his people.

War also promised profit. The call brought subsidies from the Cortes, shrunken to the compliant representatives of 17 towns called at the king's pleasure. Contributions too came from everyone—the nobles, the towns, the clergy and religious establishments, and all of them paid levied assessments as well. The king got from the pope, Calixtus III—who was a Valencian, Alfonso de Borja—three concessions: indulgences for men-at-arms like those granted crusaders against Turks and bent on recovering Jerusalem, the right to sell in Castile indulgences, known as bulls of crusade, to help finance this crusade within Spain, and a share of Castiliian contributions toward reconquering Constantinople. Enrique sent Sánchez de Arévalo to Rome to make arrangements, and at home his new *contador mayor*, or chief comptroller, Diego Arías de Avila, oversaw the profitable business; and when after two campaigns the papacy approved Arías' suggestion that those soul-redeeming licenses be guaranteed to cover the dead in purgatory as well as the living, the royal treasury did even better. So did everyone involved in their sale, which was handled, as was the collecting of revenues in general, by taxfarmers. The king also got from the pope the lucrative right of appointment of proxies to the masterships of the military orders of Santiago, Calatrava, and Alcántara, and thus an enhanced control over the power and wealth stemming from their vast domains of towns, lands, knights, and sheep. What he got, as we shall see, was a two-edged sword. Isabel would find both precedent and caution in all aspects of Enrique's policies and campaigns against the Moors. Her chroniclers would find great fault with how he had proceeded.

Enrique raised an army. His chancery having made all arrangements in Arévalo during the winter, he led south the flower of Castilian nobility in April 1455 and in three subsequent years, to its increasing disgruntlement. That first year, he devastated the Granadan countryside, but seemingly reluctantly, and nobles marveled, Valera recounted, because he would order no sieges or battles. (Marvel would be a favorite word of Isabel's, for unpleasant surprises.) Palencia left to posterity the view of Enrique as seen by unhapppy nobles, as the antithesis of a warrior king. Four years in a row, he wrote, the army saw the king turn that holy war into feints and cattle raids. He was loath to destroy olive groves and vineyards, and decreed any man who cut down even one fruit tree—"so slow to take root and grow, so quick to die"—would lose an ear, and some did. And though it was customary to lay waste to fields, he did it reluctantly and badly. For four days he sat the army down within view of Granada, supplies and funds dwindling while he refused battle and lectured his men on the preciousness of each

life. The sense emerges that Enrique, while he may have been an early envi-
ronmentalist, was having great fun by goading Castile's nobles through
belittling their hallowed concepts of waging war.

The campaigns, it appears, were adequately waged, but barely so. Provisioning was a large and never resolved problem. And, while it was more
than a token war, a principal royal goal was to make money. A time-honored method resorted to was by not spending on war all funds raised for it;
another was by harassing the enemy into renewing customary tribute payments through threatening but not destroying his sources of income. The
latter was a sound policy, except that in pursuing it the king exhibited
impatience with the temper of his most powerful subjects, and no respect
for traditions revered by Castilians.

In Seville with Enrique in 1456 was Sánchez de Arévalo, who alluded to
that situation in a treatise presented to the king, written in that accepted
genre of advice to rulers, the *Mirror of Princes*. Echoing Juan II's counselors,
who had been his mentors, that worthy reminded his prince of the great
realm entrusted to him: Castile he assumed was head of the five kingdoms
of *la nación española*; and he urged that Enrique take up his extensive inheritance from the Goths: "May your kingdom expand over infidel barbarians
and to the Great Ocean and the Mediterranean sea, your virtue not rest
until your name and power spread to the darkest parts of Africa and your
money is coined [in those places] and you recover these provinces which
. . . your progenitors . . . possessed in peace." Enrique must "change dis-
honest peace into . . . praiseworthy war," for kingship comes from heaven
and war against the infidel is not only just but a divine obligation. The king
is God's instrument.[7] Then he got to the point. While the hunting and
music to which Enrique devoted himself were suitable royal pastimes,the
pursuit "which will excite hearts and acts of virtue . . . the primary royal
exercise or sport, is the magnificent pursuit of military glory," the best form
of it war against the Moors.[8] Enrique, that is, had to get serious about the
war.

Enrique was known to have scoffed at similar advice. He neither showed
interest in distinguishing himself in arms nor appreciated the intensity of
the commitment of young nobles to chivalric values essentially medieval
but reinforced by renaissance emphasis on the pursuits of fame, honor, and
glory. It was true that traditional chivalric ways of warfare were becoming
outmoded; the English at Agincourt had demonstrated heavy cavalry and
single combat to be inadequate against crossbows. And Enrique did know
personally the advantages of riding with light armor and arms, for he himself rode Muslim fashion, *a la jineta*. Yet it was less his awareness of modernity that earned him a pusillamious reputation than that he took pleasure
in flaunting values held dear by his most powerful subjects, the entrenched
nobility. In refusing to besiege towns or join battle, and in issuing orders
against single combat with no adequate explanation, he ran counter to the
grain of the society he governed, and he set no acceptable example of his
own. (It is worth noting that not only were Isabel's chroniclers at pains to

emphasize all this, but that she herself would ostentatiously counter it, if in conformity with her own diametrically opposed bent.)

In those first years of his reign and unlike his more passive father, Enrique did assert his authority, but in ways appearing arbitrary and chimerical. *Caballeros,* knights, felt his rage, wrote Palencia, if they managed to get into skirmishes. And when the very noble youth, Garcilaso de la Vega, challenged, fought, and killed a Muslim horseman before Málaga, the young bloods saw Enrique, furious, award the Moor's charger to a current and lowborn favorite. On campaign two years later, Garcilaso died of a poisoned arrow in the neck, and the king again outraged tradition and its adherents by giving the rents of an *encomienda,* the royal grant Garcilaso held of certain lands and villages, to that favorite's brother, rather than, as was customary, to Garcilaso's son. The boy's uncle, the renowned Moorfighter, Rodrigo Manrique, and his Mendoza cousins, Santillana's sons, protested vehemently but futilely. Manrique and his numerous and powerful clan became leading dissidents. The Mendoza remained loyal, committed to the principle of monarchy if not pleased with the encumbent; their support would be decisive in Isabel's attaining the crown.

Year after year, the king returned north in the fall with a surplus of treasure, some of it from taxes on the huge amount of provisions the campaign required, some from Muslims grateful for his having spared towns and crops, and with valuable gifts from the king of Granada as well as treaties with him promising yet more gold in tribute. No one else except the recipients of royal largesse made expenses. There were few customary spoils of victory for the lords and their men, few deeds permitted to their *caballero* sons. Dismayed aristocrats saw Enrique divert war funds and present *mercedes*—the royal offices, titles, money, towns and villages, and rights to royal taxes and customs—that is, all the entrees to wealth and power, to his young companions of inferior birth. To Pedro Girón, Pacheco's brother, went the captaincy of the entire Muslim frontier. They saw Enrique favor recent converts from Judaism such as his treasurer Diego Arías, and lavish gifts and attention on his Muslim guard, 300 strong, who went richly dressed and magnificently horsed while the rank-and-file grumbled about scarcity of necessities.

Throughout his reign, Enrique would continue to antagonize his barons in one way or another to the point of revolt, and then, to avoid conflict, mollify the disaffected with large gifts of jurisdictions, rents, and honors, so that a pavotte of rebellion and reconciliation, rather than loyal service or war against the Moor, became recognized as the most certain route to wealth. That he was suggestible and volatile both deepened the prevailing atmosphere of insecurity and heartened opportunists of the sort observed during Juan II's lifetime, whom "it no doubt pleased to have such a king, because in turbulent and disordered times, in the troubled river rich fisherman are made."[9] In the resulting, escalating, jockeying for power and warring over jurisdictions, ordinary peoples' lives and livelihoods became ever more hazardous: towns endured siege, highwaymen proliferated, crops and herds were lost, and law and order belonged to the strong. Enrique liberally dispensed as *mercedes* royal jurisdictions and revenues, or nobles took them, charged excessively, and harmed merchants; ordinary people suffered most.

Underlying much of the criticism of Enrique at the time was high irritation at his capriciousness, at that mordant playfulness and delight in flauting convention. In Andalusia, while restraining his knights, he also encouraged the Queen and her ladies to stand on the battlements and pretend to shoot arrows at the foe; Palencia railed against that frivolity as indicative of Enrique's near-profanation of the serious, indeed sacrosanct, enterprise of war against the Moor. And an extended practical joke played on the Archbishop of Toledo, Alfonso Carrillo de Acuña, helps to explain why that grande, "the second person in Spain after the king, not only in dignity but in vassals," who held hundreds of cities, towns, villages, and castles, enjoyed huge revenues, had at his call an army, and who was Alvaro de Luna's close associate, became the soul of the opposition to Enrique that was ultimately responsible for Isabel's succession.

The Archbishop, known to be "of tenacious character and robust temperament," although left by Enrique during his initial foray south as a viceroy to oversee the royal chancery in Valladolid, repeatedly saw his decisions overridden by royal directives. Carrillo, a principal advocate of the reconquest of Spain and the conversion of all Muslims, complained of Enrique's taking no action against the Moor. In 1457 he protested against Enrique's misuse of the funds from the bulls of crusade. And he smarted too from the king's having undercut his jurisdiction in Toledo and generally chipped away at ecclesiastical immunities and privileges, which Palencia claims Enrique referred to as "sheepskins and goatskins, witnesses to the ridiculous."[10]

Carrillo, never known to suffer in silence—"he was a man of great heart and his principal desire was to do great things and to have great standing, fame, and renown"[11]—made known his unhappiness to the extent that Enrique (advised by Pacheco, who was the Archbishop's nephew) resolved to get him away on the pretext of having him lead a campaign to retake Baza and Guadix, Granadan strongholds claimed by the see of Toledo, and also Málaga, Granada's major seaport, and he added the offer of an advance for men-at-arms of monies from the sale of indulgences, bulls of crusade. Of course, if the Archbishop did not take those towns he was to return the money, and Enrique and Pacheco knew full well that on such short notice their conquest was impossible. Carrillo, bellicose by nature, with Rodrigo Manrique and the Count of Alba rode south immediately, to Ecija, where Pacheco met them. The game was joined. It was early September. First Pacheco must go scout out Málaga. He would return shortly. Weeks passed. Carrillo awaited him, impatience mounting. Near the end of the month, Enrique arrived from Córdoba. Besiege Málaga? Alas, it was too late and too cold and too few provisions remained. Carrillo and the Counts must ride with him to Jaén. They went, arguing for the siege, and the game continued in Jaén, until, well into October, three furious nobles realized they had been had, and had concluded that "the king would not war on Muslims but on his vassals, good customs, and the old laws."[12] Shortly thereafter Carrillo, with Manrique's support, formed a league to curb Enrique. Juan Pacheco often connived with it, for Pacheco intensely disliked the competition he met in the king's newer favorites, especially the latest one, the dashing Beltrán de la Cueva.

AT COURT

It is now that Isabel enters this picture. In 1457 to counter the weight of those nobles, or anyway to neutralize their natural ally, Juan, King of Navarre, regent of Aragón, and almost certain to become its king, Enrique, accompanied by his queen, met Juan and his second wife, Juana Enríquez, a daughter of the Admiral of Castile, and arranged a double wedding. Isabel and her brother Alfonso were to marry the Aragonese regent's children, Fernando and Juana. But when in 1460 Carrillo set up a formal coalition of nobles intent on getting control of the royal council and having young Alfonso proclaimed heir to Castile, and Juan, by then king of Aragón, leagued with those dissidents, Enrique offered Isabel in marriage to Juan's elder son, Carlos of Viana, who had joined Catalans at odds with his father. Carlos, accordingly, sent a messenger to Arévalo seeking Isabel's hand who reported her very content, *muy contento*, with the prospect of marrying the heir to Aragón. Its king, Juan, was far less content, and detained Carlos' subsequent emissaries until, on September 23, 1461, Carlos died suddenly, rumor had it poisoned by his stepmother, Juana Enríquez, in order to clear the way to the crown of Aragón for her own son, Fernando. If so, Carlos' engagement to Isabel was a contributory factor in his death.

Enrique from then on kept the Catalans stirred up against his uncle their king, Juan. And Juan Pacheco, on whom Enrique had bestowed the marquesado de Villena, which contained much of Juan of Aragón's recently foresworn inheritance in Castile, prodded and abetted Enrique in inciting those rebels, while he simultaneously negotiated with Juan for the marriage of Fernando to one of his own daughters. Pacheco had ten children, six of them daughters. Although Fernando got away, Pacheco's machinations achieved what was undoubtedly his great goal: his childrens' marriages assured his family powerful position within the interlocking directorate made up of Castile's great nobility, whose members were to be known as *grandes*.

In 1461, Juana, Queen of Castile, was pregnant. Enrique reconciled with Carrillo and at his urging, and that of Pacheco, he brought the *infantes* Isabel and Alfonso to live at court. Just how it was arranged is unclear, seemingly through Carrillo, who on occasion could display an exquisite sense of the apposite, as he did in reportedly arguing they had to come to court "because there they will be better raised and learn more virtuous customs."[13]

Isabel was in the queen's entourage when on February 28, 1462, Juana went into the labor of childbirth, an event attended by the grandes and much of the court. While the queen, supported by the Conde de Alba de Liste, squatted, the customary position for giving birth, she was flanked on one side, in strict order of rank by the king, the Marqués de Villena, the commander of a military order, and a royal secretary, and on the other by the Archbishop of Toledo and two other dignitaries. After a hard labor she gave birth to a daughter. The child was also named Juana and was baptized by Carrillo, assisted by the young Bishop of Calahorra, Pedro González de Mendoza, whose rise at court had begun. The *infanta* Isabel, now 11, was godmother.

The Sunday following, Enrique elevated his *mayordomo*, Beltrán de la Cueva, to Conde de Ledesma, feeding scandal, for Beltrán was rumored to be the child's true father and to have been urged upon the initially recalcitrant queen by Enrique himself. Whether or no, Enrique celebrated the child's arrival royally. On April 12 fifteen bulls were run and, on May 6, a joust was held (in which one knight died). Valera recalled Enrique being as happy as though she were indeed his daughter. It is not certain she was not, although, probability triumphing, she has come into history as Juana *la Beltraneja*. At court, Isabel's education was proceeding apace.

Isabel stayed in the town of Aranda with the Queen and the newborn infant from February until at least July, while a coalition supporting her younger brother Alfonso swelled. She and Alfonso were both present in Madrid on May 9 when Enrique had the nobles, some of them very reluctantly, take the customary oath to the infant Juana as hereditary princess, Princess of Asturias, and in July in Toledo the children heard the delegates to the Cortes repeat that pledge. Afterward they traveled with the court to Guadalajara, the seat of the Mendoza, to celebrate Beltrán's wedding to Santillana's granddaughter, Mencia de Mendoza. That marriage signalled the rise of a new faction, its true head the bride's uncle, the bishop Pedro González de Mendoza, who was Santillana's ninth and most remarkable child and who had recently entered the Royal Council. Although Santillana had been a critic of his government, he had died in 1458, and now Enrique sought in the powerful Mendoza family, in their numbers, their talent, and their widespread domains, a counterweight to Carrillo and the nimble Pacheco. And well he might, for Juana's birth had escalated tensions. The dissidents more stridently asserted Alfonso's claim to succession. And Pacheco was more than ever determined to topple Beltrán.

For the next few years, Isabel remained in the Queen's suite, living principally in Segovia. Within its *alcázar* was the grandest of royal residences in northern Castile, described by a traveler as "a most elegant palace adorned in gold, silver, and the heavenly color called azure, and with floors of alabaster." On view within it was the collective majesty of Castile, in the stat-

ues of its kings, thirty-four of them—all the kings of Castile and León "after
the destruction of Spain," beginning with the quasi-legendary Pelayo and
ending with Enrique himself, and with them stood El Cid and Castile's
founder, Count Fernán González, "because of their nobility and great
deeds." All were seated on thrones and held sceptres, and all, it was said,
were made of pure gold. They were in fact of wood, carved and polychrome,
painted in silver and gold. Alfonso X had had those of his predecessors
restored; Enrique had added ten. And as for the seven proprietary queens,
Alfonso and Enrique had put them behind and to one side of their husbands. Whatever Isabel's reaction to that positioning, she now lived among
those evocations of Castile's mighty past, whose histories were to be found
in the palace library by a young woman with great curiosity who was fond
of reading. Moreover, the daily sight of those numerous, illustrious, indeed
resplendent, royal forebears had to point up the contrast with the all too
human qualities displayed by the current monarch, her half-brother,
Enrique.

Isabel had as well other sorts of encounters significant for her own reign.
In late 1463, the royal family heard a series of sermons preached at court
by Franciscans on the theme that "in these kingdoms there is great heresy
by those who judaize, keep Jewish rites, and give children Christian
names," one friar vowing he could produce 100 foreskins of circumcised
sons of highly placed *conversos*. The argument was that no *converso* was to
be trusted to be a sincere Christian. It had precedent 14 years earlier, in
Toledo, in a statute denying public office to all converts and raising the
question whether any of them could ever be wholly Christian. One
response, based on the erroneous notion that Jews constituted a race, was
no, and that their blood was forever tainted; another yes, that all Christendom is one; moreover, since *conversos* had married into many of Spain's best
families, "who knows who are descended from them?" Yet from 1449 on,
Spanish Christendom was generally not assumed to be a single body in that
known *conversos* were distinguished from Old Christians.

In 1463 Enrique, annoyed, possibly bored, possibly amusing himself,
even possibly concerned with the issue, told the preacher his allegations
were a grave insult to the Catholic faith, one whose punishment belonged
to himself, the King, and he demanded to see the foreskins and know
whose they were. The evidence was not forthcoming. Enrique, though
leaguing with anti-*converso* exponents when it suited his purposes, was sufficiently nondoctrinaire in anything to resist propagandists who condemned all New Christians of Jewish lineage and, accordingly, he invited
Alonso de Oropesa, the venerable prior of the Hieronymite order, to come
preach at court against such libels.

Oropesa had written a tract defending most *conversos* as sincere Christians, distinguishing between true converts and heretics, and urging a
union among all Christians, declaring that "Christ receives whatever race
of men."[14] At the same time he condemned Jews, for resisting the grace of

God in Christ, for 'using all their astuteness and diabolic means to corrupt Christians,' and for causing suspicion of all people belonging to what he spoke of as the Jewish *raza*. (The term *raza* has meaning midway between 'lineage' and 'race.') His solution was that New Christians and Jews should be separated, and Jews induced to become Christian, if possible through love, if not through whatever coercion was necessary.

Enrique, approving, urged Oropesa to take charge of the usual process of having the bishops institute an inquisition to root out and punish heretics and apostates and exonerate true converts. Although civil war and Enrique's aversion to consistency intervened, the introduction of an inquisition had been broached, to a court wherein resided a girl who would one day implement that proposal on the basis of those same arguments, but in a revolutionary new fashion. And a principal advocate of an inquisition during Enrique's reign was Carrillo, to whom Oropesa dedicated his treatise and who would soon become a mentor of hers.

PROPOSITIONS

After the death of Carlos of Viana, the Catalans had proposed to Enrique that he, rather than Juan of Aragón, rule them and he had accepted. Pacheco, playing both sides and fearing that if Enrique waged war with Juan he might win, had talked him into foregoing the expense of armed combat by having Louis XI of France, whose reputation for guile should have deterred Enrique, mediate the matter. When, in April 1462, Louis did not decide Catalonia should be his, Enrique quickly realized that Pacheco had not only lost him territory and standing, but that through secret negotiations with Louis XI and Juana Enríquez he had arranged to keep power in precarious balance, requiring his own services. Enrique realized too that though Louis could keep Juan of Aragón busy protecting mutual frontiers, France was not to be trusted, and from 1463 negotiated with England, leading to a treaty in 1467 and to Castile reaching new heights of trade within that new alliance. Even so, Enrique's offer of Isabel's hand to Edward IV was refused; instead the English king married an English commoner, a slight Isabel was not to forget.

By 1464 Enrique was determined to marry Isabel to Afonso of Portugal, who was recently widowed, 32 years old, and his wife's brother, and whose revenues and prestige were continuing to swell from trade in the gold and slaves of Africa. Afonso, having in 1458 taken the port of Alcázar-Seguer in Africa, became known as *O Africano*, the African. From Enrique's standpoint it was an appropriate match: it would remove Isabel from the kingdom permanently, and Afonso already had a son and heir, virtually precluding that a powerful child of hers wearing Portugal's crown would ever muddy dynastic arrangements in Castile.

In April he took his Queen and Isabel, just 13, to Puente de Arzobispo to meet Afonso, who was then wreathed in the glory of having laid siege to Tangiers and was on his way to the shrine of the Virgin of Guadalupe to fulfill a vow he had made beforehand. Afonso was much taken with his young cousin Isabel; he would consult his nobles on the marriage. Although Pulgar had it that Afonso suggested they become engaged and she replied that the laws of Castile said she must seek the counsel of its *grandes,* Palencia is probably closer to reality in stating that "under the Queen's seductive influence" Isabel was ready to accept him, for her mother had told her always to prefer a Portuguese marriage.[15] And from what is known of her later, surely she was impressed by Afonso's African goals and exploits.

However that may be, when Carrillo and Pacheco heard of the meeting only afterwards, they laid having been kept in the dark to the Mendoza—that is, to Pedro González de Mendoza and Beltrán de la Cueva—and, on May 16, they and Pedro Girón, now Master of Calatrava as well as Captain General of Andalusia, signed an accord, their stated intent "to ensure the security of Alfonso and Isabel," because "some persons of damnable intent" had gained control of the *infantes* and were planning to kill Alfonso and have Isabel marry "where she ought not, not complying with the good and honor of the royal crown of these kingdoms and without the accord and consent of the *grandes* following custom. . . . all this to the end of giving succession in these realms to [one] to whom by right it does not belong."[16] They meant the princess, Juana; they also had a silent partner, Juan of Aragón.

The court went on to Madrid where Enrique, sensing something was afoot, lodged Alfonso and Isabel in the *alcázar's* keep, the *torre de homenaje.* Shortly thereafter, his guards drove off a band of armed men attempting to break into the royal residence to seize the king and the *infantes.* Enrique, well aware the men had been hired by Pacheco and not amused when that master dissimulator urged him to find the unknown assailants and avenge the insult, was said to have responded in exasperation: "Does it seem good to you, Marqués, this that has been done to my doors? Be assured that this is not the time for much patience."[17] Even so, when the court moved on to Segovia, Pacheco went along, now insisting to the king that the mastership of Santiago belonged to Alfonso, not Beltrán on whom Enrique had bestowed it. And one night, while Pacheco himself was in the royal apartments of the *alcazar* conversing with Isabel, another attempt to seize king and *infantes* was foiled, only just in time. In so bizarre a series of events, the most incomprehensible is that Enrique, to placate the dissidents, capitulated to Pacheco, recognized Alfonso as his heir, and agreed to hand the boy over into his keeping. On September 6, two days after the king and the leagued nobles had signed an agreement, yet a third attempt was made, to seize Enrique, this one impeded by archers of the *hermandad,* or brotherhood, local vigilantes, dedicated to upholding law and order, funded by towns, and notoriously loyal to the crown.

TWO KINGS FOR CASTILE

From at least 1457, Enrique had been criticized widely for moral and religious failures by preachers espousing traditional concepts of good kingship. And in a letter of 1462 Diego de Valera, as ever doing his duty as he saw it, informed this king that the greater parts of the three estates of the realm were discontent with his having ceased to war on Muslims, giving posts to unworthy men, even selling offices, and being hard of access, paying badly, and not doing justice; and Valera warned him that a number of kings in the past had been deposed and killed, and that he must "Guard these kingdoms that God has commended to you."[18]

Nor did it help Enrique's standing when Gibraltar was taken from the Muslims that year by Andalusian nobles rather than by the King. Sánchez de Arévalo then expressed widespread sentiments in writing to the pope, Pius II, that "in the west the sun of righteousness has risen," that is, that Castilians were counterbalancing Christian losses through Turkish advance in the east.[19] Harking back to the theme of the messianic role of Castile in world history, it was an equation heightening among Castilians feeling against Muslims and all non-Christians and it put Enrique on the spot as shirking the oft-prophesied role of savior-king and neglecting his obligation to take Granada.

Having set the stage by promoting such criticism and bent on young Alfonso's succession, on September 28, 1464, the league of dissidents sent a circular letter throughout the kingdom. It expressed shock at Enrique's perversion (implied was homosexuality), and at his consorting with Jews and Muslims and mocking the reconquest. It explicitly asserted Juana's illegitimacy and claimed as Alfonso's by right the mastership of Santiago, held by Beltrán, whom it accused of controlling the king and the *infantes* against the public good. The dissidents now wanted Enrique and his partisans— they meant the Mendoza—seized, and they demanded he have sworn delegates called to Cortes to take the oath to Alfonso as heir to the crown.

Enrique continued to temporize. The aged Barrientos, now high chancellor, urged him to fight. Instead, in November he gave Pacheco custody of Alfonso and a seat on the royal council, Pacheco having promised him that in exchange there would be peace. King and dissidents then agreed that Alfonso was to marry the princess Juana and receive the administration of the Order of Santiago, which Pacheco as his *mayordomo* might exercise for him. As for Isabel, she was not to marry without the consent of the three estates, nor was she to be considered as promised to anyone. Her mother was to send her five or six ladies and she was to have her own household, the king to maintain her in proper state. Beltrán and his people would quit the court. A commission of arbitration was ordered to draw up recommendations for reform of the kingdom. Each side appointed two members to it; the fifth was to be Alonso de Oropesa, the General of the Hieronymites. Enrique now, for the first time, presented sworn medical testimony to his ability to engender children. In December, increasing the pressure on him, a document ostensibly made up of petitions from high clergy, grandes, and knights was circulated, reiterating the September charges but going further, to condemn the godlessness of his reign.

On January 16, 1465, the arbitral commission made its report, a long one, known as the *sentencia* of Medina del Campo. Enrique had it circulated throughout Castile. Its 129 clauses addressed the full range of complaints against his government and prescribed remedies, often radical and in the main consistent with the demands of his opponents. Among them: royal judges and officials must be curbed, and the clergy unhindered. Finances were to be put right, and nobles to be tried by peers. Enrique's intervention in Catalonia was illegal and must end. There were to be free elections to the Cortes and no taxation without its consent. Offices were not to be inherited. Royal men-at-arms were to be reduced from 3000 to 600 lances—a lance signifying an armed knight and his attendants. The Royal Council was to be made up of three nobles, three bishops, and three representatives of the towns. Here was a new constitution for Castile, vesting power in the council, strengthening the Cortes, reinforcing the power of nobles and clergy, and circumscribing royal authority.

Yet more incendiary was its insistence on religious exclusivism, holding up Enrique's toleration as sinful: Muslims and Jews must be expelled from the kingdom and their property confiscated; an Inquisition should be established. The *sentencia*, combining personal interest and public appeal, reflected the intent of Enrique's opposition and the spectrum of grievances that united it. There was yet one other stipulation: Isabel was not to marry the Portuguese king without the consent of the Cortes.

Isabel was in fact the subject of the *sentencia*'s first clause, which substantially reiterated the earlier agreement: Her mother was to send five or six women of her own to attend her; she was to have her own household; until she married she should reside wherever her mother and grandmother were, and until that was arranged, she was immediately to be sent to a separate residence in Segovia with her ladies "and two or three honest men." Enrique was to pay her maintenance, as stated in Juan II's will. She was, that is, to be made more accessible to the dissidents. To that end, the implication was that the court was no fit place for a young *infanta*, such was the behavior of the king and the queen, whose ladies were portrayed by the opposition, and within it Palencia, as laughing and gossiping amid the constant comings and goings of go-betweens carrying indecent messages, and as "devoured night and day by a restless craving" more common to brothels. At least one of them, Mencia de Castro, was known to have a liaison; she would have three sons with Pedro González de Mendoza.

One courtier, casting his net wider, spoke of the misery of court life, telling of ferocious undercurrents, pressure to conform, and the fashion to dress with vulgarity. Another, playing upon the current issue of who was or was not circumcised, in satiric verse suggested: Circumcise the gallants and the pages, but do not circumcise the clothing worn at court, it was so short already. Isabel had, since September, been with the Queen at Segovia.

Whatever her exposure at the time, she was very careful afterwards to exemplify propriety.

Two weeks after circulating it, Enrique revoked the *sentencia*. Ever since the commission first met, he had been ordering loyal nobles, forts, and town militias to ready, and now he also renounced Alfonso as his heir and commanded Beltrán to prepare for battle. It was civil war. On June 5, by Avila's stern walls, Carrillo, Pacheco, Rodrigo Manrique, and other dissidents assembled. They drew upon a mélange of tradition that included the old Visigothic practice of notables choosing a king, the popular rite of acclamation, and political theory claiming it the right of the body politic to depose a tyrant, and above all they invoked their own right to make and unmake kings as Castile's nobility and thus spokesmen for the body politic. They then declared Enrique an unfit ruler, deposed him in effigy, and had the assembled crowd acclaim the 11-year-old boy, his half-brother, as king Alfonso XII. Palencia took credit for dissuading Pacheco and Girón from charging Enrique with heresy by reminding them that, once the quarrel was on religious grounds, Enrique had more money for bribes for Rome. At Avila too was at least one Castilian who proudly claimed descent from the king-electing Goths, Rodrigo Manrique. Manrique devices boasted: "We are not descended from kings, but kings from us," and "Manrique, blood of Goths, defense of Christians and terror of pagans." Glorying in his reputation as another El Cid, Manrique wanted a king of similar values, both a more king-like king and one who would smile on hereditary barons such as himself.

In marked contrast, his cousin, Pedro González de Mendoza, in appealing to Alfonso's adherents for reconciliation, argued that Castile was best served by royal legitimacy; he did not try to defend Enrique himself but instead argued that when the body politic finds itself sick, it is not wise to try and cure it by cutting off its head. Kings are anointed by God, said Mendoza, and not subject to human justice. The Scriptures warned that a divided kingdom is worse than a bad monarch; if the rebels were well intentioned they would not put up an 11-year-old boy as king. Rather, they showed a prime concern with their own interests and not with the well-being of the many; and if indeed their cause were just they would pursue it by juridical means.

Steeped in Castilian values and assumptions held dear by earlier advocates of strong monarchy, including his father, this Mendoza had been educated in canon and civil law at the University of Salamanca. In 1465 the law he chose to invoke was the Holy Scriptures which, he said, decreed kings be obeyed, even though they be unlearned. And he put disobedience on a religious plane, echoing the *Partidas*: those who did not obey the king were schismatics. Yet the fused national and religious grounds on which this noble prelate chose to stand, advocating monarchy as the institutional key to national unity and continuity, were forward-looking in the extreme.

The opposition much preferred its own interpretation of political theory and its own king, and it too appealed to scripture. Circular letters full of moral outrage went out immediately under Alfonso's signature, the first of many. On June 6, an order signed by Alfonso XII instructing the Count of Arcos to take the oath of homage to him recited a litany of Enrique's sins, its tenor being that the Count well knew that "the great harms all these my kingdoms and their three estates have received" had come "from my predecessor [Enrique], in whose time the holy Catholic faith of our savior and redemptor Jesus Christ has received unprecedented detriment." A long list of accusations followed, detailing how Enrique had brought God's wrath upon the land: Enrique had attacked the immunities of the church, dishonored knights, robbed citizens and peasants, violated privileges of towns and cities, and not done justice but sold it. His crimes and excesses were notorious. The enormous and ugly impieties occurring in his palace were certain to ruin the kingdom. He had evilly given Doña Juana, called his wife, to Beltrán de la Cueva, and made a daughter of hers heir to the kingdoms rightfully belonging to himself, Alfonso, as son of King Juan. Implicit was a questioning of Enrique's own legitimacy.

More explicit was the insistence now upon Enrique's impotence as manifest and upon his intent toward the *infantes* as evil. He had given, it said, Alfonso and his sister Isabel into the hands of the queen and the traitor Beltrán, their plight moving many prelates and lords to support their legitimacy. A circular letter of August 2 to the city of Palencia added the charge that Enrique sustained Muslim enemies of the holy faith, kept them in his palace as guards and gave them double pay, and that he had no will of his own. In yet another letter, to the council of Burgos on July 22, Alfonso spoke of expelling Enrique from the kingdom and redeeming his sister, Isabel, in language usually used to refer to Christians held captive by Muslims.

Alfonso was fighting his own version of holy war. A variant manifesto of August 2 promised: "the sins of heresy, sodomy, and blasphemy, which were as prevalent as they were notorious in the reign of my predecessor Enrique, will be uprooted from my kingdoms and destroyed by me."[20] Enrique was willfully bringing on the (second, and final) destruction of Spain. Alfonso's charge was to save the realm. At bottom, Alfonso's stance was militantly apocalyptic, and effective. A traveler from abroad then observed that most people were partisans of the young king, because of his greater inclination to the Christians, and it was generally believed that he would triumph completely.

Behind this war of words lay a longer-standing criticism of Enrique's rule. Begun with the rosy hope that beginnings tend to engender, his reign had soon drawn rebuke even from his partisans, criticism appealing to a political morality and concept of kingship common to the *Partidas*, the books of advice to princes, and the attempt to fortify Juan II: the king was head of the body politic, his conscience the conduit of God's will; his kingdom was dependent for its health on his good government. The highest purpose was war against the Moor. Such criticism came from earnest men seeking to set Enrique on the right path, from Juan of Castile's old counselors, Barrientos and Valera; from Sánchez de Arévalo and Pedro González de Mendoza, who were protégés of Santillana and Alfonso de Cartagena; and from other followers of theirs who were Alfonso's supporters: from the chronicler Palencia, and Gómez Manrique, who was Mendoza's cousin and Rodrigo Manrique's brother. The criticism, raised by a previous generation of Castile defiled and evil abroad, became increasingly strident and shrill, Enrique's supporters, as had Juan's advisors, blamed the entire body politic; Alfonso's held Enrique personally responsible. Both sides consulted theologians.

By 1465, anonymous, biting, thinly veiled satires attacked Enrique. In one, the *Coplas de Mingo Revulgo*, he was the bad shepherd who let the wolves, the nobles, devour his sheep. The people have lost the four cardinal virtues—justice, fortitude, prudence, and temperance, the four dogs who had guarded the flock. It ends by warning that the king may be overthrown. In another, the *Coplas del Provincial*, the superior of the corrupt monastery that is Castile reports on the previous nine years—that is, Enrique's reign—describing Castile's mighty: the men as incestuous and as sodomites, cuckolds, and Jews, and the women as adulterous and devoid of virtue. Some *conversos* were vilified: Diego Arías, the royal comptroller, when asked why his coat of arms bore not a foreskin but a cross, was said to reply it was because he had been at the crucifixion and put Christ on the cross. Homosexuality was given the full religious weight of an abominable sin, of violence against God, rather than, as was at the time often the case, viewed leniently. Those couplets and the manifestos of Alfonso's supporters counted upon those conditions being widely understood as apocalyptic signs of the dreadful times preceding the last days.

Enrique was blamed for bringing on a second destruction of Spain, which was equated with the end of the world. He was held up as that antithesis of the Good Shepherd, Antichrist. Common in apocalyptical literature were animal allegories, and disaster foretold on the basis of astrological predictions and revelations in a dream, as in the *Coplas de Mingo Revulgo*.

Strong criticisms of society as a whole, leveled in verse, were couched as timely warnings of disaster in a world turned upside down. *"Mundo ciego, mundo ciego"*—"blind world, blind world"—lamented Hernán Mexía, a municipal councillor of Jaén; for such was Enrique's realm, embroiled in discord and tyranny.[21] What had become, he asked, of the virtues and the good men, the worthy governors, the priests, knights, and *letrados*? *Ubi sunt*? The sins of the powerful infected the entire body politic. It was, he said, like the fall of Rome or the dreaded coming of Antichrist. Mexía and other poets who told of evil abroad and predicted disasterous consequences in similar, scriptural terms were by and large *conversos*, their verses infused with the additional, mounting insecurity of their own situation.

Their anguished vision was not far from that of Alfonso's devoted follower, Gómez Manrique, in poems where the chivalric convention of courtly love dominated but grim reality intruded. "The immense turbulence of this Castilian kingdom makes my hand heavy," he wrote.[22] For, though the world itself was, "quicker to change than February," though fame was "fleeting as brandy flame," yet conditions in Castile went beyond the usual turns of the world, to a world turned completely topsy-turvy, in stanzas revealing on several counts: "In a village where a Moor is stupidly made mayor, iron will be worth more than gold, and silver given away."[23]

Nor was Enrique's camp immune from sentiments of disorder, of morality upended as a plague on the land. In March 1466 his chronicler and secretary, Diego Enríquez del Castillo, writing in Enrique's name to the vigilante league, the *Hermandad*, commended all towns and cities for, as inspired by God, forming such brotherhoods, for robbery and murder were commonplace, no road nor house was safe. In rousing tones he called on the *Hermandad* to rally for the common good and to free the land, for "the glory and crown of Spain is in your hands." The dreadful state of the realm, he went on, "comes to us for our sins," employing the collective, not the royal, we. Hellfire threatened; and he made appeal to the clemency and grace of God, cited David and Jeremiah, and as had earlier Castilians, compared "the destruction of Jerusalem to the destruction of our afflicted Spain."[24]

Enrique's partisans had adapted the apocalyptic imperative also favored by the opposition. By 1466, they were emphasizing crisis, common cause, and God's wrath having descended on both king and people, conveying a sacred duty to cleanse the land of defilement. Both sides viewed the other as its cause. Such language proved highly efficacious in sanctifying civil strife as just war. Nor were the widespread and increasing sense of anarchy and distress under Enrique IV and the terms in which it was expressed, as is sometimes claimed, simply manufactured subsequently by Isabel and her apologists. Whatever the extent to which chronicles may later have been doctored, Enrique's reign increasingly inspired little confidence at the time.

CIVIL WAR

For four months after Avila, the two sides clashed, *guerra guerreada*. It was a war waged on small villages, on crops and cattle, and through fear; its principal zone was the *meseta*. Enrique, offering a general pardon on July 12, bitterly noted that not withstanding the *mercedes* he had granted, "*los cavalleros mis rebeldes*" were "so many they could not be counted."[25] All Castile felt the effect of lack of authority: of bandits and guerillas and forts seized or besieged in local contests, *guerras chicas*, waged ferociously.

Isabel by then had from Enrique the semblance of her own household, with Gonzalo Chacón as *mayordomo mayor* and an income in the form of *juros*—royal bonds—and rents from jurisdictions. Enrique named her lady of the towns of Trujillo and Casarrubios del Monte and he was still determined she marry Afonso, the king of Portugal; Queen Juana was making the arrangements. Even so, in April 1466 he received from Pedro Girón, who was then a 43-year-old-widower, an offer, made with Pacheco's consent, to provide men and money—3000 horse and 60,000 gold doubloons—and to turn over Alfonso, in exchange for permission to marry Isabel. Enrique told him to come quickly and take her, and as a precaution he dismissed Beltrán and Mendoza from court. Immediately, Girón set out from Almagro, his stronghold in Extremadura, "with great power, in men as in money," bringing finery, for the wedding and the obligatory accompanying tourneys.

Isabel, on being told just beforehand of his imminent arrival and why he was coming, for a day and night neither ate nor slept, but prayed to God that, says Valera, He kill either one or the other of them in order to stop the wedding. When Girón, suddenly striken with quinsy or croup, died on the way, how could she not think that heaven had answered her prayers? While the later celebrants of her piety do not date it from that deliverance, they make much of its efficacy in that crisis. And, with Girón seemingly having been struck down by God's hand, it is highly unlikely that, however devout she may have been before, she was any less so afterwards. Her chroniclers emphasized not simply divine action but its interplay with her exercise of free will in adjudging her reprieve to have been 'a victory wrested from fortune by patience and fortitude.' The chances are good that someone poisoned Girón, and the people with most to gain from his death were themselves at odds. They were Juan of Aragón and the Mendoza.

Pacheco again left court. The contest dragged on. The Mendoza returned to favor, and the princess Juana, again heir-apparent, was given into the keeping of the Mendoza in August 1467, chiefly as a hostage against Enrique's vacillation. Enrique also promised them to make no accords with Alfonso's followers for at least three months, nor to turn over the Queen or Isabel to anyone. He accepted the suggestion of the papal legate, one earlier made by Pedro González de Mendoza, that Juana be betrothed to Alfonso. He also renewed the offer of Isabel's hand to Afonso of Portugal, now in exchange for military aid. It was too late. For on September 15, with the help of Pedro Arías, who in 1466 had lost an eye during an attempt made on his life by Pacheco with Enrique's complicity, Alfonso's partisans occupied Segovia and, while the Queen fled, Isabel stayed, to be reunited with Alfonso and in November to celebrate his fourteenth birthday.

At Isabel's request, Gómez Manrique wrote a *momo*, a masque, for the occasion, redolent with classical allusion and moral injunction, its theme good kingship. In it Isabel and seven of her ladies performed, as muses bearing gifts, and, implicitly, as analogues of the seven (known) planets, with Isabel in the role of beneficent Fortune, making predictions of the sort received upon accession by their father, Juan II.[26] Alfonso's birthday presents were virtues, skills, and a glorious future: he would be liberal and just, a Hercules in strength, yet a gentle knight, well loved and well feared. As climax, Alfonso's sister promised him triumphs and victories, glories both earthly and celestial. Isabel, as in much else, was consistent in continuing to commission *momos* to celebrate family occasions, in relying on Gómez Manrique, in her penchant for political theatre, and in her view of what the future must hold for Castile and its monarch.

Isabel and Alfonso rode back to Arévalo and their mother, but not before Isabel got a document from Alfonso and his supporters stating she was not to be forced to marry against her will. They were there on December 7, when Alfonso presented her with the jurisdiction and estimable rents of Medina del Campo and its fairs, which neither side in that civil war had wanted closed down.

For Isabel, life at Enrique's court had been far from secure, her position uncertain, the times turbulent, and events potentially overwhelming. Still, the impression is left that she remained self-possessed, even self-contained, and from the outset evinced a quiet firmness, and a strong moral character. To whatever extent she may have enjoyed life at court, what comes through is that she presented to the world a measured demeanor, that her temperament was such to make the best of her surroundings, and that it was also such that patience and forbearance were learned qualities she assiduously cultivated.

She had come to court not as a poor relation but as an outsider with a distinctly different moral code and she appears to have retained it. She also demonstrated the wisdom to take on the protective coloration necessary for survival at court. She appears to have got on well enough with the king, and they had happy moments together when, it is recorded, Isabel danced and Enrique sang, even while learning from his example how not to rule. She gravitated toward the dissidents, who courted her, who were people esteemed at home and, whatever their motives, whose cause bound them to her brother and herself. She would not, though, personally employ the impassioned apocalyptic rhetoric they favored, the sort going out under Alfonso's signature. Her style would be exactly antithetical: rational, that of a monarch determined to set matters to rights; yet it too would be self-righteous and finally imperious, and she would understand and rely upon the appeal of such doomsday rhetoric. During her years at court there was a growing demand for social and religious order. Subsequently, she would display a penchant for order of all sorts, a faith involving a direct relationship with an ordering, just God, and a firm belief in the efficacy of her prayers.

4

The Right Marriage
1467–1469

". . . it has to be he and absolutely no other."

Isabel

ALFONSO XII

ALFONSO was 14 years old, and he was upright and vengeful. Three stories are told of him. Alfonso saying he would suffer what he must patiently until he was of an age to punish injustices. Alfonso responding angrily to a request from men in Toledo for authority to take the posts and property of *conversos* and to exile them. And Alfonso concerned about the effect on Isabel of the immodest dress and behavior of Juana's women; "although he well knew her great virtue and honesty, he would have enjoyed seeing her leave such company."[1] An impression builds of dogmatic chivalry. Yet there is something else: a vindictiveness, evident in his slaughter of the animals Enrique had collected and cherished in Segovia: deer, bearcubs, leopards and ocelots; Pacheco got him to spare one huge mountain goat, "knowing Enrique loved it."[2]

Palencia provides extenuating circumstance. Enrique, he says, had kept the boy confined for some time in the *alcázar* in Segovia, where, "Alfonso, wrenched from his mother's arms, existed as though buried, exposed to perversity and in danger of a very cruel death."[3] (By perversity he meant homosexual enticement.) And, he went on, it was said that while he was jailed in the tower the Queen often tried to poison him with herbs but the keeper of the *alcázar* prevented it, until Enrique at length freed him. Whether or not accurate, Alfonso most probably believed it. Moreover, Juan II, his father (and Isabel's), had had, it was said, a cruel and vengeful streak, but in his case along with insufficient spirit to do much harm. And many years later, a great-niece of Alfonso's who also felt persecuted when young would, forcefully, wreak sufficient vengeance to become known as Bloody Mary. Her reign, too, would be truncated.

In March 1468, when Gonzalo Chacón, on Isabel's behalf taking possession of Medina del Campo, encountered resistance, it was symptomatic of a wider movement. In the eternal pendulum swing caused by rival urban factions seeking outside support against one another, towns that had gone over to Alfonso, among them Burgos and Toledo, were returning to Enrique. In Toledo, Alfonso, who had earlier lost the support of the *converso* faction on the rumor that he was disposed to persecute such New Christians, subsequently lost the backing of the opposing faction when he would not agree to removing *conversos* from the town council. Enrique, more obliging, did some fishing of his own in troubled waters and won back Toledo; on June 16, 1468, he issued a general amnesty, and on July 3 he abolished the city council seats held by *conversos*. In Toledo the previous year trouble had begun among *conversos* and Jews competing to farm taxes. Feeding into it was a contest between the cathedral council and the principal royal official there, the *alcalde*, between, that is, Carrillo, Toledo's archbishop, who supported Alfonso, and Enrique IV. Subsequently, *conversos* there were attacked, robbed, and killed. It was another example of a religious issue put to use for other purposes, and there would be more of them.

At the end of June 1468, Alfonso, with Pacheco and Carrillo and a number of his people, set out from Arévalo to arrange a siege of Toledo to regain the city. Alfonso had accompanied Isabel to Medina del Campo in May when she had expressed a wish to go to the fair and now she rode with him. On July 2 near Avila, at Cardeñosa, he fell ill. Within three days he was dead, purportedly of plague. Palencia says he collapsed immediately after lunching on a trout *empanada*, and asserts that he was poisoned by Pacheco. True or not, in the preceding weeks, Pacheco had raided the treasury: Alfonso had signed an unusual number of *mercedes* to him and his family and also, on May 14, an oddly belated order to the *contadores mayores* to reimburse him for expenses incurred in liberating himself and Isabel.

Palencia averred that Alfonso, ever since he had been proclaimed king at Avila, had tried to get Carrillo to discuss in council the need for "reforming palace life," and recalled that he himself had been approached by the boy-king for help in escaping Pacheco's care, for Alfonso could not tolerate the *hombres infames* Pacheco had surrounded him with, the same sort of men (snorts Palencia) who had been introduced to rouse Enrique to licentiousness, to make him effeminate and thus to dominate him.

While Enrique had few policies, domestic or foreign, except to put out brushfires as they occurred, Juan Pacheco, Marqúes de Villena, had a dynasty of his own to establish, a purpose generally counter to the interests of Isabel. Pacheco strove to be mayor of the palace in the tradition of Charles Martel or the powerful al-Manṣur of Al-Andalus. His early plan may have been to join the dissidents, gain Alfonso the succession, then have the princess Juana marry a son of his, having seen to it that aspersions on her paternity ensured that she was not a desirable match for royalty, then again switch sides and restore her good name and standing. It was not beyond him. There was a secret agreement with Louis of France that Juana would wed one of Pacheco's sons. And in June 1467 he was negotiating for his daughter Beatriz to marry Fernando of Aragón; while Alfonso lived, Isabel was only Juan of Aragón's second choice for his son. Still, by August of that year, Pacheco had decided Alfonso XII of Castile would be a preferable match for Beatriz.

Plainly though, there was little congeniality in the natures of the suave Marqués and the young martinet. And Alfonso had become ever more truculent. Now, with the boy gone and Isabel about to be married out of the kingdom, it was possible that one of Pacheco's brood might both marry Fernando and wear the crown of Castile for, barring Isabel, and with Juana's paternity discredited, the Prince of Aragón and his father were as closely related to Enrique as anyone: for in Juan I of Castile they had a common progenitor. So matters stood when Alfonso fell mortally ill.

PRINCESS

A letter to the kingdom under Isabel's name went out from Cardeñosa on July 4, 1468, while Alfonso still lingered. A copy directed to Murcia survives, stating that should he die she was his legitimate heir and that the city should be held in her name as its rightful lady, its *señora natural*, and deputies be readied to take the oath to her in Cortes. The following day she signed another, announcing his death that very afternoon: "at three, it pleased Our Lord, for the sins of these kingdoms, to take from this present life the lord king my brother."[4] The wording, recalling biblical explanation of death from plague, also echoed current rhetoric in implying that Alfonso's demise was both a sacrifice for the realm and a sign of God's displeasure with its condition. In years to come, Isabel would hold to the view of God she expressed that day, a stern judge putting matters to rights, personally meting out merited punishment, and reward, to the monarch and the body politic indistinguishably, and not only through plague, although to its persistence was undoubtedly owed something of the virulence of that punishing concept of divinity.

There is no way of knowing how Isabel felt at the time. She spoke of founding a convent in her younger brother's memory at the place he died; and, although she never did, she did have him sculpted in a wall niche by their parents' tombs in Miraflores, his image conveying youthful promise personified, and blighted. Her adherents lamented Alfonso's death in similar terms, Jorge Manrique, Rodrigo's son, seeing it as a blow of fortune, leaving unfulfilled a promise of justice and virtue.[5] And Gómez Manrique, reiterating the themes of Alfonso's birthday masque, eulogized him as a young Caesar who, had he lived, would have established an empire overseas and conquered barbarous nations.[6] Palencia went yet further, or perhaps higher, in speaking of Alfonso as "that monarch born in the old age of his father to give hope to the people," thus presenting him as another young Isaac, and even as Christlike, as "the holy boy" who had given up "his immaculate soul."[7] Diego de Valera added that as Alfonso lay dying, in many places in Avila and Segovia other people on their deathbeds and especially children spoke of going to glory in the company of the blessed king *don Alfonso.*[8] As to the niche at Miraflores, the strongest impression it conveys is that of a harbinger, announcing the reign that would be Isabel's.

Isabel was not present when Alfonso's body was interred, on the night he died, in the convent of San Francisco at Arévalo. Carrillo and Pacheco had taken her to Avila, where they squabbled over what to do next. Pacheco insisted that she declare herself not Alfonso's heir but Enrique's, not queen but princess. Carrillo wanted her immediately proclaimed queen as Alfonso's successor, arguing that he did not trust Enrique: had he not put her in his wife's care so that she would grow up unfit to rule? Pacheco then insisted that she marry Afonso of Portugal. Carrillo was determined that she should marry Fernando of Aragón. Pacheco threatened to take her from Avila. Carrillo retorted he assuredly would not, for the garrison was his. Pacheco pleaded the presence of plague. And Carrillo assured him that it only attacked boys.

Two weeks later, she signed a letter to Chacón, "Isabel, by Grace of God Princess and legitimate hereditary successor to these kingdoms of Castile and León."[9] She would be Enrique's heir. With disagreement between her mentors the decision had been hers. At court, within the royal council there was recognition that she herself had made the choice and that she was extremely astute, that for an unmarried 17-year-old *infanta* to have claimed the crown would have been foolhardy.

Too, everyone knew that support for Alfonso and his faction had eroded, that nobles and towns had deserted to the extent that strength remained only in Extremadura and Andalusia, whose great lords were always quick to acknowledge the least constraining superior authority. Enrique, that is, could not be dislodged. Yet there was very broad consensus that since Enrique must have a successor, a woman of marriageable age was preferable to a young girl. As for Enrique, however he had felt about Alfonso, he interpreted his death as a prospect for peace. The *grandes* were tired of civil war. Queen Juana was in disgrace, having had a son by her keeper. So it was that Isabel and Enrique jointly signed a document on September 18, stating it had become publicly manifest that for the past year *"la reina doña Juana* had not used her person cleanly as complies with the service of the king nor her own," and that the king had been informed "that he was not, nor is, legitimately married to her."[10]

King and rebels reconciled, meeting in an open field in Avila's countryside, outside a Hieronymite monastery in a place known as Toros de Guisando. Isabel arrived on a mule with Carrillo walking beside her, holding its reins, a gesture an archbishop would only make for the highest dignitary in the land. He had come reluctantly and he refused to kiss Enrique's hand as a sign of obedience until after the rebels had been forgiven and Isabel promised succession. The promise was given, and she in turn pledged to marry no one without the king's consent. The papal envoy absolved everyone of the oath taken to young Juana.

As mute witnesses to this reconciliation, which would not last, stand to this day the ancient *Toros de Guisando*, a row of stone bulls hewn ages ago, similar to the ones in Arévalo attributed to Hercules. If, as learned opinion has it, they were set up initially to delineate cattle paths and ensure fertility, their primordial symbolism remained potent. Though it was Isabel who proffered homage to Enrique, it was at bottom her victory: for hers was the inherent power, of youth and fertility. She was soon, too, to concern herself with delineation of boundaries, to push against limits in exercising her new authority as Princess. For as heir-presumptive to the crown of Castile, she would in the months to come receive her own council, jurisdictions, and household. She would be introduced to governing and receive her own sources of income. And it was imperative she marry.

For the next nine months, Isabel was in Ocaña, where Enrique too spent much of his time. It was a stronghold of Pacheco, who again dominated the Royal Council; the Mendoza had gone home to Guadalajara, but not without having received custody of Queen Juana and her daughter. Isabel lived in the house of Gutierre de Cárdenas, Chacón's cousin, whom she made her *maestresala*, in charge of her household, and, like Chacón, a member of her council. Cárdenas had been in Carrillo's household—"he was with Carrillo for a great while, with no more than a mule"[11]—and both he and Chacón had adhered to the dissident league, worked with Pacheco, followed Alfonso, and now gave to Isabel a primary loyalty, never to be withdrawn.

At Ocaña, with her people around her and Carrillo nearby in Yepes, she organized a staff and began to enjoy the stature and power of Princess of Asturias. Enrique granted her the jurisdiction and revenues of Medina del Campo, as Alfonso had, of other towns as well, and he assigned to her all royal authority over the mint at Avila. She bestowed *mercedes* and she embarked on another politic occupation, writing innumerable letters to nobles, high clergy, urban councils, and religious houses, couched as keeping Castilians informed of her situation and consulted on whom she should marry, thereby adroitly testing the temper of the realm, strengthening her own position within it, and displaying an awareness of the worth of wooing public opinion.

Some advice she had not solicited also came, on or about her seventeenth birthday, in the form of a guide for young ladies, a *Garden of Noble Maidens*. Its author was Martín de Córdoba, an Augustinian friar, a renowned preacher who had been a preceptor to Alfonso. Her mother may have commissioned it. Urging upon her the usual maidenly desiderata—chastity, modesty, a sense of shame, and a guarded tongue, it was, although it does mention some commonplaces of good monarchy, obviously a manful attempt to put the best face possible on expectation of a woman ruler. And its litany of ideal feminine attributes had as little to do with the lives and qualities of the remarkably strong women who had recently been Spain's queens as did the virtuous precepts of the Mirrors of Princes with the behavior and character of Castile's fifteenth-century kings. At bottom, it was an extended Augustinian essay on original sin and on the descent of women from the original sinner, Eve, the product of Adam's rib (the friar went into a learned disquisition on just which rib), on Eve who was also held up as the source of all feminine weakness and inferiority. That is, Isabel was informed that she was among the best of the worst and must work very hard to be virtuous, since, having high position, she would be an exemplar to other women.

Martín de Córdoba clearly did not have Isabel in mind as reigning monarch when he wrote that God had put the seat of the king of Spain in the West, "wherefore it appears he is sharing the reign of earth with our king."[12] The advice he gave her was limited to behaving as befitted a cynosure of ideal feminine traits. The qualities he enjoined upon her could do no harm in ruling, but neither were they those considered to be of most value to a monarch. Even should she become queen, the author did not expect the queen to be the one who ruled. Birthday wishes came too from the faithful Gómez Manrique who, after wishing her happiness, added a hope "that God will give you a king for a husband."[13] Whoever might rule, she had first to become queen, and for her to do so in fifteenth-century Castile a husband was imperative.

SUITORS

Isabel, who throughout her life was indeed mindful of the wisdom of displaying among other qualities those of an exemplary woman, while in Ocaña did guard her tongue. And there was dissimulation in the letters she sent, for though she did not say so she had already chosen a husband, possibly even before meeting Enrique at Toros de Guisando. He was Fernando, Prince of Aragón, whose father had in June enhanced his stature by an additional title, King of Sicily. Immediately after Alfonso's death, that old fox Juan had broken off negotiations for Fernando's marrying Beatriz Pacheco and intensified his concurrent campaign for Isabel. Through deft diplomacy, promises of greater position and power to influential Castilians, and well-placed applications of Aragonese gold in Castile, he gained sufficient acceptance among Castilian nobles and ecclesiastics; importantly, from the Mendoza came a secret promise in May not to stand in Isabel's way to inheriting the crown. Juan's chief allies in those negotiations were his father-in-law, Alfonso Enríquez, Castile's Admiral, and Carrillo, Archbishop of Toledo. Carrillo in turn worked closely with Rodrigo Manrique, that stalwart of the old nobility who headed a formidable clan.

Other suitors as well were seeking out Isabel now that she brought Castile in her dowry. Louis XI of France requested her hand for his brother and heir-presumptive, Charles, Duke of Berry and Guienne. Although Edward IV of England had married elsewhere, one of his brothers, possibly the future Richard III, was another prospect. And Afonso of Portugal demanded she marry him as redress for the affront suffered by his niece, young Juana. Pacheco continued to vigorously support the Portuguese match: not only would it free Fernando to marry his daughter Beatriz, but, aside from his own good claim to the Castilian crown, the new king of Sicily would be far more acceptable to Castilians than a queen married to the powerful king of Portugal. With Pacheco back at his side, Enrique, shortly after reconciling with Isabel, without her permission and seemingly belying his renunciation of the queen's child, accepted Afonso of Portugal for her and Afonso's promising son and heir, João, for young Juana, and an embassy from Lisbon arrived at Ocaña to make arrangements.

Behind those formal negotiations, messages flew back and forth to Carrillo at Yepes. "All the exquisite vigilance of the Master"—Enrique had confirmed Pacheco as Master of Santiago—"was ineffective," says Palencia, who was then a secretary of Isabel's, to avoid secret envoys entering Ocaña and talking quietly to her.[14] Documents preliminary to marriage with Fernando were signed secretly in January 1469. That same month Isabel affirmed to her confederates that she would marry only the king of Sicily, that "it has to be he and absolutely no other."[15]

It was in recounting those events that Pulgar argued the decision was hers to make since she was in effect an orphan, and he then added that she also believed that if she did not marry Fernando, Enrique would ultimately choose him for Juana and disinherit her. Carrillo, in close concert with Chacón and Cárdenas, arranged that Isabel formally consent to marry Aragón's prince and Sicily's king before witnesses by proxy, with Carrillo's son, Troilos, standing in for the groom. Isabel was promised by Juan an engagement gift of 40,000 gold florins. That consortium also, since she and Fernando were second cousins, secured a dispensation for marrying within the third degree of consanguinity, not from the pope but from the bishop of Segovia, Juan Arías, who based his decision on a bull Juan of Aragón presented as having been received during earlier wedding negotiations. Juan had most likely forged it.

The complicated arrangements necessary to clearing the way for a surreptitious royal wedding progressed. Pacheco, it was surmised, knew of them and was planning to spring a trap. With Carrillo was Pierres de Peralta, Juan of Aragón's trusted counselor and his constable, who informed him in cipher that Pacheco was increasingly unpopular and that "when he decides to jump, [everything is ready] to jump ahead of him."[16] Enrique, at Ocaña on and off that spring, was uneasy, as well he might be, for in the streets children playing at being knights on stick horses would sing-song, *"Flores de Aragón/ dentro en Castilla son,/ Flores de Aragón/ dentro en Castilla son"*—"Flowers of Aragón are inside Castile, Flowers of Aragón are inside Castile"—and then, laughing and waving small banners, they would shout: "*¡Pendón de Aragón, Pendón de Aragón!*"—"banner of Aragón! banner of Aragón!"[17] There was no doubt that the populace preferred an Aragonese to a Portuguese king, especially a young, robust prince.

When Enrique, ever more suspicious, had a nobleman threaten Isabel with arrest if she did not leave the decision of her marriage to him, she broke into tears. Enrique, unswayed, had the Portuguese emissaries swear to use force if necessary to see to it that she married their king. And he did not, though he had promised he would, declare her his heir in the rump Cortes, of ten cities, he called to Ocaña. She later accused him of having had to intimidate those tame delegates into agreeing to the Portuguese marriage. He next tried to have her carried off to the *alcázar* of Madrid, and, although he desisted for fear that Carrillo would send troops to oppose it, the hubbub he had created in Ocaña caused the Portuguese to decamp.

And so matters stood when, at Pacheco's behest, Enrique went south to assert his authority in Andalusia. Isabel excused herself from accompanying him on the grounds of having to stay to escort Alfonso's body from Arévalo to permanent interment in Avila. Before he left on May 7, Enrique had her swear she would make no innovation concerning her marriage. Leaving her behind on oath was Pacheco's idea; it should flush out her intentions. Pacheco had arranged she be closely watched and left with her his nephew, Luis de Acuña, Bishop of Burgos. He had also ostensibly convinced her ladies, Beatriz de Bobadilla and Mencia de la Torre, of the folly of the Aragonese suit, and he had placed on alert nearby at the castle of Coca his ally, Alfonso de Fonseca, Archbishop of Seville, with a large garrison. Although it was a fine point, since Isabel had previously vowed to wed Fernando, she could construe plans forwarding the Aragonese match as not being innovations.

She left, as planned, for Arévalo, hoping while there to reclaim the town for her mother, for Enrique had granted it to the Count of Plasencia, Alvaro de Stúñiga, but she was stopped in no uncertain terms from entering Arévalo's gates by Stúñiga's lieutenant, an insult that rankled and that would be avenged. She nonetheless collected Alfonso's body from the Franciscan convent outside the walls, went on to Avila, and then to her mother, who was at Madrigal. There in late July a French embassy, forwarded by Enrique, found her.

Louis XI, hoping to encircle Aragón and concerned about Castile's pact with England and with Enrique's keeping Castilian merchants out of France, had sent the Cardinal of Albi to him in Andalusia to renew friendly relations and to present to him the suit of the Duke of Guyenne for Isabel's hand. Enrique obligingly broke the pact with England and signed one with France, but, unable to get the *grandes* to support the French marriage and anxious to get rid of the long-winded Cardinal, had suggested he go and convince Isabel herself of its advantages. She responded to the Frenchman, according to Pulgar, that "she waited for God to show His will, and would do that which was to His service and and the good of these kingdoms . . . and nothing without the advice of the *grandes* and knights."[18] Most of the *grandes,* of course, were known to be opposed to the match. Assuredly she had learned to say no while seeming to say perhaps.

She had reason to put off the French. Palencia added that she had recently sent her chaplain on the pretext of business, to France, to look over Charles, and to Aragón to observe Fernando. He had reported to her that in all excellence the Prince exceeded the Duke, for the Prince was very gallant and he was handsome in countenance, body, and person; he was of noble air and very disposed to all she would wish, while the Duke was soft and effeminate, with spindly legs and weepy half-blind eyes, so that before long he would have more need of someone to support him than of horse and arms for knightly endeavor. And he reminded her that the customs of the French were repugnant to Castilian gravity. Isabel was delighted with his report.

She had had a letter from Fernando; her reply survives. Addressed "to the lord my cousin, King of Sicily" and carried to Fernando by Peralta, it guardedly expressed her commitment:

> Lord cousin, now that the Constable goes there, it is not necesessary that I write as well, except to ask your pardon for so late a reply. And because it has been already so delayed, he will give it to Your Mercy. May it attest to my word, and now you shall inform me what you wish to be done, for that I must do. As for the reason that most elicits it, you shall learn it today [from Peralta] because it is not to be written. From the hand that will do as you may order, *La princesa.*[19]

It is an early instance of the mix of courteous formality and heartfelt commitment that she would retain in writing to him, and she would make similar avowals of service and obedience. Yet beneath is discernible, and imparted, her own sense of self-worth, indeed of how fortunate he is that it is she who addresses him so. That style of hers has been well described as 'meek grandeur.'

Far less meek was a letter she wrote several months later to Enrique, an open one, widely circulated, explaining her recent behavior and laying it to his bad faith. While in Madrigal, she began, she had discovered that he had ordered the town council to keep her there forcibly. Although the town fathers had wavered, she had found too that some of her women and servants had been set to spy on her, that her disapproving ladies, Beatriz de Bobadilla and Mencia de la Torre, had left for Coca, and that its lord, Fonseca, on Pacheco's orders, was to come in six days to seize her. It was then she found it necessary, she told Enrique, to send for Carrillo and the Admiral, her uncles. She did not tell him that her emissary, her confessor, Alonso de Burgos, had so insolently asked their help that Carrillo, incensed, nearly did not come. Moreover, it would be surprising if her seemingly disaffected ladies with whom she soon reconciled were not in reality her spies.

Arriving with 600 horses, the Archbishop and the Admiral had proposed to escort her out of Madrigal in order, she informed Enrique, to quit the fears of the townspeople. She left with them (she omitted that she had first gleefully said farewell to Pacheco's factotum, the Bishop of Burgos, telling him she was going where she wished). It is recorded that she then rode off in that company, "with great joy and to the sound of many trumpets and kettledrums," first to Fontiveros, where the people feared the king's wrath, then to her city of Avila, where they found that pestilence was growing worse daily, and so finally to Valladolid, which was healthy and secure and adhered to the Admiral. She had, as Juan of Aragón was informed, taken the leap.

That she had not simply acted impulsively is manifest in her having, prodded by Chacón and Cárdenas, insisted that before committing herself she receive, as earnest of Fernando's intent, the 40,000 gold florins promised in January. Palencia, sent by Carrillo to fetch them, had instead returned with some gold pieces and a golden necklace set with spinel rubies and pearls that had belonged to Aragón's queens worth, he says, the 40,000 florins. Just before coming, Carrillo had sent it to her along with 8000 florins in cash, with which, said Palencia disapprovingly, she had been prodigal, in giving 2000 each to Chacón and Cárdenas, and another 1000 to Clara Alvarnaez, "as her most obedient servants." Palencia notwithstanding, her confidence would prove well placed.

In Valladolid she stayed in the house of Juan de Vivero, whose wife, María de Acuña, was the daughter of the Count of Buendía, who was Carrillo's brother, and his Countess, who was Fernando's aunt. From there, on September 8 she wrote Enrique that long letter in which she explained, and justified, her independent course of action from Ocaña on. She reminded him of her moderation on Alfonso's death in refusing the title of Queen, indicated that it was he who had broken their agreement at Toros de Guisando in arranging marriage for her against her will; and it was now that she complained of his insistence she marry the King of Portugal and of the threats made to her and the delegates to the Cortes of Ocaña. The tone she took in writing—bordering on righteous indignation, hovering between disappointment in him and recrimination, certain of her own moral position—she would resort to frequently in all variety of communiques and situations. Now she chastised Enrique for following bad advice and declared her own decision to be based upon the collective will and best interests of the kingdom. So she reminded him that, when faced with the Portuguese marriage, he had, "condescending to the will of some individuals," wished her forced to consent. Then, "I, alone and deprived of my just and proper liberty and the exercise of free will that in marital negotiations after the grace of God is the principal requisite, secretly made inquiry of the *grandes,* prelates, and *caballeros,* your subjects, concerning their opinion." They responded, she went on, that the Portuguese marriage "in no manner complied to the good of your kingdoms . . . but all praised and approved the marriage with the Prince of Aragón, King of Sicily." That union, she assured him, would add to the glory of his realm.[20]

As for the French marriage, his subjects desired she should not marry in parts so far from her own land and customs, and they believed that that alliance would turn his kingdoms into dependencies, allowing France to accrete power, take Aragón, neighbor Castile, and "to occupy the dominions [*señoríos*] of our close relatives." Throughout, Isabel put emphasis on the usual royal practice of mentioning family relationships, repeatedly reminding him their differences were a family matter: so she spoke of Alfonso as 'our brother'; of Afonso of Portugal as 'my cousin'; of the kings of Aragón as 'your near relatives,' as well as alluding to their mutual royal progenitors. She listed the benefits of the Aragonese union, and recalled that their common grandfather, Enrique III, in his will had counseled his descendants to it. She presented herself as "a younger sister desirous of your service and the peace and tranquility of these your kingdoms," implying contrast to his non-related and sinister advisors who had little interest in the welfare of the realm. She was right about public opinion concerning France and Portugal, but she did overstate the popularity of the Aragonese match.

Palencia and Cárdenas were sent in haste to Aragón, to escort Fernando to Castile before Enrique and Pacheco returned to the *meseta*. She soon received disconcerting news from them, that many of the clergy and nobles they had been counting on for assistance had changed sides and, worst of all, that the Mendoza, from whom they had expected neutrality, had gone over to Enrique, so that their great castles and forts along the entire frontier from Almazán to Guadalajara stood between Fernando and Valladolid. Cárdenas voiced concern that Fernando would not attempt the trip; Palencia was certain he would. He had been with him in Valencia, while getting the ruby necklace for Isabel out of pawn, and had then to dissuade him from setting off immediately to rescue her.

THE PRINCE OF ARAGÓN AND KING OF SICILY

Palencia and Cárdenas reached Zaragoza at the end of September and there, in great secrecy, in a cell of the Franciscan convent, they rendezvoused with the Prince of Aragón and King of Sicily. The 17-year-old they met was of medium stature, with bright, smiling eyes, straight dark-brown hair, and "he had so singular a grace that everyone who talked to him wanted to serve him."[21] Although twice deathly ill as a child, he was now strong and fit, having "been raised at war and endured many hardships and dangers."

Fernando was born on March 10, 1452, in the village of Sos in Aragón, where his mother, Juana Enríquez, had gone, foresightedly, to establish her child's claim to the kingdom his father might well inherit. He had grown up close to this strong, indeed headstrong mother, whom her much older husband—in 1452 she was 28, he was 54—loved and indulged. She had brought up her son to succeed to Aragón's crown, beginning by putting off his baptism for nearly a year, until Juan was regent in Aragón and it could be held in the cathedral in Zaragoza. There, with royal magnificence, the child was named for his paternal grandfather, Fernando de Antequera, a king of Aragón who was as well the foremost Castilian hero of the wars against the Muslims in recent memory.

The child was five when his father, becoming Aragón's king, was immediately immersed in wars. Juan waged them personally, even though half-blind from cataracts until 1466, then completely so for three years, until an operation performed by a Jewish doctor restored his sight. Juan fought the French and from his accession there had been civil war, chiefly with the Catalans. Catalonia, with Barcelona at its heart, Aragón's largest and wealthiest province, had declined from its golden age of trade and been hard hit by related economic woes and recurrent plague. Propertied Catalans, unsympathetic to the dynastic and imperial adventures in the Mediterranean of his brother and predecessor, Alfonso the Magnanimous, did not trust Juan from the outset. In Barcelona, artisans and guilds looked to Juan for economic redress and support against proprietors and landlords; proprietors and landlords wanted to take charge of stabilizing conditions themselves. In the countryside, Aragonese peasants, suffering from plague and hard times, opposed nobles who were seeking to extract more work from fewer laborers and to renew lapsed seignorial dues. Particularly onerous was the *remensa*, a money recompense exacted from peasants for leaving the land. When they appealed for relief to the new king, he, in trying to steer a moderate course, pleased no one. *Remensa* peasants rebelled; their landlords raised armies against them.

The Catalans rising against Juan took his elder son, Carlos of Viana, as king, and when Carlos died in 1461 they claimed the queen, Juana Enríquez, had had him poisoned. Juan, busy rebuffing opportunistic French attempts to seize territory, did not soothe them when he immediately convoked Aragón's parliament, the *Corts*, and appointed Fernando, then nine years old, his lieutenant in Catalonia, delegating authority to the Queen. The Catalans, declaring her arrogant and intrusive in their affairs, soon forced her to leave Barcelona and renounced Fernando as governor; it was then they appealed to Enrique IV of Castile. Juana Enríquez retreated with her son to Gerona, where she oversaw the repulse of a Catalan siege. Three years later, at age 12, Fernando squared accounts, at the head of royal forces defeating in battle the Catalans. Subsequently, Juan, without calling the Corts, named his son lieutenant-general of the realm. The civil war wore on.

When the Corts convened at Zaragoza on February 6, 1468, Juana Enríquez, suffering from cancer of the breast and neck, was too sick to preside. Fernando went instead; he was 16 years old. When two weeks later she died—Valera insisted that a wonderful odor arose from her corpse, implying she was a saint, which was unlikely—the king was as usual battling the French in the north, and it was Fernando who saw to her funeral. Then, in Valencia, addressing the city's notables with tears streaming down his face, he paid her a tribute she would have appreciated: ''Lords: You all know with what hardships my lady mother has sustained the war to keep Catalonia within the house of Aragón. I see my lord father old and myself very young. Therefore I commend myself to you and place myself in your hands and ask you to please consider me as a son." The town councillors responded satisfactorily, promising a truce to factional strife until the war's end and donating to the crown the realm-wide receipts from taxes on bread and wine. "And so console yourself," they told their prince, "because we have confidence in Our Lord, and that you will recover our lands."[22]

Valencians had lionized him since his victory over the Catalans, their arch competitors. With Barcelona in revolt, Valencia was thriving as Aragón's chief port, and it stood to benefit further from a marriage ensuring freer interchange with Castile. So it was that in July 1469 they turned over to him, with exuberant pomp and ceremony, the ruby necklace so that he might give it to Isabel, overlooking its being held as surety for a loan made to the king his father, and they advanced him an additional 30,000 *sueldos* to pay for his wedding, since Juan's wars with the French and greasing of Castilian palms had exhausted the Aragonese treasury.

Fernando had been raised in the parental household. By ten, when he was given his own staff, he had received the initial training in letters, arms, and horsemanship usual to a noble's education. If the exigencies of war had brought him more experience in the saddle, under siege, and in council than familiarity with arts and letters, yet his native intelligence and curiosity ensured a lifelong respect for knowledge and the learned. Among his preceptors were Alfonso de la Torre, who wrote Dantesque and erotic verse and who at Juan's request had produced didactic poems for Fernando's instruction, and Joan Margarit, Bishop of Gerona, some of whose advice he seems to have taken to heart. Margarit advocated Spanish unity. He also told him that administration of a kingdom required exercise of prudence rather than an unbending morality: the prince might, he conceded, choose the moment for revealing truth, and he might make promises in war he need not fulfill. Fernando, as Pulgar knew him later, displayed the princely virtue of seeking out good counsel and the gift of listening. "It can not be said that he was frank. He was a man of truth, although the great need in which wars put him made him sometimes deviate."[23] Pulgar, incidentally, said much the same of Isabel.

In his last year in Aragón, a dashing young hero-prince, Fernando displayed yet another quality Pulgar would mention, "he gave himself to women." He then fathered two children: Alfonso of Aragón, born in 1470, who would become Bishop of Zaragoza, and Juana of Aragón, born in 1469, whom Isabel would one day welcome to her court and would marry to Bernardino Fernández de Velasco, Constable of Castile. Two more daughters of his born later would be less welcome.

Now in the fall of 1469, Fernando was resolved to marry the Princess of Castile. He left Aragón with only a few retainers. They traversed hostile countryside disguised as merchants and their servants: Fernando served supper and curried the mules. And there was cheer when along the way Palencia spotted a good omen, a pair of eagles, soaring high. At the border town of Burgo de Osma they found Gómez Manrique waiting; Isabel had sent a squadron as escort.

On October 9, in Valladolid, she received Palencia and Cárdenas, who had ridden ahead to let her know that Fernando had arrived at nearby Dueñas where he had been royally received by its Count, Carrillo's brother, and its Countess, his own aunt, that he was safe and on his way. Her happiness was intense, recounted Palencia, not least because while waiting she had had to fend off arguments against the wedding put to her by envoys of Queen Juana and of Pacheco, who were by then certain something was in the wind, as well as those of her own courtiers, who insisted that the dignity of the royal house of Castile and the excellence of the Princess so exceeded that of the King of Sicily and Prince of Aragón that it was unfitting that, because of his sex, he should have any advantage whatsoever over his spouse.

On October 12 she wrote to Enrique: "By my letters and messengers I now notify Your Highness of my determined will concerning my marriage," which at her age she adjudged to be a very reasonable act. In view of who she was, she went on, and whose daughter and whose sister, she had made the most suitable match possible, after having consulted the principal people of the realm. She had waited to write until then because she had been informed that he, "following the counsel of some," had sought to impede Fernando who, she wanted him to know, had arrived at Dueñas. Have him as a good vassal, she urged Enrique, and approve her intention. Then came that phrase so frustratingly oft-repeated: Her secretary who was bringing that letter would inform him further.[24]

TO WED

Two days later, she and Fernando first met. He came to Valladolid from Dueñas, secretly, with only three retainers, in the middle of the night, and entered the house by a postern gate. Carrillo greeted him—he tried to kiss his hand but Fernando instead embraced him—and led him inside to Isabel. As they entered the room, Cárdenas excitedly pointed him out to her: ¡ése es, ése es!—that is he, that is he!—linked esses Cárdenas ever after bore with pride emblazoned on his coat of arms.

Isabel was 18, plump and auburn-haired, comely, her blue-green eyes steady, her bearing regal. She saw enter the room a gallant youth, eyes sparkling, taut with energy, a cousin, and a very welcome one. They talked for two hours. "The presence of the Archbishop repressed the amorous impulses of the lovers," observed Palencia, "though they soon enjoyed the licit joys of matrimony." Theirs was an instant attraction, and, remarkably, it proved a passionate and long-lasting love.

A notary took down their formal promises to marry. Fernando gave Isabel customary, if unspecified, gifts and that night he returned to Dueñas. Through the formality of that first meeting is discernible delight and the sense of triumphal and momentous encounter, of danger and complicity heightening sensibilities. There is about that meeting too something calling to mind that chivalric and religious feat, a favorite in Catalan art in particular, of St. George slaying the dragon and rescuing the maiden. Even so, this was not only a romantic encounter but also a formal meeting of state concerning the union of Castile's princess with Aragón's prince and Sicily's king. There were final contractual stipulations and there remained to be decided the many questions of protocol so vitally important to the rites of royalty.

Fernando returned on the eighteenth, this time riding into Valladolid royally with a company of knights. At dusk, surrounded by a large group of well-wishers in Vivero's great hall, they heard the Archbishop read first the bull dispensing with the impediment of consanguinity and then the marriage agreement signed by Fernando and his father. They may have secretly wed that night, but whether or not they did, Fernando went to stay with the Archbishop. The next morning they wed publicly, in the same hall, the Admiral and María de Acuña standing with them. The faithful were there in force: the Enríquez, Manriques, and other lords, and knights, royal justices, priests, and, say the chronicles, 2000 people of all estates. The Archbishop assisted a priest, one Pero López de Alcalá, who the previous January had heard Isabel's promise to wed and who now performed the ceremony. The couple presented him with the dispensation of consanguinity and asked him to marry them. He read it out and declared them absolved, then, having said mass, he gave the nuptial blessings.

Public festivities went on all day. The marriage was consummated that night. Immediately upon that event, says Valera, witnesses, stationed at the door of the bridal chamber, entered, took the customary bedsheet, and, to the fanfare of trumpets and flutes, and the beat of kettledrums, displayed it to the throng waiting expectantly in the hall below. Valera, implying its condition was to their liking, adds that the witnesses surveyed the room, surely to satisfy themselves that they were not being duped. Celebration went on for a week, at its end the Prince and Princess of Aragón and King and Queen of Sicily attended mass, said by Carrillo, and received his benediction. Their standing in Castile was not so clear. Enrique arrived in Segovia by October 20, a stormcloud. Pacheco, reportedly ill with a quaternary fever made worse by the news, retreated to Ocaña.

The terms of the union Carrillo had read out on the eve of the wedding had been agreed upon nearly a year beforehand, on January 7, 1469. Those terms appeared in *capitulaciones*, not within a contract signed by both parties but as an offer by one of them based upon a previous mutual agreement. In this case it was Fernando who with his father, Juan II of Aragón, promised certain things to Isabel. He would, it was promised, behave himself fittingly, obey Enrique, observe Castile's laws and customs, respect its grandes, appoint only Castilians to office, and live in those kingdoms; he would not take Isabel from them nor any of their children, the arrival of children being "no less than should be expected."[25] Neither of them would make *merced* of any city without the other's consent. They would sign everything jointly and share all titles. He promised to honor her appointments of officials and respect her grants of lordships and to make "no movement" or any war or confederation in Castile without her counsel and consent. Fernando was to inherit his father's realms as well, and Isabel to rule in them should he die before her, but in lifetime tenancy, redounding to his heirs. Everything his aunt, María, regent of Aragón, and his mother had held as dowry should belong to Isabel. When she and he had in their joint power those kingdoms, they were obliged to war against the Moors, enemies of the holy Catholic faith, as other Catholic kings, their predecessors, had done.

The *capitulación* employed the royal plural, accentuating the joint nature of this arrangement and tending to obfuscate just who was being referred to in a given instance, whether it was Fernando himself employing the royal we or he and Isabel jointly. What emerges more clearly is the expectation that Fernando was thereby empowered to join Isabel in her inheritance, to take charge in Castile if observing certain stipulations. Too, Juan had hit upon an arrangement satisfactory to her partisans, still nervous about his claims within Castile, and first among the eminences whose honors and prerogatives the signers promised to respect was "the Archbishop of Toledo, primate of Spain, *canciller mayor,* high chancellor, of Castile and our dear and very loved uncle." It was after all Carrillo who had made this bargain with Juan.

Allaying fears of an Aragonese takeover or any attempt to settle old scores, this document, the closest thing to a marriage contract, was not so much about Isabel's exercising authority as about Fernando gaining it. He expected, it said, "to command, govern, reign, and *señorear* as one with her" in her kingdoms. Her envoys, still concerned, had additionally extracted an oath from him before leaving Zaragoza, that he would never make a *merced* in Castile without her assent. For all that, he could still envision himself as becoming, at Enrique's death, the king who ruled Castile. He did not yet know Isabel.

5

To the Crown
1469–1474

¡Castilla, Castilla, Castilla, por la muy alta poderosa Princesa e Señora, nuestra Señora la Reyna Doña Isabel, y por el muy alto e muy poderoso Principe Rey e Señor, nuestro Señor el Rey Don Fernando como su legítimo marido!

Acclamation, Segovia 1474

ROYAL IRE

IMMEDIATELY after the wedding, Isabel and Fernando went to work, in concert. Together, on October 22, they held the first formal meeting of a council of state incorporating their chief advisors, then dispatched letters to elicit support from everywhere and everyone that mattered. A conciliatory embassy to Enrique reiterated their loyalty, informing him they had married on the advice of the kingdom's prelates and grandes, and asking he receive them as his true children; the tone was one of family misunderstanding, Isabel relying on her standing as designated heir. They decided to send an envoy to Rome to obtain papal dispensation for their marriage; there is no record of when Isabel found out that none existed. And Palencia was sent with a request for 1000 lances to Juan of Aragón, who, ever hard-pressed by the French and the Catalans and penniless, sent back only advice: Fernando should listen to his grandfather, the Admiral, and especially to Carrillo.

Their respective advisors, principally Carrillo for Isabel and Peralta for Fernando, negotiated the details of their formal relationship, while they themselves established a more personal one. They discovered immediate affinity in working together. Cousins, both of them born and bred Trastámara, while having the same dynastic frame of reference, nevertheless also had temperaments which, while very different were yet remarkably complementary. Isabel was decisive, indeed resolute to the point of intransigence, and very serious, if with a gift for irony. She gave her trust sparingly but when she did, wholeheartedly. Fernando was deft of mind, affable, and cocksure; his gallantry softened her edges, and won her and the Castilians. Her earnestness reinforced an intensity latent in him. Both of them were quick to take a stand; and both had the gift of self-monitoring, curbing impetuosity, and especially they both had the ability to reassess whatever the other thought unreasonable. Nothing in Isabel's remarkable life is more remarkable than the love and respect she and Fernando demonstrated mutually, immediately, and ever after.

From the first, they were passionately attracted to one another. When they were apart in those early years, Fernando repeatedly braved danger in order to see her, said Palencia, "in visiting his most beloved wife obeying impulses of duty and desire." And Fernando himself later wrote to Isabel of looking forward to seeing her and to being "as we were in our first love."[1]

That initial devotion, coupled with a mutual trust, overcame divisive plots hatched within their court and mitigated the problems arising from their sharing power. Fortunately, Fernando had become accustomed to making decisions of state together with a stong-willed woman, his mother. And Isabel, although very much in love and always careful to express wifely subservience, stood by her punctilious sense of royal prerogative and asserted what she considered her rights as heir to Castile and now as Queen of Sicily. She could anger him with her intransigence when, as happened more than once, exasperated with her counselors he threatened to leave, and then disarm him by dissolving in tears. The images that have come down of the stoic queen and Machiavellian king are stick figures, not drawn from life.

In February 1470, having heard nothing from Enrique since Isabel had notified him of their wedding plans, they wrote to him jointly, presenting their union as a *fait accompli*, recalling Isabel's right to succession and that it had been sworn to at Toros de Guisando, respectfully informing him that they could not be denied justice for—and here the threat, or the appeal to his more responsible counselors—great turmoil would result, irreparably harming the realm, even most of Christendom. They asked that a conclave of grandes and high clergy adjudicate, and should it not reach a decision, a commission be appointed made up of the superiors of the Franciscans, Dominicans, Hieronymites, and Cistercians. Enrique replied only that he would take it up with his council. By June, having heard nothing more, they wrote again, warning him against bad advisors and against putting "enemies of nature above dutiful and loving children" to such a point that they would have to seek violent means to resist such minions.[2]

It was a war of words. Those letters, conveying their own sense of solidarity achieved, they caused to be circulated throughout Castile and abroad. Isabel, courting public opinion to an extent not seen in Castile since Enrique II had fought his half-brother, Pedro I, for the crown a century ago, appealed to the nobles, the clergy, the towns—that is, the realm—and although, unlike that founder of the dynasty, she sought to be recognized not as monarch but as heir-apparent, the line was thin and the parallel plain.

Enrique's immediate answer to the wedding was indirect but pointed: he formally granted to the Count of Plasencia Isabel's mother's town of Arévalo, with its million *maravedís* of annual revenue. And when in September Enrique's powerful supporter, the Count of Benavente, having taken Valladolid, Fernando set off to regain it with 200 lances, he had to desist, for Enrique was riding to defend it with 1000. By then they retained only Medina del Campo, held for them by Gonzalo Chacón, and Avila, by his son, Juan. Both towns, fortunately, produced substantial rents.

Still, it was a bleak winter. They retreated to safe but dismal Dueñas, a stronghold of Carrillo's family. Tempers grew frayed: Carrillo having told Fernando that he was a youngster needing to be directed, Fernando responded that he did not intend to be governed by anyone, and that that was how many of Castile's kings had come to grief. Relations between them were patched up; thereafter more frequently it was Carrillo and Isabel who were at odds. The plan to seek a papal dispensation was dropped: they well knew that there was truth in the saying that in Rome the victors are crowned and the vanquished excommunicated. Nor did they want their adversaries to take up the issue of the legality of their marriage, especially under the circumstances.

For Isabel was with child, and their brightest hope lay in a male heir. She gave birth on October 2 in Dueñas, to a daughter. Her letter of announcement, recalling that of her own birth, spoke ambiguously of the arrival of an *infante*. The child was, not surprisingly, named Isabel, and, if her mother was initially disappointed in her sex, she came to cherish her at least as much as any of the children who followed. Too, that birth signified, to Isabel and everyone else, that more children could be expected. Still, the strain told on Fernando, the sex of his child disappointing, and the place obscure and dreary. He would not hear out his advisors, insisting on making all decisions on his own. He jousted furiously. He soon developed so high a fever that Isabel feared for his life, as did his physician, who attributed his illness to too many falls from horses. Yet he rallied quickly; within days he informed his father that he was recovering, to the extent that he had dressed and attended mass.

A COLD WINTER

The opposition was delighted the child was female. Now Medina del Campo went over to Enrique, a conspiracy developed in Avila, and Enrique sent a manifesto throughout the kingdom disinheriting Isabel and once again naming Juana, his beloved daughter, his heir. The proclamation declared Isabel a dissolute woman who, acting without the king's counsel and disdaining Castile's laws, had lost her shame and coupled with Fernando, Prince of Aragón, who was so closely related they could not wed without papal dispensation, which she had scorned. She had married an enemy for the perdition of Castile; she was no wife, but a concubine. Juana, he declared, would wed the Duke of Berry and Guyenne. He signed this proclamation together with the Queen, the need to present the child as their joint progeny outweighing her indiscretion in having had by then two sons who it was known were not Enrique's. On November 26, 1470, in a reversal of Toros de Guisando, with the Queen and young Juana attending, Enrique repeated the substance of that manifesto in a solemn ceremony; and a papal bull (which may have been forged) was read out, releasing all present from the oath to Isabel. No one was aware that the Duke of Guyenne had died three days earlier, in a tourney celebrating his engagement to Juana. His death, however, in leaving her a single, unaffianced woman, weakened her position in relation to that of Isabel.

Isabel waited until early spring. In March 1471 she circulated a rejoinder, her prose riper than it would ever be again, fueled with moral indignation and a sense of righteousness she would continue to express, but in more restrained fashion. "Without doubt"—she immediately established her own reactions of outrage against false accusation—"I can say with *Santa Susana* that I am greatly anguished, because I can not remain silent without offense or harm to myself nor speak without offending and displeasing the King, my brother, and both [courses] are very grievous to me."[3] She and Alfonso—and here she reproached the king more strongly than she ever had before, and in language Alfonso had used—had been wrested from their mother's arms and brought to court. Yet there, she claimed, omitting several years in the telling, "I remained in my palace in order to be rid of your immorality, taking care for my honor and fearing for my life . . . [persevering] through the grace of God, which was for me greater protection than I had in the King, or in the Queen." She again recounted his failure to keep their pact at Toros de Guisando, by not divorcing his wife and by attempting to force herself, Isabel, to marry against her will. She had kept her word. She had wed Fernando with the advice and consent of the greatest and most rational of the kingdom's *grandes*. The king had said she had married without papal dispensation. She had satisfied her own conscience and in time would be able to show Catholic approval, and she added that Fernando would bring Castile prosperity, that Enrique's impotence was notorious, and that he had previously sworn to the Queen's brazenness, so that his measures were illegal.

Her prose undoubtedly owed something to her circumstances. At the end of the year, in a breach with Carrillo, Isabel and Fernando had left Dueñas for Medina del Rioseco, the seat of Fernando's maternal grandfather, Fadrique Enríquez, Admiral of Castile. Gruff, clannish, great of heart, and with a deep love of family—who included the Mendoza and Manrique and most of the high nobility of Castile, for he had nine sisters all of whom married well—Fadrique Enríquez equally strongly hated his enemies: it was said he would gladly give up an eye if Juan de Vivero would lose two. Revelatory of his impatience, sense of moral rectitude, and respect for tradition as he saw it, was a knuckle-rapping letter he wrote to Pacheco and his cohorts. Why, he inquired of them, do you want to set a bad example for all nobles, so that we [*grandes*] may lose our souls forever and our fame in the chronicles? So that we will suffer worse destruction in our time than did Don Rodrigo [the last Visigothic king]? And so that greed and upstarts may destroy the most honorable reputation that a Christian kingdom could ever have?[4] Clearly, Isabel and he were kindred spirits. The Admiral, who had undoubtedly influenced the tenor of that letter of hers to Enrique, died within a few years, but not before having had good indication of having been instrumental in assuring a bright future for his grandson and his grandson's wife.

Enrique, buying loyalty and time, continuing to court the barons by giving away much of what remained in royal domain, courted disaster. For not only had he ever less left to give, but his grants exacerbated local factionalism and economic malaise and were widely viewed as resulting from his pusillanimity, and from his opportunism and that of Pacheco. Everywhere, lawlessness and local warfare flourished: magnates battled over control of Seville and others fought in Extremadura for the mastership of the military order of Alcántara. In Salamanca factions both fought one another and opposed the lord to whom Enrique had granted the town. Isabel's Avila was not exempt; there the townswomen, said Valera, fought in the streets *virilmente* beside the men. Pulgar then lamented, "If there were more of Castile, there would be more wars."[5]

Slowly, the tide turned toward Isabel and the prospect of better times. Basque mountaineers and seamen who felt threatened by Enrique's friendship with France and prohibition of trade with England came over, as did the town of Bilbao. Other towns announced for her and Fernando, much as they had in 1465 for Alfonso, protesting against domination by nobles or against the royal overseers, the *corregidores*, whom Enrique had imposed over municipal councils; and with those municipalities came their valuable militias, the *hermandades*. Very heartening was the declaration for Isabel by Sepúlveda, a gateway between Castile and Andalusia, and a recent *merced* of Enrique's to Pacheco, which rose against its new lord in mid-February 1472. Pacheco's greed and power, coupled with his intrusiveness in local affairs, and with poor crops, were also turning powerful Andalusians to Isabel and Fernando, or to playing a double game. Enrique's new *mercedes* also escalated old rivalries. The lord of Murcia, Pedro Fajardo, seized the opportunity to declare against any king whomsoever.

Enrique having allied with France, Isabel and Fernando, monarchs in their own right, of Sicily, arranged alliances with Burgundy and with England. They thereby both abetted the France-encircling policy of Juan of Aragón and demonstrated to all Castilians that they had sovereign standing in international affairs. And on appeal from his father, Fernando left for Aragón in late February 1472, word having arrived that Juan was besieging Barcelona and wanted his help. Isabel had resolved differences with Carrillo and was staying with her daughter in his archepiscopal palace at Alcalá de Hénares.

It would be the first of many separations. Fernando returned only in time for Christmas, having entreated leave of his father through, says Palencia, "employing the most efficient solicitude to return to his conjugal marriage bed."[6] That in the interim he might well have had sexual relations with other women was within the mores of the time. When Pulgar observed that, "although he loved the Queen his wife greatly, he gave himself to other women," it was simply a statement of fact, one he made frequently of other notable male contemporaries. And when Fernando left again the following May, Gómez Manrique, in a plaintive poem, told of how

> In looking at the royal face of the Princess
> of Spain which is sad, beautiful, and honest,
> we feel an almost pleasurable grief.
> She flees the meadows like a turtledove.
> She is undone by her desire. . . .
> The music which used to be her greatest joy is now her worry
> Because the melody adds troubles to the troubled one.
> The great sadness which sickens this second Diana
> Saddens and worries all of us
> Enough to say right now that
> the ladies-in-waiting and the lady herself
> are as lonely as the empty city where no one dwells.[7]

She surely missed him, and Manrique said so, his allusions, both chivalric and classic, congenial to Isabel.

QUEEN OF SICILY

In Aragón that year, Fernando was hailed by the official chronicler, Fabricio Gauberto de Vagad, in terms recalling prophecies of the redeemer-king, as the prince awaited by the Spanish kingdoms. He had become a charismatic young paragon as well to many Castilians, who were caught up in a seemingly eternal shortage of food, law, order, and heroes. He evoked in both realms the stored memory of the daring exploits and popularity of those earlier *infantes* of Aragón, his father and his uncles, and the hope conjured up by the name of his grandfather, the Moorfighter, Fernando de Antequera. He was even likened to El Cid. Isabel, then less known, was generally thought of as that gallant's wife and lady, much as Manrique then portrayed her. Yet Castilians did not lose sight of the fact that it was Isabel who was Castilian-born. And she herself never forgot that, though lady and wife, hers was the claim to the crown of Castile, nor that, by the terms of her marriage, she was entitled to jurisdiction in her own right in parts of Sicily.

Certainly Juan of Aragón had come to appreciate the qualities of his daughter-in-law, and to know her persistence firsthand. Immediately after the wedding, she had requested him to turn over to her as promised the *Cámara de la Reina* in Sicily, a rich revenue-yielding area centered on Syracuse, to which he had agreed, in a document of May 1470 that went on to extol her "virtue and incredible constancy," maintained through wars, revolts, and misfortunes in order to marry Fernando, and to laud her resistance to contrary counsel and pressures. Hers, he told her, were liberality, integrity of customs, decorum, prudence, magnanimity, composure, and perfect beauty. No doubt he admired her; no doubt too he meant to keep his own administrator in the region. For, that July when Juan de Cárdenas, Gutierre's son, enroute to Sicily to complete the transfer, stopped to receive from Juan the necessary executive order, he had had to assure him that he would not take over as Isabel's governor; even so, once in Sicily he did just that. A foreigner imposing a new stringency, he soon angered the Syracusans, and a battle of wills followed, conducted in more or less measured tones, between Juan and Isabel. Upon sending Cárdenas, she had written to Juan sternly that she expected him to fulfill the contract without any change whatsoever ("*sin mudar una sola jota*"). In November she acceded to the extent of ratifying Syracuse's privileges, but had insisted that Cárdenas remain. Nonetheless, in January 1471, Juan annulled his appointment. She would not have it, and, in June, she obliged her father-in-law to revoke that order and reinstate his prior agreement. In July 1472, she wrote Aragón's king with courteous salutation, that she kissed his hands, but asked that from then on he do nothing without her knowledge and that he allow her to act in what he gave her and to do what it seemed to her she should do, "for it is certain I will do nothing unless it is just."[8] The Queen of Sicily was confident her heart was in the hands of the Lord. The King of Aragón, while unused to being bested, was assured he had a daughter-in-law of royal caliber.

As the balance of power within Castile shifted favorably, Isabel took care to assert her proprietary rights there. Devoted to Fernando, she was yet mindful of her advisors' worries about his growing popularity, his hereditary claims, and his giving every indication of equaling in strength a father who, among his considerable achievements, was semi-legendary for his penchant for making mischief in Castile. Thus when the town of Aranda, exhausted by bloody factional wars stirred by an official imposed by Queen Juana, recalled that by hereditary right it belonged to the King of Aragón and declared for the young couple, it was, pointedly, Isabel who sent a garrison to claim it in her name alone.

Wise in the ways princes were evaluated and in the symbols of position and power, she had understood from the outset the value of courting the populace, as well as the worth of regal display in that pursuit and in impressing everyone else as well. She well understood the power and authority implied by a show of splendor. Thus while she was at Alcalá ambassadors from Burgundy arrived seeking alliance, in the late spring of 1472 and again a year later. On one of those visits, she was described as welcoming them in velvets, satins, and jewels. Then, holding audience surrounded by her ladies and courtiers, she was dressed yet more elegantly and expensively, and wore the great ruby necklace. She entertained them equally sumptuously, with drinking and dancing, though she herself never touched wine and, as was customary when Fernando was absent, she danced only with her ladies. Their visit wore on and her finery mounted, seemingly no matter the occasion. Thus, she arrived at a bullfight held in their honor wearing a crimson dress, its skirt stylishly hooped on the outside in circlets of gold, and a coat of pleated satin, a gold necklace, and a great crown ringed by yet another crown encrusted with jewels. Her horse's harness was of gilded silver; the Burgundians estimated it weighed over 120 marks. Suitably impressed, they concluded that she was indeed a great lady of noblest rank. Nor would her stay with the extravagant Carrillo have done anything to diminish her penchant for such display, or the wherewithal to achieve it.

The Archbishop of Toledo had lived in Italy, from 1423 to 1439, and had returned to Castile with a taste for intrigue and warfare, a proclivity for magnificence, and a thirst for grandeur and fame. As was the style in Italian courts, including that of the papacy, that prince of the Church became a patron of both arms and letters, and was drawn to those aspects of Italian classicism and learning reinforcing his own stature and his view of the world, which centered upon Spain and a dedication to its reconquest. Archepiscopal palace life reflected those interests and attitudes.

At Alcalá during Isabel's two-year stay was Gómez Manrique, who was Carillo's *mayordomo*, and who exchanged verses with another resident, Pero Guillén de Segovia, accountant and poet, whom Carrillo commissioned to chronicle his valorous deeds in battle in behalf of Alfonso and Isabel. Guillén's account of the archbishop's feats said little of Carrillo being an ecclesiastic but made many flattering comparisons to heroes of classical history. Manrique and Guillén shared an admiration for the earlier generation of Castilian classicists, those moralists of Isabel's father's court whose advocacy of strong personal monarchy and the royal obligation to the war of reconquest they took up, now charging Isabel and Fernando with fulfilling them. Manrique, who had repeatedly voiced nostalgia for older aristocratic values lost under Enrique, proclaimed them embodied in the young pair, whom he saw as rightful successors to Castile and who seemed to him sprung from chivalric romance. The company of those articulate, informed, and admiring courtiers could only have broadened Isabel's education and reinforced her values. Nor were they alone in stating their admiration for her and her cause.

It was perhaps inevitable that Isabel would evoke comparison to another heroine of clear vision and singleminded purpose held to be divinely inspired, one who battled mightily in just cause against great odds, Joan of Arc, the Maid of Orleans. Isabel received a chronicle of the warrior maiden, dedicated to her by an author whose identity is unknown. It spoke of Joan's inspiration from heaven, but dwelt upon her chivalric ethic and rockribbed sense of morality. The Maid had redeemed and restored the crown, ran the dedication, so it was not so incredible that a powerful and excellent queen might recover those lost kingdoms; the most difficult things are possible to God. In the greatness of Isabel's own will, it went on, was known to reside the desire not only to recover what was hers but to make large inroads into the lands of "the damned sect"—the Muslims—so that in her time all faith and law would be one.[9] It was a point of view, too, in keeping with that of an archbishop who saw himself as warlord and kingmaker, who had striven to regain territory from the Muslims and who supported an Inquisition, and of his household. And it was one his young guest would implement.

THE CARDINAL AND THE BISHOP

After speaking to Isabel, in June 1472, the Burgundian envoys sought out Fernando in Tarragona, their mission to have the princes of Castile and Aragón and *reyes* of Sicily join the alliance of Charles the Bold, Edward IV of England, and Juan of Aragón against Louis XI of France. The King and Queen of Sicily figured importantly too in the policy of the new pope, Sixtus IV, who was sending legates throughout Europe to rouse enthusiasm and raise funds for a renewed crusade against the Turks. It was known that Isabel and Fernando, to counter Turkish advance, were drawing closer to Genoa and Venice; and that with Mehmet II threatening the Balkans, Sicily's position, wheat, and revenues were of great consequence. The papal envoy dispatched on that business to Spain was a native Valencian, Cardinal Rodrigo de Borja, who arrived at that port on June 18 in two galleys and with a suite of bishops, all of them greedy, insists Palencia, and aware that Spaniards would spend freely for honors. Borja himself Palencia describes as insolent and given to pomp, luxury, "and other unbraked passions," and notes that he freely advertised his faculties of papal investment and dispensation and his stock of papal bulls, that "he held the nets to catch many fish." Borja also brought the desired bull absolving Isabel and Fernando for marrying without papal dispensation; reassuringly, it referred to Isabel as *Princesa* of Castile. Palencia aside, Borja was both fisherman and prize catch.

Isabel, who had moved to Torrelaguna on report of plague in Alcalá, kept informed of Borja's talks with Fernando and Juan; she heard that he and Fernando met again in Valencia, in mid-September, and that joining them was Pedro González de Mendoza, who was then Bishop of Sigüenza. Indeed, Torrelaguna lay within that bishopric, indicating a rapprochement. Mendoza, sent to greet the papal envoy by Enrique, nevertheless had his own agenda: the bishop wanted a cardinal's hat. Fernando wanted both his support and Borja's. Borja wanted both men in his debt, the promising young king of Sicily and prince of Aragón who aspired to the crown of Castile, and the bishop who was among Spain's most powerful nobles and was distinguishing himself as also among its most perspicacious.

Borja's ceremonial entry into his native city was brilliant. It was eclipsed by Mendoza's. Pedro González de Mendoza rode in—on the afternoon of October 20, the eve of the feast of St. Ursula—on the customary episcopal mule but, commented an eyewitness, "with more entourage than common to kings," and with trumpets blaring and drums rolling.[10] Two blacks beating kettledrums preceded him on horseback. The Bishop on his mule was flanked by 30 knights, among them two of his brothers and various nephews, all richly attired, with chains of heavy gold gleaming about their necks. Behind them wended 200 light cavalry and an army of falconers and huntsmen, footsoldiers and servants, and a long mule train heaped with baggage. Fernando and Mendoza met, with bargaining counters already in play. Fernando had from his father a promise that Mendoza's brother, the second Santillana and Duke of Infantado, might keep what had been a great chunk of Juan's Castilian inheritance, and Mendoza had written Fernando a few days beforehand that he would support Isabel as Enrique's successor.

Five days later Borja, not to be outdone, invited Fernando and Mendoza and his clan, eight visiting bishops, and the notables of the city to dinner. The banquet hall was hung with damasks and silks. A huge centerpiece of sweet-smelling herbs spelled out "Ave Maria, gratia plena"—"Hail Mary, full of grace"—Mendoza's motto. Hands were washed in large gilded silver basins. The courses were many and calculated to impress: there were peacocks, cooked and then reconstituted, their heads gilded, and hanging about their necks the Borja coat-of-arms. There were pies of fowl, veal, kid, and bacon, with sauces. There were yet more peacocks, perfumed water spouting from their beaks, and, finally, condiments and sweets.

Yet, impressive as it all was, the occasion belonged neither to Mendoza nor Borja, but, despite his relatively small retinue and extremely small resources, to Fernando. For word had arrived two days beforehand that Juan of Aragón had at last entered Barcelona, in triumph, and Valencia had erupted in a week-long celebration, centered on its prince. So Borja's departing and satiated guests passed only with great difficulty through streets filled with jubilant crowds, singing and dancing, ecstatic at catching a glimpse of their prince. And the city fathers, also anticipating increased Flemish trade as a result of Juan's recent treaty with Burgundy, voted Fernando 18,000 *sueldos* and lent him another 30,000. By November, when Borja and Mendoza left together for Castile, a secret three-way bargain had been struck, of great consequence for Isabel.

She had written immediately to congratulate her father-in-law, saying she was certain that taking Barcelona brought him great happiness, for the great honor and service he derived from it, and for "the revenge that you can have because of it on all those who did not want the prosperity and augment of Your Majesty; undoubtedly it is for them a defeat."[11] Here was an early but not isolated display of an assumption of hers that would have substantial application, that vengeance was an expected and estimable motive. Her mother had, to great acclaim, taken revenge on Luna. Her father had a reputation for being vindictive. Her brother Alfonso had viewed vengeance as a knightly quality, and, in a predominating medieval tradition, God was admired as full of vengeance. It was considered another face of fairness and justice, of recovering one's own, of restoring balance to the world.

At the same time, she indicated something of what was to be a preferred *modus operandi*. Immediately, she pushed the advantage in writing to the chastened council of Barcelona demanding that it turn over to her the Catalan places promised in her dowry, not knowing that at the moment those places were highly sensitive issues in dispute between Juan and the city. So on December 29, having been reunited with Fernando and undoubtedly apprised, she wrote again to those councillors, but now graciously felicitated them for some matter or other. Then, considering her gaffe smoothed over, on February 2 she again insisted on her dower rights.

She was back in Alcalá when Borja visited her at the end of February. He stayed three weeks and came away favorably impressed with her; she had formed no high opinion of him, nor would she ever. And she would not then, as Borja urged her to do, put herself completely in the hands of the Mendoza and accept their hospitality in Guadalajara, although he promised that if she and Fernando did so he would support them and that they then might take charge of young Juana. Not only was Carrillo dead-set against it, but the deciding factor was that since Pacheco currently had custody of Juana he must be in on the plan. Still, word of papal warming toward herself and Fernando, as well as the overtures of the Mendoza, were both welcome in themselves and as increasing their standing among Castilians.

Fernando again left for Aragón in early May 1473. Isabel agreed he must go when word came that Juan had gone to retrieve Rosellón and Cerdaña, Aragonese provinces held by Louis XI as surety for a debt, and, having taken Perpignán, was besieged there by the French. Isabel wrote to her father-in-law on April 29 to say that Fernando was about to depart; she added that she felt such great anguish at the news of the new French invasion that, if affairs allowed, she would come with the prince to his aid, for the journey would be less onerous than the separation; still, she had great consolation and hope in the Lord and His blessed mother that Fernando's journey would go well and result in glorious victory.[12]

That invocation was less a prayer than an expectation, that heaven was with them and abetting their armies. And so it was. The French, aware that Fernando was coming with a sizable force, decamped. As a result, he was welcomed handsomely in Barcelona, and in an anonymous poem received another prophecy: he was the Bat, the hidden one now revealed as divinely called to universal monarchy. Yet, from August through October, his mortality was all too apparent: he lay feverish and gravely ill. Then, barely recovered, he received a message from Isabel urging he hurry back to Castile. Obtaining Juan's permission to go, he left his sister, Juana, as royal lieutenant in his stead, and, on December 1 in a handwritten note, notifying Isabel of his imminent departure, he did not resist lamenting that: "I have not been with Your Highness in seven months."[13] In June he had had from her a highly confidential message, interpreted as "all the business of Castile is in the hand of its princes."[14] In Castile, the meaning of that message was now clear to everyone.

RECONCILING

When Pedro González de Mendoza received from the pope his cardinal's hat the previous spring, it was celebrated by a procession through the streets of Segovia to mass in its cathedral, and that hat was carried by Andrés de Cabrera. Cabrera, who as Enrique's *mayordomo mayor* held the *alcázar* of Segovia and the royal treasury it housed, was also a leader of Segovia's *conversos*. Although he was with Pacheco at the *acto de Avila*, he had subsequently broken with him for his highhanded activities. And when in Segovia the following year "a great uproar in the city and factions [clashing] in the streets," was incited by Pacheco as preliminary to an attempt on the *alcázar* and its treasure, Cabrera, warned by the second Marqués de Santillana, had closed the city to the inveterate trouble-maker and calmed the populace. As a result, Pacheco had withdrawn to Madrid, where he turned instead to planning the same maneuver elsewhere: to incite townspeople against Jews and *conversos,* then come in to restore order and so take control of the town. From the trouble in Toledo in 1449, he or his cohorts had had a hand in bringing about most major anti-*converso* groundswells. (An exception was Valladolid, where an adherent of Isabel's had set in motion an anti-*converso* rising resulting in a slaughter that she and Fernando condemned but could not stop.)

Cabrera, who had been influential in reconciling Isabel and Enrique after Alfonso's death, had recently married Isabel's longtime favorite lady-in-waiting, Beatriz de Bobadilla. On June 15, Isabel signed an accord with Cabrera, promising, in return for his seeking reconciliation between herself and Enrique, to name him Marqués of Moya, near Cuenca, his birthplace. Involved in those negotiations, too, was Beatriz de Bobadilla, who was somehow on intimate terms—*muy de gracia,* as Palencia put it—with both Cardinal Mendoza and the powerful Rodrigo Alfonso Pimentel, Count of Benavente. Cabrera then discussed the succession at length with Alfonso de Quintanilla, Isabel's *contador mayor*, and Quintanilla made thirty-six trips between Segovia and Alcalá to arrange a reconciliation between the king and his sister. Here was the context of Isabel's letter to Fernando of that June.

Throughout 1473, amid unrelenting civil strife, towns and cities continued to come over to Isabel. And all the *grandes* came to favor her reinstatement as *princesa* with the exception of Pacheco and Alvaro de Stúñiga, the new Duke of Arévalo. On November 4 Isabel had signed an agreement with Benavente: she would meet Enrique in Segovia to resolve their differences, with the understanding that she was to succeed him. It was then that she notified Fernando to hurry home. He joined her in Aranda in time for the feast day of St. John the Evangelist (December 27), Isabel's patron saint, a happy augury. Beatriz de Bobabilla and Carrillo came to fetch her the next evening; they rode through the night and were in Segovia on the 29th. Enrique was terrified of Pacheco's anger, but Pacheco was away, and Enrique was being bolstered by Benavente, Cardinal Mendoza, and Beltrán de la Cueva.

It was all very festive: Isabel and Enrique were delighted to see one another. They dined together and, says Palencia, he took her into the treasure chamber of the *alcazar* and told her she might choose from it whatever she wanted; unfortunately Palencia did not record her response. They talked a good deal and attended a banquet the next day. Isabel danced and Enrique sang, as they often used to do, and they rode through the city together so people might see their amity. Enrique invited Fernando to come immediately; he arrived on New Year's Day and after dinner Enrique came to visit. They had never met but got on well. On January 9, all three rode through the city together and dined with the Cabreras.

Cabrera had sworn, says Palencia, that if Enrique did not fulfill the compact made at Guisando he would immediately turn over to Isabel and Fernando the *alcázar*, the treasury, and the keys to the city gates. Now Benavente and Mendoza convinced Beatriz, who convinced her husband, to ask a surety of the young couple: custody of their daughter and of the fortress of Avila, and she did so. Isabel resisted; she did not want to give over her child as a hostage and she was indignant that her word would not suffice. Cabrera, trying to persuade her otherwise, fruitlessly, held his temper with difficulty, but Carrillo, incensed at her jeopardizing everything, reminded her of the danger and sacrifice he himself had endured for her cause and the cost to him of troops. Fernando, inclined to meet the conditions, told her she was being obstinate. By January 11 she had yielded, reluctantly, and all was agreed.

Then occurred one of Palencia's many fortuitous happenings. He had entered Segovia secretly—he was *persona non grata* with Enrique—with a message to Fernando and Isabel from Fernando's uncle, Alfonso Enríquez, now Admiral of Castile, to be wary, and, having gone to nap in a small room, he happened to overhear just outside the door the voices of Benavente and two other men, conspiring to seize Fernando, Isabel, and their child. He informed *los principes* immediately and suggested, as he tells it, that Fernando leave; Isabel would be safe in Segovia since she was viewed as only half the problem. Palencia thought Benavente was in league with Mendoza. Other accounts say that the Cardinal, when he became aware of the plot, warned Enrique that the kingdom so strongly believed the couple to be rightfully his legitimate successors that to seize them might endanger his own life.

However that may be, Isabel too advised Fernando to go, but she insisted on staying. She had made the decision to face danger for high stakes, perhaps trusting to her own influence on Enrique—while with him, anyway. So Fernando left, on January 16, on the pretext of going hunting, and immediately transferred their daughter from Aranda to Sepúlveda, secure under the Admiral. Enrique, with no stomach for such business, indeed suffering from an intestinal ailment since the day after the Cabreras' banquet, left for Madrid. Isabel herself was running a low fever. She stayed and put herself and the city under heavy guard. She was in possession of Segovia. At bottom, it was a coup, and a victory for her strength of will. There would be many more.

THE PRINCESS IN SEGOVIA

Fernando returned soon after, says Palencia, for "he could not resist the desire to visit Isabel," then left again quickly, to stay in the village of Turégano, several hours' ride away. In Segovia Isabel increasingly relied on Mendoza, to Carrillo's mounting chagrin. Her affection for her longtime protector and her sense of indebtedness to him had been eroded by his intransigence, his lack of political vision, and his increasing involvement with other worlds. For the Archbishop of Toledo, primate of Spain, had come under the influence of an alchemist, one Alarcón, an unsavory adventurer, who, says Palencia, had traveled in Sicily, Rhodes, and Cyprus, had everywhere married, and who in Barcelona and Valencia "had corrupted clerics to incest and all sorts of obscenities." This unscrupulous necromancer had convinced Carrillo that he, Alarcón, could fly through the air and, most compelling, that he knew the secrets of the philosopher's stone and could produce for him mountains of gold. The Archbishop, in thirsting to possess the greatest splendor and wealth Castile had ever seen, spent most of his huge rents—Palencia averred that "his natural largesse reached prodigality"—on Alarcón's attempts to manufacture for him yet more wealth. In seeking to make gold of iron, it was said, he made iron of gold. Pulgar, ever more circumspect, spoke rather of Carrillo's pleasure in knowing the properties of waters and herbs and other secrets of nature, and of his desire for gold for alms; he also said that Alarcón was a creature of Pacheco.

Isabel, while at Alcalá, had encountered the alchemist and had—her chroniclers say—reluctantly, to please Carrillo, granted him 500 Aragonese florins on the rents of Sicily and daily entrée to her on a par with members of her council. Was she intrigued by his rooms full of arcane equipment and his visions of far places, terrestial and heavenly, and of mountainous riches? Years later, she would respond cautiously but more positively to another visionary seeking to make a marvelous discovery. She abhorred, says Pulgar, sorcery and divination, and from the outset Alarcón encountered a formidable and voluble opponent in her confessor, the blunt-spoken fray Alonso de Burgos. In Segovia, the halls rang with arguments between the friar and Alarcón; at one point they went at each other with staves. In Segovia Isabel at length—Palencia says bored with him— threw Alarcón out of the palace. Even so, at bottom Carrillo's infatuation with alchemy was less damning than that he looked backward, to ecclesiastical and baronial autonomy and to king-making and other moribund medieval arrangements. Mendoza faced forward, to a future as first minister atop the expanding bureaucracy of an emerging nation-state.

Carrillo left Segovia. He broke with Isabel and convinced Enrique, who was considering calling the Cortes to recognize her, to remain loyal to Juana. Mendoza, becoming Archbishop of Seville that May, within the month declared himself in suggesting to the Duke of Alba and the Admiral that they join him against the coalition of Stúñiga, Benavente, Pacheco, and quite possibly Carrillo. In June, Isabel actively enlisted military support, promising *mercedes*. It was once again civil war. Fernando took Tordesillas from a partisan of Enrique's. Isabel happily informed him of hearing that Enrique "took the business of Tordesillas very hard and showed great fury, not by deed, but by word, as usual."[15]

Fernando again left for Aragón when that month the French again invaded Rosellón. Yet there in September he demonstrated that he shared with Isabel a primary interest in Castile in refusing Juan's appeal for Castilian participation in an offensive against Castile's traditional ally, France. Isabel then wooed French support, sending an envoy to Louis XI suggesting his newborn heir Charles and her daughter Isabel marry. Juan of Aragón, unfazed, offered to mediate in Castile.

So matters stood when, on October 4, Juan Pacheco died, of the same catch in the throat, it was said, that had borne off his brother, Girón. The news was slow to get out, for only servants were with him at the time and they had stolen as much as they could, thrown his body in a wine vat, and run off. Neither Mendoza nor Carrillo showed any interest in attending his funeral.

The realm, Gutierre de Cárdenas wrote Fernando in Barcelona (God pardon it) looked on the death of the Master of Santiago as a happy miracle. Isabel, he related, showed a little sentiment, as was fitting, in being rid of an enemy, hers and everyone's, although recently they had been becoming more friendly, as at first. The king had taken it harder than he had ever taken anything, saying he had lost a father, that Pacheco had been as a father to him since he was very young. Cárdenas went on to intimate that great things were about to happen, that all the world was pregnant and pressing to give birth, and that it would not wait nine months: "I believe that there will be very grand and new happenings in these realms in which I expect Your Lordship and the Lady Princess will be well-served."[16]

Isabel immediately wrote Fernando proposing they get papal bulls vesting the now-vacant mastership of Santiago in the crown, and that, meanwhile, she would show benevolence to those grandes who asked her support in seeking it but make them no promises. Enrique, less wise in view of the numerous disappointed aspirants thereby created, bestowed that mastership instantly on Pacheco's son and heir, Diego López Pacheco, now also Marqués de Villena, thereby swelling adherence to Fernando and Isabel.

"The king," recounted Palencia, "who before had suffered some intestinal attacks, began to weaken with his repeated excesses; he was incontinent in eating as in all else, only obeying his caprice and never the dictates of reason."[17] Enrique did not consult doctors, considering them inept or acting on whim. "When sick he cared only for purges." Ill since January, he increasingly vomited blood and suffered bloody stools. Worse in late November, on December 1 he attempted to ride to a favorite hunting lodge outside Madrid but was too weak. At the end, he neither requested last rites nor made a will, and he may or may not have named Juana his successor; no one says he named Isabel. Palencia states that when the attending physician told him he had only a few hours to live, Enrique said, "I declare my daughter heiress of these kingdoms," even though a priest had arrived and tried to dissuade him. Was it proof she was indeed his, or a last stab at dignity and dynasty? We do not know. That he was fond of the child comes through solicitous letters he wrote to the Mendoza in 1470; they should attend to the Princess' diet; she should not have fruit nor anything made from milk. At his deathbed were Cardinal Mendoza, Benavente, young Pacheco, and other council and household members.

Enrique IV died in Madrid sometime during the night of December 11. He was 49 years of age and had reigned nineteen years and five months. As he requested, the Cardinal had his body carried to the shrine of Mary at Guadalupe, where his mother was interred. He had a proper but miserably attended funeral. As the news went out, one of Fernando's counselors wrote to Juan of Aragón of how remarkable it was that "the deaths of the Master and then the King, obstacles of that succession, had occurred in such a short space of time."[18]

LA REYNA DOÑA ISABEL

In Segovia, Isabel received word of Enrique's death by the evening of December 12. She cried, donned mourning—white serge was customary—began sending out letters to the realm, and called together her council. Only Cabrera, Cárdenas, and a few others were in the city. They argued no delay, that awaiting the grandes was like bestowing on them what was owed only to God and nature; Isabel, her political theory obviously having altered greatly, agreed. The next day she went, dressed in mourning, to the church of San Miguel, where Enrique's standards and those of the city had been lowered and draped in black. She attended the customary mass and rites for the dead. Then she changed her clothes and, to the roll of kettledrums and to clarinets and resounding trumpets, she reappeared, in the *plaza mayor*. She was richly, dazzlingly dressed, jewelry of gold and precious stones "accentuating her singular beauty."[19] And there, in the portal of the church of San Miguel, upon a hastily constructed platform covered with brocade, she was literally and figuratively raised to the throne as Queen of Castile and León.

She did not neglect to have a notary set down the details of the ceremony.

He recorded that present were the papal legate, some knights and nobles, a number of Franciscans and Dominicans, Segovia's notables, and a crowd of townspeople. The cry went out: The king was dead. A *letrado* of Isabel's council on behalf, he said, of all her subjects, informed her that by law the succession and inheritance and right to reign were hers; that she had been recognized by the previous king in September 1468 and been sworn to by the realm. Placing her right hand on the Bible, she then swore by God and the sign of the cross and the words of the holy evangel that she would obey the commandments of Holy Church. She would honor its prelates and ministers, defend the churches, look to the common good of the realm and to the good of its royal crown, and do her utmost to aggrandize those kingdoms and maintain her subjects in justice, as best given her to understand it; and, in accord with the custom of her glorious progenitors, she would not pervert but would guard the privileges and liberties and exemptions of the *hidalgos*—the nobles, and of the municipalities.

The clergy, the nobles, the knights, and her councillors kneeled before her and, speaking both for themselves and in the name of the kingdoms, they took an oath to her as their Queen and the proprietary *Señora Natural* of the kingdoms and to the King Don Fernando, her legitimate husband. The town notables followed their example, then handed to her their staffs of office; she gave them to Cabrera, who returned them to the officials. Cabrera then turned over to her the keys of the *alcázar* and the treasury and she returned them into his keeping as her *alcalde*. He swore homage to her, placing his hands between those of Gonzalo Chacón. Her daughter, the *infanta*, now four, was lifted up, and heralds made the proclamation: '¡*Castilla, Castilla, Castilla, por la muy alta poderosa princesa e Señora, nuestra Señora la Reyna Doña Isabel, y por el muy alto e muy poderoso Principe Rey e Señor, nuestro Señor el Rey Don Fernando como su legítimo marido!*'[20] It was a cry customarily taken up by the assembled throng; Castile's monarchs were usually installed by acclamation rather than coronation. Even so, it was recorded for her as proclamation, not acclamation, and it can be interpreted as a form of self-coronation. The royal standard was raised and music swelled. Isabel descended, entered the church, prayed before its main altar, and then, taking up the royal banner suspended on a lance and placing it in the hands of a priest, she thus offered it to God.

As she emerged from the church, a procession formed. Isabel rode, surrounded by nobles on foot, some carrying the canopy of state sheltering her and others holding the train of her gown. Segovia's dignitaries (dressed as fittingly as possible on such short notice) marched behind. A throng followed. Ahead of everyone rode a single horseman, Gutierre de Cárdenas, in his right hand a naked sword, held by the pummel, point up, "as in Spanish usage," so all could see even at a distance that the bearer of royal authority who could punish the guilty was approaching.[21] "And that night she slept in the palace."[22] Palencia wrote of murmuring at the insolence of a woman appropriating attributes rightfully belonging to a husband, but that it ceased "before the adulation of those who proclaimed that the inheritance of the kingdoms in no way belonged to don Fernando, but legally exclusively to the Queen."[23] From there, he added, derived the germ of more of those contests so enjoyed by the *grandes.*

Three things, ran a Castilian saying, maintain the kingdom: the king, the law, and the sword. In a guide to princes dedicated to Isabel, a favorite poet and courtier of hers, fray Iñigo de Mendoza, in declaring that she had come by grace of God to do justice, war against tyranny, and kill the corrupt few to save the entire kingdom, made extended use of the sword as metaphor. There was too her chivalric bent, the memory of Joan of Arc as sword wielding, and the popularity of Arthurian romance and its magic swords. Her brother, Alfonso, had ordered coins, *alfonsíes*, minted depicting him on horseback, armed, wearing a crown, and with a naked sword in his hand.

Still, in Castile the traditional monarch's symbol was a sceptre, a gold orb topped by a golden cross and held in the left hand; Enrique IV had referred to it as symbol of justice at the Cortes of Ocaña in 1469, and so did Gómez Manrique in his *Regimen for Princes.* The tomb effigy of Juan II at Miraflores held a sceptre. Isabel at her accession chose to revive an earlier usage. In 1484, a traveler, watching while Isabel and Fernando rode in the annual Christmas eve procession in Seville in remembrance of its reconquest, was surprised to see an age-blackened sword being carried before them, and, upon inquiry, was informed it was the symbol of justice. More precisely, it stood for a militant justice and a militant faith, for it was the sword of Seville's conqueror, Fernando III, and it had been carried as well, as a talisman with symbolic intent, by a namesake of his, Fernando de Antequera, both in campaign against the Moors and in his own ceremonial entry into Seville. It was to that sword and ceremony that Isabel surely chose to refer. It spoke of power and that the queen and not her consort, another Fernando, was the heir-proper of those Castilian heroes of the reconquest. At the same time, it did allude to the fact that her king-consort was another Fernando. Surely more than coincidence, among her most splendid tapestries would be one of Fame showing a queen holding a sword.

There was yet more: there was the prophetic vision honoring her father's birth, of the advent of an angelic redeemer prince, sword in hand. And, over a century later, the imagery of the sword would be taken up in behalf of another queen, Elizabeth I of England, in a reference to the old prophecy that in the last days "the Emperor [was to have] a responsibility for supporting the entry of Christ into the world with the sword of justice," and that through that monarch justice would flow from God to the world.[24] Elizabeth herself was held to personify a prophecy found in Virgil's fourth *Eclogue,* that a golden age was about to return and with it the Virgin, Astraea, or Justice, implying Astraea was to herald that great just age: "now return the ages of Saturn." There were those among Isabel's people who knew their Virgil; and some years later she would be explicitly compared to Astraea. Yet, as shall be seen, the most potent reference was surely to the Book of Revelation as the prophecy of "the one who has the two-edged sword" (2.12).

On another level, how her town of Avila celebrated her accession is also telling. On Saturday, December 17, municipal officials and her *corregidor*, Juan Chacón, gathered in the choir of the church of San Juan, at the toll of its bell as was customary, to hear read out her letter requesting their oath. They relatively quickly agreed to give it; their chief concern was how to finance the usual ceremonies. That decided, the following day they attended requiem mass for Enrique, while "all the Jewish and Muslim men and women made their laments amid the crowd" of *los enjergados*, literally those dressed in serge, gathered outside the church.[25] The notables in their finery emerged, gave the cry, "Castile, Castile for the very high and powerful lady, our lady the Queen *Doña Isabel*," three times, and then "Castile, Castile for the very high and very powerful Lord, our lord the King *Don Fernando*, her legitimate husband." That cry, much like that of Segovia, went up for both monarchs, Isabel first and foremost, undoubtedly as orchestrated by Juan Chacón. A procession formed at the church while canons sang the *Te Deum laudamus* and Muslims performed *momos* and sword dances. Then the usual participants moved forward, among them Jews carrying two torahs, trumpets and timbrels resounding, and a standard-bearer on horseback holding aloft the royal banner. They traversed the town, through the fish market to the gate of the alcazar, where everyone watched while Chacón and Avila's worthies ascended the tower and affixed Isabel's banner atop it. The acclamation came again, from the tower, and the populace below gave it back. The banner flew for nine days. On January 9, the council convened and took the oath to Isabel and Fernando.

In Zamora, receiving the same letter from Isabel, the situation was more complicated, for the city was split between former partisans of Enrique and Enrique Enríquez, the Count of Alba de Liste and Fernando's uncle. The Count, along with his brother, the Admiral, disapproved of Isabel's solo accession; their position was that Juana was indeed Enrique's daughter but that women could not succeed to the crown, so that, since Fernando descended in male line from Juan I of Castile, the crown most properly belonged to him. It was an argument making even more legitimate, although no one mentioned it, the succession in Castile of Juan of Aragón. Here was additional explanation of Isabel's decision to take the crown quickly and alone, and of the rationale she later gave to Fernando, that since they had but one child, who was female, her own accession would be setting precedent highly important to their daughter. In view of the response in Zamora, the argument had merit.

Arriving in Segovia a few days after the ceremonies were the Cardinal and his brothers, and the Admiral, the Constable, Benavente, Beltrán, and Carrillo, to kiss their queen's hand and take the oath of allegiance. Many other nobles and knights came. Yet others sent deputies. Isabel heard nothing from Stúñiga nor young Pacheco nor Girón's sons. Nor did Pacheco's Madrid or Stúñiga's Plasencia recognize her; but neither was there any mention of Juana.

II

LA REINA

6

Contests
1475

Between the King and Queen there was no discord . . . they ate together in the public hall, talking of pleasant things as is done at table, and they slept together.

. . . . where affection, bravery, and *gentileza* are found, they are always more pleasing to the god of love than to [the God] of heaven.

Crónica incompleta

KING AND QUEEN

To Fernando, at Zaragoza presiding over the Corts of Aragón, Isabel sent a concise message: Enrique had died; Fernando's presence would not be useless but he should do what he thought best, depending on circumstances in Aragón. He had already had the news: Carrillo's messenger had outsped Isabel's. Castile's new king left for Segovia, the second day enroute receiving additional letters from Isabel and also one from Gutierre de Cárdenas describing in detail Isabel's taking the crown, and making much of his own role in having ridden before her with upraised sword.

Fernando—says Palencia, who was with him—was surprised at not hearing of that ceremony from Isabel and amazed at its having taken place. When, Palencia wondered, had a Queen ever been preceded by a symbol threatening her vassals with punishment? It was a rite of kings; he knew of no queen who would have usurped that male attribute. Neither Palencia nor another companion, the lawyer, Caballería, had heard of it. Caballería, concerned, immediately advised Juan II that he, as he alone could, should do his best to enamor Fernando and Isabel of their union and of concord and its benefits, that it was very necessary for the situation in Castile "was not without suspicion of something sinister," and that Castilians were acceding to the succession only because they could do nothing else, but with their ears open, ready to take advantage of discord between the King and Queen.[1]

Fernando was confident. He confided, says Palencia, "in conquering with patience and felt certain he would triumph through satisfying assiduously the demands of conjugal love, with which he could easily soften the intransigence that bad advisors had planted in his wife's mind."[2] So he traversed Castile in high spirits, banners flying and trumpets proclaiming the presence of royal majesty "so that vassals might know it was their king who was in the land." And although he continued to marvel at Isabel's behavior, still he did not expect that she would hold him rigidly to the terms of the prenuptial *capitulación*.

On January 2 he rode into Segovia, kingly indeed in a flowing coat of cloth-of-gold lined in Russian marten fur, to be met by Mendoza and Carrillo and a host of other dignitaries, clergy bearing crosses, and a great throng of townspeople. Before the portico of the church of San Miguel, where Isabel had stood two weeks earlier, a formal ceremony of accession again took place, but with a difference. Would he, Fernando was asked, reign in those kingdoms as the legitimate husband of the Queen? Yes, he responded graciously, he would. Thereupon Segovia's councilmen swore "that they would obey and receive His Highness as legitimate husband of Our Lady the Queen for their King and Lord."[3] Their language was construable as relegating him to king-consort and revelatory of the stance being taken by Isabel and her counselors. Theirs was an interpretation of her authority in Castile in relation to his that was at great variance with what had been expected by the Aragonese. For in Aragón women could not succeed to the crown; nor in Castile had any woman reigned in several hundred years.

And Isabel? Afterwards, when the procession arrived by torchlight at the *alcázar,* she greeted Fernando just inside the gates, in the patio. The message was clear: the occasion was a formal one and she was now Castile's Queen. Legal arguments to that effect, citing queens who had ruled in Spain in their own right, were reviewed by Pulgar. In the old chronicles was found precedent in women who had governed Castile and its parent kingdoms of León and Asturias, beginning with Ormisinda, daughter of the semi-legendary chieftain Pelayo (whom Pulgar referred to as king of León); since Pelayo had no son Ormisinda had inherited León and the man she married had become its king, Alfonso I *El Católico*. Odisina, sister of Froyla, King of León, succeeded as queen in the same situation. Doña Sancha, sister of King Bermudo, succeeded in León and her husband became King Fernando *El Magno*. Doña Elvira, Queen of Navarre, suceeded in Castile, then a county, and her son, Fernando, became its first king. Urraca, the daughter of the conqueror of Toledo, Alfonso VI, married to Count Raimundo of Burgundy, succeeded in Castile and León, and, after the Count died, she married Alfonso, king of Aragón, known as The Battler, yet she continued to rule Castile and her son, Alfonso VII, succeeded her. Similarly, Berenguela,

mother of Fernando III, married to Alfonso, king of León, when the kingdoms were separate, ruled in the lifetime of her husband and continued to
be called Queen of Castile. Never, was the conclusion, when there was a
legitimate daughter descended by direct line should a male born into the
transverse line, as was Juan of Aragón, inherit the crown. Beyond dispute,
the government of the kingdom belonged to the Queen, as its legitimate
proprietress.

All this Isabel explained to Fernando, assuring him that what he as the
Queen's husband commanded must be done in Castile; and that afterwards,
pleasing God, those kingdoms would go to their children, his and hers. God
until then had given them no other heir except Princess Isabel. She
explained that after their days, "should a male come descended from the
royal house of Castile claiming the kingdom by the transverse line, or
should the Princess Isabel marry a foreign prince who wants to take over
Castile's fortesses and royal patrimony, the kingdom would come into the
power of a foreign dynasty, which would weigh heavily on their consciences and be a disservice to God."[4] For those reasons, she had taken the
crown alone.

Fernando's adherents emphatically argued against both her sole proprietorship and succession passing not to him but to a child of theirs. Palencia,
agreeing with them, stated their position: By natural, statutory, and divine
law, the man held the prerogative and should have precedence, as was customary in those kingdoms and elsewhere. Moreover, there existed an old
Castilian law stating "that in the marriage of a female heir to the kingdom,
although her husband may be of lesser rank he is jointly to wield the sceptre
and have the name of king, and to receive the other distinctions given the
man everywhere."[5] Moreover, through the male line of the royal house his
was the first claim on the throne and, assuredly, he was legitimate heir to
Castile and León should his wife die. Be that as it may, in view of the numerous deaths without which she would not have come to the crown, it is
understandable that Isabel's supporters would frown on making Fernando's sole succession an outcome of her death.

Palencia, himself fanning discord, warned Fernando that "the Cardinal
and other principal *caballeros* ceaselessly fomented in the womanly mind of
the Queen the petulance that had begun to form there," that fawning courtiers insisted she defend her hereditary rights and that she avoid the conjugal yoke that the king would try to impose upon Castilian necks. Yet he also
reported that, although swayed by such advice, the Queen, "a wife after
all," had assured them that the rights of matrimony had no bearing on
those of lordship and royal power.

Underestimated initially was Isabel's ability to put out of her mind, as her
religious advisors urged she do, all such talk and insinuation "when receiving her husband," her ability "to proceed to all conjugal concord" and only
afterwards to speak with Fernando of the conditions of governing, "which
from the most remote centuries have favored the man." Confessor to them
both was Alonso de Burgos, whom both Isabel and Fernando would reward

for his great services, surely that welcome advice among them. Alonso de Burgos has been described as coarse and immoral; yet it is worth speculating what brakes on passion the more austere confessors who followed him might have counseled—and their consequences for that marriage.

Somehow, Isabel asserted her political supremacy while not challenging the commonplace assumption that the male was by nature dominant in marriage. Her personal relationship with Fernando did parallel the known philosophy of one churchman, a mentor of her father's, Alfonso de Madrigal, *El Tostado*. He had proposed that, since a man could not escape love's trammels, he had best find one good woman, that love and friendship linked individuals most deeply to one another and to God, and that 'to love is to have a friend who is another who is oneself.' Castile's Queen would manage to maintain a semblance of traditional private role while working as an equal with her husband in public life. Fortunately, such was his own family history that Fernando would not find that sort of relationship outlandish.

So Isabel and Fernando left the working out of an agreement on their respective authority and functions to their arbitrators, and "between King and Queen there was no discord . . . they ate together in the public hall, talking of pleasant things as is done at table, and they slept together," the only friction occurring when one would want to do something for a loyal adherent, but usually "their wills coincided through intimacy born of love."[6] And both undoubtedly realized that separately neither would be very powerful, that neither of them alone could rule in Castile. Ambition there was, and passion, and something more: as Pulgar put it, "love held their wills joined."[7] It is, after all, the soundest explanation. And its course did not run smooth.

Initially, they charged the settling of the terms of their reign to Carrillo and Mendoza, but, in conversations with Carrillo, Fernando was disconcerted to hear little else except praise of Alarcón, and Carrillo saw his own people losing out to the "evil *grandes,*" as Palencia would have it, and "the instilled pride of the Queen." In those circumstances, when he discovered that the chancery had returned letters of homage to Seville for correction because they named the King before the Queen, he informed Isabel that he was deeply offended in honor and reputation, that people saw his virility undercut, and that he was leaving for Aragón. She, "protesting that she would never for any reason have wanted to cause the least humiliation to her most beloved consort, for whose happiness and honor she would sacrifice willingly not only the crown but her own health," insisted that it was all a formal legal matter. And she pleaded with him passionately "not to leave his beloved wife, for she would not or could not live separated from him." He did not go.[8]

It was Caballería, Fernando's counselor, and Mendoza, overseeing the *letrado,* Rodrigo Maldonado de Talavera, who produced a formal accord, on January 15 signed by Isabel and Fernando and ratified by the *grandes* then at court. The *capitulación* signed by Juan and Fernando in 1469 had envisioned Isabel as adjunct, Fernando exercising rule. The accord of Segovia, while permitting him wide latitude, reversed the balance. It established proprietorship of the crown as Isabel's alone. They might jointly issue documents, coins, and stamps: the King's name was to precede the Queen's, but her coat-of-arms was to come first; homage was sworn exclusively to the Queen, as it had been up until then; the castles were to be obedient to the Queen. She would appoint all Castile's treasurers, and other officials, although the King might also apportion revenues. She would concede *mercedes* and posts; both could propose appointments to masterships and church offices but at her volition. The Queen was to name governors of castles and forts, *alcaides*, but the King was to distribute garrisons and, "because of his skill in war, since accustomed to bearing arms from his youth," he would have supreme command of the armies. Orders of the King alone referring to war, crime, and authorizing expeditions were also valid, but not those treating of other affairs, particularly the collection of revenue. They would administer justice when together and each might do so when apart, always mindful of the Royal Council. Revenues of Castile, Sicily, and Aragón were to pay the expenses of the realm, with any surplus to be distributed by joint accord. They were jointly entitled *reyes*—that is, dual monarchs—of Castile, León, and Sicily, and *principes,* Prince and Princess, of Aragón. The order of succession was fixed so that the Princess Isabel might inherit the crown.[9] Remarkably, nothing was said of foreign affairs.

Fernando, though he signed it, was so irritated by the arrangement that he again proposed to leave. And it was now that Carrillo performed his last great service: he berated them both and declared he was quitting the court. Isabel, alone with Fernando, sobbed; Fernando must not go. All the dissension had been Carrillo's fault. She would have the terms modified. As Palencia tells it: "The love of his wife, whom he loved deeply, calmed the King's ire and, obeying his feelings, he assented with good grace to his wife's entreaties."[10] Some adjustments concerning collecting rents, doing justice, and rewarding services, ensued; the two agreed to use one seal, join coats-of-arms, and that both of their portraits were to appear on the coinage. And so it was that their coins showed both monarchs, their shared coat-of-arms, and such mottos as "whom God has joined let no man separate."

Jointly, they set up a household staff, filling the traditional positions: among them chaplains, an armorer, a chief barber, a quiltmaker, jewelers and silversmiths, a foundryman, a butler, and a first huntsman. They confirmed the Cardinal as principal chancellor of the secret seal, the post he had risen to under Enrique. They named Gonzalo Chacón *contador mayor*, or principal comptroller, Gutierre de Cárdenas second *contador*, and Rodrigo de Ulloa, who had been a *contador* of Enrique's, the third. Gabriel Sánchez was charged with household finances. Sánchez alone was from Aragonese realms, and he was a *converso,* as were many, perhaps most, of the royal administrators and the jurists who increasingly predominated in the royal council and the chancery.

While rewarding people of proven loyalty, they retained many of

Enrique's appointees, and they confirmed many *mercedes* he had made, although not that of Arévalo to Alvaro de Stúñiga, and not Pacheco's having invested in his son, Diego López Pacheco, the *marquesado* of Villena. The Cardinal, Alba, and the Admiral dominated the Council. And, once again disaffected, Stúñiga, young Pacheco, and his twin cousins, Rodrigo Téllez Girón and Juan Téllez Girón conspired. Stúñiga not only held Arévalo, but dominated northern Extremadura. Pacheco and the Giróns had extensive domains in Andalusia, the *marquesado* of Villena, the mastership of Calatrava, and the county of Ureña, near Valladolid.

RUMBLINGS

Isabel and Fernando postponed calling Cortes, although Isabel had initially spoken of doing it as soon as possible. Rather, on January 18 they held a full council meeting. Then immediately, invoking the royal responsibility to mete out "Justice, to which—as an anonymous chronicler puts it— more than any other principle they were inclined," they called to court outstanding jurists, who, conscious of setting tone, sentenced a number of middle-level malefactors of the previous reign swiftly and harshly. And in towns and villages, royal corregidores, although their own anterior behavior might not bear examination, sniffed the wind and emulated the court's draconian measures. The imposition of respect for law and order, however, was soon undercut by the departure from court, on February 20, of the Archbishop of Toledo, signaling a return to factional strife which one observer sadly laid to "our sins growing greater." The time of troubles was not over; heaven was not yet smiling on Castile.

Carrillo, although his influence and revenues had been diminished, could take with him into the opposition a great central chunk of the domain's sharp and rents. And young Pacheco had custody of Juana, then ten years old, and he and Stúñiga took up her claim to the crown; she should marry her uncle, Afonso, King of Portugal; he must come claim her kingdom. The stage was once again set for civil war in Castile, and with Portugal as well, but now its crowned heads were a close knit pair mated by no one, but advised primarily by a lawyer, cleric, and soldier, Pedro González de Mendoza, a man with an ability and ambition in promoting sovereign power equal to Alvaro de Luna's, but with a well-established power base of his own and with greater and more far-ranging and a strong sense of *noblesse oblige*.

Afonso of Portugal had recently had great success. In 14—, [Afon]so had taken Arzila in 147[,] a terminal of the Sahara. In eight days later he himself was in Tangier. Portuguese reached Atlantic coast under Afonso's stamp. Fernão Gómes had licensed in 1469 to explore 100 leagues of coast each— referred to as Guinea and to pay the crown handsomely— had arrived at the Costa da Mina, the Gold Coast, thirty sh—

sioned Isabel as adjunct, Fernando exercising rule. The accord of Segovia, while permitting him wide latitude, reversed the balance. It established proprietorship of the crown as Isabel's alone. They might jointly issue documents, coins, and stamps: the King's name was to precede the Queen's, but her coat-of-arms was to come first; homage was sworn exclusively to the Queen, as it had been up until then; the castles were to be obedient to the Queen. She would appoint all Castile's treasurers, and other officials, although the King might also apportion revenues. She would concede *mercedes* and posts; both could propose appointments to masterships and church offices but at her volition. The Queen was to name governors of castles and forts, *alcaides*, but the King was to distribute garrisons and, "because of his skill in war, since accustomed to bearing arms from his youth," he would have supreme command of the armies. Orders of the King alone referring to war, crime, and authorizing expeditions were also valid, but not those treating of other affairs, particularly the collection of revenue. They would administer justice when together and each might do so when apart, always mindful of the Royal Council. Revenues of Castile, Sicily, and Aragón were to pay the expenses of the realm, with any surplus to be distributed by joint accord. They were jointly entitled *reyes*—that is, dual monarchs—of Castile, León, and Sicily, and *príncipes*, Prince and Princess, of Aragón. The order of succession was fixed so that the Princess Isabel might inherit the crown.[9] Remarkably, nothing was said of foreign affairs.

Fernando, though he signed it, was so irritated by the arrangement that he again proposed to leave. And it was now that Carrillo performed his last great service: he berated them both and declared he was quitting the court. Isabel, alone with Fernando, sobbed; Fernando must not go. All the dissension had been Carrillo's fault. She would have the terms modified. As Palencia tells it: "The love of his wife, whom he loved deeply, calmed the King's ire and, obeying his feelings, he assented with good grace to his wife's entreaties."[10] Some adjustments concerning collecting rents, doing justice, and rewarding services, ensued; the two agreed to use one seal, join coats-of-arms, and that both of their portraits were to appear on the coinage. And so it was that their coins showed both monarchs, their shared coat-of-arms, and such mottos as "whom God has joined let no man separate."

Jointly, they set up a household staff, filling the traditional positions: among them chaplains, an armorer, a chief barber, a quiltmaker, jewelers and silversmiths, a foundryman, a butler, and a first huntsman. They confirmed the Cardinal as principal chancellor of the secret seal, the post he had risen to under Enrique. They named Gonzalo Chacón *contador mayor*, or principal comptroller, Gutierre de Cárdenas second *contador*, and Rodrigo de Ulloa, who had been a *contador* of Enrique's, the third. Gabriel Sánchez was charged with household finances. Sánchez alone was from Aragonese realms, and he was a *converso*, as were many, perhaps most, of the royal administrators and the jurists who increasingly predominated in the royal council and the chancery.

While rewarding people of proven loyalty, they retained many of

Enrique's appointees, and they confirmed many *mercedes* he had made, although not that of Arévalo to Alvaro de Stúñiga, and not Pacheco's having invested in his son, Diego López Pacheco, the *marquesado* of Villena. The Cardinal, Alba, and the Admiral dominated the Council. And, once again disaffected, Stúñiga, young Pacheco, and his twin cousins, Rodrigo Téllez Girón and Juan Téllez Girón conspired. Stúñiga not only held Arévalo, but dominated northern Extremadura. Pacheco and the Giróns had extensive domains in Andalusia, the *marquesado* of Villena, the mastership of Calatrava, and the county of Urueña, near Valladolid.

RUMBLINGS

Isabel and Fernando postponed calling Cortes, although Isabel had initially spoken of doing it as soon as possible. Rather, on January 18 they held a full council meeting. Then immediately, invoking the royal responsibility to mete out "Justice, to which—as an anonymous chronicler puts it— more than any other principle they were inclined," they called to court outstanding legists, who, conscious of setting tone, sentenced a number of middle-level malefactors of the previous reign swiftly and harshly. And in towns and villages, royal *corregidores*, although their own anterior behavior might not bear examination, sniffed the wind and emulated the court's draconian measures. The imposition of respect for law and order, however, was soon undercut by the departure from court, on February 20, of the Archbishop of Toledo, signaling a return to factional strife which one observer sadly laid to "our sins growing greater."[11] The time of troubles was not over; heaven was not yet smiling on Castile.

Carrillo, although his influence and revenues had been depleted, still could take with him into the opposition a great central chunk of the kingdom's places and rents. And young Pacheco had custody of Juana, now 13 years old, and he and Stúñiga took up her claim to the crown. She would marry her uncle, Afonso, King of Portugal; he must come claim her and the kingdom. The stage was once again set for civil war in Castile, and war with Portugal as well, but now its crowned heads were a close-knit pair, dominated by no one, but advised primarily by a lawyer, cleric, and statesman, Pedro González de Mendoza, a man with an ability and ambition for promoting sovereign power equal to Alvaro de Luna's, but with a well-established power base of his own and with greater and more far-seeing vision and a strong sense of *noblesse oblige.*

Afonso of Portugal had recently had great success. In 1471 his Portuguese had taken Arcilla, in Fez, a terminal of the Saharan gold route, and eight days later he himself was in Tangier. Portuguese ships too had reached Atlantic coasts under Africa's hump. Fernão Gómez, whom Afonso had licensed in 1469 to explore 100 leagues of coast each year in the area referred to as Guinea and to pay the crown handsomely for the privilege, had arrived at the Costa da Mina, the Gold Coast; there the Portuguese were advantageously exchanging trinkets, old clothes, and the conch shells of the Canary Islands for potential slaves and, most profitably, gold. Having taken Ceuta in 1415, they had diverted gold there from the old hubs of exchange along the Mediterranean coast of North Africa and now they were were exporting it from the Guinea coast as well. In the process, they had disorganized Catalan trading patterns with Egypt and North Africa, and they were affecting the gold flow into Castile and challenging its seamen. Conversely, Aragón and Castile in concert posed a threat to Portugal in Africa and the Atlantic.

None of this was lost on the King of France. And though one historian has overstated in saying "Afonso V of Portugal was a peon in the hands of Louis XI," yet nothing could suit Louis better than that his ally Portugal take on Aragón's ally, Castile, and he kept up unrelenting pressure on Afonso to enter Castile. While in January Isabel and Fernando had promised Juan of Aragón 2000 lances, yet they had also resolved to send an embassy to France, traditionally friendly to Castile, important to their control of Sicily, and now linked to rumblings from Portugal. The lances never left; in February Fernando explained to his father it was because of Carrillo's defection and the threat of civil war. Implied was *los reyes*' accepting that Perpignán again fall to the French—as it would do in March—and that the primary and immediate concern of them both lay not in Aragón but in Castile, though that Aragón retain Cerdaña and Rosellón was to Castile's interest. In March too Isabel and Fernando reached an accord with Louis.

Juan of Aragón, heretofore claiming those provinces and competing with Louis for influence in Navarre, had also allied with England, Burgundy, and the Trastámara in Naples in order to encircle France. Fernando and Isabel, before their succession in Castile, as *reyes* of Sicily had been part of that essentially defensive system. Yet Castile's Trastámara dynasty had a tradition of good relations with France, and upon her accession Isabel had sent Pulgar to Paris to confirm Castile's friendship. Pulgar was a protégé of the Cardinal's, and Mendoza strongly favored the French connection. Most recently, Isabel had offered, in response to Louis' claiming Rosellón, to sell it to him, and had instructed Pulgar to discuss the transaction. Louis' response to her was that there had been few cases of offers by individuals of sale of things jointly held, but how much did she want for it? She should send *grandes* to negotiate. By then, Pulgar had discerned that the French king was playing for time while preparing to invade Castile in support of Afonso of Portugal.

Isabel, if a novice, had become actively involved in foreign relations. That March Fernando, recognizing that they both had to sign international agreements, urged that beforehand she understand thoroughly one made with Louis. Thereafter international affairs remained a sphere of joint competency, and Isabel learned quickly. She continued to tred a careful course between Louis and her father-in-law, whom she wrote to regularly, and, together with Fernando, she exchanged formal promises of friendship with Edward IV of England. Behind this diplomacy lay interest in Castile's burgeoning commerce, for despite internally chaotic conditions the export of wool had climbed, from the 1460s on; so had long-distance trade, in the produce of Andalusia, the iron of Bilbao (especially sought after in London), and the exchange in precious metals, all swelling royal income through customs receipts and sales taxes—their retrieval by the crown, however, dependent on respect for royal authority.

THE KNIGHT AND HIS LADY

In late January, Isabel and Fernando had sent an embassy to Afonso, hoping to dissuade him and offering him the hand of Fernando's sister, Juana, but to no avail. They then sent a second, whose members argued that the war was unjust and Juana illegitimate and that in Spain Enrique's impotence and his queen's lewdness were common knowledge, and they reminded Afonso of the ancient hatred of the Castilians for the Portuguese. Their ambassadors on that occasion were two friars, a Franciscan and a Dominican, who also claimed that their sovereigns possessed the realm by the grace and will of God and by the right of succession belonging to the Queen. And Isabel, said Pulgar, then prayed that God would show where justice lay through granting them victory.

Their choice of emissaries was astute, for word came from Portugal that Afonso felt an equal certainty of divine favor, that he avowed he was impelled by destiny, that he had convinced himself that the prophecies of the Church Fathers revealed that Spain must obey the king of Portugal, and that the conquest of Castile would be just, glorious, and preliminary to waging war against a valiant foe, the kingdom of Granada. More concrete, he told his council that he had received guarantees of support signed by Castilian *grandes* and sealed with their secret seals, and that the papacy would provide, for a sum, the dispensation he needed to marry his niece, Juana. Afonso expected too that Louis XI of France, who had suggested the project to him in the first place, would be a powerful ally.

Isabel and Fernando went on progress through the *meseta* in mid-March. Alba turned over to them Medina del Campo and its fortress of la Mota. Benavente gave them the great house in Valladolid in which they were wed. They reconfirmed the privileges of the cities but still did not call Cortes. They heard from Afonso: he would marry Juana and reclaim Castile on her behalf, and Stúñiga and Pacheco announced their support for her.

Although war loomed, in Valladolid on April 3 Pedro de Velasco, Lord of Haro, held a lavish spring tournament. Fernando jousted. Isabel presided, elegantly attired and wearing a crown, from a throne on a raised dais; her 14 ladies-in-waiting all wore coronets. She had arrived on horseback, the harness of her mount trimmed in silver and adorned with flowers of gold. The *grandes* attending had spent prodigiously in vying with one another in attire and in the size and magnificence of retinues, down to pages dressed in embroidered cloth-of-gold trimmed with furs of marten and sable. Beginnings are wonderful and that handsome young couple exuded hope and promise, commensurate with the season, and not least because Isabel was again pregnant. "It seemed," an onlooker later recalled, "that God had come to the world to entertain us lavishly."[12]

All the *caballeros* did splendidly, mindful of evoking the Knights of the Round Table, responding to the joint imperatives of chivalry and courtly love, and although at odds with religious obligations. It was after all Eastertime, but the attitude was "where affection, bravery, and *gentileza* are found, they always are more pleasing to the god of love than to [the God] of heaven."[13] No heed was paid to censure such as that leveled by the poet Iñigo de Mendoza at troubadours: for invoking the god of love for the service of the Devil. Each contestant so gloried, the chronicle says, in seeking to serve his lady that, though covered in sweat and receiving great blows, none felt much pain.

Isabel was married to such a knight, whose gallantries survive in his letters to her, their phrases of devotion more usually found in love letters directed to an *amiga* than to a wife. Fernando jousted with distinction that day, and throughout April he continued to participate in jousts and tourneys, prodded by companions who, deriding the Portuguese, assured him that Afonso would never dare to enter Castile. There was criticism: "These ridiculous inventions, jousts," snorted Palencia, who thought Fernando lured into them by nobles who did not want to see him exert authority. But tourneys were also war games, and political theatre wherein to demonstrate strength, magnificence, and disdain for opponents, and to make known the temper of both Castile and its new monarchs: "And there was shown how little was thought of the king of Portugal and his cohorts . . ." And especially did those tourneys provide opportunity for calculated self-expression.

Fernando's chivalric device at Valladolid was an anvil, *un yunque*, its first letter the Y of *Ysabel*. And it stood too for his motto: "Like an anvil I keep silent and endure, because of the times." It spoke to the threat of civil war, recent unhappiness with the limitation of his authority in Castile, and inability to counter Louis XI in Aragón. Silence and endurance were also aspects of his father's favorite virtue, *the* most royal one, prudence. Fernando's device was that of the blacksmith who forged and shaped, and it recalled the smith Vulcan or Mars, the god of war. Yet its message was none too heartening, and he would soon exchange that device for another more sanguine one also beginning with Y, a *yugo*, or yoke, a double one most patently emblematic of their working in harness; moreover, a yoke of oxen was known to signify the worldly riches of love. Isabel's device was a bundle of arrows, *flechas*, which returned the compliment in beginning with an F. Arrows were prime missiles of war and execution of justice: in Castile common criminals were traditionally dispatched with bow and arrow. Significantly gathered in and bound, they seem to evoke as well Ceres' bundle of wheat, transformed. They convey her love of imposed order, and of war. Isabel and Fernando would throughout their lives continue to pay attention to the celebratory and ceremonial values of chivalry and its particular fusing of ritual and war; and war there would be.

As Afonso's forces gathered on the border, Castile's Queen and King mobilized. On April 28, they granted a general pardon for past crimes to all volunteers and, knowing they would have to work apart, Isabel, in effect modifying the arrangement agreed upon in January, yielded to Fernando powers "to provide for, decree, make, and organize" all he saw as necessary and complying with the interests of them both and the welfare and defense of their kingdoms. He might make *mercedes* of cities, villages, and forts, or name officials to them. His authority in all matters was to be joint with hers. It was not a full equality, for she remained sole proprietary ruler of Castile, but one indicating increased necessity and also deepened trust. They would work in tandem, although often separated, and they would be constantly in touch by fast couriers.

Isabel favored verbal communication. Thus, in a letter of May 16, Fernando, who was at Tordesillas, chided her roundly, saying that, although messengers came and went between them, she did not write to him, "not for lack of paper and not for not knowing how to write but for insufficient love and haughtiness, and because you are in Toledo and I in the provinces," and then the courtly *coup de grace*: "but someday we shall return to our first love."[14] And he closed: "If you do not want me to kill myself, you should write and tell me how you are." Here was a playful intimacy, bespeaking a mutual consent to his cutting through her natural reserve by teasingly pointing it up.

On May 25, Isabel had war cried throughout the land. At about the same time, Afonso entered Castile through Alburquerque with a formidable army. He came with 3600 to 3700 horse, 8000 to 10,000 foot, 200 carts of provisions, heavy artillery, cannon and lombards, and, as Fernando informed his father, with gold and silver crosses gleaming aloft and with hymns resounding in praise of the God of Armies. He brought too, much engraved silver plate and gold and silver coin. His *grandes* and knights were splendidly equipped; that the wherewithal came of exploration and trade was not lost on their opponents. The treasures of Guinea, says Palencia, had turned the old pride of the Portuguese into great display of unbridled arrogance. And it was reported that Afonso was being carried in a litter, perhaps because of a complaint of the liver but more likely to have his arrival comply with a well-known version of the prophecy of the coming of the messiah-king. The hidden one, *El Encubierto*, would, it was predicted, arrive on a horse of wood; and he would sweep Spain clean of Jews, locusts, bloodsuckers, robber-wolves, and the friar-cats—the *conversos*. *El Encubierto* was synonymous with the Bat; it was, as Isabel hoped, to be a war to determine where God's choice lay.

Afonso, joining Pacheco and Stúñiga in Extremadura, tarried, while proclaiming Juana legitimate queen—he claimed the Cortes had sworn fealty only to her and that Isabel and Fernando had poisoned Enrique—and lavishly celebrating his engagement to the lady Isabel now referred to as La

Beltraneja, thus giving Isabel and Fernando crucial time to prepare. They held a council of war and afterwards Isabel rushed to Tordesillas with reinforcements for its garrison, certain that Afonso must come to nearby Arévalo, held by Stúñiga. In Tordesillas, which would be her principal base for much of the next two years, her penchant for meticulous detail would manifest itself, and not only in organizing and deploying resources; there survives from that period a directive of hers to the Clares, nuns attached to the Franciscan order, whose convent abutted the royal residence, an emphatic request to the sisters that their courtyard be cleared of dung. Throughout her life, she was to demonstrate an order and tidiness she associated with godliness.

Isabel stayed in the *mudéjar* palace housing both the royal quarters and the convent of Clares. Alfonso XI had had it built with Muslim booty taken at Salado, by Andalusian workmen who had brought from their homeland its tiles, the gilded *artesonado* ceilings, and the traditional baths. In its vestibule a mermaid, a siren, evoked a Muslim fable of the sea; and etched on the facade of that mostly Moorish palace were the keys to Paradise. Isabel, amid one war, had a foretaste of the more exquisite spoils of another. But at the moment her mind was on other things.

Tirelessly, she garrisoned and readied other *meseta* towns, while Fernando secured Salamanca, then Zamora and Toro, or so he thought, by confirming in their positions the men who held those towns and their forts. Embassies arrived at Valladolid, from England and France, Brittany and Burgundy; the French dissimulated; the others promised support. Castile's great lords were sent home to gather their *mesnadas*, and the Cabreras were reminded of their promise to turn over the royal treasure they guarded in the *alcázar* of Segovia. They complied, but only after finally being given custody of the royal child, Princess Isabel.

Isabel proposed to visit Carrillo, who was thought to be sulking in Alcalá de Hénares, hurt particularly by her lack of gratitude. Accordingly, she wrote to him on May 10 that the Queen of Castile would much appreciate the pleasure of dining in the Archbishop's company. He responded, irony palpable in his mimicking of her royal tone, that should the Queen enter Alcalá by one gate the Archbishop would leave by another. It had become a hopeless clash of imperious temperaments. Convinced of his defection, she hastened to the core of his archbishopric, Toledo, and arriving on May 20 to a reassuringly hearty welcome, she made certain of the loyalty of its key administrators. But the strain told, and on May 31, en route to Avila, she miscarried; the stillborn child was male.

She stayed in Avila for several weeks recuperating. Too, Avila possessed a mint and she was lady of Avila. Then she sent word to Fernando, who was in Burgos, expecting Afonso to march on that principal city on the road to France in an attempt to link up with Louis XI, that she would come confer with him if he thought it essential. On June 12 he responded: "To me it seems that it is very necessary and that Your Ladyship ought to come, because in getting together we help each other more than anything in life, and now is the time that all our power should be jointly exerted."[15] They met in Valladolid on June 25. Three days later, she skirted the enemy rear-guard to reinforce Madrigal and then rode on the same mission to Medina del Campo. By July 9 she was again in Tordesillas.

ADVERSARIES

Afonso was in Arévalo. He had arrived at that stronghold of Stúñiga's with his intended on the first of June. There the news that Enrique IV's widow, Juana, had died in Madrid on June 13 evoked no show of mourning from her daughter or anyone else; indeed, throughout Castile it was rumored that Afonso, embarrassed by her flouting of convention, had had her given poison, *hierbas*. Afonso, says Palencia, was certain that he would meet no resistance on the Castilian *meseta*, that Fernando had lost the opportunity to ready for combat by frittering time away in vain distractions. And while Burgos had proclaimed for Isabel, Stúñiga's son held the fortress towering over it and with its huge lombards lobbed stones at will into the city. As for Isabel and Fernando, they had the treasury of Segovia, and Isabel, in Tor-desillas, awaited the results of having sent the Admiral to rally the nobles and their *mesnadas*, their armed companies, and of having called on the towns to confront the traditional enemy for the common good and for the glory of Castile.

By July 12, most of the *grandes* bound by oath to the crown had brought their squadrons into the royal encampment outside that town; Palencia says they were afraid not to, even though having accepted sums from Por-tugal, because so popular was the cause. Preachers had inspired large num-bers of volunteers and the general pardon brought in others. From Vizcaya, famed for its archers, and the mountains of Asturias came over 20,000 men, the bulk of the infantry. Beatriz de Bobadilla arrived with 100 lances and 1000 foot. Even so, that army was ill trained and ill coordinated, with each *grande* retaining command of his own men. And numbers proved a mixed blessing, for so great was the host that expenses quickly outran resources. Isabel arranged for the Segovia treasure to be coined, but it could not be done rapidly enough, so that men had to be paid with small bits of silver cups, or so says Palencia.

It was a blow when the news came that the Portuguese had left Arévalo, where food had become scarce, for strategically vital Toro, impregnable atop an escarpment; that the town of Toro had been turned over to Afonso by its *corregidor*, Juan de Ulloa; and that the Portuguese were besieging the fortress, held by Aldonza de Castilla, wife of its *alcaide*, Rodrigo de Ulloa, who though he was Juan de Ulloa's brother rode with Fernando. In council *los reyes* resolved that Fernando should lead the armies to the relief of Toro's *alcázar*, and they hoped to bring Afonso to a decisive battle.

Yet they delayed, awaiting with some anxiety the Mendoza under Santillana, Beltrán de la Cueva, and Benavente, and their complements of heavy cavalry, uncertain of their loyalty; for, with Villena, those *grandes* possessed much of the former domain of Juan of Aragón and his family. And while waiting, Fernando made a will, its provisions opening a window on his sentiments and policies. In it he affirmed Isabel's sole right to the crown of Castile. He commended to her together with his father the raising of his natural children, Alfonso and Juana, as well as the care of their mothers. He called upon, as his special patrons, the Virgin Mary and St. John the Baptist, and he made the sort of charitable bequests customarily associated with saving one's soul: he designated 500,000 *maravedís* for redemption of Christians held captive by Muslims and an equal sum to dower poor orphaned girls for marriage or nunnery. And he stated that he must be buried wherever Isabel chose for her own tomb: "I very much desire that as we were united by marriage and singular love in life, that we may not be parted in death."[16] His daughter Isabel was to be his successor in Aragón and Sicily, notwithstanding any impediment in Aragonese law; he requested his father arrange matters. He designated her, he stated, not through ambition, but because he loved her as much as could possibly be, "especially for being the daughter of so excellent a queen and mother"; and because he foresaw the great good, "the public good," that would result through the unity of Aragón with Castile and León. To draw up that document he chose a Hieronymite, Hernando de Talavera, despite that friar having recently scolded him for not seeking assiduously "the perfection and excellence obligatory for a prince."[17]

On July 15, Santillana, with three of his brothers and Beltrán, arrived. Fernando, although he and Isabel were still uneasy about Benavente who, if he chose, could tilt the balance of power toward Portugal, marched the next day with the massed might of the realm, an estimated 2000 heavy cavalry, 6000 light horsemen, *jinetes*, and 20,000 foot. On the eve of his departure he had written Isabel a note; she was in the palace, he in camp across the Duero river: "God knows it weighs on me that I will not see Your Ladyship tomorrow, for I swear by your life and mine that never have I so loved you."[18]

He was wrong, for that morning she appeared in camp, spoke in council, and went among the men readying for departure, "with heartening words and cheerful face." Then from atop a hill she saw them off: the grandes on horseback at the head of their hundreds-strong *mesnadas* of cavalry and infantry; Pedro de Manrique, Count of Treviño, leading thousands of Asturian foot and Biscayan archers; the recruits come in from the cities; and her own guards, bearing her banner embroidered with her bundled arrows. The massed splendor of the great lords and their mounts, the brilliant brocades and velvets, the shimmering gold and silver, calls to mind French magnificence at Agincourt a half century earlier, as does the prose of the anonymous chronicler who told of that day; yet those Castilian lords, unlike the earlier Frenchmen, were aware of the value of light armor and light cavalry. Watching those thousands wend their way alongside the Duero river and disappear over the horizon, "the Queen saw herself *señora* of this powerful fighting force." She had been dissuaded only through much effort on the part of the King and the *grandes* from riding with them.

Next day, on the heels of Isabel's having received word that Zamora, key to provisioning her army at Toro, had defected, Benavente at last arrived, and magnificently accoutered, on a mount equally superb in armor of silver platelets. With him he brought 1800 lances, nearly all light cavalry. Hiding her unhappiness at Zamora's loss, she greeted him warmly and flattered him extravagantly: he was so welcome, so great a lord, so young yet so renowned for bravery and virtue, grand even among the *grandes,* and so highly important to the service of God and the good of the kingdom. And she confided to him her own suffering and shame at the Portuguese presence in Castile and entreated him to lift her grief, "waiting every hour to be avenged," and to go where his valorous heart might have a chance to outdo itself, and she made him great *mercedes* for the numerous excellent people he had brought to serve her.[19] Within the hour, he found himself again in the saddle, on the way to report to Fernando.

Toro was a disaster. Afonso would not come out to battle. Fernando sent Gómez Manrique, twice, to remind the Portuguese king that he had declared he would engage in personal combat. On the second try, Afonso accepted the challenge, on condition that the *grandes* hold Juana and Isabel as hostages during the contest. Manrique refused, reminding him that the two women were not of equal stature nor legitimacy, and that Isabel possessed realms and a superior army.

That army itself was large and unruly, funds and provisions ran out, and with Zamora lost Toro had become for Fernando a secondary position; there was, too, suspicion that the nobles were reluctant to have him emerge as the hero of that contest. Accordingly, on July 23, the king and council lifted the siege, though not before Fernando had formally elevated the second Marqués de Santillana to Duke of Infantado. The retreat was disorderly; the troops drifted away. Isabel, coming out from Tordesillas, encountered forces greatly diminished and in disarray, far different from the proud host that had left less than two weeks before. Vehemently, she insisted they return at once to Toro. They continued on to Tordesillas. And she, all through that night, furiously berated the *grandes* for serving her badly, "and she spoke to the King with audacity, her words fitting her state of mind; and that night no council met because of the anger of the Queen." And when it did convene next day, she was there to address it.

A DEBATE

"Her womanly nature did not allow her to hide her anguish" at the army returning without glory, wrote Palencia, with most uncharacteristic restraint.[20] For that morning at Tordesillas, the 24-year-old Queen delivered an impassioned harangue. And if an anonymous chronicler took license in setting it down verbatim, the gist appears to accord with what else is known of the personalities involved. "Although," she began, "it may be that women lack discretion to know and strength to dare, and even a tongue to speak"—thus did she perfunctorily dispense with rhetorical protestations of modesty—she had found that they have eyes to see. Certainly, she had seen a great host depart from Tordesillas. "And what greater honor, what greater benefit, what greater service to God, could there be than joining battle? . . . if you say to me that women, since they do not face such dangers, ought not speak of them . . . to this I say that I do not know who risks more than I do, for I risked my King and Lord, whom I love above all else in the world, and I risked so many and such noble *caballeros,* and so many men and riches that, they lost, what more would I have to venture?"[21] Woman she may be, she implied, but she was also Castile's reigning Queen, delivering to her subjects a deserved tongue-lashing.

"I would wish," it is said she went on, "to pursue uncertain danger rather than certain shame. . . . There must first be a battle in order to have a victory." Never would Hannibal, the famed Roman general, have crossed the frozen Alps nor won the great battle of Cannae if his heart had deferred to the weak advice of his brain. Some see as best the rules of philosophy and others those of the sword, said she, but in the highest affairs it is impossible to have compass or measure, but only to take risks boldly and let God guide as He will. War wants more advice from audacity and less from *letrados,* "so that we may commit ourselves to doing things that afterwards the brain may marvel at in contemplating," and it may still find impossible after the deed that which, if judged rationally beforehand, we would never have dared to do. "For that which seems most difficult the hands and heart may accomplish, and especially kings in defending their land."

She then held out as example to those knights her own womanly introspection:

> I find myself in my palace, with angry heart and closed teeth and clenched fists, as if, seeking revenge, I am fighting with myself, and if, *caballeros,* you took unto yourselves such anxiety, the greatest danger from your enemies would be less than that from yourselves. Of my fury, being a woman, and of your patience, being men, I marvel. And excellent king, my lord, and virtuous knights: if more than I reasonably ought I have extended my words, your virtue pardon such an error, for with daring to complain I have quieted the passion that naturally grows in the heart of women. The ill-effect on your service, on the kingdom, on foreign opinion and on the honor of our honors hurts. I bare my soul, because it is not within myself, suffering in spirit, that I can alleviate the pain, nor drive it out; for it is certain that the best rest for the afflicted is to vent their ills to those who commiserate with them.

Even allowing for the uses of rhetoric, that morning in Tordesillas her impetuosity and emotion overstepped the propriety usually ascribed to her. Yet the impassioned sentiments she voiced there had parallel in other of her displays of strength of will and calls to vengeance, and in plumbings of her own conscience to ascertain divine intent.

After much discussion among those assembled about who should reply to the Queen, all agreed it must be the King, as most credible since best informed about why they had left Toro. So Fernando was said to have answered her, with equal conviction: "the grace with which you, My Lady, complain to us and the sweetness of how you say it, may make the very just very guilty, and though we were right in the doing we may lack in the telling. If you have been maliciously informed, hear the truth, and then we want you to judge." Our adversary, he went on, has equal numbers of men and sits on a high palisade, its sides like sheer towers, impossible to scale, and he has artillery to defend it and hoists and blankets and provisions which we do not have. Those who have to gain honor, have to undertake things in which they are equal to their opponents, and although they may see some disadvantage, "it can not be so great as to be so hopeless that God may have to open the sea to the width of 12 galley strokes in order to save them." Strength and time gain victory, madness hinders it. As Hannibal had crossed the Alps, so he himself would cross mountains though even more frozen, if Hannibal's enemy, snow, was the only danger. And as Hannibal won the battle of Cannae, so Fernando would win, or at least fight, if his adversary would come out into the field.

> Give repose, My Lady, to the anxieties of your heart, for the time and days to come will bring you such victories that, even if they defeat us in this one, for a thousand won you will pardon us this one lost . . . I had believed that returning in despair I would hear from your tongue words of consolation and encouragement . . . Women are always malcontent, and you especially, My Lady, since the man who could satisfy you is yet to be born, They are guilty who feel shame in the recesses of their will; but I and these *caballeros* are well satisfied in our own wills, and no blame hidden in our souls cries out, nor are we shamefaced. No one is as obliged to content women or to benefit the world as he is to his own honor. . . .

The time was past, he told her, when walls fall to earth, as they did for Joshua at Jericho, after prayer and seven turns around a besieged town and the sun turning back twenty-four hours so that the battle might be won; rather, "today one conquers with strength, diligence, and men. . . . In equal affairs we ask God's help, but without expecting a return to the marvels of the Old Testament." She must not think that with many men one performs great deeds, but with few, acting in concert. "Prudence is the God of the battles; and, above all else let us trust ourselves to that High Judge, without whom, as San Juan said, nothing is done. . . . And he in manner least expected will give us vengeance, as a just Judge. . . ." God was humbling them, Fernando concluded, but charging them to persevere, and to show piety.

In his emphasis on prudence, Fernando was his father's son. In his reliance on the God of Battles and on judgment from on high he touched on traditional royal themes taken up as motifs by himself and Isabel. Vengeance too was important to them both. Yet his words also convey a sense of dawning modernity; he expected no miracles. And it is noteworthy that it was in his mouth, not Isabel's, that the well-informed chronicler writing for contemporaries put expressions of piety. The time had not yet arrived to fashion Isabel as stolid and pious, nor Fernando as devious and machiavellian. Rather, the author portrayed them rightly in the spring of 1475 as lord and lady of chivalry. Similarly, their exchange after Toro was a variant on courtly love, wherein passion and reason always war with one another.

Worse was to come. In August Toro's fortress fell to Afonso, and Carrillo swore homage to him and Juana as King and Queen of Castile. Isabel, declared the Archbishop, he had raised from the distaff, and he was going to send her back to it. Spirits lifted when Enrique Enríquez, Conde de Alba de Liste, who was Fernando's great-uncle, arrived from Andalusia with fresh and experienced troops. Isabel had sent emissaries to Seville in February to see to collection of its sizable revenues and to extract funds from its wealthy, including the resident Italian merchants, but all that took time. And, desperate for money, rather than take Juan of Aragón's advice to give *mercedes* on expected income, she instead followed the counsel of the Cardinal and of her confessor, Hernando de Talavera, in appropriating from the churches half of their silver and their revenues from lands given them for upkeep, promising to repay everything within three years; her father, or Luna, had done the same thing in preparing to go against Granada. She had the silver made into coins that both attested to and disseminated a sense of joint royal mission: the silver *reales* then minted at Toledo bore a crown under intertwined Fs and Ys and the legend: "The Lord is my help and I do not fear what men may do to me." Other coins depicted on one side Isabel and Fernando, wearing crowns, facing each other, and, on the other, the arms of Castile and León, Aragón, and Sicily under the outspread wings of the great eagle of St. John the Evangelist and bearing the legend: "Under the shade of your wings protect us, Lord." Both mottos suited the metal's provenance as well as its purpose.

A war of sovereign titles ensued: Afonso appropriated those of Castile and León, Fernando and Isabel affixed Portugal. Both sides further reinforced their *meseta* garrisons, and Burgos was now seen by both as the key to the war.

7

Resolutions
1475–1477

See, Your Majesty, to what you are obliged, and why you were placed on
the peak of honors and sublime dignities.

Hernando de Talavera

Lady, I swear to you by Jesus Christ . . . you cannot spur your horse in that
posture, you must take one leg and put it over the saddle bow.

John Marshal to Matilda of England[1]

BURGOS

IN August and September 1475, Isabel reinforced garrisons important to
the defense of Burgos while Fernando laid siege to its fortress. Afonso of
Portugal left Toro on September 17, with Carrillo, Villena, Stúñiga, and
Rodrigo Girón, ostensibly for Burgos, only to hear on reaching Peñafiel that
the road to the north was closed, that Isabel and the Cardinal had got to
Palencia ahead of them with reinforcements, blocking the way. Afonso
returned to Toro, and in October moved to Zamora, where he planned to
lay over for the winter.

Meeting in November in Dueñas, Isabel and Fernando determined to
regain Zamora by burrowing from within, "for its people [had been] awakened to love of patriotism by rumor Afonso will expel them all and resettle
the town with Portuguese."[2] While Fernando returned to Burgos, Isabel
went to Valladolid, from where she dispatched troops to him, others against
Portuguese depredations on the *meseta,* and yet others to Rodrigo Manrique,
attacking the strongholds of Pacheco and the Giróns in Extremadura.

So matters stood when Isabel sent word to Fernando that entry into
Zamora has been arranged with partisans inside the town; he must come
quickly and secretly to Valladolid. He did, leaving in command in Burgos

his half-brother, Alfonso de Aragón, an illegitimate son of Juan's. That expert in siege warfare, having recently arrived in Burgos, looked over the work that had been done there and, having pronounced that while the double moats and stockades passed muster, the mines were inefficiently laid and the lombards so placed that the shot could not hit the fortress walls, had his engineers hard at work. In Valladolid, Isabel and Fernando conferred for three days, then Fernando, gathering men—Isabel had written to the authorities in Salamanca, Medina, Segovia, and Avila, charging them to send troops at once—left for Zamora, to learn enroute that the town had declared for them and the Portuguese had decamped for Toro, although leaving a garrison. From early December to March, Fernando lay siege to Zamora's fortress; he was supplied by the townspeople and those of its outskirts who offered him the provisions they had denied to Portugal, including "all the grain in their silos, and they sold it very cheaply."

Isabel traveled north, informed that, Alfonso de Aragón having systematically destroyed its walls, the *alcaide* had on December 2 agreed to surrender Burgos' castle within the 70 days' waiting period decreed by chivalric courtesy. Accompanied by the Cardinal, she entered the city in a heavy snowstorm to a warm reception: a great crowd cheering, children dancing and singing. The *alcaide*, young Stúñiga, surrendered to her early, on January 19. While dismissing him from command, she commended his valor. And she gained an adherent, his father, who, impressed at her magnanimity and disenchanted with Afonso, announced his own neutrality and opened negotiations with her.

SERMON FOR A QUEEN

For Isabel, victory in Burgos marked the end of the first year of her reign, begun with audacity, and of war waged with determination, yet also a year of uncertainty and vulnerability, of the mental and physical toll attendant upon miscarrying a much-desired male heir, and of an awareness imposed of her own lack of experience. She was 24 years old. She had functioned as joint ruler and asserted her legal position as sole proprietor of Castile in the face of strong competing claims; nor could she be certain, though she might refer to her as *La Beltraneja*, that young Juana was not Enrique's rightful heir. War persisted; there was no certain indication of where the right lay. And while she had recently been compared to Joan of Arc, surely she needed exemplars other than the peasant virgin of noble spirit who had led a French army, nor were women saints or the ladies of chivalry appropriate models for a reigning queen.

At the end of 1475, in an age when what one did and who one was were assumed synonymous, she expressed a desire to fortify her developing sense of what it was to be queen, and she did it by requesting of Hernando de Talavera, her new confessor—Alonso de Burgos was elevated to Bishop of Córdoba—a copy of the sermon he had delivered to his Hieronymite brothers on "How all loyal Christians should renew their spirits during Advent." (Advent occurs four Sundays before Christmas.) Talavera quickly complied, with a version especially adapted for her, a devotional tract at once spiritual and political, blending piety and power. He made of that sermon a guide for a reigning monarch, a mirror for a queen.

Its point of view and its author would have life-long influence upon her. Talavera, his father unknown, his mother a *conversa*, had shown sufficient ability to gain a chair of moral philosophy at Salamanca and come to the attention of the Cardinal. He had drawn Fernando's will and suggested expropriating church silver; now he sat on the Royal Council and was increasingly looked to by Isabel for counsel. As a Hieronymite he belonged to a religious order inaugurated in Castile by earlier royal ministers who had forsaken the world to become its founders, and the rule he followed was that of a Church father and saint, Jerome, renowned for being both mystical and practical, a scholar and a hard worker who had striven for personal perfection and salvation, had valued asceticism and direct communication with God, and had manifested a modulated apocalypticism. Jerome has been portrayed as both a penitent and a scholar in his study— beside him the lion from whose paw he has removed a thorn. He and his followers in Spain never resolved the tension between the pull of a life of rusticity and one of learned piety; the latter had gained an edge during the fifteenth century. Talavera was too a nephew of another Hieronymite, the learned Alonso de Oropesa, whose good offices had been relied upon by both Juan II of Castile and his son Enrique IV.

In January 1476 Talavera offered Isabel not simply an inspirational tract for a devout queen, but a politically astute guide to royal morality and devotion, indeed a vision of herself within the divine scheme. It built upon Spanish traditions of kingship and advice to princes within the usual religious framework, apocalyptic and eschatological. In it he bound royal power to virtue, urged she seek moral perfection, and employed some time-honored exemplars culled from the Bible, the church fathers, Castilian law and history, and from what has been called 'the moral zoo,' the ascribing of laudable qualities to beasts and birds. Isabel had elicited an updated version of a body of intertwined religious and political theory long associated with and enjoined upon Castile's rulers. Yet, unlike her immediate predecessors, the monarch receiving such advice was young and receptive and female. It contained, moreover, counsel congenial to her own cast of mind as she had revealed it to date: thus Talavera urged she strive for perfection of character and he assumed that "it is a calling to aspire to perfection of your estate. If you are Queen, you ought to be a model and stimulus to your subjects in the service of God."[3]

Isabel had shown on more than one occasion that she set for herself very exacting standards and that she subscribed to the principle that the best guide is one's conscience, that virtuous rulers follow the will of God and discern it through heeding their own conscience or heart. Pulgar attributes to her in those days a frequent prayer to that effect, as well as one indicating the great responsibility she felt, and also a lingering doubt as to the justice of her accession:

> You, Lord, who know the secret of every heart, you know of me that not by unjust means, not with cunning, nor tyranny, but believing truly that these kingdoms of the King my father by right belong to me, I have sought to have them so that what the kings my forebears won with so much bloodshed may not pass to a foreign lineage. And you, Lord, in whose hands is the right of kingdoms, through the dictates of your Providence you have put me in this royal state in which I am today. I implore humbly, My Lord, that you hear now the prayer of your servant, and show the truth, and manifest your will with your marvelous works. If I do not have justice, may there be no room for me to sin through ignorance, and if I do have justice, may you give me intelligence and strength so that, with the help of your arm, I can pursue and achieve my charge, and bring peace in these kingdoms, which have suffered so many evils and such destruction.[4]

Talavera was therefore on firm ground in beginning by addressing her as a wise monarch who was seeking divine guidance in ruling and its analogue, meting out justice. And he both flattered her and showed his awareness of her aspiring to a clear and discerning conscience in remarking that, although ordinarily what is addressed to clergy for their edification is not what secular people ought to hear, yet "I, who know the excellence of your enlightened intellect and the perfection of your devotion and disciplined will (*ordenado desseo*), find no difficulty in communicating it to Your Royal Majesty." For her request, he went on, was surely inspired by some ray of divine light which, though it may touch all people, especially touches and illuminates the royal heart. He recalled Biblical kings, David and the wise Solomon who sought above all an educated heart with which to judge his people. And he repeated to her what Christ had told his disciples: "that to you is given to know the mysteries of the kingdom of God." Although elsewhere Talavera spoke of women disapprovingly, as weak and greedy for knowledge, the Queen was clearly a special case, a woman but, more important, a monarch who must be strong and have knowledge. His attitude toward women was not far from that of Jerome, who both spoke of women in general as weak and inferior and sympathized with and admired certain individuals to whom he dedicated works; on occasion too Jerome said that they had the knowledge and intelligence he sought in men, and that God valued not gender but heart. Talavera, moreover, had an extremely elevated concept of monarchy. He assumed the ruler modeled upon and in direct contact with the sovereign of heaven.

He discerned the natural embodiment of laudable royal qualities in that most imposing of birds, the eagle, which he referred to throughout as female. His inspiration, he told Isabel, was a copy of a medieval bestiary she herself had given him. Nor was it a coincidence that the eagle was the symbol of John the Evangelist, whom she had taken as her patron saint. Thus Talavera announced his theme: "how we seek renewal in this holy time in the manner of the eagle, and of the conditions and properties which morally conform to that manner. For as [the eagle] may be queen of the birds, to whom St. John the Evangelist, because of the height of his elevated evangel and his other lofty revelations, worthily is compared. . . . it is worthwhile that Your Highness know these same conditions and properties and the significance and application of them." He ended that prologue by reminding her that Advent was a holy time of renovation and soul-searching, a time for reading "the holy evangel that mentions the universal justice that we await, in which all the world will be renewed" and we believe that time to be "nearer rather than far off." Approaching, that is, were the last days, the prophesied final age of justice.

The eagle was commonly believed emblematic of Christ and the sun. It was thought to symbolize resurrection, salvation, renewal; and in medieval Europe it stood as an allegory for, among other things, legality of royal descent, rejection of intruders in lawful succession, and "the undiminished vitality of the race."[5] Moreover Talavera, in noting elsewhere her desire to read spiritual things that would enlighten her and inform her will and her decrees, commended Isabel as the daughter of an excellent father who spent more time in reading than in any other pastime. That reference went beyond compliment to allude to her legitimacy and rehabilite, even make exemplary, someone so crucial to her who had up until then been dismissed as a weak king. Henceforth, she was to associate the attributes of Saint John and his eagle with his namesake, her father, Juan II of Castile, whose heir she could in those terms proudly claim to be.

Isabel, in exalting the memory and reputation of her father and assuming herself his lineal heir, also bypassed the reign of her half-brother, Enrique, and lessened the need, her own included, to think about his purported daughter. And the idealization of Juan II of Castile was especially politic in view of the presence of Fernando's dynamic father of the same name, who had a claim of his own to succession in Castile. Her growing sense of identification with a father who gave her the legitimacy of succession that Enrique's sometime oath could never do of itself was reflected in Fernando's writing to her that past June from Burgos of his care to visit Juan's tomb at Miraflores and that he had "kissed his hands" for her.[6]

Talavera developed the analogy of the eagle, through metaphor elucidating the fusion of religion and political authority. The eagle nests on the highest cliffs. Christ is a high and firm mountain top and from him all the faithful receive virtue as members of the body receive it from the head. Another very high peak is the holy virgin, our lady, Mary, and others are the saints, though less high. Lofty too are the kings and princes, dukes and marqueses. He listed as exemplars the patriarchs—Noah, Abraham, Isaac, Job, Moses—whom he called princes and dukes, and then the kings, Saul, Solomon, and David. Kings, he mentioned, should love reading and books and they should be surrounded by good counselors, for—and here he made explicit the link between faith and power—"the lord of all will prove to be he who is the true servant of piety." Isabel would concur with that sentiment. She had begun to court and to gain a reputation for piety; she would soon demonstrate that she too interpreted temple-building as a way of displaying it.

Kings, Talavera continued, clearly placing her within their company, "are viceroys of the King of Kings delegated to rule and govern realms and peoples and to command [their subjects] so that they will know and serve God," and kings should always think more than other men of how to do His will. God commands them to keep the book of holy law [the Bible] at their right hand and each day to study and read it and to consider their great responsibility. And, like the eagle, they should show their young how to fly. "For you, excellent Queen of so many and such great kingdoms by vicarate of God placed as one with the most serene King, your equally worthy husband," he told her, there was reason to know those properties of the eagle.

He then discussed the qualities good princes and kings, prelates and governors must have, through referring to Old Testament kings, to Aristotle, Augustine, and Jerome, and to Spanish legal and political theory. Liberality was the prime quality, but combined with powerful and sharp sight, for they must always be watchful; next, charity, constancy, and firmness—for princes must have the love of their subjects, "not as lords to servants through self-interest, but as parents to children for their own good." Rulers had to be constant and firm in the execution of justice and conservation of the laws. They should be courageous and hale, never idle nor indulge in frivolity or gaming—a proclivity of Fernando's—and queens, he emphasized, should always be well occupied. Those very qualities he prescribed for good rulers others would come to cite in describing Isabel, though sometimes with the exception of liberality.

He next considered exemplary queens, princesses, and ladies, adding ideal feminine qualities to those associated with kingship. Isabel ought to raise her children in good works and noble customs, and be conversant with certain women praised in the Scriptures: He cited the chastity of Sarah, revered by her husband Abraham, "the father of our faith," the modesty and diligence of Rebecca, Leah's hard work, Rachel's devotion and contemplation, the discretion and judgment of Deborah, and so on. Above them all he placed the virtues of "the Queen of Queens and Lady of the Angels, the glorious Virgin, our advocate and lady, Mary," citing her perfect humility and compassion, and admonished Isabel to avoid "the laziness, chatter and light life of our mother Eve." It was one of the few instances where his advice coincided with that which Isabel had received in the *Garden of Noble Maidens*.

Then Talavera returned to the eagle, finding among her admirable qualities love of God and "concern for our salvation and that of those near to us." Teach eaglets to fly, he enjoined Isabel, as our Lord did the Jewish people when he took them from Egypt (Jews who lived before Christ being widely considered spiritual progenitors of Christian Spaniards). Isabel, that is, he charged with developing strong character, behaving and governing in accord with the highest of standards, and with the triple task of emulating patriarch kings, Mary, Queen of Heaven, and the good women of the Scriptures. And he ended by exhorting her to

> Rise, rise in the air and contemplate the crown of glory . . . for through these works and considerations you will achieve like the eagle the strength and vigor of your youth. . . . Renew through God your noble spirit and gain perfection, for you have the estate . . . of mistress and lady so perfect and so full of all virtue and goodness as has the eagle among birds, in which perfection all kingdoms and domains and principally all those of yours, have to participate, as do the other birds of her flock. See, Your Majesty, to what you are obliged, and why you were placed on the peak of honors and sublime dignities.

It was, at a critical juncture in her life, an exhortation to ascend to the heights of soverignty and authority on earth, to exercise absolute rule as divine designate, an exhortation meant to demolish doubt. It was a politically astute interweaving of religion and statecraft, an injunction to an indisputable queen to soar free, and, through aspiring to it, do heaven's will. Moreover, Isabel who, as comes through the reconstruction of her tirade on retreat from Toro, had been at pains to bridge the chasm between the demonstrated certainty demanded of a monarch and the conventions of femininity, even noble femininity, here found them reconciled. Subsequently, her reign bore out just how congenial she found that advice; and she kept its profferer close to her through the years, not only as confessor but as one of her two most trusted counselors in affairs of state, relying on him in matters of policy as well as in delicate and detailed financial and diplomatic concerns. Talavera gave Isabel other written advice as well; he drew up a detailed schedule for most efficiently organizing her time in attending to matters of state, which she followed, to gain a reputation for "prodigious regularity." In accord with his counsel too she was well read. She also continued to rely on him to keep her on the path to the personal righteousness both of them considered inseparable from right rule and, a concomitant, on the path to personal and national power, fame, and glory. The consequences for Spain would be multiple.

In those initial years of her reign, she received advice from other courtiers as well who tended to praise her qualities and to look forward to a reign of justice, so desired after years of strife. And Gómez Manrique told her that while prayer was well and good, it was firm rule and stern justice that were now vital.

PELEAGONZALO: MARCH 1476

For the war had yet to be won and the Portuguese driven out. Indications were promising. With the securing of Burgos, Afonso was fast losing his Spanish allies. Rodrigo Girón asked reconciliation and Villena began talks with the Cardinal. Alvaro de Stúñiga's formidable wife, Leonor Pimentel, sent envoys to begin negotiations, as did most of the late Juan Pacheco's brood. Only his bastard daughter, Beatriz, Countess of Medellín, remained resolutely hostile; she was a force in the war fueled by factional strife that wore on in Extremadura and Andalusia. But in Castile matters were coming to a head.

Isabel, expecting a Portuguese offensive in the spring, and perhaps a clash with the French as well, reinforced Burgos immediately after its surrender and sent Alfonso of Aragón to clean out the lairs of neighboring robber barons. She then took her court to Tordesillas and, on February 9, sent on to Fernando at Zamora the Cardinal, Alba, the Admiral, and Alba de Liste with their men. For word had come that Portugal's prince, João, though the Portuguese treasury was exhausted and the gold supply from Africa disrupted by war, had raised sufficient funds for 2500 light cavalry and 15,000 foot and had brought them to Afonso. The reinvigorated Portuguese first marched on Madrigal, to be surprised by a rain of arrows from the garrison Isabel had reinforced, then proceeded to Medina del Campo, only to encounter Alfonso de Aragón, who came out against them with 700 lances, his trained eye leading him "to have more confidence in the troops than in the walls." After a skirmish or two, the Portuguese moved on, to make camp across the Duero river from Zamora. Fernando was encamped on the other side of that river, just outside the walls, thus situated uncomfortably between its fortress garrison and his adversary. Yet Afonso, low on funds and with the Castilians withholding provisions, was losing to desertion or dismissing most of his foot soldiers, while cities and towns from Aragón to New Castile sent cavalry to the monarchs, and Benavente and Treviño with their *mesnadas* swelled the subsidiary force under Alfonso de Aragón. Afonso offered Isabel peace in exchange for Galicia, Toro, Zamora, and money. She replied that, while she would be willing to discuss a cash settlement, she would not part with a bit of Castile's territory.

On March 1 Afonso decamped, before dawn, and before the day was out the only pitched battle of the war was fought, the last major contest in Castile to be decided by light cavalry and the individual valor of nobles and kings. Late that afternoon, overtaken by Fernando's forces at a place known as Peleagonzalo outside Toro, Afonso drew up his squadrons in battle formation. Although the Portuguese were superior in numbers and the Castilians were tired and strung out along the route, their artillery absent and the hour late, Fernando, as he afterwards told it, chose to join battle, confident in the right "that I and the most serene Queen, my beloved wife, have to these realms, and in the mercy of Our Lord and of his blessed mother, and in the help of the apostle St. James—Santiago—patron and *caudillo* of the Spains."[7]

Castilian pride and the habit of centuries did the rest, overcoming the calculated recalcitrance of the nobles. The Cardinal, in full armor, stung by Portuguese taunts and mindful of the death on a Portuguese battlefield of the great-grandfather whose name he bore, raised the battle cry. The nobles attacked furiously. Mendoza led his cavalry at a gallop against the foe and fought undauntedly, even after his coat of mail was pierced by a barbed spearhead. Rain and darkness ended the contest three hours later, without a clear-cut victory but leaving the Castilians in control of the field. Yet, with nightfall, the Castilian soldiers hunted spoils, not the enemy, and the remains of Afonso's army reached Toro over the old Roman bridge. Afonso was thought dead, until the next day he was found to have fled to the safety of the nearby castle of Castronuño, leaving the army to Prince João. Fernando later remarked to Isabel that "if it had not been for the chick, the old cock would have been caught." No matter, Castilians afterwards referred to that battle near Toro as divine retribution for defeat suffered in their last contest with the Portuguese, at Aljubarrota in 1385, and as a sign of heaven's favor returned to their land.

Isabel, at Tordesillas, received the news from Fernando, sent off even before he regrouped the pillagers, She had had no word since the battle was joined and, as Palencia put it, "to describe the joy of the Queen would be impossible."[8] She ordered bulls run, celebrations held, and, in the March cold and damp, she went barefoot to give thanks for so marvelous a victory before the altar of the two Saints John in the convent of the Clares. The triumphant *Te Deum laudamus* rose up. Victory had come, above all, as a sign that hers was the just cause.

The fortress of Zamora capitulated within weeks; at Toro, although Juan de Ulloa had died, his widow, María de Sarmiento, in control of the town and the fortress, continued to hold out, if in isolation. For the center of the contest had shifted to Extremadura and Andalusia, where support for one side or the other had most to do with local struggles among urban factions leagued with the great lords, and where the most bitter contests of all were those for the masterships of the military orders.

CORTES AT MADRIGAL

In mid-April 1476, Cortes was held at last, significantly in the town of Isabel's birth, Madrigal de las Altas Torres. At the outset, the assembled representatives of the by-then-customary sixteen or seventeen municipalities were instructed "to consider what things comply with the reform of Justice and the good government of our kingdoms," and procedure was stipulated:

> They shall give us their petitions so that, providing we see they comply with God's service and our own and the common good of our kingdoms, then we, in accord with Cardinal Mendoza, our very dear and very loved cousin, and with the Duke of Infantado, our uncle, and with the Duke of Alba, our cousin, and with Alfonso Enríquez our uncle and cousin and our Admiral, and with the Count of Benavente and the Bishops of Avila and Segovia, and the other viscounts and knights, *ricos hombres*—men of substance—and the *letrados* of our council, will respond to each petition and will decree as law."[9]

She and Fernando spoke as one at Madrigal, as a single sovereign entity, employing such phrases as "my royal crown" and "my patrimony." The petitions they received even when echoing grievances directed to Enrique in 1465 were a great deal more respectful, and unquestioned there were either the monarchs' right to reign or that of their daughter, Isabel, to succeed them. Conversely, royal statements were couched in terms reminiscent of the most absolutist claims put forth under Juan II. Thus, the invocation stated that as God made kings his vicars on earth, He gave them greater power than others. They were obligated to repay in administration of justice, because for this was the power bestowed upon them, for this God made kings and for it they reigned, as the *Siete Partidas* stated. "For this we were given don Fernando and doña Isabel."

Reiterated from Enrique's reign were complaints of the power of nobles and clergy, and of the great diminution of the royal patrimony, particularly of towns and villages. It was asserted that the royal right to make knights was being usurped, that ecclesiastical judges were infringing upon royal justice, and that finances were in chaos: silversmiths defrauded on weight, precious metals continued to flow out of the kingdom, the currency was unfathomable, and Enrique had left accounts in a mess.

To all of those enduring issues, the royal response was a hope to provide remedy in more peaceful times. Finances, the monarchs promised, would be examined. They issued regulations for collecting revenues. They responded, to a request that judicial officials for court and chancery be well paid and that they appoint men proposed by the delegates, only to the extent of decreeing that the royal chancery must include a prelate, two knights, six *letrados*, and six secretaries, and stating what each official should earn.

Still, at Madrigal they gave indication of where they were heading. Thus they agreed to revoke the law that forbade jailing Jews and Muslims for monies owed to Christians, and they agreed Jews and Muslims must wear insignia and not have communal officials, *alcaldes*, of their own. A sign of things to come was the argument presented by delegates against Jews exercising jurisdiction in their own communities: "Well you know, your highness, that following divine law, by the coming of the Holy of Holies [the Messiah] the authority and jurisdictions of the Jews cease."[10] The deputies, their grievances delivered, voted a hefty subsidy.

The most vigorous royal action was taken on instituting a national brotherhood or *Hermandad*, a principal reason, together with the oath to Princess Isabel and the need for a subsidy, for having called the Cortes. The deputies dutifully suggested that the time-honored remedy "to bring security to travel and trade, most certain and without cost to you, would be to make *hermandades* in all your kingdoms," in each city and village, and that royal ordinances should establish that all the cities league "one with another, and others with others, and all together, some with others." It was a bit after the fact: the minutes of the Burgos city council include a message from the crown of March 30 announcing that a nationwide council of *hermadades* was even then being set up.

In late 1475 Alonso de Quintanilla, a royal councillor sent out to pave the way for such a national league met with strong resistance. The *grandes* objected to what they saw as interference in their jurisdictions and to being joined by *populares* and clergy in their traditional function of providing the monarch with men at arms. Unspoken was their dismay that through such an association the crown could directly control a powerful fighting force, expand its influence in municipalities, and open a broad avenue to royal taxation. Towns too resisted, often incited by the nobles who dominated them, unhappy at the expense and at royal interference in what they considered their internal affairs. Yet Quintanilla had prepared the ground well enough that at Madrigal deputies made the well-orchestrated request.

And there the monarchs graciously complied. The ordinances for an overarching body, a *Santa Hermandad*, were attached to the proceedings of the Cortes. They stipulated that, much as previously, each municipality was to organize a highway patrol within its borders, with jurisdiction over a range of crimes; execution too was to be traditional, by bow and arrow. There is a traveler's description of how *hermandad* archers executed a rebel: they put a target on his left breast, offered a prize of 24 *maravedís* for a bull's-eye and a fine of a *castellano* for missing, and only afterwards did they hold a trial. In 1476 it was decreed that every municipality was to have in place such an association of vigilantes within thirty days, and each *hermandad* to keep on hand operating funds raised by taxes—thus Burgos had by June levied a tax on the entry of specific goods to support its brotherhood.

Deputies from the towns met with royal functionaries in May and June to work out finances and set the numbers of armed men each should send to their majesties. Provincial councils were held and, at the end of July, delegates from them arrived at a general assembly convened at Dueñas, which the Queen and King, many nobles, and the court attended in great state. Awe helped, but not enough. The deputies, hearing the extent of funds and men required, balked. Pulgar has Quintanilla make a day-saving speech, urging defense of the homeland against Portugal, reminding them of the ever-lurking Muslim threat, exhorting them to a campaign against evil: and declaring that the good are also punished when God punishes since they have permitted evils to endure unopposed. And he promised that the *Hermandad* would be temporary.

The deputies came around. Earlier ordinances, envisioning an institution functioning from urban units up, were adjusted to guarantee control from the top down by the national brotherhood's general assembly, and of that body by royal authorities. Locally, *hermandad alcaldes* received much greater jurisdiction, enabling them to override local justices.

Institutional mechanisms were in place; members were enrolled from central Castile and, over time, more municipalities were cajoled or coerced into joining what became a combination of national police force and rudimentary national army, its titular head that siege expert and tactician, Alonso de Aragón, who was now the Duke of Villahermosa. The *alcaldes* of the local brotherhoods levied tarriffs and fines, collected by taxfarmers overseen by Quintanilla; *hermandad* receipts also maintained companies of cavalry organized as royal guards. All in all, its establishment was preeminent among royal measures obviating the calling of Cortes from 1480 to 1498; it would make possible fielding an army against Granada, and its introduction would serve as model for that of other centrally directed institutions initially unpopular.

ALARUMS

One other matter of importance was placed before the Cortes of Madrigal: Isabel and Fernando requested it ratify an agreement of marriage, of the Princess Isabel to Ferrante, heir to Naples, whose king, Ferrante's grandfather, was Fernando's cousin. The match was sought to strengthen the coalition against the French, who had invaded Castile in February 1476, been repulsed, and would return twice more during the next four months. French hostility had much to do with *los reyes'* desire to associate with Naples, an aggressively ascending Italian power not only close to their Sicily but also in the very good graces of the papacy, and thus crucial to Afonso of Portugal's not getting the papal dispensation to marry Juana. At issue too was the trade and strategic control of the Mediterranean. And ever present was the threat of the Grand Turk, Mehmet II, who, as Palencia noted, was "always interested in promoting discord among Christian princes and favored by the avarice of the Roman pontiffs." Moreover, Princess Isabel was six years old, and her parents well aware, especially in view of the numerous arrangements made for themselves, that this might be only her first engagement.

Yet, as the Cortes ended successfully, tension was visible between the Queen and the King. Throughout early May, Isabel seemed annoyed and Fernando repeatedly "went off to hunt with falcons." Since it was to be the only falling out recorded during their lifetimes, it is tempting to hypothesize that then occurred that extramaritial activity on Fernando's part which would produce two daughters, and that Isabel had discovered it. Both daughters were named María de Aragón and both would become nuns in Santa María de Gracia, an Augustinian convent on the outskirts of Madrid, and be told of their paternity only after Isabel's death. Whatever the cause, Fernando, who had repeatedly put off conferring with his father in the past few years, at the end of the month left to do so, going by way of the northern coast.

Cantabrian ships, by cutting communications, had forced the French to leave Castile and Louis XI to sign a three-month truce at the end of June. Louis also commissioned a fleet of his own, for France had long relied on Castilian seamen and ships. Fernando ordered a squadron outfitted at Bilbao in expectation of its arrival. Then, on July 30, he went to Guernica where he took the traditional royal oath to respect and defend the privileges of the Basque *vizcaínos*, who had stayed clear of domination by any noble, and where he was received as lord of Vizcaya under its great oak tree, the symbol of age-old Basque liberties. Those liberties notwithstanding, underlying all his activity in Vizcaya was implantation of royal authority.

It was mid-August before he and his father met, in Vitoria, their first reunion since Fernando had become king of Castile. Juan insisted, despite his son's protests, on deferring to him as the more powerful king. Juan was then 78 and apprehensive that his son had come to dissuade him from his passion for one Roxa de Barcelona—who was rumored to have been introduced to him by enemies in order to wear him out. Instead, he received criticism on another count, and from Isabel. For at his old ally Carrillo's behest, Juan had ordered the Valencians besieging the town of Villena to change sides and put themselves under its Marqués, young Pacheco. Consequently, Fernando had brought his father a letter from her, conveying her unhappiness at his intervening in Castile's affairs. Juan was certain someone had put her up to it; his implication was that it had been the Cardinal, Mendoza.

The conversation at Vitoria, however, centered on larger issues of policy, concerning France, Navarre, and the relationship between Aragón and Castile. Juan was brought around from what had been Aragonese priorities to giving thought to a joint, Spanish policy. Increasingly, Fernando himself worked in broadly Spanish terms that alone made sense of his own dual allegiance. Although Juan had vowed to fight France until Rosellón was restored to Aragón, Fernando persuaded him to sign a truce with Louis and also to agree to seek peace in the independent kingdom of Navarre, where a contest for political supremacy went on between two factions—one backed by Aragón, the other by Castile. Subsequently, Fernando and Isabel, through astute diplomacy, would make that principality into a Castilian protectorate.

Jointly, Castile's monarchs were realigning its international relations: while not abandoning friendship with France they were moving closer to the newer dynasties surrounding it: York in England, Habsburg in Burgundy, and their Trastámara cousins in Italy, and they established connections in Brittany. In 1477 they would hold long secret talks with envoys of England and Burgundy, a combination of political and economic interests at issue. In October 1478 they would arrange a treaty with France and the Aragonese claim to Rosellón be arbitrated.

The kaleidoscope of international affairs was to increasingly constitute an integral part of their policies and influence domestic measures, and both monarchs would evince great skill in diplomacy. Yet while Fernando concerned himself with the diplomacy of both Aragón and Castile, Isabel's activity was largely restricted to the interests of Castile where, in late 1476, foreign affairs were less pressing than were some internal considerations.

Within Castile after the battle of Toro, there were many changes of heart and *grandes* who recanted were well received by their Queen. Old Alvaro de Stúñiga, in particular and as the first, was permitted to keep the bulk of his estates, including Arévalo. And, within a policy of leniency, Rodrigo Girón was confirmed master of the military order of Calatrava; Isabel compensated Alfonso of Aragón, his hurt and angry rival for the honor, by giving her blessing to his marriage to Leonor de Soto, one of her ladies, of whom he was greatly enamored. It was at bottom a victory for Cardinal Mendoza, who had advised winning over the powerful Girón and who did not want to see an Aragonese in so elevated a post. For his signal service to date, the Cardinal among other *mercedes* then received legitimation of his three sons; the oldest, Rodrigo, was to be Marqués de Ceñete. As for Carrillo, a petition to the Roman curia to remove him from his archepiscopal office availed nothing, though the monarchs did relieve him of his numerous forts. Isabel would see to it that from then on the papacy paid her more heed.

That August, trouble came from another quarter. Isabel, governing Castile from Tordesillas, sped to Segovia to rescue her daughter. For Cabrera and Bobadilla, who were with the Queen, had left the Princess Isabel in Segovia's *alcázar*, in the keeping of its *alcaide*, who was Beatriz' father, and word had come that the man he had displaced in that post, seeking revenge, had entered and seized the fortress but that the Princess' guards were holding out in the keep. Isabel arrived at a gallop, with the Cabreras, the Cardinal, Benavente, and a troop of cavalry, to learn that, upon hearing the Queen was on her way, the assailants had retreated. Even so, she found the city in an uproar. Its bishop, Juan de Arías, exiled by Cabrera, had seized the opportunity to return and to exploit widespread grievances against the high-handed administration of the Cabreras and their clique, and the Bishop's partisans, among them eminent *segovianos*, were holding a number of the city's gates. Arías' adherents now appealed to the Queen, condemning the Cabreras and requesting she not enter with them nor by the gates they held. Pulgar has her respond: "Say to those knights and citizens of Segovia that I am the Queen of Castile and this city is mine, left me by the King my father . . . I shall enter by the gate I wish . . . Say too that all may come to me and may do as I command them as loyal subjects, and that they must stop making uprisings and scandals in my city, for from them can come harm to persons and property."[11]

Isabel proceeded without incident into the *alcázar* but a mob soon gathered outside, demanding entry. Against everyone's advice, she had the gates thrown open, had heralds proclaim that the Queen wished as many people to enter as the courtyard would hold, and then told the throng that surged in: "Now you, my vassals and subjects, are to say what you want, because what comes from you that is good and to my service it will please me to do for the common good of all the city."

They made clear that they wanted Cabrera removed. She assured them that she would consider their petition and the shout went up, "*¡Viva la reina!*" She stayed six weeks in Segovia, put Gonzalo de Chacón in charge of the *alcázar*, listened to arguments on all sides, and, ultimately faced with either reinstating loyal despots or finding untried replacements for them, she returned Segovia to the Cabreras. All in all, it was a response to crisis and a style of adjudicating popular disputes that would persist. The attempt confirmed the Queen's belief in the human urge for revenge. And it was arranged that thereafter the Princess Isabel would stay close to her mother.

From Segovia, Isabel rode to Toro. She had sent Benavente and the Admiral in July to direct the siege of its fortress and, having ordered Quintanilla to bring *hermandad* reinforcements, she arrived herself on September 28, with supplies. She observed everything keenly: at one point as Alfonso de Aragón deployed artillery and siege engines for an attack, to get a closer look she made her way through the tunnels up to the moat of the enemy stronghold. When on October 19, convinced that longer resistance was useless, María de Sarmiento, who commanded its garrison of 80, surrendered to her, Isabel assured her she might retain her titles and property; she was after all the sister of Diego Pérez Sarmiento, Count of Salinas and chief commander of the valuable Basque foot soldiers.

Of Toro's fall, an admiring chronicler commented, "Not only did the Queen take charge of governing and dispensing justice in the kingdom, but even in affairs of war no man could show such solicitude and diligence."[12] And he added that when women become active in matters of war, men are happier to serve them for the possibility of shame through failure prodded them into greater desire to exert themselves. Happiness, one gathers, was the result of that process. However that may be, Isabel continued to wage war, and to inspire her fighting men in her cause.

Toro had special significance for her. It was the site of the great humiliation of that war, now avenged; it was also her father's birthplace; and at its shrine of Santa María de la Vega her mother had, 26 years ago, arrived barefoot in fulfilling a vow made should she conceive a child. The child was Isabel. Ironically, victory at Toro would blot out that association, for from that war came the local memory that, when a Castilian sentry left his position near that shrine to woo a young lady of the town, the Portuguese would have taken advantage of his absence and Toro been lost but for Christ himself standing in for him; consequently that same shrine became known as dedicated to Christ of the Armies.[13] Most immediately, Isabel wrote Fernando happily announcing Toro's fall; and he was exultant in passing the news on to the councillors of Barcelona. In October he was back in Castile, all strain between them seemingly gone; he was not to leave again for several years.

Afonso of Portugal had decamped in June. In September he went to France, where for a year he vainly sought the aid of Louis XI. At its end, despondent, he withdrew to a French monastery and abdicated in favor of his son, João. Five days after João's formal accession, Afonso reappeared in Portugal. He had changed his mind.

UBI SUNT?

While Isabel and Fernando had waged war on the *meseta*, in Extremadura that intrepid old knight, Rodrigo Manrique, had cut deeply into the vast holdings of the Order of Calatrava, controlled by Rodrigo Girón. Manrique had seriously eroded the opposition's power in taking Almagro, a bulwark of Girón's, and Villena's Ocaña. For such services Isabel confirmed him as

Master of Santiago, and when, in November 1476, he died, his son Jorge reviewed his life and death in an elegaic poem, which, although concluding that fame lasts longer than life but that it too ultimately dies, gave his father a kind of immortality, achieving in his couplets what others wrote entire chronicles to accomplish. As Isabel secured the crown, Jorge Manrique advised: 'Forget the Trojans, forget the Romans, we have forgotten even yesterday': "What has become of the King Don Juan? / The *infantes* of Aragón, / where has become of them?" What became of them was that, in looking back on a fleeting past, Manrique's verses achieved fame sufficient to gain to this day an immortality for evanescence, and to place both kings Juan among the immortals. And he did much the same thing for the creed of the reconquest, in restating it for his generation, which was Isabel's: "Lasting life is not gained by worldly estates, nor with pleasant living in which lies the sins of hell. But the good monks gain it by prayers and tears, and the famous knights by labors and hardships going against the Moors."

Upon hearing of Rodrigo Manrique's death, Isabel rushed to the headquarters of the Order of Santiago in the convent-fortress of Uclés, riding the 200 miles from Valladolid in three days. Arriving in a December downpour just as a new master was about to be chosen, she managed to postpone that election until she had secured the lucrative administration of the mastership for the crown. From then on, the monarchs would oversee that military order, approving Alonso de Cárdenas, *comendador* of León and uncle to Gutierre de Cárdenas, as its new master, tapping its armed might and its vast wealth, garnered from 83 commanderies, two cities, 178 boroughs and villages, 200 parishes, five hospitals, five convents, and a school in Salamanca.

Fittingly, that January in nearby Ocaña, which held memories for her and which she had just taken over from young Pacheco, Isabel received the great crown she had, immediately upon her accession, ordered from Valencia. Made of 48 pearls, eight rubies, seven diamonds, and gold from her treasury in Sicily, it was "worked in branches and leaves honeycombed in bright enamel, its eight sections each joined by a small eagle."[14] With only a relatively few pockets of resistance remaining, she could wear it securely, recognized as Queen throughout the realm.

BUILDING

At the end of January 1477 Isabel and Fernando entered Toledo in triumph, displaying royal pomp and conquered battle standards, riding through the Bisagra gate hand in hand. Toledo's archbishop was not to be seen. The city turned out to greet them, as Isabel had ordered, its notables for the first time donning bright clothing after a generation of strife, gloom, and mourning.

Isabel attended a victory mass in the cathedral, wearing the crown of eagles, and she and Fernando "gave alms and did other pious works which they had promised for the victory that it had pleased God to give them. And especially they founded a monastery of the Order of San Francisco . . . which became that magnificent edifice . . . which today is called San Juan de los Reyes."[15] Meant as royal pantheon, soaring in aspect, the richly emblazoned interior walls of its church would proclaim the legitimacy, the valor, the aspirations of the Queen and the King, and their inseparability.

Today, as completed (and restored), everywhere are Fs and Ys, everywhere the bundles of arrows, the yokes, and the motto that was to exemplify their inseparability, *tanto monta*, "as much one as the other." And everywhere too, indeed predominating, is the eagle of San Juan, sheltering under its outspread wings both their coats of arms, becoming the national standard of Spain. The image of that eagle carries the bundle of meaning Talavera had conveyed to her, and her subsequent activities evidenced her having taken his injunctions to soar to heart, reinforcing proclivities of her own. The very commissioning of San Juan de los Reyes attests to such activity.

She involved herself directly in the raising of that church. Initially, she proposed to call it San Juan de la Reina—Saint John of the Queen. As its master-builder she chose Juan Guas, who had worked on the cathedral of her Avila. In late Gothic borrowed from northern Europe, a style known today as Hispano-Flemish, or Isabelline, he achieved a structure visually imparting triumph and expansive thrust, upward and outward, in God's service and to His glory and the Queen's as well.

From 1477 too, she dispensed monies to construct the Cartuja de Miraflores in the same style. At Miraflores, the entire building serves as a long approach to her parents' tombs, built a decade later. Everywhere in that church the royal coat of arms bearing the lions of León and the castles of Castile, now hers, crowns the ceiling vaults. Both that charterhouse and San Juan de los Reyes—its change in name attesting to the royal couple's deepening identification with one another—were material evocations not only of Talavera's injunction to her, but of a desire to place herself firmly within an unbroken line of Castile's monarchs, to quiet the uneasy memory, held by the public and herself, of Enrique IV and the woman who claimed to be his daughter. They were born of a need to efface the recent years of civil war and the divisions within the realm, to heal the rift with the nobles, especially with the Pachecos who honeycombed the ranks of the aristocracy. They were a bolstering in stone of her moral position and testaments to her determination, that of a female ruler bent upon asserting her preeminence over all rivals, her barons, Fernando's faction, and the strong presence of Juan of Aragón.

Her intent too was manifest in the dedication of the Toledo church to *San Juan el Evangelista*, her patron saint and her father's, the author of the Book of Revelation. The Word of Saint John, symbolized by the eagle, was generally understood as the weapon by which the sin of the world, often symbolized by the snake or serpent, was conquered; and the eagle in besting the serpent signified setting to rights mischief done by Eve. So the glorification of San Juan and his eagle, there and elsewhere as well, bore the additional message that Isabel would wreak vengeance on the serpent, and it also carried the suggestion that Isabel represented she whose role it was to offset Eve's bringing of original sin upon the world, Holy Mary. San Juan de la Reina announced its sponsor's commitment to the battle against evil in this world, as prophesied prelude to the final age and Last Judgment. The Queen would dedicate herself to those ideals enjoined upon her father, to the enterprise associated with Castile's greatest monarchs.

And it was during that stay in Toledo that opportunity offered itself: for word then arrived that the King of Granada would no longer honor the treaties made with Castile's sovereigns. Yet for the time being, it had to be put off, for the land was not yet hers.

8

To the Sea
1477–1478

Andalusia, above all, was a species of new world for the Castilians of the
fifteenth century and continued being fundamentally a new and promising land during the following, the richest and most open zone of the Castilian crown.

Miguel Angel Ladero Quesada[1]

. . . I have come to this land and I certainly do not intend to leave it to flee
danger nor shirk work, nor will I give such glory to my enemies nor such
pain to my subjects.

Isabel

THE QUEEN GOES SOUTH

IN March 1477, with the *meseta* largely assured and Fernando coping
with remaining pockets of resistance, Isabel went southwest and then
south, to Extremadura and Andalusia. There great lords and the military
orders had long held sway with little royal control, although the endless
contests among them had allowed the crown to exert leverage. Civil war,
however, had decreased that royal effectiveness at mediating and permitted
escalation of baronial autonomy and baronial conflict, if in the name of one
royal aspirant or another.

In Extremadura, dangerously situated along the Portuguese frontier,
opposition still simmered. There the Marqués of Villena had vast holdings
and his redoubtable half-sister, Beatriz Pacheco, held Medellín as its countess. In Andalusia, other sisters were wives of some of the foremost *grandes,*
and Pedro Girón's twin sons, the Master of Calatrava and the Count of
Urueña, "had carved out a state" between Seville and Granada.

Isabel was determined to restore respect for authority in all places and at all levels. But first, enroute to Extremadura, she stopped, from late April until mid-May, at Guadalupe, at "the holy and very magnificent house of Our Lady of Guadalupe," as Talavera put it. Within the church of that beautifully situated monastery constructed in warm *ladrillo,* stands the small, age-blackened image of the Virgin of Guadalupe, among the most revered in Spain. Her chapel is a national shrine, her cult connects nationality and religion.

In 1477, Guadalupe had been for 130 years—since the days when Alfonso XI had fulfilled a battlefield vow to Holy Mary by endowing her shrine there—a devotional center, but also a bulwark guarding the Portuguese frontier and a royal resource. Kings were wont to consult its Hieronymite friars—many well-born, many *converso,* some both—noted for their piety and their learning.

Guadalupe had many attractions for a reigning monarch. It was not only a haven of peace and a center of the fine music Isabel cherished, but served as a depository for valuables and performed some functions of a bank; it housed a school, a library, and monks trained as lawyers. With perhaps 15,000 sheep and 2400 head of cattle, manufacturing cloth and leather, possessing mills and timber, and beehives, and feeding over 800 people a day, it was a model of administration and as such greatly admired by Isabel, who is said to have remarked that anyone wanting to fence in Castile should hand it over to the Hieronymites. Moreover, it was a leading medical center, with friars renowned for their knowledge of medicines, anatomy, and surgery, and Isabel, fervently desiring a son, then consulted doctors of Guadalupe. In years to come, she would return there periodically, for rest, reflection, and medical attention. To her Guadalupe was, in modern terms, a spa, a retreat, especially at Eastertime, and a clinic. She would refer to it as "my paradise."[2] In 1477, it was also an ideal place to stop and make plans, first among them to secure Extremadura's unruly towns.

Having persuaded the Marqués of Villena to put nearby Trujillo under royal jurisdiction over the objections of her advisors, she resolved to stay next in that recent scene of violent warfare. "Well," she is said to have told them, "I have come to this land and I certainly do not intend to leave it to flee danger nor shirk work, nor will I give such glory to my enemies nor such pain to my subjects."[3] And so in Trujillo the royal presence was made known and royal jurisdiction imposed. By the end of June she was in the fortress-town of Cáceres, where she dictated what were becoming usual measures for imposing effective royal control over both urban factions and local lords: she established a *hermandad,* ordered strongholds and towers of local robber-barons (usually defined by having been on the other side) demolished, and put an *alcaide* over the fort. In Cáceres some 300 *caballeros* organized in two *bandos* had feuded incessantly, so to restore internal peace she abolished the battleground that was the annual election to the city council, instead ordering lots to be drawn for lifetime tenancy of council positions and current vacancies to be filled by crown appointment. It was a reminder that elections do not of themselves necessarily mean freedom, and that for Castile's people in the 1470s it often seemed a relief "to escape into royal liberty," given the alternative.

While almost everywhere her attempts to make royal control effective in municipal affairs at first were strongly resisted, yet the universal need for peace and order, some individual hopes of bettering fortunes in a new state of affairs, and her personal ability to evoke respect and fear achieved an unparalleled imposition of royal power within cities and towns, which, in turn, generally dominated surrounding countrysides. By such measures and in particular by enrolling all Extremadura in the *Hermandad General*, she imposed recognition of royal sway and instilled new respect for the monarchy.

Boys would grow up in those same Extremaduran towns, to recreate overseas the ambience of their turbulent youth. The *conquistadores* of Peru, the Pizarros, came from Trujillo. That town was taken for Isabel by the powerful Alonso de Monroy, a leader in factional warfare, whose young cousin, Hernando Cortés, from Beatriz Pacheco's Medellín, would carry the family tradition across the Atlantic Ocean. Cortés' father, Martín Cortés, had allied with Girón against Isabel and wed Catalina Pizarro, the daughter of Beatriz Pacheco's *mayordomo*. In Mexico with Cortés, Bernal Díaz del Castillo would recall one of his fellows "always telling stories about Don Pedro Girón and the Count of Urueña." And, from wherever they came, most likely they had sailed from Seville.

SEVILLE

On July 24 Isabel made a solemn entry into Seville. With some 45,000 people, it was the most populous city of the realm, and one of the most tumultuous. When Fernando III conquered the Muslim kingdom of Seville, he had gained with that port-city a vast hinterland. Seville had continued to dominate those lands, rich in flocks and herds, wheat, olives, vines and fruits, and the timber vital to shipbuilding, a vast area extending along the Gulf of Cádiz to Huelva on the west and southward to Gibraltar. In 1477 Seville was Castile's greatest port and its southern terminus, linking the Mediterranean and the Atlantic, an emporium of both internal and foreign trade.

An administrative, mercantile, and financial center, Seville was cosmopolitan, home to a diverse populace which included enclaves of the Genoese, Florentines, Bretons, English, and Catalans who joined the crowds welcoming the Queen. The city had been an important source of royal income during the war, and its Italian residents, especially forthcoming in lending the crown money, had in turn been wooed with privileges; thus the Genoese were exempted from paying the *almojarifazgo,* the customs duties.

Present at Isabel's entry too, by express request of the city council, were representatives of the large *aljamas* of Muslims and Jews and some of the growing number of black Africans, who were mostly household slaves and artisans. Many of Seville's blacks spoke Portuguese and were known as *ladinos*, born in Portugal. Others came from Guinea: they were Wolof, from the banks of the Senegal river, near the factory of Arguim, or Mandinga, from Gambia, often by way of Palos and Moguer. All social classes but especially aristocrats and ecclesiastics owned slaves.

Above the disparate throng, the city's banner flew from Seville's ramparts, on it a likeness of Fernando III, who had entered the city with his armies as a conqueror. Even though Isabel had come purposely without her army, it was a precedent not lost on that descendant of his. And, army or no, she rode into Seville in state, grandly, having sent ahead her *aposentadores*, whose function it was to make proper arrangements for receiving and housing the monarchs. For she intended to stay awhile and to tame Seville's great lords, who since her accession had ruled the city as their own, and finally to counter the independent-minded traditions of a frontier region never fully incorporated into the crown of Castile.

Chief among Seville's magnates was her viceroy, Enrique de Guzmán, the Duke of Medina Sidonia. Married to María de Mendoza, a sister of the Cardinal, Medina Sidonia, viceroy or no, had dominated the city since ousting, after five bloody years of *bando* warfare, his arch-rival, young Rodrigo Ponce de León, the Marqués de Cádiz, married to a Pacheco, the frequently engaged Beatriz born in wedlock. Isabel was now resolved to bring that viceroy of hers who was also the strongest and wealthiest of Andalusia's great barons, into line, to reimpose effective royal authority over that proud and cantankerous city, and to set an example for her other noble subjects, particularly those of the region.

No one in all Castile had ridden higher during the years of civil strife than the Guzmán and Ponce de León of Seville and their neighbors, most prominent among whom were the Aguilar and Fernández de Córdoba of Córdoba. Guarding the southern frontiers, at times raiding, at times cooperating with Muslims and Portuguese, exercising jurisdiction over rich lands and towns, collecting revenues, and engaging in a host of entrepreneurial activities, they had amassed tremendous fortunes and reached an apogee of near-independent power. Indeed, those border lords of the Muslim and Portuguese frontiers had profited immensely not only from urban revenues, the spoils of war, and royal *mercedes*, but also from the land, its rents and its products, the olives and cereals, wines, fruits and nuts, and salt, silk, hides, and wool, and, from the sea, accumulating capital as exporters of artisanry and commercial crops. They engaged in large-scale business and long-distance trade both directly and through agents, both throughout Castile and abroad. And they owned ships for military reasons, prestige, and profit, for lading, lease, and plunder. The high clergy and the heads of the military orders belonging to that Andalusian nobility demonstrated similar enterprise.

A prime source of income for them was coastal fishing, and deep sea fishing was also important, the catches sold locally or shipped great distances salted or preserved in oil; thus the longstanding rivalry between the Guzmán and the Ponce de León over Gibraltar was linked to prospects of huge fishing revenues. Isabel herself had, on the eve of the battle of Toro, thought it sufficiently worthwhile to write Seville's council of her concern about how to restore the royal tithe on salted fish, diminished during the war. And fishing, while profitable of itself, provided a cover for a complex of unsanctioned economic activities, such as the Guzmán getting around usury laws by selling future catches to Genoese merchant-bankers, and, above all, it gave excuse for raiding, trading, and exploration along African coasts and in the Atlantic. The best fish were taken from the offshore Moroccan banks and off the Saharan coast and the Canaries. Rights to fishing went along with asserting Castilian territorial claims, and undoubtedly with expectations of trade and penetrating Africa, as they had in the grant Isabel's father, Juan II, had made in 1449 to an earlier Guzmán of a monopoly to fish and to explore the African coast to Cape Bojador, itself a response to the Portuguese having founded a factory at Arguim the year before.

Other sorts of royal *mercedes* had further empowered and enriched Medina Sidonia and the others. For some time the Guzmán had enjoyed a delegated fifth of such royal revenues as the *almojarifazgo* and the *alcabala*, or sales tax, in places they controlled, among them Seville, and they had enjoyed lucrative influence in Palos, Moguer, and other subsidiary ports. Even so, they faced competition from the other great families who had interests and authority in Seville: notably the Stúñiga, who played balance of power politics, and the Enríquez, who enjoyed perquisites as hereditary admirals of Castile.

Castile's monarchs had long understood that their own fortunes were bound to those of this southern nobility, in turn tied to business and finance and the sea. The enduring problem was one of control. So it was that, within days of taking the crown, Isabel had expressed a concern to Seville's council, which was dominated by Medina Sidonia, over the sparse returns, ever since the re-establishing of royal revenue-collecting in 1475, to her treasury from the *alcabala*, the greatest single source of royal income. Yet the problem was dual: not only a siphoning off of taxes but revenue lost through smuggling.

Over time, some of the same Andalusians who fought the Portuguese and the Muslims also traded with them, forming close connections to Granada and Africa, mainly clandestine and so avoiding imposts. Leading culprits were seamen of Andalusian towns, employed by nobles or on their own, who had fished, raided, and traded along Granadan and African coasts for generations, whatever the political climate or whoever controlled the territory. Although Enrique IV had ordered Portuguese rights be honored, from the 1450s, as Portuguese exploration and commerce broadened, Castilians too had sailed the Atlantic and made the long and difficult voyages required to raid along Africa's Atlantic coast—taking two or three months outbound, seven or eight on return—although they much preferred to seize Portuguese cargoes at sea. So in 1452 seven men and seven women were taken by a fishing caravel from a Portuguese ship off the African coast and sold in Rota, with the consent of Ponce de León; and the following year Dom Henrique of Portugal—Henry the Navigator—requested of Medina Sidonia that his vassals of Palos and Moguer return 66 enslaved blacks they had taken from a Portuguese ship. In particular Sanlúcar, Palos, Niebla, and the town of Medina Sidonia became trading stations, principally in Africans coming from Guinea—today's Senegambia in the main—and by way of the Canaries.

Yet commerce in gold was more profitable, less difficult than that in spices or slaves, and largely *sub rosa*; gold was especially scarce and so especially valuable in the 1460s and 1470s. Even so, Seville's mint produced most of Castile's gold coins and yielded much revenue both for the crown and for those enjoying its *mercedes*, in mint fees, customs duties, and business in coins as a commodity. Nobles, too, minted, albeit illegally, although Enrique had on occasion sold or granted them licenses. Temptation was great in all quarters to debase coins, and counterfeiting was profitable. Profit could be made on metal imported and on coins exported, through differential in currency prices. Thus in June 1477, to repay war debts, Fernando sought, though unsuccessfully, to have foreign coins minted at night in Valencia to profit both from the minting itself and from the differential between market value elsewhere and metal prices in Spain.

Europeans, despite centuries of effort, had not penetrated Africa to the source of its gold, which was in the West African Sudan and in the lands of the Ashanti. Lying beyond the Sahara, the Bambuhu, Buri, and Lobi goldfields had enriched the Sudanic empires: ancient Ghana, Songhai, and Kamen-Bornu; and in the early fourteenth century the first African Muslim emperor, Mansa Musa of Mali, was known to have taken 40 large camelloads of gold with him on a combined trading venture and pilgrimage to Mecca, so much gold that it devalued the currency in Cairo on the way. Abraham Cresques' Catalan atlas of 1375 acknowledged the renown of his wealth in portraying him seated on a throne holding a sceptre in his left hand and contemplating a large gold nugget in his right, his figure dominating all North Africa "within the arc of Niger and Guinea."

Spaniards, Genoese, and Portuguese had long competed both in the search for those goldfields and for control of terminals of exchange on or near the coast of the Maghrib (Northern Africa), and recently the Portuguese had coaxed gold caravans to West African coasts as well. Spain's Andalusian ports had especially profited from proximity to North Africa and imports of gold, and they and all Spain benefited from the exchange of relatively cheap gold for silver coming in from northern Europe. In that commerce, Genoese and other Italians often acted as middlemen, as carriers and merchants in ports throughout the Mediterranean, moving westward with the Ottoman advance and as Europeans pushed outwards in that direction. For Isabel, control of the gold supply, from the mines onwards, was connected to control of Andalusia and its ports, and to expansion and its financing.

WAR AT SEA

From the outset of the war with Portugal, she had paid particular attention to promoting Castile's maritime presence in the south. In May 1475 an armed fleet was ordered to patrol sealanes. By September, on royal orders four Aragonese galleys had arrived at the Guadalquivir river, downriver from Seville, to discourage the Portuguese. And, having appropriated Afonso's titles to Africa, Isabel encouraged Atlantic expeditions from Andalusia but only under strict royal supervision; that May she had sent to Seville a *letrado* of the Royal Council expressly to assert royal authority in maritime matters. He was, among other duties, to issue letters of marque, permits to privateers, against Portugal, and to license voyages to Guinea and collect the royal fifth on their return cargoes. It was more than coincidental that at the same time she moved to stabilize and regulate coinage and collection of taxes. In December she ordered each caravel that sailed to have on board a royal official to look to the royal fifth.

Her rationale went beyond the exigencies of the current war. In a decree of that August, she stated that "the kings of glorious memory, my progenitors, from whom I come, always had [the right to] the conquest of the parts of Africa and of Guinea, and they received a fifth of the merchandise that was recovered [from those places], until our adversary of Portugal, interfered by consent of the king, Don Enrique, my brother."[4] She was, in keeping with her claim to legitimacy as her father's heir, asserting her lineal right to territories once under Spain's Visigoths. "Merchandise" included captured Africans. She also awarded, as a *merced*, the lucrative concession to license such voyages to the faithful Gonzalo Chacón, and subsequently she granted rights to specific sailings to Benavente, Beatriz de Bobadilla, and to a retainer of Cabrera's, all of whom in turn sold them to merchant-adventurers.

Yet those Andalusian magnates, Medina Sidonia and Cádiz, were not to relinquish their freedom at sea readily. Indeed, Rodrigo Ponce de León, the Marqués de Cádiz, while maintaining contact with Isabel and Fernando was also in touch with his brother-in law Pacheco and with Afonso of Portugal. As Palencia put it, he and his *gaditanos* wanted to share in the wealth so long denied them. So did other Andalusians, especially since the Portuguese had recently established a West African factory so promising it was known as *Eimina* or *Mina de Oro*, the gold mine. In 1476 several expeditions from Palos and Puerto de Santa María had gone slaving to Guinea without royal license; one, backed by the *alcaide* of the fort of Palos, Gonzalo de Stúñiga, employed a ruse that would work again later, in America.

Palencia tells the story. The king of the region, who was most likely

Wolof, was accustomed to exchanging his prisoners of war with the Portuguese and such he assumed those ships to be, especially since on boarding one he was greeted in Portuguese. And so he traded with them: Africans for brass rings, small daggers, and colored cloth. Then, invited to dine aboard, having sent ahead sheep and a calf, he arrived, as arranged, with his brothers, his friends, and his chief people. All of them soon found themselves prisoners. Whose ships were these, he wanted to know. Who had so cruelly deceived him? Told they belonged to Spaniards, he asked if they obeyed any king and when answered yes, a most noble one, he expressed confidence that his fellow-monarch would soon free him. When, ashore in Palos, he refused to walk, instead demanding a horse or mule in accord with his dignity, Gonzalo de Stúñiga, struck by his regal bearing, or thinking of future expeditions, ordered a mount for him; and so he rode to Seville, majestically, at the head of the column of Africans destined for sale. Isabel, informed of so overt an act of smuggling, ordered Stúñiga to turn over king and people to her commissioner there in order to be returned home. Initially delaying, he complied only in sending back the king. Yet once home that monarch managed to capture some old enemies and to exchange them for his relatives enslaved in Andalusia.

By spring of 1476 Isabel's policy and Andalusian enterprise together had had effect, for among the reasons Afonso then gave his nobles for his returning to Portugal was that he had to arrange for a fleet to safeguard sailings to the source of so much of his wealth, Guinea. Yet now France was also a factor in war at sea, so that Isabel that spring ordered both more ships armed in Guipuzcoa and Vizcaya and a fleet readied in Andalusia for Guinea, its goal to raid Portuguese settlements in the Cape Verde islands, and especially the island of Antonio (now Santiago), named for its Genoese lord, Antonio de Noli. Noli had resided for a time in Seville, gone to Lisbon, contracted with Dom Henrique to join expeditions to Guinea, and once there convinced the Portuguese to populate that island. The settlement had prospered and Noli built a large house and engaged in the slave trade—that in gold was reserved to Fernão Gómez, the private concessionaire whose large annual payments to Afonso had helped finance his venture into Castile.

Testifying to the royal goals of countering both Portuguese and Andalusian freebooting, Isabel and Fernando had sent a watchdog of tried loyalty, Diego de Valera, to oversee the strategically vital royal enclave and customs station on the riverine coast up from Cádiz, at Puerto de Santa María, and had appointed his son, Charles, *alcaide* of its fort. And to Charles de Valera they now gave command of an expedition to Guinea. Speed was important, for it was known that Fernão Gómez had dispatched 20 ships from Portugal to load African gold.

It was decided, says Palencia, that the royal fleet should consist of 30 light ships, for the great ones were unsuitable for the navigation of those seas, while—and here he attests to the flow of traffic—caravels crossed rapidly from the Cádiz coast. In addition to Basques and to other Andalusians,

Valera recruited from neighboring Palos seamen as well as ships, for, as Palencia explained, "only those of Palos knew from old the Guinea sea, since accustomed from the beginning of the war to combat the Portuguese and take from them the slaves they had acquired."[5] Yet assembling and outfitting the fleet lagged, its overseers, one of whom was Palencia, hampered by inexperience, lack of funds from the crown, and the machinations of Andalusian magnates, particularly those of Medina Sidonia and Cádiz. Medina Sidonia had *sevillanos* withhold all necessaries until the King and Queen promised him jurisdiction over the island of Antonio when taken; and the Marqués of Cádiz sent two *gaditano* captains to Fernão Gómez to warn him the Castilian fleet was readying, and to request for having done so a share of his profits. In Palos, Gonzalo de Stúñiga had seized sole control and was doing his best to stop its caravels from joining the fleet.

Nevertheless, in late May or early June Valera sailed, with 30 caravels and three Basque ships, for the Cape Verdes, to carry the war to Portugal's lucrative Atlantic fringe and gain for Castile a base for expansion to the nearby African mainland. He raided 13 places in those islands, brought back Antonio de Noli, and, having missed the Portuguese treasure fleet, on the way home sailed for the source of its cargo, the African coast, where he seized two ships belonging to the Marqués of Cádiz loaded with 500 Africans. Yet, thereupon, the men of Palos sailed off, with Cádiz' ships and cargoes, and Medina Sidonia, on hearing, insisted the island of Antonio and the spoils taken from it were his; and both he and Cádiz, who was intent on reclaiming his cargoes, harried Valera's Puerto de Santa María until they got the greater part of the booty and the slaves. Medina Sidonia did free, on royal orders, the Genoese, Noli, who came to Medina del Campo to thank the monarchs personally, undoubtedly summoned because they wished to hear of West Africa and its potential. In years to come, Isabel and Fernando having fined for such dereliction the *paleños*, another Genoese familiar with Guinea and the Western Ocean, Cristóbal Colón, or Christopher Columbus, would reap the benefit.

Oddly enough, then surfacing was another Colón, one Louis—also referred to as Luis Coulon or Guillermo de Casanove—the erstwhile privateer whom Louis XI had commissioned to assemble and command the French fleet. In 1476, on Louis' orders, Colón escorted Afonso and his fleet from Portugal to France, sailing through the Strait of Gibraltar and up the Mediterrean coast. That fleet stopped to reinforce and provision the Portuguese garrisons at Ceuta, Tangier, Alcázarquivir, and Arzila, Afonso fearing the Moors but even more the Andalusians, and with good reason, for those reinforcements were just in time to repulse an attack on Ceuta ordered by Medina Sidonia. The Duke, meanwhile, was attending to other business, on strategic Gibraltar. Having received royal funds for its garrisoning, he had instead manned it with *conversos* escaping persecution in Córdoba, indeed charged them for refuge there; but now, having exhausted all their resources in paying for overpriced provisions, new construction, and his maritime expeditions, he forced them out and took charge of Gibraltar personally, hoping possession would buoy his chances of selling it to the crown.

As for Colón's fleet, upon leaving Ceuta in August it attacked five ships just out of Cádiz, three of them Genoese galleys, with great losses—Valera reported 5000 dead, mostly Portuguese, and that six great ships were lost: four by Colón and the Portuguese, a Genoese galley and a Flemish *urca*. Consequently swimming to shore from a vessel involved, whether Genoese, French, or one of the others is unknown, and into history was Christopher Columbus, and at the moment his destination was Portugal.

THE CANARY ISLANDS

Key to the Spanish presence in West Africa were the Canary Islands. A juridical inquiry Isabel had ordered in November 1476 affirmed Castilian sovereignty over them, on the basis given legal standing in her father's reign, that those islands were hers by lineal descent, having belonged to the last Visigothic king, Rodrigo. Nor is it surprising that signing that opinion were Hernando de Talavera and the royal jurist, Rodrigo Maldonado de Talavera. Isabel confirmed, as lords of the four Canary Islands they had conquered, Inés Péreza, whose father had bought the rights to them all from Medina Sidonia, and her husband, Diego Herrera, a councilman of Seville. By that act Isabel asserted her own sovereignty, and she then bought from them the rights to the Canaries not yet colonized, Tenerife, La Palma, and Gran Canaria, viewing those islands as bases against the Portuguese and for West Africa, way stations "to the mines of gold of Ethiopia,"[6] the name Ethiopia then redolent of King Solomon's mines, the kingdom of Prester John, and the hope of outflanking the Muslims. From the Péreza-Herrera, she also got devolution of rights to the Torre de Santa Cruz de la Mar Pequena, a fortified coastal station or factory commanding the valleys of the Draa and Nun rivers, frequented by caravans from the interior. And she licensed more ships for Guinea, to be organized in annual convoys. All those measures were steps toward the traditional royal goal of extending reconquest into Africa, now intensified by competition with Portugal.

Isabel was to continue to support with people and provisions the conquest of the Canaries. Expeditions sailed in the summers of 1478 and 1479; merchants were lured into joining them by permits to ship stipulated amounts of that prohibited export, wheat. While she herself was in Seville in 1478, a fleet of 35 caravels sailed, most of the crews from Palos, its stated goal to collect *orchilla*, a precious dye, and the conch shells so valued in La Mina, its fate to be captured by the Portuguese on the return voyage. And during that stay in Seville, Isabel forbade sale of any other merchandise before that belonging to the crown. When Inés Péraza attempted to sell some natives of Gomera, Isabel opposed it; she had merchants of Palos and Moguer who trafficked in them sued and the islanders freed. The point made was that they were the Queen's vassals, the royal prosecutor commenting that, though baptized Christians, they had been treated as though they were Moors. Nonetheless, conquest of Gran Canaria and dominion over its inhabitants was the purpose of the expedition of 1478 and it was achieved, ruthlessly, by 1483.

From the outset of Castilian ventures overseas and at sea, Isabel insisted upon royal control. Within that policy, she wanted not only her sovereignty acknowledged but either a monopoly on trade goods or a percentage of all profits. Native peoples were to be either royal subjects or royal merchandise. And when in 1478 the pope, Sixtus IV, dedicated monies received from sale of indulgences to converting the Canary Islanders, Isabel and Fernando interpreted his bulls as supplying funds not only for conversion but also for conquest by Castile. For to the Queen, bringing souls to God and vassals to the crown was of a piece. And in practical terms, the religious state of the conquered was crucial to wielding sovereignty effectively.

THE DUKE AND THE MARQUES

Before coming to Seville, Isabel had had words of her own for the Andalusian lords, and there too the underlying issue was effective dominion. She was unhappy not only at their having delayed Valera's expedition and then appropriating its profits, but also at their unwillingness to help her during the war. Seville under Medina Sidonia had made excuses in response to her urgent letters requesting light cavalry to guard conquered castles and towns, and in Jérez she understood that the Marqués of Cádiz had, most recently, assessed levies of wine and bread for the royal armada and then used them for his own ships. Yet whatever the degree of royal exasperation, she knew too that much royal power resided in arousing competitive spirit among *grandes* for honors and preeminence and accordingly an envoy had gone with stiff letters, first to Medina Sidonia, ordering he move against the Portuguese on the frontier and telling him "that both the King and Queen marvel that Portuguese soldiers have marched from the confines of Sevillian territory to the far provinces of New Castile."[7] When he refused to comply, the envoy informed him he was instructed in that event to carry letters to the Marqués of Cádiz requesting he take command of gathering Andalusian forces against the enemy. Medina Sidonia having remained adamant, and Cádiz having accepted graciously, Medina Sidonia retaliated by revoking an agreement guaranteeing Cádiz' lucrative right to fish freely for tunny off the coast. And, confirming his reputation for arrogance, he requested that the monarchs uphold that revocation, while Cádiz sought their permission to challenge his longstanding and less militant rival to single combat for having broken his oath.

Isabel did not want her *grandes* bashing one another in Andalusia. The war was not over and the frontier with Granada required vigilance. Rather, she wanted her own authority accepted indisputably by those border lords. She also wanted to regain the royal rents Medina Sidonia in particular had long usurped, to recover the ability to tax effectively and to restore royal authority in Andalusia, and especially in Seville. Toward achieving those objectives, Palencia had been instructed to sound out people in Seville on forming a *hermandad*, which could both rival and confront Medina Sidonia's own forces and loosen his hold on the city. At one stroke, Seville would have a police force dependent ultimately on the crown, not the Duke, along with a reserve of manpower, and its populace would know that he had bowed to superior royal authority. Medina Sidonia, upon hearing that a friar had come to town who was exhorting *sevillanos* to institute their own armed peacekeeping constabulary and already smarting at being passed over as Master of Santiago, angrily convened the city's authorities, threatened to hang or behead all royal officials, depending on rank, and he terrified the many *converso* notables by telling them that a publicly sponsored *hermandad* might well result in their extermination. Yet, unable to overcome the increasing appeal the *hermandad* had for the populace, he soon did an about-face and began to praise it publicly and highly. Córdoba's principal lord, Alonso de Aguilar, confronted with the same situation, behaved similarly. So matters stood when Isabel arrived in Seville.

She was received with due ceremony by Medina Sidonia, exhibiting no trace of his recent ill temper and making his own show in being accompanied by the city's knights, all its municipal and royal officials, and all the clergy. Then she rode, beneath a canopy of scarlet brocade embroidered with her arrows, its gleaming gilded supports borne by eight councilmen, through streets lined with spectators, past balconies hung with householders' most precious tapestries, to Santa María la Mayor, the cathedral, to hear mass, and afterwards to the royal palace in the *alcázar*; she would henceforth live for relatively long stretches in that grand warren. For days she was feted with ceremonies, jousts, bullfights, and dances. She admired the city, confessing she had never imagined such grandeur.

Accounts differ on her relations with Medina Sidonia from then on but, although he along with other magnates was said to think it a mistake that the Queen had come to Andalusia without her husband, that a woman alone could not do what was necessary there, especially given the threat of Muslims and Portuguese and even though she was a queen of great spirit and valor, he was soon to look forward to the King arriving to soften her impact. Isabel's first move was, whether with or without the Duke's free bestowal, to have the *alcázar* and the shipyards taken over from him by her administrators.

While asserting her prerogative or negotiating with the powerful for regaining control of royal perquisites alienated by Enrique or simply appropriated in the laxity and disorder of his reign, Isabel was also determined that the entire city should respect and fear the royal presence as never before. This she set about to do chiefly by being seen to dispense personally the justice whose symbol she had had carried at her accession. Having informed Medina Sidonia that the principal reason she had come to Seville was to rid the land of tyrants and criminals, that through her understanding and with the help of God she would work until it was made secure, every Friday she held an *audiencia*, a court of law, in the great hall of the *alcázar*. There she presided from a seat covered in gold cloth, upon a raised dais, central and high, flanked on one side by her prelates and *caballeros*, who sat a bit lower, and on the other by the learned doctors of her council and the royal secretaries. Judiciary officials, the *alcaldes* and *alguaciles*, were seated in front of those dignitaries; a corps of crossbowmen stood guard. Isabel heard individual petitions and assigned them to the proper legal experts, instructing they reach decision within a few days' time. If they bogged down in technicalities, she often took it upon herself to render a swift verdict; and on other days she continued to adjudicate in her apartments. Within two months numerous civil and criminal cases long pending had been settled and those adjudged guilty sentenced, usually harshly.

Her audiences were in the tradition of the first Castilian monarch to govern Seville, Alfonso X, and her sense of justice owed much to his *Partidas*. Through rendering justice, writes Pulgar, the Queen became loved by the good and feared by the bad, a great number of whom left the city for Portugal or Muslim lands. He indicates that overall those Friday sessions had the desired political effect, creating awe of royal majesty, even going so far as to bring eminent Sevillians to fear that if justice continued to be dispensed with such rigor no one would be left untouched, for "considering the great dissoluteness of the recent past, there were few in the city without guilt."[8]

The Bishop of Cádiz, Pedro Fernández de Solís, who managed the see of Seville for its archbishop, Cardinal Mendoza, on behalf of the citizens one Friday pleaded with her to proclaim a general pardon. Before a throng of *sevillanos*, among them women whose husbands, sons, and brothers had fled, Solís, tears streaming, argued that, while all mortals are worthy of punishment, if everyone who deserved it received it, "the world would perish in an instant." Justice, he told her, always includes clemency. Isabel, moved, agreed to forgive all civil crimes with the exception of personal injuries, thereby again demonstrating the high value she placed on honor avenged; however, when Solís questioned that exclusion (noting that many such litigants were also frequently defendants in other cases), she withdrew it and issued a general pardon for all crimes except that of heresy, which was both a civil and religious offense. Whether or not that scene had been staged, more than 4000 of those who fled her wrath, says Pulgar, returned, and people tended to resolve their differences privately, through fear or shame of appearing before the Queen. Whatever the other effects of her public hearings, Seville had gained respect for the authority of the crown.

Her show of strength had reverberations beyond the city. Late one night, after she had retired to her chambers, Rodrigo Ponce de León, the Marqués of Cádiz, slipped undetected into the city he had lost to his arch-adversary and appeared at a side gate of the *alcázar*. Agreeing to receive him, she saw before her a redheaded giant of a man, in his thirties, known to be hotheaded, ambitious, and shrewd, and also more intelligent and certainly

more decisive than Medina Sidonia. He offered her his service, pled innocent to ever having been allied with Portugal, or anyway formally, and
offered her his fortresses of Jérez and Alcalá de Guadaira. Isabel was *"muy
contenta"* with his proposal and his gallantry. While it was true, she
informed him, that she had had no good report of him—she had been talking to Medina Sidonia—his trust in coming and putting himself in her
hands obliged her to treat him benignly, and she assured him that once he
had actually turned over to her "those my forts of Jérez and Alcalá, which
you hold," she would adjudicate in his quarrel with the Duke, guarding his
honor.[9] He assigned those strongholds to her; and other holders of Andalusia's forts, who had originally seized them, as had Cádiz and Medina
Sidonia, during Enrique's reign, then emulated those two great lords in
relinquishing authority and, in the few instances where they did not, Isabel
had those places besieged and their garrisons brought to Seville and hung
as rebels. She had indeed reconquered the old kingdom of Seville.

9

Signs and Revelations
1478

Clearly, we see ourselves given a very special gift by God, for at the end of such a long wait He has desired to give him to us. The Queen has paid to this kingdom the debt of virile succession that she was obligated to give it. . . .

It seems clear that this Queen was moved to do things by some divine inspiration.

Fernando del Pulgar

A PRINCE IS BORN

THE King arrived in Seville in September of 1477, to great festivity, and to the *sevillanos'* vain hope, quickly dashed, that he would soften his wife's draconian measures. He remained until early October, or as Pulgar puts it: "he stayed some days in which the Queen became pregnant," a pregnancy, the chronicler adds, much desired by all the kingdom. It was known that Isabel, worried, for her only child was seven years old, had consulted physicians. Whatever their advice to her had been, a child was expected in late spring. That fall she and Fernando made celebratory visits to Medina Sidonia in his town of Sanlúcar de Barrameda, and its Marqués in Cádiz, and then wintered in Seville.

They held court grandly in the palace within the *alcázar*; and they lived there as well, amid the accretion of the Islamic centuries and the assertively Christian additions of Alfonso X, whose stout Gothic both proclaimed dominance and a defensive stance against the ongoing Muslim threat from Africa. Isabel's private quarters were in yet another addition at the core of that royal enclave, in the *mudéjar* palace built by Pedro I, its very presence a visual reminder that relations between Castile's rulers and Muslims in

Spain had long been far from simple. That palace recalled Pedro's friendship with Granada's Muhammad V, who had sent to Castile's king in Seville workmen from his own Alhambra. Its relative openness was a reminder too that, Pedro's father Alfonso XI having won the battle of Salado, the threat from Muslim Africa had diminished. Isabel would later make additions of her own, among them a very *mudéjar* chapel; by then too she would be the Queen of Granada.

In March, a letter from an agent of Juan of Aragón to Fernando conveyed a general atmosphere of expectation and the widespread hope that the royal child would be a boy: "It is good, Your Excellency, for here is the most grave and grand matter of Spain, and nothing is more necessary or desired."[1] The hope was fulfilled. On the morning of June 30, 1478, Isabel gave birth to a son and heir. Present as the child was born were a midwife and, by royal order, numerous courtiers and city officials; it was a state occasion and there was to be no question that the child was the Queen's. Court and city celebrated for three days and nights. That Isabel's second child was male crowned the successes of those years and was widely interpreted as a sign from God of his approval, and of yet greater victories to come.

Seville resounded with fiesta. On July 9, the baptismal procession made its way from the palace to the cathedral through thronged streets, the prince nestled in brocade cloth in the arms of his wellborn nurse, María de Guzmán, the mule she rode flanked by eight councilmen bearing staffs of office and wearing greatcloaks of black velvet "provided by the city." Alvaro de Stúñiga, the late great rebel, walked directly behind. Three of the Queen's pages strode along at the head of the procession. One held a gold jar, another gold cup; the third, carrying the customary candle, babycap, and money offering on a tray, was "so small that he bore the tray on his head, holding on to it with both hands." All the *grandes* at court accompanied child and nurse, on foot; so did many knights and other people. Silver crosses gleamed aloft, and trumpets, hornpipes, and sackbutts played ceaselessly.

The Prince was baptized Juan in the cathedral, "very triumphantly." That obervation was made by a new chronicler of a new sort, Andrés Bernaldez, a militant Andalusian chaplain much less concerned with political relations, much more uncritical of anyone both orthodox and powerful than his predecessors, and exuding a crusading patriotism.[2] Officiating was Seville's Archbishop, Pedro González de Mendoza, chief among courtiers. The godparents were the Constable, Benavente, Nicoló Franco, the papal legate, and Leonor de Mendoza, Duchess of Medina Sidonia.

A second procession, even grander, took place a month later, on August 9, when the Queen went "to present the Prince to the temple as was the custom of Holy Mother Church." She had waited until then as was also customary, for a woman was not to enter a church after childbirth until "being purified of her blood." Fernando headed that cavalcade on a small silver-grey horse. He was opulently regal in heavy brocade lined in gold and trimmed in gold and black velvet, wearing a broad hat also lined in cloth of gold. (It was sweltering midsummer in Andalusia; little wonder that Fernando reputedly said that all he wished to his enemies were winters in Burgos, summers in Seville.) At the center of that procession was Isabel, in brocade shimmering with pearls, mounted high upon a white trotter, its saddle of gold encrusted with more gold and with silver. Accompanying her on foot were most of the city's council and all the *grandes* then at court. On her right, the Constable held the bridle rein of her horse; Benavente held the rein on her left. The infant prince, again swathed in brocade, was carried in the arms of his nurse who rode a mule upon a saddle of velvet. Musicians kept pace, playing trumpets and hornpipes and many other instruments.

The symbolism was patent and glorious. In that solemn, glittering procession Castile's might showed itself subservient to the Queen, the King, and the royal infant, in that order, to, that is, the flourishing of dynasty. The royal couple demonstrated that it now held Castile through strength and respect, love and fear. In that city until recently so proudly autonomous, where the Queen in particular had effected a second Christian reconquest, those monarchs were showing themselves to be worthy successors of their common ancestor, that earlier conqueror, Fernando III.

No one spoke much afterwards of the total eclipse of the sun that occurred within the month, the reactions to that darkness at noon ranging from fear that the end of the world was at hand to a prescient foreboding concerning the royal infant. Rather, the mood continued joyous. From Barcelona's council came especially hearty felicitations, for an heir who, since male, could succeed to Aragón's throne and so become "the unifier of the kingdoms and lordships."[3] And Castilians concurred in rejoicing that Heaven, so long displeased, was at long last smiling upon them. The Desired One had arrived, as one chronicler put it, "the true promised spouse of these kingdoms, descended from its monarchs and of the noble line of the Goths," he who had come to redeem Spain from evil.[4]

HEAVEN'S SMILE

Some articulate and well-placed Castilians went still further, to see universal significance in the birth. Pulgar, in a letter to a friend whom he assumed to be of like mind, the jurist Rodrigo Maldonado de Talavera, invoked the prophecy customary to a royal birth, but he forsook earlier allusions to Merlin and Dante to rely upon the weightier authority of the Bible and to convey a more earnest piety. "We here have very great pleasure," he wrote, concerning the birth of the Prince and the good health of the Queen,

> Clearly we see ourselves given a very special gift by God, for at the end of such a long wait He has desired to give him to us. The Queen has paid to this kingdom the debt of male succession that she was obligated to give it. As for me, I have faith that he has to be the most welcome prince in the world, because all those

who are born desired are friends of God, as were Isaac, Samuel, and Saint John. . . . And not without cause, then, were they conceived and born by virtue of many prayers and sacrifices. Look at the Evangel that was preached on the day of St. John; [see] it as reproduced so that this appears nothing but a model of the birth of the other. The other Isabel is another Isabel. The other in these days is in these themselves, and also so that the populace and relatives may have joy, and that he will be a terror to those of the mountains. Because God rejected the temple of Enrique and did not choose the tribe of Alfonso: but chose the tribe of Isabel whom he preferred.[5]

The other birth was that of Jesus Christ, and Pulgar here inferred that the Messiah would come among Spaniards. The other Isabel refers to the mother of John the Baptist, Elizabeth, which is the Latin equivalent of Isabel. Further, Pulgar's reference was probably meant as a conflation of St. Elizabeth with Christ's mother, Mary, just as St. John the Evangelist—whom according to Luke [1:5–17] was born to be a terror to those on the mountains—on occasion was substituted for Christ. "Those of the mountains" then generally referred to the Muslims of Granada. Yet Ezekiel [7:17], prophesying an end come for Israel except for a remnant, reads "they that shall at all escape shall be on the mountains like doves of the valleys, all of them moaning, every one in his iniquity," and Isaiah frequently spoke of mountains in connection with the Jewish people, so that Pulgar could well have implied in mentioning "those of the mountains" not only travail for Muslims but both the coming of the last days and a time of terrible suffering for a chosen people who had come acropper of God. And, throughout, Pulgar had compound purpose in mentioning Saint John.

The Prince bore the name of both his royal grandfathers, Juan of Castile and Juan of Aragón, and had as patron San Juan. One chronicler, Gutierre de Palma, writing in 1479, compared the newly arrived prince, "the Desired One of the people" with San Juan, then went on to parallel the mystical union of Prince Juan and Spain with that of Christ and his church.[6] Well attested to by then was Isabel's predilection for Juan the Evangelist, and that she had indeed striven to emulate the qualities Talavera had ascribed to that saint's symbol, the eagle. St. John the Evangelist, Christ's cousin, was often visually depicted as his twin or surrogate; in a poem Gómez Manrique has him say: "I am Juan, that *privado* of my Lord and cousin."[7] He was even spoken of as "the firstborn of the adopted sons of Mary."[8] That Isabel connected St. John to her reign and dynasty and their divine charge in those years is apparent in those two great churches she then commissioned: San Juan de los Reyes in Toledo and the Charterhouse at Miraflores.

Yet, as Pulgar indicated, there was another allusion in the naming of the Prince. For Fernando's patron was Saint John the Baptist. Indeed, Pulgar does not say just which of the two was the Prince's patron saint, yet he was born closest to the day of San Juan Bautista, June 24. Closely identified with Christ, the Saints John, heralding the first and second coming of the

Messiah, were often coupled; a painting, donated by Isabel and Fernando to a church of San Juan in Granada, would depict a *Piedad*, or *Pieta*, with San Juan Bautista on one side and San Juan Evangelista on the other. Under the Baptist appeared the portrait of Fernando and under the Evangelist that of Isabel, who held a tablet inscribed "Make me passionately virtuous in your image and zealous for the faith."[9] The two saints together signified the dual aspect of a single crown worn by the two *reyes*, and its promise, come to fruition in a third Juan, whose birth augured fulfillment of the hopes both announced, promising a Spain united, and in holy mission.

In the intensity of response in 1478 to the confluence of peace regained, the promise of a just and strong reign, and an heir come to unite Spain, the King was lauded extravagantly. Fernando had become the warrior hero; he was another Charlemagne, as Valera hailed him, destined to be monarch of all Spain, "to reconstitute the imperial seat of the illustrious blood of the Goths, from whom you come."[10] Other commentators, among them a mentor of his, Joan Margarit, Bishop of Gerona, broadened that tribute in speaking of both monarchs as restoring that lost Spanish unity of the Goths.[11] Pulgar remarked to Isabel in sending her his completed chronicle that "to write of times of such injustice converted by the grace of God into so much justice, of so much disobedience into so much obedience, [and] so much corruption into so much order, I confess, My Lady, requires a better head than mine to produce a lasting memorial of them all for they are worthy of it."[12] And Valera, while earlier praising Fernando, went on to write of seeing in the advent of both monarchs the beginning of a golden age for all Spain; and he recognized where power resided when, in 1481 dedicating a concise history of Spain to Isabel, he addressed her as Very Powerful Princess, to whom "Our Lord has given, not without great deserving on your part, little less than the monarchy of all the Spains."[13]

He had written that summary on her command; it was centered on the accomplishments of those distinguished rulers, her forebears "in these Spains," so that through their example she might become better informed "of everything it was possible to do to govern and administer these so many and so diverse peoples that our Lord has placed under your royal sceptre."

Pulgar's chronicle was confined to the reign. Valera again placed Spain and its rulers within the universal and providential context favored by chroniclers in the reigns of Fernando III and Alfonso X. Valera began similarly, with the world as divided into Asia, Africa, and Europe, then moved to Spain and its earliest peoples, descended from Tubal, grandson of Noah. He told of Hercules and Hispan, the Romans, the coming of the Goths, Spain destroyed except for the Christian remnant under Pelayo, and so on down through its rulers, ending with Juan II and Enrique IV. Isabel received from him a version of her national and dynastic past presented as insight into God's design and stressing her responsibility for fulfilling it. In that sense it was a form of guide for a prince. Valera was 74 and still speaking his mind to his sovereign, if much more happily, for this ruler was listening attentively.

Isabel had once again sought and received a variety of inspirational tract. This one, though, went beyond injunction to place her within a line of illustrious monarchs. It provided her with a version of the universal past viewed as prelude to her own reign, a view of history offering insight into the divine plan to which Spain's monarchy, if the propitious signs were to be believed, was ever more central.

QUEEN OF HEAVEN, QUEEN OF EARTH

The anonymous author of an incomplete but incisive chronicle of those years praised the joint reign: "and so marvelous a happening was not the work of men but a grand divine mystery, that men might see the marvels of God and his power . . . God wished that, in return for their diligence and virtue the works of [the King and Queen] might appear marvels to men, and extremely different from those of the King, don Enrique."[14] No longer, said he, are we bound in servitude, but now children "of the free Jerusalem that is above," liberated by the King and Queen. Fernando had come to Castile to free its peoples, yet it was Isabel who was heaven's particular instrument. Reflecting on the surrender of Toro to her, he concluded, "how great in excellences was the Queen, the most accomplished person in the world; it was the belief of many that she was born *maravillosamente* for the redemption of kingdoms so lost."[15] All was God's marvel—prudently, he eschewed miracle—accomplished through the Queen.

Diego de Valera made explicit what was there implied, if as simile: "It can in truth be said," he wrote to Isabel "that just as our Lord wished that our glorious Lady might be born in this world because from her would proceed the Universal Redeemer of the human lineage, so he determined that you, My Lady, would be born to reform and restore these kingdoms and lead them out from the tyrannical government under which they have been for so long."[16] And it was a poet, Anton de Montoro, who removed the veil: "High sovereign Queen . . . preceding you the daughter of St. Ann, from you the son of God will receive human flesh."[17] Here was blasphemous hyperbole more usual a generation ago when Isabel's mother could hear from a poet that "You are my only God in this present life." Indeed, Montoro was an aging *converso,* his verses a relic of that earlier freer expression now frowned upon and soon to be condemned as dangerously heretical. Still, his inference was quite timely.

To be seen on the walls of the Hall of Justice in Seville's *alcázar* are the insignia of the *Orden de la Banda,* founded by Alfonso XI, purportedly on the battlefield of Salado. The symbols of that prestigious honorary society are a jar and lilies, those of the Annunciation to Mary of a heaven-sent son. Holy Mary was to Castile's monarchs both mother of armies and mother of an awaited redeemer. She was both Mary, *La Virgen de las Batallas,* bringing victory and remembered as putting the keys of Seville into the hands of Fernando III, and she was the Virgin Mary, the purest, the *más limpia,* of all women, lily-white, increasingly extolled as conceived without blemish, untainted with original sin. The ideals that Isabel was now seen to represent paralleled qualities associated with Holy Mary: she was exemplar of motherhood and embodiment of purity, virtue, piety, and compassion, those found in Alfonso X's *Cántigas de María*, those identified with Holy Mary, mother of armies, and with Holy Mary, mother of an awaited redeemer for Castile's sins and herald of its glory.

Now Isabel was also the mother of a son, and neither were ordinary. The statement that Isabel herself was born *maravillosamente* could only have been an allusion to the immaculate conception of Mary, free of the stain of original sin particularly associated with women through Eve, the first woman and mother. That contrast had been made to her pointedly in her youth in *The Garden of Noble Maidens*, its very title alluding to the lost Garden of Eden. Latent in that tract and in Isabel's society was the notion of woman's unworthiness, personified by Eve and surmounted only by Mary, mother of Jesus Christ; it had urged her to become the best of the worst.

That not very useful advice had been supplanted by Talavera's, whose enjoining Isabel to emulate the eagle, known as the nemesis of the serpent, carried with it the suggestion that she strive to counteract all that Eve stood for. Equally, the Franciscan Iñigo de Mendoza had interpreted her charge in an instruction for princes. He addressed her as High Queen, "come by grace of God to remedy our ills, as when our life was lost by the sin of a woman," so that God wants us to restore our health by the means that brought our fall—in other words, through a woman. She had been sent, that is, by heaven to redress the sin brought on by Eve—just as the first High Queen was sent, who was Mary. Hers, he inferred, was a second coming of sorts, enabling the whole Castilian people to progress from past infirmity to present good health. Like Mary, he said, Isabel had come to the world to restore what was lost.[18]

All those admirers of Isabel's brought a Biblical cast of mind to what they said, and, with the probable exception of Gómez Manrique, all—Pulgar, Valera, Montoro, Palma, and Iñigo de Mendoza—were of *converso* lineage, culturally steeped in assumptions of direct relations between monarch and God of the sort found in the scriptural Books of Kings, and all of them relayed prophetic expectation of the coming of a new age and saw it heralded by the birth of a son to this admirable queen. They alluded to the eschatological and apocalyptic themes of Daniel and Ezekiel in particular, themes John the Evangelist and subsequent interpreters had taken up and which became attached in 1478 to this mother and son. The strong Jewish messianic strain had, like so many Jews, become converted, Castilian and Christian, with much significance for Castile's queen.

Thus, with the birth of Prince Juan, Isabel was hailed by contemporaries as Mary's earthly counterpart and a spiritual virginity was claimed for her, a moral purity, a *limpieza*, that was the *sine qua non* of divine approval and choice. As royal head to body politic, she was obligated to extend that *limpieza*, to cleanse her realm of the stain, the defilement, infection, and impurity associated not only with original sin, but in Castile during the recent past with heaven's displeasure and, increasingly, linked to the presence of peoples of other faiths and, by some, to their supposedly Christian descendants. And that *limpieza* attributed to the Queen and expected of the land was assumed of universal significance: "now we are children of the free Jerusalem that is above, which is the mother of us all."[19] Spain was analogue for the earthly city. And Isabel, as mother of a male child, represented the conflation of motherland and monarch, heaven's queen and the redeemer of earth.

To what extent did Isabel share such views? She approved their being set down and disseminated, commissioning the chronicles that relayed them. And her mounting interest in Castile's past conveys not only a desire to know and profit from the experience of her progenitors, but the sort of history she solicited, and her desire to have that of her reign chronicled, points beyond self-aggrandizement to a belief in history as revelation. Too, she appreciated the contrast, often pointed out to her, between Mary and Eve. A theme also common in church representations, she would commission and own a number of paintings of Mary and Christ, and of Eve and Adam. She showed a particular devotion to the Virgin of the Immaculate Conception, founding three chaplaincies in her service, in Guadalupe, Toledo, and Seville. At Guadalupe in 1477 she had assigned 40,000 *maravedís* (on rents from Trujillo) to an annual *solemne fiesta* on the day of the Conception of Our Lady (December 8). She honored *La Inmaculada* together with San Juan and the Holy Trinity, explaining that in so doing she was giving thanks for the victory over "our adversary of Portugal . . . where divine providence was pleased to show me justice."[20] That year too she pledged funds to the Franciscans caring for Christ's tomb in Jerusalem.

Unquestionably, she sanctioned the vision of her reign and its successes then being put forth and welcomed the statements of what her son's birth portended. His arrival gave additional impulse to her commitment to cleansing the land. Whatever the timetable of God's universal design, or the extent of her own role in it, she felt she had to ready Castile. Certainly her success in pursuing that goal could not but allay doubts, hers and others, of her right, and that of her son who was to succeed her, to rule Castile; and, ultimately, that it would be success in the doing that would confirm her right-mindedness.

THINGS TO COME

As sign of things to come, St. John's Book of Revelation offered the Woman of the Apocalypse: "And a great sign appeared in heaven: a Woman clothed in the sun, and the moon was beneath her feet, and upon her head a crown of 12 stars." A popular medieval figure, she was frequently depicted with a child in her arms, and trampling underfoot a serpent.

The association was close between the Woman of the Apocalypse holding the child and crushing the serpent and the Virgin Mary, Mary conceived without stain of sin. So the sisters of that order much favored by Isabel, the Immaculate Conception of Mary, were coming, by the late fifteenth century, to have *la Inmaculada* portrayed. Then too the Woman of the Apocalypse appeared in miniatures in the choirbooks at Guadalupe illustrating the Immaculate Conception. That *conceptionista* imagery made the connection between Holy Mary and The Woman, between motherhood, morality, triumph over the Devil, and the divine promise of freedom from original sin, a promise to be fulfilled with the second coming of Christ.

As Juan II of Castile was born, his mother cried out "Oh, Sweet Mary!" or so wrote a poet wielding prophecy, seeking to establish that prince's august provenance and destiny through relating his birth to the Woman who, the Book of Revelation goes on, crying out, gives birth to a son.[21] Within the tradition of Christian prophecy that child was the World Emperor heralding the last days, which could not arrive until all peoples had accepted Christianity, until all infidels and heretics had disappeared, until the serpent was crushed.

It was an image again associated with the mother of a newborn son in 1478.[22] Isabel, mother of the child who was both heir and sign, was then hailed as earthly counterpart of the Queen of Heaven, and seen as God's instrument, the heroine whose virtue overcame the divine disfavor brought on by her predecessors, who was chosen to guide Spain out of error and from threat of destruction into light. She was the anti-Eve, even the new Eve, destined to recover Spain and to restore the loss of Eden.

It all fit within a providential and apocalyptic view of past and present that carried with it a program for the future. God's design for Castile was believed manifest through history; God's system of reward and punishment, God's sending of an ideal monarch for His purposes, in Castile in 1478 permitted seeing recent happy events as sign of and prelude to even greater things to come. Isabel, however near she believed the last days to be and however she construed her own role in their arrival, surely did not question their imminence, nor did she fault such interpretation.

Pulgar, in chronicling the birth of the royal child, employed further Biblical allusion: "And with the great supplications and offerings and pious works that she [the Queen] made, it pleased God that in that city she conceived and gave birth to a son who was named the Prince Don Juan."[23] And he immediately went on: "In those days that the King and Queen were in Seville, the King of Granada sent his ambassadors." Again the Biblical ring, this time recalling the visit of the three kings to Bethleham, heightening by contrast and lending significance to what he wrote of next, a Muslim demand for a renewal of truce. Gladly, Isabel and Fernando answered, tell your king, just as long as he agrees to pay the customary annual tribute. The response, attributed to Granada's king, Abū' al-Ḥasan' Alī, was the stuff of legend; indeed, it was legend: the kings of Granada who were accustomed to pay tribute were dead, he retorted, and the mints that had coined it were now forging lances for defense against further payment.

What is thought to have been Isabel's bedchamber in the *alcázar* of Seville, the room now known, improbably, as the Harem, has on its walls scenes influenced by *romances de la frontera*; those Castilian ballads exuded respect for Muslims brave and gallant enough to qualify as chivalric adversaries. It was an attitude underlying Pulgar's account and current in 1478, as was an awareness that the years of strife within Castile had heartened Granada; so had word that Portugal was planning to renew the war against Castile. The exchange he reported suited the image of chivalric Moor, and the royal outlook. At the time however, Isabel and Fernando acquiesced to a truce of three years without tribute, principally in order to rule out Granadan help to Andalusians in concert with Portugal. For they had still to conclude the war with Portugal.

And it was not unrelated that, amid jubilation at the birth of the Prince that summer of 1478, in Seville's streets and churches crowd-pleasing preachers took up the theme of what Pulgar referred to as combatting "those of the mountains," of war against the infidel, but chiefly and most urgently they inveighed against heresy within the realm, among *conversos* of Jewish lineage.

10

Inquisition
1478–1485

This Queen was she who rooted out and destroyed the heresy that existed
in the kingdoms of Castile and Aragón, of some Christians of the lineage
of the Jews, who returned to Jewish practices, and she made them live like
good Christians . . .

Fernando del Pulgar[1]

MOUTHS OF HELL

ISABEL had a son, the significance of his birth reflected back to her by
well-wishers in congenial terms, as a promise of the realms becoming
one; and its importance was such as to call forth prophecies in which his
role was crucial and time was of the essence. She had, as well, imposed her
authority on Andalusia, and, not unlike the kings of its first conquest, having done so she entertained ideas of expansion outwards and consolidation
within. Yet where Alfonso X had been both intrigued by Andalusia's cultural and religious diversity and seen it as a potential threat, she saw principally the threat.

Reports from her recently-introduced officials did not reassure her. From
her *alcaide* in Palos came word of "two or three mouths of hell," frequented
"by addicts of witchcraft and sorcery," where the Devil was worshipped
and "our Lord and our Lady, his mother," were not, and of renegades and
subversives living openly, with little fear; nor would he speak of matters
yet uglier but asked remedy "before this land is alienated."[2] In the telling
he coupled religious deviation with resistance to royal authority, and he
blamed on that combination a loss in royal revenues. Another informant
warned that religious laxity was widespread: "In these kingdoms are many
blasphemers, renegades from God and the Saints." He proposed as antidote
focusing on one outstanding aspect, heresy among converts. He was Tómas
de Torquemada, prior of the Dominican monastery of Santa Cruz of Sego-

via, himself probably a *converso*. Torquemada first suggested a statute to stop Jews from influencing *conversos,* then advised an investigation, an Inquisition, to uncover and punish heretics.

In Seville, Isabel was discovering that *conversos* in Andalusia were not like those at court or on the *meseta,* that they were more numerous, more overtly powerful and close-knit, and less indoctrinated in Christianity, and that they retained more openly at least residual Jewish customs. Seville had over 2500 of them. They lived, as Pulgar observed, neither within one law or the other. That they had tended to favor Alfonso and then Isabel against Enrique, boded not so much continued loyalty as that they would support the least pressing authority, which she was striving to ensure would not be her own. Their questionable loyalty was especially worrisome in view of the proximity of Muslim Granada and Africa and of the resurgent danger from Portugal. Thus she ordered, within weeks of Juan's birth, the property of some *conversos* known to have supported the Portuguese confiscated. Moreover, had not Medina Sidonia recently counted upon Seville's leading *conversos* in opposing the crown-sponsored *hermandad,* known to be a wedge to increase royal control?

In the initial years of her reign, Isabel had honeycombed the major urban councils, Seville's among them, with appointments of *conversos.* It too was a way of gaining control within towns, and also of rewarding her *letrados* and administrators, for *conversos* tended to function as tight-knit families, satellites orbiting their star who was usually a court figure, dependent upon royal service. And that she had, in Seville, recently ordered public offices restored to *conversos* dispossessed by application of local statutes of purity of blood was surely a measure taken toward recapturing the city and raising funds while at it. But now those who once appeared part of the solution seemed to have become a part of the problem and the solution to lay elsewhere.

By the later 1470s municipal councillors, their seats inheritable and their salaries minute, customarily made money through accreting land, selling influence, and both setting tax rates and farming taxes. That is, municipal councils, no longer representative, were becoming closed enclaves of privilege and within them factions frequently formed around Old and New Christians, so that she faced a challenge to maintain control of her old *converso* supporters, to not alienate Old Christians, and to keep the peace between them while dominating both. For those purposes, an Inquisition seemed just the thing, useful to sort out the spurious from the faithful, keep powerful *conversos* in line, and foster religious and political solidarity. What is more, an Inquisition, ran a strong argument, would monitor religious life; it would not only uncover religious deviance and mete out punishment, but also head off recurrences of the populace taking that royal attribute, justice, into its own hands. It would literally instill the fear of God and of the monarchy as well, indeed reinforce the inseparability of the two among the populace. By 1478, she was sponsoring measures to investigate and separate true from false converts in Seville. Preachers were arousing the public to the threat of heresy; the parallel to the royal sponsoring of crowd-pleasing sermons preceding the *hermandad* was unavoidable.

Chief among those alerting Isabel when she first came to Seville that heresy was rampant there was a Dominican friar, Alonso de Ojeda, who was only the most active and ardent among public proponents of an Inquisition. During her stay he thundered publicly against *conversos per se*, much as had Espina and other Franciscans over a decade earlier at Enrique's court. Ojeda quickly earned the reputation of being a *"Fray Vicente el segundo,"*[3] even though Vicente Ferrer had sought to have Jews convert to Christianity while Ojeda and the others excoriated *conversos* who, in part due to Ferrer, numbered in Spain perhaps 250,000. Seville itself had relatively few Jews and many wealthy and well-placed *conversos* who retained Jewish customs and formed a powerful faction in the city. Ferrer had alluded to prophecies that Jews must vanish before the Last Days; Ojeda extended that stipulation to New Christians. Moreover, it was exactly Espina's earlier wholesale condemnation of all *conversos* as crypto-Jews that some of the most vociferous advocates of an Inquisition disseminated, along with the old hate-rousing stories of atrocities committed by Jews, but now extended to *conversos*. It was the same stance the first proponents of a statute of *limpieza de sangre*, of purity of blood, had taken at midcentury in Toledo, and it had gained adherents. More recent violence in Andalusia had carried with it the conviction that all *conversos* were secret Jews, members of a race, as Bernaldez said, whose survival was an offense to God, polluting the land.

In Córdoba, where *conversos* were numerous, wealthy, ensconced in city government, and protected by its lord, Alonso de Aguilar, Old Christians, considering themselves "pure" or "clean Christians," mostly artisans, had formed a brotherhood. During Lent of 1473, as the members of that *Cofradía de la Caridad* marched in procession through the streets, a young girl emptied some water from a window, as often happened, but the house belonged to *conversos* and the liquid splattered an image of Holy Mary. There were shouts that it was urine and thrown on purpose, that it was an insult to the faith that must be avenged, that all *conversos* were traitors and heretics. The cry went up of "Death to the *conversos!*" The populace and a majority of the knights and squires and many foreign merchants responded "fast and violently," inspired, wrote a witness, "with more greed to rob than zeal for the service of God." Within days, all Córdoba's *conversos* had been thoroughly fleeced, their houses demolished, and many of them killed. Girls and women had been raped and dishonored. "And from the uprising a fiery spark leaped out from the city to all the neighboring places,"[4]

Conversos fared worst in jurisdictions of nobles hostile to Isabel. Aguilar, beholden to the *conversos* for past support, protected them at first but subsequently came to agree that everyone of Jewish lineage must leave the city and forever be forbidden public office. Some Cordoban *conversos* fled to Seville, and it was with anti-*converso* rumblings there as well that Medina Sidonia had sent them to garrison Gibraltar, then ousted them. Now, four years later in Seville, on street corners and in plazas preachers, particularly Dominicans, provoked public outrage against *conversos* by depicting them as secret Jews who had insulted images of Christ and crucified Christian children.

Isabel, it is worth noting, became a tertiary sister of the Dominican order in 1477. Still, she must then be counted with those, among them many *conversos*, who hoped by an Inquisition to put suspicion of true converts to rest, to protect the sincere Christians by separating out those who were not. New Christians were after all numerous among the nobility and among her most valued advisors and administrators, and they predominated among her chroniclers. Indeed, she and Fernando were both of Jewish ancestry. Fernando had *converso* forebears through his mother, Juana Enríquez, and Isabel's paternal grandmother Catalina, Catherine of Lancaster, was the daughter of a *conversa*, María de Padilla. Also descended from Jews was Leonora de Gúzman, mother of the first Trastámara, Enrique II, and a common ancestor of them both. Even so, the term *"converso"* usually referred only to a descendant of those Jews who had converted during the mass baptisms of 1391 or thereafter.

STEP BY STEP

Nicolò Franco, the papal legate who was Prince Juan's godfather, had been charged by the pope in 1475 with looking into the *converso* problem in Castile. That same year Isabel and Fernando had named a Dominican, Filippo de Barbieri, as Inquisitor General for Sicily, signalling their joint interest in invigorating the tribunal already existing in that kingdom of theirs.

Sicily and its parent kingdom, Aragón, had long had a none-too-active Inquisition, under the authority of bishops and the papacy. Castile had none. And in 1477 first Isabel and then Fernando confirmed a privilege (a forged one, supposedly originally granted in 1233 by the Emperor Frederick) allowing Sicily's new Inquisitor General to retain a third of all confiscated property. They referred to Barbieri in that confirmation as a confessor to them both, and the grant sounds most like a *merced*. It indicated that at the outset they recognized that profit was to be had from an Inquisition and that they considered inquisitorial procedure to be under royal aegis. Barbieri, in turn, vigorously advocated to them an Inquisition for Castile as well; the fear it would arouse, he told them, would be greatly beneficial to the faith.

On November 1, 1478, *los reyes* received a papal bull conceding them the faculty to appoint two or three priests as Inquisitors in Castile. Isabel's name must have of necessity been attached to its solicitation. There is every reason to believe that the decision to introduce an Inquisition and to do it as a royal endeavor was a joint one, and that it paralleled royal purpose and strategy in establishing the *hermandad*, and that it was meant, besides instituting religious conformity, to heighten popular adhesion and internal control and stability and to bring in funds. Moreover, its introduction flowed so naturally from the climate pertaining ever since Isabel had arrived in Seville that it could well have appeared to Isabel to be the Queen's royal and sacred duty.

Still, the enabling bull was secured with such secrecy that no mention of an Inquisition appeared in the proceedings of the Castile-wide ecclesiastical assembly held in Seville during the summer of 1478. And, once obtained, that bull was not implemented for two years. For, while Isabel left Seville that October cognizant of *converso* strength and doctrinal laxity and of factions with worrisome connections to the great nobles and the Portuguese, most immediately she faced a contest with the papacy over control of Castile's clergy, and possibly another with nobles and ecclesiastics from whom she was determined to regain Enrique's and Alfonso's grants of royal property and income. All in all, the time was not opportune to install a tribunal as a crown enterprise and an Inquisition under the bishops was not to her purpose, especially since its principal proponent was Carrillo. Moreover, it was always her tendency to innovate by degree, to impose her programs gradually, building consensus; thus did she proceed in the quest for religious conformity.

Accordingly, in 1478 she appointed not inquisitors but a commission to look into the religious condition of Seville's *conversos* and to try to persuade shaky converts to wholeheartedly embrace Christianity. Her nominees indicate the scope of her thinking: Cardinal Mendoza, represented by the Bishop of Cádiz, he whose tears had gained *sevillanos* a general pardon in civil matters, but also Diego de Merlo, on the rise as the royal deputy facing down Andalusian nobles, and fray Ojeda, the prime proponent of initiating a Holy Tribunal or Holy Office, as the Inquisition was more formally known. And Hernando de Talavera, whether or not a member proper, was highly influential in the workings of that commission.

Mendoza, as archbishop of the vast province of Seville, began by circulating to all churches and having posted in all parishes a pastoral letter insisting upon and detailing the proper forms of the sacraments and observances of Christian life. It stated, among other necessities, that Christian houses were to have "a painted replica of the cross on which our Lord Jesus Christ suffered, and some painted images of our Lady and some *santos o santas* which will provoke and awaken those living there to have devotion."[5] Charged by him, clergy, preaching in public and instructing in private, strove to show deviating *conversos* "how much perpetual damnation of their souls and perdition of their bodies and possessions" they were bringing upon themselves by practicing Jewish rites.[6] The criteria of orthodoxy was heavily weighted to outward observance and habits of everyday life, considering them sure indicators of interior disposition. Eight months later, that commission not surprisingly reported such measures insufficient. The predisposition of the commissioners aside and no matter what the religious preference of individual *conversos*, in view of the generations of habit those instructions sought to eradicate so quickly and completely the result was a foregone conclusion. As Pulgar observed to Mendoza:

> I believe that there are some there [in Seville] who are bad [Christians], and others, the largest number, are so because they follow those bad ones, and would also follow good ones if there were any. But since the Old Christians there are such bad Christians, the New Christians are such good Jews. I believe without a doubt, My Lord, that there must be 10,000 maidens in Andalusia from 18 to 20 years of age, who since they were born have never left their house, nor heard or knew of any other doctrine than that which they saw their parents do.[7]

Yet had the criteria of orthodoxy applied been Jewish, the great majority of Seville's *conversos* would have been found equally wanting. Rather, Jewish custom and Jewish law were so intertwined and had for so long so permeated every aspect of daily family and communal life that converts lacking solid indoctrination into Christianity, whatever their religious preference, tended to remain at least culturally connected to their age-old faith, and the practices so retained were the very ones now being flamboyantly denounced and equated with apostasy.

Bernaldez, who was chaplain to an Inquisitor, echoed the sentiments disseminated by street-corner preachers. Judaizing he considered inseparable from the customs "of the stinking Jews themselves."[8] Secret Jews, he went on, were recognizable as gluttons who never lost the Jewish habit of eating foods containing onions and garlic, refried with oil, and meat stewed in oil in order to avoid bacon, so that their breath reeked and their houses stank and they themselves smelled like Jews because of those dishes and not being baptized. (Baptismal water, it was said, removed that stench instantly.) Hernando de Talavera listed among customs identifying secret Jews the keeping of Saturday sabbath, circumcision, and washing the dead before burying them very deeply and outside Christian cemetaries, which he was certain gave heretics a good start on their journey to hell. As predictable, *conversos* did not mend their ways sufficiently; rather, they fled Seville in droves, particularly to places within seignorial jurisdiction.

So matters stood when, in September of 1480, a treaty with Portugal in hand and the nobles having shown themselves more tractable, Isabel and Fernando named two inquisitors, Dominicans, for Castile; they were probably at work in Seville by mid-October. When the immediate response was riots and a great exodus of *conversos* (some of whom went to Rome to appeal to the pope), Isabel ordered the provocateurs of such outbreaks and subjects who neglected to denounce fugitives punished and their goods confiscated. One of the two receivers of confiscations then named was the trusted Merlo, his appointment another indication of her awareness that political and financial value attached to orthodoxy. In January 1481 the inquisitors banished all Jews from the city and its hinterlands, and the two friars, armed with the Queen's edicts and in a bravura display of royal might, summarily ordered the Marqués de Cádiz and all *grandes* to seize and return to them in Seville within 15 days the emigrants they harbored.

Within Seville, on February 6, 1481, six men and women who had been sentenced by the inquisitors for judaizing, after secret denunciations and without public trial, were burnt at the stake. Such was the inaugural *auto de fe*. (Ojeda preached a sermon that day that was to be his last, for he died of plague a few days later.) Shortly after, in a second *auto*, three *conversos* who had plotted to kill the inquisitors were similarly executed; such had been their prominence that Isabel had in April 1478 confirmed to their ringleader, Diego de Susán, a seat on the city council. That *conversos* had formed a sizable militia in Seville during the troubles of 1473 and had subsequently been alerted by Medina Sidonia to resist the *hermandad* by force were good reasons why Susan's group was prepared with weapons and thinking in terms of resisting by arms another royal institution, the Inquisition. That by hindsight their plot seems suicidal attests to the great change they suddenly faced in confronting royal power, the upending of regional power relations wrought by the inquisitors and by royal determination.

On March 26, 17 more people from all walks of life went to the stake and yet more in April. Outside Seville's walls a great field was designated as the *quemadero*, literally "the burning place," and there statues of prophets were erected to which the condemned were tied when executed. Those figures silently spoke of the Messiah having come and been denied by Jews, and reminded the crowds of onlookers that the second coming would occur only after the world was rid of heretics and Jews. That popular spectacle, the *auto de fe*, itself served as metaphor for purifying the land through fire and it offered the assembled an implicit and graphic representation of both judgment day and hellfire, palpably reinforcing an atmosphere of expectation and dread.

Within Seville plague reached epidemic proportions. More *conversos* fled. So did the Inquisitors, for several months, in August. Yet before they departed several hundred people had died at the stake; many others been imprisoned. As many as 1500 penitents had been paraded through the streets at one time, with calculated effect on both participants and onlookers, offering entertainment and warning, enhancing fear and awe of royal majesty. The Holy Office was soon extended to Cádiz, Jérez, Puerto de Santa María, and Córdoba, all jurisdictions of nobles who, through the 1480s and 1490s, nonetheless tended to protect *conversos*, including those penanced and 'reconciled' to Christianity. In the archbishopric of Seville, by 1488, 700 men and women had been sentenced to burn, and 5000 more been punished.

At the heart of inquisitorial procedure was what has been described as "a rapid, severe, and inflexible justice, appealing in its simplicity."[9] The inquisitors and their staff, working from reports of informers, secretly investigated, judged, and sentenced converts for heresy. Those who repented received lesser sentences and wore *sanbenitos*, yellow tunics inscribed with their names and crimes, and *corozas*, high conical caps, for a designated period, highly visible reminders to everyone of the awesome reach of church and state. The progeny of both those executed as heretics and those reconciled to the church were excluded from public office and much else for at least two generations. It is instructive that in Spain today the expression 'to wear a *sanbenito*' connotes unjust condemnation.[10] And while the Holy Office was licensed to function only against heretics, it claimed jurisdiction over proselytizing Jews as well.

The *auto de fe* was a joint venture of the Inquisition and the crown, popularly recognized as such, enhancing the sacred attributes of monarchy. Ostensibly the church sentenced the prisoners, then turned the condemned over to the state for execution. That, as the Spanish historian Luis Suárez Fernández concludes, was the operative fiction. For church and state cooperated in every aspect of the Spanish Inquisition. Thus, against strong pressure, Isabel and Fernando supported keeping secret the identity of those making denunciations. Isabel is said to have believed that otherwise the *conversos* would wreak vengeance upon such witnesses; it was a stand consistent with her conviction that seeking vengeance was an acceptable and a pervasive human trait.

OPINIONS

How did Isabel regard the Inquisition in those early years? We have no personal statement, but we do have some opinions of men then close to her, whose outlooks shed a good deal of light on her own. One of the few who did not welcome an Inquisition was Pulgar, who early on wrote to Mendoza that "the Queen Our Lady does what she ought to do as a most Christian queen is obliged to do, and her duty to God requires no less." Still, he asked, might she not be misguided in executing essentially ignorant people instead of having them penanced and instructed in Christianity? For, while he has seen "the great extent of the blind stupidity and stupid blindness of those people"—the *conversos* who judaized—that did not mean they should be burned alive.

Pulgar's stands nearly alone among surviving statements in its spirit of Christian charity. It recalls the principle of jurisprudence he wrote of the Bishop of Cádiz's having expressed to Isabel in urging she make an example of Seville's foremost culprits, but not punish everyone in the city. Her response then had been forward-looking: she was persuaded to grant a general pardon, to all except heretics. Now it was to her that Pulgar attributed the introduction of the Inquisition, an institution of retributive justice, rather than one based upon the premise that the exemplary punishment of a few outstanding culprits would suffice. That institution, and the queen who introduced and sustained it were, rather, dedicated to extirpating heresy, root and branch, and to having it known that such was the case.

Pulgar's comments drew a heated response from an anonymous *familiar*, or functionary, of the Inquisition, addressed to the queen and more consonant with her own views on wielding justice. While, he insisted, the Inquisition might punish some innocent people, "the harm from ignoring sin and withholding punishment is greater than the harm that would follow from administering it, for from that error would ensue the breaking of the faith, the corruption of true doctrine, and the destruction of virtuous life; and even though the punishment [of the innocent] create a scandal, it is the doctrine of Christ to punish, and not to open the door of pardon either to the few or to the many; for it is better to enter Paradise with one eye than to suffer in Hell with two."[11] That reference to one eye would remain a favorite one with proponents of wholesale punishment by the Inquisition, as would the remarkable notion that "it was the doctrine of Christ to punish." The Christ of the Inquisition, and surely of Isabel at its inception, was not the Christ of the Sermon on the Mount.

"In this punishment," he continued, "we are dealing with the common good, the preservation of which lies in punishing obstinate sinners, and disregarding their distress, for that must be subordinated to the common good, which is considered divine; just as for the survival of the body it is advisable to cut off the rotten limb." He concluded that the Biblical books were full of acts of God's vengeance and that "God, once the evil men are eradicated, will bring His mercy." Now, was his message and that of the Inquisition, must be a time of purge, of cleansing the body politic of every bit of infection. Underlying it was an apocalyptical vision of a world where good and evil clashed, of a world at war as Castile had been for so long, but no longer at civil war; rather the good, directed by heaven, were battling the Devil's adjutants, those judaizing *conversos* who had outstayed their welcome on earth. "And if you do not know their name, read the last part of the first letter to the Corinthians, where the Apostle calls them *marrantha*, which in our language means, plainly and simply, *marranos*"—that is, pigs.

Pulgar refuted the charge that he had impugned the Inquisitors; arguing from Christian compassion, he defended minorly erring *conversos* and forgave his attacker, for "I believe that he who seeks vengeance rather tortures himself than avenges, and becomes so greatly changed that he tortures his body and does not save his soul," and him he will leave to heaven.[12] Yet his opponent had inferred that in attacking the Inquisition he was attacking the Queen, and to that he responded indirectly: Her Highness the Queen, he said, had thought that she was doing right when she entrusted the fortress of Nodar to Martín de Sepúlveda, but he rebelled and turned it over to the King of Portugal. Similarly, he implied, it was no great wonder that she may have been wrong in setting up the Inquisition, thinking that she was doing right.

His views in that exchange may have got Pulgar exiled from court, but not permanently, for he was sufficiently in Isabel's good graces to have her accept a completed chronicle in 1484. But thereafter he was silent regarding the Inquisition. No one criticized it. Among the last who did so publicly was the outspoken *converso* poet, Montoro, who, in ending a poem addressed to *la reina* Isabel, both indicated the increased social tenuousness of New Christians and displayed great confidence in the Queen's protection, even in her ironic sense of humor, in requesting that he not be burned at the stake at the moment, that it wait "at least until Christmas when fire is welcome."[13] Such levity was no longer tolerated in the 1480s.

Christians of Jewish lineage generally retained their posts at court. They remained prominent among Isabel's most trusted lawyers, and valued advisors and administrators. While the Inquisition did condemn some high-placed *conversos*, in those years none close to the Queen were publicly prosecuted by the Inquisition, although some royal functionaries and other prominent people were secretly reconciled. And, clearly, she retained the older view that baptism made a Christian, and did not then endorse the concept of *limpieza de sangre*.

Yet, as time went on, court figures were not exempt from public punishment and the attendant humiliation and loss of reputation. Shortly to be called before the Inquisition was Juan Ramírez de Lucena, a diplomat and her sometime chief notary, who had written that lapsed *conversos* were not heretics, for their baptism was not valid since forced, and who had scored inquisitorial violence and urged clemency rather than burning. Another courtier, condemned some statements of Lucena's, among them, that "the monarchs our lords do not imitate God," and in countering them presented what had become the preferred royal image and the one projected by the Inquisition: "Heaven must be praised," he wrote, "for wishing to give us monarchs who follow the heart of God."[14] Heresy was treason, and the other way around.

ON BEHALF OF THE QUEEN

Hernando de Talavera, like Pulgar, ardently defended sincere *conversos* as true Christians and was himself one. A seventeenth-century historian caught his spirit: "he detested the evil custom prevalent in Spain of treating members of the sects worse after their conversion than before it . . . so that many refused to accept a faith in whose believers they saw so little *caridad* (charity or love) and so much arrogance."[15] Yet he also supported death for judaizers, equating judaizing with practicing Jewish customs, and he claimed a good deal of credit for bringing the Inquisition to Seville. In 1481 he once again wrote a tract at Isabel's request, and once again she would give every indication of endorsing his sentiments.

The Queen had come to him, he recounted, with a tract by an anonymous *converso*, "a malicious heretic," who defended the old within the new, straddling Judaism and Christianity, and whose assertions had upset her. They infuriated him, as the refutation he quickly wrote entitled "Catholicism Impugned" attests.[16] Although claiming to be moved by prophecies, authorities, and God's inspiration, the man was, Talavera declared at the outset, but a schismatic and sower of discord who divided old and new Christians. He had the temerity to assume all New Christians to be of his own cast of mind, of his *patria*, nature, disbelief, infidelity, heresy, and apostasy, not seeing that the day was coming of anger, vengeance, calamity, and misery for sinners, when he and his fellow-thinkers would descend into hell. He was, Talavera declared, an obstinate and malicious Jew, a heretic of the sort warned of by Daniel and St. John, akin to the apostate friars and priests recently burned in Seville.

Contemporaries described Talavera as Christlike in appearance, way of life, and attitude. It was a comparison most enlightening as to notions of Christ at the time. For that confessor of the Queen's viewed God as mostly vengeful, stern, and terrible, his judgment *cruel*. He and his God expected from human beings a striving for perfection and for redemption from original sin; and he saw the good life as ascetic, a life of the soul and not the body; stating that the time was approaching in which all the world would be renewed, he spoke of "the universal justice which we await" coming soon rather than later. That being so, heretics such as this madman were intolerable. He had been influenced by Satan, "the old enemy of the human race who spoke through the serpent that deceived our mother, Eve and, through her, our first father, Adam." He was a subject of the Devil who, as Job said, was the king of the arrogant and the father of liars, and who was too the destroyer-king of the Apocalypse of San Juan.

Still, Talavera was careful to defend sincere converts, writing that the saints stated and the civil laws desired that New Christians be honored and treated well. All of them were not to be known as *marranos*, but only those who, although baptized and showing some signs of Christianity, kept the ceremonies and rites of Muslims and Jews. Such people in truth ought to die.

Jesus Christ, according to "that madman," was a Jew. Talavera demurred, arguing that lineage commonly came from the father, that Christ was of no human lineage but was the Son of God. He then went on to provide explanation for his own attitude, and for inquisitorial proceedings seemingly directed against what was simply residual habit. God, he said, had detailed in the Law of Moses that conduct was one with religious observance and faith, so that behavior signified belief. Indeed, he himself had preached in Seville that the law of Moses had had no force since the fulfilling of the prophecies through the coming of Christ, the messiah, and that it was old and black and dying, not bad in its time but that time was past. Any Christian holding to it sinned gravely and was an apostate or heretic; even Jews sinned more in holding to it than in breaking it. The new law was the Holy Evangel and all the New Testament; it was God's will concerning how human beings must live. For a new covenant had been made with a new Israel. Now "the people of Israel" signified those Christians whom the holy apostle called Israel-in-spirit.

The Jewish people were no longer the people of Israel, nor were they true Jews; rather, they were the synogogue and *ayuntamiento*, council house, of Satan, as the Lord said to St. John in his Apocalypse [3.9]; for although of the blood of Abraham, Isaac, and Jacob, they were not their chldren, nor of their line, for they had not their faith nor had they performed their works; they were but dry branches without yield. He despised, he said, those who insisted on being Jews. They were anomalies of history, which revealed God's plan, and hindrances to the second coming, and they insisted on claiming exclusivity as Israel, the chosen of God, when the chosen, the true Israel was, rather, the people of the Christian church militant.

Talavera also indicated how the religious climate contributed to royal stature. Ten years ago the law had not been obeyed. It had been due to the malice of the people or the defect of the ruler, as became clear in the improvement after "Our most serene Lord and Lady" came to rule. There was now so much justice and good government in those kingdoms it was as if they were monasteries. The Lord had enhanced the monarchs' virtue and lives as his very excellent and fitting vicars, and, doing the Lord's work, they had brought reform.

"Catholicism Impugned" closed on Talavera's old theme of self-perfection: all people desire perfection, the true good that is discernible only to those with a healthy, clean, and enlightened heart. The true good of human beings and their true and principal perfection is the glory of heaven that is to see God, to know him clearly and love him with all one's heart, and to do so a very clean heart is necessary as well as the very clear light of the holy Catholic faith. Those who abhor the light and who, like bats, love the darkness of night reach their desired end, the everlasting and consuming fire of hell. Seen from Talavera's vantage point, an official one, the *auto de fe* efficiently and relatively humanely dispatched those allies of darkness who insisted upon awaiting Antichrist as their messiah. It was to continue to do so for 300 years.

WHOSE INQUISITION?

The pope, Sixtus IV, had authorized the Inquisition in Castile expecting the usual procedure, the Tribunal to be put under episcopal jurisdiction with appeal to Rome. Isabel's instructions to the first inquisitors, while supposedly based on the papal bull, declared the Holy Tribunal a royal institution. Soon, his holiness was hearing from fugitive *conversos* and irate clergy of such uncanonical procedures as secret denunciation, false accusation, unjust imprisonment, unusually severe torture, and inquisitors appropriating the goods of the condemned. Accordingly, the pope made a stab at exerting papal and episcopal oversight. Yet while in January 1482 Sixtus chided the monarchs in recommending less inquisitorial severity, in February he conceded to them yet more control—the faculty to name the eight more inquisitors they had proposed for Castile, preeminent among them Tomás de Torquemada.

Similarly, Fernando and Isabel had named Inquisitors for Aragón in December 1481. Sixtus that January denied their request to extend the Holy Office there, then in April changed his mind, although at the same time he complained of inquisitors already at work there and in the Aragonese provinces of Valencia, Majorca, and Catalonia as moved to torture and condemn Christians by a lust for wealth. Juan of Aragón died in January 1479 and Fernando, succeeding him, took charge of the decrepit medieval institution in his lands; he was reinvigorating it and extending its reach despite protest from clergy, town councils, and *conversos*. Still, to all opposition to royal incursion and a Castilian inquisitor, Fernando responded that the Inquisition had nothing to do with infringement of customary provincial rights, that it was a creation of the papacy.

In October, when Sixtus suspended inquisitorial procedures in Aragón, it was Isabel who responded, writing by hand a long explanatory letter. She knew, she said, that His Holiness had received complaints of the Inquisition and been told that she wanted *conversos'* wealth, but such charges were untrue. In late February 1482, Sixtus reassured her that he had not heard any such criticism and that no one could persuade him of anything against her religious devotion and that of her royal spouse. "We rejoice in our heart, beloved daughter," he told her, "at the determination and diligence you put into things so desired by us. We should always put diligence in applying the necessary remedies to such pestilential harm."[17] Accordingly, he approved and thanked God for her so holy endeavor and exhorted "that you take upon yourself this cause of God, because in nothing else can you serve him better than in this." She was to carry on the work underway and he would deny her nothing he could honestly concede.

Patently, Sixtus had backed down—he needed the monarchs' aid against France in Italy—and the Inquisition was theirs. It was a victory for both Isabel and Fernando. It gave them the first institution cutting across the heretofore-separate administrations of Castile and Aragón, and greater leverage regionally and within the towns. In August Sixtus sanctioned secret reconciliation and in October he approved the naming of Torquemada as chief inquisitor for Aragón. Within Castile, more tribunals were established, one in Córdoba in 1482, and others the next year in Jaén and Ciudad Real. The latter in 1485 moved to Toledo despite the protest of Toledo's corregidor, Gómez Manrique. And inquisitors went to work as well in Segovia, Avila, Sigüenza, and Valladolid. Torquemada, as Inquisitor General, headed a growing bureaucracy that he staffed in collaboration with the monarchs, and, when a realm-wide council of *la Santa Inquisición* was established (by 1488) he worked increasingly closely with royal *letrados*, until his death in 1498; his initial appointment had been suggested by Cardinal Mendoza. Untiring and remorseless, Torquemada extended the Inquisition throughout Spain. He himself lived, as did Talavera, as a ascetic, although surrounded by pomp.

Isabel and Fernando were present when, in November 1484, Torquemada assembled the Spanish inquisitors in Seville, and drew up a regulatory code. Another such assembly they organized and attended, in Valladolid in 1488, produced additional ordinances, in sum declarations of inquisitorial power and autonomy, condoning great secrecy and brooking no criticism. Isabel sought economic security for the inquisitors and got them ecclesiastical benefices and some of the most secure rents of the kingdom, for which some of them paid large sums coming from confiscated goods.

The monarchs saw to it that the Inquisition expanded, authorizing tribunals particularly for places with concentrations of *conversos*. Those tribunals prosecuted heresy vigorously and on little evidence. Torture was normal procedure. Cases commonly began with secret denunciations. Denunciation was ordered as the duty of all good Christians, and denouncers and witnesses remained secret. Two of the early tribunals, in Avila and Guadalupe, were unusually shortlived but active. In Guadalupe within a year's time seven *autos de fe* were held in which 52 Judaizers, 46 dead bodies, and two effigies of fugitives were burned at the stake; 16 people were imprisoned for life, and yet others were sent to the galleys or sentenced to wear the *sanbenito* perpetually.

When the Inquisition arrived in Toledo in 1485, a group of *conversos*, as in Seville, plotted "to raise a tumult and dispatch Inquisitors, and seize the city" as Henry Charles Lea put it. They were betrayed and six hung. There too, as in Aragón and Seville, Jewish rabbis were ordered to have their people, although legally forbidden to testify against Christians, report on Judaizing *conversos.* In Toledo, on Sunday, February 12, 1486, there were reconciled 750 men and women, after having been made to march in procession from the church of San Pedro Mártir to the cathedral in freezing cold, the men without hats and shoes, the women naked, all carrying unlit candles and taunted by a great crowd, for people had come from miles around to see them. The reconciled wept and wailed. "It was believed more for their dishonor than for their offense to God."[18] Their prescribed penance was to repeat that procession, flagellating themselves as they went, on the five Fridays of Easter and on Holy Thursday. Again on Sunday, April 2, some 900 other men and women were reconciled in similar fashion (if warmer weather). They were then forgiven one Friday's repetition and instead fined a fifth of their wealth for the war on the Moors. Another 750 were similarly reconciled a month later. And, on August 16, 25 men and women were burned at the stake, among them a member of the city council and other notables, all wearing conical hats and yellow *sanbenitos* bearing their names followed by the words "condemned heretic." On December 10, 900 more people were reconciled; thereafter *autos de fe* were held periodically. It is estimated that 3200 people out of Toledo's population of 18,000 to 20,000 were punished for judaizing, and there is no record but strong evidence of many additional secret and undoubtedly paid-for reconciliations. Throughout Spain, Pulgar estimated, 2000 men and women were condemned and 15,000 penanced in the decade after 1481.

In Zaragoza in 1485, *conversos* did kill an inquisitor, Pedro Arbués, while he prayed in the cathedral. Apprehended by the civil authorities, one had his hands cut off, then was dragged alive to the marketplace and hung. His body was afterwards cut down, decapitated, and quartered, his hands affixed to the wall above the door of the regional deputation, and one quarter of his body hung along each of the four highways out of town. Several of the others were executed similarly. Two committed suicide. But a brother of Gabriel Sánchez, the royal treasurer, somehow got away, and Sánchez himself, although implicated, was not charged; nonetheless, he did leave court for a while. On hearing of the assassination, the monarchs ordered every supposed Christian performing Jewish rites throughout Aragón burned, "and all their property applied to the *cámara* of the king and queen, of which," it was said, "there was a great quantity," for there were many *conversos* in Aragón and they abounded in wealth.[19]

Did the desire for such wealth motivate Isabel? The Queen supported the Inquisition, Pulgar wrote, even though aware that *conversos* had fled Andalusia to the point that its great commerce had diminished, and thus her rents been very greatly reduced. Seville's revenues are estimated to have dropped by a third, with the flight of thousands of families, including those of numerous merchants and taxfarmers. Isabel, Pulgar averred, gave little consideration to the diminution of her rents, for, putting "all interest aside, she wished to cleanse her kingdom of the sin of heresy, for she knew it was to the service of God and herself. And the supplications and pleas that were made to her in this affair did not make her change her mind about it."[20]Palencia concurred (after making what was becoming the usual vituperative comments on judaizers, thereby ensuring that no one thought his opinions a criticism of the holy tribunal): "The establishment of the Inquisition, indispensible recourse to punish the depraved heresy had also augmented penury"; yet the royal course held steady:

> It is certain that this was considered trivial in respect to eternal happiness, since true riches are the possession of the true Catholic. Thus Don Fernando and Doña Isabel put before any inconvenience whatever the ripping out of the multitude of judaizers from among the Andalusian people, so that those infected by error would return to the road of eternal health by means of a true reconciliation or would perish among the flames if they remained obdurate.

Accordingly, many had been burnt, "for among *conversos* most women practiced Jewish rites." And most men fled, carrying their wealth or hiding it, so that "Andalusia remains exhausted of gold and silver."[21]

That may be so, but Andalusia found sufficient resources to serve as principal supplier of men and material in the war soon to come. Further, over the years funds from confiscations, fines, and reconciliations flowed in to royal coffers, or should have: the first receiver of confiscated goods was called up in 1487 for siphoning off a million and a half *maravedís*, and he was not the last. Still, Fernando got papal consent to take a large part of the income of those condemned in Aragón.

Miguel Angel Ladero Quesada, the leading historian today of Isabelline Spain, states that in Andalusia between 1488 and 1497 confiscations reached 50 million *maravedís*. And Pulgar noted that in Andalusia the property confiscated from the condemned was "applied to the royal treasury of the King and Queen, and there was a great quantity," and that Fernando and Isabel directed the belongings of the many who fled and were tried in absentia go "to the war against the Moor, and other things."[22] Among those other things were the construction of San Juan de los Reyes, the Dominican convent of Santo Tomás in Avila, and the royal residence, the *hospedaría,* in Guadalupe. And they continually made *mercedes* of such confiscated property.

Initially, Isabel had sought the imposition of an institution long delayed by circumstances, then from the outset employed it as a royal vehicle, and ever after, despite knowledge of its ruthlessness and abuses, and aware of the dread it engendered—indeed, viewing engendering fear as well as love as necessary for a monarch—she endorsed it and profited from recurrent, secret, paid reconciliations as well as confiscation of properties. That the Inquisition ushered in a secretive, distrustful world she could not have foreseen clearly; still, a part of her had always viewed the world in those terms. Another part, however, could temporize, as in mediating between Torquemada's zeal and the remarkably lenient inquisitors at work in that mercantile hub and source of substantial royal revenues, Medina del Campo. Too, Pulgar tells a story of the moral maze resulting from inquisitorial activity and of one way Isabel threaded through it, of Jews in Toledo, forced to testify, bearing false witness, causing death sentences, and then, the truth becoming known, Isabel commanding the liars be tried as perjurers, so that eight of them were tortured with pincers and stoned to death. Within today's morality, it appears a spiralling of injustice.

There remains, too, an account of the sort of inquisitorial influence, surely widespread, but in this instance within the royal household. One day in the 1480s, Prince Juan and his pages played Inquisition, drawing lots for who would be the judges and who the accused. The judges then read out the sentences, stripped the condemned, and were tying them to the stake when an older page, realizing the game had gone too far, ran to the Queen's apartments. Isabel herself, interrupting her siesta, hiked her skirts and hurried out, to find the boys at the point of garroting their victims. Zeroing in on the Prince, she gave him a resounding thwack, then untied the prisoners and bore them off, wrapped in hastily found capes. It is further instructive of her attitude to such matters that at least one of their parents, her secretary Fernán Alvarez de Toledo Zapata, a *converso*, was compensated with royal *mercedes*.

There is no question that for Isabel the Inquisition was a means to fused political, religious, and economic ends, to extending, heightening, and maintaining monarchical authority and to building a broadly Spanish consensus based upon religious orthodoxy and the social superiority of long-time Christians. In its vigorously and highly visibly pursuing the goal of cleansing Spain of heresy were reinforced and shaped not only religion but also patriotism and political conformity.

As time went on the Queen became—as in other projects once embarked upon—ever more obdurate in its support and convinced of its efficacy, brooking no argument and moving toward a closed mind on the matter and a closed society for Spain. Still, it was only after her death that the worst excesses occurred. And she did on occasion attempt to mitigate its abuses, those that could be construed as disrespectful of royal authority, and after a decade she sought to call inquisitors to fiscal accountability, but she certainly did not put full energy into either. The Inquisition endured into the nineteenth century, reaching a peak in activity and executions in the later sixteenth century under her great-grandson and great fan, Philip II.

Readying
1478–1481

1480. This year *los Reyes* held Cortes in Toledo, and made laws and ordinances, all so well-appearing and ordered, that it seemed a divine work for the remedy and the organization of the past disorder.

Galíndez de Carvajal[1]

Experience shows that if one foresees from far ahead the designs to be undertaken, one can act with speed when the moment comes to execute them.

Richelieu[2]

There law goes, where kings command.

Proverb, cited in couplets to Isabel[3]

TREATIES WITH PORTUGAL

WHEN Isabel joined Fernando for Christmas at Guadalupe in 1478, peace had been made with Portugal's ally France and with Carrillo. Soon after, the defeat of a last incursion by the Portuguese and of their supporters in Extremadura, along with the unpopularity in Portugal itself of the war, signaled its end. France remained at war with Aragón; that contest was soon Fernando's responsibility, for on January 19, 1479, his father died, in his eighty-first year.

At the last, Juan II of Aragón could claim vindication for his reliance on prudence (as he understood that virtue) and for his foresight in deftly engineering the marriage of Fernando to Isabel. Juan, born in Castile and king in Aragón, was indisputably *the* architect of a unified Spain. His son and daughter-in-law represented its unity in their marriage, and it was Juan who had been the mastermind behind that union. His son was king of Castile; his grandson was heir to both Castile and Aragón. To the end of his long life he had governed his kingdom strongly and personally. His example, followed selectively, would earn Fernando a reputation as Europe's most astute statesman-king.

From June through October 1479 Fernando was in Aragón. Isabel, in Castile, personally took charge of peace negotiations with Portugal. On invitation of Beatriz of Braganza, the powerful dowager Duchess of Viseu who was also Isabel's maternal aunt, the two women opened negotiations in Alcántara in March. Agreement foundered on the very first clause the Portuguese proposed: that Isabel's son Juan marry Juana, once referred to as *La Beltraneja* and now known in Portugal as the Excellent Lady; she was now 17 years old and her diminished prospects had dampened the ardor of Portugal's king but not his desire to save face. Isabel remained adamant that the potentially troublesome girl must go to a convent: she would, she declared, sooner break off all conversation than listen to any more on the subject. She also refused to have her daughter Isabel marry Afonso's son and heir, João. She had firm support; there is an annotation in her hand in the margin of her report on the talks: "The King conferred with the Cardinal on all this and sent to say they agreed entirely."[4]

Matters went better in June. Isabel sent to Portugal the jurist, Rodrigo Maldonado de Talavera, with full powers to negotiate a treaty, but not to do it without getting Juana to a nunnery and arranging that the *infanta* Isabel marry not the widower João but his son and heir, Afonso. The Queen did not like nor trust João, who had fought her in Castile; his son was more personable and closer in age to her daughter and should she marry him a child of that union might well one day wear Portugal's crown.

Maldonado wrote to the queen daily, as instructed, and Isabel, foreshadowing the diligence of her great-grandson, Philip II, personally read and annotated the copious memoranda he sent, including the reports she had ordered on Portugal's military strength. On September 4, 1479, the treaty of peace—which was signed in Alcáçovas, the residence of the infanta Beatriz—essentially reestablished the *status quo ante bellum*. Castile renounced all claims to Guinea, the Mina de Oro, Madeira, the Cape Verdes, and the Azores, and to any lands yet to be discovered between the Canaries and Guinea.

But Isabel retained the Canaries. And on July 26, 1480, a complementary accord guaranteed that Castilians might trade in Barbary and the Portuguese in Granada. The road was cleared for Castile to extend its influence along the North African coast and to expand westwards into the Atlantic (except "between the Canaries and Guinea"), with the Canaries as a base. Thereafter, maritime expansion was pursued. The natives of the Canarian island of Gomera had rebelled in 1478, with the aid of the Portuguese; within a year of the treaty a royal expedition was dispatched there under Pedro de Vera Mendoza. In 1480 too, the tame deputies to the Cortes suggested the monarchs order galleys and *naos* constructed in Vizcaya or

Seville, "so that they might be powerful at sea as on land and surpass all other kingdoms in seapower."

Isabel confirmed the treaty in September 1479 and also signed a second pact, stipulating that Juana was to enter a nunnery or be otherwise confined. So concerned was she that she agreed to send her daughter to Portugal as hostage to the peace, for she well knew that Juana's marrying anywhere could raise the spectre of disputed succession. Juana entered the elegant convent of Santa Clara in Coimbra as a novice, and although Isabel strove to see that no loophole should enable her to leave, she came and went as did many highborn ladies, and her cousin, João, after becoming king—on the death of Afonso, of plague, in August 1481—had her stay at the palace, despite Isabel's admonitions. Isabel pressed on, sending Hernando de Talavera to Portugal charged with seeing to it that Juana took the veil. And a secret treaty was arranged with João, guaranteeing that she would not marry nor leave religious life or Portugal. (She did not, and she lived until 1530.) A papal bull guaranteed that treaty, and it was seen as reinforced by the marriage of João's son and heir, Prince Afonso, to the *infanta* Isabel in 1490.

TOLEDO: 1480

After peace with Portugal was confirmed, Isabel immediately went to Toledo, where the Cortes, postponed from June 1479, at last met, from mid-January through May 1480. Toledo, hallowed as the old Visigothic capital and as a principal staging area of the reconquest, was also perennially a major seat of unrest and revolt. Its population fluid and cantankerous, it was overdue for a royal stay entailing a mighty display of royal power. Moreover, by such obvious command of the center of his archdiocese, Isabel could further serve notice on Carrillo. Nor was it happenstance that the convocation coalesced with the work underway on the great monastery of San Juan de los Reyes.

On October 14, 1479, the Queen made a brilliant entry into the city with her infant son, Prince Juan; the swearing of the oath to him as her heir was the ostensible reason for calling Cortes. Isabel was also then again well advanced in pregnancy, and in Toledo in November she gave birth to an *infanta*, Juana. Fernando entered the city nine days after she did, his entry equally solemn but more exotic. For in his entourage was an elephant, the gift of an embassy from Cyprus, its presence evoking the imperial grandeur of Alexander the Great, the world conqueror who swept the East, as well as alluding to Hannibal's crossing the Alps and pointing up the sometime comparison of Fernando to Charlemagne, the Holy Roman Emperor, who had also received a gift elephant and who himself had consciously emulated both Alexander and Hannibal.

In Toledo the royal governor, or *corregidor*, who was Gómez Manrique, staged a very different spectacle with not so different a message. Fernando de Alarcón, Carrillo's alchemist and advisor, having confessed to "having caused many scandals in the kingdom and disturbing the peace," was beheaded so that his severed head dropped into a garbage basket, in order (says Pulgar) to engender the fear that leads to peace.

In yet another sort of ceremony, in Toledo's cathedral *grandes,* prelates, knights, and *ricos homes* assembled. And, while the Queen, the King, and the Prince stood before the high altar, one by one, on a missal held by a priest, they solemnly swore "to have for king of those kingdoms of Castile and León the Prince Don Juan, the first-born son of the King and Queen, after the days of the Queen, who was the proprietress of those kingdoms."[5]

Those spectacles but raised the curtain on the assertion of royal power that was to come. Isabel and Fernando meant the Cortes to serve not only, as was customary, to confirm succession and raise money—it voted them a subsidy of 104 million *maravedís*, huge even taking inflation into account—but also as a forum for unveiling their full program for reconstituting the realm. That program, while on all points carefully citing precedent and largely emanating from measures conceived in the previous two reigns, was an innovative one in that it would, as implemented in the years to come, bring about a revolution in the scope and efficacy of central government, converting realm to state. It incorporated the vision of strong personal monarchy propounded at midcentury, the orthodoxy demanded by the critics of Enrique's reign, and promises made in response to issues raised in 1476 at the Cortes in Madrigal. It was invested with the same vigorous spirit of straightening up morally, spiritually, and administratively then also propelling a royal scheme of ecclesiastical reform (of which more later) and the Inquisition, as well as contributing to the spread of rapidly hardening attitudes toward Jews and Muslims.

The Cortes was made up of the now-usual delegates from 16 or 17 royal towns, their selection itself strongly influenced by the crown. From the outset, the monarchs convinced them to sanction a great increase in royal authority and power by convincingly presenting their measures as long desired by everyone present and as highly beneficial to the realm as a whole. As usual, petitions of the cities were received and their representatives deliberated and were formally consulted, but for the last time in Castile. For central administration was fast becoming organized and procedures being worked out to put royal finances on such a firm basis that the crown could and would become more independent of all the estates, of nobles, clergy, and propertied townspeople—in effect dooming the Cortes. The very ordinances approved in 1480 helped to ensure that for the remainder of Isabel's reign the Cortes would have to be called solely to recognize changes in the order of royal succession.

Vital to efficacious central administration was the Royal Council. For decades its control had been the focus of contests among the great nobles, but all that was being changed. "In that Cortes of Toledo, in the royal palace

1. *Isabel, Queen of Castile. The Prado Palace, Madrid, attributed to Juan de Flandes. (Arxiu Mas, Barcelona)*

2. *Fernando of Aragón. (Staatliche Museen Preussischer Kulturbesitz zu Berlin, Gemäldegalerie)*

3. *The Tombs of Isabel of Castile and Fernando of Aragón, by Domenico Fancelli (1508–17). Royal Chapel, Granada. (Arxiu Mas, Barcelona)*

4. *Tomb of Juan II of Castile and Isabel of Portugal, by Gil de Siloe (completed 1495). Cartuja de Santa María de Miraflores (Burgos). (Arxiu Mas, Barcelona)*

5. *Miracle of the Loaves and Fishes. Juan de Flandes, court painter from 1496, places a younger Isabel on the ground listening to Jesus Christ; Fernando stands behind her. From the polyptych of Isabel of Castile. (Arxiu Mas, Barcelona)*

6. *Pedro González de Mendoza, Cardinal and Archbishop of Toledo, with Prince Juan and the* infantas *Isabel and Juana. (Arxiu Mas, Barcelona)*

7. *Juana, or possibly Catalina, by Juan de Flandes (circa 1496). (Thyssen-Bornemisza Collection, Lugano, Switzerland)*

8. *Francisco Jiménez de Cisneros as Archbishop of Toledo. Painted by Juan de Borgoña between 1509 and 1511. Sala Capitular, Toledo Cathedral. (Arxiu Mas, Barcelona)*

9. *The King and Queen praying before the Virgin and Child, with Prince Juan and the infanta Isabel, or perhaps Juana. Dominican in conception, behind them stand Saints Dominic and Thomas Aquinas. From the Convento de Santo Tomás, Avila, built by Tomás de Torquemada. The Prado, Madrid. (Arxiu Mas, Barcelona)*

10. *Joint coat-of-arms, held in the talons of the eagle of Saint John and flanked by the devices of the yoke and bundle of arrows caught in the Gordian knot. Detail of interior of San Juan de los Reyes, Toledo, by Juan Guas (before 1492). (Arxiu Mas, Barcelona)*

11. *The archangel Michael slays the dragon or apocalyptic beast, by Juan de Flandes. Diocesan Museum, Salamanca. (Arxiu Mas, Barcelona)*

12. Entering Granada. Relief by Felipe Bigarny, 1520–22. Royal Chapel. Granada. (Arxiu Mas, Barcelona)

where the King and Queen stayed, five councils sat in five apartments," wrote Pulgar, describing five subdivisions of the Royal Council, several of which would become completely separate entities by the end of the reign. One group handled affairs of state including relations with other monarchs and the papacy; its decisions were binding. It included some *grandes,* some royal advisors, the royal secretaries, and the King and Queen when matters warranted. A second, devoted to justice, heard petitions and cases and passed sentence. It was composed of prelates and *letrados.* Both of those subdivisions were to remain within the Royal Council, although justice would be shared with the royal chancery or *audiencia.* Two others would become separate councils. One of them was made up of knights and *letrados* native to Aragón, Catalonia, Sicily, and Valencia, and handled the business of those kingdoms; it would become the Council of Aragón. In the other sat the representatives of the *hermandades* of all the kingdom under their royal overseers. In the last chamber, which was to remain in the Royal Council, there gathered "the *contadores mayores* and officials of the books of the treasury and royal patrimony," who estimated revenues and assessed taxes, arranged for their farming, and received and recorded payments; these were at the core of the *Real Hacienda,* the royal treasury. Shortly too, another separate council would appear, that of the Inquisition. "And all these councils had recourse to the King and Queen with anything doubtful come before them. And their letters and provisions were of great importance, signed on the back by those of the councils, and signed inside by the King and Queen."[6] Isabel's loyal minions controlled each of those conciliar divisions; the Cardinal presided over those of state and justice.

That Royal Council, which advised the monarchs and was the highest court in the land as well as their secretariat, would henceforth, it was stipulated at Toledo, be made up of a prelate who would preside, three *caballeros,* and eight or nine *letrados,* its councillors to be joined on Fridays by the King and Queen. Only those ten members might vote, though other *grandes* or counselors might continue to attend. Thus, while monarchy and nobility in tandem continued to dominate the realm, their spheres of authority and power were more clearly delineated, and the nobility were kept at a remove from affairs of state. The days of Isabel's insistence on consulting the *grandes* on all matters of some moment had passed; indeed, she relied most heavily on a smaller, private *cámara,* a cabinet, made up of certain members of the Royal Council.

Lawyers were not only a majority on the council of state, but staffed the expanding administrative bureaucracy, which included too some lesser nobles as well. The royal secretaries in particular constituted an embryonic ministry and were influential through direct and continual contact with the King and Queen and through enjoying their favor and confidence. A later Mendoza would comment that the sovereigns "put the administration of justice and public affairs in the hands of *letrados,* whose profession was legal matters, middling people between the great and the small without offense to one nor the other."[7] Such people, he added, lived quiet, simple, honest lives. They did not visit nor take gifts nor form close friendships. They neither dressed nor spent extravagantly. They were moderate and humane.

While hindsight idealized his outlook, its substance was corroborated by Isabel's chroniclers. One of them, Lorenzo Galíndez de Carvajal, himself a *letrado* and member of her council, recalled that the Queen kept in a book the names of meritorious men of middling social background, talent, and moral rectitude, as a pool of worthies for all vacant posts, civil and ecclesiastic. Moreover, seeking trained administrators, she supported those prime sources of well-educated bureaucrats, the *colegios mayores*, schools within the universities. Thus later that year she and Fernando toured the University of Salamanca and the favor they showed it was commemorated on its facade, by a medallion bearing their portraits surrounded by a Greek inscription that translates as: "the Monarchs for the University; the University for the Monarchs."

LAWS AND PROFITS

Some couplets dedicated to *la reyna doña Isabel* sagely referred to an old saw in order to state a pairing becoming common throughout Europe, "There law goes, where kings command." For Castile, the ordinances of the Cortes of Toledo were in effect the constitution of an emerging nation-state that was also a near-absolute monarchy, and they were the work of royal lawyers experienced in promoting royal interests. Thus Alfonso Díaz de Montalvo, one of Isabel's two secretaries, who three decades earlier at the behest of her father had found law to support royal authority as absolute and drawn up the crown's indictment of Alvaro de Luna, in 1480 was ordered to prepare a single compendium of Castilian law. His compilation, completed in 1484 and printed in eight large volumes in 1485, proved less a collection of existing laws than a regalist code with imperial Roman origins. For as Montalvo himself explained it, he had gathered royal ordinances and pragmatics, but omitted "laws superfluous, useless, revoked, derogated, and those which are not or should not be in use, conforming with the use of the court and royal chancery."[8] Each municipality was ordered to have a copy. That code, put in force as supplementary law by Isabel, became a basis of juridical action for over fifty years. Such a body of ostensible precedent was to both obviate having the Cortes promulgate laws and elevate reliance upon royal decrees. Similarly, administration of royal justice was subsequently expanded by introducing a second *audiencia*, or tribunal of justice (which sat first in Cuidad Real, then in Granada), and through reinvigorating the original royal chancery at Valladolid which, from 1480 on, sat permanently in the mansion where Isabel and Fernando were married.

The greatest coup of 1480 was reclaiming the royal patrimony, the numerous territories and revenues so generously dispensed as *mercedes* by both Enrique and Alfonso, a move valuable to the crown both for the revenues regained and the principle imposed. Most such grants existed in the form of *situados*, liens on specific indirect royal imposts yielding income, or as *juros*, which were annuities, transferrable rights presented to individuals or institutions, for term, life, or in perpetuity. Both types were royal permits to receive annual sums on revenues produced by a stipulated *renta pública* such as specified *alcabalas*, sales taxes. Those outstanding obligations cut deeply into the funds at royal disposal. Moreover, by 1480 some *rentas* were mortgaged so far beyond what they produced that Isabel had ordered payments to bondholders confined to a proportional distribution.

At Toledo, all such grants made by Alfonso were rescinded, and those adjudged bestowed from 1464 through force or deceit exercised upon Enrique were ordered separated from those awarded properly by him. That formula had been proposed by the Cardinal. Among other things, its adoption says something about Isabel'a attitude to the recent past, for it assumed that the civil war had been an assault of nobles on monarchy. The *mercedes* reform was in fact just the reverse, and, in signalling no high opinion of the validity of either Enrique's nor Alfonso's reigns, it buoyed the idea of Isabel's reign as the one most validly stemming from that of her father.

At bottom, the arrangements of 1480 were presented as an exchange. The monarchs pardoned all nobles and high clergy on the wrong side in the late war, assured to them their property and positions, and in 1486 would guarantee their holdings in perpetuity through confirming the institution of *mayorzgo*, the right to entail estates. Nobles were to return part of the rents acquired from 1464 on; the crown would recognize and legitimate all the rest. In accepting that arrangement, the nobility acknowledged royal authority and jurisdiction as superior to its own and the royal right to create law and administer justice centrally; the crown affirmed the economic and social sphere of the nobles, who retained much *de facto* local and regional power, and broad political influence. At Toledo, Isabel both reassured and constrained the nobility.

In implementing the retrieval of *mercedes*, she left to the many-faceted Talavera the sorting out of licit from illegal titles. He sent out royal *pesquisidores*, investigators, who traveled for three years ascertaining who held royal territories or enjoyed usufruct of royal rents and in what amounts. He then scrupulously applied the criteria decided upon and his report became the basis of final settlement. In the end, roughly half the grants were allowed to stand. Notable among those losing least was the Cardinal. Conversely, Cabrera and Bobadilla gave up an amount in *juros* only exceeded by the loss sustained by Beltrán de la Cueva, but the Cabreras were granted the *marquesado* of Moya and Beltrán did well as a leading lieutenant in the Granada campaigns. Isabel opposed in general revoking grants made to monasteries, hospitals, and the poor. That subsequently nobles, treasury officials, and taxfarmers connived to circumvent some royal decisions then taken and that they continued to siphon off some royal income did not heavily detract from the impact of the exercise of authority demonstrated at Toledo and accepted in that restructuring of crown debt.

That the three-pronged basis of power in Castile—monarchy, nobility, and towns—was well understood by the monarchs was indicated there as well, in the extension of royal control of municipalities. Castile's cities, experiencing with peace greater well-being and a surge in growth, and seeing in the crown their best insurance of continuing protection against encroaching nobles, when given the choice of relinquishing their *juros*, often uncollectible, or of facing new exactions, gave up most of their *juros*. Concomitantly, royal *pesquisidores* were sent out to municipalities in order to restore old boundaries encroached upon by nobles and to hear complaints against *corregidores*. And *corregidores*, those royal watchdogs who played balance of power between urban councils and the lords or abbots often dominating them, were in 1480 ordered situated in all cities of the realm, "so that nothing may be done to our prejudice and that of our jurisdiction without it then being remedied or reported to us."[9] Talavera was put in charge of those investigations too, and Isabel ordered he also have his agents recompense individuals for wartime losses of horses and other goods, and provide for the wives and children of men killed in the late war.

Currency reform also received attention. The stay in Seville, that center of the trade in African gold, may have influenced Isabel to prefer gold to silver. Whether or no, the monarchs imposed a gold standard, justifying it as holding down prices after years of currency clipping, devaluation, inflation, and loss of confidence in Castilian coinage. They confirmed in Cortes prohibition of exports of both gold and silver, setting a death penalty for taking out of Castile over 500 *doblas*. In 1481 they ordered *excelentes*, equivalents of the Venetian ducat, coined in Valencia, both to promote international exchange and as a way to strengthen the money of account, the *maravedí*. Minting, it is worth remembering, was a regalia of the crown and itself a producer of income, including a fee for coinage. They also had currency devalued. One effect was to raise the value of gold and so benefit the royal treasury since it had, foresightedly, put in reserves of that precious metal. Finances, it should be noted, had remained in the hands of those three time-tested stalwarts, the *contadurías mayores* Cárdenas, Chacón, and Rodrigo de Ulloa; Chacón, moreover, held the post of *mayordomo mayor*, head of the royal household, which included oversight of the royal *hacienda*, or estate, that was indistinguishable from the treasury of Castile.

Outlined at Toledo, the reorganization of Castilian finances afterwards resulted in a great increase in royal revenue; on the rise since 1477, it had more than doubled by 1482. Ordinary royal income was, increasingly, coming from commerce and additional monies from the *tercias reales*, two-ninths of the ecclesiastical tithe, and from levies on Jewish and Muslim communities; two-thirds of all royal income came from central Castile and Seville. Still, leaks occurred: there remained the thorny problem of the many nobles who considered the *alcabala* in their jurisdictions their own, and a third of Castile's population resided in noble jurisdictions. In addition, among the consequences of the measures of 1480, the *Mesta*, the association of owners of great flocks, became extremely powerful, especially from 1485 when a royal councillor was made *juez pesquidor* of the sheepwalks, succeeding the Count of Buendía, Carrillo's brother.

THE QUEEN AND THE CHURCH

Repeated at Toledo was the familiar assertion that the monarchs had the place of God on earth and were to function as His viceroys. Coupled with that assumption of divine mandate was a belief in the Queen's right, indeed responsibility, to intervene in religious matters. Not only had the decision to hold Cortes in Toledo signaled the containing of its archbishop, it had also accorded with Isabel's larger program of ecclesiastical reform, with its dual purpose of cleansing the church in Spain and tightening royal control of it. That program involved redrawing the boundaries of bishoprics, notably Toledo but others as well, and, although she could not seize ecclesiastical property as she had that of great nobles, she battled with the papacy for the right to name bishops.

Through the centuries of reconquest, Spanish clergy had loyally supported the crown, in close working relationship and mutual reliance. Her father had let the pope know that by custom the king had the right to name masters of religious orders, and that church *cabildos* could select bishops and customarily took into consideration royal preferences. That was one custom that Enrique IV strove to uphold. As for Juan II of Aragón, he had simply and arbitrarily named bishops at his pleasure, among them both a son and a grandson of his own born out of wedlock. The agreement between Isabel and Fernando immediately after she took the crown had stated that archbishoprics, bishoprics, masterships, and so on be requested in both their names but "at the will of the Queen" and that those put forth be *letrados*. Six months later they jointly took a firm stand in instructing their ambassador to Rome to make certain the pope bestowed no Spanish benefices save at their request, as in accord with ancient custom. They would take much the same line in negotiations concerning naming a new bishop for Toledo on Carrillo's death in 1482, and would then make the additional argument that the sees held castles that could not be put in the hands of untrustworthy persons, especially foreigners. Isabel, having stated that innovating concept as hallowed tradition, would then seek juridical basis for it, charging a *letrado* of her Council to find canonical titles.

Hernando de Talavera had in 1475 drawn up for her criteria for provision of bishoprics. They were to go to honest, lettered native Castilians of middle-class background, that is, no longer to foreigners or powerful nobles. He then presented that view as the royal one in July 1478 to the Castilian clergy meeting in Seville. In turn, its being accepted there without demur provided a valuable endorsement and a basis for future precedent; some ancient custom began at that point.

Before the issue of ecclesiastical patronage was raised at Toledo, tension with the papal *curia* had broken into open conflict. In 1479 when, without consulting Isabel and Fernando, Sixtus IV bestowed the bishopric of Cuenca on a cardinal-nephew of his, Isabel sent an embassy insisting that bishoprics and benefices given to foreigners be revoked, and that no episcopal appointment should be made in the future without having been proposed by *los reyes*. "And this," she directed her envoys, "you must procure with all insistence because we do not intend to accept anything else."[10] The following year in Cortes her argument was made equally aggressively: it was claimed that the pope would not make appointments in Castile's interest and that absentee foreigners kept worthy Spaniards out of sees; and she added that the monarchs knew better than the popes who was worthy. The ordinance of that Cortes forbade foreigners to hold benefices in Castile.

Two years later a concordat with the papacy was signed, demonstrating royal will having effect: the long-time royal confidante and sometime confessor, fray Alonso de Burgos, then became Bishop of Cuenca, the papal nephew received Salamanca as consolation, and Rodrigo Borja was named Bishop of Cartagena. Victory was not total: the pope, while conceding he would receive the royal preferences for episcopal appointments, retained the right to provide them. Yet Isabel did then get from him the *Cruzada,* the permission to sell bulls of crusade, indulgences, in Spain, with the proceeds to go to the war there against the Moor, and she got a tithe on the rents of the clergy as well; within the agreement, she then ceded back a third of each for the war against the Turks. That accord was signed in Córdoba on July 3, 1482. Within days Carrillo died, evoking from the sovereigns little show of grief but another rapid shifting of ecclesiastical personnel; they immediately sent a list of candidates back to Rome with the papal envoy. Everyone agreed that Pedro González de Mendoza become Archbishop of Toledo. Both crown and papacy were beholden to him for mediating the dispute over Cuenca and most other matters.

Defense, control of great revenues, and residence in the diocese were arguments Isabel made for choosing as bishops Spaniards by birth. Conversely, bishops, including Mendoza, were told to reside in their sees. The queen also wanted bishops celibate, although here tradition was strongly against her; the Cardinal himself had three recognized sons. Undaunted, looking ahead, and enlisting his aid and that of Talavera, Isabel encouraged establishing seminaries to train Spanish clergy, who were in turn expected to exemplify and instruct the populace in morality, and she chose for ecclesiastical offices earnest and obscure but gifted friars who lent tone and swelled the ranks of the upright and the loyal.

Yet, despite her hewing to the principle that bishops reside in their dioceses, they were expected to appear at court and some were employed there. And those not trusted, notably the Bishop of Burgos, Luis de Acuña, Carrillo's brother, who had been on the other side in the civil wars, was in fact kept with the court for years, running royal errands and thus away from making mischief in his base of power, until his death in 1495. She also had assemblies of Castile's clergy meet periodically, the first that at Seville in 1478. That council not only supported the royal prerogative, but also expressed great concern, as did the crown, at the dismal moral state of the Roman curia.

Throughout her lifetime, Isabel worked to develop a national church dependent on the crown, at the expense of regional, episcopal, and papal power. She would increasingly promote clerical reform, and she and her people were to continue to come into conflict with clergy in matters of jurisdiction: in disputes between clergy and royal *corregidores,* in attempts to make royal justice superior in civil cases, and in conflict over competence in cases mixing civil and religious elements. They would clash over a host of jurisdictional boundaries: in bringing temporal cases to ecclesiastical tribunals, in ecclesiastical authorities imprisoning laymen, in cases of commercial debt, in the excommunicating and interdict of royal officials and municipalities for defending the royal prerogative, and in cases involving the finances of churchmen. For, although sincere in desiring a morally upright clergy, she was moving the crown into what had been ecclesiastical and papal territory, and the most efficacious manner of doing it was in the name of reform. While there is no doubt that Isabel was devout, her thrust for ecclesiastical reform went beyond personal piety. From the next pope, Innocent VIII, she and Fernando extracted high appointments for native sons, favorite ones: the Archbishop of Seville for Diego Hurtado de Mendoza, a nephew of the Cardinal, and Alonso de Burgos proceeded from Cuenca to Palencia, while Talavera was confirmed as Bishop of Avila.

FIRST, THE TURKS

In Spain, the papacy had campaigned in the 1460s and again in the 1470s to sell those indulgences, bulls of crusade, for war against the Ottoman Turks. And as Isabel came to the throne, Rodrigo Borja had been enforcing a subsidy on the clergy of a third of their tithes for that crusade. The preaching of crusade against the Turks at that time, and again by the papal legate in 1479 when preachers were also advocating an Inquisition, contributed as well to intensifying feeling against Jews, *conversos*, and all Muslims, as did restrictive measures, particularly against Jews, emanating from the Cortes of 1476 and 1480.

The opening of a campaign for religious reform and exclusivity was paralleled by the soliciting of support for holy war. It was time to reconstitute Spain, to pursue the reconquest. The royal intention to go to war against the kingdom of Granada was announced dramatically at Toledo in 1480, the occasion presenting itself in the investiture of the new master of the order of Santiago. He was Alonso de Cárdenas, a valiant captain in Isabel's cause during the late war and the uncle of Gutierre "who had reached great *privanza* with the Queen." One day soon after the the Cortes had convened, the new master arrived for solemn mass at the cathedral, striding in with

400 commanders and knights of Santiago, a veritable army in white habits emblazoned with red crosses, who marched down the main aisle to the high altar between the two choirs of the church. Then Cárdenas alone entered the choir where the King and Queen waited, and fell to his knees. Isabel and Fernando solemnly gave into his keeping the banners of Saint James—"in that bestowal was given to understand that they made him Captain and standard-bearer of the apostle Santiago, patron of the Spains"—and they enjoined him "to go with God against the Moors, enemies of our holy Catholic faith."[11] The Master kissed their hands and promised that indeed he and all his knights would go to the land of the Moors and war on them, thereby to serve God and themselves and to fulfill the statutes of his order. The monarchs then assured him that they were planning to declare war against the Moors soon, but that first they must send an armada against the Turks.

Mehmet II, "a great prince of the Muslims, lord of a great part of Asia," on his death in May 1480 was poised to invade Italy. Since taking Constantinople in 1453, the Ottoman Turks had spread over the Crimea and the Black Sea, into the northern Aegean and the Balkans, and they had moved westward in the Mediterranean. The Grand Turk having, as Bernaldez construed it, "died and descended to hell," his successor, Bayazit II, immediately launched a double offensive, by land into Trieste, and by sea laying siege to the island of Rhodes. But, says Bernaldez, it did not please God [that Rhodes] should fall, "and some Turks confessed that in that battle a very frightening knight, dressed in white, had vanquished them, and they said it was San Juan, the glorious apostle, whose order held that city, come to defend it."[12] In August came dire news: the Turks had seized Otranto, in Naples, establishing a base in western Europe and putting to the sword most of its Christians and all its priests, although taking into captivity the young people, male and female. They had sacked the city, left a garrison of 5000, and were thought to be preparing a fleet to invade Sicily.

A great terror gripped Europe. Sicily's sovereigns, Fernando and Isabel, "ordered daily prayer to God in the churches of their kingdoms, because it should help to lift His anger and free the Christians from the forces and power of that enemy."[13] And they immediately requisitioned from merchants of Burgos arms and ammunition—lances, and large shields, body armor, helmets, and crossbows, artillery, and military stores. Receiving from the national council of the *hermandad* a petition, surely solicited, to form an "armada for the [Mediterranean] sea for the service of God and the exaltation of the faith and the royal service," Isabel ordered allocated to that purpose all the *hermandad* contributions of Galicia, Cantabria, the lands of Medina Sidonia and Cádiz, and the towns of Moguer, Palos, and Santa María del Puerto, as well as confiscations made by the Inquisition. And she immediately sent Quintanilla, the *hermandad's contador mayor*, and its governors north to Vizcaya, Guipúzcoa, and the mountains of Asturias, to commandeer ships and gather men, supplies, arms, and artillery, to ready an armada to protect Sicily and support the Neapolitans in retaking Otranto.

The inhabitants of those northern places, suspicious of that royal delegation and zealous for their traditional liberties, were brought around by Quintanilla, his rhetoric as reported by Pulgar an indication of royal tactics to come. "He changed suspicion into pride and their excuses into extreme diligence," convincingly arguing that he and the others had in fact come to protect their liberties. He exhorted them: how holy the enterprise, how ungodly the Turk shedding Christian blood, how great the honor of serving king, country, and religion. He praised them: how wise they were in navigation, how valiant in battle at sea. And he appealed to their honor: surely they were better than the Portuguese, so why would they remain sulking at home and allow the Portuguese to reap honor at sea? Seventy ships sailed for Naples on June 22, 1481. They arrived with their crews decimated by plague, and to find Otranto retaken and its Duke selling the vanquished garrison into slavery—many of them into the galleys—and also selling back to the Turks their artillery. Although Bayazit's energies were deflected by court intrigue, halting for the time being the Turkish advance, there remained the pervasive sense of threat to Christendom, a great fear, which Isabel and Fernando directed masterfully against Granada.

CLAIMING AND RECLAIMING

The King and Queen, explained Pulgar, "knowing that no war should be started except for the faith or for security, always had in mind the great thought of conquering the kingdom of Granada and of casting out from all the Spains the rule (*señorío*) of the Moor and the name of *Mohamat*."[14] War against Granada had been promised in their wedding *capitulaciones* and civil war been justified as prelude to that highest of goals: it had been argued, in proposing the *hermandad* be extended into a national military force, that such a marshalling of soldiers along with supporting funds, even a general mobilization, was necessary to prepare the country for war against the Moor. Readying for that enterprise had been proclaimed too in the measures proposed at Toledo against heretic and infidel, and of course in negotiations with the papacy for retaining crusading funds in Spain.

Palencia, in the preface to his chronicle of the war of Granada, echoed royal cognizance of the general satisfaction felt that so lofty an aspiration so long advocated by Castile's monarchy had become an immediate project: "The pleasure with which I begin the narrative of the campaigns against the Granadan Moors, long interrupted and today at last industriously resumed, is only comparable to the repugnance with which in other times I saw myself obliged to write the annals of happenings sufficiently shameful." Castile had progressed from ignominious civil strife, a sure sign of the frown of divine providence, to glorious endeavor: "Nevertheless this same misfortune awakened the beneficient energies of the illustrious couple, Don Fernando V of Aragón and Doña Isabel, renowned heir to León and Castile. On them Providence appears to have bestowed the gifts necessary to dispel the inveterate habits of anarchy of the natives and to vanquish the tenacious enemies of Christianity in Spain."[15] Palencia had at last come to respect the Queen. Yet it was a sign of the times too that in 1480 during Cortes in Toledo, Isabel dropped that outspoken curmudgeon as official chronicler and named the more subtle and attuned Pulgar instead, the reason given that Palencia would not present his writing for official review.

Toledo had been a triumph for the King and especially for Castile's proprietress Queen. Leaving that city in August, it was time to carry out three projects necessary for completing royal domination of the peninsula: to implement the ordinances of that Cortes in Castile, to firmly attach Aragón, and to gain Granada. Portugal was assured through the engagement of the *infanta* Isabel to João's son and heir, Afonso. Fernando would go to Aragón, Isabel to Medina del Campo. But beforehand the royal family stopped at Arévalo, to visit her mother and carry out the pleasant task of reclaiming that town of her youth, bestowed by Enrique on Alvaro de Stúñiga, whose lieutenant had so humiliatingly turned her away that day in 1469. Stúñiga's widow, the redoubtable Leonor de Pimentel, now relinquished it in exchange for Plasencia and the mastership of Alcántara for her underage son, if with the proviso that the crown would retain legal authority over the Order.

From September through January Isabel stayed in Medina del Campo. Attributed to her is the conceit that she would be glad if God were to give her three sons so that one could inherit her kingdom, another be archbishop of Toledo, and the third become an *escribano*, a notary, of Medina del Campo, for such people validated all business contracts and Isabel well knew a great deal of lucrative business was transacted in Medina del Campo. It was an ideal headquarters for preparing financing and provisioning for the upcoming campaign against Granada. And as the year ended she fulfilled, far less enthusiastically, the wrenching obligation of sending off her elder daughter to Portugal as hostage to the peace.

On April 9, she joined Fernando, who was now Fernando V of Aragón, in Calatayud to open the Corts of that kingdom. Although no woman could succeed to Aragón's crown, Isabel became co-regent, governor, and general administrator there, designated by its new king as an *"otro yo"*—"another I"—whether he was present or absent. And on May 19 she saw her son sworn heir to Aragón's crown. That month too, presaging events to come, there arrived at court some leading, captive, and ostensibly converted Canarians, *guanches*, whom the monarchs declared to be under their protection, free from enslavement, and parallel in privilege to their Castilian subjects.

In June, the royal family solemnly entered Zaragoza, the venerable heart of Aragón, then while Fernando progressed through his new realm Isabel remained in Zaragoza's splendid *mudéjar* Aljafería palace, of special importance to her. For it was the birthplace of her ancestor, Santa Isabel, who had been *infanta* of Aragón, Queen of Portugal, and first in the long line of its Isabels. Isabel of Castile and her husband would give attention to restoring that palace so evocative of their ancient, honorable, and intertwined heritage. She rejoined Fernando in Barcelona on June 28, her presence during the next three months helping to finally bring that most recalcitrant of cities to obedience and even affection. From there they proceeded through Tarragona to Valencia where, at year's end, they heard that the Granadans had stolen a march, that they had taken by surprise the frontier fortress-town of Zahara.

Palencia told of Zahara's *alcaide* having gone to Seville, "where he was giving himself up to a licentious life," so that "the sagacious Moors, advised of this negligence" on the dark and stormy night of December 27, 1481, scaled the wall of a part thought inaccesible, overpowered the fortress without the least resistance, and before dawn were masters of the village. They carried off all its inhabitants and left a strong garrison "for the grave harm and ruin of the Christians in those regions."[16] The news was received in Castile—said Bernaldez who thus began what is the most complete chronicle of the war—as a spark to kindling gathered in a basket of dried straw and heaped high.

Retaliation was swift: "knowing the desire of the monarchs to seize some place or fortress of the Granadans before declaring war on them openly," and resolved to satisfy them—as Palencia put it—on February 28, Diego de Merlo, the Marqués of Cádiz, other Andalusians, and some knights of the Queen's guard seized the treasure town of Alhama, thirty miles from Granada itself.

By then, Isabel and Fernando were back in Medina del Campo, turning the surrounding fields into barracks and exercise grounds for footsoldiers and light cavalry, chiefly men mustered by the *hermandades* of the towns. They were dispatching orders for gunpowder and military provisions, and for great lombards. And now they had war against the Moor cried along the entire frontier from Lorca to Tarifa.

To Granada, they sent a *pro forma* demand for the customary tribute owed by its kings to those of Castile, although in March 1481 they had renewed the treaty with Granada for a year, without tribute, and although it had in fact been paid only sporadically from the time of Fernando III and never to Isabel. There had been three treaties with Granada's king since her accession; none had mentioned tribute; now Abū al-Ḥasan not surprisingly refused to pay it. Bernaldez has attributed to him yet another memorable response of doubtful veracity but enduring legend, its tone appropriate to sentiments current on both sides: the Granadan ruler replied that those who had paid tribute were now dead, and so were those whom they had paid.[17] He was right, but it did not matter.

In 1480 at Toledo the monarchs had, while reclaiming *mercedes* and announcing effective extension of royal authority, promised to Castile's nobles, cities, and people the imminent probability of material and spiritual national enrichment in taking up the conquest of Granada. Now the climate was propitious, and divine sanction was assumed.

12

The Queen's War I
1482–1485

By the solicitude of this Queen was begun, and by her diligence was continued, the war against the Moors, until all the kingdom of Granada was won.

Anonymous[1]

. . . the towns suffered great fatigues, both because they favored the war against the Moors and because the Queen was very feared and no one dared to contradict her orders.

Pulgar[2]

GRANADA

IN February 1482, Isabel called to war all knights holding royal lands and subsidies. Footsoldiers and light cavalry from the *meseta* towns and from the north arrived at Medina, as did Aragonese and Swiss mercenaries. Some of the Queen's jewels then went to Valencia, to be held in the sacristy of its cathedral under triple lock as surety for loans; she would send yet others over the years of war. Fernando left for Andalusia in mid-March. Isabel tarried, not feeling well. She was expecting twins in June. Should one be a son, he was to be named King of Granada.

In early April, having sent *corregidores* into key towns and cities and left the Admiral with royal powers in Castile, she too went south. Stopping in Toledo at Easter, she presided over the ingathering of magnates and their *mesnadas* customary to royal campaign, welcoming Gutierre de Cárdenas, Chacón, Cabrera, the Cardinal, and everyone important who was ever on any side of a Castilian embroilment. Jubilation was general at the news of Alhama; Pulgar wrote of everyone seeing in the destruction of its populace God's wrath and justice, a warning to sinners.

It was from the outset Isabel's war. Aware of her great sufficiencies, Pulgar wrote, "gave over and entrusted to her all things," relying on her proven ability and good natural intelligence. With Otranto rid of the Turks and France and Portugal declared allies, their majesties could go against "the ferocious enemy of Catholicism" who for centuries had dominated so much territory properly claimed by Castile. As Isabel observed, it would also keep her nobles busy.

The city of Granada and its surrounding *vega*, countryside, constituted "one of the richest irrigated places in Europe."[3] A town under the Romans, Granada came into its own as an emirate or kingdom only in the thirteenth century when Muslim power in Spain splintered and the Christians streamed into Andalusia. With the fall of the kingdoms of Córdoba and Valencia, Muhammad I al-Ghālib firmly established the Nasrid dynasty, Granada's greatest, after negotiating a treaty with the Castilian conqueror, Fernando III, promising him tribute and military aid, and providing it during the conquest of Seville. His successor, backed by the sultan at Fez, reversed course by attacking the Christians. Thereafter, relations seesawed. They were at their friendliest in the later fourteenth century, when Muhammad V sent workmen from the Alhambra to Pedro the Cruel for his palace in Seville's *alcázar*. He also sent Pedro three galleys to use against Aragón and 1500 *jinetes* to employ against his half-brother, Enrique de Trastámara, who nevertheless triumphed.

The kingdom of Granada embraced the present provinces of Granada, Málaga, and Almería, the southernmost area of Spain. Two hundred miles long and 65 miles wide, the size of Switzerland, it was protected by mountains on three sides and the Mediterranean sea on the fourth. It had 14 cities, 100 fortified towns, and in 1481 perhaps 300,000 people, many of them refugees originally from places taken by the Christians. The 50,000 inhabitants of the city of Granada were so crowded in, it was said, that 'three men had to share the ownership of one fig tree.' It housed not only Iberian Muslims, many of them refugees, but Africans, Christian renegades, many Jews, and some Genoese merchants; there was a larger community of Genoese in its principal port, Málaga.

Above this densely packed last Islamic refuge in Iberia, emblematic of "the distilled splendor of al-Andalus," stood what a contemporary described as the stupendous towers and marvelous walls, harmoniously constructed, of the fortified administrative complex, the Alhambra. Dominating the city, the Alhambra contained not only the palace but also the mansions of courtiers and high functionaries, as well as mosques and schools, workshops, markets, grain warehouses, barracks, stables, and an armory.

Granada was part of an intricate network of trade and communications uniting east and west. An Egytian cotton merchant, 'Abd al-Bāsiṭ, coming to the city from Alexandria aboard a Genoese ship in 1465–66, wrote of his delight in this western emporium which conserved the heritage of seven centuries of al-Andalus. It reminded him of Damascus, so rich in splendid buildings and monuments and in religious congregations, literary culture, and technical skill. It had running water, and poets, scientists, and artists, "among them the best men of our time," and an impressive garrison with (an exaggerated) 80,000 archers.[4]

On the hill opposite the Alhambra, he climbed winding streets and admired the wares of the Albaicín, an autonomous urban area with its own governors and justices, a quarter where artisans produced brocades and taffetas, woollens and linens, leather, ceramics, jewelry, and weapons—all shipped from Málaga or carried overland into Castile, destined for other European lands of the eastern Mediterranean or traded to the Maghrib (northwestern Africa) in exchange for Sudanese gold. From the heights of the Alhambra, 'Abd al-Bāsiṭ admired the *vega* abounding in fruit, vines, and fig trees, irrigated by the Genil river, and the soft and agreeable odors rising from vegetable and flower gardens along the river Darro. Yet he sensed uneasiness among Granada's inhabitants, for the nearby infidel had taken the greater part of the land of al-Andalus and many of the fortified cities renowned throughout Islam.

Frontier raids, ambushes, and skirmishes were part of everyday life. Towns on both sides of the extensive frontier, Muslim and Christian, retained justices specially charged with negotiating with their counterparts concerning stolen people or cattle or other grievances. It was a *de facto* and edgy coexistence punctuated by spurts of hostility, which at times took on the aspect of sporting contests between members of two societies geared for war. Muslims and Christians alike excelled as warriors, subscribed to the ideal of a chivalric code of behavior, and participated in games honing military skills; both celebrated special occasions with bullfights and *juego de cañas*, a tourney of two teams on horseback fighting with reeds and leather shields. Popular frontier ballads conveyed sincere respect for one another's chivalric qualities, affirming the adage that a worthwhile enemy was one equal in valor.

Even so, Granada was far weaker than its neighbors. It had endured chiefly by playing off Morocco against Castile, and it was beset internally by factional struggle. Since the days of Fernando III, Castile had viewed Granada as by rights a tribute-paying vassal kingdom and it is never clear whether royal sallies against it, including the campaigns of Isabel's predecessors, Juan II and Enrique IV, were designed as steps to its conquest or pressure to keep friendly dynasts on its throne and extract tribute from them. Tribute or no, Granada profited Castile's crown by contributing to the flow of trade; it sent Castile silk, sugar, leatherwork, and African gold. Yet recently the warrior-emir, Abū al-Ḥasan Alī, had attacked bordering Christian settlements during civil war in Castile, raiding, burning, and carrying off many Christian captives, undeterred by treaties he made with Isabel and Fernando in 1475, 1478, and 1481. Those treaties, after all, did not cover such minor incursions; customarily, sieges of three days or less and forces not publicly called up did not count, and such indeed were the taking of Zahara and Alhama. By 1482, however, Isabel was determined to complete the Christian reconquest and considered that the best defense against advance of the arch-foe, Islam, both Moors and Turks, was ridding the peninsula of the Muslim presence and moving into Africa. The situation within Granada was propitious.

Abu al-Ḥasan Alī, though esteemed as a brave warrior, also delighted in sensual living, imposed burdensome taxes, and neglected government, or so said his opponents. On becoming king in 1463 he had renounced his wife Fatima, the daughter of one previous ruler and the widow of another, for a young Christian captive, Isabel de Solís. Fatima, who had borne him two sons, became the soul of the opposition. The depth of distress within Granada at the loss of Alhama—its impact finding echo in a ballad of lament, *"ay de mi Alhama"*—allowed Fatima and her supporters to seize the moment, evict the old king, and replace him with her elder son, Muhammad XI, known as Boabdil. As a result, Granada was rent by civil strife through the 1480s to the advantage of Castile. (It is worth mention that remarkably similar, and at least equally useful to Castilians, would be the political situation later encountered among Aztec and Inca in America.)

MUSTERING: 1482

In the Christian camp, there was worry whether Alhama, so deep within Granadan territory, could be held. Isabel refused to listen to any suggestion that it could not. She well knew, Pulgar explains, that since she and Fernando had decided to proceed with conquering the kingdom, "and since that city was the first that was won, that it would be imputed to cowardice if it were abandoned."[5] Accordingly, in mid-May 1482 Fernando provisioned and reinforced Alhama's garrison--of 400 *hermandad* lances and captains, and 1000 foot, according to Pulgar—and 40,000 mules carried in enough supplies for three months.

In Córdoba, a council of war, overriding a suggestion by Cádiz to invest Málaga, decided to besiege the smaller town of Loja. Isabel made ready. Immediately, she assessed all cities, villages, and religious orders a stipulated number of knights and foot and told them to bring lombards and much gunpowder. She also assessed them specific quantities of bread, wine, cattle, salt, and pigs, commanding that half be delivered to the encampment before Loja by the end of June and the other half in July, adding the inducement that "each might sell at the best price he could get." Hearing the Granadans had sent messengers throughout Africa seeking aid, an armada, including some Genoese carracks, was sent to patrol the Strait of Gibraltar. Short of money, yet desiring the greatest control possible, she and Fernando relied on the *hermandades* and the municipal councils to provide soldiers, for the armies of the *grandes* were costly, heavily weighted to cavalry, and ultimately not the crown's to command. She found the cities and towns disappointingly reluctant to comply with royal quotas, and the army assembled in Córdoba smaller than planned.

On June 28, as Fernando prepared to depart, Isabel went into labor, at the council table. She gave birth to a third daughter and a stillborn female twin. The surviving child, in a marked departure from giving family names, was baptized María, demonstrating devotion to the cult of Holy Mary, most likely in her guise as Protectress of the Armies.

Many people, said Palencia, saw in the death of one twin a bad omen. And hindsight once again did not fail him, for from the time Fernando left two days later, Isabel received nothing but bad news. Cádiz had warned that their force was too small to invest Loja, and on making camp he informed Fernando that the site chosen was too low and too narrow. Another seasoned warrior, Alfonso de Aragón, commanding the *hermandad* recruits, warned the king that the men were undisciplined, that no provision had been made for an attack from Loja, and that food was in short supply. When Fernando ordered camp moved, the Moors attacked and the Castilians, panicking, ignored Fernando's order to hold their ground. He, refusing to retreat, fought furiously and nearly alone, until Cádiz rode in and pulled him to safety. Some 1000 Christians were taken prisoner, many more died. Fernando returned to Córdoba, sadder but wiser.

Isabel was immensely distressed, "because with great diligence she had worked to provide all necessary things, and for the pride the Moors took in seeing themselves so soon free." Nonetheless, recounts Pulgar, she hid her feelings, so that "no one could tell from her words or actions."[6] She now knew much more of war than she had six years ago when she berated all concerned for retreating from Toro. From then on, says Bernaldez, rancor mounted against the Moor, and great engines of war were ordered, including many catapults. Fortunately, Spanish artisans, profiting from the European-wide increase in metal production and technological improvements in mining, were even then shifting from the casting of bells to bronze guns and from the forging of iron utensils to wrought-iron ordnance.

If there was bitterness at court over defeat by the infidel at Loja, there was satisfaction at the extirpation of heresy in nearby Seville. During August and September the Inquisition "burned in Seville or submitted to diverse tortures many *conversos*, and from day to day their perverse errors became more patent and the punishments were repeated."[7] In 1483, the monarchs and the Inquisition ordered the Jews expelled from all Andalusia.

Late that summer, Fernando again reinforced and provisioned Alhama and he laid waste swaths of Granada's countryside, already suffering from poor crops, as was all Andalusia that year. He and Isabel moved north in October, stopping at Guadalupe, and that winter, from Madrid, they gave attention to international matters, arranging a league with Milan, Florence, Ferrera, Naples, and the papacy, against France. Negotiations to have England join, while unsuccessful, did affirm Isabel's tenacity in their course. Her envoy then told Richard III that she "was turned in her heart from England in time past" for the unkindness shown her by the late king, Edward IV, "whom God pardon, for his refusing her and taking to wife a widow of England."[8] Moreover, while exploring closer ties to Flanders, which would offset France and establish an Atlantic connection desired by

Burgos merchants and Basque seamen, the monarchs opened discussion with an envoy of Maximilian of Habsburg about the possibility of marriage between one of their daughters and his son Philip, the heir to Flanders.

Looking toward the next spring's campaign, Isabel was cheered by a subsidy voted by the clergy and by promise of receipts arriving from what was to prove the greatest source of royal revenue, returns from the sale of bulls of crusade. In Castile, the business of those indulgences was turned over to the new Bishop of Avila, Talavera. A Valencian, Luis de Santángel, received that same charge in Aragón. Then named too, as a collector for the papacy of both the tithe and *cruzada*, was a Genoese resident in Castile, Francisco Pinelo, associated with the papal envoy, the Genoese Dominico Centurione, and the bank of Centurione, which handled papal finances. By the spring of 1483 bulls of crusade were being printed—an example survives from the press of a Dominican convent in Mendoza's new see of Toledo—and distributed. The hawking of the bulls by salesmen-preachers deepened the public sense that this was a holy crusade against unbelievers—Turks and Moors—and waging war a religious duty.

A ROUT AND A PRIZE: 1483

Isabel, accompanied by Cardinal Mendoza, spent most of the spring of 1483 in Madrid and the summer in Santo Domingo de la Calzada, an old town, comfortably near Aragón's border—Fernando was in Aragón—with dynastic significance: there Enrique II, the founder of the Trastámara dynasty, had died in 1379, and there his heart was buried. Even while raising troops for that year's campaign against Granada, she paid great attention to family and dynastic affairs. Talavera was again sent to Lisbon, where he convinced King João to accept the *infanta* Juana in exchange for her sister, Isabel, whom he brought back to her mother that summer. The Queen also sought to tighten the Spanish hold on Navarre by arranging the engagement of Prince Juan to its child-queen, Catalina. Isabel now faced the probability that she might not bear another son, that Juan was not strong, and that it was her namesake, the *infanta* Isabel, who might inherit the crown. Nor, marriage alliance notwithstanding, did she ignore the rivalry with Portugal in the Atlantic for territory, strategic advantage, the wealth of Africa, and, ultimately, a route to the east. To that end, she then sought people and provisions to support the conquest and settlement of Gran Canaria.

Certainly her own star was rising, her reputation growing for intrepid diplomacy and passionate waging of just war. In connection with her formal reception by the Basques as queen, one Basque diplomat then opined her greater than Esther or than Judith, who had killed Holofernes to liberate her people, that "like Our Lady the mother of God she has protected the human line, for by her virtue she has saved all Spain, and even all Europe, especially since the militant enemy of humankind"—he meant the Devil and his minions—"was striving to sow discord in order to be able to throw off their highnesses from the very holy project on which they are embarked."[9]

A heightened respect was obvious too when, that March 1483, many more of Castile's magnates responded to the call to war against the Moor. Most of Andalusia's young knights now sought to join one or another border lord, hoping to repeat the *hazañas* of Alhama and to gain booty as rich. And now the captains and men of the *hermandad* came in in greater force. With the monarchs absent—Isabel was in Madrid arranging the Portuguese marriage and Fernando was attending to factional strife in Galicia—Alonso de Cárdenas and the Marqués of Cádiz had joint command. Once again Cádiz proposed a swift attack on Málaga, having had word that its *alcázar* was then poorly garrisoned and counting on Castile's ships to prevent its provisioning by sea, and once again he was overridden. Instead, Cárdenas' proposal to lay waste the lush countryside around Málaga was approved, despite Cádiz' warning of the savage, broken terrain of the approach to it, a region known as the Ajarquía.

A great host departed the forward base at Antequera, 3000 light cavalry and relatively few, perhaps 1000 foot; bringing up the rear were the usual merchants ready to buy booty. Castilians pillaged and burned Muslim towns and villages until, on March 21, in the narrow defiles of the gorges of Ajarquía, as the sudden mountain darkness fell this inexperienced force was ambushed and massacred. Ringed round by watchfires seeming "10,000 candles aflame," arrows and rocks hurtling down upon them, their horses stampeded, entangling riders as they fell. Cárdenas spurred ahead, giving no command. Cádiz, in the rear and cut off from the main squadron, relying on his skilled *adalides*, guides, retreated to Antequera. Most of the others, weighed down by armor and spoils and terrorized by Muslim war cries, were killed or captured as they attempted flight.

The monarchs soon heard that nearly 800 Christians, the flower of Andalusian knighthood, had died, and 1500 been taken captive, including 400 nobles. "Our Lord consented to it," concluded Palencia, "because it is certain that most of those people went with intent to rob and to do business, rather than serve God"; he noted that many knights had carried money from friends to buy slaves and silk clothing.[10] Similarly, Cárdenas, not mentioning his own lapse of judgment, laid the debacle to God's wrath, which had turned "against us for our sins so that it has pleased Him to punish us at the hands of the infidel."[11] Certainly, Castilians from then on displayed a heightened animosity to the Moors, a more intense dedication to holy war, and a strong desire to avenge that rout and regain honor. The official reason given was bad guidance by the *adalides*, and the monarchs immediately resolved on a new expedition. Isabel's response was to quickly have security tightened along Castile's borders and to see to it that thereafter Fernando would command the armies and Cádiz be his chief lieutenant and principal counselor.

Rodrigo Ponce de León, the Marqués of Cádiz, was "a man of great heart." In his late thirties, that redheaded giant was determined to live up to if not excel the deeds of El Cid, an earlier Rodrigo whose relations with his sovereign and with Muslims had some similarities. Cádiz' allegiances had varied before submitting to Isabel in Seville. He had come to war young and in his first major battle, at the age of 17, been given up for dead after a lance traversed his arm, yet by that August had sufficiently recovered to join his father, Juan, Count of Arcos, in taking Gibraltar. Like El Cid, the Marqués was an outsider, in his case since born out of wedlock. Yet having no legitimate sons, his father at length married Leonor Núñez, Rodrigo's mother, and in 1469 Rodrigo inherited his title and his most valuable single jurisdiction, the port of Cádiz. In 1471, driven out of Seville by Medina Sidonia, he fortified Jérez and through the good offices of his father-in-law to be, Juan Pacheco, received the higher title of Marqués de Cádiz. Though his past relations with Muslims, Pacheco, and Portugal did not bear scrutiny, Cádiz was to demonstrate amply that he considered his personal honor to be bound up with the royal recovery of the kingdom of Granada.

Exactly a month after the rout at Ajarquía, everyone's sense of honor was partially assuaged when the Count of Cabra and his nephew, the *Alcaide de los Donceles*—the noble youths educated at court to be knights—both of whom were named Diego Fernández de Córdoba, fortuitously captured Boabdil. Coming upon a Muslim raiding party at Lucena and though having far fewer men, they had trumpets sounded on either side of the Granadans, "who thought all Castile was there" and who fought fiercely but only briefly. Among their 700 prisoners was one who at first claimed to be a certain captain's son, then admitted, after having nearly died because that captain had killed his captor's brother, that he was Boabdil. Fernando advanced the prize prisoner funds for appropriate raiment and retinue, had all Córdoba's streets cleaned, and welcomed him there in May. It was agreed Boabdil was to receive 14,000 ducats and turn over his brother and son as hostages, and in September he was freed, as a Castilian vassal committed to warring against his father, Abū al-Ḥasan. The combination of war and diplomacy, of frontal attack and fomenting internal division was to serve Castile well.

Isabel, rejoined by Fernando at Vitoria in late September, thanked Boabdil's captors, the Fernández de Córdoba. She had them join the royal family at table and honored with "a stately and cadenced dance" to the music of trumpets and flutes. She granted Cabra the right to place on his coat of arms the nine Muslim battle flags he had taken, as well as the head of a king on a chain. A month or so later she heard from Cádiz. Not to be outdone, he and his companions wild at recognizing the armor, horses, and trappings of relatives or friends killed or captured in the Ajarquía, had fallen upon a squadron of Muslim *jinetes*. Then, having exacted vengeance of a satisfactory sort through killing most of them, he had gone on to scale and regain Zahara. Fernando's response to Cádiz was a high compliment, the promise of an annual gift of royal clothing. Isabel wrote congratulating him and urging him on. She would make it a habit to write him hortatory notes, and he to inform his queen of his estimable deeds in her service.

That winter, spent in Vitoria and Tarazona, was again a time of attention to international European matters. Isabel's plans for Prince Juan's marriage were disrupted by Catalina of Navarre's engagement instead to a French lord, and although Louis XI had recently died and the new king, Charles VIII, was a child, the French would not yield the provinces of Cerdaña and Rosellón; accordingly, Spanish troops were stationed on borders with both France and Navarre. At the same time, in order to restore Barcelona's trade, in decline for a century, and reassert the former Aragonese hegemony in the Mediterranean, impossible without Alexandria, it was decided to reestablish relations with Egypt. Those decisions fit within the larger policy, thought imperative after Otranto, of establishing cooperative relations with the Muslim rulers of Africa against the common enemy, the Turk. Within that overall plan, Sicily was viewed as a bulwark and Italian equilibrium was vital.

Most pressing, as ever, was the need for funds. It was now that, as Pulgar put it, the flight from the Inquisition augmented royal penury so that "Andalusia remained exhausted of gold and silver." However that may be, the four *brazos* or estates of the Corts of Aragón—ecclesiastic, noble, military, and popular—were summoned to Tarazona for a vote of subsidies. And a head tax was imposed in Castile, for Isabel was determined to pursue the war.

GAINING THE VEGA: 1484

She vented that determination in no uncertain terms in Tarazona that April. She had had word that Andalusians had for forty days been ravaging Muslim lands, taking immense satisfaction in successfullly traversing Ajarquía. Although the Corts was still in session, "that war against the Moors was much on her mind." She had, she told Fernando, resolved to go to Andalusia—"because," as Palencia has her say to him, "it was so just and holy an enterprise, that among all the Christian princes nothing was more honored, nor could be; because pursuing it truly had the help of God and the love of the people."[12] He argued that they must suspend the war with the Moors, for it was voluntary "while war with France was necessary, to recover what was theirs," the counties of Rosellón and Cerdaña. Isabel, having graciously conceded his points, reminded him that they had fought the Moors for two years on sea and land at immense cost. He should remain in Aragón with some Castilian men at arms and do as he wished. She was going to carry on the war against Granada.[13]

Taking with her the Cardinal and her children, she was in Córdoba by May 15, organizing that year's campaign. Nobles and knights, especially from Seville, answered her call, and infantry as well. French and German engineers arrived to make guns, cannon, and siege machines. Hundreds of carts brought wood and iron for weapons and stones for catapults; and some 13,000 *bestias*, donkeys, mules, and oxen, were hired to pull them and to bear provisions. "Following the Queen's opinion," says Palencia, a small armada was fitted out, for the Genoese and Venetians, well paid, were ferrying troops sent by the Muslims of Morocco to the Granada coast. That fleet of *naos*, galleys, and carracks would guard the Strait of Gibraltar and blockade Granada's ports. And warnings went out to the senates of Genoa and Venice and to their notables who resided in Seville and Cádiz, that if they did not desist from aiding the enemies of Christianity, they would be made to suffer more terrible vengeance than that inflicted by the Mohammedans.

Her dedication and perseverence, her very presence, writes Pulgar, set an example causing her ministers and servants to work extremely diligently. She had the army readied within two weeks and, with Fernando absent, she gave command to the Cardinal. Moreover, the council with Isabel present unanimously favored the proposal of "that noble and powerful *caudillo*, as practiced in affairs of war as fecund in plans to wage it," the Marqués of Cádiz, that they besiege Alora, midway between Antequera and Málaga. His opinion was also approved by Fernando, who arrived on May 29; the Corts of Aragón had refused to fund a campaign against the French.

On June 9, Fernando departed, this time with an army that was well provisioned and marched in good order, one that carted more and better artillery, siege weapons, and firearms than ever before. Isabel sent with it six great tents for the wounded, and bedclothes, physicians, surgeons, medicines, and male nurses. Chronicles and subsequent histories never fail to mention that field hospital and tend to celebrate her principally for womanly compassion. No matter that Isabel had shown herself to be the guiding force behind the war and had overseen all arrangements for the armies. Compassionate she was, but to a point. For to the queen, while suffering during war was to be allayed to the extent possible, it was to be borne, for the cause was the highest and most imperative.

Alora surrendered within nine days, after lombards had demolished two gate towers and pierced a great wall heretofore considered impregnable. Such fire power as had never before been seen leveled the town and terrified Alora's people into submission. Seeking refuge at Málaga, they were vilified as cowards, for the *malagueños* would not believe their account. On May 20 the banners of the King and Queen and the pennon of the *Cruzada*, the holy cross, flew over the highest tower still standing in Alora. Neighboring towns surrendered rather than face similar destruction. Fernando, satisfied and ever low on funds, prepared to return to Córdoba.

Isabel had daily dispatched money and provisions, relentlessly dunning everyone for more men, more mules, more food. In letters to Murcia's council she marveled at its notables' tepid response to the royal call to war and warned them that rumors had reached her of their trading with Granada. Now, upon hearing Fernando was planning to come back, she sent to tell him that, if it pleased him, he ought first to lay waste the *vega*, or besiege some other town, for enough of summer remained. It pleased him. And, on her orders, Medina Sidonia and Cabra led separate expeditions with the same purpose. To Fernando too she sent 5000 *bestias* laden with provisions for Alhama. In August she conceded to Rodrigo Ponce de León the titles of Duke of Cádiz and Marqués of Zahara. In September Fernando, on Cádiz' advice, besieged and took the fortress town of Setenil not far from that bulwark of western Granada, the town of Ronda.

The monarchs, in Seville from October into February, refused the belated offer of Abū al-Ḥasan to pay them tribute, and they spurred Boabdil to keep Granada embroiled in civil war. That they then received an embassy from the King of Fez, traditionally a mainstay of Granada, bringing gifts of horses and harness for the king and silks and perfumes for the queen, indicated a growing awareness abroad of Castile's new strength, and the efficacy of their naval blockade. The mood that winter was reflected in a romance, recited to musical accompaniment in the royal chapel and indulging in grandiose prophecy. It spoke of the royal desire to reconquer Granada and then annihilate from end to end all the sect of Muhammad, "and to regain the Holy House [in Jerusalem], as is prophesized, and place on the Holy Sepulchre your royal crusading banner."[14]

Readying for a major strike against Granada, Isabel and Fernando then took steps to tighten their grip on the towns, sources of so much wherewithal. They put into effect the ordinance of 1480 ordering the investigation of all *corregidores*, their conduct in office to be reviewed within the year through *residencias*, the taking of evidence within their jurisdictions. *Pesquisidores*, those most onamatopoeic of royal functionaries, were dispatched to investigate complaints of municipal lands having been usurped by nobles. Moreover, by then at royal bidding was a staff of several hundred *continuos*, retainers who served the monarchs as personal envoys, and spies. Often of noble blood, they were constantly on call to travel on crown business, especially to notify municipalities of amounts of money, men, and funds they must provide; and they were empowered to confront local and private authorities in securing them. *Continuos* traveled with the armies as well, gathering provisions and keeping an eye on their distribution and on monies collected.

Through such men were conveyed to the realm a royal order of November 23 stating that, in addition to the royal guards, the *hermandad*, and the prelates and grandes, all *caballeros* with their arms and horses and all *hidalgos*, also with arms and mounts, or at least bows and lances, were obliged to present themselves in Córdoba in March 1485, or to send a deputy. Military service was inherent not only to nobility but also to position on municipal councils. Excepted were the clergy, friars, Jews, and Muslims, all of whom were assessed special war taxes. Those men who came and served were promised a salary and certificate of service. Those who did not, without just cause and without sending a deputy, would lose all exemptions of *hidalguía*, that is, nobility. It was the first general call-up of Castile. Individual *hermandades* now came closer to meeting assigned quotas of men and provisions, and the *hermandad's* national council, overseen by Quintanilla, Alfonso de Aragón, and fray Alonso de Burgos, conceded for the war the great sum of two million *maravedís*.

Artisans were attracted to Ecija, which had become a foundry, by tax exemptions and in some cases at least by grants of property confiscated by the very industrious inquisitors. In January 1485 in Seville, while the monarchs were in residence, 19 men and women were burned at the stake, bringing the total so executed to 500. It is not known whether or not their highnesses attended that *auto de fe*; it is known that a captain of artillery, an expert in gunpowder, and a trumpet-player—the monarchs made certain that musicians, so important to morale and to discomfit the enemy, were always with the armies—received houses and corrals confiscated from *conversos* condemned for heresy.

RONDA: 1485

The court remained in Andalusia that winter. In January, against Isabel's advice Fernando attempted to take Loja, and failed. Still, there was the consolation of diversion, hawking and hunting. Medina Sidonia set up suitable accommodations in the forests then surrounding the city for the King, the Queen, the *infanta* Isabel, and all their retainers. And Seville's *alcázar* received attention: an order survives from Isabel and Fernando to Valencia for gardeners to tend its grounds; they were to bring trees with them. (Valencia had a large Muslim population, and *mudéjares* were known as the best gardeners in the Spains.) Yet respite was brief, for late in January some people in the palace fell ill of plague, and the royal family, the Cardinal, and those knights and functionaries permanently attached to the court immediately left for healthier towns. By late March the monarchs were in Córdoba for the general muster.

That spring Isabel was more determined than ever to impose upon the expanding army a high moral tone consonant with holy endeavor and conducive to better behavior and tighter control. The *grandes*, or their sons or nephews whom they sent with their *mesnadas* to Córdoba, arrived to a literal dressing down from the Queen and the King; they were scolded for spending too extravagantly on their clothing, their persons, their retinues of people useless in war, their tables, and their paraphernalia, especially torches and torchbearers, on everything, that is, that seemed necessary to them to show great estate. They were, they were told, setting a bad example to other knights. The monarchs, it was clear, had in mind a new sort of army, wherein what counted most were numbers, efficiency, discipline, and economy.

Leaving Córdoba in April were perhaps 11,000 horse and 25,000 foot, Heading the large Sevillian contingent were veterans of Ajarquía rescued or ransomed from Muslim prisons. Engineers and *maestros*, some of them

Frenchmen and Bretons, went along to tend the lombards and other siege engines, and with them were specialists in making shot of rubble and the new iron balls. There were experts in gunpowder, carpenters with their tools, and blacksmiths with their anvils. A thousand wagons carted the artillery and siege machines. Corps of foot with pickaxes and hoes accompanied them, to clear the way. There were oxen conscripted from Avila and Segovia, mules that had been requisitioned and others that had been hired, and cattle for food; scavenging in Christian-held countryside was punishable by death. There were the six commodious tents of the Queen's hospital and all it required. Isabel sent along Gutierre de Cárdenas to dispense funds for provisions and pay, and to keep an eye on the tremendous amount of money carried. The lombards just founded at Ecija and a conscript army were making obsolescent heavily armored knights and their chivalric conventions; a straight line would run from there to Don Quixote. Within decades, this new-model army would evolve into the most powerful in Europe and from it would come the indomitable captains of Europe and America.

The objective for 1485 was to isolate Málaga through taking its satellite towns. In early May, Fernando having taken Coin after a week's siege and hard fighting and Cártama having fallen to him within another week, Isabel sent off one of her congratulatory notes, mentioning that should he wish to pursue conquest elsewhere, there was suffucent summer remaining and she would send the necessary provisions. Now it happened that Cádiz, who was with Fenando, had had a letter too, from an old acquaintance, the *alguacil*, or bailiff, of Ronda, informing him that the town's populace was depleted, disheartened, and an easy target, that civil strife in the city of Granada meant no relief would come from there, and that he himself was ready to serve their majesties if they would show him their gratitude. Fernando, Pulgar recounts, accordingly had a Muslim prisoner first tricked into thinking that he had overheard plans to besiege Málaga, then allowed to escape and spread word that the Castilian army was headed for that port. Fernando then marched off in its direction, but, on May 8, Cádiz left camp after nightfall and, as day broke, *rondeños* awakened to find their town encircled by his army and much of the garrison just gone to defend Málaga. Fernando, doubling back, soon joined Cádiz before Ronda's walls.

Ronda, Granada's western bastion, enjoyed a situation magnificent but daunting: escarpment and strong walls on three sides, and, on the fourth, a gorge, its floor a swift mountain stream, the river Guadalevín. As an Arab visitor, Abū al-Fiḍa, saw it, Ronda had clouds for a turban and torrential rivers for its swordbelt. The Guadalvín was Ronda's chief water supply and so deep was the gorge that to obtain water from it required traversing 130 steps down a narrow zig-zagging passageway cut into the cliff inside the walls; fetching water was generally left to Christian prisoners. Control of that river was crucial to victory, and Cádiz, more than once, waist-deep in the swift current, led his men in battling those of Ronda's small but fierce garrison. Commanded by a doughty old warrior, Aḥmad al-Taghrī, its men were mostly African mercenaries, Gomeres, "whose whole business was to fight."[15] It was Taghrī who had been chiefly responsible for harrying the Christian forces at Ajarquía, and, so it was thought, for that disaster itself.

Isabel had relay stations established, and she sent massive supplies—3400 mules and 600 pairs of oxen as transport are recorded, and there were more—and much light artillery and projectiles. To pay for it all, she pressed everyone for funds with a high degree of success; when they lagged, her royal order was followed by her royal ire: "I marvel greatly," she wrote Seville's council, "that in so needy a time, the King My Lord being where he is, that you should delay sending the aforesaid *maravedís*."[16] And she insisted all *aljamas* of Muslims and Jews in Spain immediately pay all war taxes in arrears.

Ronda surrendered after two weeks of siege, on May 22. Its capitulation was due to a number of factors. The new siege engines—the giant lombards, their thunder terrifying—battered the town, and fireballs were employed for the first time. There was too the King's generalship, the Queen's unrelenting support, the essentially traditional, chivalric derring-do of the Marqués of Cádiz, and some citizens who had no interest in heroism. Ronda's inhabitants were expelled with what they could carry; *continuos* arrived from court to see to apportioning houses and property to Castilians wanting to settle there or in the other captured places; the monarchs drew up meticulous ordinances for each town. The exiles went to Granada and Africa, Isabel ordering that they be protected enroute and that anyone who robbed them be punished, with—says Pulgar—some degree of success. Excepted were perhaps 100 leading families—the group who had preferred surrender to loss of life and property—who removed comfortably to Carmona or to Alcalá de Guadaira, outside Seville, receiving property the Inquisition had confiscated. Fernando, after leaving Ronda, took the port of Marbella and 40 neighboring places; in those surrendering promptly, he permitted the populace to stay as *mudéjares*, tribute-paying royal subjects, "promising them on his royal word to conserve the law of Muhammad."[17]

Conquered mosques were ritually purified and rededicated as churches, to Santa María de la Encarnación, the Spíritu Sancti, Santiago, San Juan el Evangelista, and San Sebastián, the last quite possibly a barbed response to the Muslims increasing use of poisoned arrows. As for the mystery of the Incarnation, that from Mary Christ took human form, it was the theological principle on which Muslim and Christian diverged most sharply, to the extent that Muslims considered Christians polytheists, in this way rubbing in victory. Bernaldez tells the story of Juan de Vera who, when on embassy in 1482 to Granada, overhearing a Muslim nobleman say "Our Lady the Virgin Mary did not remain a Virgin after she gave birth to Our Lord Jesus Christ," had instantly called him a liar and gashed his head with a sword stroke, and that Fernando rewarded Vera handsomely for that deed.[18] To all those churches Isabel sent crosses, chalices, silver censers, silk and brocade vestments, and altarpieces, images, books, and bells. (The Muslims hated bells.) And she graciously received the 400 Christian captives discovered in the dungeons of Ronda: emaciated men, women, and children wearing rusted leg irons, hair and beards waist-length, in rags or naked. Many of the men had been taken at Ajarquía. Now they were redeemed, a phrase alluding to their delivery from captivity as analogue of a wider redemption of Castile from evil through so just a war. Isabel had them fed and each given eight *reales* with which to get home. Their fetters she had sent to Toledo, to be hung on the facade of San Juan de los Reyes.

On June 28, Isabel greeted Fernando at the entrance of the palace in Córdoba, ceremoniously, with their daughters and many women attendants, all of them in brocades and silks "and other rich fabrics." He had returned in triumph and throughout all Spain, indeed throughout Christian Europe, the fall of Ronda was acclaimed. In Seville, a procession of thanksgiving was immediately organized by the councils of church and city. Rome too celebrated; on June 3 Fernando had written of Ronda's fall to the pope, "so that Your Holiness should see and know on what Spain spends its time and money."[19] Heaven did not smile on a second campaign mounted that year. Fernando failed to take Moclín in September; losses were high. Boabdil's formidable uncle, Muhammad ibn Sa'd, known as al-Zaghal, who had attained supremacy in Granada, enhanced his standing by having a war party of *jinetes* return with 11 Christian captives, 80 trophy heads, and 90 warhorses.

In Córdoba Fernando came down with fever and Isabel, who was pregnant, suffered a spell of uncharacteristic despondency, as Pulgar reports equally uncharacteristically, for he has heretofore accentuated her steadiness and resolve, and now he describes her as appearing perturbed, indecisive about resuming the campaign, and, although greatly concerned with how to provision Alhama, refusing the Cardinal's offer to go in person to do so, "for since his company was a great consolation and his council a great relief and remedy for things as they occurred, she would not permit him to leave her."[20] Thus too does Pulgar, perhaps as a nod to the mentor he esteemed so highly, offer a rare glimpse of the *privanza* enjoyed by Mendoza, affirming that he was Isabel's constant and chief counselor and that she relied on him greatly, although he did not dominate the royal will nor the government as had the *privados* of the kings who preceded her. That fall Mendoza remained at her side; captains provisioned Alhama. Fernando, recovered, took two castles threatening Jaén, Cambril and Alhabar, in rugged terrain where Pulgar saw over 6000 men leveling a mountainside to permit passage of the artillery. And the monarchs, who had kept Boabdil at court, now released him to combat his formidable uncle and rival.

In late October, the court went north to Alcalá de Hénares, for Isabel a return to a place she had known well under vastly different circumstances; Alcalá, once Carrillo's seat as Archbishop of Toledo was now Mendoza's. Again there was plague in Seville, and, rather than strain Andalusia's resources further—the court now numbered in the hundreds and the four royal children each had a court in miniature—the monarchs chose to spend the winter accepting the hospitality of the Archbishop. Her bout of weakness past, Isabel was a demanding guest, insisting that royal justices and jurisdiction must pertain in Alcalá during her stay. Mendoza argued for his own archepiscopal jurisdiction as customary and prevailing. She, obdurate, declared her jurisdiction superior to all others everywhere in her kingdoms, even in church lands. Neither would budge; each appointed five *letrados* to meet and settle the dispute. They could not. Argument over principle persisted throughout the winter while in practice sometimes royal and sometimes ecclesiastical officials did justice, and the Queen and the Cardinal conferred on state business as usual.

In Alcalá, on December 15, 1485, what was to be her last child was born, the *infanta* Catalina. "The birth of a son," says Palencia, "would have caused the King and Queen greater happiness, for a succession depending on an only son inspired no small fear, and the fecundity of their daughters boded difficulties for future relationships."[21] That is, the birth of another daughter only increased the dreaded possibility of disputed succession. Even so, of all the children, Catalina would most resemble her mother. She too would be a queen, but her circumstances would be far different.

Castile having gained with Ronda the countryside all the way to Gibraltar, and with seamen of Jérez and Puerto de Santa María industriously raiding African coasts, grandiose visions of Castilian expansion were abroad. In seeking recruits for the next season, Cádiz reminded Castile's nobles of old prophecies about to be fulfilled and the *Encubierto*—the Hidden One—truly revealed. For, said he, the King and Queen having been jointly elected and sent by the hand of God, and "the heart of the king [being] in the hand of God," the prophecy that a great prince would appear was about to be fulfilled. He would destroy the Moors of Spain and all renegades, conquer Granada and all Africa, raise his banner in Jerusalem, and become emperor of Rome and monarch of the world, destined to rule it until its foretold end.[22] It was a vision in accord with romances current at court, and with the operative royal ideology of the Granada war. It fit with royal aspiration to powerfully influence affairs in Africa and the eastern Mediterranean and to be viewed as protectors of Jerusalem. It had visual parallel in those years in the lions, the eagle, and the wildmen chosen to adorn Cádiz' castle facade at Marchena and the ubiquitous *salvajes* of the Mendoza palace in Guadalajara. That year too Gil de Siloe designed the flamboyant Gothic tombs of Isabel's parents in the Cartuja de Miraflores, and construction in similar style began on Cardinal Mendoza's *Colegio* of Santa Cruz in Valladolid.

At the same time, late in 1485 or early in 1486, occurred the first event in a chain that would bring Isabel and her descendants much advantage and lasting renown. She and Fernando gave a brief audience that was of little moment to them at the time: "Thus Christopher Columbus brought himself to the court of King Fernando and Queen Isabel and made them relation of his imagination, to which . . . they did not give much credit, and he talked with them and said he was certain of what he told them, and showed them a map of the world, so that he aroused in them the desire of knowing those lands."[23] It was an ideal time to lay before them a map of the world.

13

The Queen's War II
1486–1492

With armor well burnished, and lances all flashing,
And banners all waving, and one golden standard
In front of the general, the King, Don Fernando. . . .
She also comes riding, Fernando's great Queen,
So powerful to hearten the hosts of Castile.

Muslim ballad[1]

The dead weigh on me heavily, but they could not have gone better
employed.

Isabel to Fernando. May 30, 1486

CRUSADERS: 1486

IN the spring of 1486, having stopped at Madrigal and Arévalo, the monarchs again came south by way of Guadalupe. There Cardinal Mendoza had prepared festivities, but Isabel opposed them since it was Lent. She was no longer the young Queen who would reign over a tourney in Lententime. At Guadalupe, she had an oratorio built above the choir where she prayed the canonical hours; and tradition has it that when the choir sang she sang along. There too she commissioned a royal hostelry, described as a true palace, paid for by Inquisition funds.

Since her last visit, the Inquisition had had other impact in Guadalupe. Three friars had been burned at the stake and its Hieronymites, declaring themselves shamed and dishonored, in chapter meeting had ordered all houses investigated and decreed that no New Christian could take the habit until the kingdom was cleansed of heresy. They also sanctioned a statute of purity of blood in proposing that Hieronymites who were *conversos* be excluded from the offices of prior and vicar. That proposal elicited from the monarchs a messenger warning of carrying matters too far. Still, Cardinal Mendoza's own advice to its proponents was telling: Have patience.

That spring the armies at last took Loja—from Boabdil who had reconciled with al-Zaghal—and also Illora and Moclín, west and northwest of Granada, commanding those approaches to the city. Isabel had called up a greater force than ever, perhaps 12,000 light cavalry and 40,000 archers, lancers, and musketeers. She had requisitioned 70,000 *bestias* with provisions and artillery, and sent along some 6000 foot to clear the way and build bridges. She was ill with fever when, on May 13, Fernando left Córdoba with the armies, but wrote to him five days later. In one of those very few personal letters of hers that survives, she thanks him profusely for the great concern he has expressed about her health. She is completely well, rid of the fever and feeling fine. Let her know where the siege will be. The children are all well. It is a note reflecting cognizance of their royal station and her wifely status, and the due form of both—she addresses him as Your Lordship, and yet it is warm and loving.[2]

She wrote again on May 30, giving rare insight into her state of mind. She could not know that Boabdil had just surrendered Loja, so she cheered Fernando on. She prayed to the Lord to continue granting victory "until He gives you the city and all the kingdom. This has been a marvelous thing and the most honorable in the world. . . . The dead weigh on me heavily, but they could not have gone better employed"; and she mentioned in particular one Velasquillo, who, because "he was afraid of dying even so honorable a death, had to show he was no coward, that he knew how to live and to die." She was dispatching reinforcements and, although it would take more time to send them provisioned still she would do it, for she did not know how well provided the camp was. He was to tell her what he needed and on what day and she would see to it, "because we do not want to err in anything." She marveled that the Muslim kings put themselves at such great disadvantage; "they would do better to concert with us." And she suggested promising Baza and Guadix and their lands to Boabdil as his own, then caught herself. "Pardon, Your Lordship, because I speak about what I do not know." The iron fist in the velvet glove. More advice nonetheless followed. She closed by telling him that they were all well. May the Lord guard him and bring victory, as she desired. In that letter, too, she observed of the politics of the Moors that "they are fickle and they rise and fall quickly." It implied the very opposite of her own steady determination and the high value she put on constancy, and it was a transference to the enemy of qualities associated with that disavowed but still potent alternative to Divine Providence, pagan Fortune.

Her blending of authority and subservience were reconcilable within the canons of chivalry; above all, she and Fernando wrote to one another, and demonstrably treated each other, as lady and knight. In their conduct and elsewhere as the age of modern warfare dawned, chivalry was making a last grand stand, along with individual armies. In one notable instance, although most Castilian *grandes* were tiring of the war, the Cardinal's brother's son, the Duke of Infantado, did arrive, with some 600 lances and 2000 foot, and not disposed to heed their majesties' condemnation of extravagant attire. Infantado came to war draped in cloth of gold, man and mount, with 50 of his *caballeros* and their horses nearly equally resplendent and all the rest, from head to hoof, in silks. Yet he fought bravely, and when his men flagged he rallied them with "Hear, *caballeros*, if you show yourselves in rich trappings, you must distinguish yourselves even more in great deeds."[3]

The possibility of doing great deeds while crusading within Europe attracted to Spain some of that disappearing breed, knights-errant, from France and Ireland and, most memorable, an English noblemen, Lord Scales, related to Isabel through her Lancastrian great-grandmothers, Catalina, Queen of Castile, and Philippa, Queen of Portugal. Scales had fought for Henry VI against Richard III on Bosworth Field, says Palencia, who then went into one of his tirades; a century before Shakespeare, he recounted the horrible deeds of Richard III, terming the contest between Lancaster and York bloody and seditious, and lambasted all the English: "This nation is so inclined to cruelty that it appears never satiated with seeing bloodshed; this fever takes so many devious forms, especially among the nobility, that among the English he is reputed happiest who is at the point of exposure to the most atrocious death."

Scales, was Palencia's point, now wanted to engage in just war. He had come to gain pardon for his sins and to serve God by making war on the Moors, "those tenacious enemies of the Christian religion." He had brought with him some 300 knights, musketeers, cross-bowmen, and foot with lances and battleaxes. He insisted on being in the thick of skirmishes and, in leading a scaling operation he lost, besides some men, two teeth. Fernando, offering what was meant as consolation, told Scales he should rejoice, for his virtue had knocked out his teeth. Isabel, commiserating with him later, received the gallant reply "I have opened a window so that through it Christ, who built this structure, may more easily see what is hidden inside."[4] Before he left, she presented him with expensive gifts: two beds with linens and bedcoverings, one embroidered in gold thread, twelve horses, and some field tents. The memory of her great-grandmother, Catherine of Lancaster, Palencia explained, sufficed. And she grieved when Scales died soon after, fighting in Brittany against France.

Yet after a bloody battle had secured the outskirts of Loja, it was not chivalry nor scaling operations but a single day's heavy pounding (on Sunday, May 28) by the lombards and other machines—*tiros e cortaos e pasabolantes e cebretañas e ribadoquines e pasabanías*—"the rigor of the gunpowder, that vanquished the fury of the Muslims" of that fortress-town. Boabdil, although wounded, rode out, dismounted, and in token of surrender kissed Fernando's feet. Fernando insisted he remount and that sometime vassal rode away, to do more mischief within Granada. Loja's inhabitants were permitted to resettle as *mudéjares* in Castile, Aragón, and Valencia. On word of Loja's surrender, the Queen, with her daughter Isabel and her ladies, went on foot from Córdoba's cathedral to the church of Santiago; she gave alms to churches and monasteries and had constant prayers of thanksgiving for victory said; and she prepared to depart for the front.

On June 11, having visited Loja, she reached the camp before Illora, some 20 miles from Granada and "called by Granadans their right eye," to find Fernando had gained the city. He had arrived five days earlier, fired the artillery on June 7, and, on June 9, its populace had left for Granada; what fighting there was had taken place within the Christian camp, between the Asturians and the *Sevillanos*, and terrible punishment had been meted out. The next day the entire, chastened, camp turned out to greet Isabel. She rode in, not disappointing expectations of how the Queen should look, in a scarlet cloak of Moorish design, velvet outerskirt, velvet and brocade underskirts, and wearing a broad-brimmed black hat, thickly embroidered, and under it her hair caught in a silk net. She rode a brown mule, blanketed in gold embroidered satin, its silver saddle richly gilded. She was accompanied by 10 ladies and some 30 male retainers; and she was met with an unprecedented display of respect and enthusiasm. Fernando—equally on display, astride a fine horse and wearing a crimson vest, a loose brocade robe over short yellow satin skirts, a plumed hat, and a scimitar—greeted her with both ceremony and warmth. Immediately behind him was Lord Scales. To the Castilian eye "he looked very pompous and strange." For Scales was in full armor and over it wore a short French cape of black brocade; sweeping plumes adorned his white French hat, and he carried on his left arm a small round shield banded in gold. Odder still, his stirrups were long and his horse covered from head to hoof in azure silk ablaze with gold stars and edged in mulberry. His five pages were equally exotically fitted out, in silk hose and suits of brocade. What is more, as the monarchs progressed into camp, Scales rode back and forth, alternating drawing up alongside them to offer gallantries with showing off the gaits of his steed, his antic behavior even more astounding to the sedate Castilians than his outlandish costume.

It did not hurt the Queen's standing, on going with the army on June 16 to besiege Moclín—another bulwark, perched high, extraordinarily difficult of access—that on the first night *una bomba* fired by mortar directly hit the town's stores of powder, sulpher, nitre, and provisions—that fireball, said Pulgar, appeared to have been carried by Divine Providence—and Moclín capitulated three days later. Seeming equally providential, Castilians entering the town singing the *Te Deum* heard voices join in, soon realized that they came from below, and found dungeons with Christian captives, none more thankful than they.

Upon Moclín's surrender, Isabel visited some wounded knights and *continuos* of her household. While solicitous, she told them that they should be happy to have been offered such dangers to strengthen their faith and aggrandize their land, and that if they were not repaid in this life God would not forget them in the next. She also had her treasurer give expense money to each, according to his estate. By the end of June, Fernando had raided the *vega* and taken several more towns and the monarchs were back in Córdoba. What before had taken a year had been done in a month.

Maintaining internal order was necessary to planning for war. Isabel had made clear her determination to keep Castile on a war footing, administrators efficient and as honest as possible, nobles obedient, clergy compliant, everyone fearing and respecting the crown, and the realm strong and united in high purpose. Accordingly, that summer she and Fernando brought under royal sway the last regional cluster of recalcitrant nobles. She had, the year before, on receiving word of insurrection in Galicia—the Conde de Lemos had seized Ponferrada, a royal town—become so exasperated that she had spoken of going personally and instantly to put it down. But the war had come first and she had sent Quintanilla instead, with a *hermandad* force and, when he failed, Benavente, who did no better. Now, a year later, the audacious young Count of Lemos having in flouting royal authority inspired other Galicians, the situation was not only infuriating but dangerous to the internal peace of a realm at war.

Both monarchs went north. Leaving Prince Juan and his younger sisters in Jaén, they took with them the *infanta* Isabel, who had become her mother's near-constant companion. The royal presence proved sufficient. Since the rebels insisted that Lemos had told them he was defending Ponferrada for the crown against the attempt upon it by Benavente, Lemos had no recourse but to surrender that town, and his own castles as well. He was called to account, fined, and exiled. Isabel and Fernando then entered Santiago de Compostela on September 15. Galicia's nobles flocked to court to proffer service. Graciously accepting apologies for past behavior, the monarchs took away the biggest troublemakers, then toured Galicia, where they ordered over 20 castles demolished, and, on departing, left a royal governor instructed to reclaim towns, monasteries, abbeys, and lands grabbed over the years by the aristocracy, and to ensure the *gallegos* contributed liberally to the Granada campaigns. While in Santiago for the first and last time, Isabel visited the shrine and tomb of the apostle Saint James, Santiago, for five centuries the patron saint of the reconquest. After that journey he loomed larger in the pantheon of saints to whom she dedicated religious establishments, but well below San Juan and Holy Mary.

Isabel and Fernando wintered in Salamanca, that center of legal studies, an appropriate place to implement further the program presented at Toledo in 1480. There too, a great preaching of crusade and sale of indulgences was forwarded. Talavera, assisted by Santángel as *contador*, and associated with Pinelo who was to oversee Rome's portion, enrolled hundreds of people to print the bulls, send them to each treasury, sell them, and keep an eye on one another. The monarchs showed no great zeal for the one-third interest of the papacy in this business. Rome would repeatedly protest abuses in collections of receipts from the sale of bulls of crusade and from a tithe Isabel in effect requisitioned from the clergy. Cardinal Mendoza, who had established strong financial bonds with the Genoese bankers of the papacy and had negotiated the *cruzada*, himself saw to farming that tithe.

Isabel exerted other pressure on the papacy. With the campaigns against infidel and heretic going well and the new pope, Innocent VIII, valuing Spanish support in Italian affairs, Isabel seized the moment. She secretly ordered her ambassador in Rome to obtain a bull enabling her alone, if need be, to administer the military orders. It was, her envoy reported, the most difficult business he had ever done in Rome, "because the Pope and all the cardinals held it as contrary to law and as a monstrous thing that a women would be able to have administration of [military] orders."[5] She was granted only co-administration with Fernando of the masterships as they fell vacant. To Isabel, it was but a first step, and it did provoke admiration at home. Thus that court wit, fray Iñigo de Mendoza, is credited with saying that if St. Helena was to be esteemed for finding a cross—the Holy Cross on which Christ was crucified, our Queen should be all the more so, for finding three: Alcántara, Calatrava, and Santiago—for all of them had crosses as their insignia.

When word came of the Turks, possibly in alliance with Egypt, preparing another attack in the West, Fernando and Isabel thought it in support of fellow Muslims in Granada and against themselves. It was, they concluded, imperative they take Málaga.

MALAGA:1487

Municipalities and grandes were notified to have specific quantities of cavalry and infantry at Córdoba by March 27, a general call went out to all knights, and amnesty was offered to all fugitives from justice who presented themselves. And Isabel now decreed that, although heretofore customary, no campfollowers and prostitutes might go with that army. The *hermanded* approved a mammoth levy of 10,000 foot with salary for 80 days. A host similar in size to the previous year was assembled, calculated to take advantage of the renewed strife within Granada between al-Zaghal and Boabdil, whose partisans incessantly fought through its narrow streets. Money came in from the bulls of crusade, and through huge individual loans: 11.3 million *maravedís* from Medina Sidonia, 8.3 million from the *Mesta*, five million from Benavente, and a million and a half from Cádiz.[6]

Isabel was in Córdoba with all her children by March 2. Arrangements were made with partisans of Boabdil within Málaga, a brief campaign was expected, and in early April she saw the army off to the base camp at Antequera. The plan was to invest first the outlying town of Vélez Málaga, to cut Málaga off from Granada. The campaign began inauspiciously; there was an earthquake the following day. She heard from Fernando of his having spent an anxious, sleepless night, so concerned was he for her safety, and of his wish that "Our Lord guard you above all others."[7] Then came torrential rains, and word of floods washing out roads and pasturelands, slowing the host to five leagues a day. Vélez Málaga sits behind a daunting barrier of mountains a half league from the sea. Into that rugged mountainous terrain went 2000 foot and carpenters to build bridges over *arroyos* and fill in deep pools of water, while another 4000 *peones* wielding iron pikes and poles leveled and paved the ground.

Once Fernando was encamped before the town, on April 16, more bad news soon followed. Only a part of the artillery had arrived and the giant lombards remained mired down in Antequera. Twelve hundred sick and wounded lay in the field hospitals. The *gallegos*, Asturians, Basques, and other paid foot were proving unruly. And rain had ruined a great deal of food. Still, ships brought more to the coast, and people from Málaga provided some, until Málaga's *alcázar* was taken from Boabdil's *alcaide* by partisans of al-Zaghal.

Isabel, hearing through her swift couriers that al-Zaghal had himself left Granada relieve Vélez Málaga with 1000 horse and 20,000 foot, urgently called upon knights from all Andalusia—the Cardinal offered to pay personally all cavalry volunteering—and she ordered all its men from 20 to 60 "to take arms and go to the King and serve him." Al-Zaghal indeed arrived, by April 25, but his plans went awry after a small group of his men in fleeing from a skirmish induced a general panic. He retreated, to find himself locked out of Granada in disgrace and Boabdil proclaimed king.

Boabdil had had help. At his urgent request, Fernando and Isabel had sent him Spanish cavalry, under Gonzalo Fernández de Córdoba, and arms, money, and provisions. Granadans, the monarchs had assured him, might leave the city to sow their crops and travel to Christian lands to get provisions, anything but arms. In response, Isabel had a letter from Boabdil of April 29, announcing his triumph and reaffirming the obedience he had sworn at Loja. And an agreement was reached in which, much as Isabel had suggested, he would turn over Granada, when he could, in exchange for places in the eastern part of the kingdom, which was then loyal to al-Zaghal.

Vélez Málaga surrendered on April 27, followed by all the places between it and Málaga, their people were permitted to retain their religion and customs, a calculated leniency. On May 6, Fernando was encamped before Granada's great Mediterranean port, Málaga, renowned, as Palencia says, for the opulence of its inhabitants and "its decided commercial inclination," and known to be harboring numerous Christian renegades and many fugitive *conversos* and expelled Jews. His initial hope for its speedy surrender was soon dashed; within days, negotiations foundered.

Two weeks later Isabel arrived, to an impressive panorama. The Castilian camp sprawled over beaches and countryside on three sides of the city. Her fleet stood off the fourth, blockading the port, firing upon it, and ferrying provisions to her armies. Málaga itself, beautiful and apparently impregnable, its fortifications designed to protect its sizable populace (then over 11,000) and tremendous wealth, was situated, as Pulgar explained, "nearly at the end of the Eastern Sea and at the entrance of the Western Sea,"—

between Mediterranean and Atlantic—"near the Strait of Gibraltar which separates Spain from Africa."[8] Málaga had three strong fortresses, two of them just seized by Aḥmad al-Taghrī, that fierce partisan of al-Zaghal and his Gomeres—Palencia estimates a garrison of 5000. That he was master of the city was an unexpected blow.

Isabel had come, with her usual entourage, at Fernando's urgent request, to allay the rumor rife within Málaga that the Queen so feared the pestilence afflicting nearby villages that she had ordered the Christians to decamp. Her presence attracted more knights and foot, for everyone "thought that with the arrival of the Queen the Moors had to surrender."[9] Beyond the firm intent her coming conveyed, such was the conviction she personally exuded that a treasurer of hers, one Ruy López de Toledo, a man of business and finance, was transformed into an ardent soldier and captain, and at Málaga was seen to fight so boldly and valiantly and so to inspire others that the Cardinal told the Queen that in him she had another Judas Maccabeus. That comment reflected both an easy familiarity with the Old Testament and alluded to the fact that the treasurer was, like so many of Isabel's staff, a *converso*.

She and Fernando then demanded that Málaga surrender immediately or they would promise captivity—a euphemism for slavery—for all its inhabitants when it did. Al-Taghrī refused, expecting rains that would make Málaga's unprotected harbor so dangerous an anchorage that ships could no longer provision the Christians daily, and he awaited help from Africa. Consequently, his Gomeres killed or terrorized all dissenters, and a holy man buoyed Málaga's increasingly hungry populace, prophesying that one day they would feast on the mountains of food in the Christian camp.

Within a month of Isabel's arrival, another Muslim holy man came into the Castilian camp and, brought before Cádiz, convinced him that he had information on how to take the city that he could give only to the king. Fernando, however, was asleep and Isabel would not then see him, so he was taken to a nearby tent, where, seeing a Portuguese nobleman and Beatriz de Bobadilla, he mistook them for the king and queen. As Bobadilla, frightened by his expression, hurried to the entry, he lunged at her companion with a dagger. Ruy López de Toledo seized the assassin from behind and other men, running in, hacked the assailant to pieces. Those pieces were then catapulted into Málaga—where, says Pulgar, they were gathered up, sewn together with silk thread, washed and perfumed with oils, and buried with great ceremony. Al-Taghrī retaliated in kind, killing a principal Christian captive, disemboweling the corpse, tying it to an ass, and driving the animal into the Christian camp. God, was the interpretion, had wished to protect the sovereigns. Thereafter, Isabel had a guard of 200 men at arms.

Summer wore on. Fernando and Isabel, hoping not to destroy the town, had initially subjected it only to the fire of the middling artillery, if several hundred pieces of it. Yet after a month passed the seven great lombards arrived and were brought into play. And in a move both practical and emblematic, Fernando ordered to be carried from Algeciras, "now depopulated, all the lombard stones that the king Don Alfonso [XI] his great-great-grandfather had fired against [Algeciras and Gibraltar] when he laid siege to them."[10]

Still the starving *malagueños* held out, and within the Castilian camp, tempers frayed, many of the men were sick, desertion was endemic, and rumor was rampant. The monarchs banished all *mudéjares* from the camp, for it was being said, in a time-honored accusation made against outlanders, witches, and infidel, that they were poisoning the wells; and severe and summary punishment was meted out for all offenses.

The sea proved of crucial advantage. Fernando and Isabel, low on gunpowder, quickly procured some by sending a galley to Valencia and a caravel to the king of Portugal. And when they called on Medina Sidonia for aid, he came in person with all his knights, a loan of 20,000 *doblas de oro*, and 100 ships as well. Proving their blockade and privateers effective, ambassadors arrived from North Africa, from the king of Tlemcén (Oran), opposite Granada, offering service and requesting the sea be opened to his subjects. They graciously complied, for Africa's Mediterranean coast figured in royal plans, economic, political, and religious.

Isabel and Fernando had solicited and received papal permission for keeping open both African trade and that of Málaga. Málaga had formerly traded heavily with Barcelona and more recently with Valencia, in Granadan and re-exported African products—saffron, wax, hides, sugar, fruits and nuts, silks, and gold—and in spices and other Eastern wares brought by caravan or ship to the Barbary coast. The ships involved were often Genoese. It is tempting to tie such Genoese activity to the fact that Christopher Columbus was sent funds to come to the royal camp before Málaga, and to speculate that he may have served as a contact with resident fellow-Genoese within that city in arranging continuation of trade, or even Málaga's surrender. More will be heard of all this.

In the third month of the siege, in August, when Fernando offered a reward for information on conditions within the town, a group of *gallegos* hid among the tombs in a Jewish cemetery outside the walls, waylaid five men who came out to find grass for their goats, and managed to take one of the fellows alive to the king, who at length induced him to reveal that the inhabitants were eating dogs, rats, and weasels; that few horses or burros survived; yet that the holy man was inciting the populace to resist and that the Berbers, renegades, *conversos*, and apostates, who could expect no mercy from the Castilians, would hold out to the death.

Even so, a leading *malagueño* merchant, Ali Dordux, partial to Boabdil, sounded out the monarchs, who insisted now on unconditional surrender; the siege had been unexpectedly long, hard, and costly. The city fathers forthwith threatened to kill the 600 Christian prisoners, and Fernando told them that should one die he would kill every Muslim in Spain. Dordux continued to negotiate, with Gutierre de Cárdenas, and on August 18, overcome by starvation, Málaga capitulated, followed by al-Taghrī and his garrison two days later. As the royal standards and Holy Cross appeared on Málaga's ramparts, the Queen, the *infanta*, and the entire camp knelt and prayed to *"nuestro Señor e la Virgen Santa María gloriosísima,"* and to *el Apostól Santiago*, while the *Te Deum laudamus* rose up. Isabel and Fernando were in command of the chief port of Granada, its second city; Málaga had been Muslim for 770 years.

When the corpses had been cleared away, the stench abated, and the mosques made churches—Talavera headed the clergy reconsecrating the principal mosque, to Santa María de la Encarnacíon—they entered the city gates. Even before, to their tent beside the walls came the Christians released from Málaga's dungeons, over 600 men and woman, emaciated and yellowed from hunger and disease.

Looting was forbidden and Málaga placed under heavy guard. Dordux had not revealed to his fellow citizens the full terms of surrender. Isabel and Fernando had resolved, and Dordux knew, that renegades would die by sharp pointed reeds, *conversos* and judaizers be burned alive, Gomeres enslaved, and most other inhabitants held for a near-impossible ransom, of 30 *doblas* for each man, woman, and child, to be paid within 16 months.

Street by street, the inhabitants were registered individually, under the direction of Gutierre de Cárdenas. They were divided into three lots. One was to be exchanged for Christians held by Muslims. Another was to be parceled out to all knights, council members, captains and other *hidalgos*, officers and soldiers, whether Castilian, Aragónese, Valencian, or Portuguese, who had come to the war, in accord with their rank and services. A third, "to help meet the expense of the siege," was reserved by the crown and to be held for ransom. The crown requisitioned all valuables as an initial ransom installment, and set a period in which the captives had to complete payment or be enslaved. As for Málaga's Jews, they were allowed their moveable property and transported to Carmona where they were to be locked in the castle until the ransom set for them was completely paid; there too were incarcerated al-Taghrī and the demagogic holy man. Some of the *malagueños* held for ransom were sent to Seville, to serve householders there or in Córdoba, Jérez, and Ecija, as hostages until the debt of all should be paid in full. It never was.

Most *malagueños* became and remained slaves. They were in effect, "corralled and counted and enslaved and sold."[11] From 2500 to 3000 Muslims were distributed among Christian nobles and prelates: the Cardinal was given at least 70. Fifty young women went to Juana, Queen of Naples, Fernando's sister, and 30 more to the Queen of Portugal. Isabel bestowed a great many on ladies of Castile and took others to serve in her palace. And royal account books list nearly two million *maravedís* received from the sale of 192 "heads of Moors." The Pope received a gift of 100 of the surviving Gomeres, who arrived in Rome during a consistory in February 1488 where he doled them out: one, two, or three apiece to the assembled clergy. Many other captives remained in Andalusian cities, and in Málaga itself over 3000. Ali Dordux had arranged exception for himself and some relatives, between eight and 40 households, with permission to stay in the city as Castilian subjects. Málaga's Jews—450 souls, mostly women speaking Arabic and dressing in Moorish style—were ransomed for the huge lump sum of 10,000 *castellanos de oro*. It was raised by Abraham Señor, the high judge of Castile's *aljamas*.

Ransom of the Muslims of Málaga could not be met and sales of 4363 people are documented, sold with their goods for over 56 million *maravedís*; moreover, the crown customarily collected sales tax on the transfer of such slaves of war.

NEW FACES: 1487–1489

That fall Aragón required attention. Isabel and Fernando left their younger daughters in Montoro, safe from the plague raging in Córdoba, took with them the *infanta* Isabel and Prince Juan, and stopped enroute to be royally entertained by Infantado in Guadalajara. In Zaragoza from mid-November through mid-February, they held Corts. And there and elsewhere in Aragón, they introduced the *hermandad*, that proven remedy for factional disturbances and guaranteed enhancer of royal authority. They diverted some Aragonese revenues to the war, and made certain the Inquisition was doing its job.

After that summer's campaign, a highly successful one in eastern Granada, Isabel was particularly diligent in organizing the Inqusition for all the realm. The inquisitors were called to Valladolid, and either Isabel alone or both monarchs—Fernando joined her in December—oversaw their assembly and the issuance of those ordinances (mentioned earlier) reinforcing inquisitorial power and autonomy, condoning great secrecy, and brooking no criticism. Isabel, aware of the scope of Inquisition activity, reconfirmed its power and procedures. Those abuses she then considered worthy of regulating had to do with major peculation—it was then a receiver of confiscated goods was called to account for siphoning off a million and a half *maravedís*.

With rising reputation abroad came offers of marriage alliances. Ambassadors from Burgundy sought a pact against France and the hand of the *infanta* Isabel for the widower, Maximilian of Habsburg, whose inheritance included present-day Austria and Flanders, and that of Juana for his son, Philip, heir through his mother to Burgundy. Yet it remained to be seen whether or not the Habsburgs could gain effective power in those domains. The Queen, temporizing, replied that the *infanta* Isabel was promised to another and Juana not yet of age, but agreed to reopen the conversation when she was. She and Fernando also begged off joining Burgundy against France because of the war with Granada, but sent to it a manned fleet.

There followed that spring a month-long stay at Medina del Campo by an embassy from England's new king, Henry VII. He had proposed that his infant son and heir, Arthur, marry the *infanta* Catalina and so well had preliminary discussions in London gone, their resident ambassador reported, that at their conclusion Henry had joyfully broken into a *Te Deum laudamus*. The reception of that embassy provides comparison with similar earlier occasions. The Queen "made [the ambassadors] very particular honor," for she prized her Lancastrian kinship with Henry, and saw a connection with England, as with Burgundy, important to preeminence in Europe. The envoys were to be impressed. Summoned on March 14, at dusk, they were brought by torchlight before "the kings" (as the English referred to them) who were seated in a great hall against a cloth of gold emblazoned with the quartered arms of Castile and Aragón. Isabel and Fernando sat side by side, both robed in cloth of gold trimmed with sable. Isabel, not underdressed, wore too a riding-hood of black velvet, slashed to reveal the gold cloth beneath and trimmed in solid gold and jewels "so rich," reported the awed emissaries, "that no one has ever seen the like." And over one shoulder she had thrown a short cloak of crimson satin fringed with ermine. A large Balas ruby "the size of a tennis ball" decorated her girdle. Her golden necklace was enamelled with white and red roses, at the center of each a large jewel, surely a reference to the reconciliation of England's Tudors and Yorks. And "suspended on each side of her breast" was a ribbon studded with large diamonds, rubies, and pearls. The visitors estimated the value of her attire at 200,000 crowns of gold. "Seated nearest to the Queen on the same seat" was the Cardinal. Many great lords and ladies were in attendance. The ambassadors presented their letters and made the expected speeches in Latin. The Bishop of Ciudad Rodrigo made reply. "But the good bishop was so old, and so toothless, that what he said could be made out only with great difficulty."[12] No matter, it was only the beginning.

The next evening the ambassadors stated their business to the monarchs, and found them again extravagantly attired. Isabel had on one of the several ruby necklaces they described her as wearing during their stay. At their request they saw Prince Juan (in rich crimson velvet) and the *infanta* Isabel (in cloth of gold and a green velvet robe with long train). Four days later at royal invitation they joined the monarchs for complines in the chapel and then sat with them to watch young courtiers dance, among them the *infanta* Isabel. As protocol dictated, she danced with one of her ladies, the one she liked best, who was Portuguese. Several days after that the Englishmen attended a tilting match, to find Isabel more richly bejeweled than ever and escorted by the Cardinal; then came minstrels, dancing, and dinner. They next met the *infantas* María and Catalina, also opulently dressed and attended. Finally, a bullfight was held in their honor, and afterwards 100 knights "skirmished and ran with dogs in the way they fought with the Saracens." The Englishmen sat with the royal family in the scaffolding, "and it was beautiful to see how the Queen held up her youngest daughter, the Infanta donna Catherine, [who was to be] princess of Wales; and at that time she was three years of age." Again dancing followed, mother and daughters not lacking in rich jewelry. Culminating those festivities was the treaty of Medina del Campo, promising mutual aid and defense and the marriage of Catalina and Arthur; it would guide relations between Castile and England until their deterioration in 1525 when Spain's king, Charles, jilted England's princess, his cousin Mary.

BAZA: 1489

Threading through that fall and winter were preparations for the upcoming campaign against Baza, key to hemming in al-Zaghal in Almería and the costliest to date. In November the *junta* of the *hermandad* agreed to again provide 10,000 infantry and 80 days' pay. Again the city councils were assessed and, in February, a forced loan levied on them, amounts specified for each place, payable in a year, and *continuos* instructed to see to their collection. Nor were Jews and Muslims, who paid other levies annually, exempt from new extraordinary imposts. The *Mesta* too was charged a special tax, to be handed over to Talavera. Individual nobles and bishops once more loaned large sums. The clergy voted a subsidy as well as paying a tithe, each amounting to over 13 million *maravedís*. And tremendous returns came in from the *cruzada*. A royal pardon was promised to criminals in Galicia and Asturias who would volunteer for a year. In February, orders went out to buy grain, wheat and barley, at set prices.

Isabel visited her mother in Arévalo, then went to Guadalupe, and, in mid-April she and Fernando were in Córdoba and, in May, in Jaén. There she remained until late fall with her children, the Cardinal, Talavera, and most of her council, while the siege of Baza began. Lasting from mid-June through December, it would be among the longest, the hardest, and the last campaigns of the war.

Baza is surrounded by jagged mountains on three sides and in a river basin on the fourth lay the *huerta*, the irrigated farmland, protected by a low wall. Although Fernando had 13,000 horse and 40,000 foot, the rains were prodigious, the city well garrisoned and fortified, and when a fierce 12-hour battle ended in a draw, a long siege loomed. He considered raising camp and attacking some other place. Council opinions varied. Cádiz wanted to stay, Gutierre de Cárdenas to go. "And about all this, says Pulgar, the King "decided that he ought to consult the Queen, who had charge of arranging all provisioning, to get her opinion about the things needed if the siege was to continue." She had his account of how matters stood, carried by relays of couriers, within ten hours. Nor is her reply unanticipated. She responded equally quickly that her council did not know enough to give an opinion, he should decide, but if he did resolve to continue the siege, which at the beginning all had agreed to, then with the help of God she would arrange that they should be well provided with men and money and provisions and all the other things necessary until the city was taken. The King chose to continue the siege, for, says Pulgar, "those things the Queen offered are the principal ones that sustain wars."[13] And he added that, her resolve known, the rank and file now wanted to see it through, that men who were originally reluctant or simply bent on booty had adopted the royal cause as their own.

Isabel pressed everyone for more funds. Luis Santángel, who had arranged international loans, made advances against them. Cádiz and other magnates accepted seignorial jurisdictions in exchange for loans. The Genoese merchants of Seville contributed handsomely; and one of them, Francisco Pinelo, associated with Talavera and Santángel in the *cruzada* and other financial activities, lent three times as much as did the others together. And it is now that, the ransom period having expired and the need for funds pressing, Málaga's people were being sold into slavery; handling that business too were Santángel and Pinelo.

However difficult, Isabel punctiliously sent Boabdil money monthly. Granada remained torn by factional strife. Appealed to by Granadans, the sultan of Egypt, Qā'it Bay requested of the pope that he inform the King and Queen of Spain that they must end the war and, if not, Christians in his domain, which included Jerusalem, would be treated as they treated Muslims. The Sultan's unlikely envoys were two Franciscan friars of Christ's tomb in Jerusalem; the pope sent them on to Fernando and Isabel, whose response was that their progenitors had held those lands the Muslims now ruled unjustly, that those Muslims had warred on Christians, and that they would treat the many Muslims in their realms as the Sultan treated the Christians in his. Yet they wrote directly to Qā'it Bay as well, in more conciliatory terms: it was not a religious war, rather these were vassal states of theirs that had tried to break away. They themselves had always respected the religion of the vanquished, as their agreements upon surrender attested. And to show the Sultan their good faith they suspended preaching of the *cruzada* for the moment. They were not greatly concerned, for the Sultan also requested the help of an Aragonese fleet against the Turks. His friar-emissaries had found Isabel in Jaén. She talked extensively with them about the Holy City, pledged them 1000 ducats annually from her revenues on Sicily for maintenance of Christ's tomb, "and she gave them a veil that she, moved by devotion, had made with her own hands, to cover the holy sepulcher."[14]

Isabel kept the camp at Baza well supplied, as she had promised. For five months she continually sent money and provisions, bread and wine and meat, and armorers, saddlemakers, harness-makers, and other necessities. That encampment attracted merchants, from Castile, Aragón, Valencia, Catalonia, and Sicily, selling brocades and silks, cloths and linens, hangings, and other things then welcomed by men at war with pay and booty to spend. But no merchant would carry provisions on his own account. So she ordered wheat and barley to be purchased in Andalusia and the lands of the military orders, and with dearth and doubled prices in Andalusia that year, she permitted shipment of more from the Barbary Coast. She readied men to transfer it to the muletrains which went daily to the camp, and had the grains sold at a fixed price. She also arranged for milling grain and then carrying flour there.

In July, she decreed stiff punishment for desertion and absence without leave, and, with a long siege likely, in August she coaxed reinforcements and their pay out of the cities, and additional loans. She dunned towns in arrears, levied further forced loans upon them and on prelates, knights, and ladies as well, and urged merchants to lend all they could. The response was good, indicating staunch patriotism and confidence in the Queen's credit. She drew relatively heavily on Talavera's see of Avila and on the *cruzada*, Talavera as its *comisario general* having recourse to its huge revenues. She also sold bonds payable on the rents of municipalities directly under the crown. And she sent jewels into pawn; the ruby necklace was again in Valencia in August, surety for a loan of 20,000 florins. In December, a crown of gold and diamonds followed it, to ensure a loan of 35,000 florins arranged by Santángel. Meanwhile, within Muslim Baza, the women's jewels went to pay the soldiers of the garrison.

Although the fall was extraordinarily mild, Fernando prepared for the winter snows and winds habitual to the region. He and the great lords had houses built, mud walls covered with tile and wood; over 1000 went up, laid out along streets, within four days. The foot soldiers built sheds of branches or huts for themselves. No sooner was this tour de force completed than it was hit by a deluge; houses were ruined and roads rendered impassable. Yet only one day's supply trains failed to arrive. For the Queen immediately sent workmen and 6000 *peones* to repair roads and build causeways and bridges. From then on one route was kept open for supply trains going to the camp and another for those returning. Other provisions came by sea, through the port of Vera, transported principally by Andalusian ships. Overseeing those supplies and their distribution within the camp were a formidable team, testimony to the importance of that task: two royal secretaries, Hernando de Zafra and Fernán Alvarez de Toledo Zapata, and the *letrado* Rodrigo Maldonado de Talavera of the Royal Council.

Letters from Cádiz kept Isabel informed of the campaign, and she received repeated requests, from Fernando, from *grandes*, from knights, that she come to camp, for should the Moors but see her they would surrender. She hesitated until she heard that within the war council one faction, which included Fernando, was again ready to raise camp. She was at Baza on November 7, with her daughter Isabel—from whom, Pulgar observes, she was never parted—and her Cardinal and ladies, everyone coming out to greet her except the posted guards. Pulgar, who was there, admits that to men bored after a siege of six months, her arrival at the very least brought welcome novelty. And among the besieged, it had immediate impact; all artillery fire and skirmishing ceased and shortly thereafter Yaḥyā al-Nāyyar, the military governor of Baza, was ready to negotiate, and so was Isabel.

After Gutierre de Cárdenas had assured the governor that should he not come to terms they were prepared to stay all winter, Baza surrendered. The royal forces entered the city in blinding snow on December 4. The terms were among the most lenient of the war: the garrison might leave, the inhabitants might stay but they must move outside the walls, pay tribute, and become royal subjects, *mudéjares*. Fernando and Isabel swore they might keep their faith, their laws, and their *fueros* or customary rights. Surrender of other settled places from Baza to Almería quickly followed, under the same terms, with forts to be turned over to Castilian *alcaides*. Then came word from al-Zaghal; he also would surrender for, as it is said he explained, "it appears that the will of heaven is to take this land from me and give it to you." The Christians too saw as a marvel attributable to the divine will that such strong cities could be had without further effort. On December 10 al-Zaghal signed a capitulation, and he turned over Almería on December 22. Isabel was detained by heavy snow and arrived on the twenty-third, in time for the reconsecration of its mosque. He surrendered Guadix on December 30. The monarchs, too optimistic, wrote to Seville that the war was over.

A great number of Christians died in that campaign, up to 20,000, the great majority of them from sickness and cold. Isabel turned her attention to the families of the dead and wounded, decreed them exempt from future war exactions, and granted them funds from fines levied on deserters and no-shows. And, with the end of the war at least near, Cardinal Mendoza gave orders for the carving of a scene commemorating the surrender of each of fifty-four Muslim towns and cities on the choirstalls of Toledo's cathedral.

ROYAL WEDDING: 1490

Isabel had tried in vain to have the Portuguese accept another of her daughters but Prince Afonso, it was said, wanted only Isabel; with her, too, might one day come all Spain. In February Portuguese ambassadors arrived, urging the celebration of the marriage. Afonso, five years younger than his intended, was now of age. The *infanta* Isabel was 20 and had become her mother's companion. As a child she had been placed in the care of Teresa Enríquez, the wife of Gutierre de Cárdenas, renowned for her devotion and piety, and as an adult she appears to have been closer in character than was her mother to their ancestress, Santa Isabel. Intelligent and dutiful, she had been hostage to the Cabreras and then to the peace between Castile and Portugal. She knew Afonso well, for both had lived as hostages to peace in the castle of her great-aunt, Beatriz. She was, in effect, still a hostage; she must marry, and her choice of husband had been limited, either to Afonso, a boy she knew and liked, or Maximilian, a stranger and a middle-aged widower in a far land. Her mother would have her marry the prince of Portugal because he was closer to her in age and customs, and of a shared border and lineage, and also as a way to keep relations sweet in matters of Africa and the Atlantic.

Isabel's relations with Portugal's king, João, who had taken the title Lord of Guinea and was reaping from Portugal's African enclaves the gold that had once gone to Algiers, Tunis, and, hence, often to Spain, were never good, especially since 1483 when he had executed his most powerful noble, the Duke of Braganza, on suspicion of plotting with herself and Fernando, which he well may have done. Now, having to send her daughter off once more, she would show the world how valued was her firstborn, and how powerful Spain's royal family had become.

Arrangements were made with the Portuguese by Talavera and Cárdenas. Isabel, accustomed to supplying an army, in providing a handsome dowry and in everything else having to do with the wedding manifested a war-reinforced habit of thinking on grand scale. Her daughter's silver and gold plate alone cost over three million *maravedís*. She paid for splendid public festivals in May lasting 15 days, including over 500,000 *maravedís* for the trappings of the mounts of the court ladies attending the jousts, over 100,000 *maravedís* for the harness of Prince Juan's horse, and 26,554 of them for the stage sets for the customary *momos*, which were ostensibly commissioned by 12-year-old Juan in honor of his sister, much as his mother had once done for her brother. The wedding arrangements and celebrations demonstrated, as they were meant to, both the closeness of that thriving dynasty and its ability to mobilize funds.

On Easter Sunday 1490 Cardinal Mendoza officiated, at the proxy ceremony; the actual wedding would take place in Portugal. Knights were there from Aragón, Valencia, Catalonia, and Sicily; the *grandes* shone in cloth of gold and precious chains; the 100 *caballeros* of the royal household appeared everywhere in silks and cloth of gold. The Queen too wore cloth of gold and she and the soon-to-be Princess of Portugal were accompanied constantly by 70 women in brocade and jewels, who were each escorted nightly by eight or nine torchbearers. A great jousting field was set up between the shipyards and the Guadalquivir river, just outside the city walls (assumedly a sufficient distance from the *Quemadero*). In short, it was November before the *infanta* Isabel left, her parents and her brother riding with her as far as Constantina, where everyone shed many tears at farewell. Then the Cardinal and a large escort accompanied her as far as the border. In Portugal the marriage was celebrated with another month of extravagant festivities. Pulgar, ending his chronicle in 1490, will not have Castile outshone: although the Portuguese strove to outdo in grandeur the King and Queen of Castile, he sniffs, they showed themselves of a greater mind to spend than of a sufficient faculty for doing it in good taste.

Six months later, in July 1491, Afonso was galloping on uneven ground along a river bank when his horse slipped and, in falling, crushed him to death. Isabel, upon receiving word of the tragedy and that her daughter, overcome by grief, was neither eating nor sleeping, determined that she must return to Castile. And so young Isabel came back, in deepest mourning, to rejoin her parents, her sadness unallayable, her tragic figure by hindsight a portent of greater woe to come.

MURMURINGS

Isabel, preparing to move against Granada itself, sought yet more funds. Although the years at war had forged in the people of Castile a sense of unified Christian purpose, and success had enhanced the prestige of the monarchy to the point where towns, cities, religious bodies, and individuals paid monies requested of them on demand, support was not unalloyed. Indicative of opposition was criticism by one Hernando de Vera, who was angered by tremendous subsidies demanded of Jérez, where he sat on the town council. Vera's vehicle was a reprise of the scathing couplets of *Mingo Revulgo*, popular in the 1460s, berating a shepherd for poorly tending his flock. The shepherd meant had once been Enrique, now it was Isabel. Also scored was a poor friar who had become tremendously rich, possibly Talavera or Alonso de Burgos, and "the old dog who runs always at your side," undoubtedly Mendoza.[15] "The seven rapacious serpents," with a dragon at their head and another behind, signified the closest royal cohorts and linked them to the monster of the Apocalypse. Vera foresaw an eclipse of the moon, "an eclipse like *Luna*," and indications of evils to come, possibly influenced by a comet appearing in 1490 and considered an ominous sign. Badly misjudging what was then permissible, he was sentenced to death for those verses, but managed to avert execution until 1497, when they were no longer topical and he was pardoned.

THE END OF THE WAR

It was time to lay siege to Granada. Boabdil, although he had promised to turn over the city when the eastern provinces fell, did not, for he was leery of the strong war party made up of the military and the refugees, nor would Isabel and Fernando grant him the lands he wanted in exchange. He attacked some Christian forts. The Castilian monarchs termed it rebellion. In the spring of 1491, Isabel called up all nobles and knights and ordered all men of Castile between 18 and 60 to enlist in companies under captains. In April and May Fernando raided the *vega* from the camp at Los Ojos de Huécar, on the outskirts of the city, joined by the *caudillo* of Baza, who came with 150 horse "and took the most dangerous place," and al-Zaghal, with 200 *jinetes*.

Isabel arrived in early June, with Prince Juan, the *infanta* Juana, and a large entourage; her widowed daughter Isabel rejoined her at the end of July. In the interim, Prince Juan had a birthday. That February, Fernando had ordered him turtles from Valencia, to delight a boy. But Juan was 13 years old in June; he had come of age. And so, encamped before Granada, Fernando knighted his son. His *padrinos*, godfather-sponsors, were Medina Sidonia and Cádiz. Juan received a helmet and a coat of mail, campaign breeches and a dagger. Isabel handed him the coins for the liturgical ceremony, twelve Castilian doubloons. The Prince was now a *caballero* with horse and armor who accompanied his father on expeditions and in turn knighted the young sons of *grandes*.

That June too, fulfilling a longstanding desire, Castile's queen first saw Granada's walls and towers, from a high window in a house in the hamlet of Zubia, an occasion of sufficient moment to her to commemorate by the construction of a Franciscan monastery on the spot. She had ridden there accompanied by Fernando, their children, and a number of courtiers, and escorted by Cádiz leading a detachment of cavalry. There was to be no skirmishing, she had instructed him, no responding to taunts should the Granadans come out of the city; she wanted no one killed because of her caprice. Yet the regal procession passing before Granada's walls went beyond caprice; it was a defiant show, flaunting strength and embodying determination, made even more provocative by Cádiz' men galloping back and forth in high spirits. When hundreds of *jinetes* streamed out of the city, those knights, resisting goading only so long, engaged, with losses on both sides. Ballads would tell of it, and of Muslim noblewomen watching from the Alhambra's towers.

Such encounters were indeed the stuff of ballads, and chivalric doings were frequently indulged in during that final siege, for expectations were high, there was not too much else to do, and capitulation seemed only a matter of time. Redolent of chivalry too was the behavior of Cádiz in faithfully escorting his Queen whenever she was in "the lands of the Moors, because he was so feared by them."[16] Heroic indeed was his presence until Granada fell, although suffering from a painful wound received in a skirmish, a lance thrust that traversed his right arm, from which he was never to recover fully.

Looking back with nostalgia on it all as a simpler time before the more deadly and less idealistic Italian wars, a Venetian ambassador, Andrea Navagiero, who was there, recalled the conquest of Granada as the last war waged as giant tournament, with challenges to single combat on both sides and chivalric rules respected:

> It was a beautiful war, with [relatively] little artillery as yet, and brave men were readily seen to be brave. There were daily encounters, and every day there was some fine feat of arms. All the nobility of Spain was there, and all were competing in the conquest of fame. The Queen and her Court urged each one on. There was not a lord present who was not enamored of some one of the ladies of the Queen, and these ladies were not only witnesses to what was done upon the field, but often handed the sallying warriors their weapons, granting them at the same time some favor, together with a request that they show by their deeds how great was the power of their love. What man is so vile, so lacking in spirit, that he would not have defeated every powerful foe and redoubtable adversary, risking a thousand lives rather than return to his lady in shame? For which reason one can say that this war was won by love.[17]

He was wrong in that Granada was won over the long haul by unified effort, superior technology, manipulation of internal factions, money, and tenacity. Yet, especially during the siege of the city itself, resurgent chivalry, fed by a righteous sense of Christian purpose, had a field day, and throughout the campaigns a spirit essentially chivalric had inspired the knights and the captains who inspired the men. Crucial to the chivalric code was service to a lady, and in that war the lady served universally was the Queen. Chivalric and religious attitudes overlapped, mutually reinforcing her prestige. Isabel contributed to that conjunction by behaving as Joan of Arc might have had she been a married queen, and by demonstrating her own dedication to both chivalric virtues and holy war.

Both chivalry and an act of God figured in the most dangerous event of the final siege. In the early hours of July 14, Isabel, who had left a candle burning beside her bed, awakened to a tent in flames. Shepherding Juana and her servants outside, she encountered Fernando running out of his tent in his nightshirt, dagger and sword in hand, cuirass on his arm, thinking it a surprise Muslim attack. Then, while Isabel and her daughter, escorted by a page in nightshirt went to Cabra's tent, Cádiz, gathering (it is said) 3000 men, rode out to make certain that Muslims did not indeed take advantage of their plight, and his Marquesa sent the Queen clothes and all necessaries; on return he himself relinquished to her his own tent. Nothing availed; despite the efforts of the entire army, the fire, fanned by wind, consumed much of the camp.

The Christians rebuilt. They raised tiled houses, constructed principally by the men of the towns and the military orders, with the experience at Baza standing them in good stead, so that "it appeared a well-ordered city." Isabel sent a painting of it on cloth to the Portuguese court, showing it replete with walls, moats, battlements, and towers. Its orderly streets conformed to the shape of a cross (visible as such from Granada's battlements) and it was called Santa Fe, the Holy Faith. Everything was in abundance: silks, cloths, brocades, and all the rest "as though it were a good fair." Isabel saw to its provisioning. In Granada, eight miles distant, there was great unhappiness at such strong indication that the Castilians had come to stay.

Within Granada, although a holy man incited a popular outcry against surrender, Boabdil at length prevailed, convincing his council that with no hope of rescue from abroad, they could not hold out. The formal documents of surrender, the *capitulaciones*, were signed on November 25, and he was given a customary chivalric period of grace, 65 days. The terms were relatively lenient. Granadans might remain. Isabel and Fernando guaranteed to them their lives and property, promised to respect existing laws and religious institutions, and acknowledged their right to practice their religion freely. Education was to remain under Muslim *doctos* and *alfaquies.* Inhabitants would receive three years' exemption from taxes. Boabdil and his family were to have ample domain, in the Alpujarras, and he was to receive 30,000 *castellanos de oro* upon surrender. Granada was to be subject to Castile and to have a Castilian governor. Henceforth its peoples would be *mudéjares.*

Events surrounding the surrender itself further attest to chivalry at work, and to planning awry. Formal surrender was set for January 2, 1492. But, along with the 600 noble Muslims Boabdil dispatched as hostages to the camp at Santa Fe on January 1, he sent a message: a force must come into the Alhambra, secretly that night, to secure it against any trouble during the next day's formalities. The monarchs accordingly dispatched Gutierre de Cárdenas with a contingent of men-at-arms, and in the Torre de Comares Boabdil turned over to him the Alhambra's keys, though not without getting a written receipt for them. Cárdenas stationed guards at all towers and doors, then had Granada's new governor, Iñigo López de Mendoza, the Count of Tendilla, a seasoned warrior and diplomat, come quickly. It is unclear if it was then or the next day that the banners of Castile and León and of Santiago were hoisted on the Tower of Comares and his uncle the Cardinal's great silver cross was raised on the highest tower, the Tower of the Winds. Whenever it was, Isabel was watching and waiting; when she saw the cross and her banners flying atop the Alhambra and heard the shout go up, "¡*Castilla! Castilla*! for *Don* Fernando and *Doña* Isabel!" she fell to her knees and gave thanks to God, and her chapel resounded with the *Te Deum*, "everyone crying with joy."

The official surrender took place next day as planned. The King, the Queen, Prince Juan, one of the *infantas*, the Cardinal, and the court, everyone splendidly dressed, proceeded to within a half-league of the city, stopping by the bank of the Genil river. Fernando forded it to meet Boabdil, who rode out of the gates on a mule, accompanied by 50 knights on horseback. Beforehand, in negotiations on protocol, Boabdil and his indomitable mother had been adamant against his kissing any hands, Isabel and Mendoza equally so in refusing to cede on any bit of due ceremony. At length it had been agreed: Boabdil was to take one foot from the stirrup and to doff his hat, then Fernando would signal he need do no more. And so it went. The two kings then rode to Isabel, who also refused Boabdil's kissing of hands in submission but did admonish him henceforward to behave himself. Boabdil gave the keys of the city to Fernando who passed them to Isabel. They went farther, but there is no agreement as to just where: either from her to Prince Juan, and finally to Granada's governor, Tendilla, or from Isabel to Tendilla and then to Gutierre de Cárdenas. Whatever the progression, the city was hers. Tendilla and the new Archbishop of Granada, Hernando de Talavera, led a contingent of 1000 horse and 5000 foot up to the Alhambra. They met, coming the other way, a straggling procession, Christian captives just released from the dungeons in the rock below the Alhambra. Ragged and malnourished, dragging their chains, they walked in file behind a cross and an image of the Virgin Mary, singing to the God of Israel, to the Old Testament God of war and Deliverer from captivity. He seemed the most appropriate deity.

There is the story of Boabdil returning to the Alhambra in tears, to meet his mother's reproof that he should not cry like a woman for what he could not defend like a man. And there is another, often told and equally suspect: just beyond the Alhambra is an eminence known as the Moor's Sigh where Boabdil is said to have turned to look back sadly as he left Granada. However that may be, Boabdil went with his family to Val de Purchena in the Alpujarras, where he had been granted three towns. He was not to stay long.

Isabel and Fernando made solemn entry into the city on January 6, Epiphany, the Day of Kings, an event commemorated in yet another unreliable but telling anecdote. Against the monarchs' specific prohibition, a knight, spurring ahead, preceded them into the Alhambra. They ordered him beheaded, then—and here the transition from war to peace began—they reconsidered, for he had fought in all the campaigns ever since Toro, and so "they forgave him and made him *mercedes* in that city and kingdom."

AFTERWARDS

They stayed for three months more in Santa Fe, going into Granada during the day only, until advised that the city was safe; after some rapid repairs in the Alhambra they spent the night there in early April. They took over the palace and, while leaving most mosques in the city intact, had the royal mosque converted into a Christian church. Although they ordered all arms in the city collected, uprisings were attempted and a large cache of weapons found, "about which they made much justice." They also had Granada's Jewish quarter demolished; its estimated 20,000 Jews were cast out with the realm-wide expulsion.

Throughout the predominantly Muslim region, they had fortifications erected or strengthened and garrisoned, and new construction techniques employed to counter new artillery technology. In the Alhambra itself, walls were reinforced and gates reconstructed. The *puerta de hierro* is still emblazoned with the royal coat of arms then prominently placed upon it, and their Fs and Ys, yoke and arrows, are visible on the ceilings.

Tendilla, although showing himself acutely sensitive to the disposition of Granada's inhabitants, was essentially a military governor of occupied territory whose difficult assignment it was to incorporate the still-Muslim city within the crown of Castile. To achieve it, he worked in tandem with Granada's first archbishop, that mainstay of royal government and the royal conscience, Talavera, who made or reviewed decisions of every kind. Isabel stayed through May, assuming major responsibility for transforming the Muslim kingdom into a province of Castile, counting on both men and also upon the experienced royal secretary and administrator, Hernando de Zafra, who continued to work with them closely after she left, and to keep her informed.

Throughout the campaign the monarchs had placed large, important subjugated areas and their towns and cities in *realengo*, that is, directly under royal jurisdiction. Others, usually of great size but very rural, they ceded to powerful nobles in return for wartime services. Thus, Cenete became the head town of the *mayorazgo* of its new Marqués, Rodrigo de Mendoza, a bold captain and one of the Cardinal's sons. Muslims of Guadix,

Baza, Almería, and Almuñécar were allowed to settle there, for to their noble proprietors much of the value of such *señoríos* was the presence of Muslim peasants, so hardworking and so experienced in cultivating mountainous regions. Such aristocratic proprietors preferred Muslim subjects; Castilian veterans or emigrants settled mainly on royal domain, usually receiving small holdings. They came principally from Andalusia, New Castile, and Murcia. They also settled along what had been near-deserted frontier. The crown parceled out to them lands and goods through *mercedes*, through purchase, or in *repartimiento*—the division of lands in places where Muslims had been expelled, as in Málaga, Ronda, and Baza. In those towns royal officials had inventoried moveable property and real estate, grants were made from their lists, and it was anticipated that through this system royal revenues would soon be large. Settlers were attracted by initial freedom from taxes and greater social mobility. Castilians gravitated to the city of Granada as well. Though no reapportioning of land occurred there, they enjoyed the advantage of belonging to the dominant faith and culture, an advantage that would increase with time. In 1495, when the three-year moratorium ended, heavy taxes were levied on all Spanish Muslims and the heaviest on those of the former kingdom of Granada. The Muslims of Granada were indeed a subject people by then; worse was to come.

From Granada, the monarchs instructed anyone holding Muslim captives or slaves to turn them over to royal officials, disclosing their cost under oath, and the crown would see that they were reimbursed. Yet such slavery endured. Several years later a traveler wrote of seeing numerous Muslim slaves on the estates of the Marqués de Cádiz. Isabel herself had female Muslim slaves in her domestic service. The suspicion arises that, especially with peace, exceptions were made to general regulations.

The tithes of benefices in churches established as conquest proceeded had been assigned, a third to the parishes and two-thirds to the crown. To endow such new churches, the goods and rents of mosques, hospitals, and religious groups were simply taken over, serving a double function in strapping Muslim institutions. Her account books reveal Isabel's own ongoing donations to those churches, a long list of bells, organs, benches, images, missals, candelabra, monstrances, chalices, ornaments, altarcloths, vestments, and other necessaries. In many of the churches dotting the former kingdom of Granada, a piece of velvet altarcloth or an embroidered vestment is today revered as having been embroidered by Queen Isabel herself; the tradition is an old one, the fabric usually of more recent date.

Crown and Archbishop constructed monasteries for the principal religious orders. Above all, religious dominance was made manifest through continuing to dedicate new establishments to those aspects of Christian belief most repugnant to Muslims: the divinity of Christ and the virginity of Mary. On royal order an artillery engineer was instructed to recast the alarum bells of fortresses for churches. The victors continued to ring out the old with an incessant pealing of the new church bells so much a symbol of Christian triumph and so despised by Muslims. "We hear the cowbells all right," the besieged *malagueños* were supposed to have said in disdain, "but the king has no cows."

Bent upon convincing leading Muslims to become Christian, Isabel made them dozens of gifts including sums of money. Her archbishop, Talavera, true to his principles, was determined to convert all Muslims and to do it without force, through the force of reason, example, and persuasion. Opposed to mass baptism, seeking sincere Christians, and well knowing the dreadful results of forcing Jews to convert, he undertook to understand Muslim customs in order to battle old ways and introduce Christianity more compellingly, and he learned to speak Arabic. Among those won over he strove to eradicate customs equated with Muslim ceremonies, including traditional ways of celebrating birth, marriage, and death. Bathing, since considered a ritual, was discouraged. He expected heads of families to learn Christian rudiments, make the sign of the cross, kneel in church, revere the images, and recite the *Pater noster*, the *Ave Maria*, and the *Credo*. Infants were to be baptized within eight days of birth. Marriage bans and wedding ceremonies had to be the province of priests. The dying had to receive last rites, and the dead be buried in consecrated cemeteries. Families had to attend mass and vespers and family heads go daily to church to pray and receive holy water; the church was to replace the mosque as place of daily gathering. Such converts were to form *cofradías*, mutual aid societies, and send their children to church schools, ideally to learn to read, write, and sing, but at least to learn prayers. And they were to sustain one or two hospitals for their poor and sick. Talavera, with Isabel's help and at his own cost, founded in Granada a seminary for priests, the *Colegio de San Cecilio*. He also put up *segundones*, younger sons of the high nobility, in his own house, teaching them *ciencia y virtud*. All of this accretion of experience would be carried to the New World by missionaries and royal officials, some of them trained by Talavera and Tendilla in Granada.

III

TOWARD EMPIRE

14

The View from Granada.
The Grand Design
1492

As God did his deeds
defense was unavailing
for where He put his hand
the impossible was nearly nothing.

Juan del Encina, on the fall of Granada[1]

"TO SING UNTO GOD A NEW SONG"

We write of the great mercy that Our Lord has shown us in giving us this city. . . .
We assure you that this city of Granada is greater in population than you can
imagine; the royal palace very grand and the richest in Spain.[2]

So read the bailiff of Valencia in a letter of January 1492 from their majesties. They wrote much the same thing to their bishops and to the pope but omitted those mundane details meant to impress the inhabitants of a mercantile port city, and they instructed all their subjects to say prayers and hold processions of thanksgiving for a Spain restored after 780 years; God had given them victory, to His own glory and that of the faith, to their honor and the increase of the realm, and to the honor of their loyal subjects.

They informed Europe's other kings as well. Very detailed letters were received in London from Spain's king and queen, as Francis Bacon recalled, "signifying the final conquest of Granada from the Moors; which action, in itself so worthy, King Ferdinando, whose manner was never to lose any virtue for the shewing, had expressed and displayed in his letters at large, with all the particularities and religious punctos and ceremonies, that were observed in the reception of that city and kingdom."[3] Henry VII, Bacon continued, "naturally affecting much the King of Spain, as far as one King can affect another, partly for his virtues, and partly for a counterpoise to France" sent all the nobles and prelates at court and the mayor and aldermen of London to St. Paul's church, where the Lord Chancellor told them that they were assembled "to sing unto God a new song"; that for now, through "the prowess and devotion of Ferdinando and Isabella, Kings of Spain, and to their immortal honor," were recovered the great and rich kingdom of Granada, for which all Christians must thank God; and that this conquest was obtained "without much effusion of blood. Whereby it is to be hoped, that there shall be gained not only new territory, but infinite souls to the church of Christ, whom the Almighty, as it seems, would have alive that they may be converted." And throughout Europe the victory was seen too as a step toward redressing the loss of Constantinople.

The prestige of Isabel and Fernando soared, and that welcome state of affairs was reflected back to them in lofty prose by ambassadors: from Henry of England, from Venice, and from the pope. Hieronymus Münzer came "on behalf of Maximilian and other Germans" and to see with his own eyes the marvels of which he had heard. He told the King and Queen that their noble deeds were known throughout the universe and that they filled the princes and lords of Germany with admiration, especially for having turned discord and civil war into peace and prosperity. "We see," he wrote of saying to them, "the rulers through whose arm God has caused regeneration of their vassals and the submission of kingdoms and men of other races." Now were the chains of captives broken, the peasant secure, the traveler confident, and Spain in tranquility.

In such accolades the monarchs were jointly spoken of, as Isabel had long insisted they be, as one sovereign head, *los reyes*, or, as Bacon put it, "the kings of Spain." Even Münzer, with no high idea of woman's place, conceded that Isabel had proven herself impossible to overlook: "Such is her counsel in the arts of war and peace, that nearly all hold it above what it is possible the female sex can do . . . I believe that the Omnipotent on high, on seeing Spain languishing, sent this most admirable woman, so that, in union with the king, it might be restored to sound state."[4] Pedro Mártir stated what "*los reyes*" implied, that they were "two bodies animated by a single spirit, for they rule with one mind."[5] Their motto, *tanto monta, monta tanto,* alluded both to their expediency—if something cannot be done one way, try another—and, above all signified joint sovereignty: "as much one as the other."

THE NEXT STEP

True to her usual mode of operation, with one grand-scale enterprise completed, Isabel contemplated a project of yet broader scope: advance into

Africa and the Atlantic. The Spanish claim to the domain of the Visigoths in Africa and the Canary Islands, that claim which in her father's reign had passed from hortatory rhetoric to legitimate enterprise, metamorphized once again, into current program. Recovering *lo suyo*, her own, that which Christian Spaniards had once held had, with her prompting, in the late 1470s provided justification for the seaborne ventures whose goals were territory and gold, security against the Muslims, and besting Portugal. The treaty with Portugal in 1479 had distinguished between eastern and western Barbary, divided by the Strait of Gibraltar, and had recognized Spanish economic interests across from Andalusia in eastern Barbary, nearly coterminus with the kingdom of Fez. Castile's African commerce had accelerated since. Isabel had asserted royal oversight, and though instructing her subjects planning to trade along the western coast to Cape Bojador to seek license from Portugal, she insisted the seas off that coast were free. She also claimed a monopoly of her own and collected fees for fishing in those waters.

The Canaries continued to offer a base to Africa and beyond, and gold to remain a magnet. With Gran Canaria under Castile's jurisdiction, on July 13, 1492, she and Fernando signed an agreement with Alonso Fernández de Lugo for the conquest of La Palma and Tenerife, "to be gained at his own cost and expense." Funded by some Genoese and Florentines and by Medina Sidonia, he sailed in 1493 with 1200 people and 20,000 goats and sheep. The monarchs also garrisoned a small enclave on the Guinea coast itself, at Torre de Santa Cruz de Mar Pequena (Mar Pequena was the name given the waters between Africa and the Canaries), which did a brisk business with Melilla, a Saharan gold terminal. And they profited from a monopoly on Canarian products, principally *orchilla* (a red dye stuff of mediocre quality), and cowrie shells, which sold well to the Portuguese since they were used as a medium of exchange on the Guinea coast.

Although rulers of North Africa had proffered friendship, still there was good reason to be concerned about Granada's extensive coastline, so exposed to expeditions from the opposite shore, especially those of Barbary pirates. Accordingly, Isabel made it her business to bring all major ports in noble hands under the crown. Through a combination of firmness, diplomacy, cash, and exchange she took over as crucial to defense, as naval bases, and as points of enforcing royal customs collection, Cartagena from Juan Chacón, Gibraltar from Medina Sidonia, and, most important, Cádiz.

When that mainstay of the war, Rodrigo Ponce de León, died in August 1492, not yet fifty but having achieved the victory and glory he sought, she and Fernando put on mourning for him; they also extracted from his widow the port of Cádiz. At the intersection of two trading routes, from the Mediterranean to Flanders and England, and from the Barbary coast to Atlantic Andalusia, Cádiz from then on superseded Puerto de Santa María as the royal port of entry for cargo from North Africa and the Atlantic. Thereafter, any merchant might go to Africa but had to stop at Cádiz on return and pay to the crown a fifth of the value of goods brought back, which were usually slaves and gold, the gold estimated as then worth over 200,000 *ducados* annually, the principal shipments of it received by Europe.

By 1492, Bartolomeu Dias had rounded Africa's Cape of Good Hope. But there remained other routes to Asia, through Africa—where Prester John was to be contacted—or through the Mediterranean, although Muslim dominated; and there was the scheme of the Genoese, Columbus, to out-flank Portuguese and Muslims by sailing westward to reach Asia. Yet other plans were afoot. Isabel and Fernando then sent spies to North Africa, among them the chronicler Lorenzo de Padilla, who explained that "As the souls of the King and Queen were great, not contenting themselves with having conquered Granada, they then planned to conquer Africa."[6] In 1494 Münzer noted the readying of ships, men, and provisions, that the King was to go with the armies, that no doubt Africa would soon belong to the Crown of Castile, and that with Africa conquered, it would be easy for *los reyes* to take Jerusalem.[7]

In 1492 an envoy was dispatched from court to that holiest of cities, often depicted on maps as at the center of the world. Jerusalem was seen by Isabel and Fernando not simply as a spiritual center but as heaven's analogue and the ultimate goal of Christians, as it had been viewed by crusaders through-out the centuries, and surely as not impossible to retake to monarchs who had seemingly reversed the Muslim onslaught, or at least as possible to their dynasty. Longstanding was the analogy of the destruction of Spain to that of Jerusalem, and the pairing of the restoration of both.

During the war, prophecy and popular romance had celebrated the royal desire to reconquer Granada, annihilate the sect of Mahomet, and take Christ's tomb. "Nothing remains to Your Majesties except to add to your victories the reconquest of the Holy Sepulchre of Jerusalem," Münzer told them when received at a royal audience soon afterwards, undoubtedly aware his words would be welcome; "this triumph is reserved for you, to crown your triumphs. . . . Now we see the saviors of all Spain."[8] His rhet-oric, if overblown as customary in such circumstances, also attested to a wide cognizance of the grand, visionary design of which Granada's con-quest was but a piece. Similarly, and even earlier, Pedro de Cartagena, a *continuo* at court who had died at Loja, in verses he directed to *la Reina Doña Isabel* had observed: "You will not be well content until the royal standard is raised in Jerusalem."[9] The I in Isabel, he said, stood for *Imperio*, empire. Talavera too had addressed her in a poem as Queen of Jerusalem. The mon-archs of Aragón had indeed long included Jerusalem among their titles.

Certainly the war had been fought within a Spanish sense of purpose transcending gaining Granada. So Diego de Valera had looked forward to unbounded Christian conquest, Spanish led; and successes by 1486 could be advertised by Cádiz as signalling the advent of the warrior-emperor of the last days come to redeem Jerusalem. In 1492, the prophesied world emperor seemed associated with *los reyes* jointly. And Innocent VIII, in writ-ing to Isabel in 1489, had spoken of the eleventh hour as near. Theirs, it seemed eminently possible, was that eleventh hour, the time of the Last

Days, of, as one prophecy had it, "the Age of Triumph, when peace and material goods would abound, Jew and infidel be converted, and Jerusalem would be glorified."[10]

A treatise published in 1493, congratulating both monarchs for restoring lands lost for 800 years and retrieving infinite souls captured by the Moors, spoke of another aspect of the last times, that "Heaven must be praised for giving us monarchs who follow the heart of God" and that they had done everything to the glory of Jesus Christ "and so against Satan, who in the form of a dragon through snares had sown in in your lands . . . *tanta ziza-nía*," meaning, roughly, "so much confusion."[11] Victory over Granada immediately stimulated pent-up expectation of Satan's imminent defeat, that necessary prelude to the second coming and the final day of judgment. A prophecy then circulated too of the eagle having ascended and the lion having roused to combat the serpent, much in the same spirit as a popular *Book of Antichrist* that also appeared in 1493 spoke of a great conflict immi-nent: Antichrist, Muslims, and Jews against all Christendom—which would win, led by a Spanish king; the world would then convert, and the golden age arrive.

Whether or not the last days loomed, God had clearly been with Spain's monarchs recently and continued to obligate them to do their utmost. This point of view was practicality in Granada in 1492, the very fact of being there confirming the great responsibility they continued to bear as Chris-tendom's divinely designated champions. Whatever the intensity of Isa-bel's own apocalyptic or messianic outlook, she and Fernando knew the value of such pronouncements and believed themselves directed by God; certainly the conquest of Granada had confirmed that they were on the right course, that the hearts of *los reyes* were in the hands of the Lord.

In 1492 then, the vision of Jerusalem as ultimate goal gave cohesive reli-gious and dynastic meaning to victory and to continuing campaign, to all the various royal initiatives embarked upon shortly thereafter: expansion into Africa, the Atlantic, and the Mediterranean; the expulsion of the Jews, the sponsoring of Columbus, even involvement in Italy and the further Por-tuguese marriages; and to an alliance with Egypt (which, handily, Merlin was said to have stated would precede the world's end). That sweeping ongoing vision also imbued their past accomplishments with greater glory, and higher purpose. Those enterprises were to be the stuff of the last decade of Isabel's life, parts of a grand, indeed grandiose, dynastic and imperial scheme to expand Spain into empire and achieve hegemony over Christen-dom. To Isabel, in 1492 residing with Fernando in the Alhambra, holding sway over that symbol of the heart of Muslim Iberia, that Islam could be vanquished throughout the world and Christendom's heart be liberated, at least by her progeny, would not have seemed impossible.

It was in 1492 also that the humanist, Elio Antonio de Nebrija, recalled that when, during a visit of hers to Salamanca, he had told the queen of his plan to write a Castilian grammar, the first in any European vernacular, she had asked why, and that Hernando de Talavera had answered before he could "that after Your Highness subdues beneath your yoke many barbarous peoples, and nations with foreign tongues, with conquest they will have to receive the laws conquerors give the conquered and, with them, our language." It was a sentiment that Nebrija himself, in dedicating a Spanish grammar to her, expressed as "language has always been the companion of empire."[12] To Talavera and Nebrija, and to Isabel and other Castilians in 1492, reconquest had become synonymous with lofty purpose and an empire beyond Spain, their grand design encompassed dominating and converting other peoples; it was to be a compound enterprise combining national and religious expansion, its composite goals to gain territories yielding material and spiritual profit, and glory.

THE FRUITS OF WAR: MONARCHY AND THE ECONOMY

War had proved a stimulus to implementing the royal program unveiled at Toledo in 1480. The monarchs and great noble families had established a mutually satisfactory relationship. The nobility had gained wealth and aggregated titles. At the same time, those nobles by birth who held court posts in 1492 did so very respectfully and alongside *letrado* administrators and men more recently ennobled by Isabel, preeminent among them Chacón, Cárdenas, and Cabrera, all of whom were tremendously wealthy by the end of the war. The monarchs had granted to the 15 great lines a third of all royal *mercedes* and (from 1489) those *grandes* had in turn bought royal *juros*, and they had enjoyed an expansion of their holdings. Spain's aristocrats now bridged two worlds, those of medieval barony and modern court. And if their baronial autonomy and military function had diminished, their militant ideals had not, but, reinforced by war and taken up by the new men, their essentially chivalric values had become imbued with greater patriotic and religious content and now permeated society.

War too, had been kind to lesser nobles, the urban *caballeros*. They had gained power locally, directing town councils and *hermandades* and prospering within the growth attendant upon a wartime economy. Greater cooperation and more direct relations with the crown had brought them a good deal of freedom from the high nobility and a greater preeminence over *el común*, the four-fifths of the populace who alone paid taxes. And population had mounted. Initially, war had also elicited a census, taken by Quintanilla in 1482, who came up with 1,800,000 householders, translating into perhaps five million people in Castilian lands (not counting Granada) and another million or so under Aragón. With more people than ever before, towns and surrounding rural areas grew, as did the domination by both towns and the nobility of hinterlands, their land and their villagers. Still, it all went on under the watchful eye of *corregidores*, who had become generally accepted in towns, fixtures, overseeing everything, symbols of the royal presence.

The war had contributed to royal goals in some ways most likely not anticipated. During it, heightened demand and the use of money had expanded the production of goods and services, stimulated transportation and communication, and furthered the economic integration of Spain's regions. War had promoted the navy and merchant shipping, production of cotton and wool and their working into cloth, and the output of foodstuffs. The bulk of royal income, which had until 1480 derived from sales taxes (the *alcabala*) and customs duties (the *almojarifazgo*) had thereafter vastly increased through extraordinary imposts that consequently the monarchs sought to retain: the *cruzada* receipts and church tithes, subsidies voted by ecclesiastical assemblies, the levies on prelates, the *hermandad*, and municipalities; gifts, loans, and forced loans (some repaid, many others covered by *juros*); the mortgaging of future income, and the funds coming through the Inquisition. Isabel and Fernando were successful in that exactions initially levied as emergency measures would continue to generate most royal income, which was to double by the century's end. Even so, expenses outran it, and from 1490 on the crown sold *juros*, mortgaged future returns, and built public debt.

War had not only brought Isabel and Fernando greater and more direct control of society, but invaluable experience in financial management. And while it was not yet the time of comprehensive economic programs, many of their specific decrees had to do with economic matters and their diplomatic and political measures had a large economic component: thus vying for African gold as metal, merchandise, and money was a large factor in the rivalry with Portugal, and access to the port of Alexandria, a hub of trade with the east, was a primary reason why good relations with Egypt's sultan were deemed vital.

Just what Isabel's economic interests and priorities were can only be pieced together. Overall, the economy was to benefit the royal treasury to the greatest extent possible, and seen as crucial to that end was effective collection of taxes, in turn based upon duties and sales, preponderantly of raw materials, so that much depended upon a thriving commerce. Nor can the suspicion be dismissed that Isabel and Fernando knew that accreting gold in the royal treasury was not necessarily the same thing as not allowing any bullion to leave the country. Decrees against gold leaving were issued seemingly to discourage its export *per se*, but other reasons readily present themselves: to curb smuggling, to encourage profits being exported in products of the land, to have as much gold as possible go through royal mints, and to make money through sale of exemptions to that ordinance. It was also most desirable that the gold and silver that was reexported be in coins, yield royal customs returns and sales taxes, and that their exchange for one another profit the treasury. While bullion was a prime desiderata, the most advantageous way of procuring it had proven not necessarily to be the most direct. Theirs was an outlook that can be characterized as early mercantilist.

The monarchs took some specific measures to stimulate the economy in accord with their priorities. In 1491, among other steps toward more efficient customs collection, they had a list drawn of *almojarifazgo* charges. They limited export of cereals, arms, and iron, thus keeping them more affordable internally (and enabling a good business in selling royal licenses for their export), promoted better flow of silver, demanded sounder silver coinage, and in 1497 legislated to make Castilian gold coinage uniform with Europe's best. Isabel herself invested in ships on the Flanders route, both sent olive oil there, and Fernando took a personal interest in large-scale wheat trading. They licensed corsairs, and their fleets guarding Castilian shipping also dabbled in piracy; thus in 1484 royal ships seized two Venetian galleys off the Maghrib laden with gold. The Venetians were known to be in league with the Turks and suspected of supplying the Granadans, but, equally explanatory, Sicily minted gold coins, exported them and re-exported ingots, and Sicily's King and Queen were to receive a royal fifth on confiscated cargoes.

Chiefly interested in distribution and only secondarily in production, they protected their merchants abroad and foreign merchants in Spain, and encouraged both sorts of traders, as well as the production ultimately most lucrative to commerce and so to the royal treasury. They promoted production of iron, so vital to war and so profitable an export. They encouraged shipbuilding, especially of the large vessels preferred for war. And they protected Granada's silk industry and its much sought-after high-quality satins, damascenes, and velvets. And while their ordinances outlined the economic functions of municipalities, they left agricultural production and localized distribution to the town councils and the nobles. They frowned on internal customs barriers, for such revenue redounded chiefly to localities and magnates. And, spurring them to exercise control of the military orders—they took charge of Calatrava in 1487, Alcántara in 1494, and Santiago in 1499—were the great revenues of those august bodies, for the orders owned huge flocks of sheep and held sway over a tenth of Castile's land and its population.

Los reyes, in the process of promoting those elements of the domestic economy that they perceived as integral to profitable foreign trade, assisted nobles involved in producing for and distributing to expanding overseas markets. And especially did they increasingly favor the owners of large flocks, who were usually the nobility and the military orders, and they smiled upon the distributers of wool as well. Thus in 1492 they confirmed the exclusive privileges of the Mesta, which had supplied funds to the crown during the war, its wool a staple of trade with Flanders, Brittany, and England. The crown continued to collect revenues on the sale of Mesta wool and the seasonal migrations of its vast transhument flocks which had doubled in numbers within the century, to somewhere close to three million sheep. By 1492 great nobles were consolidating control within it, and owners of smaller flocks dwindling. And in 1494 Isabel would license an exclusive *consulado* or guild for Burgos merchants, who sent wool to England and the continent in Basque ships and had their own communities in key ports abroad. In Isabel's reign wool became *the* export of Castile, its production to prove so disasterously inhibiting to both agriculture and industry. Those verses derived from earlier ones attacking Enrique IV and now accusing her of extracting *tanta lana,* so much wool that a mantle made from it could cover the country, while alluding to her favoring of wool interests, had as their primary point that she was squeezing her subjects unmercifully and indicated that "wool" was thought of as synonymous with wealth.

During the war, buying and selling with money had surged; and the vast wartime operations and their funding had brought sophistication in the uses of credit. Royal ordinances accordingly made credit easier and, in doing so, stimulated the economy. In 1492 a complex banking and money system was evolving, with mechanisms, including various sorts of bonds, to get around condemnation for usury. Barcelona, once a center of banking and commerce, was recovering. Valencia was at its height and prospering from relations with thriving Castile. Within Castile, greater economic integration among its diverse regions paralleled the expansion of exterior trade. More merchants and great numbers of oxcarts and mule trains plied an extending network of roads. Isabel and Fernando personally kept an eye on the royal fairs of Medina del Campo, among Europe's largest, which they continued to enjoy visiting, and which, despite devastating fires in 1491 and 1492, were more popular than ever as centers for internal exchange and long-distance commerce and banking. The monarchs had made certain that all nobles holding competing fairs had ceased doing so. From 1492 until Isabel's death in 1504, though with fluctuations, Castile flourished, particularly the south. Seville was Spain's leading commercial and banking center and Castilians increasingly profited from Granada's wealth and commerce. In 1492 it was assumed at court that all subjects must in some way or other benefit from the realm's prosperity.

The monarchs relied in economic and financial matters on Quintanilla and Cárdenas, and ultimately on Talavera and Mendoza, who in turn made use of Genoese, Florentine, and Venetian merchants and bankers. Venice had been a traditional ally of Aragón, but the Genoese were increasingly favored by both monarchs as merchants and bankers, as they were by the pope. Whatever the extent of Jewish and *converso* funds and services, the Genoese, among whom also were *conversos,* had come to either compete or collaborate in providing them. At the end of Isabel's reign there would be 300 Genoese merchant companies in Spain. Although Spanish *conversos* and other Spaniards continued to engage in commerce and finance, the Italians had the advantage in established international networks permitting large transactions and long-distance trade.

Fitting within her devotion to order, Isabel's economic instinct was toward thrifty and efficient management of resources; thus the remark attributed to her, that anyone wanting to put a fence around Castile should hand it over to the Hieronymites, whom she knew at firsthand to be hardworking, productive, and skilled in administration. In 1492, it was to her a moral imperative that all her subjects should become more industrious, and devout as well.

CLEANSING THE REALM

With peace at hand, Isabel shifted some wartime (and warlike) energies to eradicating corruption throughout society, beginning by endeavoring to reform the institution responsible for propagating, upholding, and policing morality, the Church. Such reform she expected would improve the learning and morals of the clergy, filter outwards to most Castilians, and strengthen respect for authority. Thus, as Granada capitulated, royal decrees signaled an escalating severity toward erring friars, their prevalence soon to be commented upon in a "tragi-comedy," La Celestina, wherein the procuress, Celestina, remarks: "The clergy were so numerous that there were some of all kinds: some very chaste, and others whose duty it was to support me in my profession. There are still some of these, I think."[13] (Indeed, La Celestina depicts the postwar society Isabel sought to reform.) Royal orders went out that concubines of clergy, until then commonly accepted as a fact of life, were to be publicly scourged, and heavy penalties were levied as well upon laymen who kept concubines.

Some other sorts of behavior deemed highly immoral were punished savagely. Munzer wrote of seeing, on leaving Almería in 1494, the bodies of six men dangling from a tall post. Italians, convicted of sodomy—that is, homosexuality—they had been hung first by their necks, then by their feet, but only after "their genitals had been cut off and hung around their necks, because in Spain they hate this sin greatly." Three years later Fernando and Isabel, concluding the existing penalties "insufficient to eradicate such an abominable crime," decreed conviction for sodomy carried with it guilt of heresy and high treason.[14] In the last decade of Isabel's reign royal authority reached ever more persistently into private life to impose an orthodox morality. Interestingly, some offenses punished severely were ones once linked to royal behavior, to Fernando's often commented upon fondness for gambling, and to Enrique IV's purported homosexuality. That homosexuality was associated with Antichrist was not lost on Enrique's opponents nor on publicists in the 1490s coupling orthodoxy, prophecy, royal absolutism, and the imminence of the Last Days.

Nor was the papacy exempt from Isabel's penchant for propriety. Her opinion of the new pope, Alexander VI, who succeeded Innocent VIII in July 1492, had never been high. Even though as a Valencian he might favor Spain, to her he remained Rodrigo Borja. The doctrine of papal infallibility lay in the future. She confided to the papal nuncio that if His Beatitude had heard of her censure he should know it was made not through animosity but through love, for it distressed her to hear said that the wedding festivities of his daughter Lucrecia were scandalous, and she wished he would show less heat in the affairs of his son the Duke Caesare and his brothers. A chronicler, the newcomer Alonso de Santa Cruz, echoed her sentiments in summing up Borja's reputation: the pope was ambitious and greedy and his two sons were thought not very good Christians. Santa Cruz's inference was that his monarchs were much better ones. They thought so too.

Affirming the royal championing of orthodoxy and contest for power with the papacy, spoken of ever more respectfully, and attracting crowds to its public events, the Spanish Inquisition continued to ensure in its battle against Satan that cohesion through an apocalyptic faith and the unity born of wartime commitment was perpetuated. In 1491 the monarchs confirmed the ascending power of the Holy Office in sanctioning an accusation of heresy made against the powerful and esteemed bishop of Segovia, his parents and relatives, and against other ecclesiastics as well. And since trials of bishops were reserved to the papacy, another contest with Rome ensued, which the monarchs would win, emerging as the most assiduous of Christians.

It was patent that in the cleansing and consolidating of the body politic and the campaign for moral regeneration there was no room for cultural or religious plurality. The Inquisition both continued to impress that point and to intensify belief in its validity, in the process making appear ever more anomalous Spain's mix of faiths and peoples. The Muslims were seen as a problem on its way to eventual solution through baptism or emigration. As for the Jews, their value to the crown had diminished as had their numbers and wealth and, ever more unpopular, they were viewed as a threat to that orthodoxy of New Christians now equated with internal peace. To Isabel by 1492, Spain's Jews were a remnant of a people whose time had come and gone. Her decision to expel them that year (of which more presently) attested to the continuation of a war-reinforced crusading spirit and to a recognition that the presence of Jews made Spain look old fashioned and heterodox, and so was a hindrance to its assuming what had become so important to her, a rightful position of primacy in Europe and all Christendom.

Primacy in Europe appeared very possible in 1492. Her son would inherit a united and expanded realm (although one not yet referred to as Spain out of deference to Portugal and Navarre), indeed an empire extending overseas. The marriages arranged for her children were expected to cement alliances with Atlantic Europe, but they also looked beyond immediate European concerns. She had had the *infanta* Isabel marry in Portugal not only because of shared border and lineage and for strategic and economic reasons, but also to merge dynasties, so that one day a grandchild of hers would come to its throne. Equally, the marriages planned with England and the Habsburgs confirmed dynastic power and stature. They were also useful to surround France, Spain's chief competitor in Europe. The ambitions of the new young French king, Charles VIII, in Italy were of particular concern in 1492; they would soon derail Spanish plans to move into Africa.

By 1492, Isabel herself had achieved a standing unheard of for a monarch who was female. She had made her mark in foreign courts and with the papacy as well. The war had proven one of those situations of crisis, change, and innovation in which the impact of individuals is greatest, and none had been greater than that of the Queen, Isabel.

THE QUEEN AT 40

In 1492 Isabel, at 40, was at a height of power and prestige. Pedro Mártir was not alone in thinking that she surpassed all woman and all of the ancients in rectitude, constancy, and "the valor to commit great enterprises," nor in realizing that she was dowered with many more and more powerful kingdoms than possessed by the king, nor that "in everything, whatever she orders is done." And, as he told an Italian friend, "she commands in such a way that she always appears to do it in accord with her husband, so that the edicts and other documents are published with the signature of both. . . . These virtues, unheard of in a woman, together with the magnanimity of her strong heart, have won her merited fame." As for Fernando, "The king does not disagree with this [verdict], for with her counsel she alleviates for him many preoccupations and cares."[15] Lucio Marineo Sículo, at court in 1497 on Isabel's invitation and eventually Fernando's secretary, would concur, in saying that although both showed a true majesty, "in the judgment of many, the Queen was of greater beauty, more lively intelligence, a heart more grand, and greater gravity."[16]

Isabel was not small, she was becoming stout, and she was reckoned a force. Münzer in 1494 thought her most imposing, and that she looked no more than 36. With Fernando she had established a highly effective *modus vivendi*, sharing a history, indeed a universe, a highly developed mutual understanding and appreciation, a working partnership in exercise of authority, and a mutual love and reliance upon one another, fully confident of together personifying sovereignty and dynasty. As Pulgar said, love held their wills joined. Their closeness and trust, there from the beginning, had become accepted and admired, indeed was being written of as a marvel of the world.

Even so, Isabel was jealous. She loved the king her husband so much, said Marineo Sículo, that she continually watched for signs he might love another. And if she felt he was looking at some woman of the household with any sign of love, she prudently found a way to remove that lady. She had cause; Fernando had had children by other women. Loving him intensely, respecting him highly, she was at once a jealous wife and a queen regnant, consummate in matters of state, where she always stood her ground tenaciously.

She guarded too against rivals to her faith; husband and faith were monopolies, to be preserved from poachers. Her will, always strong, iron, had been forged by inculcated moral principles and religious beliefs into steel in the crucible of war, so that it had become well tempered, even slightly flexible when necessary. She was not known to smile readily. Reserved, she nonetheless showed a maternal warmth convertible as the occasion might demand into a matriarchal concern, and she demonstrated a compassion for individual suffering, although it was allayable in the aggregate or in consideration of ends she viewed as highly principled and desirable, or if the individuals in question were not Christians.

And to Isabel, vengeance remained a fact of life and exacting it always sweet, as though revenge restored balance, even harmony. She was a stickler for retributive rather than exemplary justice, as well as for being loved and feared, a stern judge in the manner she most admired, that of Old Testament kings. She thought of herself as highly reasonable, delighted in being proven right and, as Pulgar admitted, although she listened to advice, she altered her opinions only with great difficulty. There is the story that when Fernando wanted to dispatch a certain knight on important business, although she suggested the man not be sent because he had poor judgment, he was, and he did well. But, when again sent on business and he botched it, she had her secretary award him a *juro* of 30,000 *maravedís*. The mystified secretary asked why she gave that fellow *mercedes* now, when she had not done so when he had performed well? Answered Isabel: Because now he had done what was reasonable in going wrong, as he had not before in getting it right. Yet, if tending to equate what she expected with what was reasonable, indeed with what should be, Isabel retained a gift for surrounding herself with very loyal and very capable people, as well as a great penchant for irony.

Münzer spoke of her as extremely devout, pious, and sweet, qualities he obviously admired highly in women; and Marineo Sículo, himself a court chaplain, noted that she had many chaplains and collected about her the wisest priests.[17] He did not say that they were the most observant or the holiest. He also recalled that from his arrival in the late 1490s every Thursday of Holy Week both monarchs imitated the apostles: they had twelve paupers brought in and they washed their feet, fed them and served them at table, and give them new clothes and a gold ducat apiece. Yet it was Fernando whom Marineo singled out as punctilious in personal devotions. As to Isabel, he was more struck by the display she made of religious diligence and he also noted that she was reputed "to follow more the way of rigor than of piety."

She was, he observed in high praise, "a great lover of virtue." He used the word virtue not only in a moral sense, but also in the fashion of humanists, as individual excellence, among its components sterling character, mastery of letters and of one's self, and right living as well as right relationship to God, and he perceived her correctly as esteeming that quality greatly. Nor were fame and glory outside the purview of such virtue, so that he could add admiringly that she "was desirous of great praise and illustrious reputation." She had always been; but now in the 1490s she could in good conscience see those pursuits as eminently virtuous. And certainly she had, as she acknowledged to Talavera in 1493, achieved greatness and prosperity.

Pulgar had earlier admitted that while she was naturally inclined to be truthful, "wars and changes" made her sometimes deviate, and he corroborated her reliance on inspiring a combination of love and fear in stating that, while she made many bountiful grants, she said that queens should conserve lands, because in turning them over they lose the rents with which to make *mercedes* in order to be loved, and so diminish their power to be feared. She also valued ceremony and wished to be served by great noblemen, with great reverence and much humbling. Pulgar made excuses: it was said to be a vice that she displayed too much pomp, but *el rey* is superior and ought to shine above all the estates, for he has divine authority in the land. *El rey* was she, a woman of great heart.

She had remarkable stamina and a strong constitution and had suffered but few illnesses. Yet sometime in 1491 she wrote to Torquemada saying she had not responded to his letters, hoping each day to write by hand, for she had been indisposed with eye trouble and tertiary fevers and was unable to write, but that "now, thank God, I am better."[18] She also suffered while encamped at Santa Fe with swollen legs, then attributed to too much riding. Eye trouble, fevers, and swelling would all recur. And while there is a story that she took an oath not to bathe until Granada fell, and another that she did not bathe at all, it would be very odd behavior in someone so fastidious in all else, who so intensely endorsed other sorts of cleanliness as holiness. Yet bathing was associated with Muslim and Jewish rites and customs, and the Inquisition, having made religious issues of cultural habits, considered frequent washing of the body among the most blatant indications of heretical behavior; and from the twelfth century on the Church had held that bathing aroused erotic notions. Moreover when, years before, Sánchez de Arévalo had praised her half-brother by stating he bathed little, it was then understood not as a compliment to Enrique's orthodoxy but as evidence of his lacking "Roman effeminism." In 1492 Isabel did restore the Alhambra's baths but, with public baths in severe disrepute and anything resembling ritual bathing a matter for the Inquisition, whatever the fastidious Queen did privately, she did not publicize that she bathed.

Isabel, as she so often demonstrated, loved music and valued it tremendously in devotions, public display, war, and court life. Musicians had always accompanied her processions and her armies. A chapel traveled everywhere with her, composed of 20 singers, two organists, and a choir of 15 to 25 boys, among the best in European courts, as were her composers and musicians. Notable still are Juan de Anchieta, who among other pieces composed a mass for her on the surrender of Granada, and Juan del Encina, who not only wrote music but collected in his *Cancionero del Palacio* of 1496 over 300 songs of the court, among them many ballads sung to lute and viol. And Isabel enjoyed theatre, as was observable from the time she commissioned and played in Gómez Manrique's *momo* and, ever after, in her calculatedly superb performance as Queen of Castile.

DYNASTY

In everything she did there was the sense of dynasty. When visiting her mother in Arévalo she waited on her personally and thought it instructive to her children to see her do so. To them she showed strong maternal love and in them she found a promise of continuity. She centered much affection and her dynastic hopes in her son and heir, Juan. She paid great attention to his upbringing and did not stint on his court, his activities, his clothing, and his retinues, nor on his participation in court pageantry and festivities. He was given his own household and there waited upon as befitted a great prince, with exact protocol maintained from rising to retiring, with a hierarchy of servants to dress and undress him and *grandes* to attend him. She attached to his household her own mentors: Gonzalo Chacón, now known as *el viejo* and whose grandson of the same name was one of Juan's companions, and Gutierre de Cárdenas, as his *mayordomo mayor* and *contador*. Juan's tutor, Diego de Deza, was a nephew of yet another of her long-time comptrollers, Rodrigo de Ulloa. She arranged her son's daily routine. Each morning there were prayers with Deza, then mass, then lessons. Since he particularly enjoyed music, she would often send to him during his daily two-hour siesta her music master and four or five choirboys, and he would sing with them, tenor. He was given his own musicians as well and he owned and played a number of instruments, among them the first *claviórgano*—a combination of organ and plucked string instrument—in Spain, made by a Muslim grandmaster artisan from Zaragoza; it was a present from his half-brother, young Alfonso de Aragón, Archbishop of Zaragoza, Fernando's son.

Yet Juan's health was always delicate, his diet and regimen carefully monitored. Each morning doctors visited and he reported to them on how he had slept, and on his digestion and bodily functions. Münzer, indicating physical disability, wrote of having saluted the prince in Latin and of Juan's understanding it but ordering Deza to reply for him since, said Münzer, he suffered from a weakness of the lower lip and tongue which impeded his answering plainly. Isabel spoke of her son as "my angel," and had him sent treats considered good for digestion: strawberry conserves, lemon blossom candies, sugared sweets, and jars of quincemeat from what she referred to as "Valencia del Cid."[19]

Juan's upbringing tells a good deal about Isabel. One of his pages later recalled that in his education the Queen had cared "as much for letters as for other abilities and, above all, for virtue."[20] Manly virtue included proficiency in arms. Juan was given a master of arms, and he slept with a sword at the head of his bed and was instructed in its use. His father had knighted him before Granada. His mother had even earlier provided as companions for him ten knights, five mature, five young, "a species of *colegio*." One, who fought at Granada, dedicated to the boy a translation into Castilian of Caesar's commentaries; his purpose, he informed him, was patriotic, for arms would not benefit his prince without good counsel. Juan corresponded with Lucio Marineo and with Juan del Encina, who adjudged him as learned in *sciencia* as in empire. He was, that is, raised in an atmosphere, permeating the court, composed of apocalyptic Christianity, resurgent chivalry, and a rising vogue for Roman classicism.

Isabel gave much thought to Juan's education, designing it as an ideal upbringing for a Christian prince, its principles derived from the *Siete Partidas* and the mirrors of princes as glossed by current usages and humanism, yet with a basic emphasis on religious orthodoxy. Her unusual attention to his education. and her ideas about what constituted it, were reflected in a treatise written by a courtier close to her, Alonso Ortiz, in the form of a dialogue between herself and Cardinal Mendoza. Surely echoing her own concerns, the principal question raised in that treatise was how to achieve the spiritual health of the prince and the answer given was through learning good habits in childhood. In it, Mendoza presented a highly traditional rationale with some humanistic overlay. He cited the Platonists' and Pythagoreans' understanding of purification in stating that the stars incline us and the wiles of the demons push us toward vices, that original sin infected all, corrupting the flesh weighing on the soul; that the flesh submitted to the influence of the stars but the will remained free, subject only to God, and accordingly needed instruction, in order to gain wisdom. Training in will power, he explained, would develop natural abilities and correct bad inclinations. Accordingly, he advised an education consonant with the stages advocated by Plato and Aristotle, one leading to virtue, both moral and intellectual, to the happy mean. Virtue and vice he declared within human power, life a pilgrimage toward blessedness and bliss, toward the eternal life of which San Juan speaks. It was a guide for a prince's education, simply assuming much of what such guides had heretofore customarily stated, that the monarch's spiritual health was the same as the common good. It concentrated rather, on that specific prince's personal development of wisdom and justice, moral qualities and high character, as the route to his individual salvation.

In that treatise, and mirroring Isabel's outlook by all indications, was the observation that fables have the purpose of teaching children good customs easily and pleasurably, although the examples given seem not to have much to do with good customs; they are those of Hercules and the pagan gods: "all the theology of the ancients [that] brings with it the lightning, the shield, the trident, the battle-axe, the dragon, and the staff of Thyrsus [carried by Dionysius and his attendants]."[21] Indications are that Isabel shared such views and found in them a rationale for her own enjoyment in reading fables, fabulous history, and historic romances. She also saw to it that humanistic philosophy was not absent from Juan's own education, and she established on similar principles a school at court where the sons of nobles were educated by Pedro Mártir to be loyal future leaders and suitable companions for the prince.

Yet while she approved of her son being instructed in the humanism, the combination of Greek and Latin classics and Christian philosophy then in vogue, she placed closest to him his tutor, Deza, a Dominican theologian whom she would later appoint Inquisitor General, who reputedly "neither in words nor deeds ever indicated he knew nor even suspected anything lewd or indecent," and who, unlike most of his peers, was said to be a virgin. It was a choice promising a grounding in Christian morality and scholasticism and an emphasis on the value of purity in life and faith. Monies went out for Thomas Aquinas' *Summa*, for a book by St. Bonaventure, for a breviary and a Bible, "and a book on ethics." In 1493 she commissioned the Bishop of Coria to write a manual of Christian edification for the young nobles at court. Nor was statecraft forgotten: "In order to learn to make justice," at 18 Juan received his own court and council, and from the age of 10 on his parents had him sit with them from time to time in deliberation on affairs of the realm. Mártir in praising Juan effusively relayed his mother's hopes for him: "for us you are a *vice-díos* on earth.'[22] Too, Isabel carefully saved some of her son's Latin copybooks.

Nor did she, mindful of her own inadequate preparation, neglect readying her daughters to become queens, if in their cases most likely queens-consort, although she was well aware that Juan's health was delicate. When the humanist, Luis Vives, at Catalina's court in England, counseled that young women be educated in letters, spinning, and handwork, and observed that "they are honest exercises that remain to us from that golden century of our predecessors," he was referring to the upbringing Isabel had given her four daughters. All of them had letters, that is, Latin, instructed by friar-tutors and also by the humanist brothers, Antonio and Alexander Geraldini, invited to court by Isabel.

The *infanta* Isabel was in 1492 a widow devoting herself to good works, but she was also welcomed into her parents' discussions of state matters. The *infanta* Juana, Münzer reported, was highly learned "for her age and sex" in reciting and composing verses. Later, in Flanders, she would speak the French of her new court as well as some Latin. She enjoyed dancing and her passion was music; Juana played several instruments, among them the clavichord. Catalina was proficient on keyboard and harp; moreover, she was learned in philosophy, literature, and religion, and had Latin, Castilian, French, English, and German. During her years as England's queen, between 1509 and 1527, Catherine of Aragón attracted to court the learned and the wise, her piety and erudition praised by Vives and Erasmus. María, who would become Queen of Portugal, if apparently the least gifted of Isabel's offspring, would be known for her own seven children and the education she provided for them, so like her own.

THE QUEEN STUDIES, THE QUEEN PRAYS

During the war, Isabel herself began studying Latin. Within a year she thought that she understood enough that, should any preacher or choirboy err in pronunciation, she would take note and afterward correct him. It had bothered her that she had not the learning prescribed in mirrors for princes and by her closest advisors, the letters thought to complete an aristocrat's education and to burnish a royal image, the Latin believed necessary to read what were considered the best and most useful writings on law and government and war, the Latin her father had, and, determined to set an example, she did. Asked the humanist, Juan de Lucena, rhetorically, "Do you not see how many have begun to learn, admiring your Highness? What kings do, good or bad, we all try to do. . . . When the king gambles, we are all gamblers. When the Queen studies, we become students."[23]

Isabel was well read by all accounts and she encouraged the new art of printing; thus Valera, praising a German who with several of his compatriots was responsible for having introduced printing into Spain, referred to him as "a familiar of Your Highness."[24] The printing press arrived in 1478, in Seville, the same year as the Inquisition and, like it, was a boon to the royal reach. In the early 1480s Talavera had some presses set up to print bulls of crusade; and printing ensured that the royal laws Montalvo compiled were, as ordered in 1480, available to every town, and facilitated a wide dissemination for his edition of the *Partidas*, printed in 1491. And, much as Isabel set the tone for study, it is obvious that even where she did not commission a book herself, her policies and her taste in reading influenced what was printed.

She owned, in manuscript and in print, in Castilian and in Latin, nearly 400 volumes, many of them additions made during her reign to the royal library she had first encountered in Segovia. From the various guides for princes she knew, as Talavera had reminded her, that monarchs should love reading and books. Most of that royal collection was as expected. There were the traditional treatises on the education of the prince, some of those in manuscript possibly inherited, others only recently printed. There were numerous religious works, Bibles, books of hours, psalters, commentaries, and the philosophy adjudged Christian of Aristotle, Seneca, and Boethius. Assuredly, most books printed were religious, and of an approved sort. A papal injunction of 1487 ordered the clergy to keep an eye on what was being printed in theology, and, among the other events of 1492, it was forbidden to publish entire Bibles in the vernacular.

Yet she also owned and is said to have especially enjoyed those chivalric romances that were among the earliest of published works: *The Prison of Love*, a courtly romance appreaing in 1492 (and going through 20 Spanish editions) and *Tirant lo Blanc* (1490), the adventures in Africa and Asia Minor of a white knight steeped in the fortitude and forebearance of courtly love. And she had several copies of the prophecies of Merlin. If her serious opinion was akin to an informed one of the day, that "it is said the Devil was

Merlin's father and I would not advise anyone to waste time in such read-
ing,"[25] yet by classifying such stuff as fables she could read it with clear conscience. Far places and distant times interested her; she owned Sir John
Mandeville's book of his travels, surely approached as partially fabulous.
And there is something else. Isabel was earthy, not of delicate sensibility,
and if decorous also passionate. Two of her favored courtiers, both priests,
Alonso de Burgos and Iñigo de Mendoza, were renowned for being ribald.
Some erotic works she owned also reflected the late medieval delight in
playful obscenity; such were the *Decameron*, the tales of the Archpriest of
Hita, and a purported biography of Aesop illustrated with "scabrous
engravings."

That Isabel found the past highly instructive, as evidenced in her commissioned histories, is corroborated in her large collection of histories and
chronicles. She owned Livy's *Decades*, morally reinforcing and instructive
in chivalry, military strategy, and patriotism; she owned chronicles of Troy,
often claimed as cradle of Spain's own classical antiquity, which were full
of heroic exemplars; so too were her several copies of the life of Alexander
the Great and the *Labors of Hercules*. She would have known that, Livy aside,
such histories were part fact, part fantasy. Among her 300-odd tapestries
there were five bedhangings depicting the conquests of Alexander the
Great, six wallhangings of the Labors of Hercules, three illustrating Arthurian legends, and others taken from chivalric romances. Whether pur-
chases or gifts, they surely entered the royal collection as pleasing in subject
matter to the Queen.

She did, however, put greater faith in some other histories with mythical
elements; they were the royal chronicles, ranging from those of her distant
forebears to those she herself ordered written. And how those of her own
reign varied over time provides insight into her own changing vision of the
significance of that reign. Her initial chroniclers, Pulgar, Palencia, and
Valera, concentrating on Castile's Queen, King, and nobles, and on character, personality, and morality, chiefly wrote of current events, if within
an implicit framework of providential history. Bernaldez brought a righteous post-Inquisition spirit to his account, more sharply depicting the
reign as the working out of providential design. Yet that early in her reign
she also sought something grander in scope is reflected in her commission
to Valera for a history of Spain within a universal context. From 1492 on,
all the histories she commissioned were more universal. They tended to
integrate Christian and classical background in establishing Spain's pedi-
gree through Troy and the Goths, and to stress its divinely assigned role as
culmination of human history. Yet if their scope was that of the old universal chronicles, notably those written in the reign of Alfonso X, and
equally providential, there were significant differences, as Robert Brian
Tate shows by comparing Pulgar's chronicle with Nebrija's history of 1495,
dedicated to Isabel. In their accounts of speeches "Pulgar argues either
from Biblical example or immediate political exigencies whereas Nebrija
debates against a background of ethical humanism. . . . Where [in Pulgar

the Duke of Medina Sidonia] calms a quarrel over the distribution of booty by warning his men against the power of the devil, Nebrija puts in the duke's mouth a Ciceronian proverb and a condemnation of *'auri sacra fames.'*''[26] As for Isabel herself, the young queen can be found in Pulgar, yet, like the evolution of the histories she commissioned, she came to take on a universalist outlook and a veneer of classical humanism.

She particularly, say her own chroniclers, enjoyed the chronicles of her father's reign. Certainly by 1492 she saw herself fulfilling the program of moral regeneration they told of having been urged upon him. Indeed, Lucena and Mártir then wrote of Spain entering a glorious classical period, a golden age; and in all the histories undertaken from 1492 in Spain while they lived, the reign of Isabel and Fernando was seen as the culmination of the monarchy, restoring empire and promising to return Spain to the more virtuous time of the Visigoths. "In you begin the golden centuries," declared Juan del Encina.[27]

Mártir and Marineo Sículo and Geraldini, the men who then brought a new wave of Italian humanism to her realms, were priests and devout, although Mártir admitted to becoming a priest in Spain since convinced that it was the only way to win respect for a man of letters. They put late fifteenth-century humanistic classicism to the service of reinforcing values compounded of chivalric ideals, Christian virtue, divine monarchy, and patriotism. That blend was noted by Marineo Sículo in speaking of "our Christian sovereigns, who in the beauty of their lives and the glory of their deeds surpass ancient and modern alike."[28] And all of them, stung by the consensus in Italy that Spain was uncivilized, concluded that there was something corrupt about Italy and its Romans, and that Spain was purer, *más limpia*.

In Spain, they declared, a golden age was dawning, one both providential and classical, implicitly fulfilling the apocalyptic belief in the coming of the Last Days —spoken of by Talavera as the last Age of Justice predicted by St. John—and realizing the dream, at once classical and modern, of an Age of Gold. It was the prophesied era of the World Emperor when life would again be as before Eve ate the apple; it was the utopia already envisaged in classics studied by humanists. In both versions it was paradise on earth, the return of the first, Edenic golden age told of by Alfonso X in his *General History*, when human beings knew no evil and Adam was a just world ruler. Inherent in those visions was the return of the Messiah.

Isabel was given prominent place within those predictions. She was acclaimed as both another Minerva and "the very resplendant Diana." The goddesses of wisdom and of the hunt and the moon, that is, had supplanted earlier paragons; Biblical heroines were becoming outmoded, birds passé, although one sort of beast, the lion, was not. She was in one instance addressed as *"Diana, primera leona,"*[29] blending allusion: to classical deities, to Christian prophecy, that of the Lion-King, and to the primordial earth goddess of folklore who had become associated with Diana. Isabel was also compared, not unfavorably, to the Queen of the Amazons, as well as to

Astraea, come down from the sky—the Virgin Astraea, or Justice, whose descent Virgil, Ovid and Dante saw as heralding the return of the golden age an imperial one.

At the fall of Ronda, Valera had written to Fernando of Isabel that "she fought no less with her many alms and prayers and by giving order to the things of war than you, My Lord, with your lance in your hand." Talavera later similarly stated that "the restoration of this city [Granada] was also the work of the counsel, strength, and labor of the Queen."[30] Juan del Encina, in his *romance* on Granada's surrender, hailed Isabel as a strong, brave woman: "¡*Viva* the very grand lioness! High Queen prospering." He continued, "Victory was owed to *La Reina Doña Isabel*, the most feared and loved," but then went on, partially echoing Valera, "she with her prayers," and the King "with many armed men." Some years later, Marineo Sículo, commissioned to write a chronicle emphasizing Spain's civility, located the source of regeneration precisely in Isabel's piety, stating that because of her prayers, merits, and holy works, God had looked benignly on her kingdom and helped, defended, and exalted it. That is, Encina and especially Marineo in mentioning Isabel's piety now saw in it the extent of her efficacy. Clearly, the image of the Queen and the ideals of queenship were altering from 1492 on. Talavera's soaring eagle and Gómez Manrique's injunction to leave off prayer were being ever more firmly replaced by an ideal of piety, the civilized virtue of women, within a tendency to fit Isabel's image to more modern, peaceful times, as well as an attempt to strengthen patriotic, civic religion. She was now to exemplify the pious woman, the repository of the gentler virtues, responsible for the humane, cultured, and civilized ordering of society. The ideals offered Isabel long ago in the *Garden of Noble Maidens* were again germane; and indeed that treatise was published in 1500.

As the moment of victory receded, within joint rule a division of male and female types of activity between King and Queen was being seen as the accepted norm and, with the war over, it was not thought civilized for the Queen to be hailed as dunning towns for funds and soldiers or riding off to war. She should, rather, be an exemplar of civic virtue and the power of turning to prayer, and so she soon was. In Granada, in the *Pietà* portraying Isabel directly below John the Evangelist, it will be recalled that the tablet she held read, "Make me passionately virtuous in your image and zealous for the faith." And that image of her piety endured. It was not the piety of the good monarch obligated to be energetic, moral, and devout conveyed to her by the mirror for princes, the *Partidas*, and Talavera's advice, the monarch she had striven to be, her own piety, but a more spiritual, more humble sort of supplication bringing to mind the piety idealized in female saints. Confusion about the nature of her piety would take over completely; she would be buried beneath it for 500 years.

Still, gone were the days of her calling back Fernando for a tourney on Passion Sunday. After 1492 she would in fact become more contemplative. In the war years, even while expectation heightened of the Messiah's militant second coming, the cult of Holy Mary was joined by a spreading devotion to that of Christ as exemplary human being, come to the cross for human sins. A devotion spread to the living, suffering Christ, to be emulated in simplicity and contemplation as in the golden age past and in order to achieve personal salvation. Isabel treasured a Flemish book of hours originally belonging to Juana Enríquez, beautifully illustrated with the life of Jesus. She commissioned paintings of Christ's life and death and a manual on Christian life, and she promoted the translating and publishing an *Imitation of Christ*, a handbook of spiritual exercises and private contemplation. And, as the decade wore on, amid newer currents of pietism and mysticism and under press of events, her religious sensibility altered, assimilating the new but not shedding the old.

WRIT IN STONE: VIRTUE RESTORED

Skilled *mudéjar* artisans were summoned from Zaragoza to repair the Alhambra immediately after Granada's fall, and Isabel refused to let the great mosque in Córdoba be altered. A Granadan *morisco* —a Christian of Muslim culture—reminded her great-grandson, Philip II, of that patronage and its reason: *Los reyes* "sustained the rich *alcazares* of the Alhambra . . . as they were in the time of the Muslim kings, in order always to manifest their power through the memory of the triumph of its conquerors."[31]

Isabel and Fernando too, as customary for European royalty, had religious institutions constructed, their number and grandeur expected to reflect their own stature and their vision of their reign. Among those structures were not only the royal hospice at Guadalupe but the monasteries of St. Thomas in Avila and Santa Cruz in Segovia, a hospice for pilgrims in Santiago, and a church of St. Francis in Rome. Isabel founded two convents of Saint Isabel, one in Toledo and one in Granada. Even so, most striking, and telling, were the two monuments she commissioned earliest, San Juan de los Reyes and the charterhouse at Miraflores with its royal tombs. Both were churches in late Gothic, Hispano-Flemish style, both dedicated to dynastic splendor, and both completed in the years around 1492. Both sought to allay mortality. Grandiose and full-blown, they spoke of her illustrious heritage and her commitment to surpass it.

The tombs at Miraflores and the surrounding sculpture, built between 1489 and 1493, reveal a good deal about Isabel. In a wall niche there her brother Alfonso is sculpted kneeling in prayer, his face young and fresh and remarkably like portraits of her, his hat a mass of spring flowers; these signs are of a new beginning and that hat sidesteps the problem of a crown. Above him and to one side is a pulled-back curtain, the whole conveying not death but promise. Juan II of Castile and Isabel of Portugal lie below the altar within a great, raised, star-shaped confection, ringed by the cardinal virtues personified—outstanding among them the figure of Justice, who has been given two swords, undoubtedly temporal and spiritual. Saints surround them, and Old Testament prophets, angels, and a great array of flora and fauna. Birds and beasts abound, and most frequent are eagles. The four evangelists guard the corners of the tombs and, among them, San Juan is most carefully carved, and his attendant eagle has each feather delineated. High above are the eagles ending the ceiling vaults, their wings sheltering the royal coat-of-arms. The whole bespeaks a dynasty chosen to forward God's design.

The choice of a star shape to encompass the tombs has been described persuasively as referring to heaven and divinity, and as standing as well for another astral body, the sun, connoting Christ, so that Isabel's parents are ringed round by God, the equivalent of a halo implicit in the circle around King Juan's head.[32] Yet the allusions are multiple: to the phrase of St. Jerome taken up by Sánchez de Arévalo: "In the West the sun of righteousness has risen"; and to Jerome's own implicit contrast in seeing the East as contaminated by Lucifer and his demons—whom Spaniards from time to time explicitly identified with the prophet Muhammad and the Muslims. By extension, it commemorates as well the crusade of Juan and his daughter against the influence of Oriental ways of thought in Spain. The star recalls too other stars, those surrounding the Woman of the Apocalypse, who stood for the church, for the Queen of Heaven, Mary, and for her temporal counterpart, Isabel. It calls to mind Astraea, equated with the constellation Virgo, a classical analogue promising empire and a golden age of justice. It recalls Alfonso X's astronomy (translated from the Arabic) wherein in the constellation *Aquila*, now known as Altair, the brightest star is called "the flying eagle."[33]

The star at Miraflores has eight points. To Francisco Imperial, the poet who had offered prophecy to Juan II, the number eight had special symbolic value in that king's birth.[34] It was, moreover, the symbol of new life, surely that of Juan's daughter. Imperial also spoke of "the Star Diana" in undoubted conflation of Diana, the goddess of the moon, who was thought to help women in childbirth, with the Virgin Mary, whom Imperial saw as having a similar responsibility, and the Woman of the Apocalypse, standing upon the moon and surrounded by stars. Nor can it be happenstance that all of them had become analogues of Juan's heir, Castile's queen.

Juan of Castile holds a sceptre, explained in Mena's verses: "Justice is a sceptre that the sky created."[35] And it is an orb, symbol of the globe and, more precisely, of its center, Jerusalem. Above the tombs, in the glittering altarpiece, the splendid, powerful, and devout patrons, Isabel and Fernando, kneel in prayer. Miraflores is a visual reclamation: here Isabel has aggrandized her parents and, implicitly, herself. Miraflores speaks of her own dedication to meeting his responsibilities, and to fulfilling the blighted promise of another Isabel, her mother. Miraflores was too an attempt to surpass all other funerary structures, especially the recent ones built by nobles.

Palaces, religious institutions, and public buildings, reflecting the royal aesthetic, with their patrons often employing the same people to build, sculpt, and paint them, were commissioned by obviously prospering *grandes,* bishops, and chief courtiers, particularly by Cardinal Mendoza who was all of those things. He had a hand in the splendid Mendoza palace in Guadalajara with its facade and great hall embellished with *salvajes,* was responsible for the expansion of the cathedrals of Seville and Toledo, for their altarpieces, Spain's most spectacular *retablos,* and for having the choir-stalls of Toledo's cathedral so decorated as to commemorate the campaign of Granada and thereby endow that conquest and its perpetrators, himself included, with high sacral purpose. In Valladolid the progress of his *Colegio de Santa Cruz,* the College of the Holy Cross, parallels the changing outlook at court. Begun in 1487 in Gothic style, it was completed by 1492 as the first major Renaissance structure in Castile. The Cardinal, bald-pated, looking more banker than *grande,* appears on its tympanum. He is on his knees before St. Helena, the discoverer of the holy cross. In that dedication to the *Santa Cruz* of Jerusalem, he made a sweeping bow not only to his title proper, Cardenal de Santa Cruz, but to his close connection to the monarchs and royal goals.

In Valladolid too, another longtime associate of Isabel's, Alonso de Burgos, Bishop of Palencia and president of the *hermandad,* between 1487 and 1496 built the church of San Pablo, and, adjacent, the *colegio* of San Gregorio, both their facades as flamboyant as a prophet's vision. The two Saints John grace that of San Pablo, while over the central portal of San Gregorio the royal escutcheon is "borne aloft in the branches of a huge pomegrante tree." The pomegranate, conveniently symbol both of Granada and resurrection, was added in 1492 to the royal coat-of-arms. The tree is also a Tree of Jesse, a messianic genealogy, amid its branches a chivalric panoply of pages, heralds, and knights and, at the bottom, a row of naked hairy wildmen.

In common with Mendoza and Cádiz, Alonso de Burgos employed *salvajes,* whom Luna had placed over the entry to Escalona and who appear on his brother's tomb in Toledo, whom Henry the Navigator claimed as worthy adversaries, who showed up in sentimental novels and at royal fetes, and who were emblematic of Hercules and the Visigoths, guardians of heritage and moral values. Thus one noble, Gómez Manrique, in his masque for Alfonso's birthday and in the subsequent prose and poetry he addressed to Isabel, presented the Visigoths as savages come to Spain but quickly become humane, magnanimous, liberal, and devoted to the arts and sciences, much like the then-popular Livy and Tacitus had praised the rustic simplicity of Germanic tribesmen or as Sánchez de Arévalo had lauded the ancient Hispani as robust and avoiding "the effeminate pleasure" of hot baths.

Noble savages and knights alike, both inherently chivalric and alluding to a lost golden age of virtue, had great appeal to such aspiring and ambitious aristocrats, God's warriors and the Queen's, for they spoke of their aspirations to lineage and their own position, achieved or envisioned. Like Manrique and Mendoza, those nobles often took pride in pure Gothic descent, that is, in *limpieza de sangre*, *limpieza* eliding with pristine virtue. Isabel too favored chivalric imagery: on the exterior of San Juan de los Reyes are kindred armed knights, *maceros* or *reyes de armas*, guards literally of honor, sentinals, as the wildmen are also, heraldic and emblematic; and similar armed warriors guard the tomb of Alfonso in Miraflores.

Such buildings, conceived from the late 1470s on to commemorate idealized origins and announce arrival, convey a great surge of assurance and prosperity, and a broadly shared sense of a divinely ordained national mission and destiny under the monarchy. The queen commissioned some and inspired others of them; she had come to personify their common message.

THE COURT

In 1492 the court was swelling, its offices proliferating, its habitues alert to positions coming open as chief ministers aged and some stalwarts died. Still peripatetic, now numbering over 1000 people, including the royal guards, the chapel, and the many servants, it was a traveling city. More than ever the center of social and political power, attracting *grandes* as the place to be, it was as well the hub of a growing administrative apparatus. Within that administration, the ascending value to the monarchs of the *letrados* was apparent. Mendoza's *Colegio de Santa Cruz*, had been founded for their education. At the University of Salamanca, which in 1494 had 5000 students and no rival in Spain, and was also principally dedicated to legal studies, the core of the university as well as a new cathedral had been recently constructed at royal expense.

While competition for position intensified after the war, a haphazard system of rewarding secretaries and jurists endured, so that in 1493 Isabel could hear from Talavera that some especially worthy, loyal, and hardworking men were grossly underpaid, and his comments leave the impression that rivalry within court circles was fierce and intensifying. Nobles, while no longer dominating the royal council, retained power in the council of state and influence at court, as well as enjoying resurgent power in the towns and the economy. In the 1490s titles escalated and dukes in particular proliferated; there had been few at Isabel's birth. The nobility was closing ranks, procreating apace, intermarrying, and entailing estates. Sons succeeded fathers, and younger sons more often received titles of their own. Isabel favored families who had rendered great service during the war, and she tended to back them in their numerous disputes with town councils over municipal lands. Those councils themselves—offices proliferating, more often sold and becoming hereditary—were increasingly the property of a few families, little responsive to popular interest. And royal *corregidores*, with longer terms and less oversight by the crown, were accreting local property and power. Yet if nobles throve in a decade of economic expansion, so did propertied townspeople. A postwar society, more mobile, less idealistic, greedier, and more urban was, as mentioned, reflected in *La*

Celestina. Within it behavior was very much at odds with royal injunctions, very non-Isabelline. Münzer, touring Spain, described a conjunction of prosperity, ostentation, and moral laxity. People dressed very showily, he observed, in gold, brocades, and silks, even though the monarchs prohibited such excesses.

The court partook of that expansive postwar atmosphere. Expenses soared for the royal household as the monarchs displayed an ascending opulence they considered appropriate only to themselves and their children. Castilians had long expected their rulers to dress and live splendidly, befitting their station, and Isabel, although avowedly opposed to superfluity and extravagance, when the occasion merited was happy to follow that counsel. Yet for Spain as a whole her goal remained a highly moral, Christian society and, as the next step in that direction, she now adddressed the matter of the presence of Jews.

The Expulsion of the Jews
1492

And the kingdom and the dominion, and the greatness of the kingdoms
under the whole heaven, shall be given to the people of the saints of the
Most High; their kingdom is an everlasting kingdom, and all dominions
shall serve and obey them.

Daniel 7:27.

For behold, I create new heavens
And a new earth,

. . .

And I will rejoice in Jerusalem.

Isaiah 65:17,19

THE DECREE

WITH triumph over the Muslims, the moment was at hand to put into
effect another, related, policy: ridding Spain of Jews. The royal
decree of expulsion of all Spain's Jews was, appropriately, given in Granada. Dated March 31, 1492, but not made public until the end of April, it
gave them until the end of July, three months, to leave the country. They
were not to take out of Spain gold, silver, money, arms, or horses.

The decree explained the expulsion as evolutionary: that since there
were bad Christians in the realm, and a great cause of their condition was
communication with Jews, segregation of Jews from everyone else had
been ordered in the Cortes of 1480 and the Inquisition been established.
Nevertheless, great harm to Christians had continued from contact with
Jews, subverting "our holy Catholic faith." Jews held meetings where they
read and taught. They managed to circumsize *conversos* and their sons and
gave them books of prayer. They informed them of the history of their law,
and notified them of holy days and instructed them in their observance,

even taking to their houses unleavened bread and ritually slaughtered meat. Partial, exemplary expulsion, based on royal clemency, had been tried: "We, knowing that the true remedy of all these harms and inconveniences is separating the Jews from all communication with the Christians and expelling them from our kingdoms, had wished it to be enough to order them to leave all. . . . Andalusia where it seemed they had done the most harm." It was thought that it would suffice to warn all others to leave off proselytizing. It had not: "Each day it is found that the Jews increasingly continue their evil and harm."[1] It was an explanation according with the process usual to Isabel of piecemeal imposition of dire measures, and one of reassuring herself and convincing everyone else that she was proceeding judiciously.

Whatever the date a nationwide expulsion was first conceived, to Isabel in 1492 emptying Spain of Jews was a necessary next step, taken much like a logistical decision to cut off the enemy from allies and provisions; in that sense it was an extension of a war-nurtured ruthlessness. War had accustomed her to uprooting great numbers of people; war and the Inquisition contributed to her thinking dispassionately of people en masse. And by 1492 the Inquisition had found some 13,000 converts guilty of Jewish practices. Even so, a more neutral analogy was made in the decree: "if, when some grave and detestable crime is committed by some members of some college or university . . . the entire body may be dissolved and annihilated . . . and those who perturb the good and honest life of the cities and towns and by contagion can harm the others may be expelled from the towns and even for other less serious causes that may harm the Republic, then how much more [should they be expelled] for this greatest and most dangerous and contagious of crimes." Invoked, that is, was the old organic metaphor of cleansing the body politic of disease. All Jews, by their very existence, were assumed guilty of such contamination.

A sense is conveyed of royal patience at an end, and something more: "Because of the weakness of our humanity, the diabolic tricks and enticements that continually war against us could quickly triumph if the principal cause of this danger is not removed," which is the Jews. Inquisition language spilled over into the royal decree, and carried with it an assumption of endless warfare against the Devil and those instruments of his, the Jews. It is hard to conclude anything but that Isabel herself believed in the this-world venue of the contest between heaven and hell. Although on occasion she expressed disdain for the *opinión del vulgo* concerning the Devil's power, she denied only its potency in relation to God's might. Concerning the Jews too she was acutely attuned to the public temper, and, once again, had had much to do with molding it.

Relatively early in her reign, she had employed the traditional royal formula in insisting: "all the Jews of my kingdoms are mine and they are under my protection and power, and they belong to me, to defend and protect and maintain in justice."[2] It was as much an assertion of royal authority as anything else. In 1476 she had signaled the direction of her thinking

in statutes emanating from the Cortes at Madrigal, catering to urban deputies and popular prejudices and proclaimed throughout the realm. They
had resurrected discriminatory ordinances fallen into disuse: Jews and
Muslims were to wear special badges or signs, Jews to wear on their right
arm a six-pointed star. Neither were to dress in luxurious fashion. Debts to
Jews were excused if usurious. And at Madrigal and thereafter, in policies
toward the Jews Isabel spoke as one with Fernando.

PROPHECY AND PRECEDENT

The expulsion decree affirmed adhesion to a European-wide and centuries-
long animosity toward Jews as a clannish people of different religion and
culture, as foreigners among Us, and with antipathy to Them found to be
immensely valuable in defining Us. That hostility had long and adroitly
been played upon by Castile's kings, who had kept it both alive and tamped
down. Alfonso X's *Partidas* had laid down the established relationship:

> Jews are a manner of men who do not believe in the faith of Our Lord Jesus
> Christ, but the great lords of the Christians have always suffered them to live
> among them. . . . And the reason why the Church and the Emperors and the
> kings and the other princes suffer the Jews to live among the Christians is this:
> because they shall live as in captivity forever and shall remind men that they
> come from the line of those who crucified Our Lord, Jesus Christ.[3]

Elsewhere the *Partidas* spoke of Jews as helpmates of the Devil in connection with the belief that in the last days, Antichrist, archdevil and tyrant,
was expected to arise. He was there viewed as it was believed Daniel had
dreamed of him and the Book of Revelation portrayed him, a horned monster, a serpent, the principle of destructive power, indistinguishable from
Satan. There was allusion to this assumed relationship of Satan and the
Jews in the words of the edict of 1492: "the tricks and enticements of the
Devil could quickly triumph if the cause of this danger is not removed."
Such doomsday assumptions, enshrined in royal law, fed hatred of a large
and distinct group whose chief protection lay in the same people who spoke
that way of them, the monarchs. Isabel on becoming Queen had claimed
the customary guardianship and exhibited the customary disdain.

Yet she knew that, even within that legal and social situation, one of the
largest, if not the largest, communities of Jews in Europe had lived and
worked in Spain for centuries, providing its monarchs with counsellors and
revenues within a relationship where separate largely self-governing
enclaves of Jews within towns throughout the realm were considered
directly under royal authority. She also knew that *conversos* were both providing services previously the province of Jews and arousing similar popular hostility, so that Jews had become less valuable and more problematic
to the crown. Having at Madrigal indicated a desire to restrict Jewish activ-

ity, she had done so a few years later, within the eschatological atmosphere thickened by the birth of her son and the preaching of friars sent out by the court. She had in 1478 supported the Cardinal in pressuring Seville's Jews to convert as prelude to introducing the Inquisition. And, although in theory limited to prosecuting Christian heretics and apostates, the Inquisition, introduced to discover Jewish backsliders, connected apostasy and heresy to the presence of overt Jews. Yet at the time, Isabel's more immediate concern was judaizing converts.

She was certainly aware that most *conversos* dated from 1391, when, after mob violence against Jews had broken out in conditions of weak royal control, thousands of Jews had converted, perhaps more than had not. And she surely knew that in 1412 during her father's minority such widespread violence had flared again, when, fanned by the incendiary warning of Vicente Ferrer that the Last Judgment was not far distant, that Jews must disappear as soon as possible, popular "wrath had burned . . . as a sea aflame." Nor had it done so without royal compliance, for Ferrer had been favored by the regents, Fernando's grandfather, Fernando de Antequera, and her paternal grandmother, Catalina. Many additional Jews, coerced mightily, accepted baptism, and received little or no instruction in Christianity. Yet, with his majority Juan II, and Luna, had eased pressure on Jews until, at midcentury, it was again applied, if indirectly; now Luna's opponents made use of the sort of tracts, sermons, and demonstrations previously directed against Jews, but this time against *conversos* supporting him, in accusing them of being secret Jews.

Some eminent *conversos*, put on the defensive in 1449 by the Toledo statute of purity of blood coupling them with Jews on the basis of lineage, had then argued that in accord with God's plan, all Jews should convert. While proud of their highborn Jewish ancestry, several bishops and royal secretaries then declared that the Jewish people had been chosen to announce and produce the Messiah, but that with his coming they had outlived their place in the divine scheme and that those Jews who refused to see it were obdurate, stiff-necked, perverse, and must be malicious for their God had wished them to become Christian through all the intervening centuries.

Isabel had been with Enrique's court in the 1460s when, after a quiescent period allowing partial recuperation for *aljamas*, spokesmen for an Inquisition had clashed on whether or not *conversos* remained Jews but agreed that Jews were despicable and a threat to Christianity. One position was established in a tract of 1459 by Alonso de Espina, who, bent upon showing that all New Christians continued to be Jews by blood and so belonged to a depraved race, had repeated old slanders: Jews sacrificed innocents on Good Friday, they profaned the host, and they poisoned wells; even more ominous, since the fall of Constantinople they were making astrological computations calculating just when their messiah would appear; moreover, they equated the Jewish messiah with Antichrist. Opposing Espina's condemnation of all *conversos* was Alonso de Oropesa, who gave his opinion at court. He declared all Christians to be the new Israel, defended Christian *caridad* and the right of *conversos* to Christ's faith, yet thought it estimable to belong to the race of Abraham, for Christ was born into it. Israel, imperfect beforehand, had by His coming been offered perfection. Those Jews who had not accepted Him were an anomaly, the source of all the difficulties confronting New Christians and the greatest danger to Christianity, a contamination. It was, Oropesa concluded, necessary to afflict them so that vexation and pain might open their eyes to understanding, for Jews were to suffer before their own redemption, as Isaiah had prophesied. Although divided on their opinions of converts, Espina and Oropesa agreed about Jews.

By Isabel's accession a number of *conversos* had joined those old Christians who viewed contemporary Jews both as a bad influence on converts and malevolent in resisting conversion themselves. Isabel's decrees indicated she coincided in sentiment. Among people she trusted, Gómez Manrique loathed and insulted Jews. Hernando de Talavera, in the tract of 1481 written at her request, in affirming the work of the Inquisition and declaring damned all converts holding to any custom prescribed in Mosaic law, also demonstrated how much the court attitude toward Jews had hardened. Drawing upon arguments put forth in previous reigns, and particularly since the wholesale conversions of Jews to Christianity, he declared that he despised Jews, that they were vestigial, anomalies of history, and no longer the true Israel, which was the Christian church militant. Rather, they were the synagogue of Satan (and there he cited the Apocalypse of St. John), and it was to protest their keeping of the Law of Moses that Christ had not yet come again; yet so blind were those people that they even awaited a messiah of their own, who was in reality Antichrist. Jews, he concluded, either too thickheaded to see the truth or too malicious, were damning their own souls and putting others in jeopardy. Moreover, the prophets had announced some oppression or captivity that the Jewish people were to suffer for their sins as the Day of Judgement drew close.

Talavera, both royal ideologue and administrator, demonstrated the relationship between hardening attitudes and legislation. In a letter he addressed to Burgos when drought had left that city without bread, he linked heaven's wrath to the presence of Jews. God, he informed the town fathers, was punishing sin; in order to regain His favor no bread nor meat nor wine nor fruit were to be sold on Sundays—that is, a day holy to Christians but not to Jews—and Jews and Muslims had to wear distinctive symbols and no silk "or any other noble fiber."[4] The message conveyed was that official sufferance, and so the Queen's, for such people was wearing thin.

QUARANTINE

That message was corroborated within the royal program set out in the Cortes of 1480, in the severe restrictions then imposed. Jews were to live segregated in *aljamas* and no longer subject to their own justices but to municipal and royal officials. Magistrates were to be named in each urban unit, whether under crown or noble, to establish places Jews must live, and to see to it they were resettled in them within two years. Jews were forbidden to sell goods during Christian holidays, to spend the night outside their *aljamas*, to have shops in plazas or Christian streets, or to build synagogues larger than existing ones. From 1481, those measures were applied with rigor and they were sanctioned by a bull of May 31, 1484, that the monarchs secured from Sixtus IV. It also authorized their expelling Jews from Seville, Córdoba, and Cádiz—that is, from most of Andalusia; it was issued after the fact, for that expulsion had been ordered by the Inquisitors on the first of January 1483. Probably many then paid and stayed, for many Jews left Andalusia only in 1492.

In the process of implementing segregation, Isabel and Fernando jointly, conscientiously, and conspicuously, performed the royal function of supreme mediator. And mediation was very necessary, for their stance had by then encouraged a spate of local anti-Jewish measures resulting in appeals to the crown. Thus, Jews of Avila complained of being robbed on the basis of the ordinances of 1476. And those ordinances had put Jews who lent money in a particularly difficult situation, for war, inflation, and fluctuation in currency had brought increasing recourse to borrowing, yet made lending risky and thus subject to high interest rates. In that volatile economic climate, the laws against usury emanating from Madrigal were wilfully misinterpreted by Christian borrowers. Again in Avila, both sides appealed to the crown when Jews, who had initially reacted to those laws by refusing to lend and then relented upon the urging of the town council, found their debtors would not repay the sums borrowed, citing usury, and would not heed the *corregidor*'s orders to do so. Isabel sent mediators who in turn evoked new Jewish protests. It was a state of affairs highly inflammatory, advantageous to demonstration of royal authority within municipalities, and conducive to bolstering the royal treasury. Thus, in June 1485, the monarchs accepted an offer from Castile's *aljamas* of 4000 *castellanos de oro* for a decree freeing their residents from any suit to reclaim usurious interest.

By the later 1480s, towns were enforcing proscriptive ordinances so overzealously that the monarchs whose laws were being abused intervened. In 1486 they annulled a new ordinance of Burgos that limited the number of Jews who might live there and directed any who had married in the past three years to leave. Yet at the same time, they left undisturbed the prohibition, consonant with their decrees and Talavera's injunction, against Jews selling food in the *aljama* on Sundays and Christian holidays. And when Segovia in 1488 forbade Jews to sell salted or dried fish in the plaza, or to buy fish on Fridays or meat or poultry on Thursdays until afternoon, and its Jews appealed, the monarchs demonstrated a talent for exquisite fine-tuning in having that decree modified to the extent that Jews might buy meat on Thursday mornings beginning at eleven. They did, however, completely revoke an ordinance of Medina del Campo which in 1489 prohibited sale of firewood, charcoal, and bread in the Jewish quarter; even so, the next year they approved Medina's prohibiting Jews having shops in the plaza, thereby cutting them off from both local trade and the fair, but then again changed their minds after hearing an envoy from Medina's *aljama* (in such appeals, a gift to their majesties was not unusual). So it went. When Plasencia's council complained Jews would not stay in the new *judería*, then admitted that it was not fit to live in, a royal official supposedly sent to better their situation made it worse. Although he was replaced and a royal edict of May 18, 1491, promised security to that *aljama*, it was not to last long.

That the royal tone had altered a great deal since 1476, from an emphasis on royal jurisdiction over Jews to one on sufferance of them, was evidenced in a decree of 1490 prohibiting inhabitants of Bilbao from harassing the Jews of the village of Medina de Pomar, which ran: "By canon law and in accord with the laws of our kingdoms, the Jews are tolerated and suffered, and we command you to tolerate and suffer them, that they may live in our kingdoms as our subjects and vassals."[5] Conveyed was an impatience to have done with the Jewish presence, although not quite yet. In 1490 too the *aljamas* paid a special levy of 10,000 *castellanos de oro*, as well as the high ransom set for Jewish *malagueños*. Jewish communities had met extraordinary tributes repeatedly during the war; in October 1491 a last-minute extraordinary war assessment was levied on them, half due at the end of November and the rest in mid-January 1492.

As the war ended, mounting hostility to Jews, the spreading activities and influence of the Inquisition, and a professed royal stance of segregating Jews as a contagion to be contained, set the stage for perhaps the most notorious of Inquisition cases in which, in 1491, five Jews were sentenced to burn at the stake. The resulting *auto de fe* preceded the decree of expulsion by only four months. In 1490, the Inquisition had charged a *converso* of La Guardia, near Toledo, with possessing a consecrated wafer and plotting with five other *conversos* and six Jews to use it, along with a human heart, to cast a spell in order to bring insanity and death to all Christians. A year later additional arrests and torture brought confessions that the heart was that of a Christian child the plotters had crucified at La Guardia. Though no child was anywhere missed and the confessions impossibly inconsistent, at Avila in November 1491 three Jews, deceased, were burned in effigy, two others, alive, were torn apart with redhot pincers, and the six *conversos* were reconciled to Christianity (and so mercifully strangled) and then burnt at the stake.

Testimony extracted by the inquisitors had it that it was the spectacle of the initial *auto de fe* at Toledo that had frightened those people into recourse to black magic; yet at the same time, the sentence passed by the inquisitors viewed such murder as a ritual usual to Jewish proselytizing and to *conversos* who judaized. That sentence was widely disseminated, even translated into Catalan; a cult of the martyrdom of the holy child of La Guardia sprang up and still endures, although not sanctioned by the Church. Other than malicious gossip, there is no evidence that this type of crime had ever occurred, it was then a recurrent and widespread false accusation often accompanying other sorts of attacks on Jews in Europe, a slur that has continued to be repeated across the intervening centuries.

Immediately after that *auto de fe*, the monarchs received from the Jews of Avila a request for guarantees that they would not be slaughtered. The publicity attending that case was so intense and so successful in raising anti-Jewish sentiment to boiling, that it is hard to escape the conclusion that outrage was purposely fanned as prelude to expulsion. Conversely, an inquisitor and others declared that that ritual murder had much influence on the monarchs' decision to exile the Jews. Certainly within a month of that execution, in December 1491, legislation reserved to the crown the right to supervise the taxfarming system and cancel contracts "inconsistent with reorganization plans of the state."[6] Since there were still some Jews among principal taxfarmers, it may well be that the expulsion was even then contemplated. Still, given Isabel's *modus operandi*, the suspicion lingers that it had been planned even earlier.

WHOSE DECISION?

Historians tend to see the decree of 1492 as principally the work of Fernando, basing their opinion on his correspondence endorsing it, influenced by the Machiavellian reputation he acquired later, and noting that in 1486 when an inquisitor in Zaragoza was murdered by *conversos* and riots ensued, he had ordered Zaragoza's Jews expelled. Yet ringing true is an account that lays that edict at least equally to Isabel. Its author was Isaac Abravanel, who in 1492 shared with Abraham Señor the leadership of Castilian Jewry, and who was both a writer of philosophy and Cardinal Mendoza's chief taxfarmer. He had been called to court in 1484 and had subsequently, together with Señor, loaned Isabel millions of *maravedís* for the war and become a trusted financial advisor. In March 1492 he was proud of having gained royal favor, appreciation, and esteem and completely surprised by the edict of expulsion. As soon as he learned of it, he later recounted, he quickly went with the octagenarian Señor and Señor's son-in-law and successor as chief taxfarmer, the rabbi Mair Melamed, to urge the King to cancel the decree. Fernando agreed only to delay it. Abravanel and Señor then offered him a great sum, possibly 300,000 ducats, and he had reconsidered but finally refused, telling them that it had been a joint decision of *los reyes* and was irrevocable. And so Abravanel went to the Queen. Clearly he knew Isabel, and he chose to meet her on her own ground, moral certitude. If (and here Abravanel's biographer paraphrases his reminiscence) "she thought that, by measures like expulsion, the Jews could be brought to surrender and to extinction, she was greatly mistaken. He pointed out to her the eternity of the Jewish people, that they had outlived all who had attempted to destroy them, that it was beyond human capacity to destroy [them], and that those who tried to do so only invited upon themselves divine punishment and disaster."[7]

Her reponse, as he gave it, was consistent with what we know of her and is fundamental to understanding her reasons for expelling Spain's Jews: "Do you believe," she asked him, "that this comes upon you from us? [Rather,] the Lord hath put this thing into the heart of the king." Abravanel, plunging ahead, asked her to influence the King to withdraw it. "No, she could not . . . even if she desired it. 'The King's heart,' she said, 'is in the hands of the Lord, as the rivers of water. He turns it whithersoever He will.'" It was an instance of the value to *los reyes* of their subjects having to deal with two crowned heads rather than one; and, as Isabel did not choose to say to Abravanel but had so often demonstrated that she believed, her heart too was that of a monarch and directly in God's keeping.

Abravanal and Señor came to the conclusion that in fact Isabel, rather than Fernando, was chiefly responsible for the edict and the refusal to cancel it, and they were convinced there was no recourse. She insisted, moreover, that the two convert and stay. Señor accepted baptism, at Guadalupe, his sponsors the sovereigns and the Cardinal. But Abravanel, despite cajoling, threats, even a plot to kidnap and baptize his grandson, would not consent and in early August took ship at Valencia for Italy.

Isabel's exchange with him was at bottom a confrontation of competing claims to being God's elect, a contest of wills concerning God's will. Her implication was plain: it was the Lord who viewed the Jews as anachronistic and that, as Talavera and others had put it, her own Christian people were the New Israel, the spiritual heirs of the initial chosen ones and that, the Messiah having arrived, it was past time for Jews to disappear. To the extent possible, the Spanish monarchs were implementing the divine timetable for the Second Coming. At the very least they had been chosen to set an example to the world by cleansing Spain.

CONSEQUENCES

Abravanel had made his stand by affirming that it was the Jews who were and would remain God's elect. Later, in exile, in the first of three messianic works, he took pains to establish Jewish triumph soon to come, to prove Jews were the fifth kingdom of Daniel, the select people of the saints of the Most High. During Isabel's reign, as their numbers shrank and pressures upon them had mounted, a growing sense of impending disaster among Jews was channelled into a rising messianic expectation. Upon learning they must leave Spain, such people most often reacted with panic, hysteria, and despair then, once past the initial shock, came to see exile as an ordeal set by God preliminary to total triumph and boundless prosperity, as the prophesied Day of Wrath, to be followed by entry into the Promised Land or the coming of the fifth kingdom. And faced with conversion or expulsion, most chose to leave.

The chronicler Bernaldez described the impact of the decree on Spain's Jews. Wholly sympathetic to the Inquisition, indeed a functionary of it, he yet wrote compassionately. Much like Isabel, he sympathized with individual suffering even when believing it necessary for a higher good; he reiterated the old saw: it is better to enter heaven with one eye than go to hell. Like Oropesa and Talavera he believed the Jews had to suffer before the Last Judgment. And with his sovereigns he shared the equally-essentially eschatological assumption that it was past time for Jews to go. The spirit of his chronicle is much like that of the 1492 decree, of whose consequences he told, events Isabel set in motion.

"Having seen the very great harm proceeding from the obdurate opinion and perpetual blindness of the Jews, and how they nourished the depraved Mosaic heresy," he began, "and being at the camp of Granada in 1492, [the King and Queen] commanded and decreed that the Holy Evangel and Catholic faith and Christian doctrine be preached to all the Jews of Spain and all its kingdoms."[8] The monarchs sent out yet another of those friar-vanguards such as they had dispatched before imposing the *hermandad* and the Inquisition, this time to convert all of Spain's Jews. It was not successful. Although, said Bernaldez, it was preached to the Jews that the Messiah whom they awaited was Jesus Christ, yet they ignored it, fearing the truth, and "having been deceived by the false book of the Talmud," which, he declared, was "filled with lies and abominable crazy things against the law of God and against the law of nature and against the law of the Scriptures." Indeed, "the wise men among them were intoxicated as much as the simple . . . although they saw before their eyes their own exile and perdition, and although they were importuned and threatened," yet "they remained pertinacious and unbelieving, and though forced to hear, never have they willingly received in their hearts a thing that benefited them."

Apologists for the expulsion until today adhere to that same argument, that it was after all by choice that the Jews left, for they had only to convert in order to stay. Bernaldez blamed their rabbis for so misleading them: "Even before they left off hearing the evangelical preaching, their rabbis preached to them the contrary, and strengthened them and gave them vain hope, and said to them that they were to know for certain that that [impulse for their expulsion] came through God, who wished to take them from captivity and carry them to the promised land and that in this exodus they would see Israel."

Bernaldez gave historical explanation. The Jews had not recognized nor received Jesus Christ, nor given ear "to the great miracles and marvels he worked, before maliciously persecuting and killing him; and the error made, never did they repent of it." The chronicler compacted time and bent scripture to find the origin of the dispersion of the Jews in that refusal, as his contemporaries tended to do. He and they also held out the Roman emperor Vespasian, responsible for the Jewish diaspora, as an instrument of divine vengeance sent because the Jews did not repent the crucifixion. There was no reason for Isabel, whose library included Josephus on Vespasian's destruction of the temple in Jerusalem, to think otherwise.

After that dispersion, as Bernaldez explained it, "many came to Spain at many times" and "from them come those who live now, in lineage as in contumacy," of which there were over 30,000 households. Scholars tend to accept his figures but disagree on the proper multiplier, seeing it as between three and five. At the most, then, it stands for 175,000 Jews in Spain in 1492. Most lived in the lands held by lords, he said, "and all were merchants and vendors and farmers of the *alcabalas* and stewards of nobles"; they were also "cloth-shearers, tailors, shoemakers, tanners, weavers, spice merchants, peddlers, silk dealers, silversmiths, and of other similar occupations," that is, "people who never broke the earth nor were farmers nor carpenters nor masons, but all sought easy jobs with little work." Still, they prospered, for "they were very subtle people and people who lived commonly by many profits and usuries with the Christians and in a short time many of the poor became rich." He omitted some occupations, particularly physicians and proprietors of landed estates, nor did he indicate that most Jews were artisans. And then, as from time to time occurred, the observer overcame the polemicist: "Among themselves they were very charitable. Although they paid tribute to lords and kings. . . . they never became very needy because their councils, called *aljamas*, supplied their necessities."

Returning to the Jewish reaction to the decree of 1492, Bernaldez imparted the pervasive sense of the time having arrived for being led by God in another exodus to the promised land and told of how that exodus was organized:

> The rich Jews paid the cost of departure of the poor Jews, and they treated each other with much *caridad*; so that none wished to convert, except for very few of the most needy. The Jews, simple and lettered, in that time commonly held the opinion, wherever they lived, that just as God, with stong hand and arm extended and much honor and riches, had through Moses led the people of Israel from Egypt miraculously; that thus He would return to them and lead them from these parts of Spain with much honor and riches and without any loss of belongings to possess the holy promised land, which they confessed to having lost through their great and abominable sins, which their ancestors had committed against God.

Yet, he went on, they were sadly mistaken, for the Jews who left Egypt had been good and humble, and the Egyptians bad and gentile and idolators. "And now, on the contrary, the Jews are bad and unbelieving and idolatrous, and not sons of Israel, but sons of Canaan [Cain?], and of perdition, and the Christians are good and sons of God, of law, of benediction, and of obedience, and people of God." The Christians, to Bernaldez as to his queen, were the true successors to the Old Testament Jews; they were the new elect, the people of God.

And so the Jews prepared to depart Spain:

> In the time of six months [effectively three] allowed by the edict, they sold and sold cheaply what they could of their estates. . . . The Christians got their very

rich houses and heirlooms for little money, for they encountered no one who would buy them and so gave a house for an ass, and a vineyard for a little cloth or linen, because they could not take out gold or silver; although it is true that they took infinite gold and silver secretly, and especially many *cruzados* and *ducados* embedded in their teeth. They [also] swallowed them and carried them out in their stomachs, and the women swallowed most; it was said that one person swallowed thirty *ducados* at once.

The chronicler's pride in accurate observation, and belief that it was necessary that Jews suffer as preliminary to the redemption of humanity, produced sympathetic counterpoint. "And, before leaving, they married to one another all the young men and women who were over twelve, so that all the women would be accompanied by a husband; and they began to leave Castile in the first week of July." All of them, he continued,

confiding in their vain blind hopes left the lands of their birth, children and adults, old and young, on foot and in wagons, and the *caballeros* on asses and other beasts, and each journeyed to a port of embarkation. They went through roads and fields with many travails and [mixed] fortunes, some falling, others rising, others dying, others being born, others falling sick, so that there was no Christian who did not feel sorry for them and always invite them to be baptized. And some sorrowfully converted and stayed, but very few. And on the way the rabbis heartened them, and had the women and youths sing and play tambourines to cheer the people, and so they went through Castile and arrived at the ports. . . .

When those who went to embark through Puerto de Santa María and Cádiz saw the sea, they shouted loudly and cried out, men and women, great and small, in their prayers demanding mercy of God, and they expected to see some marvel of God and that he would open a path through the sea for them.

Instead, they encountered hardship and suffering. Some were seized by corsairs upon leaving and sold as slaves in Cádiz. "Many were robbed and murdered on the sea and in the lands through which they passed, by both Christians and Muslims." Many others sailed from Cartagena and other Aragonese ports; some went to Navarre, France, and Germany. Those on the Andalusian coast waited many days on the shore, then had to crowd into 25 ships. Seven sailed to present-day Morocco, to Oran, encountered a pirate fleet in port, were allowed to depart only on promise to pay 10,000 *ducados*, and went on to the Spanish port of Arcilla, their destination Fez. Some changed their minds: 150 Jews disembarked in Cartagena and 400 in Málaga and were baptized. Those who went to Portugal—Bernaldez says 700 households; most scholars think more, indeed the great majority of those expelled—were told they could stay only six months and were charged an entry fee of a *cruzado* apiece. From Portugal, some went on to Italy, others to Fez or Turkey, and many converted and returned to Castile. In March 1493, all were expelled from Portugal, but 600 of the richest households were permitted to remain for a time on payment to the king of 100 *cruzados* for each member, another 100 houses paid eight *cruzados* per person, and over 1000 other Spanish Jews were enslaved by the king because they had not paid the entry fee. João's successor, Manoel, freed them on coming to the throne in 1495; but two years later, fulfilling a stipulation made by his Spanish wife-to-be, the *infanta* Isabel, he insisted that all Jews in Portugal convert or leave.

Those who went to North Africa fared worst. Jews who had left Gibraltar for Arcilla, although once there had hired a guard of Muslim soldiers to escort them to Fez, "along the way by command of its king were robbed and the girls and women and their bundled belongings carried off, and women were raped in the sight of their fathers and husbands" and otherwise molested, so that, hearing of it, many who had remained encamped outside Arcilla went into that town and were baptized. Many others subsequently came back from Fez, experiencing even worse treatment in returning to Arcilla, for Muslims seized them and "made them open their mouths to get gold and they put their hands [into their private parts] below for it . . . or stripped them and raped the women and killed the men and cut them in half looking for gold in their stomachs."

People from both groups continued to return to Spain from 1493 to 1496. Bernaldez said he himself had baptized more than 100, among them some rabbis, whose citing of a comment on Isaiah 10 he saw as acceptance of Christ as Messiah. Isaiah also speaks of a chosen few to be saved, and for Bernaldez, a remnant saved was good reason for the Inquisition and for expelling the Jews, a sentiment also attributed to Isabel. Bernaldez did not mention that Isaiah 10 begins "Woe unto them that decree unrighteous decrees."

Many of those who returned to Spain from North Africa, he noted, "came naked, barefoot, and full of lice, dying of hunger and having been very badly treated, so that it was a sorrow to see them." On he went, chronicling the suffering he viewed as resulting from unbelief and inherently necessary to the apocalyptic scheme. Informed estimates place the number of Jews returning to Spain at between 30,000 and 50,000, most of whom were baptized preemptorily, swelling the *converso* population and providing raw material for the Inquisition. In 1499, a royal edict declared death for any Jews re-entering Spain, unless advance word was sent that they were coming to be baptized and it was done and notarized at the point of entry. Records show that the edict was enforced stringently in 1500 and 1501, and also that Jewish slaves were then ordered deported or converted. The Jews were gone, but calumnies multiplied, which justified their expulsion and served individuals as an assertion of orthodoxy to ward off inquisitors. And as the century ended, it was the *moriscos*, the new forced converts, who would receive royal attention.

CLEANING UP

While income was probably not among the most compelling reasons for the expulsion, still the crown profited from it. In Aragón, where Fernando most blatantly used the Inquisition for political ends, the expulsion was carried out by inquisitors and Jewish property was catagorized as that of heretics, and so subject to confiscation. Inquisition and expulsion, that is, were fused, to royal profit. Zaragoza, since the royal command of 1486 to expel its Jews, had received "a confusion of orders and counter-orders, edicts and threats, along with secret instructions and exceptions for individuals"; there all Jewish property was first ordered inventoried, then it was sequestered and given out by authorities to their cohorts.[9] In Castile the expulsion of 1492 was instead supervised by secular, civil officials, and there royal measures indicate an intention to continue to protect Jews as royal subjects while getting them out, and in the process to take in as much profit as possible. Thus, royal escorts went with some of those departing, following reports of others having been robbed, or subjected to extortionate duties, or having paid for protection never supplied. Yet, arriving at ports, Jews were charged a royal embarkation tax of two ducats apiece, and the crown confiscated all gold, silver, coins, horses, and arms they sought to take with them. It can be ventured that the issue was one of just who was to fleece them.

A royal edict of May 14 allowed Jews to sell their lands, although in Aragón not until royal taxes were paid and courts decided any questions of debts. Everything owed Jews was ordered paid them so that they could pay their own debts, which they were to do promptly or forfeit their lands. A subsequent decree of May 30 ordered claimants to come forward and courts to adjudicate by mid-July. Unable to collect monies owing before leaving, Jews sold rights to them cheaply to Christians, who soon found them encumbered; for on September 10 a royal order suspended payments on all such debts until the question of usury was settled, although those held by Cardinal Mendoza, the Toledo church, and the creditors of Abravanel were excepted. From October 6 on, a series of orders went out for tallying such debts, and Isabel and Fernando ordered all goods, debts, and letters of exchange Jews still owned in Spain confiscated. Italian, particularly Genoese, bankers had done well in drawing up letters of credit for much of the money Jews had received for debts and property. After the expulsion, the Crown invited the Genoese creditors to declare those letters, arguing that Jews had taken prohibited goods with them and promising their holders a fifth of their value. With those letters inventoried, in July 1494 the monarchs ordered all debts still pending collected and deposited in the treasury. In Burgos alone, the government collected an estimated seven million *maravedís* in assets left by Jews. Abravanel estimated that Jewish property was worth 30 million *ducados*. The figure is probably too high, but whatever it was, the crown did its best to get the lion's share.

The royal treasury confiscated *aljamas*, synagogues, and cemeteries, the communal property Jews left, often redistributing it as *mercedes*. Thus, Fernando and Isabel in March 1494 granted Torquemada the old Jewish cemetery in Avila on which to build the convent of Santo Tomás. Cardinal Mendoza received the Jewish goods of his *señorío* to compensate, said the grant, for vassals and rents he had lost, and other nobles received similar gifts.

And, indicative of more general practice, at the end of 1492 Isabel conceded to Toledo's cathedral the gravestones from its Jewish cemetery, and the land as commons to the city.

THE HEART HAS REASONS

The Queen had moved, slowly but inexorably, from the traditional view that while Jews were an anomaly they were the monarch's own and a royal resource, to believing it imperative that Spain have no Jewish inhabitants. They had been valuable as a source of regular income, considered a reserve much like gold and jewelry, and served as a bank of financial expertise, but their wealth and usefulness to the crown had diminished, and Isabel increasingly had other sources of funding and professional expertise. She had come to rely less and less on Jews as taxgatherers—they were no longer the only people who could get together enough capital to farm taxes—and on receipts from *aljamas*. Funds were more available elsewhere. Royal bureaucracies, with *conversos* prominent within them, by 1492 handled much of the assessing and collecting of royal revenues. Baptism over time had brought old Jewish skills and expertise into the social mainstream, as well as many of the more talented and educated Jews. Isabel no longer relied on Jewish physicians, but on *conversos*. And those other powerful states of western Europe, France and England, had long ago expelled the Jews.

Isabel's intentions were high, as usual and as she saw them. And also as usual, in casting out the Jews she saw herself doing God's will, synonymous with what was best for the realm, the faith, and the crown. She was also clarifying, amid rising and contending messianic expectation on the part of both Jews and Christians, just who were now the Chosen People. Moreover, in tolerating the Jewish presence Spain appeared benighted; court humanists bridled at those Italians who, sneering at Spain as barbarous, also referred to it as a nation of *marranos*, of secret Jews. That is, the Jews had to go for the old reasons, those of Revelation, so the golden age might arrive, and for newer reasons, those of progress, so the golden age might arrive. Yet for an up-to-date monarch, eschatological reasons would not do publicly or even, perhaps, personally, but social contamination by untrustworthy and disruptive elements was an eminently acceptable reason. Even so, the step once taken, it was justified at court ever after in religious and racial terms and with increasing emotion—as Pedro Mártir's remarks made on royal behalf to the sultan in Egypt in 1502 demonstrated.

For several years after 1492, Isabel continued to consider *conversos* of proven persuasion fellow-Christians, indicating a belief that baptism made a Christian and that Jewish ancestry was no blight, only Judaism. Yet when she and Fernando had in 1486 stopped the Hieronymites from passing a statute of purity of blood, they had in effect elicited the shame precipitating it: those friars had proposed that exclusionary measure, they said, because a friar of Guadalupe having been burned at the stake, their fear of further dishonor was great, "for they saw the warmth the King and Queen bestowed upon the business of the Holy Office of the Inquisition."[10] Cardinal Mendoza indicated where he stood on the issue when he placed a statute of *limpieza de sangre* in the founding constitutions of his *Colegio de Santa Cruz*. At the century's end, Isabel herself was to sanction such exclusionary measures, and the persisting assumption that Jews were a race would take firmer hold on queen and country. The *Partidas*, after all, had stated as much in commanding that "other Jews must not molest converts."

Praise for expelling the Jews came principally from Italy. Rodrigo de Borja, now Pope Alexander VI, termed it a fine service to the faith. Gian Pico della Mirandola, the humanist, praised the sovereigns, recounted the sufferings of the exiled, and pointed out that the expulsion had given the lie to Jewish astrological calculations connected to the arrival of their messiah. Machiavelli termed it a "pious cruelty." Guicciardini later wrote of Castile as anarchic under Enrique IV when it was full of Jews and Muslims but now it was freed of Jewish heretics, and that Spain had been on the verge of forsaking Catholicism before the expulsion, and he applauded the burning of 120 *conversos* in one day at Córdoba. Far less enthusiastic were Jews who chronicled the events of 1492; some of whom spoke of the anguish caused by the malevolent and perverse Isabel, "that she-bear."[11]

As her prestige abroad ascended with success against the Muslims, and as she sought good marriages for her children, Isabel, courting world opinion as she once had that of her subjects, expelled the Jews. It would no longer do to have those sad, benighted, stubborn, and outmoded people in the land, insufferably claiming to be God's elect. *Los reyes* were obliged to God to purify Spain, to impose order and harmony, to ready it for greater things. All Europe was aware of it. Moreover, their reputation among their Christian peers, so glowing now that it was not to be dimmed by small failures, permitted taking an occasional risk, such as sponsoring Christopher Columbus.

16

Christopher Columbus
and the Queen
To 1492

I saw the royal banners of Your Highnesses placed by force of arms on the
towers of the Alhambra, which is the citadel of the city; and I saw the Muslim king come out of the gates of the city and kiss the royal hands of Your
Highnesses and of the Prince, My Lord. . . . [and] after having driven out
all the Jews from your realms and lordships. . . . Your Highnesses commanded me that, with a sufficient fleet, I should go to the said parts of
India.

Christopher Columbus, *Journal*[1]

Cardinal Mendoza, a man equally worthy for his qualities and his wisdom,
was of the opinion that Nicholas of Lyra was a very able theologian and
Saint Augustine a doctor of the Church, renowned for his doctrine and
holiness, but that neither of them was a good geographer.

—Alessandro Geraldini[2]

THE PROPOSAL

THREE months after entering Granada, between the drafting of the
decree expelling the Jews and its issuance, Isabel and Fernando agreed
to sponsor Christopher Columbus on an expedition of exploration westwards into the Atlantic. That Genoese seamen and sometime merchants'
agent had come to them in late 1485 or early 1486 with a plan to reach the
East by sailing west, after having been turned down by João II in Portugal.
When and where they first gave him audience, and most of the facts of his
life before then, and just what he proposed, are conjectural. The combination of his learning, information on Portugal, experience at sea, including
in Guinea, and connections with fellow-Genoese and some court figures

was sufficiently rare and potentially valuable to gain him a hearing and consequent attention.

He did give some indication of what he had proposed when presenting them with his journal in 1493 on return from his first voyage:

> . . . information which I had given to Your Highnesses concerning the lands of India, and concerning a prince who is called "Grand Khan," which is to say . . . "King of Kings." How many times he and his ancestors had sent to Rome to beg for men learned in our holy faith, in order that they might instruct him therein, and how the Holy Father had never made provision in this matter, and how so many nations had been lost, falling into idolatries and taking to themselves doc- trines of perdition, and Your Highnesses, as Catholic Christians and as princes devoted to the holy Christian faith and propagators thereof, and enemies of the sect of Mahomet and of all idolatries and heresies, took thought to send me, Christopher Columbus, to said parts of India, to see those princes and peoples and lands and the character of them and of all else, and the manner which should be used to bring about their conversion to our holy faith, and ordained that I should go . . . by way of the west, by which down to this day we do not know certainly that any one has passed."[3]

The "Grand Khan of India" was generally believed to be allied with (the legendary Christian ruler) Prester John. Columbus, in alluding to the Span- ish monarchs' extending the holy work they were accomplishing within Spain worldwide, and to their taking up a labor the papacy had let drop, implied that they were greater champions of Christendom than the pope. It was an appealing formulation, one not foreign to their own. It is gener- ally assumed that at that first audience Columbus spoke of reaching Asia— the East Indies—by sailing west, hoping at least to encounter new islands enroute and possibly even an unknown continent, about which there had been speculation since classical times. Once there he would seek alliance against the Muslims.

Indicative of their piqued curiosity, Fernando had ordered from a Val- encian bookseller a copy of a prime source of Columbus' notion of the globe, Ptolemy's *Geography*, probably for Isabel, since he read little. The king and queen instructed Talavera—who had had a hand in arranging that interview—to form an investigatory commission, "to call together people who seemed to him most versed in that matter of cosmography, of whom there were sufficiently few in Castile." It met in Salamanca, many times, frequently with Columbus, who was at court often if not steadily for several years. It concluded that not only were his promises and offers weakly founded, uncertain, and impossible, but that should the queen and king sponsor him they would gain nothing, lose money, and derogate royal authority. Still, his project coalesced remarkably with their own grand design. It was another of those projects that Isabel did not forget but post- poned to a more appropriate time; and commission or no, Columbus had the support of some of her most trusted people.

With experience in the ways of the Portuguese court, somehow he had met and convinced the right people in Castile to plead his cause, especially to Isabel. He had secured an introduction to Talavera, perhaps dating to Talavera's days in Portugal negotiating the peace treaties, and he had met Mendoza. The Cardinal had obtained him royal audience; he had reported that he found Columbus astute, intelligent and able, versed in cosmography, in short, convincing, and had suggested that their majesties should help him with some ships, for they would venture little and might gain much. Concurring with him was the humanist and courtier, Alessandro Geraldini, in noting, in an allusion to the commission's attitude, that while some prelates saw manifest heresy in denying Nicholas of Lyra's views concerning the terrestrial globe and St. Augustine's conclusion that there were no antipodes, it was the Cardinal's opinion that neither of them was a good geographer. (Nor, it turned out, was Columbus.)

Columbus was kept on retainer. Talavera signed authorizations for stipends to him, the first known in May 1487 for 3000 *maravedís*, another on July 3, and, in August, 4000 mrs. for him to come to Málaga from Córdoba, "for some things pertaining to the service of their highnesses," and 3000 more in mid-October.[4] That the most active and influential merchants in Granadan Málaga were Genoese, that among them were Columbus' old associates the Centurione, that contacts within Málaga were considered all-important to its conquest, and that it was thought imperative that Málaga, once taken, should be fitted into the Castilian port system to the benefit of the crown, may well have had as much to do with that summons as the far less immediate interest in Atlantic exploration.

Granada has been described as virtually a Genoese colony, and the Centurione, sometime papal bankers, were also powerful within a Genoese network, not only there but in Seville and Córdoba, and in Jérez and Cádiz they were affiliated with the Negrón and Spínola who traded with Barbary, mostly in gold and slaves. As it has been said, "the Genoese used Cádiz like an African trampoline."[5] Columbus also had connections with Florentines, whose commerce linked the north African coast with those bases for West Africa and the Atlantic, the Canaries, the Azores, and the Madeiras, and who dealt with Muslims and Portuguese. Yet the purpose of calling Columbus to Málaga may have been even more complex, having to do with his Portuguese connections. For within Portugal's search for the source of African gold, Diego Cão had in 1486 contacted peoples up the Congo river, purportedly inhabitants of the lands of Prester John. And João of Portugal had not only been sending agents eastwards by land but in 1487 dispatched Bartolomeu Dias to find a sea route to Asia and sent two seamen to seek land to the west of the Azores. When, within the year, Columbus brought to royal attention a request from João that he return to Portugal, another subsidy of 3000 *maravedís* was forthcoming, and when Dias returned to Lisbon in December 1488, Columbus claimed to have been present; if so, quite possibly it was at the behest of Isabel and Fernando.

THE ANDALUSIAN CONNECTION

For Isabel, Columbus' proposal was a logical extension to her policy of exerting royal control over Atlantic exploration and the Canary Islands. When in 1488 Pedro Mártir had written to a friend that Queen Isabel "has brought under submission to her empire the mysterious Fortunate Islands—if such are the Canaries," the inference was that although he was skeptical of their worth, Isabel was not. However that may be, when not at court Columbus gravitated to those principal Andalusian ports of African and Atlantic endeavor, Seville, Puerto de Santa María, Palos, and Moguer, and he sought out one of the region's most powerful lords, who were also keenly interested in maritime enteprise, Luís de la Cerda, Duke of Medinaceli. Indeed the La Cerda, who were of royal blood, retained the title of "Princes of the Fortunate Isles," referring to a century-old claim to the Canaries. Is it coincidence that Medinaceli was the Cardinal's first cousin (whose daughter would marry Mendoza's son)? According to Medinaceli, by early 1489 Columbus had spent two years as his guest. Medinaceli's seat was at Rota and he shared jurisdiction over Puerto de Santa María with those royal officials, Diego de Valera and his son, Charles.

Since the time of Alfonso X, Puerto de Santa María had been a strategically vital royal enclave on a sea frontier, otherwise dominated by great barons, a port crucial to Castile's defense, to contact with Africa and the Atlantic, and to royal collection of customs duties along coasts long notorious for smuggling. Situated between Jérez and Cádiz, it could monitor the traffic of the estuary formed by the Tinto and Odiel rivers, including that of Palos and Moguer, notoriously dedicated to maritime expeditions and piracy. It was a naval yard for layovers and repairs, a fishing port, and a commercial town. In 1485 Isabel and Fernando ordered that all African ventures must go through that royal port. That year too seamen from the Puerto and Jérez raided African coasts and returned with more than 400 women and children to sell as slaves. Situated just beyond the Strait of Gibraltar, it had prominent Genoese residents (who were *converso*) and was a favorite stopping place for Italian merchant ships. Little wonder that Columbus came initially to that region of Spain, and undoubtedly with purpose beyond that of leaving his son, Diego, with Diego's aunt or with the Franciscans of Santa María de la Rábida, just outside Palos. That monastery, too, had close ties with Atlantic exploration; it had led in organizing missions to the Canaries.

Isabel's trusted *corregidor* in Puerto de Santa María, that astute and outspoken old knight, Diego de Valera, courtier, royal chronicler, and experienced proferrer of advice, (and a *converso*) was valued by Medinaceli as well: in 1486, in a grant explicitly stating his appreciation for their many services, Medinaceli turned over to the Valeras some houses whose former owners had come afoul of the Inquisition. The Valeras were also well acquainted with Genoese in the area; indeed, Charles de Valera's fourth and last wife was a Spinola. During Columbus' stay with Medinaceli, he and the

Valeras surely met, drawn by mutual interests, and Isabel would have been apprised of any worthwhile information about Columbus, for as Diego de Valera had assured her, he always kept her informed.

There was much to talk about. Columbus had sailed to Guinea from Portugal at a time when many Andalusians, especially those of Puerto de Santa María and Palos, also had a good deal of contact with the Portuguese one way or the other, either through cooperating with them or in poaching on their shipments of gold and slaves out of Portuguese Guinea. Those seamen knew the Canaries—some had sailed there with Charles de Valera, and from those islands it is possible to find winds for America. The geographer, Carl Sauer, has speculated on the speculation then occurring: "What if . . . one followed downwind from the Canaries? Were the Canaries to remain the end of Spanish venture or to become a starting point for parts unknown and promising? . . . land, current, and genial skies invited exploration."[6] Abounding too were rumors of ships out of Andalusia blown off course, to Guinea and even to other lands in the Western Ocean; tales were then told and conjecture endures of an anonymous pilot who had reached the Caribbean before 1492. If Columbus had heard of any such voyages, it is likely that so had the Valeras, and so had Isabel.

Columbus also, according to his son and biographer, Fernando, conversed at length with a mysterious one-eyed sailor of Puerto de Santa María. Men of Palos remembered Columbus staying at La Rábida in 1488–89 and frequently coming into town to talk to Pero Vásquez, or Pedro Velasco, skilled in ocean sailing, who forty years earlier had gone exploring as pilot with one Diogo de Teive, a former page to Dom Henrique of Portugal. The two had sought in vain the legendary Antilla, appearing on some maps as an island to the west of the Canaries and Azores, said to have seven cities populated by Visigoths who had escaped the invading Muslims in the eighth century, and to have been rediscovered by a Portuguese ship blown off course. Whatever Columbus knew when he arrived and whatever his purpose in coming to that region, he surely gathered, along with yarns of lost isles and of the voyages of St. Brendan and St. Ursula and her 10,000 seagoing virgins, further information on Atlantic navigation from its experienced residents, and met the Valeras.

Indeed, coinciding remarkably with Columbus' later cast of mind were the words that in 1485 Diego de Valera had addressed to Fernando on taking Ronda, "It is clear that our Lord intends to carry out what has been prophesied for centuries . . ., to wit, that you shall not merely put these Spains under your royal scepter, but that you will also subjugate regions beyond the sea." Coinciding too was the allusion made the following year, by the Marqués who held Cádiz and had long been involved in Andalusian seafaring, to the prophecy that "he who will restore the ark of Zion will come from Spain." Columbus would subsequently say much the same things. In addition, his years in Portugal had surely exposed him to Dom Henrique's goals and to King Afonso's competing claim to be *el Encubierto*, that same restorer of Jerusalem; indeed it was in Portugal in 1481 that

Columbus first expressed an apocalyptic sense of his own. He would also later speak of looking forward to an emperor-king who would subjugate far places and finally Jerusalem; and like the friar-preachers and humanists of Isabel's court, he would equate Christian unity and Jerusalem regained with the coming of the last, golden age.

A MEETING OF MINDS

By early 1489 Isabel had received from Medinaceli a request to permit him to back Columbus. She denied it, and Medinaceli, after Columbus' triumphant return from his initial voyage, presented to the Cardinal a face-saving account of that interchange, one incidentally reflecting the great esteem in which the Queen was then held: "And as I saw that this enterprise was [properly addressed to] the Queen our Lady, I wrote about it to Her Highness from Rota and she answered that I was to send it to her. I sent it to her then . . . Her Highness received it and passed it on to Alonso de Quintanilla."[7] Isabel had long ago decided all such ventures must be under royal patronage, and Quintanilla had long looked after the royal interest in them, as well as his own. In responding to the Duke, she graciously expressed pleasure in having in her realm a person, himself, of such generous spirit and such inclination to heroic endeavors, but, she told him, such an enterprise was only for monarchs.

Within two months of refusing Medinaceli, Isabel, urged by the Cardinal and Diego de Deza, recalled Columbus to court. A letter patent corroborating that summons, drawn in both royal names, survives, given in Córdoba, May 12, 1489:

> The King and Queen to the members of the councils, justices, *regidores* [members of town councils], knights, squires, officials, and honest men in all cities and villages of our kingdoms and *señoríos*: Christopher Columbus must come to this court and to other places of our realm, to concern himself with some matters to be carried out in our service; whereby we command you that when he should pass through said cities and villages, or stay in them, he be put up and be given good lodgings for himself and those with him, without charge if not at inns; and provided with maintenance at fair prices. And you must not quarrel with him or with those he may bring with him. And you must do nothing to hinder him in any way, under pain of our justice and a fine of 10,000 *maravedís* apiece.[8]

She received him at Jaén in June—Fernando was in camp at Baza—and gave him "certain hope, once the matter of Granada was settled," which was then expected to occur soon after Baza fell. She conversed with him at length. Self-avowedly unlettered but oddly cultured, courteous and entertaining, his bearing and appearance were to his credit; "He looked like a Roman senator: tall and stately, gray-haired, with dignified face."[9] He was a remarkable combination of mariner and gentleman, of the sort her Portuguese grandmother would have recalled her husband retaining; indeed, Columbus' father-in-law, Bartolomé Perestrello, a Genoese who in 1449 became hereditary captain of Porto Santo near Madeira, had been in the household of that grandfather. Perestrello had also had an interest in Atlantic exploration and was associated with Henry the Navigator. Columbus had his papers, and so surely there were familial as well as entrepreneurial matters to discuss with the Queen.

This great-niece of Dom Henrique, who had adapted his guiding vision of encircling and defeating the Muslims and regaining Jerusalem, had here a seaman of experience and imagination who might one day prove useful to Spain. Too, his moral universe aligned with hers; indeed, it became no less congruent as time passed and he came to understand hers better. Isabel remained intrigued and all accounts indicate that Columbus was intriguing, in both senses of the word. Moreover, his scheme offered her a means to challenge what Dom Henrique had begun and João of Portugal had assiduously taken up, searching for a sea route eastwards; for it was now that Bartolomeu Dias returned, having rounded the Cape of Good Hope and found that route. And Columbus had recently written to João, perhaps visited him, and he had Portuguese contacts.

Isabel would have heard from him something of his claim to have sailed everywhere; of his trading in gold and jewels, spices, sugar, and slaves; of what he had learned in Portugal and Andalusia of exploration and discovery, navigation and geography; of his reading of Ptolemy, Marco Polo, Pierre d'Ailly, John Mandeville, and others considered authorities on cosmography; and of what he had gathered from his father-in-law's papers and from other sailors about the Western Ocean. She had a copy of her own of Sir John Mandeville's *Book of the Marvels of the World and Voyage through Jerusalem, Asia, and Africa*, a compendium of earlier compendiums. Columbus attributed to Mandeville his idea of circling the globe, of going west and returning by way of Jerusalem and Rome to Seville. He also frequently cited Mandeville as an authority on such matters as the Antipodes, the kingdom of the Christian king-priest, Prester John, in India (later writers put it in Ethiopia), and the existence of the Earthly Paradise—the Garden of Eden—which Mandeville placed (conveniently) in eastern Asia; there, prophecy had it, were Amazons, hidden until the last days, Gog and Magog, and the 12 Lost Tribes of Israel. Diego de Valera, in the historical summary he wrote at Isabel's behest, had borrowed freely from Mandeville in describing the regions of the world, and in recounting the popular story of the world-conqueror, Alexander the Great, who, Valera said, encountering noble savages devoid of material desire on an eastern island, had admired them and left them undisturbed.

Surely Columbus would have taken into account the Queen's understanding of geography, informed by Mandeville and also by St. John's apocalyptic cosmography, a description influential in the legends current of her great-uncle Dom Pedro's travels around the world. He would have learned of her policies regarding the Canaries, her desire to compete with Portugal in Guinea and beyond, and the components and moral intensity of her commitment to reconquest, for they were no secret in a court at the hub of an appreciation, ascending in Spain and radiating throughout Europe, of the Spanish monarchs as religious and military bastions of Christendom.

Columbus was with her court in Jaén when Isabel conversed intently with the friars from the Holy Sepulchre in Jerusalem, promising them 1000 ducats annually and proposing to work a covering for Christ's tomb with her own hands. Residing within a court caught up in the heady atmosphere of great times, great deeds, and great rulers, Columbus deftly situated himself and his project amid all that greatness. There as well, another recent Italian arrival, Pedro Mártir, admitted to being captivated by the dedication, the moral rectitude, the effectiveness, and the sheer power exuded by Spain's monarchs. Thereafter he and Columbus displayed an affinity of outlook regarding *los reyes*, and that humanist courtier of Isabel's would be the first to chronicle Columbus' exploits, the first European historian of what became known as the Spanish Indies.

EXPECTATIONS

In 1492, Columbus, corroborating the royal stance of being poised for empire, fit his own sense of mission within Isabel's and Fernando's aspirations as he perceived them. Thus his recollection that "I saw the royal banners placed by force of arms on the towers of the Alhambra," and then that their highnesses, "having driven out all the Jews," had commanded him to go to India. In reversing the order of events—his commission had in fact preceded the Jews' leaving—he put into proper sequence the prophesied conditions for the coming of the Last Days. And he not only evoked what one commentator has aptly termed "the intermingled destinies of himself and their majesties,"[10] but also did his utmost to insert himself indispensably within the royal construction of that destiny. Much of the messianic vision he subsequently wrote of to Isabel was in terms quite familiar to her; it was compounded of elements culled from a European-wide body of belief and adapted to Iberian traditions, particularly to those previously associated with reconquest. Thus, he would repeat to her and Fernando their right to Africa and to Atlantic lands based upon the Visigothic heritage, but he would strengthen it through supposing a land bridge had existed between Iberia and Africa, so that they were once one.

Familiar with the royal vision, he would also fit and later present his own enterprise within a frame of reference consonant with it. He would not only allude to prophecies of being done with Jews and freeing the holy places associated with Christ as necessary preliminaries to a final golden age, but also state that his own ultimate goal was to bring light to the holy city and free the rest of the world from pagan darkness. Equally concordant, Columbus, mirroring Isabel's predilection for St. John and his Book of Revelation and concerned with the hidden divine plan to be revealed, as well as Talavera's speaking of "hidden things," and her father's express desire to know the world's secrets, phrased his purpose as a divinely inspired mission of revelation, to reveal the hidden part of the world as a necessary preliminary to the Last Days. He used revelatory language: *encubierto*, enclosed or hidden, and *descubierto*, discovered but also uncovered, as well as making the references to bringing to light. He presented himself, and came to see himself, as breaking a path both outwards, into the unknown, and upwards, opening toward the light, uncovering the hidden, all within God's design, fulfilling old prophecies.

A generation later, Bartolomé de Las Casas, the Dominican who took upon himself protection of the Indians and who admired Columbus and viewed him as the divine instrument enabling their evangelization, became his filter for future ages. Columbus had wanted, said Las Casas, "to disclose what was locked away—*por descerrajar las cerraduras*—to which the Ocean, from the flood until now, held the keys, and through his person to discover another world, which this world hid enclosed within itself, and as a consequence to open very wide doors for the divine doctrine and Evangel of Christ to enter and be disseminated."[11] Columbus himself would write in 1500: "God made me the messenger of the new heaven and the new earth of which he spoke in the Apocalypse of St. John after having spoken of it through the mouth of Isaiah, and he showed me where to find it."[12] It was a formulation of what he was about that satisfied both his own aspirations and those of his sponsors; indeed, in accord with prophecies associated with them, he was, in conformity with God's design, uncovering for them what had been hidden of the world. Thus, he wrote of himself as having been chosen to adumbrate, to bear the messiah, Christ; it was in this spirit that on return from his initial voyage, having uncovered unknown lands and people, he signed himself *Cristo-ferens*, Christ-bearer. His mission as he saw it was to be instrumental in fulfilling the prophesied conditions necessary to inaugurating the last great age of Christianity, for Europe outwards.

Contact with eastern Asia, he stated, was desirable for two reasons, to encircle Muslims in order to free the holy Christian city, and to find gold. Implicitly, converting peoples to Christianity was integral but secondary, just as, to fifteenth-century Europeans in general, liberating Jerusalem was more lofty a goal than converting unbelievers. Crusading had far wider appeal than missionary work; converting heathen was a means to expedite the coming of the Last Days rather than an end in itself. Among Spaniards, the impetus to bring infidel to Christ was great chiefly among friars; the rescue of Christian captives, their redemption, had in the recent war proved a rallying cry far more potent than conversion of their captors. Now the ultimate goal, his and Isabel's, was to redeem captive Jerusalem.

For Columbus as for Isabel, the principal lures of Africa had been gold and a route eastward. His fellow-Genoese in mourning the loss of Jerusalem saw in it a symbol of Muslim expansion disastrous to both their faith and their commerce. With Turkish advance, they had moved their mercantile operations westward in the Mediterranean and had avidly traded in African gold and searched for its hidden sources. The Portuguese and Isabel's subjects only received gold at its coastal termini. Could its mysterious interior source be discovered through coming westward again from eastern Asia? And what of the fabled riches of Asia itself? Yet it was prudent of him to rebut the prevalent notion, which derived from the Book of Revelation and was frequently repeated in works then being printed, that Antichrist, certain to come before the last days, would find and use hidden treasure.[13] Much more welcome was the prophecy attributed to Merlin that treasure would be revealed in the ends of the earth, possessed by pagans or infidels. For he wanted gold, he later told them, in order to pay soldiers so that their majesties might retake the Holy Sepulchre; thus he regretted having sent them so little, for God had kept it hidden. Did he believe all he professed? If not initially, certainly eventually, for he believed that in pursuing that vision lay his own fame and glory. The quest for gold, after all, fit within the concepts of exploration native to both Columbus and Isabel, even within a shared tradition of Christian spiritual quest, and it comfortably fit in with the ongoing Spanish goal, articulated centuries ago by El Cid, of "winning our bread," which assumed an earned right to treasure as booty. In short, Isabel was at home with those references made by Columbus in fusing global geography and God's design, and not at all unhappy about his dedication to searching for King Solomon's lost mines.

ISABEL'S JEWELS

Yet when, Baza and Almería having capitulated, Boabdil did not surrender Granada as he had promised, hope for immediate victory evaporated and Isabel once again dismissed Columbus from court. Then, in the fall of 1491, just as Granada's surrender was assured, she heard of him again. Columbus, back at La Rábida, had encountered a sometime chaplain and *contador* of hers, the Franciscan Juan Pérez, now its guardian. Pérez had written to her on Columbus' behalf and she responded within two weeks: Pérez was to come to the encampment at Santa Fe, Columbus to stay at La Rábida and await her good reply. Pérez went, and she sent back with him a new summons to Columbus to come to court, and 20,000 *maravedís* in florins for suitable clothing and a mule. He arrived at Santa Fe in December 1491, in time for the triumphant royal entry into Granada, which he later wrote of as prefiguring his own enterprise.

Shortly thereafter, she called a conclave of nobles, prelates, and *letrados* to reconsider the enterprise of Columbus. His project "was discussed by a Council made up of the men most eminent in rank" and opinions were divided. The wait had been too long; other projects were afoot, and Africa now of most moment. Mendoza and Talavera were no longer enthusiastic, everyone thought Columbus asked too much, and competition with Portugal had receded with João's failing health and mutual guarantees associated with young Isabel's marriage to his son. Once again, Isabel dismissed Columbus.

Then the stuff of high drama: Columbus left for Córdoba, with thoughts (he later said) of going to France or even Genoa. He was overtaken outside Granada, at the bridge at Piños, by a royal messenger: he must return to court. The Queen had changed her mind. Fernando later claimed he had had a hand in it. Las Casas says it was due to Luis de Santángel, the Valencian who "managed the accounts of the royal household." Santángel, together with Pinelo, both *conversos*, had superseded Señor and Melamed in their positions as treasurers of the *hermandad*, administrators of taxfarming, and general receivers of taxes for the Royal Council. Immediately after Columbus had departed, Santángel (according to Fernando Colón) had gone to the Queen on his behalf; he had chided Isabel, as Mendoza had once done, for not taking so small a risk for so large a possibility of glory to God and church, and glory and aggrandizement to her kingdoms and estates. He had told her that should some other prince sponsor Columbus, she would be criticized by friends and retainers, and enemies as well, and that she and her successors would regret it. But should she and Fernando back him, whatever the outcome, they would be judged as magnanimous and generous princes for having intended to know the greatness and secrets of the universe, which had brought other kings and lords great praise. And the cost was small. He appealed most strongly, that is, to her desire to appear preeminent among rulers and in royal qualities, particularly in liberality, never her strong point, as well as in one ability traditionally viewed as a sign of God's special favor, exposing what yet lay hidden of the universe.

It was an effective argument. She thanked him for his good advice, accepted it with pleasure, but suggested its execution wait until some reparations from the war allowed funding, or, if he thought it pressing, the quantity could be found quickly through pawning some jewels of her household. Santángel responded that she need not pawn the jewels, because he would be pleased to perform so small service for Her Majesty as to lend from his funds the 2500 ducats necessary to outfit a fleet of three ships. Small it was. In 1491 he had personally advanced the crown over 10 million *maravedís*.[14]

Did Isabel indeed offer to pawn her jewels? Probably, for that was one of the reasons rulers owned jewels and the sum was small and reimbursement anticipated. Her gesture need not be viewed as a tremendous commitment to Columbus' project, for in any case she was not offering prized possessions so much as customary collateral. Many of her jewels, among them the ruby and pearl necklace that was her wedding gift, were already in pawn in Santángel's Valencia, and not for the first time, as surety for three loans totaling 60,000 florins borrowed for the protracted campaign against Baza. And four years later, on the eve of her children's weddings, she would borrow back her crown, which had been in pawn in Valencia since 1489 as collatoral for 35,000 florins. In her suggestion to Santángel, therefore, she may have been indulging in some of her habitual irony, for the sum was scarcely worth her jewels. The florin was worth roughly two-thirds of a ducat; by comparison to other transactions, the 2500 ducats for Columbus was a minor outlay. Nor did Santángel respond as gallantly as to open his own purse. Rather, he advanced funds from crown monies to which he had access. Through the labyrinth that was royal financing, those funds for Columbus ultimately came from *cruzada* receipts and were dispensed by the Archbishop of Granada, Talavera.

Wherewithal assured, on April 17 Isabel and Fernando signed the *capitulaciones*, the articles of agreement drawn by the friar Juan Pérez, representing Columbus, and affirmed by the royal secretary, Juan de Coloma. They did not mention a religious mission or purpose, but dealt with territory and trade. Columbus was to be royal admiral, viceroy, and governor-general over all he might find, with rights to a tenth of any treasure and with permission to trade duty-free. A safe conduct of the same date, though, did mention religion, if rather cryptically, in stating purpose: "We send Cristóbal Colón with three caravels through the Ocean Sea to the Indies, on some business that touches the service of God and the expansion of the Catholic Faith and our own benefit and utility."[15] Columbus would sail for Castile, which, unlike Aragón, had a well-documented claim on Atlantic exploration, a reminder that Spain still remained a congeries of kingdoms, united only in the persons of its sovereigns.

Those were the concessions the King and Queen initially found exorbitant. By them Columbus would, if successful, become effective lord of eastern Asia, or of unknown lands enroute. Yet Isabel was experienced in modifying such grants, over time and in ways favorable to the crown, as she had shown in getting royal control of the Canary Islands. And neither those, nor any other documents known, specifically delineated Columbus' salary and rights.

On April 30, she and Fernando sent out directives ordering ships fitted out, confirmed Columbus' titles and offices, and provided him with a blanket letter of recommendation—meant, says Las Casas, for the Grand Khan and all the kings and lords of India and anywhere else he might discover. It said only that the object of the voyage was islands and mainland in the Ocean Sea, although secret documents of the same time referred to Eastern trade and sailing to the Indies, and to an unnamed Asiatic prince. So Columbus was dispatched, to extend empire, find gold, outflank the Muslims through reaching eastern Asia, and to link up with hidden Christians or possibly with savages, peoples *sin ley*, humbly awaiting Christianity.

Isabel and the Indies
1492–1504

I hope to God that when I come back here from Castile, which I intend to do, that I will find a barrel of gold, for which these people I am leaving will have traded, and that they will have found the gold mine, and the spices, and in such quantities that within three years the Sovereigns will prepare for and undertake the conquest of the Holy Land. I have already petitioned Your Highnesses to see that all the profits of this, my enterprise, should be spent on the conquest of Jerusalem, and Your Highnesses smiled and said that the idea pleased you, and that even without this expedition you had the inclination to do it.

—Christopher Columbus, *Journal*, December 26, 1492

My confidence in God and her Highness, Isabel, enabled me to persevere . . . I undertook a new voyage to the new heaven and earth, which land, until then, remained concealed.

—Columbus, Letter to Juana de Torres (1500)

BARCELONA: 1493

ALTHOUGH none too convinced of the soundness of Columbus' venture, Isabel, to whom vengeance was sweet, in May 1492 wreaked it on her disobedient subjects of Palos, who were so prone to smuggling, ignoring royal duties and monopolies on trade, and fishing in forbidden waters. So, in Palos on May 23, Columbus had a royal order read out before the church of St. George: "Know you that whereas, for certain things done and committed by you to our disservice you were condemned and obligated by our council to provide us for a year with two equipped caravels at your own charge and expense."[1] The Pinzóns of Palos provided the *Pinta*; from nearby Moguer, whose seamen were accustomed to joint ventures with those of Palos, the Niño family supplied the *Niña*. Columbus chartered his third, largest, and least seaworthy ship, the *Santa María*, from its Vizcayan owner, Juan de la Cosa, who had been sailing out of Puerto de Santa María. The Admiral of the Ocean Sea, that is, requisitioned ships, crews, and master mariners from Castilian ports whose men were accustomed to voyaging the Atlantic southwestward the 1000 miles and more to Guinea and the Canaries. He sailed with 90 men on August 3, 1492.

In March 1493, Isabel and Fernando, in Barcelona, had word from him: he had discovered the Indies, lost one ship, and left a settlement, La Navidad, in the island of *La Española* (or Hispaniola), where there was gold and docile people, and he had sighted the mainland of Asia, for so he thought Cuba. On March 30, they sent a congratulatory letter to "Don Cristóbal Colón, our Admiral of the Ocean Sea and viceroy and governor of the isles that he has discovered in the Indies." They took, they said, great pleasure in what he had written, "and that God has given you such a good end in what you began, whereof He will be greatly served and ourselves as well and our realms receive so much benefit."[2] And they requested he hurry to the court at Barcelona, for he had to return that year to the land he had discovered.

In response, they received from him suggestions on governing the Indies. Found three or four towns, he advised, each having an *alcalde* and clergy who would minister to the townspeople and also see to conversion of the Indians, yet his main concern at the outset was regulating goldmining and ensuring that the crown received half of all gold found. He advised too that they regulate all trade between Spain and the Indies. That letter, of highly practical content, he signed *Christo-ferens*, Christ-bearing. His sense of election, he now felt, had been confirmed.

On or about April 21, in the great hall of the old palace of Barcelona's counts, the Queen, the King, and Prince Juan greeted him; they were seated "in all majesty and grandeur on a rich throne under a gold-brocaded canopy," with a host of notables in attendance.[3] Pedro Mártir reported it all to Tendilla and Talavera: "Raise your spirits, my two wise old men! Hear about the new discovery! Remember, because you should, that he has come back from the western antipodes." Columbus had encountered seven islands, more land than Spain, and brought back remarkable things: gold, and cotton, cinnamon, pepper, and dyewoods, and nude people.[4]

Isabel was presented with *hutias* like small grey rabbits, though with the ears and tail of a rat; chili peppers, burning the tongue, sweet potatoes, and monkeys, and parrots, and some gold. "Most admired were the [six] men wearing gold circles in their ears and nostrils, who were not white, nor black, nor dark brown, "but the color of cooked quinces.""[5] Those Taínos were called Indians, and subsequently baptized, with the King, the Queen, and the Prince standing as godparents. One, named Juan de Castilla after the Prince, remained at court as a page, but briefly, "for God soon called him to Himself."

Las Casas wrote of streets crammed with people along Columbus' route, of "a solemn and beautiful reception," of the monarchs on hearing his account sinking to their knees in gratitude to God, of a *Te Deum* by the royal chapel choir, of tears of joy. Mártir related how Isabel and Fernando had insisted Columbus sit down in their presence, which "is among our kings the greatest sign of benevolence and honor that they concede for great deeds." And they urged him to sail again immediately. It was imperative he further explore and claim for them the land he had assured them must be *tierra firme*, the mainland of Asia.[6]

The information he brought was too scant to enable assessing the geographical position or economic or religious potential of those lands. Still, as to Spain's Admiral having reached India or any part of Asia, Mártir, keenly attuned to royal sentiments, was among the first to express doubt, in a letter of October 1493: "I do not deny it completely, although the magnitude of the globe appears to indicate the contrary." Yet, a year later, he recanted, in writing that Columbus had found a new archipelago—much as Columbus himself referred to an *otro mundo*, an other world—Mártir spoke of "this world unknown until now" and placed it off the Golden Cheresonese, the Malay peninsula of Asia.[7] Certainly, it was the politic opinion in terms of international standing and establishment of royal territorial claims.

REACTIONS

Pleased with her Admiral, Isabel's deepest reaction to Columbus' success was concern about instituting a Castilian monopoly over the newfound lands in anticipation of a counterclaim by Portugal. Talavera, shortly after Columbus' return, expressed similar disquiet in writing to her: "O that [the matter] of the Indies may come out certain!" And he added, chiding, "of which Your Highness has not written me one word."[8] "We are now," she replied archly, "[negotiating] with the King of Portugal concerning those islands Colón found, those same ones about which you say I never wrote you."[9] She was coupling that business with arrangements underway for her widowed daughter, Isabel, to marry again in Portugal, with Dom Manoel, the nephew João had designated his heir. Even so, on word from Medina Sidonia that the Portuguese were preparing a fleet to follow Columbus' route, on May 2 she wrote back that he was to have his caravels ready in case it was so. While she wanted her daughter to marry Portugal's heir, she did not want to share the Indies with her in-laws.

For whatever reason Isabel did not mention Columbus' discovery to Talavera, it was not because it did not create excitement at court and among the populace. Most remarkable was the speed with which its details were known, not only within Spain but all over Europe through a letter purportedly written by Columbus to Luis de Santángel. That letter was circulating in Barcelona by the time Columbus arrived there, printed in Rome and elsewhere soon after, and by 1497 had gone through 17 European editions. It emphasized those aspects of his voyage most conducive to Isabel and Fernando securing a papal bull confirming their possession of the new-found lands; it spoke of God's gift of the Indies to Castile, their proximity to the Canaries, and how very apt the Indians were to receive the faith. Whether it was written by Columbus or, as some scholars assert, was a fabrication by the royal chancery, it still fits within what is known of Columbus' own outlook, and provides no reason to lessen belief in the affinity of Columbus' interpretation to that of the monarchs concerning the meaning of his landfall.[10]

Cardinal Mendoza himself went with the ambassador, Diego López de Haro, to Rome in May. Sent officially to congratulate Rodrigo Borja on becoming Pope Alexander VI, López de Haro while there lectured the new pontiff before the papal consistory for having promoted war in Italy, corruption and venality in the curia, and the sale of benefices. Isabel and Fernando, having waged holy war and espoused religious reform at home, had their envoy speak from a position of their being at least as religious as the pope. And a week later their resident ambassador in Rome, Cardinal Bernardino de Carvajal (who was Mendoza's nephew), in a speech before the college of cardinals, proclaimed that by the will of Christ *los reyes* had subjugated to their dominion the Fortunate Islands, "and now He has given them many others toward India, until now unknown . . . and it is expected they will be converted to Christ in a short time by persons the sovereigns send there."[11] Accordingly, his monarchs requested bulls confirming the Indies to them. They also successfully sought papal permission to apply receipts of bulls of indulgence, which had gone to fund the war against Granada, to "the conversion of new found peoples"; and upon receiving the solicited document, their chancery added to it the words "and conquest."

Las Casas reported Alexander VI having received the news as of "a hidden world, full of nations centuries behind, infinite, to be led to the Church in what is, following the parabola of Christ, the eleventh hour."[12] Certainly the pope quickly issued a bull, which went to Spain on May 17, confirming to Isabel and Fernando dominion of the islands Columbus had discovered sailing toward the Indies, as well as any others found by men they had sent out, provided that such lands had never been held by any Christian prince. Two years earlier, João of Portugal had obtained bulls confirming Portugal's right to the African coast and lands south of the Canaries and west of Guinea, and the Portuguese continued to insist that that meant any lands southward, no matter how far west. The pope now limited that Portuguese claim in issuing two more bulls, which drew a line of demarcation in the Atlantic from north to south, just nicking the tip of Brazil; everything to the west was to belong to Spain. A fourth bull cancelled all previous grants to those areas, which (although it did not say so) had been claimed by Portugal. The Portuguese, unhappy, sought direct negotiation with Spain and, at Tordesillas in 1494, with Isabel and Fernando in residence, Gutierre de Cárdenas, Rodrigo Maldonado de Talavera, and a battery of *letrados* thrashed out with their Portuguese counterparts a treaty, in accord with the

papal bulls but compromising in moving the demarcation line a little further west, thereby allotting to Portugal the bulge of as-yet-undiscovered
Brazil.

It was now that Isabel and Fernando sent scouts to Africa; they received
as well a bull for African crusade and the sale of indulgences for that enterprise. Although in 1479 Isabel had agreed that Fez was within Portugal's
sphere, at Tordesillas that area was left open—thus in effect reopened—to
arbitration. The result was that the litoral of the Maghrib was henceforth
considered a field open to Castilian expansion. In 1494, Isabel and Fernando planned, once the conquest of the Canary island of Tenerife was
completed, to occupy Melilla, principally because it was near Tafilalt, a
West African hub of gold exchange between the coast and the Sahara
desert. With that aim in mind they recognized Portuguese claims to western Barbary in exchange for acknowledgment of their own right to Melilla,
which fell to them in 1497. The several treaties of Tordesillas allowed them
not only Atlantic but also Mediterranean expansion. Their terms attested
to a conceptual linking by Castile's monarchs of Africa, the Indies, and
Asia. Columbus was a piece in a global puzzle.

THE SECOND VOYAGE

Isabel and Fernando kept Columbus at court for five or six weeks, while
arrangements concerning his second voyage were worked out. Warmth
prevailed. They granted him not only *mercedes*, including a coat-of-arms,
10,000 *maravedís* annually for life, and his titles "for now and for always,"
to pass on to his children, but also the right to propose officials and name
lieutenants in the Indies. Even so, during those same weeks, rapidly, in
"document after document, directive after directive, it was the sovereigns
who were establishing the fundamentals of colonial government: naming
public functionaries, provisioning the fleet, recruiting peasants and laborers," setting up their own monopoly on the Indies, all culminating in the
Instructions of May 29.[13] The first colony in the Indies they stipulated was
to be made up of male employees, mostly laborers, salaried and provisioned
by the crown, and overseen by Columbus as their viceroy with the help of
a few royal officials. As a return for their expenditure and for promoting,
at God's behest, evangelism, they and their successors were to be overlords
to any potentate encountered. They were, as Las Casas interpreted it, to be
"as sovereign emperors over all the kings and princes and kingdoms of all
these Indies, islands and mainland, discovered and to be discovered."[14] It
was a traditional way of extending sovereignty over newly won or newly
encountered peoples and places.

This second voyage, expected to strengthen the Spanish claim through a
strong presence in the islands, to extract gold, and to encounter the Asian
mainland, was a major enterprise, of 17 ships and 1200 men. It was readied
speedily, within five months, by an obviously well-trained protégé of Tala-

vera's, Juan Rodríguez de Fonseca, Archdeacon of Seville and sometime chaplain to the Queen. As directed, Fonseca laded arms and tools, biscuit, wine, wheat, and flour, oil and vinegar, cheeses, rice, and chickens, and mares and a few stallions, as well as other necessaries for the voyage and to sustain settlement. Columbus, stopping in the Canaries, added more hens, and cattle, goats, sheep, and also eight pigs—at 70 *maravedís* apiece, from whence, says Las Casas, come all the *puercos* then in the Indies, which were infinite—as well as the seeds and pips of oranges, lemons, apples, melons, and everything grown in gardens, their yield also infinite.

Fonseca also loaded, as instructed, trading goods belonging to the monarchs; there was to be no private commerce. Most recruits were peasants, meant to labor, till the soil, and mine gold. Las Casas says that "if they had known what the work would be I do not believe that one of them would have come." There were too some artisans, some *caballeros* from Seville, 20 mounted troopers from Granada's new *hermandad*, a few men of the royal household, and a physician. There were no women. Among the *caballeros* was one Alonso de Hojeda who, in order to get the attention of the Queen during a visit of hers to the tower of Seville's cathedral, had climbed out on a ledge and dangled by one leg. Her reaction is not recorded, but Hojeda's audacity was to lead him, in 1499, to prove that Venezuela was part of a mainland. He would too be instrumental in annihilating most Indians on Española.

The monarchs sent with that fleet a royal comptroller, a bailiff of the court, an inspector, and a treasurer, all of them crown officials, their appointment indicating that the greatest royal interest lay in revenues and implanting royal justice. And upon departing, all members of Columbus' second expedition took an oath to be loyal and obedient to the king and queen and to the admiral and the justices, and to respect the royal treasury. Disloyalty to the sovereigns in the New World would be very rare; relations to resident authorities were another matter.

Two unofficial royal watchdogs went as well: an Aragonese noble and soldier, Pere Margarit, and a Catalan friar, Bernardo Boyl (or Buyl, or Boil, or even Buil), a humanist turned Benedictine monk, who had been Fernando's secretary. Boyl went under both royal and papal auspices. Stated the monarchs: "We send our devoted *padre Fray Buyl*, together with other religious . . . to procure that the Indians may be well informed about our faith and understand our language."[15] Those people were looked upon as ready to be converted, without law or sect of their own. Columbus, as Admiral, Viceroy, and Governor was to see that the natives were well treated, attracted and converted to the faith, and given gifts from the royal store of merchandise. Boyl had been empowered by the pope to choose missionaries to accompany him. Then going was a Hieronymite friar, Ramón Pané, a Catalan, who would write on Taíno life and customs and learn something of one Indian tongue; and, it seems likely, several Mercedarians and three to five Franciscans also went. A lack of interpreters guaranteed little proselytizing. Boyl did destroy what Spaniards saw as idols and, in the new Spanish town of La Isabela, in what was to be called America he dedicated the first church, to the Word Incarnate and the Most Holy Mother Mary (heretofore the customary dedication in Muslim places). Isabel herself provided its ornaments, including a velvet cloth for its chapel, preserved for years almost as a holy relic, "for being the first and for the Queen having given it."

Boyl did not stay long. He was soon at odds with Columbus; Las Casas says over the Admiral's severity in whipping and hanging Spanish miscreants, but those punished were mostly men under Margarit, and more likely the quarrel signified a power struggle in which Boyl joined a fellow-Catalan. The Friar placed the Admiral under interdict; Columbus retaliated by withholding Boyl's ration of food. In late 1494 Boyl returned to Spain to present his grievances; their majesties listened and considered their viceroy less indispensable.

Isabel had written Columbus a long letter on September 5, 1493, revealing her concern about Portuguese claims and requesting he always let her know everything that he had found and he was doing. She had a response only the following March, by way of Antonio Torres, the captain general of the Indies fleet, who had returned to Cádiz for supplies. Columbus had come upon more islands, which he named Guadalupe, Montserrat, and Antigua; he had returned to find the original settlement of La Navidad destroyed and was building La Isabela—public buildings of stone, houses of thatch—in proximity to goldmines he believed located in Cibao. He sent the King and Queen 26 of what he described as cannibals, "men and women, boys and girls, which Your Highnesses can order placed in charge of persons from whom they may be able better to learn the language while being employed, gradually ordering that greater care be given them than to other slaves." It would be good for them, he was certain, to speak Spanish, to break old habits, to be baptized, and so "secure the welfare of their souls."[16]

Clearly, they were a sample, indicating that Columbus had found little gold and a lot of people—estimated are 800,000 to 1.5 million Taínos on Española—and was adjusting his notion of where profit lay. Within Castilian and canon law, cannibalism was just cause for enslavement. Pedro Mártir wrote of seeing eight of the Caribs Columbus sent, among them (the Queen of the Cannibals) and her son, and he assumed their slavery justified in reporting that Spaniards had found in Carib huts on Guadalupe human joints ready for cooking. Isabel and Fernando, temporizing, replied to their Admiral only that they were not ready to make a decision on slaving.

Although Torres brought them relatively little gold, only 30,000 ducats worth, and inferior or bogus spices, along with an urgent request for additional provisions, still they wrote to Columbus on April 13, 1494, encouragingly and sent out his brother Bartolomé and three caravels of provisions, and they welcomed his sons, Diego and Fernando, to court as pages to

Prince Juan. That summer they heard that he had come upon Jamaica and coasted Cuba, but insufficiently to determine it a mainland. Isabel wrote to him again on August 16, beginning with reassuring cordiality:

> And one of the principal things giving us much pleasure is [what has been gained] through being invented, precipitated, and had by your hand, work, and diligence; and it seems to us that all that you told us at the beginning you have been able to achieve for the most part, that all has come out as certain as though you could have seen before what you said to us; we have hope in God that all will continue thusly with what remains to be known, so that through [further discovery] you will have much cargo of which to make us *mercedes*.[17]

There is equivocation in her "for the most part." While clearly curious, what she most desired was more information from him in order to evaluate the situation. She wanted, she told him, to hear more about what he had discovered: what names he had given each place, what he had found in each one, and about planting and seasons; he should send birds and all else, "for we wish to see everything." Each month she would dispatch a caravel to Española and one should also leave there monthly for Spain. Let her know what she should send, she wrote him, much as she had written Fernando in prodding him on. In dealing with the people there, he should give them as much contentment as possible, but not allow them to overstep in anything that they were ordered to do for her; as to problems with Europeans—she had undoubtedly heard they roved the island, looting and raping women—he must do as he thought best.

It was a month later that expectations were lowered considerably by reports from Boyl and Margarit. They reported that all Columbus claimed was a joke, that expenses would never be repaid, that there was famine and syphilis at La Isabela, that Columbus had jailed the royal comptroller, and that the tribute system he had introduced, based on having chiefs collect a set amount of gold from every Indian, was unworkable; there were no mines and little gold. (Española, Cuba, and Puerto Rico had only placer mines, and gold-bearing quartz veins.) They did not mention that by 1495 there was great starvation among the Indians, nor that terrible penalties were inflicted on Taínos who could not produce enough gold as tribute. Concerning the natives, they reported only that they were fighting the goldhunters.

Torres returned to Española by the end of 1494 with an invitation for Columbus from the monarchs to come "advise them on negotiations with Portugal," which he did not accept. Mártir, who so often reflected the royal mood, was still sanguine about the presence of gold, writing at the end of 1494 that large chunks, *"pepitas de oro en bruto"* were to be plucked from streams, but in January 1495, while still praising the climate and productivity of those lands, he for the first time failed to mention gold at all. And within weeks his emphasis shifted significantly, onto converting many thousands to Christianity.[18] Although royal hope dimmed for treasure, there was still the wealth of souls to be gained, especially important in that it was the basis of the papal confirmation of Castile's claim to dominion. The trade in bodies was another matter, neither publicized nor resolved.

Yet Columbus, disappointed in obtaining enough gold to support the colony, repay the crown, and ensure his own wealth and fame, not to mention fund an expedition to retake Jerusalem, had indeed turned to the slave trade. He had 1500 Taínos brought to La Isabela and sent the 500 he thought best to Fonseca in February 1495, as legally enslaved since they had warred on the Europeans. Two hundred died at sea, and most of the others did not live long. In April 1495 the monarchs wrote Fonseca that Andalusia seemed the best place to sell those Indians, then four days later they informed him that they wanted a commission of *letrados*, theologians, and canonists to look into if, in good conscience, they could sell them for slaves at all, and that that could not be done without letters Torres had brought from the Admiral detailing the cause of their captivity. Meanwhile, Fonseca was to sell them provisionally. That August Pedro Mártir's tone changed markedly: while "Admiral Colón supposes [Española] to be Ophir, Solomon's goldmine," had he found the Indies at all and was Cuba not after all just an island?[19]

Columbus returned to Spain in the spring of 1496. Despite reports from Española of "infinite cattle, especially pigs," and many chickens but little gold and much trouble, on July 12 Isabel and Fernando wrote him a gracious note, if understandably less enthusiastic than formerly, extending permission to join them whenever he wished. He came to court that fall, in Burgos. His son, Fernando, there as a page to Prince Juan, described the scene. His father arrived with more things of the Indies—birds, animals, trees, and plants, masks and belts adorned with gold, and gold dust and nuggets. The monarchs greeted him with affection and due ceremony. They heard a rosy account of the progress of mining and a proposal for a third voyage, requiring eight ships, two with provisions for Española and six to seek a mainland Indians had said was to the south. Yet this time they were in no hurry to accommodate him. His venture was after all proving unprofitable, unspectacular, and relatively unimportant. Nor did it help Columbus' cause when, after they had heard from a pilot-captain, who arrived from Española in October 1496, that he had brought them three ships full of badly needed gold, they discovered that the gold he had referred to was the estimated worth of Indians Columbus had shipped as slaves. Isabel, since her commission had not yet decided whether or not such people could be legally enslaved, ordered Fonseca to sell fifty of them who were between 20 and 40 years old to row the royal galleys, but to get receipts in case they had to be freed, so that if need be he could ship back the ones still living. Moreover, from January 1496, all vessels arriving from the Indies were to come only to Cádiz and there to turn over all the gold they carried only to Fonseca.[20]

THE THIRD VOYAGE

Whatever the monarchs' disillusionment with Columbus' Indies, Portugal was sending out Vasco da Gama and this was not the time to relinquish their advantage in the Atlantic. On April 23, 1497, the orders they issued to prepare another voyage clearly sought to rectify earlier mistakes. They granted Columbus the eight ships he had requested and permission to recruit 300 settlers, but those conscripts were to be salaried and to include sailors, artisans, squires, goldminers, a physician, an apothecary, a herbalist, and peasants who would double as foot-soldiers, and 30 women as well, unsalaried, their status not specified. They may have been the first European women in the Indies, although some may have gone out earlier with Torres. The monarchs advanced funds for food, stipulating they be repaid after those people had made money. They set salary scales and prices for provisions, and loaned wheat to farmers to sow, directing that from their crops they must tithe to God; and they decreed that mares, asses, and 20 yokes of oxen were to go to work the soil.

Subsequently, Columbus was authorized to take another 170 people, unsalaried, and, granting his request, criminals were permitted to go "to serve us through our Admiral." They were to work, for two years if serving a death penalty, otherwise for a year, before being pardoned; not eligible were heretics, traitors, murderers, counterfeiters, arsonists, sodomists, or anyone who had exported money from Castile. Each settler was to receive lands with wood and water, and to build a house. They were to plant gardens, vineyards, cotton, olive trees, and sugar cane, and they might construct mills and sugar mills. The crown reserved for itself deposits of gold and silver, and the valuable dyestuff, brazilwood. Financing was found with great difficulty, most of it advanced through the Genoese Centurione in Seville. Almost as a postscript, on June 15, Columbus was directed to take priests to administer the sacraments and convert the Indians.

On this third voyage, of January 1498, Columbus expressly sought the Grand Khan and Cathay, according to Mandeville the richest province in the world and close to the lands of Prester John. In late 1498 the monarchs heard from him that he had reached the mainland at last. He had coasted Trinidad, come upon present-day Venezuela, sailed into the Gulf of Paría and discovered the mouth of the Orinoco. He wrote of having encountered "an other world" in the East Indies, south or southeast of the Chinese province of Mangi (which was Cuba), and that he had reached the continent where lay the Earthly Paradise, "because all men say it is at the end of the Orient," and that it lay nearby, on a promontory he compared to "the nipple on a woman's breast" atop the pear-shaped earth.[21]

His mysticism had become more pronounced with ill health—painful arthritis and sore eyes—and diminishing esteem. In 1498 too da Gama reached the Malabar coast of India, and the monarchs heard from an envoy in London that for the past seven years Bristol had been sending ships out "following the fantasy of this Genoese Cabot," who sought the fabled isles of the Seven Cities and Brazil, and who in 1497 had reached Newfoundland and Nova Scotia. They were misinformed; ships of Bristol had explored the western sea since 1480. Fonseca, now paying no attention to Columbus' monopoly, quickly licensed Hojeda to explore where Columbus had left off, and furnished him with Columbus' charts. It was Hojeda who named Venezuela, although greater glory would accrue to his shipmate, Amerigo Vespucci.

Isabel had had as model the earlier settling of Atlantic islands by Spaniards and Portuguese, in which military enclaves were established where paid laborers or sharecropper peasants worked under a few merchant proprietors, some of them Genoese, and where urban European social strata were not reproduced. But the first Spaniards in America were either intent on making a fortune quickly and returning home or they had in mind a familiar situation, Christian settlement in places taken from Granada's Muslims. Columbus himself aspired to both the stature of the new lords of such towns and that of the merchant princes of the islands.

In 1498 Isabel received from him steady complaints of settler pretensions. It was easy to discern that he was not succeeding as either lord or merchant prince. He had returned to Española to find Europeans in revolt, 160 of them ill with syphilis, and that God was concealing the gold. He requested more men and ships. He would send to Spain brazilwood and slaves; and he wanted priests sent, as missionaries and also to reform the Spaniards, and a royal magistrate to dispense justice, "since without royal justice the religious will profit little." The chief justice had been Francisco Roldán, who had become chief rebel, and in trying to appease him, as Isabel learned only later, Columbus had instituted a system of *repartimiento*, literally a parcelling out of Indians who must work for those receiving them, and it was understood that with those natives went the benefit of their lands. It was an arrangement not only detrimental to Indians, but reminiscent of the sort of autonomous lordships the Queen had so recently combatted in Spain.

When that year Columbus again requested a magistrate, one had already been chosen. Francisco de Bobadilla was sent with the double-edged title of judge investigator, instructed as chief magistrate to look into the entire situation, including the activities of Columbus. Bobadilla was a *comendador* of the military order of Calatrava, a warrior noted for bravery in war against the Moors, and a former captain of the Alhambra guards.

INDIAN POLICY

A story Las Casas tells rings true: when in May 1499, the Queen heard that 300 settlers had returned, each with a slave presented by Columbus, she loosed her wrath: "What power of mine has the Admiral to give anyone my vassals?"[22] She ordered cried throughout Granada and Seville, where the court was, that all Indians given by Columbus must be returned home on pain of death. Some went with Bobadilla in June 1500. Her confessor, Francisco Jiménez de Cisneros, also sent with him four Observant Franciscan friars and a Benedictine as missionaries; they simply baptized Indians en masse. Isabel had concluded that Indians were royal vassals in whom Christianity must be instilled, and that enslaving them was generally unjust. Yet in Spain that order of hers was confined to Indians that Columbus had presented, and did not affect the others held there.

Once in Española, Bobadilla liberally granted Indians in *repartimiento* to Europeans; and to encourage mining he lowered royal imposts on gold, so that under his jurisdiction placer-mining began in earnest and with Indian labor. And, a veteran of infighting within his military order on the Castilian frontier, familiar with the impossibility of divided command in wartime, he had Columbus and his brother siezed and, in October 1500, shipped them to Spain for trial, in chains.

Isabel and Fernando, on hearing, sent orders by rapid post to free them, or so says Pedro Mártir; a more recent and perhaps less subjective account, that of Samuel Eliot Morison, says the order came only after they had been in a Cádiz prison for six weeks. Whatever the timing, and although Columbus' son, Diego, recalled that the Queen then declared Columbus had done all he had promised, of undoubted weight were requests from the friars on Española that Columbus not come back. He wanted no priests there, they said; he was turning the island over to the Genoese, and he would soon destroy everything, this Pharoah-king. Columbus' other son, Fernando, recalled he and his brother, with the court in the Alhambra that summer, being taunted by idlers returned from the Indies with cries of "Look at the sons of the Admiral of the Mosquitos, of the one who has discovered lands of nonsense and deceit for the misery and burial of Castile's *hidalgos!*"[23] Those men also importuned the king as he passed for monies promised and never received.

Still, just before Christmas the monarchs summoned Columbus and granted him 2000 ducats for a fourth voyage. There was further exploration to be made, and his earlier voyages, though disappointing, had had a salutary effect in reinforcing their chosen image. Thus verses written to Isabel in 1499 by an old retainer, Juan Alvarez Gato, offered a vision of peoples of all lands flocking to bow to her. Then too another poet, Diego Guillén de Avila, felt the time ripe to reiterate the prediction that she and Fernando would conquer Africa and then rescue the Holy Sepulchre from the infidel. Yet immediately some more pragmatic action was called for; on Española, they replaced Bobadilla with Nicolás de Ovando, a member of the more austere military order of Alcántara, a *caballero*-friar of Cistercian vows—poverty, chastity, obedience, and battling infidels—who had proven himself both loyal to the crown and adept at administration within his order, and who had been one of the knights making up Prince Juan's entourage.

Ovando and the *letrados* and secretaries he took with him were salaried, where before officials' income had come from a percentage of colony revenues, and 2500 colonists went in the 30 ships of his fleet, some for a specified term and some with families and assigned lands; they were expected to reside in towns and help extract gold. The monarchs directed he send them complete information on all his decisions. Ovando, arriving in April 1502, found only some 300 Europeans surviving.

With Ovando too went twelve or thirteen Franciscans and four or five priests recruited by Cisneros. At Barcelona in 1493, everyone had been cheered by the Taínos' "multitude and simplicity, gentleness and nudity . . . by their most apt disposition and ability to be lead to our holy and Catholic faith," as Las Casas put it. "Their royal highnesses, especially the holy Queen Doña Isabel" felt that with divine favor and with royal expenditure—although, he noted, little outlay was required—a great many infidel nations would be discovered and led to the universal Church in a land more extensive than Granada.[24]

The monarchs had evidently promised the pope to send missionaries to the Indies; his bull of May 1493, confirming to them the Indies alluded to that promise. Yet it was not until four years later, when it was realized that gold was scarce and Indians the greatest natural resource of the islands, that, in instructions for Columbus' third voyage, he was ordered to take clergy to minister first and foremost to the Indians. The first full contingent of friar missionaries arrived only in 1502 with Ovando, their dispatch coinciding with the monarchs' receiving from the pope in 1501 the direct use of tithes in newfound lands, on condition that they not only introduce and maintain the Church in them but also have their inhabitants instructed and converted to Christianity. Even so, once on Española those friars too attended chiefly to Spaniards, although they took in a few highborn Indian boys to instruct. Subsequently, other friars did go out seeking to save indigenous souls by example and instruction, and to find themselves allied with the crown in mounting competition with Europeans for jurisdiction over ever fewer Taínos.

ISABEL'S SUBJECTS

Earlier experience with Canarian conquest, administration, and religion set precedent for royal handling in America of conquerors, settlers, and indigenous inhabitants. It established precedent for *capitulaciones* with *conquistadores,* for adaption of *repartimiento,* for regulating slavery, for cultivating sugar cane, and for the blending of mercantile and *conquistador* mentality and activity. And much of the precedent set was attributable to the Queen.

Isabel had earlier opposed Inés Pereza selling Canarians as slaves, and had had merchants of Palos and Moguer who trafficked in them sued, ordering those Islanders, and Africans as well, freed and returned to their homelands. The Queen's interest lay in collecting import duties, prohibiting illicit slaving, and imposing the principle that peoples of newly conquered lands were royal vassals, or, in certain circumstances, royal merchandise; she did not question the legality or morality of the institution of slavery itself, indeed she employed in her court Muslims enslaved at Málaga. The norm endured of slavery as it had existed in Murcia at her birth.

In 1481, she and Fernando had treated high-ranking baptized Canary islanders brought to court more or less as subject potentates. They and their people were privileged to enjoy royal protection, "like the Christians they are," and were free to travel and trade in Castilian dominions, and not to be enslaved. Yet while the earlier success of Franciscan missionaries and such treatment by the monarchs did gain them adherents in the Canaries and made Vera's conquest there easier by dividing the natives, within two years he had provoked sufficient resistence to turn to fire, sword, and the profitable business of enslavement. In the Canary Islands, natives were enslaved and provided most labor, supplemented by black Africans. Canarians were also valuable to Madeira's sugar industry, until 1490, when the Portuguese king prohibited their use, asserting they were royal vassals and, thereby, providing precedent.

In the Indies, Isabel did not want the natives enslaved—instructions of 1493 to Columbus had been to treat them lovingly; yet she did want to make use of Indian labor to mine gold and maintain the Spanish presence. Her solution was to have the Taínos become Christian and enforce the principle that they were royal subjects, to be treated as such by resident Europeans, who might have access to their labor only with that understood. Accordingly, she rejected the essentially Aristotelian notion, presented to her early on in the Prologue to the *Garden of Noble Maidens*, that "the barbarians are those who live without law; the Latins, those who have law; for it is the law of nations that men who live and are ruled by law shall be lords of those who have no law; wherefore without sinning they may seize and enslave them, because they are by nature the slaves of the wise who are ruled by law." Yet while Isabel viewed the Indians as royal vassals rather than as slaves, she did think that "they have neither law nor sect," as instructions for Columbus' second voyage noted. That is, they did not completely lack civilized ways, as she construed them, and could become fully civilized if brought law and faith, which were inseparable. That concept of a civilizing mission served as a justification for Spanish dominion in the Indies, as the papal confirmation attested. Through Ovando, Isabel resolved to battle Spaniards in the Indies for the labor and revenues of "her vassals." In the islands she lost, for those vassals she claimed were within a decade decimated by ill treatment, overwork, starvation, and the disruption of their societies; disease was soon to follow. Yet she made her point; the legal principles and the royal authority she then imposed in the Spanish Indies endured for over 300 years.

Ovando had been instructed: "We want the Indians well treated as our good subjects and vassals" and "to pay tribute to us as they do, through their chiefs who will collect from each one; and since their work is needed for gold and other labors, they must be made to serve us through work, and be paid a just salary, nor should they live outside of villages"; he was to "make anyone who treats them badly understand that, because you will punish them in such a way that from then on no one will dare to do them harm."[25] The Franciscan missionaries who went with him were counted on to underscore that interpretation of vassalage.

In March 1503 he was further instructed, that "we are informed that, for what complies to the salvation of the souls of the Indians, they must live in villages, each in a house with a wife, family, and possessions, as do the people of our kingdoms, and dress and behave like reasonable beings." In those villages, there had to be a church and a chaplain charged with teaching them the Catholic faith as well as "a person who in the royal name is in charge of the place as though he holds it as an *encomienda*. And it would be well if the Indians mined gold for us, retaining a certain part for themselves."[26]

By 1505, Ovando had introduced a system of *encomienda*, which entailed the commending of the services of Indian communities to individual Europeans. In Castile *encomienda* had been a grant to members of military orders, commonly made in places taken from Muslims, of extensive lands and their castles and peoples, who were considered to be royal vassals; the *encomendero* received jurisdiction and the obligation to serve the crown militarily, and he was exempt from local jurisdiction, thus highly autonomous, in effect a petty king. In the castle-less Indies, where Isabel wanted no lords, *encomienda* quickly became a system having more to do with holding people than with land, and it largely replaced *repartimiento* and slavery. Under Ovando, royal government would be effectively imposed; native leaders who resisted killed, and political structure broken; and, though not what the Spanish, whose goal was use of Indian labor, desired, the population would continue to decline. Soon, extended to the mainland, *encomienda* would become the initial central institution maintaining Spanish domination of indigenous peoples in America.

In October 1503, Isabel did sanction some sorts of slavery in decreeing that cannibals might be justly warred against and enslaved "as punishment for crimes committed against my subjects." For, she said, since the Indians should become Christians and live like reasonable men, she had ordered some captains to go with clergy to preach and indoctrinate them in the faith and what was required of those in her service. Only the cannibals had resisted. They had also killed some Christians and warred on Indians in her service and eaten them, so they might be punished for crimes against her subjects. Also, although enjoined repeatedly to convert and live peacefully, they remained obdurate in their idolatry as well as "in eating the said Indians." While Isabel did not accept the hypothesis, put forth by Bernaldez among others, that the Indians were subjects and instruments of the Devil (along with the Muslims and Jews), neither did she entirely preclude its applicability to those who practiced idolatry. She decreed that anyone under her orders might try to bring those cannibals to her service and the faith and, if failing, could capture them and take them to other places and sell them, "paying the portion that belongs to us," for in serving Christians those idolators might more easily be converted and attracted to the faith.[27]

Cannibalism and idolatry, was the inference, could be construed as of a piece.

That December she further conceded that the Indians of Española "might serve the Christians" for they had to work, but they were to be paid for day labor, as the free people they were.[28] That is, she now sanctioned another sort of *repartimiento* having to do with parcelling out Indians, but unlike the former one this version while asserting the principle that those people were royal vassals conceded their labor to resident Europeans.

Ovando's instructions had raised the possibility of employing blacks as slaves, and some were sent from Spain, until he wrote that they could not be stopped from escaping and joining Indians and asked that no more come. The trade stopped, then began again after Isabel's death. As to mixed marriages, they were permitted only of Spaniards with noblewomen, daughters of *caciques*. The clause in the codicil to Isabel's last will of 1504— "if the Indians have received some offense, it must be remedied and resolved"—was very much after the fact; for most of the Taínos such had been the contact with her Spanish subjects that by then it was too late.

THE LAST VOYAGE

In 1500, Pedro Alvarez Cabral, en route to India, bumped into Brazil while on a *volta*—the wide arc required to sail southwards in navigating the West African coast. In 1501 the monarchs acceded to Columbus' request to make yet a fourth voyage and in September they appointed to go with him a gold founder and marker, a treasurer, a ranking royal official, and a commercial agent (who was one Francisco de Monroy, of the Extremaduran clan from whence would soon come another emigrant, Hernando Cortés). Columbus sailed in May 1502, with four ships and with instructions to stay away from Española. He coasted Central America, seeking a strait across what he wrote of as the Malay peninsula, then turned to goldhunting. He wrote to the pope embellishing his finds—Cuba was the Asian mainland still—and recalling his promise to the monarchs to provide enough wherewithal for an army to reconquer Jerusalem, and that he would have done it before had he not been prevented by the malice of Satan. He wrote to Isabel and Fernando in the same vein. He also told them that "Jerusalem and Mount Zion are to be rebuilt by the hands of the Christians as God has declared by the mouth of his prophet [Isaiah] in the fourteenth psalm," that "he who should do this was to come from Spain," and that Saint Jerome had shown the Holy Woman the way to accomplish it.[29] In that letter, and in similar statements he addressed to them in his *Book of Prophecies*, he was still evoking what he saw as shared views. He was making flattering allusions to themselves, the Lion-King and the earthly emanation of the Holy Woman, and putting his own activities in a light of highest importance: "I was aided not by intelligence, by mathematics or by maps. It was simply the fulfillment of what Isaiah had prophesied."[30]

He was shipwrecked for nearly a year on Jamaica. By then, his monopoly on exploration and his position in Española had evaporated. The monarchs licensed other venturers: Isabel, though ill, sent off one of her handwritten hortatory notes to the *conquistador* Pedro Arías de Avila (known as Pedrárias Dávila), and Vicente Yáñez Pinzón reached Brazil. In 1503, Isabel also instituted the *Casa de Contratación*, the Board of Trade, in Seville, putting at its head Fonseca, who, appropriately enough, later became Bishop of Burgos, for it had been due to the arguments of an earlier bishop of Burgos, Alfonso de Cartagena, that Castile had retained legal access to exploring the Atlantic and the right to lands found there. On behalf of the crown the *Casa* oversaw every aspect of the enterprise of the Indies: all commerce, justice, technology, and cartography. The government and trade of the Indies were to remain a royal monopoly. Isabel also insisted that the property Bobadilla had taken from Columbus be returned, but not his titles or authority. At the last, Columbus addressed her as his principal supporter and his inspiration. On November 7, 1504, he returned to Spain from his final voyage, bitter and worn out, not to see her again. She died less than three weeks later.

For the Indies as elsewhere, Isabel sought a symbiotic balance between God's work and royal benefit. She sought to gain souls there, and also sovereignty, monopoly, revenues, and firm royal control over both Spanish and indigenous subjects, which entailed royal justice prevailing over both, and, gold lacking, profit from indigenous labor. Royal benefit involved parceling out the business of consolidating conquest among delegated administrators, financial experts, and justices, as well as the clergy who carried on the missionary work equated with the civilizing process. The civilization sought was European and Spanish, and required organized communities with hierarchical social and political arrangements, at their heads the monarch. The concept of civilization settled on America was Isabelline.

Isabel died well before Magellan's expedition, in circumnavigating the globe, proved the West Indies were not the East Indies, and America not Asia. Even so, it had become obvious to her that the Indies had not the wealth proper to Asia, and so she treated them as a waystation to it, much as she did the Canaries in relation to Africa. Yet to the last it was politic to speak of the Indies as part of eastern Asia. And, whether or not a new continent had been discovered, it was a new world to Europeans. An implication of the term "new world," as employed by Columbus, Las Casas, and Pedro Mártir, was that its inhabitants, uncivilized though they were, like other *salvajes* had something to teach Europeans about morality. Theirs, as Columbus and Mártir agreed, was a golden world of people who lived simply and innocently without being forced to by laws, and without quarrels, judges, and libels, "content only to satisfy nature." That interpretation, implying contrast to a corrupt Europe, was consonant with Isabel's own vision of the need to reform Spain itself. The moral virtue she sought personally and for her subjects, and which those observers ascribed to the Indians of the New World, she strove to impose at home—although not the doing away with law and judges—by starting with the clergy, those supposed exemplars and disseminators of the will of God, and that of the monarchs, to the Spanish populace.

18

The Catholic Kings
1492–1499

And now, who cannot see that, although the title of Empire is in Germany, its reality lies in the power of the Spanish monarchs who, masters of a large part of Italy and the isles of the Mediterranean Sea, carry the war to Africa and send out their fleet, following the course of the stars, to the isles of the Indies and the New World, linking the Orient to the western boundary of Spain and Africa.

—Antonio de Nebrija[1]

The pope, our Lord, for the great merits of Your Highnesses in the Catholic faith and Christian religion, has deliberated jointly with the holy college to entitle Your Highnesses with the title of *Católicos*, as your progenitor is Alfonso [I] *el Católico*, and most meritoriously he has done it, and I know the French are very upset.

—Bernardino de Carvajal[2]

INTIMATIONS OF MORTALITY

IN October 1492 Isabel and Fernando had entered Barcelona in state. There Isabel saw her son received as heir-apparent by the often truculent Catalans. There too, on December 7, as Fernando was descending a staircase after presiding over a Friday session dispensing public justice, he was savagely attacked from behind and felled by a knife-thrust in the back of his neck. Only the heavy gold chain he wore, in deflecting the blade, prevented the amputation of the royal head.

So wrote Pedro Mártir to Talavera and Tendilla the next day, and he continued to keep them informed. The King's life was despaired of. The assailant, a Catalan peasant, one Juan de Canamares, was taken alive and readily confessed: he had been told by a demon to kill the King so that he himself might claim the kingdom which was rightfully his. As to the Queen, upon hearing, "she flew in search of her husband"; but fearing a plot, she first commanded that war galleys be rowed to the embankment before the royal residence in order to protect the Prince, who was heir to Aragón should his father die. "An entire battalion of doctors and surgeons has been called," said Mártir; "we lurch between fear and hope."[3]

Nine days later, Mártir wrote again to Talavera. While the King seemed out of danger, his tongue was completely swollen and his cheeks burning with fever; still, he was taking food from the Queen's own hands. On December 23 Mártir reported Fernando still housebound, and that people were undertaking pilgrimages to pray for his life, "through mountains, valleys, coasts and wherever there is a sanctuary. The entire royal family has gone on foot to [the shrine of Our Lady of] Montserrat."[4]

On December 13, Isabel had her secretary, Alvarez, inform her deputy in Castile that she had ordered an investigation by members of the Royal Council and the dignitaries of Barcelona. They had learned from the prisoner himself, through torture and otherwise, and through reputable witnesses, that he was subject to fits of temporary and violent insanity. He had confessed that a diabolic spirit had moved him, and it had been decided that he must do penance in all his erring members. On December 12, upon a high platform visible to all, punishment was meted out: the right hand that wielded the knife was removed, as were the feet by which he had come, the eyes by which he saw the way, and the heart that had prompted him. Pincers tore the flesh from all his body and then it was turned over to the people to be stoned and burned, for everyone wished to have vengeance on it. "And so that traitor met the end he merited." In truth it was a marvel that the prisoner had not been torn to pieces on coming out of the jail. The King was much better and sitting up in bed; the Queen was reading him letters and keeping him informed of affairs. Another account stated that she had mercifully ordered the assailant garroted before execution. Whether or no, a public display of retributive justice was the object. Isabel's secretary's explanation for it all was that "the Devil had sought through the hand of that man to stop the good being done by His Highness, and Our Lord had permitted it in order to show the world the King's great qualities."[5]

Isabel wrote to Talavera personally on December 30, ruefully and revealingly beginning "for since we see that kings can die of some disaster like other people, there is reason to prepare to die well."[6] While she had thought of death often before, "greatness and prosperity has made me think of it and fear it more." Still, there was a vast difference, she continued, between thinking of it and facing it. She hoped never to die in such a way, and especially not with her debts unpaid. And so the purpose of that letter: she wanted from Talavera a list of her debts. She wanted to know her literal debts, the sums she owed on loans received as *servicios*, on wartime indemnities, on old *juros* incurred when she was Princess, in regard to the mint at Avila, "and all the things that seem to you have to be repaid and satisfied. . . It will be the greatest relief in the world to have it." Tantalizingly, she mentioned that she had incurred other sorts of debts, but she did not say what they were. Sensibly, she appealed to the man who had been both her confessor and chief accountant, who could tally obligations both financial and otherwise. Yet nowhere does her no-nonsense literal-mindedness come clearer; to her, debts were primarily monetary. And, ever certain of the omnipresence of divine purpose, she had, as usual, extracted from near-catastrophe some practical lessons.

Unburdening herself to her old familiar, she spoke of her own anguish, Fernando's condition and popularity, and God's activity: "the wound was so great, according to the physician of Guadalupe, that I had not the heart to see it, so large and so deep, of a depth of four fingers, of such size that my heart trembles in saying it. . . . But God made it with such compassion [that it was] in a place where it could be done without danger." God had then sent a life-threatening fever, a night of inferno. "But believe, Father," that never was such [popular concern] seen before anywhere: everyone spontaneously prayed or went on pilgrimage for the King's recovery. Now he was up and about. "The pleasure of seeing him get up was as great as had been the sadness. We are all restored. I do not know why God shows to us this great mercy and not to others of much virtue . . . What shall I do, who have none? And this is one of the sorrows I feel: to see the King suffering what I merit, not meriting it, but paying for me"; it was this that "killed me most of all." She has prayed to God, she said, that she will serve him henceforth as she ought. Had she a guilty secret? Or was it, as has been said, that in Catholic cultures suffering tends to be seen as a sign of God's attention and love, and, if so, then about her greater deserving of suffering may have hovered not only love but competition.

She ended the letter on a note of relief; she has been reassured that the assailant acted alone and was out of his mind. At the end he had seemed to awaken from a dream, and she had insisted that a confessor be called when everyone else wanted him to lose both body and soul. There was a postscript: her secretary had found a list of her debts after all; perhaps Talavera had some additions. She hoped that she had not tired him but felt compelled to write at length and that he would suffer her daring to do so. She showed him affection and great deference, addressing him as *reverendo y devoto padre mí confesor*; and yet, as a subsequent exchange between them indicates, within the changes of the 1490s, the promptings of her conscience, on which she relied so heavily, were diverging from his views.

On January 19, 1493, the monarchs signed with France a treaty returning the long-contested provinces of Rosellón and Cerdaña to Aragón, but at a price. Fernando and Isabel then agreed that Charles VIII might traverse Italy to fight Ferrante, the King of Naples, to determine whose claim to Naples was better; they agreed to a trial by combat, a medieval arrangement that, as it turned out, was to bring Spain's army into modern times. Isabel, in writing to Talavera, mentioned that the attendant festivities held for the French ambassadors had wearied her. He replied seemingly opaquely, enjoining her to strive for her own moral perfection, reminding her that what God wills must be constantly guarded in return for His gifts. Then he became more specific: "since your very excellent prudence will not be content with this generality," he would say what she might not want to hear and what he had become tired of saying, that while he was not censuring such festivities, nonetheless certain things required prudence: among them, having the French dining with her at table, her lavishing of gifts and *mercedes*, her taking pleasure in showy military exercises, and her spending money on new clothing; and "what I see most offending to God . . . was the dancing, especially of one who ought not dance." Isabel, he knew, loved to dance. Irony unsheathed, he employed it generously: he marveled that she could dance without sinning and he lamented the mingling of French knights and Castilian ladies at supper, reminding her (as she herself had once reminded her half-brother) how far the French departed from Castilian decorum and gravity. It was a bad example to her country; how much his queen and sovereign lady had lost through it! He cited Biblical queens who had behaved far better in similar circumstances. He alluded to her daughter's widowhood of two years as though it had just occurred, and then he thundered disapproval: "And what can I say of the bulls, that without dispute are a condemned spectacle?" Assuredly, he predicted. international embarrassment would follow upon such cruelty and crudity—he was well aware of her tenderness on that point—and then the *golpe de gracia*, worthy of a master matador: "Pardon all, Lord; do not inflict the merited punishment." He closed calmly but pointedly, implying her sense of purpose had gone astray through suggesting putting more emphasis on commemorating annually the battle of Salado, in which her ancestor, Alfonso XI, had triumphed over the last Muslim invaders from Africa. He did not mention that in recent festivities he had praised her profusely, as another Deborah and another Judith. It may have been just as well, for at court then the favored analogy was to Diana or Athena.

Her response, at the end of 1493, quietly self-exonerating, indicated a distancing from his way of thinking: In entertaining the French, she explained, she had not danced nor had she worn new clothes, only a silk dress with some gold trim, the simplest possible. Men and women dining together was a French and Burgundian custom. She too was opposed to bullfights. The discussion was regally shown closed by a change of subject, to another at once alluding to their old intimacy and to her being engrossed in more pressing matters than dress and dancing: She had been in bed all day. She was not sick. She had had too much work to do to take the time to get up. Too, the tenor of her response and the months she had allowed to elapse before making it hint that she now found him out of touch with her court and a changing world, and that his influence upon her was diminishing.

FRANCISCO JIMENEZ DE CISNEROS

Isabel had a new confessor. Mártir wrote to a friend of her satisfaction with him: "The Queen, because she fears and respects God, appears to have encountered what she has so ardently desired, the man to whom she can disclose with tranquility her innermost secrets . . . and this is the cause of her extraordinary content. They say he is called Francisco Jiménez.''[7] In the spring of 1492, about to leave Hernando de Talavera in Granada as its archbishop, she had, as one chronicler put it, sought a person of honest and holy life as a confessor, and God had provided him. Once again, heaven's instrument was Cardinal Mendoza, who had known just the man, his old vicar of Sigüenza who had become a contemplative Franciscan, Francisco Jiménez de Cisneros.

Cisneros, born in 1436, his father a receiver of tithes for the crown and undoubtedly a *converso*, had early displayed several sorts of strength. He had stood up to Carrillo, showing himself equally contentious in an argument over a benefice. He had ridden into Sigüenza with Mendoza, who had had to resort to force of arms to take up his appointment to that bishopric, and once there Cisneros had proved a brilliant diocesan administrator. He then had, in 1484, retired into a remote monastery and adopted the most austere Franciscan regimen. "Fearing the inconstancy of the world," as Mártir archly explained his decision, "and the snares of the Devil, he abandoned everything in order not to become caught up in pernicious gratifications and delights.''[8] Cisneros, Mártir went on, was pale and emaciated, like the desert saints, with the acuity of St. Augustine, the abstinence of Jerome, and the severity of Ambrose. He had acquired a reputation for holiness. Reputedly, he wore a hairshirt, scourged himself frequently, experienced ecstacies, spoke with heavenly beings, and could be carried away in spiritual contemplation of the divine mysteries. Isabel, eager to sound out this paragon of everything, interviewed him on some pretext and, a few days later, invited him to become her confessor. He had accepted, on condition he reside in his cell except when summoned by her. She soon found him indispensable.

Taken together, Isabel's reaction to the attempt on Fernando, her letters to Talavera, and the policies of the years immediately following the war indicate that now imposed on her consciousness was a sense of finite time and of much still to be done. Moreover, after the attempt on Fernando, a wariness in the face of general well-being never left her. She was ever watchful for family and faith, nor did she ever after cease preparing to die well. There is a thought-provoking mention in a letter of Mártir's at the end of 1494. He recalls the comment of a former student of his, that no one was content at court, that "Even the Queen herself, whom the entire world in part respects, in part fears and admires, when you have been permitted free access to her, you find her to have become closed off in sadness.''[9] Mártir's response, that the only happiness lay in good use of intelligence, implied a disapproval of nonrational pursuits and an understanding that her new confessor, much more than her old, was given to such pursuits.

Her sadness may have stemmed from a new quest, for spiritual closeness to God, a closeness she had heretofore simply assumed resulted from being a queen who behaved and felt as she ought. Yet, just when she had thought to have come into God's good graces, He had receded, and was less knowable than ever. Marineo Sículo reported that in the 1490s she heard mass daily and prayed the canonical hours like a nun. Certainly, at a time when greater attention was being paid to Jesus Christ, to his death and resurrection and the promise of the Second Coming, and when his life and sufferings were being taken as individually exemplary, Isabel herself showed an awakened interest in meditating on Christ's life and death as a way to take the soul toward God. She was undoubtedly swayed by Cisneros, himself a contemplative belonging to a branch of the Franciscans holding as exemplary the life of Christ and his apostles. Thus in writing to Talavera in 1493 she mentioned an impatience to see printed the *Vita Christi*, the *Life of Christ*, of the Carthusian, Ludolf of Saxony, then being translated by a friar of San Juan de los Reyes; she referred to it as a book of secret consolation. She commissioned Pedro Jiménez de Prejano, who was the bishop of Coria, an inquisitor and a protégé of Talavera's, to write an inspirational manual especially for young nobles at court. He entitled it *Lucero de la vida cristiana*, the *Guiding Star of Christian Life*, and its dedication to *los reyes* reassuringly reinforced the sacredness of monarchy: "It is not you who speak, but the holy spirit who speaks through you."[10] Published in 1493, it would, a century later, after the Council of Trent had defined orthodoxy, be expurgated by censors of the Inquisition, if for its theology and not for its view of monarchy.

Still, there were other, more mundane reasons for her sadness. She was losing her old stalwarts. Gómez Manrique and Rodrigo de Ulloa had recently died. The Cardinal, mortally ill, had retired to Guadalajara. Her son's health was worrying. Her daughters must soon marry and depart. Although she had striven so hard to achieve peace and godliness in her realms, all things were becoming more complex, including Spanish society, and more immoral. Her plans were often disrupted now. The contest with the French in Italy and Fernando's rising involvement in Aragón were unplanned and meant that, although *los reyes* were more powerful than ever, she could no longer proceed according to her own priorities. She was also approaching the age at which her father, the longest lived of her dynasty, had died. Perhaps the sadness observed by Mártir stemmed from all those things: from getting older, from a new spiritual insecurity based on a revised view of God's will just when she had thought to have fulfilled much of her religious obligation, from growing complexity and a sense of less control experienced at the dying away or inefficacy of the old and the simpler, and from the side-tracking of the great single-minded mission symbolized by Jerusalem.

JERUSALEM RECEDES

For the first time since the early days of their marriage, she and Fernando were seldom apart. They spent all of 1493 in Barcelona, and there greeted

Columbus on return from his initial voyage. Until then Fernando, long embroiled in Castilian affairs and the war with Granada, had given only cursory attention to Aragón. Since succeeding to its crown in 1479, he had reaffirmed the limited monarchy traditional there and governed through viceroys. Still, he had shown himself adept at resolving some of its long-standing problems. He had gained respect in Barcelona through promoting commerce and mediating among powerful rival cliques; and in 1486 he had, by the *Sentencia de Guadalupe*, freed those peasants who had been, much like serfs, tied to the land and had made them proprietors in all but name. Now he brought Aragón's old royal council within the larger system of advisory councils, signaling the monarchs' decision to rule over separate states of varying constitution federated only under a common sovereign, *los reyes*. It was an arrangement eminently suitable for expansion into dynastic empire, allowing, in Aragón, in America, and anywhere else imaginable, the leaving in place of a facade of existing legal, political, and social institutions, the maintaining of old hierarchies of authority and taking control at the top of each and every one of them, gathering them all into a *de facto* empire.

That arrangement could not tolerate any threat posed by former heads of once-independent states. Thus when, upon hearing of the attempt on Fernando, Boabdil had sent from his dominion in the Alpujarras an emissary with his good wishes, Gutierre de Cárdenas took advantage of the opportunity presented. He paid the envoy well to agree to his master being recompensed for his Spanish holdings and transported to Africa. Although Boabdil was furious when he heard and informed their majesties such were not his wishes, they had Tendilla send three ships to Almería, and, in May 1493, Granada's last Muslim ruler "passed over into Africa where he lived miserably and was deprived of the sight of his eyes," and where, soon after, he died.[11] "Of the going of the Moor king," Isabel wrote to Talavera, "we have had much pleasure; and of the going of the *infantico*, his son, much pain." She had better luck with Boabdil's younger half-brothers. A contemporary described them as tall and courtly, good Christians who had been baptized as "don Fernando and don Juan." Isabel treated them like *infantes*; she married Fernando to a granddaughter of the Duke of Infantado and Juan to a daughter of the Count of Castro. Their mother, Zoraida, whom she had also convinced to return to Christianity, on baptism was herself named Isabel.

Returning to Castile, Isabel and Fernando spent 1494 on the *meseta*, in Valladolid, Medina del Campo, Segovia, and Madrid. And during May and June in Tordesillas, as a result of Columbus' success, the campaign for the Canaries, Portuguese rivalry, and a Valencian pope, they came to satisfactory agreement with Portugal on spheres of influence and power in areas long of great concern to Isabel and with ramifications beyond dividing up what would be America. Subsequently, the conquest of the Canary Islands was completed.

Alfonso Fernández de Lugo, having overcome fierce resistance, had at last subjugated Gran Canaria and La Palma and led expeditions to Tenerife; all were private enterprises contracted with the monarchs; one was backed by some Genoese, another by the Duke of Medina Sidonia. Tenerife offered most resistance. Lugo, needing war to acquire booty and to legally enslave, purposely stirred up its inhabitants; then, forming a mercantile company, he sold slaves. When in 1498 the monarchs sent an official to take Tenerife's enslaved Guanches from their masters and resettle them on their lands, for many of them as for their American counterparts, it was too late.

All the Canary Islands were occupied by 1496; and in 1495 and 1496, Diego Cabrera, the son of Cabrera and Beatriz de Bobadilla, headed a royal expedition from Gran Canaria to the opposite coast of Africa, got Saharians transporting gold there to agree to a protectorate by Castile, and brought back much precious metal. Then too it was arranged that a watchtower be built, as the monarchs wished, on the African coast at Santa Cruz del Mar Pequena, a toehold and contact point for Castile. In 1494, the bulls of crusade, printed and sold throughout Spain for carrying the war against the Muslims to Africa, raised funds, advertised that enterprise, and helped to keep alive among the populace the spirit of the Granada wars.

Yet the major plans involving Africa soon had to be shelved. In 1494, Charles VIII, invading Italy, argued to the pope and the world that not only was Naples his by right, but that it was a necessary base for a crusade against the Turks in which he was the emperor destined to conquer Jerusalem. Within the old French prophetic tradition, this brash young king had himself hailed as a second Charlemagne who would rescue Christ's tomb, yet another awaited warrior-king of the last days. Nor did international competition stop with prophecy. When Ferrante of Naples—who was married to Fernando's sister, Juana—died and was succeeded by a bastard son, Alfonso, both Charles and Fernando claimed a superior right to the kingdom of Naples, Fernando through his paternal uncle, its former king Alfonso V the Magnanimous.

In those circumstances, Isabel and Fernando had sent to Rome in 1493 not only to secure bulls confirming to Spain the lands Columbus found, but also to form an alliance with Alexander VI against French pretensions in Italy. To assure the pope's goodwill, they then catered to his desire for Spanish estates for his children and permitted his son, Giovanni, or Juan, Duke of Gandia, to wed María Enríquez, Fernando's niece. Isabel soon had cause to complain of the Duke's behavior. For once in Spain, chafing under the moral sobriety of the Spanish court and finding his wife a model of the discretion he hated, he quickly gained a reputation as a gambler, a womanizer, and a coward. The Queen spoke her mind to the papal nuncio. The Duke returned to Rome, and there one night in 1497 he was murdered, rumor had it on order of his brother, the then Cardinal of Valencia, Caesare Borgia. That God works in strange ways was, as has been said, in this case particularly apt, for "this bad example," as Isabel referred to him, and María Enríquez were the grandparents of Francisco de Borja, knight, founding Jesuit, and saint.

As to Alexander VI, although he called Charles VIII in against young Alfonso in Naples, he changed his mind when the French entered Rome, then changed it yet again after Charles threatened to reveal papal dealings with the Turks and to back a council on church reform. Fernando and Isabel in response drew closer to Portugal and England, and they formed a holy league—holy since, despite the incumbent's vacillations, it was formed to defend the papacy. It was composed of Spain, Venice, Milan, Maximilian, and the nimble Alexander VI. Since their diplomats had reached every major Italian city-state, the French king feared for his line of communications and left for home with half his army, perhaps 9000 men, sacking Rome on the way.

War against France was cried throughout Spain. Fernando and Isabel dispatched to Italy an expeditionary force of veteran Moorfighters, commanding it Gonzalo Fernández de Córdoba, an Aguilar second-son who had been a page to Isabel and her brother, Alfonso, and then distinguished himself in the Granadan campaigns. It was an inspired appointment. Gonzalo, initially losing several encounters with the French, soon realized that his skilled allies, Italian *condottieri*, those well-paid captains, had much to teach him. Within the year he was relying upon light infantry with great firepower and mobility and demonstrating a genius for strategy, timing, and leading men. Naples was all but his and he was celebrated as *El Gran Capitán*, the Great Captain. "From that campaign," runs the verdict of posterity, "came the Spanish army that would dictate to Europe until the seventeenth century."[12] More immediately, Spain became a power in Italy; the Spanish defeated a French fleet at sea—and regained from it the treasures of Naples accreted by that renowned patron of the arts, Alfonso the Magnanimous; and European relations became uppermost in Spanish policy.

The monarchs planned a standing army; at home they instituted a militia wherein royal captains recruited men within set geographical areas, promising to pay them monthly, thus establishing a direct line of command between crown and recruit, and superseding the *hermandad* (which was disbanded in 1498). And to offset burgeoning expenses, they levied a head tax on their taxable subjects, those neither nobles nor clergy.

PEDRO GONZÁLEZ DE MENDOZA

In September 1494, Isabel and Fernando visited the Cardinal in Guadalajara, for Mendoza was gravely ill and confined to bed; the diagnosis was an abscess in a kidney. Thereafter Isabel sent physicians and kept informed of his health, for, reported Mártir, both monarchs "are convinced that they will lose a great part of their own selves" if they were deprived of his greatness and frequent counsel.[13] Pedro González de Mendoza, Archbishop of Toledo and Cardinal of Spain, died on January 17, 1495. He was 75 years old, a prince of the church and *grande* of Castile, and, as Mártir had so often reminded him, he was "the third king of Spain," without him *los reyes* made no difficult resolutions.[14]

Instrumental in Isabel's gaining the crown, Mendoza had been for 20 years her principal minister and her closest advisor, more constantly at her side during the decades of war than Fernando. Pragmatic, learned in law, a master of diplomacy, valuing rationality in religion and temporal life, as his remark on Spain's geographers attests, he was too a militant, indeed fighting cleric. Yet his urbanity balanced the impassioned zeal of her other intimate, Talavera, whom he had introduced to court and with whom he worked closely. Between them, they had not only supported and advised the Queen, but had built and administered her apparatus of state. She could not have done it without them. Was Mendoza as moderating a force as he seems? Or is it that he too was of incremental persuasion, as in his backing the piecemeal introduction of Inquisition, or suggesting to supporters of statutes of purity of blood that they bide their time, and including such a statute in the constitutions of his own *Colegio de Santa Cruz*? He understood power, indeed enjoyed it doubly, wielding it for the monarchs and being trusted by the papacy. A prime exponent of absolute royal authority, he was ever mindful of balance, and of his own power, as when he so tirelessly contended with Isabel over jurisdiction within his see of Toledo.

Himself the son of a renowned *grande*, warrior, and eminent poet, the Marqués de Santillana, Mendoza was a lawyer and priest, statesman, patron of arts and architecture, and operative head of Spain's most powerful clan. He left his sons with titles and estates, and Isabel bereft. Their esteem had been mutual; in his will he named her his executrix, granted her full powers to emend it if she thought best, and in his own hand noted his complete trust in her judgment. Those notations serve to allay any lingering suspicion that he might have been a puppet-master. To her, he left three last pieces of advice: she should make peace with France; she should not give the archbishopric of Toledo to a nobleman; and, surely most disquieting to her, she should marry Prince Juan to Juana, "Queen Juana's daughter."[15] She would take only one of them.

The omnipresent Münzer, in attending the Cardinal's funeral was most impressed by the immense wealth he had accrued, estimating money, jewels, and moveable property as worth more than 200,000 ducats, and declaring his residence in Guadalajara as among the most beautiful in Spain and most lavish in its use of gold. The Cardinal was, said Münzer, known to have spent sparingly on his own person but exuberantly on everything else. Isabel has been credited with commissioning his imposing tomb, in the *Capilla Mayor* of the cathedral of Toledo, but it would be surprising if Mendoza had not arranged for it himself. Münzer described the royal couple and their court a week after his death, everyone dressed in black, in mourning for Pedro González de Mendoza.

Yet such were the exigencies of monarchy that even while he lingered Isabel fought the curia for jurisdiction over the see of Toledo. And at his death, despite the opposition of the cathedral *cabildo*, she quickly and for the first time imposed nominees into those offices of the vacant see she construed as secular, observing "we much marvel" at any questioning of the royal right. Equally indignant, that *cabildo* tried to seize all Mendoza's funeral paraphernalia and prohibit erecting the funeral bier ordered by the rulers, but it backed down, slowly, in response to threats and pressure exerted by a royal attorney. That in general she had advanced royal control of church administration was evidenced in her decrees on the subject having moved from the justificatory preamble—"*e porque . . .*" ("And because . . .") of 1480, to the forthright command—"*Ya sabedes . . .*" ("Now know you . . .") in 1495; and she personally supervised the inventorying of Mendoza's vast estate.[16]

Isabel took his advice regarding the social background of his successor. It had become her practice to prefer men of middling background and proven ability, and she was fully cognizant of the opportunity now presented her to extend royal control over what was also the greatest barony in Spain. So in naming Mendoza's successor, having resisted Fernando's desire to appoint to his own son, Alfonso de Aragón, Bishop of Zaragoza, she sent off one envoy to the pope with the name of a worthy Franciscan friar, and then she sent another, to say that she had changed her mind and was naming Francisco Jiménez de Cisneros as Archbishop of Toledo. Alexander VI confirmed her choice; at the moment he preferred Spanish backing in Italy to asserting papal power in Spain, and Isabel and Fernando, knowing his priorities—Italy and his children—understandingly yielded the see of Valencia to Caesare Borgia.

She did not tell Cisneros of her decision beforehand, knowing that he would be opposed to it, and when, without comment, she simply showed him the papal bull, he turned his back on her and strode out of the palace. He held out for six months. Isabel waited. She had become very good at it. In October he consented, although he refused to discard his friar's robe and put on the customary silks and ermines. He only recanted when ordered to do so by the pope, and even then with the proviso it be only in public.

At court he was respected but not well liked. "The Archbishop," as a chronicler of Aragón explained, "had a mind that soared with great thoughts more usual to a king than a friar."[17] He and Fernando had their differences. "He was a man of warlike and even disquiet condition,"[18] wrote a later Mendoza, implying Cisneros was not mentally well-balanced. Whether he was a mystic or epilectic or both, he did experience flights of ecstatic transport. Still, the meditation and solitude he valued proved no barrier to his bringing vigor to public affairs. He was to be Inquisitor General and twice regent of Spain in the troubled years after Isabel's death, and set in motion trends in political and religious life reverberating to this day. Despite his earlier demurs, he would be frequently at court, the most influential of counselors, temporal and spiritual. Cisneros was to take the place with the Queen of both Talavera and Mendoza for the rest of her life.

While his personal influence was great, Isabel, in giving the Archbishopric of Toledo, traditionally the most powerful position below the monarch's, to a non-noble friar had ended the possibility of nobles, as Carillo had, employing it as a personal power base. She also seized the opportunity to diminish its size to royal advantage and assert the royal right of patronage. She could rely so heavily on Cisneros because he owed his position to the crown.

CLEANSING THE COUNTRY

To whatever extent she thought ridding society of corruption, greed, and heresy necessary to the advent of the Last Days, she nonetheless hoped that a clergy morally uplifted would in turn uplift the populace. Mendoza and Talavera, conscious of setting precedent had sought reform of the way clergy lived, established seminaries in their residences, and favored obscure but gifted friars who lent tone and swelled the ranks of the educated and upright. Even so, as things stood there were in the 1490s perhaps 40,000 secular and regular clergy in Spain. Many had no training, had been simply appointed by bishops, were married and of bad reputation, and did not wear habits. The first church assembly of her reign, held at Seville in 1478 and dominated by Mendoza and Talavera, had ordered every bishop to make certain that each priest have a shaven crown, the size of an old *blanca*—a large silver coin—and a habit worn four fingers below the knee. Isabel, in soliciting a papal bull to that end, added her own more precise specifications: the tonsure should be "the size of the seal on the bull of his Holiness," the hair short enough to see the ears, the habit of decorous color, black or dark blue or dull tawny, or drab, closed in back and pinned at the chest, and long enough to reach the instep, and "it must be worn for four months before committing a crime"—that is, before the cleric could come under ecclesiastical rather than royal jurisdiction. She informed her ambassador in Rome that men who took clerical habit often did so to escape punishment for crimes they had committed rather than to serve the Lord, thereby compounding their guilt; that huge numbers of clergy had no religious vocation, lived with women, and went about armed; and that monastic life was particularly scandalous and she wanted to appoint a prelate or religious charged with its reform.

From 1485 on, she and Fernando had tried without success to secure from the papacy the necessary faculties for a general reform of the clergy. Once again, the royal strategy became to reform piecemeal, for Alexander VI would only authorize reform within certain religious orders. The process began in womens' convents. There is an unsubstantiated story that Isabel visited some of them personally and there plied needle or spindle, meaning to set example. And with Isabel's staunch support, Cisneros became provincial in Castile of his own Franciscan order and toured monasteries in his charge in 1495, traveling on foot, eating by begging, and assiduously imposing reorganization. Pedro Mártir wrote of one consequence. Mártir had been asked to secure a pardon for one Lorenzo Vaca, a *comendador* of the Holy Spirit and a fugitive from justice, charged with having given the habit of his own religious order to Franciscans fleeing Cisneros' rigor. "*Mis reyes*," Mártir explained, "plan to check, restrain, and return to the primitive spirit of their order the lascivious friars of the order of St. Francis." What punishment then did Vaca not merit for having thwarted that plan? Nevertheless, Mártir had asked mercy for him of Cisneros, "a man of holy probity—as they say—a man of highest integrity—as is the rumor—the Queen's confessor—as is commonly said—and the promotor of such a great enterprise." The interview was a disaster:

> Turning to me with furrowed brow he said, "Pedro Mártir, do you defend this man, who has dared to profane such holy decrees of the monarchs?" And he threatened me with the hatred of the Queen if I dared to say one more word in [Vaca's] favor. This man [Cisneros] . . . is he who through his counsel makes everything happen now in Spain. He, through the dynamism of his talent, through his gravity and wisdom, through outdoing in holiness all the cenobites, hermits, and anchorites, has so much prestige with the monarchs as no one ever achieved before. They judge it a sin to contradict his counsel, for what he says they do not believe comes from the mouth of man.[19]

It was useless in that business, he concluded, newly critical of *los reyes*, to speak to them on the subject without first placating Cisneros.

Mártir, annoyed at that recent ascendency and such treatment, and highly partisan to the supplanted Talavera, was far from objective and prone to exaggerate for effect. For when Franciscan houses resisted radical reform, Isabel did admonish Cisneros for going too far too fast. And, whatever she learned from him, she showed him the efficacy of patience and incremental advance—until, in 1499, papal license arrived to reform all mendicant orders.

There is no mistaking, however, that after 1492 and with Cisneros' ascendency, royal decrees tended to be presented as ever closer to holy writ and Spain to be portrayed in them as a battleground of good and evil, so that the language and spirit of reconquest became standard. And intrinsic to that process was Isabel's ongoing wholehearted support of the Inquisition, which ever more blatantly confirmed a symbiosis operative between crusade, personal salvation, apocalyptic hopes and fears, social control, royal power, and benefit to the royal treasury.

When in 1498 Torquemada died, he was succeeded as Inquisitor General by Prince Juan's old tutor, Diego de Deza, signaling no distancing of the Holy Office from the court. The Inquisition was firmly entrenched and the monarchs wanted it accountable, at least financially, and its activities profitable. Between 1495 and 1497, the royal treasury at last managed to extract some accounting of finances from the Inquisition, although royal investigators continued to find it difficult to tally the accounts of the many tribunals who somehow could not locate their records. There were too huge numbers of purchased rehabilitations into public life by the penanced. Moreover, the Crown then levied on all reconciled converts a general fine, explained as a one-time buying of rehabilitation. The implicit and erroneous rationale was that since Jewish influence had been removed, the levy was among final steps, and that the Inquisition was to wither away. The papal *nuncio* had another explanation: Isabel and Fernando wanted the money and were expecting so many millions that it was his opinion that the faculty to impose such a fine be granted them only in return for some extraordinary service to the curia. By 1497, it has been estimated, the Crown had received through the Inquisition somewhere near 15 million *maravedís*.

The Inquisition did not disappear. Isabel continuously defended the Holy Office to Rome. Cisneros would later tell her grandson, Charles V, with only slight exaggeration, that the peace of his kingdoms and even his own authority depended upon that institution. Rather, increasing emphasis was put on *limpieza de sangre*, carrying the message that all *conversos* and their offspring bore continual watching and were continually being watched. When in 1497 the Queen dismissed the president and all the magistrates of the royal chancery, it was said to be because "they were all new Christians and little clean of hand." And the story was told that in 1498 Isabel, on hearing that a *converso* was resisting expulsion from the prestigious *Colegio de San Bartolomé* in Salamanca, which had instituted a statute of purity of blood, responded, "if he will not leave by the door, throw him out the window."[20] By 1500 the monarchs opposed *conversos* entering the church and sanctioned the norm of excluding them and their near relatives from public position. The following year the concept of purity of blood was introduced within their government by an edict prohibiting any relapsed *converso* to the second generation to sit on the royal council. Just how those statutes were implemented remains a mystery, since some of their principal proponents were themselves *conversos*.

On December 2, 1496, as the French withdrew from Italy, Alexander VI and his curia showed their appreciation of the merits of Fernando and Isabel. A papal bull commended those monarchs for having unified and pacified their kingdoms, conquered Granada, and expelled the Jews, for having promised to carry the crusade against the Turk, and of course for ridding the papal states and Naples of the French. They were, consequently, henceforth to be known as *Los Reyes Católicos*. That specific honorific was decided upon in the curia only after much discussion of possible alternatives, among them *religiosos, defensores,* and *protectores*. Certainly it was the broadest and the most likely to offend Charles VIII. The Spanish ambassador in Rome, Carvajal, reported that the title had indeed upset the French.

ROYAL WEDDINGS

In 1495 Prince Juan was 17; at the end of January Isabel sent him as royal representative to the French frontier with a guard of 135 knights and all the nobles of the military orders. That month too, Maximilian signed a double wedding contract: Prince Juan was to marry his daughter, Margaret of

Austria; and the *infanta* Juana to wed his son, the archduke Philip. The monarchs now found Maximilian satisfactory; he had beaten the Turks at Villach in 1492 and had regained and unified the Habsburg lands of Austria and Hungary. For his part, Maximilian was well disposed to linking his dynasty with this ascendingly powerful one; it had been through his own marriage to Mary of Burgundy that he himself had risen from a minor princeling to control much of central Europe. The Habsburg luck held; for in several generations that dynasty would rule much of Europe and many lands beyond.

Isabel could in 1495 be gratified to see her children strongly connected. Catalina was to marry England's crown prince, Arthur. And when João died that year, she patiently coaxed young Isabel to remarry in Portugal, to its new king, Manoel, who had lived for several years in Castile's court and who refused to accept María instead. Yet her oldest daughter resisted, firmly. Now 24, she had, Pedro Mártir lamented, "become thinner than a dry trunk"; that since becoming a widow five years ago, she had not returned to eat at table, but mortified herself with fasting and vigils, spent her time working church ornaments, and that she blushed and became very agitated when it was suggested she marry again. Yet he felt that some day her parents would persuade "this daughter that they loved so extraordinarily to wed a good king." Actually, they had signed her marriage contract, negotiated by Cisneros, on November 30, five days earlier than his comment. And, unbeknown to her mother, the bride-to-be had made the stipulation that, before her arrival, Portugal be rid of Jews and begin to prosecute heretics.

Even though the suspicion arises that Mártir's repeated prescient remarks, such as that concerning young Isabel someday marrying a good king, may be the result of *post facto* editing, his letters are the richest of sources for the events of those years at court, for the royal weddings and what came after.

In August 1496, he reported, Isabel, saddened by separation from Fernando (who was readying an army against the French in Perpignán), went with all her children to Laredo, on the Cantabrian sea, to send off Juana to the side of her spouse. "A powerful fleet had been readied, of two Genoese carracks and 108 caravels, carrying, it was said, 10,000 armed men come from between the mountains of Cantabria and the Basque country, because it was to sail along French coasts." The Admiral of Castile, Fadrique Enríquez, was in command; many nobles, knights, and ladies were to sail with the *infanta*. Isabel spent two nights on board with her. The fleet set sail on August 22. "The Queen, after crying for her daughter, whom she thought she might never see again, left for Burgos . . . where we are now, awaiting the King with great anxiety."[21]

Although Isabel had reassuring news of Fernando every eight or nine days by relay riders, "she suffers greatly because of her daughter, for she does not know how the furious winds, immense reefs, and high seas will treat the delicate maiden and she is tormented with uncertainty as to her having escaped the Charybdis-like whirlpools of the British sea." Day and night, continued Mártir, the Queen kept at her side expert mariners whom she constantly queried about winds and possible causes of delay, and she lamented the luck of having seen herself obliged to send her daughter to remote Flanders when the sea was nearly unpassable with winter near and with communications cut by land due to the enmity of the French.

"While those preoccupations were torturing her mind," Isabel received word from Arévalo of her mother's death. Mártir says that although her death was a natural one, that she was "consumed by age"—Isabel of Portugal was in her sixties—that did not stop her daughter from crying. (Isabel of Portugal was interred in the Franciscan convent outside Arévalo; then, in accord with her daughter's orders, in 1505 her body was laid beside her husband's in Miraflores.) Fernando returned by October 21. Word came at the end of November that Juana had arrived safely; yet Isabel worried still, for Margaret was to come to Spain in the same fleet as soon as the weather broke. Before it did, most of the men-at-arms of the bridal fleet froze or starved to death at sea or in Flanders' ice and snow.

Margaret arrived at Santander, on March 8, 1497, after a stormy voyage and a near shipwreck, with a large entourage and the first carriages seen in Spain. Isabel received her in Burgos, in the palace courtyard with numerous ladies, formally. Everyone wore gold and precious jewels, according to their station, says Mártir, and they shone in them everywhere during the days of festivity that followed. Isabel had borrowed back from Valencia her pawned crown. The wedding took place on April 2, although it was Lententime. "Our prince," Mártir explains, "burning with love, got his parents to dispense with protocol in order to get to the desired embraces." There was one somber note, a knight killed jousting. Mártir, at his most prescient, worried that it was a portent of unhappiness to come.

On June 13 he wrote to Tendilla, describing Margaret: "if you saw her, you would think you were contemplating Venus herself." Yet he trembled to think that some day that beauty might lead to unhappiness and the loss of Spain. For the Prince, carried away with love of her, was pale and thin and "bore himself sadly." The doctors and the King were counseling the Queen that some of the time the two should be separated, "for too frequent copulation constitutes a danger to the Prince." Sexual overindulgence, they told Isabel, was softening his bone marrow and weakening his stomach. They got nowhere. It was not fitting, she insisted, that men separate those whom God had joined in matrimony. The Prince had from infancy been weak by nature, they rejoined, raised on chicken and other digestible foods like an invalid; she must not confide in the example of her own husband, who from his mother's womb was naturally gifted with an admirable robustness of body.

Isabel would listen to no one. She showed herself obdurate, a quality that for years she had been at pains to hide. Mártir professed astonishment: "She has been transformed into another whom never until now have we suspected in her. I always have proclaimed that she was a constant woman;

I would not have called her contumacious; I was too confident." Yet God willing, all would go well. The monarchs were then in Medina del Campo, but leaving soon, to take the *infanta* Isabel, now consenting to marry again, to meet Manoel at the Portuguese border.[22]

Clues to the queen's stubbornness lie in her strong desire for dynastic continuity, her chivalric notions of the potency of love, and in her belief in the holiness of marriage and that on no account should a man and wife be kept apart. Did she have in mind Luna's attempt at monitoring relations between her mother and father? She insisted that marriage was so holy that the Devil could not affect it, even though the pope had declared that of her half-brother Enrique and his first wife Blanca bewitched; that, rather, it was so sacrosanct that only God could have power in it. Isabel was a remarkably happily married woman.

In mid-July, Mártir sent the news of Juana to Talavera. She had been well received and was esteemed by the Flemings, for they believed her very suitable for motherhood. It was said that Philip, her husband, lacked nothing of what a woman could desire in a man: he was of admirable age, physique, beauty and habits, possessing a steady character and all natural attributes. "Our monarchs," he reported, "are content with him and with their daughter-in-law, unless her beauty harms the Prince their son." From both marriages they awaited exemplary grandchildren; "the grandest and most insatiable desire of parents."[23]

KNIVES OF SORROW

Two months later, he announced tragedy. On September 13—with ominous portents—"*con hados adversos y aves infaustas*"—the court left Medina del Campo. The King and the Queen, who was not well, were accompanying their oldest daughter as far as Alcántara, and Juan and Margaret were going to Salamanca, its jurisdiction assigned to the Prince when he married, where they were to live. They arrived to a jubilant reception; that city dedicated to letters went wild for its future king, who from his youth had loved and cultivated learning. Three days later, Juan lay desperately ill of a high fever. Relay riders sped the news. It was decided that Isabel stay to conclude the Portuguese wedding, and Fernando rush to Salamanca. There he found their son pale but lucid, and implored him not to give up hope. Juan replied he was resigned to death. Mártir, ever the humanist, praised the Prince for being so philosophical, attributing to him a marvelous exaltation of spirit due to to his having read volumes of Aristotle.[24] Still, there is something to be said for Fernando's insistence on exerting a will to live. Less than two weeks later, on October 4, Juan died.

Fernando had informed Isabel only that some days Juan was worse, some better, and now he ordered that no word of their son's death reach her until he rejoined her and they could console one another. When told, all she was heard to say was that "God gave him to me, and He has taken him away." Juan's body was interred in the Convento de Santo Tomás in Avila. Mártir relayed general sentiment: "There was buried the hope of all Spain." Yet one hope remained. Margaret was pregnant.

Ten days later, *los reyes*, "orphans of so grand a son," were trying to dissimulate their profound grief, Mártir told Talavera, "but we divine it inside them, crushing their spirits. When they are seated in public, they continually look at one another, not knowing what to do on discovering what lies hidden within," their eyes full of a grief too deep for words. He worried that they would cease being human beings of flesh and blood and become harder than diamonds if they did not give vent to their enormous loss.[25] Spoken of henceforth were Isabel's knives of sorrow, in implicit reference to Mary's suffering and Christ's passion. They went into relative seclusion, to Alcalá de Hénares with Cisneros, and resided there through April 1498.

More tragedy lay in store. Margaret miscarried: "Instead of the desired offspring, she has had an abortion; instead of the longed for heir, we have been given an unformed mass of flesh worthy of pity."[26] From Portugal, Manoel and Isabel were immediately called to take up the succession. They came, after Manoel had been guaranteed the continued separateness of Portugal and young Isabel been assured all hereditary rights as proprietary Queen of Castile. They received the oath from the Cortes, called to Toledo on March 16, and within the month were in Zaragoza, where problems arose. For by Aragón's ancient constitution no queen could bear the sceptre, yet since young Isabel was pregnant, it was conceded that the oath could be taken to her child, if male. The Queen, it is said, was so thoroughly exasperated at that disrespect shown by the Corts that she declared that a more honest remedy would be to conquer Aragón.

On August 24, 1498, young Isabel, the Queen of Portugal, had a son, and died in childbirth. She, lamented Mártir, who had the gifts of soul of her mother, her great virtue and magnanimity, but was so different physically. The mother was stout, the daughter thin, so thin she could not support the anguish of giving birth. Indeed, she had frequently predicted her own death and had had the *viaticum* and friars on hand to confess her. To her mother, she left one consolation, a grandson who could become the sovereign of those great kingdoms. The child was named Miguel and was not strong, but, a month later, the signs that he would survive were sufficient that his father Manoel, leaving the infant, returned to Portugal. Isabel lay abed, ill beforehand and now stricken with grief at the death of her favorite daughter. Yet she rallied to attend the Corts which now recognized this male heir, though with the proviso that should Fernando ever have a legitimate son, the oath was null.

Marineo Sículo, admiring the fortitude of the King and Queen, gave an explanation for the degree of resiliance they did show, that "they had from youth been accustomed to dangers and work and great changes in matters of their estates."[27] He did not exaggerate that resilience. In Zaragoza in early July, the Queen had been so sick with "tertiary fevers" that there was fear for her life. Cisneros, who was with her, informed his *cabildo* on July 6 that she had been bled twice and was feeling much better, yet also that processions were being held for her health, and masses and prayers said. Young Isabel died a few weeks later; her mother never fully recovered. Yet life went on within the ever-expanding court. With the French quiescent, attention to Africa seemed more urgent than ever with the return from Calcutta of Vasco da Gama. Then, on April 8, 1498, Charles VIII died, to be succeeded by his uncle, Louis XII, who renewed the Italian embroglio.

WINTER IN ALCALÁ

During that long stay at Alcalá after Juan's death, Isabel worked with Cisneros on projects dear to her heart. Artists designing the great Gothic extravaganza that is the altarpiece of the *capilla mayor* of Toledo each brought his maquette to Alcalá so the Queen might look them over and pronounce her opinion. With Cisneros she furthered arrangements for clerical reform. And Cisneros was then planning a university that would rival Salamanca and reverse its priorities in having theology as its crowning study rather than law. For there remained, in a Spain so assiduously championing orthodoxy, much confusion as to what constituted it.

For Isabel, Cisneros had become a mainstay; and from then on he was increasingly influential, including in making key appointments at court. He had proven energetic, authoritative, arrogant, ruthless, and politically astute, in everything demonstrating tremendous force of will and high intelligence. He had also found a way to practice both meditative spirituality and rigorous administration. Cisneros was less concerned than Talavera was with how a desired goal was achieved; he lacked Talavera's insistence on principle applied at every step of the way, and was, more like Mendoza, sometimes empirical in means to ends, if more grating in style; he did not have Mendoza's more genial worldliness or his sense of *noblesse oblige*. Cisneros did take care to express himself with great moderation, and the effort showed. He has been described as chaste and modest, and having much self-control, implying he found it necessary to curb his passions. His warnings of the emotional snares set by the Devil seem to convey firsthand experience. Nor would he stay in a dwelling where women were, although he was courtly in his relations with them. He would later show himself "a harsh prophet of Spain's messianic destiny"; nor as has been said, was he unsympathetic "to the prophetic dreams which enjoyed wide sympathy among some churchmen at this time and which foretold an imminent *Renovatio mundi* which would both transform the church and . . . introduce the Christian millennium."[28] In such a pursuit mundane affairs mattered; the readying was lofty purpose enough for engaging in government vigorously, for carrying a crusading mentality into civil and ecclesiastical administration, to say nothing of crusading itself. Cisneros was to lead an expedition against Oran in 1509 personally. Before that, he played upon an expectant atmosphere compounded of the presence of the Inquisition, royal success against Muslims and expulsion of Jews, the advance toward Jerusalem, and the advent of the year 1500. Says one scholar, "I think that people met in the streets and discussed prophecies as long as Cisneros lived."[29]

Did Isabel, under the weight of her childrens' deaths and Cisneros' influence, seek consolation in meditation and a greater spirituality? Indications are that Talavera's metaphor of reigning queen as soaring eagle was not so much displaced as joined by an inner vision of soaring soul. That is, to Talavera's pointing the way to perfection of the soul through self-confidence, self-control, and steady, diligent work, to his valuing most highly Christian practice, and to the assumption that the monarch was in contact with the divine will, was added Cisneros' concern with reform of temporal life as well as with the obligation to know God more intimately through meditation and prayer. It was then that Isabel's piety seems to have taken on more of the characteristics associated with piety today. Moreover, while, like her father in his last years, she was drawn to attempts to reconcile classic philosophy and Christianity, she went further, to favor especially those authors who saw in philosophy preparation for the imitation of Christ and his universal reign. More than ever, her library and the art she commissioned reflected those more recent and more contemplative interests, as did the books whose printing she encouraged.

Beneath all, a reinforced sense of her own mortality, with her ever since the attempt on Fernando, may well have intensified both her devotions and her already strong moral code. To ensure morality, in 1502 she and Fernando ordered books be licensed; that is, before printing royal magistrates were to examine them and authors to pay a fee. They also forbade blasphemy and gambling—"inspired by God," said a courtier, for blasphemers "say things against the honor of God," and gambling led to robbery, murder, and insanity, and gamblers would go to Hell." Homosexuals they ordered burned alive. Similar statutes were being issued in England and elsewhere, so that Isabel was also keeping abreast of European trends. And in 1499, the monarchs enacted more stringent measures against any Jews found in Spain, and others against gypsies, as well as sumptuary laws against excessive luxury in dress within one's social ranking.

Those people meant to be Christian exemplars, the clergy, proved recalcitrant. Isabel persevered. In 1500 she notified the Bishop of Calahorra that in his diocese priests still lived publicly with concubines or kept mistresses and went armed to prevent detention. In Bilbao, when the royal *alcalde* disarmed a priest, six or seven of them had entered that officer's bedroom and beat him up; and in Seville, when an assembly ordered priests living with women to be separated from them, it was a signal for gangs to eject such women and loot their houses, and those of innocent priests as well. Isabel wrote to those places prohibiting entering such houses by force, though to little avail, and she chastised officials who had joined in the looting.

Assaulting people seen to be in royal disfavor was a habit well established, in Seville and elsewhere, if earlier principally channeled into attacks on Jews.

Yet if Isabel showed herself to be less well and more devout, she did not abandon directing the affairs of this world. And if, increasingly, she left international relations to Fernando, it was also the case that they were increasingly bound up with Aragón's traditional interests in Italy. In November 1500 both Isabel and Fernando signed a treaty; they divided Naples with Louis XII, retaining the port. And Isabel remained especially concerned and involved with those northern relations that had to do with her daughters, Juana and Catalina. Matters of foreign trade and Castilian shipping continued to be important to her, and figured prominently in negotiations with England and France. She paid attention, too, to ongoing relations with Portugal. María was to marry Manoel; on October 12, 1499, the Cortes voted the tremendous subsidies needed for her dowry and for Catalina's. And Isabel did not neglect the affairs of the Indies.

In 1500, it was she who insisted that Medina Sidonia relinquish Gibraltar, "because it complied to her service."[30] Control of Gibraltar was deemed more vital than ever. There was too every indication that Italian and European policies continued to be part of a broader plan encompassing Africa, the Mediterranean, the Spanish Indies, and ultimately Asia and Jerusalem. Between 1497 and 1500, an interval in the Italian wars, she and Fernando not only occupied Melilla, but tightened their protectorate over Tunis, and sponsored an expedition that tried but failed to reach sub-Saharan gold sources. They ringed the Tyrrhenian sea with consulados, reinforced Malta, and gained Otranto and Tarentum as bases on the Mediterranean. As the century turned, they formed a league with Portugal, England, and Scotland against their strongest Islamic adversary, the Turks, who had taken Venetian colonies in Greece, threatened Sicily, Naples, and the whole western Mediterranean, and continued to stand between them and Jerusalem. And royal directives then went out for prayer and sacrifice for Christian well-being and the triumph of Christian arms against the infidel; for in July 1499 she and Fernando had returned to Granada, and once again it was war against the Moor.

19

The Queen and Her Daughter
1499–1504

The first knife of grief that stabbed the spirit of *la Reyna Doña Isabel* was the death of the Prince, the second was the death of *Doña* Isabel, her firstborn child, Queen of Portugal; the third stab of grief was [the death of] Miguel, her grandson, with whom she had consoled herself. From those times she lived without pleasure, her life and health foreshortened.

—Andrés Bernaldez[1]

. . . I wish St. Michael to receive my soul and to empower and defend it from that cruel beast and ancient serpent who will then wish to swallow me, and not to leave it until through the mercy of our Lord it may be placed in that glory for which it was created.

—Isabel, Last Will

ONCE AGAIN, GRANADA

THE court returned to Granada in July 1499, for the first time since 1492. Though Talavera and Tendilla proudly pointed out to the monarchs the city's tranquility and progress toward Christianity, they were surprised at how Muslim it still was. The Turks were again threatening the Mediterranean; Barbary pirates in league with Granadan Muslims were marauding coasts; and while Granada remained Muslim, any advance into Africa was threatened. By mid-November Cisneros had come, most likely in response to their summons, and, by the time they left for Seville several weeks later, he had launched an intensive campaign.

Cisneros and the preachers he brought in began to convert Muslims through sermons, bribes, and threats, especially pressuring notables to be baptized as examples to everyone else. The recalcitrant were locked in and preached to daily; a holdout of 20 days, as has been said, was considered a man of iron. Cisneros' special target though were Muslims baptized as Christians found backsliding, *elches*, and he baptized their children and some others without parental permission, receiving and wielding inquisitorial powers in prosecuting such renegades.

Muslims saw those activities as violations of the *capitulaciones* of 1491; one recalled Cisneros' cohorts insisting with no basis that "your grandfather was a Christian who embraced Islam."[2] On December 18, 1499, when a bailiff entered the Albaicín to arrest one such purported apostate, the quarter, fearing a general forced conversion, rose and killed him and set up a state of armed resistance. For three days the city's Christians, relatively few, feared for their lives, until, having acted speedily and in concert, the two *ancianos*, Tendilla and Talavera, personally stopped the uprising from spreading, and through their immense prestige, managed to restore order three days later. Tendilla cordoned off the Albaicín; Talavera went in to quiet it and win over its leaders with a combination of promises and threats. They had also called upon Andalusia's towns to send troops.

Cisneros, ever sanguine, informed his cathedral *cabildo* on December 23 of the uprising, reporting that he having on the eighteenth converted 300 Muslims before midday meal, the Moors had risen because "Satan always procures to overturn all good things." Yet it had been for the best, for "with the fear [the insurgents] had of what they had done, it has pleased Our Lord that where they had thought to upset conversions, that trouble had instead "been the cause that today 3000 souls are converted and baptized."[3]

Isabel and Fernando, in Seville, had rumor of all Granada having risen before an accurate account arrived and, enraged by Cisneros' provoking of disaster, Fernando at once wrote to Tendilla of "the Archbishop of Toledo, who never saw Moors nor knew them," and instructed that only the Moors who killed the bailiff be punished. Then, with report of damage contained, he and Isabel notified Cisneros and Tendilla of a change of mind: while they marvelled at not having been informed immediately, yet they were pleased with how the uprising had been handled, and had decided that, "as to what touches the service of Our Lord and the augment of our Holy Catholic Faith, our desire is that in conversion you make all the fruit you can make."[4] By mid-January 1500, Cisneros believed that all the city was Christian; that now the entire kingdom of over 200,000 souls was but awaiting conversion by the Lord. The more than 19,000 *mudéjares* throughout Castile, many of them on the *meseta*, suffered backlash; Isabel wrote to Arévalo and other places that Muslims were under royal protection and must not be harmed.

Although the monarchs had proclaimed mass conversion throughout the kingdom of Granada to be against their instructions—Isabel in January 1500 personally assured envoys from Ronda that the treaties made at the time of surrender remained in force—they also interpreted the insurrection in the city as a Muslim breaking of the *capitulaciones,* so that Fernando, at the end of January back in Granada, "made known his will and the Queen's" that everyone must convert, that "there is no salvation for the soul in any *otra ley*, only in that of Jesus Christ."[5] Tendilla had pardoned all involved who would be baptized; Fernando offered amnesty to everyone converting by February 25. Mass conversion ensued, of perhaps 50,000 people. The Archbishop of Toledo had counselled *los reyes*, says Mártir, to offer baptism or death "in order that they [the infidel] not be lost."[6] Talavera, less sanguine, warned that such converts lacked true understanding of Christianity, and that there would be trouble.

Cisneros forcibly carried the campaign to the surrounding region, to resistance. Güéjar rose. Gonzalo Fernández de Córdoba crushed it with troops that had been about to embark for Naples; Güéjar's people were enslaved. When places in the Alpujarras, fearing forced conversion, revolted and sought aid from Muslims abroad, Fernando went during the first week in March to set an example: in some villages all inhabitants were slain; in Lanjerón, "the occupants were baptized before perishing."[7]

In January the monarchs had noted that the archbishops of Toledo and Granada had had some differences, and that it was "to God's service and our own" they be reconciled. Talavera, resigned to the sovereigns' having abandoned his own patient policy of persuasion and individual indoctrination, wrote ruefully to the royal secretary, Miguel Peŕez de Almazán, a parable on his own powerlessness: "Although one swallow does not make a summer or, better said, winter, Our Lord has broken the wings that can [do so], and our wings and strength to fly to heaven." And he closed with a bitter pun: "From Granada, in truth very *desgranada*, picked over, and turned to nothing."[8] A general accord was reached on July 30, 1500; between August and October, most of the kingdom's Muslims turned Christian. Isabel, suffering as well from broken wings, had returned to the Alhambra in July and remained for over a year, until October 20, 1501.

Cisneros had left. The monarchs took charge in the city and requested more clergy to minister to the baptized, especially priests who spoke Arabic. To great effect, they assured converts they might keep their lands, and, levying a fine of 50,000 ducats on rebels throughout the kingdom of Granada, they exempted converts, so that the entire weight of that fine fell on those remaining Muslim. By September all Baza had asked for baptism; by 1501, the eastern region was quiet.

Then, early that year, Ronda and the surrounding Sierra Bermeja rose, a terrible rout ensued, and among the dead lay the *grande*, Alonso de Aguilar. The body of that veteran of so many campaigns, Gonzalo de Córdoba's older brother, was so hacked up, reports Mártir, that it was scarcely distinguishable in the immense pile of corpses of servants, familiars, and loyal friends who perished with him. Fernando is said to have replied forebearingly to a suggestion he put all Muslim rebels to the sword, responding that "when your horse does something wrong you do not reach for your sword to kill him before you give him a slap on the rump and throw a cloak over his eyes; so my opinion and that of the Queen is that those Moors be baptized, and if they should not be Christian, their children or grandchildren will be."[9] Even so, he took no captives and gave no pardons. He got a treaty by April 11th, and sent it on for Isabel's approval and signature; many of the defeated were granted the permission they requested to go to Africa and given passage there.

Isabel called Cisneros back. The royal position had crystalized. She then wrote of her resolve that all Muslims in her realms be baptized, but without recourse to force or reward, for that would be scandalous. Rather, "they must either convert or leave our kingdoms, for we can not harbor infidels."[10] To be given a choice was not to force, as Mártir, whom she then sent to the Sultan of Egypt, explained to him; it was but a variety of persuasion. In July 1501 *los reyes* forbade Muslims to reside in the kingdom of Granada, since, was the rationale, they disturbed the indoctrination of converts. On February 12, 1502, a decree to that effect was issued for Castile; by April 20 all adult Muslims of Castile had to choose between baptism or exile. Aragón, with its large, productive, Muslim enclaves, valued by crown and aristocracy, was left for later. The sale of Granadan captives and spoils brought in over five time more than royal expenses in putting down the uprisings; and anticipated were the two-thirds of tithes paid by New Christians, conceded by the pope in March 1500.

Most *mudéjares*, deeply attached to their lands, converted, to be known as *moriscos*. In Isabel's lifetime all Castile became Christian, if nominally. As guarantor, there was the Inquisition. As for Isabel, while farsighted in looking to the condition of the great-grandchildren of her subjects (although, as it would turn out, she was mistaken), she was more aware than ever of her own mortality, and of great uncertainty as to the future of the dynasty. The deaths in the family had taken their toll, and they were not at an end.

AN END TO DYNASTY

Within three weeks of her return to Granada the infant Miguel, the heir to Castile, Aragón, and Portugal, not yet two and never strong, died, on July 20, in his grandmother's arms. "Such great grief," wrote Marineo Sículo, "has swept over our most Christian princes and the whole court that no one has been able to approach the Queen, for the King and the Queen are bowed down in deep distress."[11] A month later Mártir told a friend, "The death of the small *infante* Miguel has discouraged his grandparents profoundly. They declare themselves impotent any longer to support with serenity of mind so many blows of fortune. . . . Nevertheless, they dissimulate those dark feelings all they can, and show themselves in public with smiling and serene countenance. It is not difficult, nonetheless, to divine what goes on inside."[12] Bernaldez again found comparison for Isabel's misery in Mary's sufferings: "the third stab of grief was [the death of] Miguel, her grandson, with whom she had consoled herself. From those times she lived without pleasure, her life and health foreshortened."

Fast couriers went off to Ghent immediately, to Juana, next in line of succession. Reports of her had been disturbing: that she was excessively enamored of her husband, Philip of Burgundy, Archduke of Austria and

Count of Flanders, that he was neglecting her, and that he was evidencing an obvious predilection for France. Even so, it was unthinkable to change the order of succession. Philip would, upon Juana's accession, become king-consort in Castile. To Isabel, it was not a happy prospect. He was no Fernando, but reportedly dependent upon a *privado*, his old tutor the archbishop of Besançon. And Juana was clearly no Isabel. Accordingly, arrangements were sped for the marriages of Catalina to Arthur, Prince of Wales, and María to the widower, Manoel of Portugal, hoping to establish through other powerful sons-in-law counterweights to Philip and so to France.

In May marriage had been contracted between Manoel and María, who was then 17 and whom Isabel had wanted him to marry in the first place. Extracted from Manoel was a promise to prohibit Muslim worship in Portugal. Alexander VI rushed a dispensation in exchange for yet another son of his, Luis Borja, receiving the archbishopric of Valencia. María went to Portugal on September 30, haste dictated too by Manoel's need for an heir. For with the death of Miguel, Portuguese factions were forming dangerous to internal peace and Castilian interests. And ever worrisome to Isabel was the presence in Portugal of "the Excellent Lady," Juana. Isabel soon heard that that marriage was a happy one, Manoel solicitous and giving his bride magnificent presents, María beaming and, reassuringly, spending much time with her sagacious great-aunt, Beatriz of Braganza.

Plans for Catalina's marrying England's crown prince went less smoothly, although it was obvious Henry VII wanted both the promised dowry of 200,000 *escudos* and Spanish trade. The wedding had been cele brated by proxy in 1499, nonetheless there was news that Philip had initiated negotiations to have his sister Margaret, Prince Juan's widow, marry Arthur instead. Even so, Isabel delayed sending Catalina until Arthur was 14, that is, considered of an age to consummate marriage.

In Flanders, Juana and Philip were in no hurry to come to Spain. On word of Miguel's death, envoys had flocked to them from all Christendom, among them many Spanish grandes, and Alexander VI had sent them the papal Rose of Love and Friendship. It was heady business for Philip and his advisors and signaled a loss of prestige for the Spanish monarchs. The couple had had a daughter, Leonor, in 1498 and and in February 1500 Juana had given birth to a son. Yet even that welcome news was not unmitigated, for it was known that Margaret, just arrived, had asked her brother that the child be named Juan, but that Philip had preferred he be baptized Charles, after his Burgundian grandfather, Charles the Bold. More serious was word that Juana had held herself aloof from the attendant celebrations and that her state of mind troubled her retainers. Still, Isabel and Fernando had instructed their ambassador, Gutierre Gómez de Fuensalida, to relay the pleasure they took in the son the Lord had given to Juana and Philip, that may it please God to protect him, "and that they might have of him much delight, and might see children of the children of his children, and of them more children who would give them much pleasure."[13]

Disquieting reports continued, of Juana confiding only in her husband, who relayed everything to his old tutor, the Archbishop of Besançon; of Philip wanting "the usual princely freedom from his wife"; of a policy in force among Philip's counselors to isolate Juana, especially from affairs of state; and of Philip determined to assert his superior authority over her. In that situation, the quick-tempered Juana was lashing out, not at Philip and his people, but at those about her. From Flanders one exasperated Spaniard wrote in August 1501 to the royal secretary, Almazán, "of one thing I am certain, it is attributable to her alone that she has not a living soul who will help her."[14] This daughter was in straits foreign to Isabel; Juana was far from home, mired in powerlessness, ringed by unfriendly factions, and caught in unrequited love for a husband whose political interests ran counter to much of what she represented. And she was showing little aptitude or even inclination for statecraft.

As early as 1498, her parents had instructed their ambassador that Philip be informed that he had no claim on the Spanish inheritance and counseled to be friendlier to his in-laws; that he was, that is, to be less friendly to France. By late 1500 his ministers had, instead, arranged the marriage of his infant son, Charles, to Louis XII's only daughter Claudia. Coming to Spain from Flanders shortly thereafter, in January 1501, was not the eagerly awaited young couple but Flemish envoys, one of them the Archbishop of Besançon, their stated business to get an agreement to the French marriage before Philip and Juana would set foot in Spain. Isabel and Fernando accepted the match, which could have its dynastic advantages. They entertained the Flemings lavishly for three months, Isabel patiently and repeatedly pointing out to them that the young couple should live in the kingdoms that they would one day rule. It was Juana whom she particularly wanted, with her son Charles, who was to inherit both Castile and Aragón, so that he would be raised in Spain.

The Flemings were persuaded only that both Philip and Juana had to be there in order to receive the indispensable oath in Cortes. Pedro Mártir then interpreted the situation: "there is no doubt Juana will come if her husband does, for she is lost in love of him, although she would not be moved by ambition for so many kingdoms and love of her parents and of all those others with whom she was raised. Only her attachment will drag her here, to the man they say she loves with such ardor."[15] But, as Fuensalida reported from Flanders, Juana had recently shown herself torn; she had refused Philip her power of attorney for negotiations with France and Spain with the explanation that she first had to consult her parents. He had, in response, spoken to her so abusively, said Fuensalida, that he himself, unable to hold his tongue any longer, had complained to Philip on behalf of his sovereigns. Bleakness was not unalloyed: he also reported that the children, Charles—"*Musyor de Lucenburc*"—and "*madama Leonor*," were very well, that Charles maneuvered a go-cart with the strength of a three-year-old, and that Leonor was very pretty.

From England came more cause for concern. Recent French advance in

Italy and word reaching London from some Genoese in Cádiz who exaggerated the difficulties in Granada, had made Philip's proposals more appealing to Henry VII, wrote the Spanish ambassador; Catalina must come as quickly as possible. Isabel could delay no longer and in May 1501 sent off her youngest child, from Granada, with a fittingly regal escort headed by steadfast Gutierre de Cárdenas. She could not take her herself, as she had planned, as far as La Coruña on the northwest coast. Both she and Catalina had been very ill with tertiary fever that spring, and Isabel was still not well enough to accompany her daughter. Instead she worried, hearing the fleet had sailed on August 17 only to be blown back, to Laredo by a storm. It sailed again only in October. Then came good news: Catalina had arrived and, as Henry VII wrote, been "welcomed by the whole people." A surviving anecdote corroborates a truly popular reception. Along the way to London Catalina was offered a glass of the best English beer, gamely tasted it, made the appropriate courteous remark, and then, turning to a retainer, whispered, "This is the sponge of ice and vinegar given Our Lord." She and Arthur wed in November. Isabel would not live to see tragedy overtake this daughter whose intelligence and judgment were so markedly in contrast with those of her sister Juana, and who was known in England as Catherine of Aragon.

THE HABSBURGS ARRIVE

In Flanders there was yet further delay, the explanation given that Juana was again pregnant. After the birth of a second daughter, assuagingly named Isabel, on July 15, 1501, Juana and Philip departed. His insisting on taking the land route, through France, did nothing to allay concern and unhappiness in Spain with his behavior to date, for in Italy boundaries between the French and Spanish areas of Naples were being disputed and war was again likely. And still Philip and Juana did not hurry. Rather, they lingered at the French court, staying through Christmas, when Philip, it was heard, offered Louis the customary coins in token of vassalage, but at least Juana did not, and when pressed responded by taking to wearing Spanish dress. In late January 1502, a year and a half after being summoned, the Archduke and Archduchess arrived at Fuenterrabia, where Gutierre de Cárdenas met them. Fernando joined them en route and, at last, on May 7, Isabel received them, in Toledo at the gates of the palace, and in state, although after the customary formalities she took Juana by the hand and led her off into her own apartments.

A state banquet followed, and tourneys in which Philip showed his mettle, even learning quickly to ride *a la jinete*. No one, observed Mártir, was more affable, more valiant, more handsome; but his insatiable hunger for the sceptre had clouded his intelligence. Isabel and Fernando were extremely cordial to everyone, even when the Flemings intruded themselves in negotiations between France and Spain, and even when word came that Catalina's husband, Arthur, had died of the plague, and that Philip was secretly and assiduously negotiating to have his sister Margaret marry Arthur's brother, Henry, England's new crown prince.

Isabel and Fernando, resolved to outspeed their untrustworthy son-in-law, within the month sent an ambassador whom they instructed first to talk to Henry VII of sending back Catalina along with half her dowry, then to broach as possible alternative her marrying young Henry and she and her dowry staying in England. By June, Henry VII was speaking of the match as probable. He was less interested in aiding the Spanish monarchs in Italy against France which, Isabel had written him, "has the lack of shame to make war on us."[16]

On May 22, the Cortes and most of Castile's luminaries dutifully took the oath to Philip and Juana as *los principes* of Asturias, heirs-apparent to the crown of Castile, although some among its members made known to the monarchs reservations stemming from Philip's not speaking the language, knowing the customs, nor being unwilling to remain in Spain any longer than absolutely necessary. When, in Portugal, María gave birth to a son and named him Juan, it was an irony lost on no one. Fernando and the *archduques* then went on to the Corts at Zaragoza, having been assured by the Aragonese that there would be no problems with the oath this time. Isabel was not well and remained in Toledo.

She heard from Fernando, from Calatayud; his letter of July 30 provides a rare glimpse of how undifferentiated for Isabel and himself were public and private matters, how much the stuff of their ordinary conversation, and it corroborates an enduring intimacy as well. He worried, he wrote, for he had not heard from her since she had been given a purge. He had heard from her secretary, Lope Conchillos, and congratulated her on something she had said to Besançon. Yesterday letters had come from England. Its King was well and whatever Besançon had told her a lie; however, he could not read them more closely, for his secretary Almazán, had not brought the cipher. Have Lope send it. Authorities at Perpignán reported that the French were moving to the frontier and with artillery, "a lot of it, even against us a lot." He should reach Zaragoza Tuesday or Wednesday morning. He expected her to follow, but she should avoid the bad road from Sigüenza to Monreal. He awaited an envoy from the King of France. "I close kissing the hands of Your Ladyship whom may Our Lord guard more than all others, as I desire."[17] Whatever the references to Besançon signify, that thorn in Isabel's side was removed soon after; he sickened and died in Toledo.

Fernando wrote to her again, from Zaragoza on August 15. He had heard from her and was delighted she was better, though undoubtedly still in much pain. He asked her not to work too hard. Since she was organizing financing for the defense of Perpignán against the French, he suggested that in order not to rely further on Genoese loans—the Geneoese were then handling the funding of the war in Italy—they levy *sisas*, taxes on foodstuffs, sell public property, and farm out the taxes on Seville and other places too large to handle. There would, he thought, be no peace with France until there was war. He was awaiting "my children," for he very much wanted to talk to Philip of the great harm he was doing to foreign relations and to those within their kingdoms, and to tell him that she and he could see they had no assurance that he, Philip, would act in their interests. He was pleased she had sent the Duchess of Alburquerque with Juana; it seemed good to him that the women of those kingdoms should love its Princess. Although Isabel heard rumor of French ships in the Mediterranean and had expressed fear of traveling, she should not worry; even if the French had many more ships, they would still be all right. They had next to go to Barcelona to receive the oath there. He wanted her to come.[18]

It was that September that Pedro Mártir returned from Egypt, writing to Talavera and Tendilla of having arrived at the most secure port of all, *la Reina Católica*, and that Isabel had received him four times, "with composed and serene countenance," and asked him many questions. Yet, a month later, on October 27 as, breaking tradition, the Corts at Zaragoza accepted Juana as *"primogénita sucesora,"* Fernando heard that Isabel was gravely ill. He was at her side in Madrid within three days. Philip, whom he had left to preside, followed on November 3, leaving the Corts to Juana, who stayed 20 days more and then came as well. Isabel's dire condition made succession seem an imminent possibility; the court boiled with intrigue. Yet by November 21 she had recovered sufficiently to send a letter to Manoel: such had been her health that she could not answer his letters, she told him, that she had twice improved and then had setbacks but that she was now much better, although she still could not write by hand.[19]

Several weeks later she had so clearly rallied that Philip was impatient to leave, to return to Flanders and by the route he had come, through France; after all, a five-month truce had been arranged in November. Isabel insisted that he ought not think of such a thing with French relations still so bad, that he must stay and spend time with his vassals if he wanted to be obeyed later, and that certainly Juana, who was pregnant, should not travel. Philip agreed only to Juana's staying, despite her entreaties he take her with him. If his obduracy was hard on the Queen, observed Mártir, "it was much harder on his ardent spouse, who is a simple woman, although daughter of so great a woman; she did nothing but cry. Nor did it soften Philip. He is harder than a diamond."[20] He did not mention that Besançon and some others of his entourage had died in Spain, that Philip feared for his life.

Fernando went in February to Zaragoza to conclude the Corts, then to face problems Philip had left in his wake: revolt in Rosellón and French resurgence in Naples. And, exasperated that talks between Philip and Louis of France had ended in agreement that Naples would go to Charles and Claudia when they wed but in the interim be governed for them by the French and the Flemings, Fernando sent more troops to Gonzalo de Córdoba in Italy. He spent most of 1503 in his own kingdoms of Aragón securing his position, for the French were pressing and should Isabel die he would, according to their agreement of 1475, lose all authority within Castile. In October he rushed to Perpignán to reinforce nearby Salsas against a French siege. In France, Philip sickened and lay deathly ill for two months; poison was rumored. Another event that month appeared relatively unimportant, but was not: on October 25 María had a daughter, Isabel, who would one day wed her cousin, Charles, become Queen of Spain, and give birth to its next king, Philip II.

Isabel effectively functioned as head of state, although she had not fully regained her health, and although anguished: by war with France, by her daughter's unceasing pining for her husband, and by the loss of longtime counselors and friends. Gutierre de Cárdenas and Juan Chaćon, who were cousins, died, within a few days of one another. Cárdenas, heavy and hearty, had accrued position, high trust, and tremendous wealth since the days he had escorted Fernando into Castile to wed its princess. *Comendador* of León, *contador mayor* of the royal treasury, her *maestresala*, and a force in the Royal Council, he had been entrusted by Isabel with the most delicate of missions and negotiations, and with overseeing her son's household. Cárdenas, as was said, had "always lived in the palace." Juan Chacón had long ago ensured that Isabel was proclaimed Queen in the crucial town of Avila, and in reward she had arranged he marry the daughter and heir of Pedro de Fajardo, Murcia's powerful *adelantado*, or governor, whom he succeeded in 1482; and he had proved a force in the campaign against Granada. Remarkably, his father, Gonzalo de Chaćon, who had attended Isabel since her birth, still lived; past seventy and a widower, he had recently taken a second, very young wife, in order, he explained, to warm his bed. (Upon yet another death Isabel did not grieve, that of Alexander VI, rumored poisoned at a banquet, by a drink his son, Caesare, had meant for a rich cardinal.) Mártir could only compare the Queen to a gigantic rock in the sea, pounded by waves on all sides. Early in January 1503 she went with her daughter Juana to Alcalá, the residence of the principal statesman left to her, Cisneros.

There the gloom lifted. On March 10 Juana gave birth to a second son and his grandmother celebrated it, her last state occasion. Isabel attended a mass of thanksgiving the following Sunday, fittingly elegant "in a French skirt of fur, colored scarlet, with a large jewel at her breast, a gleaming medallion on her coat, and on her right arm an emerald and ruby bracelet that reached from wrist to elbow."[21] Her ladies wore marten and ermine, gold and precious stones. One *grande* carried a gold sword, others wore gold chains and velvets, and several nobles dressed in the new style, completely in black.

In his sermon that day the bishop of Málaga praised Juana and told of the great armada that had carried her safely and so magnificently to Flanders, the husband who contented her, and the children she bore with no pain. It was an obvious allusion to Mary's having painlessly given birth to Jesus; his enumerating God's blessings to her was a dexterous attempt to present the Princess as divinely chosen to rule. Isabel and Juana dined, then they and their ladies watched from a window as the nobles and their retainers jousted in celebration.

The following week it rained incessantly, so that Isabel ordered the baptism set for that weekend put off, until she heard the bishop of Burgos preach that postponing the ceremony placed the infant in danger of mortal sin. A solemn, and soggy, procession wended through the downpour, the child so completely wrapped in brocade that only the top of his head was visible. In Alcalá's main church, with six bishops in attendence and his grandmother looking on, the primate of Spain, Cisneros, baptized him Fernando. Cisneros was experienced; he had given thousands of Muslim converts the same name. Afterwards, Isabel and Juana received well-wishers, and, the steady downpour notwithstanding, bulls were run and jousts held. That grandson of Isabel's would grow up in Spain, then leave to rule the Habsburg domains in eastern Europe.

Isabel remained in Alcalá into July. She had a daughter she must try to train in statecraft, and a healthy grandson who proved a greater comfort than did Juana's small appreciation of queenly priorities. Isabel did not call Juana "my mother-in-law" only because she looked like Juana Enríquez, but because she too was inordinately headstrong. What Isabel did not mention was that Juana showed much more disturbing signs of resembling her own mother in her mental distress. Juana now lived "with furrowed brow, not speaking except to reply rudely when spoken to," interminably insisting on returning to Philip. Her behavior, as Mártir noted in a graphic phrase of which he was particularly fond, was tearing at her mother's entrails; it was, he said, reviving the grief brought on by Juan's death and deepening her worry over what would become of the realm. Even so, Isabel continued active. Concluding the Cortes called the previous year, she got the needed subsidies for the renewed war in Italy. In May, the Great Captain took the city of Naples.

Yet Isabel's pleasure in victory was shortlived, for in retaliation Louis XII had sent a large force to besiege Salsas and Fernando had gone to relieve it. She said she was upset not so much by his being there, for she received three or four letters a day from him, as because that war was between Christians and Christian lives would be lost. She entreated him to avoid battle; she prayed and she had prayers said in churches and monasteries. Seemingly in answer, the French decamped; as to exacting vengeance for the bother they had caused the Spanish, wrote Mártir, she would leave them to God. Isabel had had enough of warfare among Christians, from which she seemed to exclude war in Italy, and more than ever she sharply distinguished them from people of other faiths, indicating a deepened commitment to a solely Christian world.

Yet while, in what was to be the last year of her life, in at least one instance she laid aside revenge, she did not neglect statecraft. Louis XII had worked against Spanish interests in the independent kingdom of Navarre, and she sought to offset his influence there through marrying her Habsburg granddaughter, Isabel, to the Navarrese prince and heir, Enrique. And, in mid-April, to bring matters to a head with England, she ordered the Flanders fleet there to take on Catalina. With that, and rumor that the Spaniards were destroying the French army in Italy, on June 23 England's king Henry signed the contract for Catalina's marriage to the son who was to succeed him as Henry VIII.

IMPASSE

In June Isabel was again very ill, and again seemed to be recovering, until on the twentieth her doctors had cause to write to Fernando. They had bled her, they wrote, she had only a low fever and little pain; but yesterday, having left her apartments to see Juana, she had returned terribly altered, her face drawn and drained of color. She had spoken of feeling cold and of great internal pain, then for four hours she ran so high a fever that they had despaired of her life. Today, praise God, though still in much pain she had sweat copiously and at midnight the fever had abated, the pain subsided, and she had eaten a little and was better. "Your highness must believe," they concluded, "that it is a great danger to the health of the Queen to have the life she has with the Princess."[22]

Isabel had good cause for being upset. Such was "the disposition of the Princess" as they described it, "that not only should it pain those who see her often and love her greatly, but also anyone at all, even strangers, because she sleeps badly, eats little and at times nothing, and she is very sad and thin. Sometimes she does not wish to talk and appears as though in a trance; her infirmity progresses greatly." The customary treatment, they explained, was through love, entreaty, or fear. Juana had proven unreceptive to entreaty, and even a little force affected her so adversely that it was a great pity to attempt it and no one wanted to try so that, beyond the Queen's customary immense labors and concerns, this weight of caring for her daughter fell upon her. Isabel's illness, it has been speculated, could have been cancer, endocarditis—an infection on the heart valve, or chronic dropsy—fluid in the lungs, or several of them combined. By the following June she had a visible tumor, though just where and what sort was not stated.

In August she took Juana to Segovia, which she had seemingly avoided for years, telling her it was a step toward the north coast and her departure for Flanders. Isabel could not get her to turn her mind to affairs of state. Juana showed little interest in her child and a good deal of disregard for religious matters of any sort, as well as for public opinion. The princess disdained or seemed to pervert the very qualities her mother valued most highly. Even so, Juana was her designated successor, and she was determined to keep her in Spain. So the arguments patiently repeated, the season, the sea, the French, that Philip should be safe in Ghent before she traveled, and did she not want to see her father before she left? The hope remained that Juana would stay and Charles come, so that Isabel might have him educated in Spain's customs and to prefer its people. And with Juana and Charles there and Philip not, should Isabel die, Fernando, still King of Aragón, could surely manage to rule as regent in Castile.

It was November. A treaty with France—arranged by the French queen, Anne of Brittany, and Margaret of Austria—had been signed, and an envoy arrived from Philip requesting Juana's return. Isabel, playing for time, responded that the Princess, although better, was not well, that relations with France were still such that it was not safe for her to travel by land nor, now that it was winter, by sea, that she had better wait until spring, and that "following her frame of mind and *la pasión* she has" that she should not be where there was no one who could quiet and restrain her for it might be dangerous for her. The implication was that Juana was emotionally out of control. Exactly what was meant by "restrain" we do not know.

Isabel, hoping to cheer her up and keep her from leaving, sent her daughter to Medina del Campo at fairtime, holding it out as a further step toward the northern coast. There Juana, receiving letters from Philip urging her to come immediately, by land or by sea, for the French had assured safe conduct, resolved to depart immediately and, as Isabel herself told Fuensalida, "against our will." Juana ordered her bags packed and her household readied. Isabel, advised, sent Juan Rodríguez de Fonseca, the Bishop of Córdoba, who had been Juana's tutor to talk her out of it, "for it would appear to everyone to be a very bad thing, of such shame for her and of so much disrespect for us." He found her outside the inner door of the castle of La Mota where she was staying, about to leave, and pleaded with her to return to her apartments and await her mother's permission to go. Juana held her ground. Fonseca, caught between duty to his Queen and ruining his future by alienating her successor, temporized, ordering in the Queen's name that no horses be brought. Juana countered; she would walk to the stables through the city streets. He, "in order to see that, in view of her authority and the estimation of her person, she did not do so unreasonable a thing in sight of the natives and strangers there for the fair," had the outer doors of the fortress closed. She threatened him with death and refused to return into the castle.[23] Fonseca went for Isabel.

Juana remained between La Mota's inner and outer gates, during one of the coldest nights of that winter and despite everyone's pleas—burning with the fury of an African lioness, said Mártir—and the next day retreated into an adjacent fruit-storage shed. Isabel sent her notes by courier, to no avail, then dispatched Cisneros and the Admiral of Castile, who could not budge her. After four or five days of stalemate, the Queen came herself, traveling the sixty miles within two days, in a litter, as she informed Fuensalida, "with more effort and speed and making longer daily journeys than good for my health." She found Juana still in the shed, under a table, suggested she return to her apartments, and met rebuff: "She spoke to me very resentfully words of such disrespect and so far from what a daughter ought to say to a mother, that if it were not for the state in which she was, I would not have suffered it in any manner."

Patiently, the Queen who had swayed thousands managed to coax her daughter back into the castle and on various pretexts to delay her trip. If she would wait, Isabel promised, a fleet large enough to protect her would be readied to sail as soon as the weather broke—that is, in the spring. Juana stayed, and so did her mother. Isabel had managed to keep her daughter in Spain for over a year until, by January 1504, Philip appeared to be disposed to take up an offer of governing Naples in exchange for sending Charles to Spain. In March she at length agreed Juana might go to the coast, and the distraught woman who would one day wear Spain's crown departed, only to await clement weather at Laredo for two more months.

MEDINA DEL CAMPO: 1504

Isabel remained in Medina del Campo, in the royal great-house on the plaza. She had come full circle; this was the closest place to home, to Arévalo and Madrigal, that could accommodate her court. It was the town that her brother, Alfonso, had given her long ago. Time and again she had come with him and then Fernando to its fairs. She had had war declared against Granada from Medina. From there she sent her grandson, the infant Fernando, whom Juana had left behind and whom Isabel pampered, to be raised as she had been, in nearby Arévalo by trusted retainers. But it was his older brother, Charles, whom more than ever she wanted in Spain.

Juana arrived in Flanders in May. Isabel received dismal reports: that her daughter did not want Charles to come to Spain and that, finding the greatly desired Philip cool, in a fit of jealous rage she had attacked one of her ladies whom she suspected of being a rival. Philip had upbraided her, perhaps even hit her, and declared "he would spend time with her no longer." Isabel, highly indignant and highly frustrated, could only instruct Fuensalida to do the best he could and to chide Philip for not treating his wife kindly, for she was of unsound mind. Isabel's health worsened. Fernando had arrived in Medina del Campo in time for Christmas, and he stayed.

A letter from her secretary, Conchillos, to Fernando's, Almazán, written early that December, revealed Isabel hard at work, getting off dispatches at midnight and permitting him little sleep. She signed ordinary documents until May 1504, then until September only those of great importance. Sometime during that period, Prospero Colonna, ally and *condottierre*, arrived from Italy, declaring that he had come to see the lady who ruled the world from her bed.

Bedridden, she had her room hung with certain tapestries: some of themes from the Apocalypse of St. John, some of God the Father, and at least one of the legendary Vision of the Mass then erroneously attributed to St. Gregory, a depiction of the real presence of Christ's blood in the host. There were too one of death and several of greenery and one of Cupid and the triumph of love. Around her, as bed hangings, were three scenes from the life of that legendary forebear of hers, Hercules, the preeminent royal exemplar of power. Exemplary too was the woman lying amid that visual potpourri so emblematic of her diverse founts of inspiration. As spring approached, she had a door and eight windows cut into the walls to give her air and garden scents and views, and light.

On April 5 a great earthquake signaled to the credulous, of which there were many, a new time of woe for the kingdom, and indeed pestilence and hunger followed. While especially devastating in Andalusia, the Queen and King felt the shock while at the Hieronymite Monasterio de la Mejorada, not far from Medina, where they had gone for Eastertime retreat. Mejorada had the feel of the royal houses in which Isabel had been born and raised. It offered familiarity and a sense of continuity with the atmosphere of Guadalupe, which was too far for her to travel now, and with the religious approach of Talavera's Hieronymites, in effect a comforting alternative to Cisneros' less accessible God. They stayed at Mejorada for over two months, ratifying there a treaty with the French; Naples was theirs. Then, within days of returning to Medina on July 26, both Isabel and Fernando developed a high fever. His illness and consequent absence deeply upset her; she once again feared for his life. He recovered fully; she did not. Even so, in August she could write Fuensalida, unhappily, that "the discontent and lack of love" between Juana and Philip "weighs on us greatly"; that he must do what he could.[24] Remarkably lucid, in the matter most important to her she was powerless.

After September 14 she signed no state papers and developed a great thirst, unassuagable, diagnosed as a sign of worsening dropsy. On the twenty-sixth Fernando sent word secretly to Philip and Juana: Isabel was dying. She had had fever since July, and serious seizures recently; they should be prepared to come. "Fever consumes her," wrote Mártir on October 7.

LEGACIES

On October 12, Isabel did sign one more document, a will; it was customary to do so only in one's final days. It reveals much of her state of mind at the end of her life, of how far she had or had not traveled mentally and spiritually. While her body was infirm, it began, "of an infirmity that God wished to give me," her mind was "healthy and free."[25] Then, as customary, she invoked God and the Virgin Mary and certain heavenly protectors, her choice of saints highly personal and unusually meticulously explained. She called upon "the powerful Father and Son and Holy Spirit, three persons and one divine essence," the trinity that was "universal creator and governor of heaven and earth and of all things, visible and invisible," the Virgin Mary, "Queen of the Heavens and Lady of the Angels, our Lady and advocate," and then she singled out certain other members of "the court of Heaven." She assumed that the kingdom of heaven was structured much like her own; she had always seen hers as its earthly counterpart.

She next invoked the archangel, Saint Michael, "that very excellent Prince of the Church and *Cavallería angelical*; and the glorious celestial messenger, the archangel Saint Gabriel," as of first rank, above the other *sanctos y sanctas* of the court of Heaven, and among whom she singled out "especially that very holy precursor and herald of our Redeemer Jesus Christ, Saint John the Baptist," and those princes among the apostles, Saints Peter and Paul, "with all the other apostles, particularly the very blessed saint *Juan Evangelista,* beloved disciple of our Lord Jesus Christ and great and shining eagle, to whom He reveals his very high mysteries and secrets. . . . This holy Apostle and Evangelist I have for my special advocate in this present life." It is fitting that the first word of her last testament is *poderoso,* full of power, and that in her regard for heaven's court she manifest the punctilious sense of hierarchy and protocol she had shown throughout her reign.

In mentioning both Saints John, in stating now a dual devotion, she voiced a very close identity with Fernando, and reconfirmed their linking her spiritually with the Juans of her life, and linking Spain's kingdoms with one another as well. They connected, too, revelation to millennial expectation and to belief in herself and her people as chosen to carry out God's plan. She had not abandoned certainty of her own direct relationship with God—quite the contrary. She assumed that he had singled her out to suffer, unquestionably with purpose, and she had borne it well in her last display of self-mastery on earth, making a good death. And such a death was very much on her mind: "For while it is certain," she had dictated, "that we have to die, it is uncertain when or where we will die, so that we ought to live as though each hour we might have to die."

It was the Evangelist whom she expected to be her advocate in the hour of her death, and "in that very terrible judgment and stringent examination, most terrible against the powerful, when my soul will be presented before the seat and royal throne of the Sovereign Judge, [who is] very just and very equal, who according to our merits has to judge us all." Moreover, that Saint John would then be one with his brother, Saint James, whom the Lord gave as patron to her kingdoms, and also with Saint Francis and "those glorious confessors and great friends of our Lord, Saint Jerome and Saint Dominic, who as evening stars shine resplendantly in the Western parts of these my kingdoms, to the eve of the end of the world."

It will be recalled that when Constantinople fell shortly after she was born, Spaniards had laid claim to having, even being, a new sun, or a new star, rising in the west to counterbalance that loss and redress it. Those guiding stars had found reflection on her parents' tomb, and, for Isabel, at the end of her life, it was those two saints John, twin evocations of the western star, who were to guide that westering movement to her realms and so to its final, golden conclusion. She invoked one more, surprising, special advocate, St. Mary Magdelene, with no explanation. A generation later, a humanist would provide enlightenment in noting "Look how we divide among our saints the functions of the gentile gods. Mars has been succeeded by Santiago and Saint George. . . . and, in place of Venus, *la Magdalena.*"[26]

Isabel had formed a very clear idea of how she must die properly and how best to arrange for reaching and entering heaven. She sought, she said, to imitate "good king Hezekiah," in disposing of her *casa*, her earthly goods, as if she had to leave this world immediately. She commended her spirit to Jesus Christ, then repeated a worry she had expressed to Talavera a decade ago:" "And if none can justify themselves before Him, how much less can we of great kingdoms and estates who have to give account?" She requested that Mary and her patron saints be her advocates when she should stand before Him. And she asked that "the blessed archangel Saint Michael, prince of the angelic knights, receive and defend my soul from that cruel beast and old serpent who will then want to devour me, and not to leave it until through the mercy of the Lord it may be placed in that glory for which it was created."

The beast and the serpent—apocalyptic creatures from the Revelation of Saint John the Evangelist (ch. 13)—were Antichrist and the Devil. Throughout her life she had battled those whom she had come to see as their minions—the Muslims, the heretics, the Jews—and had feared their vengeance, as she did now. This Queen who had spent so much of her life at war dreaded being at the mercy of old enemies and, while certain her soul was destined for glory, yet looked to a sword-wielding saint to guard her passage to it. Her view of death was an extension of her view of life; both were perilous passageways between good and evil within an everlasting war that must be waged by monarchs such as she against the forces of darkness. That battle between good and evil had been central to the religion of her childhood and then to her developing sense of what she as a queen must do and be. It had been reinforced during the conquest of Granada. It had intensified after 1492, justifying what she had done to infidel and heretic, escalating animosity toward Jews and Muslims, and reinforcing her conviction of having behaved morally, and as God wished.

In what has since been termed a messianic outbreak as the century turned, and within messianic expectation earlier, Saint Michael was often substituted for Christ militant, saving worthy souls and crushing Satan permanently as the end approached. In the Beatus manuscript Michael bound the dragon in the abyss; on a Catalan altarpiece Michael disputed the fate of a soul with the Devil; Michael was often depicted with a balance for judging souls in his left hand and a sword in his right; Michael slew the dragon on the seal Rodrigo de Borja used as papal legate in Spain in 1472; and again in a panel by her court painter, Juan de Flandes. The grandson Isabel had expected to inherit the realm had been baptized Miguel in a marked departure, for no forebear had held that name. And 30 years previously in Segovia, it was before the church of San Miguel that Isabel had been proclaimed proprietary Queen. The powerful St. Michael was an easy substitute for the saint on whose day she was in fact born, that of Saint George, whose specialty was dragon-slaying.

As her will abundantly corroborates, she had not relinquished Talavera's righteous, personal, and essentially rational deity, nor her sense of her own direct relationship with God the Father, nor her lifelong vision of heaven as organized much like the kingdoms she knew, with a monarch and court the ideal of hers. There were jousts and balls in Paradise. And there was much chivalry in her theology. Like a proper knight she had quested to find herself, valued service, striven to recover a kingdom, even to establish an empire, and she prized honor. The concept of heaven she held to was chiefly that of her royal predecessors, notably Alfonso X, whose *Partidas* spoke of God having organized his court in hierarchical order, of archangels, angels and so on, within a hierarchic universe. Nor is it unrelated that in her will she frequently spoke of her own "absolute royal power."

She instructed her body be interred in the Franciscan monastery of Santa Isabel in Granada, dressed in the habit of the order of St. Francis, "that blessed poor man of Christ," and that her tomb be low and unadorned, but if the king chose to lie elsewhere, her body was to be buried with his, "because the *ayuntamiento,* the marriage of our bodies, and that of our souls we had while living, I hope in the mercy of God we may have in heaven, and that our bodies in the soil may represent it."

She wanted no extravagant funeral honors, and that what was customarily spent on mourning instead go to pay for clothing for the poor. All her debts had be paid. She charged the consciences of her executors with everything she considered most conducive to achieving the welfare of her soul: with having masses said, 20,000 of them, in the most devout churches and monasteries; with having *maravedís* given to dower poor girls for marriage and convent; with clothing 200 poor "so that they may be special suppliants to God for me"; with redeeming 200 captives from the infidel, "so that the Lord grant me jubilee [on judgement day] and remission of all sins and blame." They were to have alms given, in the Cathedral of Toledo and to Our Lady of Guadalupe and to other pious foundations, as customary. They were also to comply with her father's last will, and to honor the tombs of her parents and brother in Miraflores. She had established, to her own satisfaction, her position as in the direct line of Castile's ruling monarchs.

To discharge her conscience, for as a monarch she must render account to God for the well-being of the realm, she criticized some recent decisions she had countenanced confirming practices she felt detrimental to the crown and the public good, diminishing both. She asked God's pardon for the accretion of offices in the realm, wanting their number restored to what it had been "in accord with the good and old custom of the kingdoms." She wanted annulled certain *mercedes* of questionable legality, revoking one such grant in no uncertain terms: "by my own will and certain knowledge and absolute royal power which in this situation I want to employ and do employ." Her heirs must never alienate the *marquesado* of Villena, nor Gibraltar; undoubtedly she remembered the mischief done by Juan Pacheco when Marqués de Villena, and she wanted to ensure dynastic control of the Strait for trade, defense against Islam, and advance into Africa. Gibraltar had been won in her youth; its conquest, highly symbolic, had prompted that reference to prophecy, that "in the west the sun of righteousness had

risen"; Gibraltar's domination was emblematic of reconquest, of royal purpose and of God's. She had, she confessed, allowed some *grandes* to collect
taxes rightfully royal; they must not be permitted to claim that tolerance as
custom in order to continue collecting them. She had heard that some
grandes and others impeded recourse to royal justice; it should be remedied.
Certain revenues of Seville that she had conceded to her daugher, María,
Queen of Portugal, were María's for her lifetime only. She warned against
making the *juros* given in exchange for funds for the war against Granada
perpetual, asking her successors to redeem them, with the revenues of Granada if possible, so that the crown would not face a perpetual debt. And she
wanted the dowries promised to Portugal and England paid.

While designating Juana her heir, she made her own lack of enthusiasm
for the prospect plain: "conforming with what I ought to do and am obliged
to by law, I order and establish and institute her for my universal heir . . .
to be received as true Queen and natural proprietress." All fidelity should
be given to Philip, as her husband; Isabel meant as King-Consort, not as
King. And, immediately following accession, all the *alcaides* of *alcázares* and
forts and lieutenants of cities, towns, and places should take an oath to
Juana, and the fortified places be held for her alone. She returned to a favorite theme in requesting that, fulfilling her obligation as Queen and in
accord with laws made by her progenitors, no royal post or ecclesiastical
dignity be given to foreigners, for they did not know the laws nor the customs and the people would not be content. She stated it twice, and commanded "the Prince and Princess, my children," to guard and comply with
that request of hers and do nothing contrary to it. Isabel, who had never
left Spain, did not trust foreigners. And she specified that "the isles and
mainland of the Ocean Sea" and the Canary Islands belonged under the
crown of Castile. America for her remained principally a waystation to the
East.

To the last, Isabel was a crusader. She commanded "the Princess and her
husband" to honor God and the faith and to take up the obligation to protect and defend the Holy Mother Church, as they were obliged, and in that
connection she coupled the expanded reconquest and internal orthodoxy,
insisting "that they not cease the conquest of Africa and the fight for the
Faith against the infidel, and that they always favor highly the things of the
holy Inquisition against the depraved heretic [now the common term for
secret Jew]."

She did as much as she could legally to see that Fernando retained power.
She instructed, as at the behest of the deputies of the Cortes of 1502 and
having consulted some *grandes* and prelates, that should Juana come to the
realm and then leave it or cease governing for any reason, that "the King,
My Lord, in such cases ought to rule and govern and administer these kingdoms for the Princess, or, if she does not wish to govern them or can not
understand governing them, the King is to do it until the *infante don Carlos*
is of age, that is, at least 20 years old," and, having tried to give him many
more years of rule in setting Charles' majority so high, she asked Fernando

to accept that responsibility. She relied, she explained, on what he always had done to increase the royal patrimony, and she requested he take an oath to that effect. She ordered her people to obey him. And, revealing doubts, she asked "the Princess, my daughter, and her husband always to be very obedient and subject to the King, and honor him as obedient children ought to honor a good father, and follow his orders and counsel, and for the good of the realm as well." She asked them all to live in love and unity and conformity. In short, she did not want Juana to rule Spain, thinking her not competent to do it, and she particularly did not want Philip ruling it for her. Isabel now did her best to give to Fernando, whose rights in Castile she had long ago circumscribed in the interests of her own authority and the female inheritance, as much power as possible. It was another in the string of ironies threading through her life. Yet the most dreadful irony was that, of her remaining children, the least competent was to inherit the crown.

She eulogized Fernando. He should, she said, be honored and respected for being so excellent and renowned a king, gifted with such virtues and so many of them. He had worked mightily "in recovering my kingdoms, so alienated at the time I succeeded," and in combating the great ills and wars and turbulent movements of the time, and no less had he risked his royal person in gaining the kingdom of Granada and thrusting from it the enemies of the faith, "and in bringing these kingdoms to good government and justice in which they are today by grace of God." She and he, she declared, had always lived in much love and concord, and she charged her children, Juana and Philip, with having between them that love and union and conformity she expected of them. She returned to what she owed Fernando, for having taken great care in administering her realm, and, because Granada, the Canaries, and the isles and mainland of the Ocean Sea must remain within the kingdom of Castile in accord with the apostolic bull, there was reason that he be "in some way served by me and those of my kingdoms, although it can not do as much as Your Lordship merits and I desire." Accordingly, beyond the masterships he held for life, she instructed he be paid annually half the revenues of the islands and mainland of the Ocean Sea and other stipulated rents.

Mercedes were to be given her servants, *continuos*, and familiars, among them the Marqués and Marquesa de Moya and Gonzalo de Chacón, for having served her loyally. And she established the order of succession: after Juana, Charles, his descendants, males to be preferred to females, conforming to the *Partidas,* down through Catalina, Princess of Wales, and her progeny. As for her possessions: the jewels given her by Juana and Philip were to be returned. "The relic that I have of the breechcloth of Our Lord" should be given to the monastery of San Antonio in Segovia; all the rest of her relics were to go to the cathedral of Granada. All the things she had in the *alcázar* of Segovia must be sold to pay her debts and bequests, and everything else given to churches and monasteries, except that the king was to take any jewels and things he wished, "because seeing them he can have more continuous reminder of the singular love I always have had for him, and because since he knows he must die and I hope it is in another century, that with this memory he can live more holy and justly."

As executors she named Fernando and four of her councillors: Cisneros, "*mi confesor*"; Antonio de Fonseca, her *contador mayor'*; Juan Velázquez, Juana's *contador mayor*; and Diego de Deza, Fernando's confessor; and also her secretary and *contador*, Juan López de Lecárraga. Once her body was interred in the monastery in the Alhambra, the body of her daughter Isabel should be carried there as well, and a tomb of alabaster be made for the burial of her son Juan in the monastery of Saint Thomas in Avila. A royal chapel should be constructed in the cathedral in Granada. (It was, and her tomb is there.) The original copy of her will was to be deposited in the monastery of Guadalupe. She signed it before a notary and seven witnesses, among them three bishops.

A month later, on November 23, she added a codicil. It principally had to do with specific matters where she might well be faulted, and so sheds light in some dark corners. The holy see had conceded bulls of crusade specifically for campaigns against Granada, the Muslims of Africa, and the Turks, all "enemies of our holy Catholic faith"; if those funds had been spent on other things, she directed, they should be paid back. She had wanted to put order in the laws, and now charged Juana and Philip with it, although nothing should be enacted against ecclesiastical immunity and liberty. She acknowledged that measures taken to reform monasteries had sometimes exceeded the powers vested in the reformers; and she worried about just pricing of the *alcabalas*, "because they are the greatest and most principal of royal rents," and of other taxes. Well she might, for administrative corruption and financial fraud had soared in the last decade, and the obvious need to reform the mechanisms of royal income had recently led to an investigation.

She wanted 20,000 masses said for the souls of her dead retainers, and that her mother's servants be provided for. And she asked that, since the Holy See had conceded the isles and mainland of the Ocean Sea in order to convert those peoples, Fernando and Juana do no harm to those Indians or their goods, but treat them justly and well, and "if they were receiving any harm, to remedy it, so that it did not exceed the apostolic letter of concession." Within context, that injunction was part of her great concern to die with a clear conscience, a requisite for salvation, and it was too an admission, in circuitous and the least self-incriminating fashion possible, of having transgressed moral and legal bounds concerning the people of the Indies. Of prime consideration was not so much the welfare of the natives as that she might have jeopardized her soul in overstepping the papal license, and also put at risk Castile's legal justification for holding the Indies.

A dispatch sent from Flanders on November 1 had arrived at Medina on

November 21, with no good news. Juana was behaving very oddly, constantly washing her hair and bathing. In allowing only her Moorish slave women near her she had so irritated Philip that he sent word that she had to dismiss them. When she refused, he came and insisted. When she asked why, he replied because she wished to do nothing he wished, that she must be served by decorous older women, and that he would not sleep with her until she complied. Within a week he had sent home those women of hers and locked Juana in, fearing she would leave for Spain. He was, in fact, considering coming to Spain without her. Heaven did not seem to be smiling on the Queen of Castile's lifetime of work. Given that situation, Isabel, by her codicil, sought to make doubly sure that she was seen to have done her best in God's sight. As for her kingdoms and her family, she could but leave them to heaven, and, as far as morally and legally permissible, to Fernando.

For 50 days her people had given themselves over to processions and prayers for her recovery; now, "seeing it the will of God to carry her to her rest," she ordered they cease importuning God for her health. She put aside things of this world, and command, and royal dignities. In her illness she could not sleep, said a contemporary; but in those vigils God gave her consolation, compunction, and understanding of his secrets, so that she said never had she so much of all of them in her life. She thought about many passages of the Holy Scriptures and she said never until then had she understood the readings from Job that are said in the office of the dead. She had, that is, prayed and contemplated Biblical texts, as advocated by Cisneros and in accord with the new spirituality, yet the texts she chose and her making a good death were highly traditional, as her will attests. A central focus of the new spirituality, the cult of Christ, was not favored by her at the last. Undoubtedly that approach to God was too far removed from being Queen as she construed it, and from the faith she had known and that sanctified reigns on earth, including her own.

She died on November 26, a Tuesday, between 11 and 12 in the morning, having received all the sacraments, although her modesty was such that in receiving extreme unction from the prior of La Mejorada she would not allow her clothes to be raised above her feet. So runs the usual interpretation. Yet extreme unction was widely feared and put off until the last minute, for it was commonly believed that once received one could have no further sexual relations, a belief responding to the custom of anointing not only the loci of the five senses but the kidneys as seat of sexual desire. Isabel expected life eternal and had precluded the anointing of her kidneys. Fernando recounted her last minutes: "she received the sacraments of the Church very much awake and with contrition, which certainly in part alleviates our work."[27] He was certain of her going to heaven and of having an advocate there. As the friar intoned the last rites, at the phrase "*in manus tuas,*" it is said, she sighed and made the sign of the cross and when he said "*Consummatum est,*" she died. "And thus the most excellent Queen *doña* Isabel ended her days."[28]

REQUIEM

Reminiscent of her device, the bundle of arrows, hers were a bundle of qualities, shaped in interaction with her world and circumstances, within what was possible. Her sense of morality, perceived as the promptings of the royal conscience, bound them firmly. It was a morality special to time and place, culturally derived. She saw herself as an absolute monarch and strove conscientiously to fulfill moral responsibilities to God, her realm, and herself.

To Isabel, morality and piety were of a piece, as were position and self. All were inseparable, mutually supportive. We know that she believed in heaven and hell, and in God's revelation conveyed by an angel to John the Evangelist of the divine schema for the end of the world. Whether or not she herself believed that the last days were imminent, she knew that that conviction was widespread and she did believe in their eventuality and that during that final age certain conditions had to prevail, notably the absence of infidel, heretics, and Jews, and the reign of a chosen few under a world emperor. She repeatedly endorsed that conviction and did everything in her power to achieve those conditions. In the doing, she condoned imposing tremendous human suffering, principally through the campaigns against Muslims and Jews, the workings of the Inquisition, and in overseas expansion. Within that climate of belief, her intentions were often good. The human suffering she caused was monstrous.

Yet if God as she conceived of him, the stern and militant God of the Old Testament, had designed a punishment for her, it could not have been greater: to lift and then dash her hopes of dynasty so indistinguishable from children well raised and well married and grandchildren in the same mold, a string of family deaths killing her, slowly, excruciatingly; and, at the end, the one child who could undo her life's work, because of the precedent she herself set, had to be her successor. Still, she never lost her sense of her own direct and personal relationship to God. Explanation for her torment she found in the tribulations of Job, and as Job we must leave her, entrusting her soul to Saint Michael to shepherd past the apocalyptical beast and the old dragon.

Epilogue

"A Queen
Has Disappeared . . ."

A Queen has disappeared who has no equal on earth for her greatness of
spirit, purity of heart, Christian piety, equal justice to all, [or for] her spirit
of conserving the old laws and putting order in the new, for the creation
of a rich patrimony and a strong economy, which is most important for
the realm and the people.

—Francisco Jiménez de Cisneros[1]

. . . she, besides being such a personage and so conjoined with us, merits
in her own right [recognition] for being gifted with so many and such singular excellences, she who was in her lifetime exemplary in all habits of
virtue and the fear of God, and who so loved and saw to our life, health,
and honor that we were obliged to desire and love her above all the things
of this world. . . .

—Fernando[2]

. . . The Queen is in Hell, for she oppressed people . . . those kingdoms
were very badly governed; and the King of Aragón and she did nothing
but rob those kingdoms and were very tyrannical.

—A denunciation made to the Royal Council, 1507[3]

HER funeral cortege traversed the realm, from Medina del Campo to
Granada, at its head a silver cross, borrowed from the Franciscan
monastery in Arévalo and draped in black cloth. Prelates and priests and
Pedro Mártir, Beatriz de Bobadilla, and many of Isabel's household escorted
the plain coffin, trussed with cords and protectively covered with calf hide.
Through Arévalo, Toro, Cardeñosa, Toledo, and Jaén they went, as though
marking off Isabel's milestones. They proceeded, for weeks, through
unceasing rain, over roads and rivers so flooded that Mártir declared he had
not encountered such perils in the whole of his hazardous journey to Egypt.

It is said the sun only broke through on the day it reached Granada, December 18. Isabel was interred in the Franciscan monastery in the Alhambra, "with such sorrow and sentiment of all the city that I never saw nor heard so marvelous a thing," Tendilla wrote Fernando, "and now this treasure lies in this monastery."[4] To that faithful lieutenant and many others the Queen's body was close to being a holy relic. Nor had the deluge been unexpected. A prophecy of Merlin spoke of an iron monarch and of heretics burned, and predicted that "a great rain will fall so that the earth will be as wet as when it lies under water."

On the day she died Fernando had written to Philip that "she was the best and most excellent wife that ever a king had, the sorrow of the absence of her is ripping my entrails . . . but otherwise seeing that she died as holy and Catholicly as she lived, is to believe that our Lord has her in her glory, which for her is a better and more lasting kingdom than that she had here." He had no doubt she would soon have status in heaven commensurate to that she had enjoyed on earth.[5] Two days before she died he had instructed Fuensalida to "say clearly to the Prince our son, and to his people, if they talk about it, that, if the Queen dies, may God protect her, the Princess has to come to take possession and governance of these kingdoms as proprietary *señora*, that they then will be hers, and that without her the Prince has no part, nor will he be received in any manner."[6]

Isabel might truthfully have said on more counts than one, "after me, the deluge." Fernando had lost not only his wife but Castile. The very afternoon of her death he gave indication of what he would do about it. He had the customary banners raised for Juana as *la reina proprietaría* of the kingdoms, and he also had himself proclaimed governor and administrator for her. Messengers carried word to the realm's dignitaries and municipalities that all Castile was to follow that formula and obey his commands and decisions and show him obedience and loyalty, as conforming with the desires expressed by the Cortes of 1502. He called a Cortes in Toro, where he had triumphed in battle nearly thirty years before; undoubtedly he meant to remind Castilians of his exertion on their behalf ever since. On January 11, the delegates heard Isabel's last will, declared it the law of the land, and, in accord with it, took an oath to Fernando as governor and administrator. And, in secret session, they unanimously agreed that if Juana was ill, Fernando should be permanent regent and that Philip was to be informed of that decision.

The week before Isabel died, Mártir had written of nobles scurrying to Philip and their openly proclaiming that by that same route their ancestors had augmented their patrimony; gain, he commented, was always to be had when there was discord about succession. Thus, notably absent at Toro were most of Castile's *grandes*. Still, Fernando counted on Alba and a few others, and on the towns (once again beset by nobles), and on Cisneros and Tendilla, who made certain Granada and all Andalusia stayed calm.

It was maliciously being said, Juana wrote to the Flemish ambassador in Spain, de Vere, in May 1505, that she has lost her wits and even that the

King her father was pleased, for he wanted to govern. "Speak to him for me, for I do not believe it." If she had shown temper, she explained, it was because of jealousy, which was not unique to her. "My Lady, the Queen, who is in God's glory, who was so excellent and renowed a person was also jealous, just as it pleased God to make me"; she added that in Isabel's case, time had amended it.[7] Unfortunately for the succession, it was one of the few of Isabel's traits her daughter Juana could claim.

Not until the spring of 1506 did Juana and Philip return to Spain, and then with an armed host. Even then, Philip was in no hurry to leave Galicia until seeing who would come to join him. In the interim, Fernando had stunned everyone by allying with Louis XII of France and, on October 12, 1505, contracting to wed Louis' niece, Germaine de Foix. He had earlier tried, unsuccessfully, to marry Juana, "the Excellent Lady." The wedding took place less than a month before Juana and Philip arrived. Now he was in León from where, having attracted many less nobles than had Philip, he sent emissaries of welcome to his daughter and son-in-law. He also sent Cisneros, who arranged an accord. Fernando and Philip met in June at Remesal, with great formality. Philip arrived with an army, Fernando with his best resources, patience and a plan. He got Philip to recognize his, Fernando's, position in accord with the terms of Isabel's will; then both agreed that Juana was incompetent to rule and that Philip was to exercise exclusive power. They had, thereby, gone against the will, as Fernando knew and stated in a secret document in which he repudiated those agreements as having been signed under duress and in order to avoid civil war; in it he swore that he would gainsay neither Isabel's will nor Juana's rights.

Fernando retired to Aragón and in September he sailed for Italy. In Castile, Philip and Juana were confirmed by the Cortes as King and Queen, and Philip took charge. He turned over to his current *privado*, the Castilian noble, Juan Manuel, a number of forts, including the *alcázar* of Segovia, and lavished upon him other *mercedes*, making him Castile's most powerful lord. Other nobles grabbed towns. Many *conversos* had earlier fled to Flanders, expecting Philip to be unsympathetic to the Spanish Inquisition, and he was, but not for long. For, having ruled for less than three months, he fell ill and, within days, he died, on September 25, 1506. There was rumor Fernando had poisoned him; but his doctors insisted it was plague and anyway Fernando was in Italy and in no hurry to come home.

Throughout Castile, factions were once again feuding violently backed by nobles now unrestrained. Mártir beseeched Almazán, Fernando's secretary, to "come save us from the wolves." Medina Sidonia was stopped from retaking Gibraltar, indeed Andalusia held, by the redoubtable Tendilla. Muslims raided the coasts; Isabel had been prescient. Juana, if lucidly revoking all of Philip's *mercedes* on a particular day, did not govern. She traveled Castile's roads, carting with her his body, though without the heart which had been sent to Flanders and the entrails which had been interred in Miraflores. She may well have feared the Flemings would otherwise steal it away to Flanders, and so was herself taking it to be entombed in Granada. And she gave birth to her fourth child, Catalina.

It was Cisneros who at 70, having emerged as the most astute and respected statesman in Castile, managed Fernando's recall. Even then, Fernando delayed another seven months, letting events play themselves out in Castile while he reintegrated Naples into the crown of Aragón, so that whatever happened, he would have a base, for influence in Italy, control of the Mediterranean, and forays into Africa and even Asia. In the process he dislodged Naples' viceroy, the Great Captain. He was suspicious of Gonzalo's ambitions and loyalties, uncomfortable with his splendor and magnanimity, uneasy at his popularity, and cognizant that had it not been for the feats of that hero, his own military exploits against Granada might well stand as the greatest of the age. Nor was it a good idea to have a powerful Castilian viceroy in a kingdom he might want to claim for Aragón. He made him great promises, of lordships in Italy and Spain, of the mastership of Santiago, and got him back to Spain.

Fernando himself returned; in August 1508 he got from Juana her power of attorney. She had been torn between father and husband; now the decision was not difficult. He saw to it that she retired to Tordesillas, where she stayed until her death at the end of the reign of her son, Charles. Castile was now Fernando's to govern as regent. For Fernando, there were echoes of the 1470s; many nobles had come to think they were better off under his firm and experienced hand, yet powerful exceptions remained. When, in Córdoba, Aguilar's son the Duke of Priego jailed and expelled his envoy, Fernando came south by forced marches and reimposed royal authority there. And, when Fernando proposed that his grandaughter—the daughter of his son, Alfonso de Aragón, archbishop of Zaragoza—marry the 14-year-old duke of Medina Sidonia and the duke's guardian, Pedro Girón, Count of Urueña, instead engaged him to his own daughter, Fernando swooped down, taking the entire dukedom into the crown.

Since 1500, in an Andalusia suffering famine and plague, an inquisitor, one Luccro, supported by the Inquisitor General, Deza, had plundered, tortured, and burned *conversos* known to be good Christians. He and his confederates, ran one report to Almazán, were "discrediting all these kingdoms and destroying a great part of them without God and without justice, killing and robbing and forcing virgins and married women, to the great vituperation and ridicule of the Catholic religion."[8] By January 1506, so unsettled was the kingdom and so great Lucero's power that he had jailed and tortured Talavera's sister, his nephew, and three nieces, and only awaited the necessary papal permission to charge with judaizing the Archbishop of Granada himself.

Talavera wrote to Fernando lamenting the great offense to God that the Inquisition had become, stating that it was separating Christians on the basis of lineage, that Isabel would never have allowed matters to come to such a pass, and terming him negligent. Even at that Talavera was being diplomatic, for it was well known that Deza and the Inquisition were in Fernando's camp. Talavera was more successful with an appeal to the pope; at length a *nuncio* secured absolution for him and his family. It was Cisneros who saw to it that Lucero and Deza were deposed, and he himself became

Inquistor General, but not before Talavera, near 80, died, on May 14, 1507, his family still in prison. Granada mourned its archbishop as a saint; the friar's robe that was his shroud was torn to shreds by relic-seekers. So departed the first Archbishop of Granada, he who, along with Mendoza, was so instrumental in organizing the realm into a modern state, and he who had confirmed its Queen in a dual reliance, on revelation and on her own conscience.

For the next two years, Fernando was at the height of power and reputation, the arbiter of Europe. His former daughter-in-law, Margáret, helped to allay tensions between him, her father, Maximilian, and Louis XII; she had married the Duke of Savoy and now, once again a widow, she took charge of raising her nephew, Charles, in Flanders. Fernando annexed Navarre, and he was at last free to turn to Africa. Yet recruits were a problem, for men were now more interested in venturing to the Indies. Even so, conforming with Isabel's injunction in her will, his armies conquered Tripoli in July 1510 and came to dominate all the African coast facing Andalusia except Tunis—which his grandson Charles would take. Fernando jubilantly spoke of going on to regain the eastern Mediterranean and making effective his hereditary title of King of Jerusalem; and with his African campaign reverberating throughout the Christian West, the pope Julius II addressed him as "The strongest athlete of Christ." Fernando, as has been said, knew how to join earth and sky.

In England, Henry VII had died, in April 1509. His strapping heir, another Henry, 18 years of age, wanted to marry Catalina, to Fernando's great satisfaction. They were wed on June 11 and, two weeks later, London celebrated the coronation of Henry VIII and Catherine of Aragón. Fernando corresponded a good deal with his intelligent, energetic, and still malleable new son-in-law; and Catalina wrote to her father: "Our English kingdoms enjoy peace and the people love us, as my husband and I love one another."[9]

That May, Germaine gave birth to a son, who was named Juan and who did not live out the day. There were no more children. Four years later Fernando, at 60, becoming gravely ill, nonetheless insisted on continuing the custom he had shared with Isabel of retreating to a monastery at Eastertime. At Mejorada, his fever soared and for a day he was delirious; he never recovered completely. Pedro Mártir explained that illness as the effect of a potion taken to enhance his potency, or perhaps inclination. Mártir said that, in order to make his wife pregnant, Fernando had for over a month taken a concoction of bulls' testicles prepared either by the Queen's French cook or two of her ladies. In November Fernando was still unwell and deeply depressed. From 1513 on, he showed little interest in politics and was irascible and withdrawn, but would not be confined to a sickbed. A holy woman had told him he would not die before conquering Jerusalem and he wanted to believe it. In late 1515, seemingly determined to outspeed his own mortality, he started for Andalusia, but having reached the hamlet of Madrigalejo, in Trujillo, he could go no farther. There he signed a last will with customary flourish, an F intertwined with a Y. It instructed he lie, as they both wished, beside Isabel in the cathedral of Granada. He died in Madrigalejo on January 23, 1516.

Fernando, wise in the judgments of history, had helped on those concerning himself and Isabel. He had the chronicles of the reign of her father, Juan II of Castile, and of her half-brother, Enrique IV "corrected and coordinated" by the royal councillor, Lorenzo Galíndez de Carvajal. Of at least equal consequence, Galíndez, who had entered the Royal Council in 1503, kept that body functioning on Isabelline lines until Charles' reign, providing continuity within it in the initial years of the young king. And, in giving his opinion to Charles on governing, he frequently cited the example of "the Catholic Queen, *doña* Isabel, and the Catholic king her husband, Your Majesty's grandparents."

In the interim before Charles arrived to rule in Spain, it was Cisneros, then in his eighties, whom Fernando had designated as regent, who governed Spain for nearly a year. Cisneros or a cohort of his then wrote an *instrucción* for Charles, urging he return the kingdom to the condition in which Isabel had put it. Although after his reign the worldwide empire of Charles V, Holy Roman Emperor, would come to be viewed as a modern state far different from Isabel's Castile, Charles himself and his son, Philip II, as well, would justify much of what they did and thought as within the tradition of that august forebear of theirs. They took those achievements as the measure for their own. In that too Isabel had set precedent, in taking up old institutions. And she had done it so energetically, extending old usages through forceful exercise of power and authority, as to transform them and Spain. She left a legacy of personal, absolute monarchy so strong that Spain had to wait centuries for representative government.

She and Fernando also transformed the old crusading spirit of reconquest into a vision of universal monarchy, one their descendants would make reality in forging a Catholic empire girdling the world, and inaugurating a golden age in Spain. Their heritage was the grand design. Especially made for Charles' baptism had been four figures from the Old Testament and three from the New, exemplifying the fulfillment of the former in the latter, and of all scriptural prophecy in Charles. In Spain, Cisneros promoted the prophecies of world emperor and second Charlemagne as fulfilled in Charles.

From high in the courtyard of Philip's palace in the Escorial, a gallery of Old Testament kings look down, appropriated by him as spiritual ancestors of Spain's kings. Philip II, among his inherited titles that of King of Jerusalem, most closely identified with the most august of them, Solomon. And it is not beside the point that his mother was yet another Isabel, the daughter of María and Manoel of Portugal.

The Empress Isabel, her cousin and husband, Charles, and their son, Philip, were all zealous for the faith. Philip celebrated receiving the crown with an extravagant *auto de fe*, and he saw the defeat of his glorious Armada as God's will, even possibly as God's favor confirmed through suffering.

Perhaps nowhere in western Europe did the power of revealed prophecy and the expectation of apocalypse so long and so pervasively affect state-craft as in Spain. There it was nurtured by the Inquisition and monarchs and nobles shared the belief of Spain having been chosen and directed by God. One concomitant was expressed by Philip's viceroy in the Nether-lands, the Duke of Alba, who is said on his deathbed to have told his con-fessor that "his conscience was not burdened with having in all his life shed a single drop of blood against it," for, was the point, all the blood he had shed was that of heretics and traitors.[10] His remark recalls Isabel's unhap-piness in her last years with war waged against Christians.

The English historian, Francis Bacon, declared her reign "the corner-stone of the greatness of Spain that hath followed."[11] During Charles' reign, one chronicler wrote of her as "honored throughout the Spains and mirror of women."[12] Another, the Count of Castiglione, papal *nuncio* to Charles' court in the 1520s, reported that while Spanish opinion recognized Fer-nando as magnificent, yet Charles and everyone else would do well to see in Isabel's reign "a mirror for princes." A principal aspiration of hers had been achieved. She had become for posterity what she had striven to be, the exemplification of an ideal monarch. Nor was it any longer her own guides to rule, the *Partidas* or the mirrors for princes or the moralistic mon-archists of her father's court and their followers, that inspired Spain's kings so much as it was this progenitrix of theirs who had taken the advice of them all in turning herself into the reigning Queen of Castile.

Yet the image of herself which she projected so successfully, so closely approximating that of an ideal ruler, set an impossible standard for Spain's monarchs and for Spain itself, overburdening her successors, from our van-tage point misdirecting them as it had misdirected her. And the hold some of the lofty ideals she fostered continued to exert evoked a world-renowned reaction, that of Miguel Cervantes and his idealistic and hapless knight, Don Quixote. The world of Don Quixote's imagination was that of Isabel-line ideals and aspiration, of Isabelline chivalry. It was a world of nostalgia for a lost golden age, Isabel's, and of lament for "this our age of iron." Golden or no, hers was an age of paradox, wherein a former page of her son's could take pride, as he declared he did, in being Spanish, because among all the Christian nations there was no other like Spain, where the best people were known as noble "and of good and clean caste," and he could do so although he himself was, though he did not say so, of *converso* stock.[13] That double-think too was an Isabelline legacy.

Yet, if Isabel's princely qualities inspired both European acclaim and emulation by her immediate Habsburg successors, as time went on that image of her gave way to another, that of a devout and pious queen, a view culminating in a relatively recent attempt to have her recognized as a saint. Her faith was not that one associates with saints; the ideal of monarchy she aspired to is not today associated with saintliness, and her piety—fusing devotion and severity, justice and revenge, love and fear—was integral to that aspiration.

Within the world as she knew it, she strove to be just and pious. She would not have understood today's condemnation of so much that she did and for which she stood. For Christianity has left behind her militant God and her intolerance for other faiths and cultures. And a morality, generally considered universal, has long condemned the Spanish Inquisition. Hers is a story of conjugal love, familial warmth, and ambition to excel, as well as a cautionary tale for the ages, having to do with the use to which are put extraordinary reserves of will, resolution, and courage. That combination in one monarch 500 years ago has left an indelible imprint on Spain, on Europe, on America, on the world.

Notes

PROLOGUE

1. Petri Martyrus Anglerii, *Opus Epistolarum*; Spanish translation by José López de Toro; and see Pedro Mártir de Anglería *Epistolario*, v.9–10 of *Documentos inéditos para la Historia de España* (Madrid, 1955).

2. Jacques LeGoff, *The Medieval Imagination* (Chicago, 1988) 5.

CHAPTER 1

1. Fernando del Pulgar, *Letras*, ed. Paola Elia (Pisa, 1982) letra 6.

2. Juan Torres Fontes, *Estampas de la vida murciana en el reinado de los Reyes Católicos* (Murcia, 1984) 321–24.

3. Jorge Manrique, "Coplas a una beuda que tenía empeñado un brial en la taberna," in his *Obra completa*, ed. Miguel de Santiago (Barcelona 1978) 188.

4. Alonso Fernández de Palencia, *Crónica de Enrique IV*, ed. Antonio Paz y Melia (4 v., Madrid, 1973–75) Déc. I, lib. 3, cap. 2.

5. Diego de Valera, *Memorial de diversas hazañas*, ed. Juan de Mata Carriazo (Madrid, 1941) cap. 33.

6. *Ibid.*, cap. 3.

7. *Memorias de Don Enrique IV de Castilla*. Tomo II: *La colección diplomática . . .* (Madrid, 1835–1913; hereinafter *CD*), doc. 96.

8. Anon., *Carro de las Donas* (Valladolid, 1542) lib.II, 43rb,44vb.

9. Gutierre Díez de Games, *El Victorial*, ed. Juan de Mata Carriazo (Madrid, 1940) cap. 19.

10. Tarsicio de Azcona, *Isabel la Católica. Estudio crítico de su vida y su reinado* (Madrid, 1964) 112.

11. Diego Enríquez del Castillo, "Crónica de Enrique IV," ed. J. M. Flores, cap. 37; in *Biblioteca de Autores Españoles* (hereinafter *BAE*) 70 (Madrid 1959).

CHAPTER 2

1. Thomas F. Glick, *Islamic and Christian Spain in the Early Middle Ages* (Princeton, 1979) 32.

2. Leopoldo Torres Balbas, *Algunos aspectos del mudejarismo urbano medieval* (Madrid, 1954) 21.

3. *Las Siete Partidas*, Partida 2: tít. 1, ley 5; also see ley 7; tít. 13, ley 26; tít. 5, ley 4; expectations of kings: I, tít. 2, leyes 1,3,4.

4. Jeffrey Burton Russell, *Lucifer* (Ithaca, N.Y., 1984) 69 n13.

5. Angus Mackay and Dorothy S. Severin, introduction to *Crónica del sereníssimo rey don Juan II* (Exeter, 1981) 6.

6. See *Cancionero de Baena*, ed. Jose María Azaceta (2 v., Madrid, 1966)I; and Charles F. Fraker, Jr., *Studies in the Cancionero de Baena* (Chapel Hill 1966).

7. Palencia, *Crónica*, Dec. I: lib. 2, cap. 9.

8. *Ibid.*, Déc. I, lib. 1, cap. 10.

9. *CD* doc. 25, p. 44.

10. Iñigo López de Mendoza, Marqués de Santillana, *Obras completas*, ed. Angel Gómez Moreno, *et al.* (Barcelona, 1988) 410–13.

11. *Prosistas españolas*, ed. Mario Penna (2 v., Madrid, 1959) in *BAE* 116:7–8.

12. *Ibid.*, 3.

13. Juan de Mena, "Laberinto de Fortuna," in *Cancionero Castillana del siglo XV*, ed. R. Foulché-Delbosc (2 v., Madrid, 1915; hereinafter *CC*) I:coplas 255, 271. etc.

14. Palencia, *Crónica*, Déc. I, lib. 2, cap. 8.

15. *CC* I:680.

CHAPTER 3

1. Palencia, *Crónica*, Déc. I, lib. 3, cap. 2.

2. Charles T. Wood, "Review article. The Return of Medieval Politics," *American Historical Review* 94 (1989) 391–404.

3. Palencia, *Crónica*, Déc. I, lib. 1, cap. 2.

4. *CD*, doc.35.

5. Fernando del Pulgar, *Crónica de los Reyes Católicos*, ed. Juan de Mata Carriazo (2 v., Madrid, 1943) cap. 1,3.

6. [Hieronymus Münzer], "Itinerarium Hispanicum Hieronymi Monetarii, 1494–1495," ed. R. Foulché-Delbosc, *Revue Hispanique* 48 (1920) 125–26.

7. Rodrigo Sánchez de Arévalo, *El Vergel de Príncipes,* ed. Mario Penna, prologue, in *BAE* 116 (Madrid, 1959).

8. *Ibid.*, 21.

9. Fernán Pérez de Guzmán, *Generaciones y Semblanzas,* ed. R. B. Tate (London, 1950) 47.

10. Palencia, *Crónica*, Déc. I, lib. 4, cap. 3.

11. Fernando del Pulgar, *Libro de los Claros varones de Castilla*, ed. R. B. Tate (Oxford, 1971) 62.

12. Palencia, *Crónica*, Déc. I, lib. 5, cap. 2.

13. Enríquez del Castillo, cap. 37.

14. José de Sigüenza, *Historia de la Orden de San Jerónimo* (2v., Madrid, 1909) I:cap. 19.

15. Palencia, *Crónica*, Déc. I, lib. 6, cap. 10.

16. *CD*, doc.92.

17. *Estudio sobre la "Crónica de Enrique IV" del Lorenzo Galíndez de Carvajal,* ed. Juan Torres Fontes (Murcia, 1946) 212.

18. Valera, letter of July 20, 1462, in *Prosistas* I:8–9.

19. R. B. Tate, "An Apology for Monarchy. A Study of an Unpublished Fifteenth-Century Castilian Historical Document," *Romance Philology* 15 (1961) 112.

20. Angus Mackay, "The Hispanic-*Converso* Predicament," in Mackay, *Society, Economy, and Religion in Late Medieval Castile* (London, 1987); *cf. CD*, doc. 119.

21. *CC* I:no. 149.

22. Gómez Manrique, "Pregunta a Pedro de Mendoza," *CC* II:no. 352.

23. Gómez Manrique, "Esclamación e querella de la governación," *CC* II:no. 415 (s.2); "Coplas . . . Diego Arías," *CC* II:no. 377 (s. 47).

24. Enríquez del Castillo, cap. 87.

25. *CD*, doc. 125.

26. *CC* II:no. 391; Fraker, *Studies*, 100.

CHAPTER 4

1. Galíndez de Carvajal, "Crónica," 316.

2. *Ibid.*, 313.

3. Palencia, *Crónica*, Déc. I, lib. 7, cap. 1.

4. Juan Torres Fontes, *El príncipe don Alfonso* (Murcia, 1971) 134; Galíndez de Carvajal, "Crónica," app. 505–6.

5. Jorge Manrique, "Coplas por la muerte de padre," stanza 20.

6. *CC* II: no. 417, pp. 149–50.

7. Palencia, *Crónica*, Déc. I, lib. 10, cap. 10.

8. Valera, *Memorial*, cap. 41.

9. Azcona, *Isabel* 119.

10. *CD*, doc. 152.

11. Valera, *Memorial*, 53.

12. Martín de Córdoba, *Jardín de nobles donzellas: a critical edition and study*, ed. Harriet Goldberg (Chapel Hill, 1974), cap. 6.

13. *CC* II:no. 390.

14. Palencia, *Crónica*, Déc. II, lib. 1, cap.7.

15. Antonio Paz y Melia, *El cronista Alonso de Palencia* (Madrid, 1914) doc. 21.

16. *Ibid.*, doc. 18.

17. Andrés de Bernaldez, "Historia de los Reyes Católicos," cap. 7, in *BAE* 70.

18. Pulgar, *Crónica*, cap. 8.

19. Félix de Llanos y Torriglia, *Así llegó a reinar Isabel la Católica* (Madrid, 1927) 163.

20. *CD*, doc. 168.

21. Pulgar, *Crónica*, cap. 23.

22. Report of Miralles, notary of the diet of Valencia, in Jaime Vicens Vives, *Historia crítica de la vida y reinado de Fernando II de Aragón* (Zaragoza, 1962) 190–91, 196.

23. Pulgar, *Crónica*, cap. 23.

24. *CD*, doc. 170.

25. Diego Clemencín, *Elógio de la reina doña Isabel* (Madrid, 1821) app. 1.

CHAPTER 5

1. *Cartas autógrafas de los Reyes Católicos (1475–1502)*, ed. Amalia Prieto Cantero (Simancas, 1971) carta 2.

2. Enríquez del Castillo, cap. 144.

3. *CD*, doc. 187.

4. Paz y Melia, *cronista*, doc. 33.

5. Pulgar, *Letras*, no. 25.

6. Palencia, *Crónica*, Déc. 2, lib. 3, cap. 9.

7. *CC*, II:no. 402.

8. Paz y Melia, *cronista*, doc. 27.

9. See Adeline Rucquoi, "De Jeanne D'Arc à Isabelle la Catholique: I'image de la France en Castille au XVè Siècle," *Le Journal des Savants* (January–June, 1990) 155–74.

10. Jose Sánchis y Sivera, "El Cardenal Rodrigo de Borja en Valencia," *Boletin del Real Academia de Historia* (hereinafter *BRAH*) 84 (1924) 149.

11. Paz y Melia, *cronista*, doc. 44.

12. *Ibid.*, doc. 49.

13. "Cartas autógrafas," 16.

14. Andrés Alfonsello, *Los reys d'Aragó y la seu de Girona desde l'any 1462 fins al 1482*, ed. Fidel Fita (2nd ed., Barcelona, 1873) I:51.

15. Paz y Melia, *cronista*, doc. 74.

16. *Ibid.*, doc. 69.

17. Palencia, *Crónica*, Déc. 2, lib. 10, cap. 9.

18. *CD*, doc. 206.

19. Palencia, *Crónica*, Déc. 2, lib. 10, cap. 10.

20. M. Grau Sanz, "Así fué coronado Isabel la Católica," *Estudios Segovianos* 1 (1949) 24–36.

21. *Ibid.*

22. Francisco Pinel y Monroy, *Retrato del buen vasallo . . . Andrés de Cabrera* (Madrid, 1677) 198.

23. Palencia, *op. cit.*

24. Frances A. Yates, *Astraea: The Imperial Theme in the Sixteenth Century*, (London, 1985) 3–4, 9.

25. M. de Foronda y Aguilera, "Honras por Enrique IV y proclamación de Isabel la Católica en la ciudad de Avila," *BRAH* 63 (1913) 427–34.

CHAPTER 6

1. *CD*, doc. 206.

2. Palencia, *Crónica*, Déc. 3, lib. 1, cap. 4.

3. Grau, 37–39.

4. Pulgar, *Crónica*, cap. 22.

5. Palencia, *op. cit.*

6. Anon., *Crónica incompleta de los Reyes Católicos (1469–1476)*, ed. Julio Puyol (Madrid, 1934) 145.

7. Pulgar, *Crónica*, cap. 22.

8. Palencia, *Crónica*, Déc. 3, lib. 1, cap. 5.

9. Jerónimo Zurita, *Anales de la corona de Aragón*, ed. Angel Canellas López (8 v., Zaragoza, 1977) lib. 19, Ch. 16.

10. Palencia, *Crónica*, Déc. 3, lib. 1, cap. 5.

11. *Crónica incompleta*, 157.

12. *Ibid.*, 166.

13. *Ibid.*, 167.

14. "Cartas autógrafas," 17.

15. *Ibid.*, 29–30.

16. Vicens Vives, *Historia crítica*, 415–16.

17. Pedro de Alcántara Suárez, *Vida del venerable don Fray Hernando de Talavera* (Madrid, 1866) 59–63.

18. "Cartas autógrafas," 35–36.

19. *Crónica incompleta*, 225–26.

20. Palencia, *Crónica*, Déc. 3, lib. 3, cap. 5.
21. *Crónica incompleta*, 239–42.

CHAPTER 7

1. Georges Duby, *William Marshal. The Flower of Chivalry* (New York, 1986) 61.
2. Paz y Melia, *cronista*, doc. 94.
3. José Amador de los Ríos, *Historia crítica de la literatura española* (Madrid, 1865) VII:541–61.
4. Pulgar, *Crónica*, cap. 31.
5. Rudolf Wittkower, "Eagle and Serpent: A study in the migration of symbols," *Journal of the Warburg Institute* 2 (1938–1939) 293–325.
6. "Cartas autógrafas," 29.
7. *Colección de Documentos inéditos para la Historia de España*, ed. Miguel Salva y Munar and Pedro Sainz de Baranda (Madrid, 1842; hereinafter *CODOIN*), 13:396–400.
8. Palencia, *Crónica*, Déc. 3, lib. 25, cap. 9.
9. *Cortes de los antiguos reinos de León y de Castilla*, ed. Real Academía de la Historia (7 v., Madrid 1861–1903) IV:51–109.
10. *Ibid.*, IV:94.
11. Pulgar, *Crónica*, cap. 78.
12. *Crónica incompleta*, 310.
13. William Christian, Jr., has written me of a response received to a questionnaire about the shrine, dated October 12, 1969, that contains the story of the young captain.
14. Amalia Prieto Cantero, "¿Dónde están el collar de balajes y la Corona Rica de la Reina Católica?," in *Homenaje a Vicente de Cadenas. Estudios Geneológicos, Heráldicos, y nobiliarios . . . Hidalgúia Madrid* (June 10, 1978) 207–208.
15. Pulgar, *Crónica*, cap. 84.

CHAPTER 8

1. Miguel Angel Ladero Quesada, *España en 1492* (Madrid, 1978) 15–16.
2. Monetarius [Münzer], 112.
3. Cited by Alfonso de la Torre y del Cerro, in *Homenaje a Isabel la Católica en Madrigal de las Altas Torres* (Madrid, 1953) 14.
4. *Documentos sobre las relaciones con Portugal durante el reinado de los Reyes Católicos*, ed. Alfonso del la Torre y del Cerro and Luis Suárez Fernández (3 v., Valladolid, 1958–63) I:doc. 30.
5. Palencia, *Crónica*, Déc. 3, lib. 26, cap. 6.
6. Alonso de Palencia, *Cuarto Década de . . .*, ed. José López de Toro (2 v., Madrid, 1970–74) lib. 31, cap. 8.
7. Palencia, *Crónica*, Déc. 3, lib. 27, cap. 1.
8. Pulgar, *Crónica*, cap. 89.
9. *Ibid*, cap. 90.

CHAPTER 9

1. Azcona, *Isabel*, 288.
2. Bernaldez, cap. 32.
3. Vicens Vives, *Historia crítica*, 489.
4. Bachiller [Gutierre de] Palma, *Divina retribución sobre la caida de España en tiempo*

del noble rey Don Juan el Primero, ed. José María Escudero de la Peña (Madrid, 1879) 73.

5. Pulgar, *Letras,* letra 9.

6. Palma, 73,88.

7. *CC* II:150–51.

8. Alcántara Suárez, 175.

9. Julio Puyol, note to Jerónimo Münzer, ''Viaje por España y Portugal (1494–95)'' *BRAH* 84 (1924) 114–15.

10. Carriazo, introduction to Diego de Valera, *Crónica,* lvii, lxv.

11. José Antonio Maravall, *El concepto de España en la Edad Media* (2nd ed., Madrid, 1964) 312.

12. Pulgar, *Letras,* letra 11.

13. Diego de Valera, *Crónica de España abreviada* (Zaragoza, 1493) dedication.

14. *Crónica incompleta,* tít. 51.

15. *Ibid.,* tít. 52.

16. Valera, in *Prosistas,* 17.

17. María Rosa Lida de Malkiel, *Estudios sobre la Literatura Española del Siglo XV* (Madrid, 1978) 294–95.

18. Iñigo de Mendoza, ''Dechado del Regimiento de Principes,''[1475?] appended to Pulgar, *Libro de Claros varones,* ed. Tate, 75.

19. Palma, echoing Paul (Galatians: 4.26).

20. Nazário Pérez, *La Inmaculada y España* (Santander, 1954) 80.

21. Francisco Imperial, in *Cancionero de Baena* (facsimile ed., New York, 1926) no. 226.

22. Palma, 72.

23. Pulgar, *Crónica,* cap. 92.

CHAPTER 10

1. Pulgar, *Crónica,* cap. 24.

2. Azcona, *Isabel,* 387.

3. Yitzhak Baer, *A History of the Jews in Christian Spain* (2 v., Philadelphia, 1966) II:324.

4. Pedro de Escavías, *Repertorio de príncipes de España,* ed. Michel García (Jaén, 1973) cap. 147; Diego de Valera, *Memorial,* cap. 83.

5. Hernando de Talavera, *Católica Impugnacíon del herético libelo que en el año pasado de 1480 fué divulgado en la ciudad de Sevilla,* ed. Francisco Martín; intro. Francisco Márquez Villanueva (Barcelona, 1961) 186–87.

6. Pulgar, *Crónica,* cap. 96.

7. Francisco Cantera Burgos, ''Fernando del Pulgar and the *Conversos,''* in Roger Highfield, ed., *Spain in the Fifteenth Century, 1369–1516* (New York, 1972) 306–308.

8. Bernaldez, cap. 43.

9. Francisco Márquez Villanueva, ''Conversos y cargos concejiles en el siglo XV,'' *Revista de Archivos, Bibliotecas, y Museos* 63 (1957) 1536–37.

10. My thanks to Vicente Lleó Cañal for calling this saying to my attention.

11. Cantera Burgos, ''Pulgar,'' 316–17.

12. *Ibid.,* 327.

13. *Poesía crítica y satírica del siglo XV,* ed. Julio Rodríguez-Púertolas (Madrid, 1981) 317.

14. Alonso Ortiz, *Cinco Tratados de . . .* (Seville, 1493) fol. 101r.

15. Sigüenza, II:306.

16. Talavera, *Católica Impugnación*, 224, 235–36.

17. Fidel Fita y Colomé, "Nuevas fuentes para escribir la historia de los judíos españoles. Bulas inéditos de Sixto IV y Inocencio VIII," *BRAH* 15 (1889) 473–74.

18. Sebastían de Horozco, *Relaciones históricos toledanos* (Toledo, 1981) 100.

19. Pulgar, *Crónica*, cap. 224.

20. *Ibid.*, cap. 96.

21. Palencia, "Guerra," Lib. 4.

22. Pulgar, *Crónica*, cap. 96.

CHAPTER 11

1. Lorenzo Galíndez de Carvajal, "Anales breves del reinado de los Reyes Católicos . . . ," *BAE* 70:543.

2. Cited in John H. Elliott, *Richelieu and Olivares* (Cambridge, 1984) 55.

3. Florencia Pinar, *CC* II:559.

4. Torre y del Cerro and Suárez Fernández, I:209.

5. Pulgar, *Crónica*, cap. 116.

6. *Ibid.*, cap. 115.

7. Diego Hurtado de Mendoza, *La Guerra de Granada*, ed. Bernardo Blanco-González (Madrid, 1970)105.

8. Alfonso Díaz de Montalvo, *Compilación de leyes del reino* (facsimile ed., Valladolid, 1986).

9. Azcona, *Isabel*, 344.

10. *CODOIN* VII:539–71; Tarsicio de Azcona, "Reforma de espiscopado y del clero de España en tiempo de los Reyes Católicos y Carlos V (1475–1558)," in *Historia de la Iglesia en España*, ed. Ricardo García-Villoslada (Madrid 1980) III:1, pp.124–25.

11. Pulgar, *Crónica*, cap. 116.

12. Bernaldez, cap. 45.

13. Pulgar, *Crónica*, cap. 119.

14. *Ibid.*, cap. 126.

15. Palencia, "Guerra," 77.

16. *Ibid.*

17. Bernaldez, cap. 35.

CHAPTER 12

1. Pulgar, *Crónica*, cap. 24; but a summarizing interpolation, not in Pulgar's manuscript, which ends by 1490.

2. *Ibid.*, cap. 134.

3. Gerald Brenan, *South from Granada* (Cambridge, 1980) 231.

4. 'Abd al-Bāsit, "El reino de Granada en 1465–66," in *Viages de extranjeros por España y Portugal*, ed. José García Mercadal (Madrid, 1952) 252–57.

5. Pulgar, *Crónica*, cap. 132.

6. *Ibid.*, cap. 135.

7. Palencia, "Guerra," lib. 2.

8. *Letters and Papers illustrative of the Reigns of Richard III and Henry VII*, ed. James Gairdner (London, 1861) I:32.

9. Vicente Rodríguez Valencia, *Isabel la Católica en la opinión de españoles y extranjeros* (3 v., Valladolid, 1970) I:249.

10. Palencia, "Guerra," lib. 3.

11. Pulgar, *Crónica*, cap. 146.

12. Palencia, "Guerra," lib. 4.

13. Pulgar, *Crónica*, cap. 158.

14. *Canción Musical del Palacio*, ed. Francisco Asenjo Barbieri (2nd ed., Buenos Aires, 1945) no. 332.

15. Washington Irving, *The Granada War* (Boston, 1899) 95.

16. *El tumbo de los Reyes Católicos del concejo de Sevilla*, ed. Ramón Carande Thobar and Juan de Mata Carriazo (5 v., Seville, 1929–68) IV:826–833.

17. Pulgar, *Crónica*, cap. 173.

18. Bernaldez, cap. 67.

19. Azcona, *Isabel*, 512.

20. Pulgar, *Crónica*, cap. 178.

21. Palencia, "Guerra," lib. 5.

22. "Historia de los hechos de don Rodrigo Ponce de León, marqués de Cádiz (1443–1488)," *CODOIN* 106:247–51.

23. Bernaldez, cap. 118.

CHAPTER 13

1. Cited in Mary Purcell, *The Great Captain* (London, 1962) 90.

2. "Cartas autógrafas," 58.

3. Pulgar, *Crónica*, cap. 188.

4. Mártir, *Epistolario*, epis. 62.

5. A. Rodríguez Villa, "Don Francisco de Rojas," *BRAH* 28 (1896) 189.

6. Miguel Angel Ladero Quesada, *Castilla y la conquista del reino de Granada* (Granada, 1987), 293; M. A. Ladero Quesada, *Los Reyes Católicos: La Corona y la Unidad de España* (Valencia, 1989) 258.

7. "Cartas autógrafas," 66.

8. Pulgar, *Crónica*, cap. 204.

9. Bernaldez, cap. 83.

10. Pulgar, *Crónica*, cap. 204.

11. Bernaldez, cap. 87.

12. "Journals of Roger Machado. Embassy to Spain and Portugal. AD 1488," in *Historia regis Henrici Septimi*, ed. James Gairdner (London, 1858) 157–99.

13. Pulgar, *Crónica*, cap. 237, 238.

14. *Ibid.*, cap. 241.

15. Rodríguez-Puértolas, *Poesía crítica*, 330.

16. Bernaldez, cap. 104.

17. Otis H. Green, *Spain and the Western Tradition* (4 v., Madison, Wis., 1963–66), I:92–93.

CHAPTER 14

1. Juan del Encina, *Poesía lírica y cancionero musical* (Madrid, 1975) no. 30.

2. Antonio de la Torre, "Los Reyes Católicos y Granada," *Hispania* 4 (1944) 304.

3. *Bacon's History of the Reign of King Henry VII* (Cambridge, 1901) 97–98.

4. Monetarius, [Münzer] 130.

5. Mártir, *Epistolario*, epís. 6.

6. Lorenzo de Padilla, *Crónica de Felipe I llamado el Hermoso*, in *CODOIN* 8:16.

7. Monetarius [Münzer], 132.

8. *Ibid.*, 126.

9. *CC* II: no.922.

10. Marjorie Reeves, *The Influence of Prophecy in the Later Middle Ages* (Oxford, 1969) 222.

11. Ortiz, f. 94.

12. Elio Antonio de Nebrija, *Gramática sobre la lengua castellana*, (Salamanca, 1492) prologue.

13. Fernando de Rojas, *The Celestina, a novel in dialogue*, tr. Lesley B. Simpson (Berkeley, 1955) 111.

14. Monetarius [Münzer], 41–42.

15. Mártir, *Epistolario*, epís. 31.

16. Lucio Marineo Sículo, *Obra . . . de las cosas memorables de España* (Alcalá, 1539) f. 181–82.

17. *Ibid.*, f. 182.

18. Azcona, *Isabel*, 735.

19. Felix de Llanos y Torriglia, *En el hogar de los Reyes Católicos y cosas de sus tiempos*, (Madrid, 1943) 38.

20. Clemencín, 221–36, 383–86.

21. Alonso Ortiz, *Diálogo sobre la educación del Principe Don Juan hijo de los Reyes Católicos*, ed. Giovanni María Bertini (Madrid, 1983) 160.

22. Mártir, *Epistolario*, epis. 61.

23. Juan de Lucena, "Carta de . . . exhortaría a las letras," in *Opúsculos literarios de los siglos XIV a XVI*, ed. Antonio Paz y Melia (Madrid, 1892) 215–16.

24. Francisco Javier Sánchez Cantón, *Libros, Tapices y Cuadros que Coleccionó Isabel la Católica* (Madrid, 1950) 24.

25. Gonzalo Fernández de Oviedo, *Las quincuagenas de la nobleza de España* (Madrid, 1880) I:535.

26. R. B. Tate, "Nebrija the Historian," *Bulletin of Hispanic Studies* 34 (1957) 127.

27. *Antología de poetas líricos castellanos*, ed. Marcelino Menéndez y Pelayo, (Buenos Aires, 1943) II:136, 141.

28. Caro Lynn, *A College Professor of the Renaissance. Lucio Marineo Sículo among the Spanish Humanists* (Chicago, 1937) 115–16.

29. Pedro de Gracia Dei, "Crianza e virtuosa dotrina," in *Opúsculos*, 381.

30. Rodríguez Valencia, I:369–71.

31. Torres Balbas, "Alhambra," 194–97.

32. Joaquín Yarza Luaces, "La imagen del rey y la imagen del noble en el siglo XV," in *Realidad e imágenes del poder. España a fines de la Edad Media*, coord. Adeline Rucquoi (Valladolid, n.d.) 269–71.

33. Owen Gingerich, "Alfonso X as a Patron of Astronomy," in *Alfonso X of Castile, the Learned King*, ed. Francisco Márquez-Villanueva and Carlos Alberto Vega (Cambridge, Mass.,1990) 32.

34. Colbert Nepaulsingh, *Micer Francisco Imperial. "El Dezir a las syete virtudes" y otros poemas* (Madrid, 1977) lcvii.

35. Mena, "*Laberinto*," copla 231; Yarza Luaces, "Imagen," 270n5.

CHAPTER 15

1. "Edicto de los Reyes Católicos," ed. Fidel Fita, *BRAH* 11 (1887) 512–20.

2. Luis Suárez Fernández, *Documentos acerca de la expulsión de los judíos* (Valladolid, 1964) 116–17.

3. *Siete Partidas*, Lib. VII, tít. xxiv, ley 1.

4. Biblioteca Nacional (Madrid) MS 1.104, f.46–52.

5. Suárez Fernández, *Documentos . . . judíos* 344–46; Fritz Baer, *Die Juden en Christlichen Spanian* (2 v., Berlin, 1936) II: 397–98.

6. Baer, *Juden*, II:doc. 372.

7. Benzion Netanyahu, *Isaac Abravanel* (Philadelphia, 1972) 55–56.

8. Bernaldez, caps. 110–11.

9. José Cabezudo Astráin, "La expulsíon de los judíos zaragozanos," *Sefarad* 15 (1955) 103–106.

10. Sigüenza II:31–32.

11. Baer, *History*, II:500–501, n. 66.

CHAPTER 16

1. Preamble to *The Journal of Christopher Columbus*, tr. Cecil Jane (New York, 1960) 4.

2. Alessandro Geraldini, *Itinererium ad regiones sub aequinoctiali plagas constitutas . . .*, (Rome, 1631) lib. xiv, f. 204.

3. Columbus, *Journal*, 4.

4. Martín Fernández de Navarrete, *Colección de los viajes y descubrimientos que hiceron por más los Españoles* (5 v. Madrid, 1825–37) II:4.

5. Antonio Rumeu de Armas, *Cádiz, metrópoli de comercio con Africa en los siglos XV y XVI* (Cádiz, 1976) 12.

6. Carl Ortwin Sauer, *The Early Spanish Main* (Berkeley, 1966) 11.

7. *Cartas de particulares a Colón y Relaciones coetanéas*, eds. Juan Gil y Consuelo Varela (rev. ed., Madrid, 1984) 144–46.

8. Navarrete II:6.

9. Bartolomé de Las Casas, *Historia de las Indias*, (3 v., Mexico, 1951) lib. I:cap. 78.

10. Pauline Moffitt Watts, "Prophecy and Discovery: On the Spiritual Origins of Christopher Columbus's 'Enterprise of the Indies,'" *American Historical Review* 90 (1985) 97.

11. Las Casas, lib. I: cap. 28.

12. Gil and Varela, doc. 41.

13. I am grateful to Sabine MacCormack for suggesting that Columbus had to prove he was not an instrument of dark forces.

14. Ladero Quesada, *Castilla 299*.

15. *Capitulaciones del almirante Don Cristóbal Colón y salvoconductos para el descubrimiento del nuevo mundo* (facsimile ed., Granada, 1980) 23.

CHAPTER 17

1. Samuel Eliot Morison, *Admiral of the Ocean Sea* (2 v., Boston, 1942) I:146–47.

2. Navarrete, II:21–22.

3. Las Casas, lib. I:cap. 78.

4. Mártir, *Epistolario*, epís. 133, 134.

5. Francisco López de Gómara, *Historia de las Indias*, in *BAE* 22:125.

6. Las Casas, lib. I:cap. 94.

7. Mártir, *Epistolario*, epís. 133, 135 142, 146.

8. Clemencín, 369.

9. *Ibid.*, 372–73.

10. Demetrio Ramos Pérez, intro. and ed., *La Carta de Colón sobre el descubrimiento* (facsimile ed., Granada 1983) not paginated.

11. José María Asencio, *Cristóbal Colón* (Barcelona 1891)I:466–67.

12. Las Casas, lib. I: cap. 79.

13. Antonio Rumeu de Armas, *Colón en Barcelona* (Seville, 1944) 38.

14. Las Casas, lib. I:cap. 79.

15. Fidel Fita, "Fray Bernal Buyl y Cristóbal Colón. Nueva coleccíon de cartas reales enriquecida con algunas inéditas," *BRAH* 79 (1891).

16. *Cristóbal Colón: Textos y documentos completos*, ed. Consuelo Varela (2nd, rev. ed., Madrid, 1984), doc. 7.

17. Las Casas, lib. I:cap. 103.

18. Mártir, *Epistolario*, epís. 146, 158.

19. *Ibid.*, epís. 164.

20. Navarrete, III:506.

21. Varela ed., doc. 24.

22. Las Casas, lib. I:cap. 176.

23. Hernando Colón, *Historia del Almirante*, ed. Luis Arranz (Madrid, 1985) cap. 85, pp.280–81.

24. Las Casas, lib. I:cap. 78.

25. *Colección de Documentos para la Historia de la Formación Social de Hispanoamérica*, ed. Richard Konetzke (Madrid, 1953) I:4–6.

26. *Ibid.*, I:9–13.

27. Navarrete II, doc. 17, pp. 414–16.

28. Konetzke I:16–17.

29. Christopher Columbus, *Four Voyages to the New World*, tr. and ed. R. H. Major (London, 1847; reprint New York, 1961) 197–98.

30. Christopher Columbus, Prologue to The *"Libro de las Profecías,"* eds. Delno West and August Kling (Gainesville, 1991)

CHAPTER 18

1. Preface to *Décadas*, cited in Ramón Menéndez Pidal, "The Significance of the Reign of Isabella the Catholic, According to Her Contemporaries," in Highfield, 401–402.

2. Azcona, *Isabel*, 720–21.

3. Mártir, *Epistolario*, epís. 125.

4. *Ibid.*, epís. 126, 127; and see 130.

5. Appendix to Gonzalo Fernández de Oviedo, *Libro de la Cámara del Príncipe Don Juan* (Madrid, 1870) 193–96.

6. Clemencín, 355–59.

7. Mártir, epís.108.

8. *Ibid.*

9. *Ibid.*, epís. 150.

10. Rodríguez Valencia, I:304.

11. Alonso de Santa Cruz, *Crónica de los Reyes Católicos (hasta ahora iñedita)*, ed. Juan de Mata Carriazo (2 v., Seville, 1951) I:99; Padilla, 21–22.

12. Luís Suárez Fernández, in *Los Trastámara y La Unidad Española*, t.5 of *Historia General de España y América*, coord. L. Suárez Fernández (Madrid, 1981), 580.

13. Mártir, *Epistolario*, epís. 143.

14. *Ibid.*, epís. 24, 29, and elsewhere.

15. Pedro Salazar, *Crónica de el Gran Cardenal de España, Don Pedro Gonçales de Mendoça* (Toledo, 1625) f.358, 362.

16. *Ibid.*, f.358; Azcona, *Isabel*, 456, 725–26.

17. Zurita, *Anales*, lib. 7, cáp. 29.

18. Diego Hurtado de Mendoza, lib. 1.

19. Mártir, *Epistolario*, epís. 163.

20. Albert A. Sicroff, *Los Estatutos de limpieza de sangre. Controversias entre los siglos XV y XVI*, (rev. ed., Madrid, 1985) 122.

21. Mártir, *Epistolario*, epís. 168.

22. *Ibid.*, epís. 176.

23. *Ibid.*, epís. 179.

24. *Ibid.*, epís. 182.

25. *Ibid.*, epís. 183.

26. *Ibid.*, epís. 192.

27. Marineo Sículo, *De las cosas*, f. 186.

28. *Spain. A Companion to Spanish Studies*, ed. P. E. Russell (London and New York, 1985) 268.

29. Linda Martz, in conversation.

30. Padilla, 79–80.

CHAPTER 19

1. Bernaldez, cap. 155.

2. Miguel Angel Ladero Quesada, *Las Mudéjares de Castilla en tiempos de Isabel I* (Valladolid, 1969) 77.

3. *Ibid.*, doc. 85.

4. *Ibid.*, doc. 86.

5. Bernaldez, 693.

6. Mártir, *Epistolario*, epís. 215.

7. *Ibid*

8. Azcona, *Isabel*, 554.

9. Ladero Quesada, *Mudéjares*, 81 n66.

10. Azcona, *Isabel*, 555.

11. Lynn, 22.

12. Mártir, *Epistolario*, epís. 216.

13. Gutierre Gómez de Fuensalida, *Correspondencia de. . . . Embajada en Alemania, Flandres e Inglaterra (1469–1509)* (Madrid, 1907) 114.

14. Azcona, *Isabel*, 718.

15. Mártir, *Epistolario*, epís. 222.

16. ''Cartas autógrafas,'' 77.

17. *Ibid.*, 81–82.

18. *Ibid.*

19. Torre y del Cerro and Suárez Fernández, III: doc. 513.

20. Mártir, *Epistolario*, epís. 250.

21. Prudencio de Sandoval, *Historia de Carlos V* (3 v., Madrid, 1955–56) I:23–24.

22. Antonio Rodríguez Villa, *La Reina Doña Juana la Loca* (Madrid, 1892)82.

23. Gómez de Fuensalida, 196–98.

24. *Ibid.*, 266–67.

25. *Testamentaría de Isabel la Católica*, ed., Antonio de la Torre y del Cerro (Valladolid, 1968).

26. Alfonso Valdés, *Diálogo de las cosas ocurridas en Roma*, ed. J. F. Montesinos (Madrid, 1956) 139.

27. Azcona, *Isabel*, 741.

28. Gracia Dei, 377.

EPILOGUE

1. Alvar Gómez de Castro, *De rebus gestis a Francisco Ximenio Cisnerio, Archiepiscopo Toletano* (Alcalá de Henares, 1569) lib. 8, f. 52r.

2. Fernando's will; Madrigalejo. Jan. 22, 1516; Rodríguez Valencia, I:8.

3. One Alvaro de Mercado citing the *corregidor*, García Sarmiento, during an investigation held in 1507 by the Royal Council; "Informe o Pesquisa contra algunos que hablaron mal de la Reina Católica y su marido." May 17, 1507. AGS. *Estado Castilla*, Leg.1 (2), fol. 192.

4. Rodríguez Valencia I:259–61

5. *CODOIN* 18:420.

6. Gómez de Fuensalida, 310.

7. Rodríguez Valencia, I:20.

8. Azcona, *Isabel*, 423.

9. Suárez Fernández, *Trastámara*, 652.

10. William S. Maltby, *Alba* (Berkeley, 1983) 305.

11. Bacon, 197–98.

12. Santa Cruz, I:303.

13. Fernández de Oviedo, *Quinquagenas*, 281.

Selected Bibliography

Works are generally mentioned only the first time they are pertinent.

The best account of the period is Miguel Angel Ladero Quesada, *Los Reyes Católicos: La Coruña y la Unidad de España* (Valencia, 1989); his bibliography may be used to supplement this one. The five volumes by Luis Suárez Fernández on *Los Reyes Católicos* (Madrid, 1989–90) focus on international relations but not exclusively. Most thorough on Isabel alone are Tarsicio de Azcona, *Isabel la Católica* (Madrid, 1964); and Diego Clemencín, *Elógio de la Reina Católica Doña Isabel* (Madrid, 1821). See too Joseph Pérez, *Isabel y Fernando. Reyes Católicos de España* (Madrid, 1988). Classic accounts of the broader Spanish context appear in J. H. Elliott, *Imperial Spain, 1469–1716* (London, 1963); Angus MacKay, *Spain in the Middle Ages* (London, 1977); and MacKay in J. H. Elliott, ed., *The World of Spain* (New York, 1990). See also Charles E. Dufourcq and Jean Gautier-Dalché, *Historia económica y social de la España cristiana en la Edad Media* (Barcelona, 1983); J. N. Hillgarth, *The Spanish Kingdoms, 1250–1516* (2 v. Oxford, 1978) II; and the collected essays of Angus MacKay, *Society, Economy and Religion in Late Medieval Castile* (London, 1987). Vicente Rodríguez Valencia, *Isabel la Católica en la opinión de españoles y extranjeros* (3 v.,Valladolid, 1970), is of great historiographical value, but accentuates the positive.

PROLOGUE. AN EMBASSY TO EGYPT: 1502

Petri Martyrus Anglerii, *Opera: Legatio babilonica* (Seville, 1511; rp. Graz, 1966); there is a Spanish translation by Luis García y García, *Una Embajada de los Reyes Católicos a Egipto* (Valladolid, 1947). See too Luis Suárez Fernández, "Las relaciones de los Reyes Católicos con Egipto," *En la España Medieval* (Madrid, 1980) I:507–19; and Antonio de la Torre, "La embajada de Pedro Mártir de Anglería," in *Homenaje a Rubio Lluch* (Barcelona, 1936).

1. ON THE MESETA: 1451–1460

The chronicles of the reign of Enrique IV are Diego Enríquez del Castillo, "Crónica de Enrique IV," ed. Cayetano Rosell, in *Biblioteca de Autores Españoles*, v. 70 (Madrid, 1953); Lorenzo Galíndez de Carvajal, "La Crónica de Enrique IV," in Juan Torres Fontes, *Estudio sobre . . .* (Murcia, 1946); Alonso Fernández de Palencia, *Crónica de Enrique IV*, ed. Antonio Paz y Melia (4 v., Madrid, 1973–75); and see Fernando del Pulgar, *Crónica de los Reyes Católicos*, ed. Juan de

Mata Carriazo (2 v., Madrid, 1943); and Diego de Valera, *Crónica de los Reyes Católicos*, ed. Juan de Mata Carriazo (Madrid, 1927). See too Juan Torres Fontes, *Itinerario de Enrique IV de Castilla* (Murcia, 1953). For Isabel's Portuguese connections: Gomes Eanes de Zurara, *Crónica dos feitos notáveis que se passaram na conquista da Guiné*, ed. T. de Sousa Soares (2 v., Lisbon, 1978–81); Fernão Lopes, *Crónica de dom João I* (Lisbon, 1980); J. P. Oliveira Martins, *Os filhos de don João I* (5th ed., Lisbon 1926); and Peter E. Russell, *Prince Henry the Navigator* (Oxford, 1984).

Arévalo's legends appear in Juan José de Montalvo, *De la historia de Arévalo y sus sexmos* (2nd ed.,Avila, 1983). For Arévalo's *mudejarismo* see Juan Carlos Frutos Cuchilleros, "Arquitectura mudéjar en el partido judicial de Arévalo (Avila)," in *Actas del I Simposio Internacional de Mudejarismo* (Madrid-Teruel, 1981); Manuel Valdes Fernández, *Arquitectura mudéjar en León y Castilla* (León, 1984); and Torres Balbas. For Muslims as worthy adversaries see: Angus MacKay, "The Ballad and the Frontier in Late Medieval Spain," *Bulletin of Hispanic Studies* 53 (1976) 15–33; and Maria Soledad Carrasco Urgoit, *El moro de Granada en la literatura. Siglos XV y XVI* (Madrid, 1965). The figures in Toledo's cathedral are explored in Angela Franco Mata, "El Génesis y el Exodo en la cerca exterior del coro de la catedral de Toledo," *Toletum* 70 (1987) 53–160.

2. A ROYAL HERITAGE: PERCEPTION AND REALITY

Leopoldo Torres Balbas, "El ambiente mudéjar en torno a la Reina Católica y el arte hispanomusulmano en España y Berbería durante su reinado," in *Curso de conferencia sobre la política africana de los Reyes Católicos* (Madrid, 1951) II, discusses Muslim architecture of the *meseta*. Castilian advance is described in J. A. García de Cortazar, *et al., Organización social del espacio en la España medieval. La Corona de Castilla en los siglos VIII a XV* (Barcelona: Ariel, 1985); and Charles Julian Bishko, "The Spanish and Portuguese Reconquest, 1095–1492," in Bishko, *Studies in Medieval Spanish Frontier History* (London, 1980). For the economy: Dufourcq and Gautier-Dalché; Miguel Angel Ladero Quesada, *Historia de Sevilla* (2nd ed.,Seville, 1980); his *La Hacienda Real de Castilla en el siglo XV* (La Laguna de Tenerife, 1973); and his *El siglo XV en Castilla: fuentes de renta y política fiscal* (Barcelona, 1982); Angus MacKay, *Money, Prices and Politics in Fifteenth-Century Castile* (London, 1981); Pierre Vilar, *History of Gold and Money, 1450–1920* (London, 1984); and Andrew M. Watson, "Back to Gold and Silver," *Economic History Review* (1967) 1–34. For Alfonso X see Evelyn S. Procter, *Alfonso X of Castile* (c. 1961; reprint Westport, Conn., 1980); Francisco Rico, *Alfonso el Sabio y la "General estoria"* (2nd ed., Barcelona, 1984): and Robert I. Burns, ed., *Emperor of Culture* (Philadelphia, c. 1990). And for royal political theory, see José Antonio Maravall, *El concepto de España en la edad media* (3rd ed., Madrid, 1981); and José Manuel Nieto Soria, *Fundamentos ideológicos del poder real en Castilla (siglos XIII–XVI)* (Madrid, 1988). The literature on prophecy is extensive: outstanding is R. W. Southern, "Aspects of the European Tradition of Historical Writing: 3. History as Prophecy," in *Transactions of the Royal Historical Society*, 5th ser., 22 (1972) 159–80; and Charles F. Fraker, Jr., *Studies on the Cancionero de Baena* (Chapel Hill, 1966), who also discusses Jews becoming *conversos*; as does Philippe Wolf, "The 1391 Pogrom in Spain. Social Crisis or Not?" *Past and Present*, no. 50 (1971) 4–18. See the editions of Juan de Mata Carriazo of the chronicles: Gonzalo Chacón, *Crónica de Alvaro de Luna* (Madrid, 1940); Lope de Barrientos, *Refundación de la crónica del halconero* (Madrid, 1946); Pedro Carrillo de Huete, *Crónica del Halconero de Juan II* (Madrid 1946); the *Sumario de la crónica de Juan II* (Seville, 1951); and Pedro de Escavías, *Reportorio de príncipes*, appended to Juan Bautista Arvalle Arce, *El cronista Pedro de Escavias* (Chapel Hill, 1972). Short but key contemporary biographies, critically edited by R. B. Tate, appear in Fernán Pérez de Guzmán, *Generaciones y Semblanzas*, (London, 1965); and Fernando del Pulgar, *Libro del claros Varones* (Oxford, 1971). Indispensable is R. B. Tate, *Ensayos sobre la historiografía peninsular del siglo XV* (Madrid, 1973). For Luna's impact: Nicholas Round, *The Greatest Man Uncrowned: A Study of the Fall of Alvaro de Luna* (London, 1986).

3. THE WRONG KING: 1461–1467

See the chronicles of Enrique's reign; and William D. Phillips, Jr., *Enrique IV and the Crisis of Fifteenth-Century Castile, 1425–1480* (Cambridge, Mass., 1978), a fine brief scholarly account. Enrique's most sympathetic and only exclusive chronicler is Enríquez del Castillo, and even he is none too sympathetic. See too Pedro de Escavías, *Hechos del Condestable don Miguel Lucas de Iranzo*, ed. Juan de Mata Carriazo (Madrid, 1940). The *Colección Diplomática* in the *Memorias de Don Enrique IV de Castilla* (Madrid, 1835–1913) II; and *El cronista Alonso de Palencia*, ed. Antonio Paz y Melia (Madrid 1914) are rich in documents of the reign. For Enrique's physical problems see MacKay, *Society* XVI. For satirical texts: "Coplas del Provincial" in Julio Rodríguez-Puértolas, *Poesía crítica y satírica del siglo XV* (Madrid, 1981); and *Las Coplas de Mingo Revulgo*, ed. Vivana Brody (Madison, 1986). For Alfonso: Juan Torres Fontes, *El príncipe don Alfonso, 1465–1468* (Murcia, 1971).

4. THE RIGHT MARRIAGE. 1467–1469

In addition to the aforementioned works on Enrique's reign, there are Isabel del Val Valdivieso, *Isabel la Católica, princesa (1468–1474)* (Valladolid, 1974); Baltasár Cuartero y Huerta, *El pacto de los Toros de Guisando* (Madrid, 1952); and Juan Torres Fontes, *El príncipe Don Alfonso y la contratación de Guisando, 1465–1468* (Murcia, 1985); for Fernando's childhood: Jerónimo de Zurita, *Anales de Aragón*, ed. Angel Canellas López (Zaragoza, 1988) VII; Julia Nuría Coll, *Doña Juana Enríquez, lugarteniente real en Cataluña (1461–1468)* (2 v., Madrid, 1953); and, principally, Jaime Vicens Vives, *Historia crítica de la vida y reinado de Fernando II de Aragón* (Zaragoza, 1962).

5. TO THE CROWN: 1469–1474

For Castile's nobles see R. B. Tate's introduction to Pulgar, *Libro de claros Varones*; and Roger Highfield, "The Catholic Kings and the Titled Nobility of Castile," in *Europe in the Late Middle Ages* (London, 1975).

6. CONTESTS: 1475

Important now, besides Palencia, Pulgar, and Valera, is the anonymous *Crónica incompleta de los Reyes Católicos (1469–1476)*, ed. Julio Puyol (Madrid, 1934), its author generally assumed to be Juan de Flores. Indispensable is Antonio Rumeu de Armas, *Itinerario de los Reyes Católicos (1475–1516)* (Madrid, 1974).

7. RESOLUTIONS: 1475–1477

The role of the towns and their *hermandades* comes out in Martin Lunenfeld, *The Council of the Santa Hermandad* (Coral Gables, Fla., 1970); Lunenfeld, *Keepers of the City. The Corregidores of Isabella I of Castile (1474–1504)* Cambridge, 1987; and José María Carretero Zamora, *Cortes, monarquiá, ciudades* (Madrid 1988). For San Juan de los Reyes, see José María de Azcárate, "Sentido y significación de la arquitectura hispano-flamenca en la corte de Isabel la Católica," in *Boletín del Seminario de Estudios de Arte y Arqueología* (Valladolid, 1971) 203–23; and his "Datos histórico-artísticos de fines del siglo XV y principios de XVI," in *Colección de documentos para la historia de arte en España* (Madrid and Zaragoza, 1983) II. There is no satisfactory life of Talavera; helpful are Pedro de Alcántara Suárez y Muñano, *Vida del Venerable don Fray Hernando de Talavera* (Madrid, 1866); Quintin Aldea, "Hernando de Talavera. Su testamentoy su biblioteca," in *Homenaje . . . Pérez de Urbel* (Madrid, 1977) I: and Francisco Márquez Villanueva, *Investigaciones sobre Juan Alvarez Gato* (Madrid, 1960).

8. TO THE SEA: 1477–1478

Juan de Mata Carriazo and Ramón Carande Thobar, comp., *El Tumbo de los Reyes Católicos del concejo de Sevilla* (5 v., Seville, 1929–68) is a trove of royal communiques to Seville and the kingdom. For Andalusia: Miguel Angel Ladero Quesada, "Aristocatie et regime seigneurial dans l'Andalousie du XVème siècle," *Annales* 6 (1983) 1346–68; and Ladero, *Andalucía en el siglo XV* (Madrid, 1973). For Guadalupe: Guy Beaujouan, *La science en Espagne aux XIV et XV siècles* (Paris, 1967); J. R. L. Highfield, "The Jeronymites in Spain, their Patrons and Successes, 1373–1516," *Journal of European History* 34 (1983); Nicholas G. Round, "Fifteenth-Century Guadalupe: The Paradoxes of Paradise," in *Medieval and Renaissance Studies in Honour of Robert Brian Tate*, ed. Ian Michael and Richard A. Cardwell (Oxford, 1986) 135–49; and A. A. Sicroff, "The Jeronymite Monastery of Guadalupe in 14th and 15th Century Spain," in M. P. Hornik, *Collected Studies in Honour of Américo Castro's Eightieth Year* (Oxford, 1965) 397–422.

For Atlantic venture: Valera; Andrés Bernaldez, *Memorias del reinado de los Reyes Católicos*, ed: Manuel Gómez Moreno and Juan de Mata Carriazo (Madrid, 1962); Pierre Chaunu, *European Expansion in the Later Middle Ages* tr. Katherine Bertram (Amsterdam, 1979); Florentino Pérez-Embid, *Los descubrimientos en el Atlántico y la rivalidad castellano-portuguesa hasta el tratado de Tordesillas* (Seville 1948); Antonio Rumeu de Armas, *España en el Africa Atlántica* (2 v.,Madrid, 1956–57); Francisco Fernández-Armesto, *Before Columbus* (London, 1987); and his *The Canary Islands after Conquest* (Oxford, 1982); P. E. Russell, "Fontes documentais castelhanas para a história da expansão portuguêsa na Guiné nos últimos anos de D. Afonso V," *Do tempo e da História* 4 (1971) 5–33; Antonio Rumeu de Armas, *Política indigenista de Isabel la Católica* (Valladolid, 1969); and Antonio de la Torre, "La política de los Reyes Católicos en Africa: antecedentes y orientaciones," in *Curso de conferencias sobre la política africana de los Reyes Católicos* (Madrid, 1951) II:157–62.

9. SIGNS AND REVELATIONS: 1478

Diego de Valera, *Crónica abreviada*, had at least six Spanish editions between 1482 and 1500. For aspects of Mary and Eve: William A. Christian, Jr., *God and Person in a Spanish Valley* (Princeton, 1972); Susan Tax Freeman, "Faith and

Fashion in Spanish Religion: Notes on the Observation of Observance," *Peasant Studies* 7 (1978) 101–22; and Nazario Pérez, *La Inmaculada y España* (Santander, 1954). For the Granadan treaty background: "Las treguas con Granada de 1475 y 1478," in *En la frontera de Granada* (Seville, 1971).

10. INQUISITION: 1478–1485

For the early Inqusition, see Ladero Quesada, *Los Reyes Católicos*; and Juan Meseguer, "El período fundacional," in Joaquín Pérez Vilanueva and Bartolomé Escadell, *Historia de la Inquisicíon en España y América* (Madrid, 1984) I. Valuable too is Juan Antonio Llorente, *Historia crítica de la Inquisicíon española* (4 v., Madrid, 1870–80)I; and B. Lorca, *Bulario Pontificio de la Inquisición española* (Rome, 1949). Henry Charles Lea, *A History of the Inquisition of Spain* (4 v., New York, 1907, reprint 1988) remains the classic and most complete overview. A recent survey in English is Henry Kamen, *The Spanish Inquisition in the Sixteenth and Seventeenth Centuries* (Bloomington, 1985). The articles of Fidel Fita are key, among them his "Nuevas fuentes para escribir la historia de los júdios españoles. Bulas inéditas de Sixto IV e Inocencio VIII," *BRAH* 15 (1889) 449–52. Among regional studies are: Francisco Cantera Burgos and Pilar León Tello, *Judaizantes del arzobispado de Toledo habilitados por la Inquisición en 1495 y 1497* (Madrid, 1969); Sebastián de Horozco, *Relaciones históricos toledanas* (Toledo, 1981); Antonio Cascales Ramos, *La Inquisición en Andalucía* (Seville, 1986); Hipólito Sancho de Sopranis, "Historia social de Jérez de la Frontera al fin de la Edad Media," *Anecdota* 3 (1959); Sopranis, "La judería de Puerto de Santa María de 1483 a 1492," *Sefarad* 13 (1953) 309–24; Fidel Fita, "La Inquisición en Jérez de la Frontera," *BRAH* 15 (1889) 313–46; Haim Beinart, *Los conversos ante el tribunal de la Inquisición* (Barcelona, 1983); and Ricardo García Carcel, *Orígenes de la Inquisición Española. El Tribunal de Valencia.* For converso history: Albert A. Sicroff, *Los estatutos de limpieza de sangre*, tr. Mauro Armiño (rev. ed., Madrid, 1985); Angus MacKay, "Popular Movements and Pogroms in Fifteenth-Century Castile," *Past and Present* no. 55 (1972) 33–67; and his "The Hispanic-Converso Predicament," in MacKay, *Society*; Miguel Angel Ladero Quesada, "Judeoconversos andaluces en el siglo XV," *I Congreso Internacional "Encuentro de las Tres Culturas"* (Toledo, 1983); Antonio Domínguez Ortiz, *Los judeoconversos en España y en América* (Madrid, 1971); Francisco Márquez Villanueva, "Conversos y cargos concejiles en el siglo XV," *Revista de Archivos, Bibliotecas, y Museos* 63 (1957); and his *Investigaciones*; Luciano Serrrano, *Los Reyes Católicos y la ciudad de Burgos* (Madrid, 1943); Adeline Rucquoi, *Valladolid en la Edad Media* (2 v., Valladolid, 1987) II: Francisco Cantera Burgos, "Fernando del Pulgar y los conversos," *Sefarad* 4 (1944) 295–348, reprinted in Roger Highfield, ed., *Spain in the Fifteenth Century, 1369–1516* (New York, 1972); and Benzion Netanyahu, *The Marranos of Spain from the Late XIVth to the Early XVth Century, according to Contemporary Hebrew Sources* (New York, 1966) The literature on *conversos* is immense and most often overly subjective, harboring the assumption either that *conversos* secretly remained Jews religiously, or that *conversos* remained Jews "racially," no matter what their religion.

11. READYING: 1478–1481

See Lorenzo Galíndez de Carvajal, "Anales breves de los Reyes Católicos," in *BAE* 70, pp. 533–67. For relations with Portugal: Rui de Pina, *Crónica de el-rei Dom*

João II ed. Alberto Marsins de Carvalho (Coimbra, 1950); Antonio de la Torre y del Cerro and Luis Suárez Fernández, *Documentos sobre las relaciones con Portugal durante el reinado de los Reyes Católicos* (3v.,Valladolid, 1958–63)I; Luis Suárez Fernández, *Política internacional de Isabel la Católica* (6 v., Valladolid, 1965–72)I; and Torre and Suárez Fernández, *Documentos sobre las relaciones internacionales de los Reyes Católicos* (6 v.,Barcelona, 1949–66)I. For the Cortes and royal government: Real Academia de Historia, *Cortes de León y Castilla* (7 v.,Madrid, 1861–1903)IV; Manuel Colmeiro, *Cortes de los antiguos reinos de León y Castilla* (2 v., Madrid, 1883–84)II; Salustiano de Díos, *El Consejo Real de Castilla (1385-1522)* (Madrid, 1982); María S. Martín Postigo, *La Chancillería castellana de los Reyes Católicos* (Valladolid, 1959); María Antonia Varona García, *La Chancillería de Valladolid en el reinado de los Reyes Católicos* (Valladolid, 1981); and Alfonso Díaz de Montalvo, *Compilación de leyes del reino* (facsimile ed. Valladolid, 1986). For church reform: Tarsicio de Azcona, *La elección y la reforma del episcopado española en tiempos de los Reyes Católicos* (Madrid 1960).

12. THE QUEEN'S WAR I: 1482–1485

See the chronicles of the reign, Juan de Mata Carriazo, *El "breve parte" de Fernán Pérez del Pulgar* (Seville, 1953); the anonymous continuation of Pulgar, and Alonso de Palencia, "Guerra de Granada," in *BAE* 70; and *Cuentas de Gonzalo de Baeza, tesorero de Isabel la Católica*, ed. Antonio de la Torre y E. A. de la Torre (2 v., Madrid, 1955) for royal expenditures from now on. Indispensable are Miguel Angel Ladero Quesada, *Granada* (2nd ed., Madrid, 1979); and his *Castilla y la conquista del Reino de Granada* (2nd ed., Granada, 1987). Juan de Mata Carriazo has a fine narrative of the war in Carriazo and Luis Suárez Fernández, *La España de los Reyes Católicos (1474-1516)*, t.17 of *Historia de Espana*, ed. Ramón Menéndez Pidal (Madrid, 1969). Washington Irving, *The Conquest of Granada*, in numerous editions, is basically sound; and see too Leopoldo de Eguílaz y Yanguas, *Reseña Histórica de la conquista del reino de Granada por los Reyes Católicos según los cronistas árabes* (Granada, 1894).

13. THE QUEEN'S WAR II:1486–1492

See the books above of Miguel Angel Ladero Quesada; his "La esclavitud por guerra a fines del siglo XV: el caso de Málaga," *Hispania* no. 105 (1967) 63–88; his *Milicia y economía en la guerra de Granada: el Cerco de Baza* (Valladolid, 1964); his "Las coplas de Hernando de Vera: un caso de crítica al gobierno de Isabel la Católica," *Anuario de Estudios Atlánticos* 14 (1968) 365–81; his *Las Mudéjares de Castilla en tiempos de Isabel I* (Valladolid, 1969); and his *Granada después de la conquista: Repobladores y mudéjares* (Granada, 1988). For Granada's surrender: Miguel Garrido Atienza, *Las capitulaciones para la entrega de Granada* (Granada, 1910); and María del Carmen Pescador del Hoyo, "Como fué de verdad la toma de Granada, a la luz de un documento inédito," *Al-Andalus* 20 (1955) 283–344. See too Hernando de Baeza, *Relaciones de algunos sucesos de los últimos tiempos del reino de Granada*,ed. Emilio Lafuente Alcántara (Madrid 1868).

14. THE VIEW FROM GRANADA. THE GRAND DESIGN: 1492

For Isabel in Granada: Leopoldo Torres Balbas, "Los Reyes Católicos en la Alhambra," *Al-Andalus* 16 (1951) 185–95. For the economy: Angus MacKay, *Society*; Jacques Heers, *Gênes au XVè siècle* (Paris, 1961); his "Los genoveses en la sociedad andaluza del siglo XV: orígenes, grupos, solidaridades," in *Hacienda y Comercio. II Coloquio de Historia Medieval Andaluza* (Seville, 1981); and there too: Enrique Otte, "El comercio exterior andaluz a fines de la Edad Media." For Isabel's sayings: Melchor de Santa Cruz, *Floresta española de apotegmas* (Madrid, 1643). For her collections: Javier Sánchez Cantón, *Libros, tapices y cuadros que coleccionó Isabel la Católica* (Madrid, 1950). For her clothing: Carmen Bernis, *Trajes y modas en la España de los Reyes Católicos* (Madrid, 1978); and Ruth Matilda Anderson, *Hispanic Costume, 1480–1530* (New York, 1979). For her children and court: Gonzalo Fernández de Oviedo, *Libro de la Cámara real del príncipe don Juan* (Madrid, 1870); and his *Batallas y Quinquagenas*, ed. Juan Bautista de Avalle-Arce (Salamanca, 1989); Antonio de la Torre, "Maestros de los hijos de los Reyes Católicos," *Hispania* 16 (1956) 256; Alonso Ortiz, *Diálogo sobre la educacíon del Príncipe Don Juan hijo de los Reyes Católicos*, ed. Giovanni María Bertini (Madrid 1983); Ottavio DiCamillo, "Humanism in Spain," in *Renaissance Humanism*, ed. Albert Rabil, Jr. (2 v., Philadelphia, 1988)II; an anonymous *Directorio de Príncipes*, ed. R. B. Tate (Exeter, 1977), written in 1493 and dedicated to Isabel; S. Rubio, *Historia de la música española* (Madrid, 1983)II; and Jeremy N. H. Lawrance, "Humanism in the Iberian Peninsula," in *The Impact of Humanism on Western Europe*, eds. Anthony Goodman and Angus MacKay (London and New York, 1990).

15. THE EXPULSION OF THE JEWS: 1492

See Yitzhak Baer, *A History of the Jews in Christian Spain* (2 v., Philadelphia, 1961); the German edition, *Die juden im Christlichen Spanien* (2 v., Berlin, 1929–36) II, for documents; and the Spanish edition, *Historia de los júdios en la España cristiana* (2 v., Madrid, 1981) for a fine bibliography by E. Cantera Montenegro. See too José Amador de los Ríos, *Historia social, política y religiosa de los júdios de España y Portugal* (3 v., Madrid, 1984); Luis Suárez Fernández,*Documentos acerca de la expulsíon de los júdios* (Valladolid, 1964); and his *Júdios españoles en la Edad Media* (Madrid, 1980); Abraham A. Neuman, *The Jews in Spain* (2 v., Philadelphia, 1942); Julio Caro Baroja, *Los júdios en el España moderna y contemporánea* (3 v., Madrid, 1961)I; Miguel Angel Ladero Quesada, "Los júdios castellanos del siglo XV en el arrendamiento de impuestos reales," in Salvador de Moxó, ed., *Estudios sobre la sociedad hispánica en la Edad Media* (Madrid 1975) 417–35; and his "Las juderías de Castilla según algunos 'servicios' fiscales del siglo XV," *Sefarad* 31 (1971) 249–64; Pilar León Tello, *Júdios de Toledo* (2 v., Madrid 1979) I; Rucquoi, *Valladolid*; and studies by Francisco Cantera Burgos. On the infant of La Guardia: Fidel Fita, "La verdad sobre el mártirio de Santo Niño de la Guardia o sea el proceso y quema (16 de noviembre 1491) del júdio Juce Franco en Avila," *BRAH* 11 (1887) 7–134; Lea, *History*, I; and Henry Charles Lea, *Studies from the Religious History of Spain* (Boston, 1890; reprint 1988). For Jewish reaction to the decree: Salomón Ben Verga, *Chebet Jehuda (La Vara de Juda)*, ed. Francisco Cantera Burgos (Granada 1927).

16. CHRISTOPHER COLUMBUS AND THE QUEEN: TO 1492

The best sources for Columbus' biography remain Las Casas and Fernando Colón, whom he edited. See Bartolomé de Las Casas, *Historia de las Indias*, ed. Agustín Millares Carlo (3 v., Mexico, 1965); Fernando Colón, *The Life of the Admiral Christopher Columbus*, ed. Benjamin Keen (c. 1959; reprint 1978); Pedro Mártir de Anglería, *Epistolario*, in *Documentos inéditos para la Historia de España* (Madrid, 1955) IX; *De Orbe Novo, The Eight Decades of Peter Martyr D'Anghera*, ed., Francis Augustus MacNutt (2 v., New York, 1912); *Cristóbal Colón: Textos y documentos*, ed., Consuela Varela, (2nd, rev. ed., Madrid, 1984); and *Cartas de particulares a Colón y Relaciones coetáneas*, eds. Consuela Varela and Juan Gil (Madrid, 1984). The standard biography remains Samuel Eliot Morison, *Christopher Columbus* (2 v., Boston, 1942). Now see William D. Phillips, Jr., and Carla Rahn Phillips, *The Worlds of Christopher Columbus* (Cambridge, 1992); *The "Libro de las Profecías" of Christopher Columbus*, eds. Delno C. West and August Kling (Gainesville, 1991); *Libro Copiador* de Cristobal Colón, with study by Antonio Rumeu de Armas and facsimile ed. (2 v., Madrid 1989); and A. Milhou, *Colón y su mentalidad mesiánica en el ambiente franciscanista español* (Valladolid, 1983). For Andalusia: Hipólito Sancho de Sopranis, *El puerto de Santa María en el descubrimiento de América* (Cádiz 1926); Sopranis, "Las relaciones entre los marinos de Poniente y del Puerto de Santa María en el decenio 1482–1492," *Estudios Geográficos*, num. 39 (1949) 675–94; and Miguel Angel Ladero Quesada, "Palos de la Frontera en vísperas del Descubrimiento," *Revista de Indias*, no. 153–54 (1978) 471–506.

17. ISABEL AND THE INDIES: 1492–1504

See Antonio Rumeu de Armas, *Colón en Barcelona* (Seville, 1944). There is no consensus on names, numbers and activities of missionaries going to America in Isabel's lifetime: for bibliography (though not interpretation) see Pedro Borges Morán, *El envío de misioneros a América durante la época española* (Salamanca, 1977). For Columbus in America: Carl Ortwin Sauer, *The Spanish Main* (Berkeley, 1966). And see entries under Atlantic venture above, Ch. 8.

18. THE CATHOLIC KINGS: 1492–1499

See Alonso de Santa Cruz, *Crónica de los Reyes Católicos*, ed. Juan de Mata Carriazo (2 v., Seville, 1951); Antonio de la Torre, *La casa de Isabel la Católica* (2 v., Madrid, 1954): José García Oro, *La reforma de los religiosos españoles en tiempo de los Reyes Católicos* (Valladolid, 1969); and his *Cisneros y la reforma del clero español en tiempo de los Reyes Católicos* (Madrid, 1971); Alvar Gómez de Castro, *De las hazañas de Francisco Jiménez de Cisneros*, ed. José Oroz Reta (Madrid, 1984); García-Villalada, *Historia de la Iglesia en España* (Madrid, 1980) III-1; Antonio Domínguez Ortiz, "Los conversos de orígen júdio después de la expulsión," *Estudios de Historia y Sociedad de España* 3 (1955) 226–431; and Narciso Alonso Cortés, "Dos médicos de los Reyes Católicos," *Hispania* 11 (1951) 607–57.

19. THE QUEEN AND HER DAUGHTER: 1499–1504

For Juana and Philip: Gutierre Gómez de Fuensalida, *Correspondencia de . . .* (Madrid, 1907); Antoine de Lalaing, *Voyage de Philippe le Beau en Espagne en 1501* (Brussels 1878) I; Philippe de Comines, *Las memorias de . . .* (2 v., Antwerp, 1643); Lorenzo de Padilla, *Crónica de Felipe I llamado el Hermoso*, in *CODOIN* (Madrid, 1846) VIII; and Prudencio de Sandoval, *Historia de . . . Carlos V* (3 v., Madrid, 1955–56)I. For Isabel's will: *Testamentaría de Isabel la Católica*, ed. Antonio de la Torre (Valladolid, 1968).

THE ROYAL RELATIONSHIPS OF ISABEL OF CASTILE

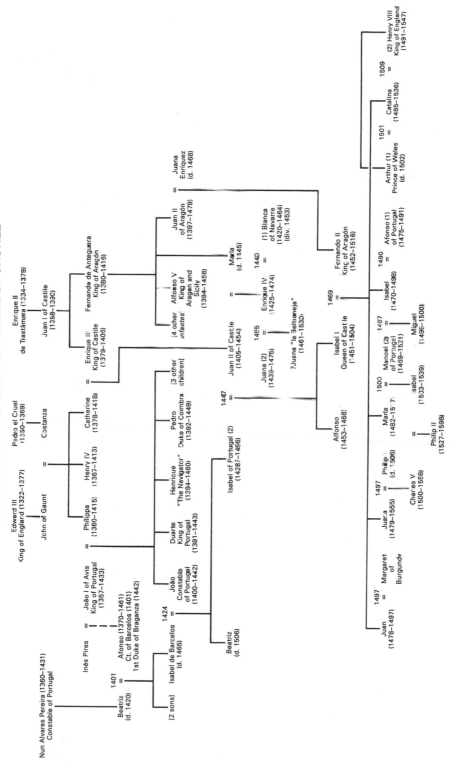

Index